Bourgeoisie, State, and Democracy: Russia, Britain, France, Germany, and the USA

Bourgeoisie, State, and Democracy: Russia, Britain, France, Germany, and the USA

Graeme Gill

OXFORD
UNIVERSITY PRESS

Great Clarendon Street, Oxford OX2 6DP

Oxford University Press is a department of the University of Oxford.
It furthers the University's objective of excellence in research, scholarship,
and education by publishing worldwide in

Oxford New York

Auckland Cape Town Dar es Salaam Hong Kong Karachi
Kuala Lumpur Madrid Melbourne Mexico City Nairobi
New Delhi Shanghai Taipei Toronto

With offices in

Argentina Austria Brazil Chile Czech Republic France Greece
Guatemala Hungary Italy Japan Poland Portugal Singapore
South Korea Switzerland Thailand Turkey Ukraine Vietnam

Oxford is a registered trade mark of Oxford University Press
in the UK and in certain other countries

Published in the United States
by Oxford University Press Inc., New York

British Library Cataloguing in Publication Data

Data available

Library of Congress Cataloging in Publication Data
Gill, Graeme J.
    Bourgeoisie, state and democracy : Russia, Britain, France, Germany, and the
USA / Graeme Gill.
      p. cm.
   Includes bibliographical references and index.
   ISBN–13: 978–0–19–954468–4
1. Middle class—Russia (Federation)—Political activity. 2. Middle
class—Western countries—Political activity. 3. Social classes—Political
aspects—Russia (Federation) 4. Social classes—Political aspects—Western
countries. 5. Political participation—Russia (Federation). 6. Political
participation—Western countries. 7. Russia (Federation)—Politics and
government—1991– 8. Western countries—Politics and government.
I. Title.
HT690.R8G55   2008
305.5′50947—dc22   2007051153

Typeset by SPI Publisher Services, Pondicherry, India
Printed in Great Britain
on acid-free paper by
CPI Antony Rowe, Chippenham, Wiltshire

ISBN 978–0–19–954468–4

1 3 5 7 9 10 8 6 4 2

Acknowledgements

Many people have contributed, knowingly and unknowingly, to this work. I would like to thank particularly all of those who have given invaluable research assistance over the period when this work was in progress: Roger Markwick, John Brookfield, Fiona Gill, Michelle Dixon, Marian Orchison, Susan Park, and Lucy Watson. I enjoyed fruitful periods of study leave at the European University Institute in Fiesole; St Antony's College, Oxford; and King's College, Cambridge while working on this book, and I owe their respective masters and staff thanks for making my stays there so enjoyable. In Sydney, my colleagues in Government and International Relations continue to make this a stimulating and enjoyable environment in which to work. In particular, Rod Tiffen has been a major supporter at all times, and his help and friendship have been much appreciated. Michelle Button was always on hand when there were computer problems, and she saved my sanity on more than one occasion. Stephen Fortescue, whose knowledge of the Russian business scene is encyclopaedic, saved me from numerous errors. The Australian Research Council has generously funded this work, and to them I am eternally grateful. And finally, Heather has once again put up with my distractions for far too long. Without her love and support, this book would never have been completed.

Contents

List of Tables

List of Abbreviations

ABCC	Association of British Chambers of Commerce
AVI	Working Community of Iron Finishing Industries
CdI	Central Association of German Industrialists
DNVP	German National People's Party
FIGs	Financial Industrial Groups
FTR	Federation of Commodity Producers of Russia
FVer	Freisinnige vereinigung
GDP	Gross Domestic Product
IMF	International Monetary Fund
KPRF	Communist Party of the Russian Federation
KSBR	Russian Business Round Table
LDPR	Liberal Democratic Party of Russia
NAM	National Association of Manufacturers
NCF	National Civic Federation
NIRA	National Industrial Recovery Act
OHR	Our Home is Russia
RddI	National Association of German Industry
RSPP	Russian Union of Industrialists and Entrepreneurs
SPD	Social Democratic Party
SPS	Union of Right Forces
TPP	Chamber of Commerce and Industry
UES	United Energy Systems
VdESI	Association of German Iron and Steel Industrialists
VDMA	Association of German Machine Builders
WIB	War Industries Board
YCL	Young Communist League
ZAG	Central Working Association

1
The Bourgeoisie: Creators of Democracy?

Throughout the 1990s, the press was full of reports about the nature of business practices in the newly independent post-Soviet Russia. Reports of the killing of business rivals, of the power of organised crime and the protection rackets with which they were associated, and of the way in which unethical businessmen (and they were almost always men) cheated and connived to gain advantages over Russian consumers, business associates, and potential Western investors filled the media. There were widespread reports of the way in which particular businessmen had been able to accumulate fabulous wealth through what was essentially a form of insider trading, making use of their personal positions and contacts to privatise state property at minimum, if any, cost. Some of these exceedingly rich businessmen, labelled 'the oligarchs', were presented as being able to exercise significant power over the country's leaders, especially President Boris Yeltsin, and were sometimes described as running the country. These reports, backed up by a number of studies, projected a picture of a business environment in which there were barely any rules and in which the state was little more than a resource to be plundered and exploited by the most ruthless of the newly emergent businessmen. Russia was perceived as 'capitalism's wildest frontier', a place of 'bandit capitalism' and the 'wild east'[1] This post-Soviet Russian experience was widely seen as unique, growing out of the circumstances of the Soviet fall and the attempt to build a capitalist democracy on the ruins of the communist system. This sort of picture has a considerable element of truth to it, although it is not the full story.

For many, the activities of Russian businessmen appeared almost pathological, and it was argued that the structures and processes that would emerge from their activities would distort the Russian economy for decades and would prevent the emergence of a firmly based market democracy. One author even suggested that the result was a criminal state.[2] The implication of much of the analysis was that what was occurring in Russia was unique, sui generis, and had no real analogues either historically or in the other former communist states. Certainly at times people did make passing reference to the American 'robber barons' as possible forerunners, but this was usually at a journalistic level and based on little, if any, historical research. One of the problems with conceiving of the Russian situation in this way is that it robs such an analysis of any comparative dimension, and thereby prevents our understanding from being informed by any appropriate yardsticks. This opens the way for exaggerated claims and for a lack of perspective. It also fails to locate this phenomenon in any continuing narrative that has any resonance within the broader historical or theoretical literature. The issue is, what sort of approach can be used to overcome these problems?

One possible approach would be to compare Russia with some of those other countries that experienced the collapse of communism and the subsequent attempt to build a capitalist democracy. Comparison with such countries would benefit from the apparent similarity of the cases, especially in terms of the structural similarities in the institutional systems from which the post-communist systems emerged and the closeness of the time periods when such transitions occurred. There have been a number of studies of the businessmen who emerged in many of these countries.[3] Such a comparison would be useful in telling us how typical the Russian experience was of this type of post-communist case, but it would not enable either the Russian experience or that of post-communism more generally to be related to the established literature on the relationship between the emergence of this type of class and the development of democracy. It would not, therefore, tell us whether the circumstances of communism's collapse produced a type of class unique in history or whether, despite some differences, the new class was similar to those which had emerged elsewhere in earlier times. For this, another sort of comparison is necessary.

In structural terms, what we have witnessed throughout the former communist world, including Russia, has been the emergence of a new class of property owners where one did not exist before. Given the collective nature of the Soviet economy, the large-scale accumulation of personal wealth combined with the power that goes with control over economic resources, which has been so evident in the post-Soviet era, propelled a new class into a prominent position within Russian society and the state. The emergence of such a class is not without historical parallel. The onset of large-scale factory industry in the West also saw the emergence of a new class of economic entrepreneurs, both industrial and financial, which was not present before the so-called industrial revolution. This was part of the fundamental transformation of society in the West that led to the modern era, and it may be that this experience can throw light and perspective on the nature and role of contemporary Russian business. Analysis of the development of this new industrial class in the West has often been conducted under the aegis of the notion of 'the bourgeoisie'.

The notion of 'the bourgeoisie' is one that is prominent in many accounts of long-term, and often not so long-term, political and social change, but surprisingly it has not been a major focus of study itself. Nor has there been significant analysis of what the term means. In part, this is because of the way in which the term has undergone change in its meaning over time, but also because it acquired a generally negative connotation; to be 'bourgeois' was for many to be an object of vague contempt. Originating in French, and at an early stage being anglicised to burger/burgess meaning the inhabitant of a borough or town, bourgeois was a formal, juridical social category in French society. It denoted an urban dweller whose life was solid and stable, and rested on income not derived from manual labour; the ideal was to live on invested income.[4] It was in this dual sense of both a category of people and a lifestyle that the notion of bourgeois has entered the scholarly lexicon.

The major means whereby this notion has been propelled into the prominent place it has occupied in social and political analysis has been the writings of Karl Marx. Although Marx never conducted a systematic and extended analysis of bourgeois, or the bourgeoisie as a class, this is a principal category in his historical explanation of the development of capitalism. His use of the term is not strictly consistent throughout his writings—sometimes it refers purely to the owners of the means of production, sometimes it includes professionals like doctors and lawyers—and his conception of who is bourgeois is not always crisply and clearly drawn; for example, the definition of class purely in terms of ownership of the means of production does not differentiate between the factory owner and the landowner. Nor is his conception of the social structure limited to two opposing classes, the bourgeoisie and the proletariat; even under capitalism he acknowledges the existence of other classes located between these two opposing camps, including the peasantry and the petty bourgeoisie, and he recognises that during the course of class struggle, these groups may temporarily ally themselves with the bourgeoisie.[5] He also recognises the existence of fractions within the bourgeoisie, including industrial, agrarian, and financial fractions.[6] Nevertheless, the bourgeoisie is, for Marx, a revolutionary class.[7] This is the class that destroyed the feudal structures of power and life, that broke the feudal hierarchy, and that, through the domination of society and its politics that it was able to achieve, ushered in a completely new set of social relations and institutional structures. It destroyed feudal, patriarchal relations and replaced them with the commodity tie that Marx saw as being the hallmark of capitalism. This was associated with the construction of a new type of society, one in which the values and way of life of the people are fundamentally transformed, and the dominant power of the bourgeoisie is consolidated. The rise of the bourgeoisie therefore not only transforms the economic processes and structure of the society, but both reshapes its politics and fundamentally reworks the structure of values that dominates in the society. Given the intrinsically expansionist nature of capitalism, in particular its need to expand in order to avoid its own internal contradictions, this sort of society spreads across the globe. But while this class is revolutionary in its destruction of feudalism and creation of bourgeois society, it is reactionary in its subsequent opposition to the proletariat which is the spearhead for the subsequent destruction of bourgeois dominance.[8] Indeed, for Marx, the bourgeoisie is its own gravedigger because the contradictions which ultimately destroy bourgeois society are produced from within that society itself.

This conception of the bourgeoisie as the shapers of modern society has been much more widely accepted than just within the Marxist frame of reference.[9] Scholars from a range of different schools have identified the bourgeoisie as fundamental to the emergence of the modern world, as being the agents for change in the construction of a new, capitalist order. This is the class that both fostered and profited from industrialisation and the transformation of finance and trade that accompanied it. This is the class that is seen as dominating political and cultural power, and using these to shape society and its aspirations in its own image. To some degree, this view would be accepted by most scholars; the shape of modernity was very much a bourgeois creation.

Part of the revolution ushered in by the bourgeoisie has been the transformation of politics, marked most clearly by the shift away from a structure dominated by traditional landowning elites. This has led to much debate about the relationship between the bourgeoisie and political forms, most usually in terms of the argument about whether there is a causal connection between capitalism and democracy, and the assumption that the bourgeoisie is in some way the natural carrier of democratic values. For Marx, the relationship between bourgeoisie and the type of political institutions was not an issue: while bourgeois revolution ushered in a shift of power from traditional landowners to the bourgeoisie, the latter could exercise dominance under liberal parliamentarism as in Britain or Bonapartist dictatorship as in mid-nineteenth century France. The traditional institutions and how they functioned were immaterial because they simply obscured the class power exercised by the triumphant bourgeoisie. But not all have accepted this view. A rich vein of theoretical writing has sought to analyse the relationship between the development of this new bourgeoisie and the emergence of new, democratic political forms. Particularly influential have been studies by Barrington Moore Jr,[10] by Rueschemeyer, Stephens, and Stephens,[11] and by Kurth.[12] While the principal task to be addressed in each book is different—Moore seeks to understand the role played by rural classes in shaping the development of different types of political regime, Rueschemeyer et al. are interested in the relationship between the development of capitalism and the emergence of democracy, while Kurth focuses on the relationship between the phase of industrialisation and type of political system—all deal with that class that is at the heart of the current study, the industrial bourgeoisie.

Moore defines the bourgeoisie as the 'independent class of town dwellers', 'the town dwellers, mainly the upper stratum that we may loosely call the bourgeoisie'.[13] This conception of the bourgeoisie seems to include not just economically based elements of the class, but also professionals like doctors and lawyers, and maybe even artisans, petty traders, merchants, and some workers. However when he is undertaking his historical analysis, he has a much more restricted view of the bourgeoisie, limiting it principally to industrial and commercial elements. This is because he is less concerned about the ideological development that accompanies what he sees as the fundamental turning points of the old regime, and is more focused upon the politico-economic power of class forces that shape political development.

Moore identifies three paths to modernity, and one cul-de-sac. In all of these the bourgeoisie plays a crucial role. The first path was the democratic-capitalist route, which came about when there was an approximate balance between the monarch/state and the traditional-landed upper class, thereby creating the opportunity for the emergence of a strong and independent bourgeoisie. The bourgeoisie was able to establish its control over the state and national policy either by allying with the landed upper class or by destroying its position. The commercialisation of agriculture, which Moore sees as fundamental to the course of future development, was carried out by the bourgeois–landed upper class alliance as in England, or by the bourgeoisie alone having destroyed the economic power of the landed upper class as in France. This path is the basis for Moore's famous axiom, 'No bourgeois, no democracy'.[14]

The second path was the route to fascism and was believed to apply to Germany and Japan. This path came about when the landed upper class sought to deal with the challenge of agricultural commercialisation through a tightening of labour repressive controls over the peasantry, a mechanism that relied substantially on the repressive apparatus of the state. The urban bourgeoisie remains politically and economically weak and dependent upon the state–landed upper class alliance, and is therefore unable to exercise any independent influence on national life. In effect, the state–landed upper class (Junker)–bourgeoisie alliance closes off the prospect of democratic development and results in a repressive, fascist regime.

The third path was the route to communism and was applied to Russia and China. The origins of this path lay in a weak urban bourgeoisie and the refusal of the landed upper class to promote agricultural commercialisation, although market relations had begun to penetrate the countryside. If the peasantry remained cohesive, the link with the landlords was weak (usually because they operated on an absentee basis), and the peasants could find allies with organisational skills, peasant revolution would lead to communist rule. If the peasantry lacked the cohesion necessary for effective action in this situation, the result was a cul-de-sac of the sort Moore identified in India.

For Moore, the key to a democratic outcome was the form in which agricultural commercialisation occurred and the consequent fate of the landed upper class and peasantry. Where commercialisation led to the destruction of conservative power blocs based in the countryside, what Moore sees as the revolutionary break with the past, the powerful bourgeoisie could assert its control over the state. Where such power blocs were not destroyed but sought to maintain their position through heightened repression, they were able to construct a conservative alliance with the state; if the weak bourgeoisie also sought the assistance of the state's repressive apparatus to keep the urban workers in check, the basis existed for a conservative tri-partite alliance between state, landed class, and bourgeoisie. Thus the destruction of the traditional rural classes was essential for a democratic outcome, but so too was the bourgeoisie. Where the bourgeoisie was powerful and independent, it was able to push through the sort of structural change that opened the way to democracy; where it was weak and dependent (or just weak), it was content to go along with continuing authoritarian rule.

Moore's work has stimulated a substantial critical literature[15] but many of the points made by his critics will not be essayed here. However it is important to note three aspects of his discussion of the bourgeoisie. First, much of Moore's argument rests upon notions of the strength or weakness of the bourgeoisie as a class, but it is not clear what criteria are used to establish how powerful a class is. Second, in the absence of such criteria, the dominance of a particular class may be judged by the realisation of its putative interests. But the problem is, how can we be sure what those interests are without the sort of close analysis of the historic details of the course of national politics that Moore does not undertake? His democratic–capitalist path makes sense if we assume that the bourgeoisie upon which he focuses possessed the values generally attributed to that class—liberalism, individual freedom, limited state involvement, and the value of individual initiative—but it is awkward for the German case. Given the absence of any measure of the German bourgeois class' power relative to the Junkers, they are held to be dependent because liberal values did not gain the ascendancy within the political sphere. However if we assume, for example, that the German bourgeoisie did not possess liberal values but were much more ideologically aligned with the Junkers, where is the evidence for their dependence? This leads to the third aspect: why should we assume that an independent bourgeoisie is always a pro-democratic force? These aspects of Moore's discussion of the bourgeoisie run through the analysis in this book.

The question of the bourgeoisie's presumed democratic orientation leads to the book by Rueschemeyer, Stephens, and Stephens. These authors use the term 'bourgeoisie' to refer to the 'capitalist class' or 'big business', excluding small businessmen, professionals, and white-collar employees.[16] Their definition is therefore narrower than the definition of Moore, but closer to the way in which he actually uses the term in his analysis. Like Moore, they also see an important role in the process of political development being played by the traditional landowning class, although while Moore describes them in terms of relying upon 'repressive labour', Rueschemeyer et al. refer to them as reliant upon a large supply of cheap labour. But in terms of their relational class model, Rueschemeyer et al. place less emphasis upon the putative strength of a class, and more on the opportunities open to it to form cross-class alliances in pursuit of their interests. In this regard, the bourgeoisie is seen not as a consistently democratic force, but as a class which will pursue its interests in the best way it sees fit to achieve their realisation. The way it acts will be structured in significant part by the alliance options open to it.

The main axis of the Rueschemeyer et al. book is the relationship between the development of capitalism and democratic political outcomes, and the principal explanatory tool is the pursuit of class interest. As a general principle, they argue that the subordinate classes fought for democracy while those benefiting from the status quo usually resisted it. This means that capitalist development has often been associated with democracy because it has led to the strengthening of the working class, which is seen as the most consistent democratic force,[17] and other subordinate classes while weakening the large, traditional landowners. However capitalist development also strengthens the bourgeoisie, the owners, and the managers of capital, but this group adopts an ambiguous, or historically inconsistent, position. As Rueschemeyer et al. declare:

Where bourgeois power came to constitute a counterbalance to the power of the nobility, the result was liberal oligarchy, possibly open to extensions toward the subordinate classes, more often closed to such an opening for long periods of time. In many cases, however, an oligarchic alliance with large landowners and the state—an alliance that guaranteed the institutional framework for continued capitalist accumulation without institutionalizing contestation—was a significant historical alternative to liberal oligarchy.[18]

The result of bourgeois power was generally liberal oligarchy, with the bourgeoisie content to operate under that structure of power. However in some cases, like Britain, the bourgeoisie was willing to agree to the further opening up of the system to integrate the working class into it and allow that class a share of power. This usually occurred only when the working class, manifested through its political representatives, seemed to pose no threat to bourgeois interests; in effect this meant when there were no *radical* working class or socialist parties. In other cases, although the bourgeoisie did not favour further opening of the system to subordinate classes, the working class was able to gain allies and force through the further democratisation of the system.

In this way, just as for Moore the destruction of the power of the landed nobility is important for a democratic outcome, so for Rueschemeyer et al. it is also important; the destruction of their power deprives the bourgeoisie of a possible partner in a reactionary alliance. Thus for Rueschemeyer et al., the fundamental class dynamic was one of situational bourgeois ambiguity within a context of consistent support for democracy by the working class and consistent opposition to it by the landed upper class.[19]

This view of the role of the bourgeoisie is much less ideological than that of those who see that class as a consistent supporter of democratisation. So too is the interpretation offered by James Kurth.[20] Kurth argues that what was crucial in shaping the attitude of industrialists to political change was the timing and phasing of industrialisation. He argues that industrialisation went through three phases: from light consumer goods (especially textiles), to capital goods (especially steel and railway building), to consumer durables. He also argues that consumer industries tend to lead to liberalisation and democratic politics while capital goods industries have often tended to lead to authoritarian politics. For Kurth, in the early industrialisers, Britain and France, the lower levels of investment required for industrial development meant that the early entrepreneurs had no need to rely on either the state or major banks for financing, and that they favoured a liberal parliamentary regime which gave them some representation and could break down the remaining restraints on their economic activities. In Britain, the heavier levels of investment required for the subsequent development of the capital goods sector came mainly from the success of the earlier consumer goods industry, especially textiles, thereby creating a process whereby industrialisation could reach the higher level without recourse to major state intervention. In France, the second stage of industrialisation was funded principally by the new investment banks (like Credit Mobilier), which needed the strong support of the Second Empire state to break the traditional banks and establish their predominance. This alliance between the state and the banks was underpinned by an ideology of 'developmentalism' which fuelled the deepening of French industry. However the industrialists, who were locked out of this alliance, soon began to seek an alternative, and shifted their support to the Third Republic, which continued to support the steel industry (e.g. through the Freycinet Plan). When the domestic market for steel was sated (the 'saturation phase'), producers in both Britain and France turned to exports to other countries, sales to the colonies, and armaments production. In the late-industrialising Germany where absolutist monarchy and the traditional landowning class had not been overthrown, liberalism and industrialism diverged from the outset. Because of the earlier development of international competitors (Britain and France), German industrialisation had to occur behind state-imposed tariff walls. The development of the capital goods industry relied on industrial cartels, large investment banks, and the state for the mobilisation of capital, thereby making industry reliant on the state in ways it was not in Britain and France. When the Empire was lost at the end of World War I and Germany was confronted by the developed economies of Britain and France, the option of selling steel to colonies disappeared and to the developed economies in Europe was curtailed. Accordingly the steel industry supported a rejection of the Versailles peace terms, re-armament, and the expansion of German interests and influence into Eastern Europe. Stronger government than that provided by Weimar was also sought. During the 1920s, two other major sectors of German industry, electrical and chemical, developed as international leaders, and they favoured free trade with the developed economies of Western Europe and domestic consumerism, and they underpinned the Weimar system. However the crash of 1929 undermined the free-trade option and led to an alliance of the steel, chemical, and electrical sectors behind Hitler.

The perception that the class would take up different positions on the basis of its interests and how those interests related to those of other forces in the society seems much more likely to be accurate than a view which ascribed to it an unchanging commitment to democracy.[21] But this view can only be sustained if the mechanisms linking industry with political developments can be shown. This means that the notion of causality, of how industrialists related to political change, which is missing in all of these accounts, needs to be addressed. This requires much closer analysis of the way in which the class, or prominent members of it, interacted with the existing social, economic, and power structures, and, in particular, the state. The bourgeoisie, defined generally in terms of the owners of capital, was a new class emergent into a situation in which power, wealth, and privilege were already distributed in a hierarchical and unequal fashion among existing actors. There were social, economic, and political structures already in place, and the new class had to break into these if its members were to achieve their aspirations socially, economically, and politically. It is the way in which the new class was integrated into existing structures that in large part determined the political trajectory of the system. Chief among these structures was the state. A detailed analysis of how such integration was brought about does not appear in the Moore, Rueschemeyer et al., or Kurth studies, and yet it is fundamental to the arguments they make. Analysis of the mechanism of such integration, by showing the nature of the relationship between the bourgeoisie on the one hand and the state and those who ran it on the other, will go straight to the heart of the explanatory power of this earlier theorising, and help us understand the role played by the bourgeoisie in democratisation.

The integration of the new class was of two types, social and political. Social integration refers to the way in which the emergent bourgeoisie was able to infiltrate, or perhaps better merge with, the existing dominant class. Its capacity to do this was related to its own social origins, the extent to which

9

new entrepreneurs came from the established privileged class groupings in the society, and the principal mechanism whereby it was achieved was through social mixing, including inter-marriage. Social integration was achieved when there was no clear line separating the new bourgeoisie (or at least its upper levels) and existing pre-industrial dominant class groups; living styles converged, social taboos dropped away, and distinct differences disappeared. But the emergent bourgeoisie sought integration not only socially but also politically. The capacity of the new bourgeoisie to gain influence in, perhaps even control over, the state was the measure of political integration. This was reflected in both the population of state offices by members of this class (or its representatives) and by the exertion of influence on the state through organisations developed with this aim specifically in mind. But while the presence of representatives of the bourgeoisie in state organs and the existence of bodies representative of bourgeois interests are important, more so is the actual political influence that could be exerted through more informal means. The higher the levels of political integration, the greater the exercise of such influence should have been. And as observers from both the left and the right agree,[22] business generally has enjoyed a very privileged position vis-à-vis the state. Thus integration of the new class into the social and political structures is the crucial variable that is missing from existing studies of the role of the bourgeoisie in political change, and it is this which the current study seeks to remedy.

It does so by analysing the mechanisms of these dimensions of integration. Chapters 2 and 3 analyse the social origins of the new economic bourgeoisie as well as the extent to which the new class became socially enmeshed with other dominant groups in the society. The following two chapters look at the levels of formal participation by this new class in the institutions of the political system. Chapters 6 and 7 explore the nature of informal influence within the political system, principally in terms of the relationship between the class and the state. By focusing on these three dimensions of integration, the capacity of the new class to bring about change, so central to the earlier theorising, will be laid bare. And by applying the same analysis to the post-Soviet bourgeoisie, we will be able to see how they compare with the earlier cases and the implications for the future of democracy in Russia.

Some Parameters

The major cases to be examined in this book are Britain, France, Germany, the United States, and post-Soviet Russia. With the exception of Russia, these are major subjects of analysis of both the Moore and Rueschemeyer et al. volumes, while Kurth focuses on the three European states but excludes the United States. By surveying the national experiences of Britain, France, Germany, and the United States, greater light will be thrown on the Russian experience, and in particular the argument that the Russian case is unique. Limited attention will also be given to the pre-1917 Russian bourgeoisie. This will provide a counterpoint to the Western examples as well as an understanding of the national precursor to the contemporary Russian situation, and although the almost 75 years of Soviet rule eliminated this class as an entity, echoes of it have extended into the present.

The initial question that arises is the comparability of these cases. The emergence of a new bourgeoisie in the first four countries accompanied the onset of industrialisation on a major scale, and began in Britain in the late eighteenth and first half of the nineteenth century, in France in the second half of the nineteenth century, and in Germany, the United States, and tsarist Russia in the last third of the nineteenth century extending into the twentieth century.[23] In post-Soviet Russia, the emergence of the new bourgeoisie dates from the late twentieth century into the first part of the twenty-first century. This is a significant temporal spread, and some may argue that the Russian case is simply too far removed from the earlier, and especially the British, to be truly comparative. This is not simply a case of the elapse of time, but of the vastly changed circumstances within which contemporary Russian events are unfolding compared with one to two centuries earlier. The high levels and denser nature of international integration, especially among the leading developed economies of the world, suggests that contemporary class formation would be much more moulded by the international environment than it ever has been in the past. This does not mean that international factors were not important earlier; the growth of the British mercantile sector based on foreign (and especially imperial) trade and the importance of the Empire for the growth of the British financial sector are clear instances of the way in which the contours of the class structure in the earlier period were shaped by factors outside the national borders. But what is new is the degree of interlocking that has taken place, especially in terms of foreign investment and of communications, and the way in which foreign economic actors can play a direct and immediate part in a country's economy and in the shaping of its class structure. The scope for this is much more extensive in the late twentieth and early twenty-first centuries than it was in the earlier periods.

The internationalised nature of contemporary capitalism is only one, albeit an important, way in which that economic system differs from the industrial capitalism that emerged at the time of the earlier cases. The variations in modern capitalism and their differences from their predecessors have been a matter of major scholarly concern[24] and will not be extensively analysed here. However it is apposite to note that the differences between the early phases of these national capitalisms and the contemporary period are immense. Such differences occur with regard to, inter alia, the organisation of the market (e.g. coordinated versus liberal), the role of government, the size of many firms, the sources and types of investment upon which they rely, the scale and mode of organization of production, internal governance arrangements, the nature of the workforce and its relationship with management, and the relationship with customers. While these differences make the earlier and contemporary systems quite distinct, the differences in the structure of the economy do not invalidate the central question with which this work is concerned: how is the new class incorporated into the existing power structure? Even if the means whereby capitalism functions have changed, the relationship between existing power holders and emergent class forces still needs to be sorted out. In this sense the increased complexity of the economic system, while it may shape the circumstances of class incorporation, does not eliminate the essential question of how that is achieved. Nor, of course, does it affect the analysis of the original cases and therefore the implications for the theory seeking to explain the earlier trajectories of political development.

Another aspect of the temporal dimension is historical learning. Each successive case of class formation took place in conditions different from those which preceded it because of the experience of these earlier cases. Major actors learnt from what went before. State elites, business groups, workers organisations, and party leaders did not act in an historical vacuum, but were informed by the experience of their counterparts elsewhere. In this sense, there is no equivalent to the case of the first-comer, the British bourgeoisie. This sort of learning also had another temporal effect: subsequent cases of industrialisation tended to be more telescoped, or truncated, than earlier ones. By learning the lessons of the pioneers, the latecomers were able to cut corners and take shortcuts, thereby reducing the time it took to achieve similar levels of development.[25] But although such learning could take place and it could affect the way particular actors acted and the length of time the process took, the essential process was the same: a new class with its potential power vested in control over industrial and financial capital had to be accommodated some way into the existing structure.

The Russian case also differed from its predecessors in the economic circumstances under which the new class emerged. In the earlier cases, it was the expansion of industrial production and the development of new industrial sectors which created both the basis upon which the emergent class could grow and the impetus for that growth. As the new economy was being born, opportunities were expanding. This had two effects on the circumstances of class formation and development. First, the prospects for capital accumulation were bright; it was much easier to make money and accumulate resources in an environment in which the economy was expanding than in one where contraction or stasis was the rule of the day. Even though such opportunities may have been more restricted for the later-comers (especially the French, Germans, tsarist Russians and, to a lesser extent, the Americans) by the growing economic power and presence of the British bourgeoisie and its quest for international markets and reach (reflected in part by investment in the economies of these states), the expansion of new sectors in the domestic economy generated opportunities for advancement that hitherto had not existed. Second, the growth of new opportunities meant that the development of new classes did not create a zero-sum economic game in terms of relations with already dominant classes, at least initially. If the emergent bourgeoisie was concentrating its activities in new sectors of economic activity, the economic challenge to those who dominated in the established or traditional sectors of the economy seemed more indirect. Such a challenge became more explicit later, when the interests of the different sectors, and therefore the classes which relied upon them, diverged, but initially such conflict of interest remained muted. Accordingly, when the newer class was at its weakest, it did not appear as significant an economic threat to established interests as it was to become later.

The conditions in which the post-Soviet bourgeoisie emerged were quite different. One important difference lay in the changes in the international environment noted above. Russia at the end of the twentieth century confronted a world in which advanced industrial capitalism was dominant and where, through the processes of globalisation, domestic developments were increasingly being shaped by broader economic and cultural forces. This had a number of implications. First, there already existed models of an economic order which could be used as a guide for those engaged in the Russian transformation. While there was significant opposition within Russia to the adoption of any of the particular models of capitalism extant in the West, the simple existence of these models meant that the path of future potential development was not a blank sheet of paper. There were historical precedents resulting in contemporary models, and given the rejection of communism and the ideological acceptance of capitalism as its replacement, such models could shape the course of Russian debates. This situation also applied, with somewhat lesser force, to all cases of industrialisation following that of Great Britain. Second, the globalisation of capital meant that domestic development could not be autarchic. Capital from the most advanced industrial, perhaps even post-industrial, economies sought new fields of investment, and the post-communist economies offered what appeared to be rich locations for this. In a range of economic sectors, from retail to metals to oil and gas, foreign capital sought to enter the Russian market, with varying degrees of success. In addition, significant numbers of Western-trained businessmen and advisers entered the ranks of Russian business, working both in Western, especially in legal and accounting firms, and Russian companies and helping to shape the developing business environment. In this way, the external impact on the domestic functioning of the emergent business environment was probably greater in Russia than in any of the other countries under study.[26] Another aspect of the external environment which was more significant in Russia than elsewhere was the integration of the

13

newly emergent capitalist economy into the world trading network. This was a network which was highly differentiated and in which the bulk of Russian-produced goods could not easily compete, although natural resources was an exception to this. This was less of an issue for the other countries: Britain and France had large imperial markets to add to their developing domestic market, the United States had an expanding domestic market, while Germany's principal focus upon heavy industry meant that for some time its production too could be substantially accommodated by the domestic market. For Russia, the domestic market was initially flattened by the economic collapse associated with the fall of the USSR and, until 1998, flooded with foreign goods.

Another important differentiating factor was domestic economic conditions. Russia at the end of the twentieth century was undergoing a process of de-industrialisation and sustained economic contraction. The crisis of the Soviet economy in the 1970s and 1980s saw industrial production decline and, especially during the early 1990s, many factories effectively cease to function. With much equipment old and outdated, established supply lines disrupted, and the domestic market shrinking as a result of both economic hardship and foreign competition, the industrial sector experienced significant contraction. The competitive pressures for success and resources faced by emergent Russian businessmen were acute. This situation was exacerbated by the fact that because Russia was already industrialised, the emergence of the new class did not coincide with the growth of new industrial sectors (although a transformed financial sector and a new private retail sector did emerge) of activity. The emergence of new, private, entrepreneurs whose power rested on economic control and private ownership constituted an obvious challenge to the political principles upon which the Soviet structure had rested.[27] This was in stark contrast to the other countries' experiences and reflects the fact that Russia was not a green field site for industrial development in the way that the other countries were. In Britain, France, the United States, Germany, and tsarist Russia, the emergence of an industrial bourgeoisie accompanied the growth of a new industrial sector whose operation generated substantial economic expansion. It was therefore easier for the new entrepreneurs to make money in an expanding market than it was for those like the Russians who were emerging into a contracting economy. Furthermore those from post-Soviet Russia had to cope with an ageing industrial infrastructure that was designed to service a command economy, and therefore was ill-suited to the needs of the newly emerging capitalist economy. In comparison, in the other countries most of the infrastructure was newly created with the industrial development, and therefore much better suited to its needs. The general situation confronted by the emergent Russian bourgeoisie was thus very different from that of its historical predecessors, but it is not clear that this dictated a different strategy for the emergent Russian business class to those followed by the other cases. This, and the situation which occasioned it, will be discussed further below.

Some[28] have sought to distinguish the Russian case from the others by arguing that Russian businessmen were different from entrepreneurs in the West. They were not seen as being the nucleus of a new class of capitalists or entrepreneurs because their main aim was the accumulation of wealth rather than the building up of their businesses. They were driven to takeovers and expansion not by the desire for profit through productive activity, but through predatory action. They were more interested in asset stripping than investing for growth, and in using their economic resources for non-economic ends. In other words, they are accused of failing to act like capitalist entrepreneurs. While it is true that during the 1990s many acted in these ways and were not driven by the search for profit in order to re-invest, which is said to be the hallmark of the classic capitalist, these people did seek to use their economic resources to generate more resources, they were in control of the principal economic units in the economy, and they certainly saw themselves as 'biznes-men'. Furthermore following the crash of 1998, there seems to have been significantly higher levels of re-investment in Russian capacity than there had been before. Moreover in the earlier cases, the extent of the diversion of newly generated wealth away from productive activity into conspicuous consumption should not be underestimated.

Another important difference between the earlier cases and contemporary Russia relates to the nature and role of the state. The twentieth century saw the massive expansion of the state, both in terms of the institutional bulk of the state machine itself and its reach into society. As the state took on increasing responsibilities, its structure became more complex and its penetration of society both more wide ranging and more routinised. In this sense, state capacity expanded in the twentieth century to such an extent that the state was a discernibly different body to what it had been earlier.[29] Both more routinised and specialised in its functioning, and staffed on a professional basis by full-time employees (although some of this was changing in the last decade of the twentieth century as state elites followed policies of reducing state functions and employment), the modern state looked very different from its nineteenth century predecessor. But regardless of these differences, the essential issue remains: the relationship between state and emergent class in control of productive resources.

The temporal dimension is also relevant in our evaluation of what is democracy and what is not. The criteria for democracy now are much more clearly defined and set much higher than was the case in the nineteenth century. What in this earlier time would have been seen as radical and democratic are today viewed as moderate and liberal. Accordingly, the contemporary Russian situation may widely be seen as authoritarian or, at best, a case of 'democracy with adjectives'[30] while, for example, the American case has been widely seen as democratic in the context of the times. The issue of contemporary context is important and is also related to the above-mentioned point about sequencing and the accelerated pace of change.

In sum, there are substantial differences between the circumstances in which the earlier cases of the emergence of a new class that had to be incorporated into the existing structure and the post-Soviet case occurred. Nevertheless, despite the problems associated with what has been called 'world historical time',[31] comparison of the nature of the respective bourgeoisies and their activities is enlightening. Furthermore the essential theoretical problem of incorporation, of how it is achieved and its political consequences, remains. When a new class in control of substantial and growing economic power emerges, it must be accommodated within the existing structures of power. An understanding of how this was done in earlier historical instances can therefore be helpful in our understanding of how that process is occurring today and the possible political implications that might flow from it. This does not mean that we expect the present to mirror the past. Rather, by assisting us to get a better understanding of the crucial role of the location of the bourgeoisie in the power structure, knowledge of the past will enable modification of the theories of democratisation and therefore a better application of them to current reality in Russia.

There is also an issue with the use of the term 'bourgeoisie'. As indicated above, this is not an unproblematic term. There has always been a certain ambiguity about what it has meant, and it also acquired somewhat derisory connotations, especially in the political rhetoric of the left. And for the right, its association with Marxism made it a term of suspicion. Many prefer not to use it in contemporary social science analysis. Much of the literature that concerns government–business relations, for example, does not focus on class, but on business and government elites, on the incorporation of particular firms into government activities, on a largely undefined entity called 'business', or on individual business people and their activities. Such a focus is unnecessarily narrow, largely ignoring the social bases of that upon which it concentrates and cutting itself off from the sweep of historical literature that both focuses upon class and has things of interest to say to this more narrow literature. Because of the broader historical and comparative advantages that flow from using the notion of bourgeoisie to describe the different groups upon which this work concentrates, that term will generally be used throughout this book.

Much scholarship has preferred the term 'middle class' to bourgeoisie when discussing contemporary social structure. However the conception of a middle class is less useful in this study because in its usage it has often had a somewhat static character, being more a snapshot of a single point in time than a dynamic view of a changing situation. Furthermore it is much broader than the group that is the actual focus of this study. In broad terms, when people use this notion, they see it as embracing three groups:

- the producers of economic wealth, principally the owners and managers of firms, the 'businessmen'; these are the people who are central in the structuring and operation of the economy and in the creation of the material basis for what was seen as a 'bourgeois style of life', and what is now accepted as the norm in the large cities of the West;

- the ideologists who generate and articulate the values that are associated with this new style of life; these include many in the professions (especially lawyers and teachers), intellectuals, and journalists/publicists;

- white-collar workers who work in the large structures of the contemporary society; these include civil servants as well as white-collar workers in private industry; these are the people who aspire to, and usually achieve, the 'bourgeois style of life'.

There have clearly been links between these three parts of the middle class in terms of social origins, values, and class location, but these groups are definably different. The primary focus of this study is narrower than this range of groups, and also narrower than the conception of the bourgeoisie as urban dwellers following white-collar occupations or pursuits and adopting a lifestyle that is generally described as 'bourgeois'. The principal focus is upon a fraction of the bourgeoisie: it is upon those engaged in economic activity, who own (or maybe manage) productive economic resources apart from their own personal labour power, skills, and talents. They own productive industrial and financial capacity and put it to work to generate income. They are the first group noted above, the businessmen,[32] principally the large businessmen but also small and medium-sized ones. Except when qualified, it is this group that will be meant throughout this book when the term 'bourgeoisie' or 'economic bourgeoisie' is used. Furthermore throughout most of this time they were an emergent class, a class in formation, rather than one fully developed.

So the main thrust of this work is to compare the trajectory of the post-Soviet bourgeoisie with those of its counterparts in Britain, France, Germany, and the United States. The four Western countries have been chosen because they became the leading industrial powers, because the relationship that their bourgeois classes developed with other class forces and the state took on varying patterns, and because they have been the focus of the classical theories of democratisation. The tsarist Russian experience will be noted because it is the national precursor of the post-Soviet bourgeoisie. The analysis will examine the social origins of the new class, followed by a study of its integration into the political sphere, both in terms of the formal institutions and the more informal aspects of the relationship with the state. This will enable us to see the similarities and differences in the Russian case compared with the earlier ones, and throw new light on the earlier theories of democratisation.

Notes

1. Respectively, Matthew Brzezinski, *Casino Moscow. A Tale of Greed and Adventure on Capitalism's Wildest Frontier* (New York, The Free Press, 2001); Martin McCauley, *Bandits, Gangsters and the Mafia. Russia, the Baltic States and the CIS* (Harlow, Longman, 2001), Ch. 8; and "Russia: The Wild East", *Granta* 64, Winter 1998.
2. David Satter, *Darkness at Dawn. The Rise of the Russian Criminal State* (New Haven, Yale University Press, 2003). In fact, the book does not analyse the emergence of a criminal state, but recounts a number of episodes of nefarious behaviour in the business sphere.
3. For example, Gil Eyal, Ivan Szelenyi & Eleanor Townsley, *Making Capitalism without Capitalists. The New Ruling Elites in Eastern Europe* (London, Verso, 1998); Michael Burawoy & Katherine Verdery (eds.), *Uncertain Transition. Ethnographies of Change in the Postsocialist World* (Lanham, Rowman & Littlefield Publishers Inc., 1999); John Higley & Gyorgy Lengyel (eds.), *Elites After State Socialism. Theories and Analysis* (Lanham, Rowman & Littlefield Publishers Inc., 2000); and Victoria E. Bonnell & Thomas B. Gold (eds.), *The New Entrepreneurs of Europe and Asia. Patterns of Business Development in Russia, Eastern Europe and China* (Armonk, M.E. Sharpe Inc., 2002).
4. See the discussion in Raymond Williams, *Keywords. A Vocabulary of Culture and Society* (London, Fontana Press, 1983), pp. 45–48. In Mann's discussion of old regime France, he refers to the way in which "the term 'bourgeois' referred as much to people 'living nobly' off rents, annuities, and offices as to merchants, tradesmen, and manufacturers'. Michael Mann, *The Sources of Social Power. Volume II. The Rise of Classes and Nation-States, 1760–1914* (Cambridge, Cambridge University Press, 1993), p. 173.
5. Karl Marx, "The Class Struggles in France, 1848 to 1850", Karl Marx & Frederick Engels (eds.), *Selected Works in Two Volumes* (Moscow, Foreign Languages Publishing House, 1951), Volume 1, pp. 109–220.
6. On this, see Victor M. Perez-Diaz, *State, Bureaucracy and Civil Society. A Critical Discussion of the Political Theory of Karl Marx* (London, Macmillan, 1978), p. 60.
7. See Karl Marx & Frederick Engels, "Manifesto of the Communist Party", Selected Works, esp. pp. 34–35.
8. For example, see Karl Marx, "Critique of the Gotha Program", David Fernbach (eds.), *The First International and After. Political Writings. Volume 3* (Harmondsworth, Penguin, 1974,), pp. 339–359.
9. For a short summary of what he calls the "myth" as central to the making of the modern world, see Immanuel Wallerstein, "The Bourgeois(ie) as Concept and Reality", *New Left Review* 167, January–February 1988, p. 99.
10. Barrington Moore Jr, *Social Origins of Dictatorship and Democracy. Lord and Peasant in the Making of the Modern World* (Harmondsworth, Penguin, 1969).
11. Dietrich Rueschemeyer, Evelyne Huber Stephens & John D. Stephens, *Capitalist Development and Democracy* (Cambridge, Polity Press, 1992).
12. James R. Kurth, "Industrial Change and Political Change: A European Perspective", David Collier (ed), *The New Authoritarianism in Latin America* (Princeton, Princeton University Press, 1979), pp. 319–362.
13. Moore (Social Origins), pp. 418 & 423.

14. Moore (Social Origins), p. 418.

15. For example, see Ronald P. Dore, "Making Sense of History", *Archives europeennes de sociologie* X, 1969, pp. 295–305; Stanley Rothman, "Barrington Moore and the Dialectics of Revolution: An Essay Review", *American Political Science Review* 64, 1, March 1970, pp. 61–82; Lester M. Salamon, "Comparative History and the Theory of Modernization", *World Politics* 23, 1, October 1970, pp. 83–103; J.V. Femia, "Barrington Moore and the Preconditions of Democracy", *British Journal of Political Science* 2, 1, 1972, pp. 21–46; Theda Skocpol, "A Critical Review of Barrington Moore's *Social Origins of Dictatorship and Democracy*", *Politics and Society* 4, 1, 1973, pp. 1–34; Francis G. Castles, "Barrington Moore's Thesis and Swedish Political Development", *Government and Opposition* 8, 3, Summer 1973, pp. 313–331; Timothy A. Tilton, "The Social Origins of Liberal Democracy: The Swedish Case", *American Political Science Review* 68, 2, June 1974, pp. 561–571; Jonathan M. Wiener, "The Barrington Moore Thesis and Its Critics", *Theory and Society* 2, 3, 1975, pp. 301–330; Jonathan Tumin, "The Theory of Democratic Development. A Critical Revision", *Theory and Society* 11, 2, 1982, pp. 143–164; Ton Zwaan, "One Step Forward, Two Steps Back. Tumin's Theory of Democratic Development: A Comment", *Theory and Society* 11, 2, 1982, pp. 165–178; Brian M. Downing, "Constitutionalism, Warfare, and Political Change in Early Modern Europe", *Theory and Society* 17, 7, 1988, pp. 7–56.

16. Rueschemeyer et al. (Capitalist Development), p. 309.

17. This is the general argument made by Therborn, although Rueschemeyer et al. argue that the working class could not bring about democracy on the basis only of its own efforts but needed allies, leading to the formation of multi-class alliances. Rueschemeyer et al. (Capitalist Development), pp. 98 & 270. For Therborn, see Goran Therborn, "The Rule of Capital and the Rise of Democracy", *New Left Review*, 103, May–June 1977, pp. 3–41.

18. Rueschemeyer et al. (Capitalist Development), pp. 58–59.

19. The Rueschemeyer et al. argument is actually much more complex and nuanced than this, involving the state and transnational power structures as major elements in the explanation, but both of these are important chiefly for the way in which they affect class relations and dynamics.

20. Kurth (Industrial Change).

21. This has been widely accepted in studies of non-European cases of democratisation. For example, see David Brown & David Martin Jones, "Democratization and the Myth of the Liberalizing Middle Classes", Daniel A. Bell, David Brown, Kanishka Jayasuriya & David Martin Jones (eds.), *Towards Illiberal Democracy in Pacific Asia* (Basingstoke, Macmillan, 1995), pp. 78–106.

22. For example, Ralph Miliband, *The State in Capitalist Society* (New York, Basic Books, 1969), p. 145, and Charles Lindblom, *Politics And Markets. The World's Political Economic Systems* (New York, Basic Books, 1977), p. 194.

23. A rough indicator of this is when industrialisation provided a greater proportion of the national product than agriculture. This occurred in 1820–1824 in Britain, 1845–1849 in France (although from 1855 to 1889 agriculture once again was the source of a greater proportion of the national product), 1890–1894 in Germany, and 1879 in the United States. B.R. Mitchell, *International Historical Statistics. Europe 1750–1988* (New York, Stockton Press, 1992), pp. 913 & 917, and B.R. Mitchell, *International Historical Statistics. The Americas 1750–1993* (Basingstoke, Macmillan,

1998), p. 788. In Russia, this did not occur until the Soviet period. In the last peaceful years of the tsarist system, 1909–1913, agriculture accounted for 51% of the national product compared with 32% for industry, construction, transportation, and communications. Paul R. Gregory & Robert C. Stuart, *Soviet and Post-Soviet Economic Structure and Performance* (New York, Harper Collins, 1994), p. 27.

24. For example, Ronald Dore, William Lazonick & Mary O'Sullivan, "Varieties of Capitalism in the Twentieth Century", *Oxford Review of Economic Policy* 15, 4, 1999, pp. 102–120 and Peter A. Hall & David Soskice, "An Introduction to Varieties of Capitalism", Pater A. Hall & David Soskice (eds.), *Varieties of Capitalism: The Institutional Foundations of Comparative Advantage* (Oxford, Oxford University Press, 2001), pp. 1–68.

25. But even given this, the short time expanse of the emergence of the Russian bourgeoisie means that conclusions about the longer term implications for Russia of the current course of class formation must be considered tentative.

26. Although the overall level of foreign investment in Russia has been much less than in many of the other post-communist countries and has not been the dominant factor in structuring Russian economic life. For some comparative figures on foreign direct investment (FDI) over the 1990s, see European Bank for Reconstruction and Development, *Transition Report 2001. Energy in Transition* (London, EBRD, 2001), pp. 105–213.

27. Although there were clearly economic aspects of the power base upon which the Soviet rulers rested, the essence inherited from the Soviet period was a structure shaped more by political than by economic concerns. This is discussed in more detail below.

28. For example, see David Lockwood, "Managers and Capitalists: The Emergence of New Class Forces in the Early Post-Soviet Economy", *Russian and Euro-Asian Bulletin* 6, 2, February 1997, pp. 1–12.

29. See the discussion in Graeme Gill, *The Nature and Development of the Modern State* (Basingstoke, Palgrave Macmillan, 2003), Chs. 4 & 6.

30. David Collier & Steven Levitsky, "Democracy with Adjectives: Conceptual Innovation in Comparative Research", *World Politics* 49, 3, April 1997, pp. 430–451.

31. For one discussion of the methodology of dealing with time, see Paul Pierson, *Politics in Time: History, Institutions and Social Analysis* (Princeton, Princeton University Press, 2000).

32. And the overwhelming majority are men, so this term will be used.

2

The Making of a Social Class: The Western Bourgeoisie

The most common conception of the development of the emergent bourgeoisie in the nineteenth century is that it generated a period of class conflict in which the old, established aristocratic landowning class was displaced as the dominant force in society by the newcomers. This picture has much to recommend it; it is clear that in many countries, the dominance of the traditional landowning class was broken and a dominant place was taken by those interests associated with the expansion of industrial production. But it is not clear that this outcome was the result of unambiguous, vigorous, and open class conflict. While there were certainly instances when the interests of the landed classes conflicted with those of emergent industrial, commercial, and financial circles, this was paralleled by a process of integration of the emergent class into the extant social structure. In all of the countries under review, Britain, France, Germany, and the United States, the emergent bourgeoisie found itself in a society in which hierarchies of wealth, power, and prestige already existed. These hierarchies within each country did not exactly match one another, thereby giving a degree of fluidity, flexibility, and ambiguity to the social structure, which provided openings the new class could exploit in its quest for position, power, and status. Such openings provided the opportunity for the integration of the new class into the social structure. This occurred without widespread violence, but as a result of the operation of processes of social adaptation, established markers of status and difference were eroded and new patterns of life and social interaction emerged. Rather than overthrowing the established social structure, the emergent bourgeoisie was integrated into it and thereby fundamentally transformed it. What is it that enabled the new class to become integrated into the existing structure while avoiding a direct and open clash with the prevailing dominant class of traditional landowners?

Important in this process is the ability of the new class to gain a degree of social integration with the dominant class in the pre-industrial structure.

The social origins of the new bourgeoisie are relevant here. If that bourgeoisie stems, as it did, from within existing productive groups, it may appear less as a new or alien force in society than as a simple extension of an existing social formation. Furthermore, if significant elements of the new bourgeoisie were to stem from within the ranks of the traditional landed class, the cause of integration, at least at the edge between the two class groups, would be facilitated because such integration will depend, in part, on the attitude of the established dominant class to the newcomers. Where the social hierarchy is relatively open and the traditional class does not seek to exclude the newcomer, a degree of integration will occur; where that traditional class sees itself in more exclusivist terms, less integration will be likely. Such integration is likely to be propelled principally from below: it is the dominant class and the lifestyle it leads that is the primary touchstone of both acceptability and prestige in society, with the result that the emergent class will aspire to take on some of its characteristics. A partial merging of the two groups thereby occurs, with this process taking different forms in Britain, France, Germany, and the United States.

Social Origins

The development of a new class is not a sudden event which crashes onto the historical stage like a thunderclap, but a slow process of growth and development over an extended period of time, perhaps even generations, before its ultimate crystallisation. This process of growth and development is shaped by both the internal dynamics of the emergent class itself and by the location of the new class in the existing class structure. Indeed, the relationship with other classes is fundamental to both the identity and location of the new class. With the exception of when a society is invaded and a new class of rulers is established by external conquest, new classes stem initially from existing classes. Historically the development of the new class has been propelled by the way in which new technologies of production are taken up by sections of the old class, and in so doing they create a dynamic which produces new means of economic production and a new set of social relations. Reflected in changed structures in the workplace, a developing consciousness of collective (class) identity, and new sets of relations with other class groups, this development transforms the existing class structure. But this transformation stems from the existing classes; the people who come to constitute the emergent class come from families which are embedded in existing classes. Their location in the existing class structure is related to the types of activities they pursue, for example, large landowner, peasant, artisan, merchant. And the type of activity in which they were involved usually, but not always, is linked to the type of activity which characterises their new class of affiliation.

This means that as the new class takes form, the boundaries between it and its class/es of origin may remain blurred.

Central to the emergence of a new class is the pursuit of certain sorts of economic activities in a way which differs substantially from that which went before. The development of what was to become large-scale industrial activity, characterised by the concentration of workers, resources, and production in large plants, was a different sort of enterprise to the small-scale production of the artisan working in his workshop or the home labourer working through the outwork system. But the two types of enterprise were not unconnected. It was but a short step for the small-scale producer manufacturing goods for sale to the market, to seek to increase his turnover and profit by expanding his activities. This could be done by expanding his workforce and increasing his resource inputs, but neither of these solutions would have lifted what he was doing out of one type of activity into another; this was still small-scale manufacturing production. However, when technological advances enabled changes in the way production was carried out, small-scale manufacturing could give way to large-scale industry, thereby transforming one form of enterprise into another. This logic would suggest that out of the small-scale manufacturer, the large-scale industrial capitalist grew. In the case of the classic bourgeoisies of the West discussed below, there is considerable truth to this view.

In all of the countries being surveyed, before the onset of large-scale industrialisation, small-scale industry existed and provided the basis from which industrial expansion stemmed.[1] Marx has identified two roads to capitalism.[2] The first is where competition among petty producers leads to social differentiation whereby the more productive producers become capitalists and employ the labour-power of their less productive neighbours. The petty producers were mainly artisans and tradesmen working in their own small workshops in the towns where they might work either alone or with the employed labour of a number of apprentices or assistants. Given the small scale of their operations, it is likely that few of them were able to accumulate substantial financial resources or to generate the sort of capital flow that would have enabled a significant expansion in their activities. However some, usually through a combination of luck, patronage, and hard work, were able to establish larger workshops or even small factories (often referred to as manufactures, many focused their efforts on producing goods for the court) and constituted the embryo of the future capitalist industrialists. But although these were larger than the artisanal workshops, they remained small in scale. Thus in this view, the source of the future capitalist industrialists were the artisans.

Marx's second road focuses not on urban workshops but on the outwork system which he sees as falling under the control of the merchants who sell the produce of that system, with mercantile capitalism the result. Marx also offers a variant of this road whereby the merchant becomes an industrial capitalist by withdrawing from the sphere of commodity circulation, purchasing the means of production, and hiring the labour-power of workers. The second road thus sees the merchant as the source of future capitalists.

This form of industrial production is referred to in the literature as 'Proto-industrialisation'. This refers to the growth throughout Europe between 1500 and 1800 of mainly export-oriented industries based in domestic premises.[3] Chiefly involved in textiles and metalwork, this sort of enterprise typically comprised workers (usually family members) working from home linked together by the activities of an entrepreneur or merchant manufacturer who both supplied the raw materials needed for production (frequently this was in the form of credit, counted against the future sale of the finished article) and collected the finished or semi-finished product for sale. The roles were clearly demarcated: the entrepreneur ensured the continuity of supplies and, when needed, the provision of credit for the workers, but was not directly involved in the manufacturing; he was the organiser and financer of production rather than a direct producer himself. The workers had no part to play in the sale of the goods they produced. Such a division was, of course, also to be evident in factory production. But what distinguished proto-industrialisation from the factory system is that in the former, the workers were isolated from one another, working in their own homes, while the entrepreneur was itinerant, following a path which regularly took him to all of his workers. Furthermore, this sort of production was spread across the countryside rather than being concentrated in larger urban centres. In contrast, in the factory system, the workers were concentrated in larger entities where they worked collectively, and although individual factories sometimes began in the countryside, if successful they soon became the magnet for the growth of an urban centre. And unlike the factory workers who worked for a wage, the domestic workers had some autonomy, selling the goods they produced to the entrepreneur.

The proponents of proto-industrialisation as a phase in the development toward large-scale industrial production see this as facilitating the emergence of conditions which stimulated factory production.[4] The growth of rural domestic industry has been seen as a means of capital accumulation, of the acquisition of entrepreneurial skills, including the knowledge of and contacts with wider markets, and as a stimulus to population growth, and therefore a potential factory labour force. While the debate about the precise relationship between proto-industrialisation and factory production remains unresolved, it is clear that the development of this style of production did assist in the process of capital accumulation and the development of entrepreneurial skills. Its small scale and dispersed location also meant that, once initial economies had been achieved compared with urban-based workshop production, if further economies were to be gained it was in the sphere of economies of scale that they were most likely. Along with the development of new sources of power generation, especially coal to add to the existing water power, this encouraged the shift to a form of factory production where large numbers of workers could be serviced through a single power source.

There is no reason to believe that either path had a monopoly on the origins of industrial capitalism. Both artisanal workshops and the outwork system could act as the basis of future capitalist development within one country. For example, some scholars of American economic history, basing their analyses upon the New England cotton textile industry in the early decades of the nineteenth century, argue that merchants were the central force for the growth of antebellum industrial development.[5] Others who base themselves on the production of iron, farm implements, machinery, and the railways argue that the principal path to industrial capitalism was through the differentiation of artisans.[6] Post concludes[7] that both schools were correct. He argues that the textile industry was unique in transforming merchants into industrialists, but also that the textile industry was much less important in the development of industrial capitalism than other sectors of the economy. While those other sectors which were crucial in shaping American industrialisation were themselves heavily reliant upon merchant capital for their development, the primary source of industrial capitalists lay in 'the social differentiation and transformation of artisanal petty producers, not in the direct transformation of merchants'. In this sense both of Marx's roads were present in the genesis of industrial capitalism. The factory system developed slowly, alongside both the small artisanal workshops and the domestic production of proto-industrialisation, with some people simultaneously being both industrialists and merchant manufacturers, combining factory production and some domestic-based production.[8] As a result the class of industrialists emerged by stages, as different sectors of the economy entered the factory system, and it was not homogenous.[9]

As this class emerged, it entered a social structure whose contours were already broadly formed. But because initially it was largely seen as an extension of its class of origin, by the time the new class has taken on its own particular class forms and distinct identity, it will have acquired a general acceptance as part of the prevailing social structure. However its precise location within that structure may be problematic. This is because the emergence of a new class based upon new forms of production and new wealth will automatically project it as a potential challenger to the class or classes that already dominate society. How the dominant class reacts to the emergent class, whether it is open to it and embraces it, or whether it rejects it and seeks to retain exclusive dominance, will play a significant part in structuring the society's course of development.

Different scholars have studied the emergence of this class in the countries under review, and although the terminology they use differs, the conclusions they draw are broadly the same: while industrial capitalists stemmed from

Table 2.1. Origins of 'the first industrialists' in Britain (%)

	Fathers' occupations	Current occupations	Initial occupations
Upper class Landed peer, landed gentry, army/navy officer	8.8	2.5	2.9
Professional middle class Clergyman (established church), lawyer, doctor, surveyor, civil engineer, land agent, architect	7.1	2.5	3.3
Merchants and traders Banker and 'capitalist', merchant (foreign trade), wholesale merchant (usually inland trade), draper or other large retailer, shopkeeper, and small businessman	23.0	19.6	11.5
Manufacturers and industrialists 'Manufacturer' in domestic system (including those who ran small mill or factory, and dealers), 'industrialist' at head of centralised undertaking, manager, clerk, foreman and other non-manual employee, independent craftsman	29.2	41.8	26.3
On the land Yeoman or farmer and manufacturer/engaged in non-agricultural activity, yeoman, tenant farmer and other cultivator, coalmaster or quarrymaster, mine-adventurer	21.7	4.1	2.5
Working class Skilled workman, domestic industry workman, unskilled workman, 'poor', servant	7.1	9.8	22.6
Various Actor, artist, journalist, government employee, non-conformist minister, sea-captain, school master, teacher	3.1	3.8	2.5
Persons who set up directly		15.8	14.8
Persons who started by working under their father or a relative as employee or partner			13.6

Source: Crouzet (*First Industrialists*), pp. 147–51. The industries included in Crouzet's sample are cotton, woollen, and worsted, flax, silk, lace, hosiery, primary iron industry, smelting of non-ferrous metals, secondary metal trades, engineering, ceramics, glass, paper, rubber, shoe-making, brewing, food and tobacco, and chemicals. p. 147.

every social class, their main point of origin was those already engaged in independent industrial production.

The major British study was undertaken by Francois Crouzet. His figures (Table 2.1) refer to the fathers of 226 founders of large industrial undertakings in Britain between 1750 and 1850, the occupations of 316 industrialists at the time they founded such undertakings, and the first post-schooling/apprenticeship occupation of these people. These figures suggest that there is a strong relationship between involvement in industry before establishment of a major enterprise and the establishment of such an enterprise. In terms of Crouzet's variables (father's occupation, and current and initial occupation), the largest proportion of these early industrialists came from within the ranks of those already engaged in manufacturing and industry, especially cognate branches of industry. Also significant are the merchants and traders. Together these two categories (manufacturers and industrialists, and merchants and traders) constitute more than 50% of both the fathers' occupations and the current occupations of large founding industrialists. Perhaps not surprisingly, these are also the two main areas (apart from land) of independent wealth creation in the eighteenth and nineteenth centuries' economies, and therefore principal arenas for the accumulation of the capital necessary to establish factory production.[10] This reflects the nature of economic development before the growth of industry, and in particular the earlier development of manufacturing, an active trade network, and the commercialisation of the agricultural sector.[11] Speaking of the entrepreneurial capitalists who emerged in Bradford between 1825 and 1850, one student has said that nearly all of Bradford's 'new parvenu bourgeoisie came from relatively modest, often Nonconformist, family backgrounds with deep roots in the protoindustrial lower middle and skilled artisanal working class'.[12] Thus although in class terms while industrialists came, in Ashton's words, 'from every social class',[13] those from established industrial, commercial, and financial families predominated. But although most industrialists came from among those sections of the middle class that were already involved in industrial activity, as the nineteenth century progressed, it is likely that there was a narrowing of the social origins of new entrepreneurs,[14] especially as the initial entry and set up costs rose in terms of capital required and education needed. According to one scholar, between 1870 and 1889, 57% of British business leaders were the sons of businessmen, 19% of public officials, 13% of farmers, and 11% of clerical workers and labourers.[15]

The traditional source of wealth creation in Britain was the land and this too constituted a source of the early industrialists. Just over a fifth of the fathers of the 226 founders of large industrial undertakings surveyed were small farmers, most of whom also ran small mining operations on the land. Many of these people were able to gather sufficient capital to help their sons become established as industrialists; very few moved into industry directly from the land, this shift being mainly a generational one. But the higher levels of land ownership, the noble peers and the gentry, very rarely either fully entered industrial life themselves or financed their sons in such activity.[16] Certainly it was common in the first half of the nineteenth century for nobles to engage in a range of non-agricultural pursuits on their estates to supplement the commercial agriculture upon which they had embarked.[17] Mining was especially common in this regard, in part reflecting the fact that, unique in Europe, British landowners also owned all minerals on their estates, except for gold and silver.[18] Furthermore, the development of such small mining enterprises often stimulated landed grandees to invest in canal and railway construction as means of getting their produce (both agricultural and

Table 2.2. Social origins of French businessmen in 1901 (%)

Economic bourgeoisie	
Large	43.2
Small	12.2
Civil servants	
High level	14.8
Medium level	4.8
Professions	16.1
Petit bourgeoisie	7.4

Source: Christophe Charle, *Les Elites de la Republique (1880–1900)* (Paris, Fayard, 1987), p. 66. For some figures that confirm the substance of Charle's view but for a slightly later period, see Pierre Lauthier, 'Les dirigeans des grandes enterprises electriques en France, 1911–1973', Maurice Levy-Leboyer (ed), *Le patronat de la seconde industrialisation* (Paris, Les Editions ouvrieres, 1970), p. 106 and Maurice Levy-Leboyer, 'Le patronat francais, 1912–1973', Levy-Leboyer (Le patronat), p. 142.

mining) to the market.[19] But this sort of activity was rarely extended into major operations directly run by the landowner. More usually, after establishing such enterprises, the landowner would lease out the mine or allow it to operate under licence to an outsider. In this sense, while the landowner might effectively be the initiator and founding financer of these enterprises, rarely did he continue as the operator. Most landowners preferred to continue their gentlemanly, landed lifestyle rather than become engaged in the travails of industrial production.[20] They remained, in the words of one writer, a rentier capitalist aristocracy.[21]

Although there does not seem to have been a systematic analysis of the origins of French entrepreneurs of the sort carried out for their British counterparts, it seems clear that most industrialists and financiers of the nineteenth century came from families that were also engaged in such pursuits (Table 2.2).

Charle's figures are not definitive on the origins of the initial major industrialists, but combined with the picture that emerges from studies of prominent individual industrialists, they suggest that, as in Britain, industrialists came principally from among those already involved in industrial and commercial activity. The most important industrialists were often from provincial families that had long been engaged in commerce or industry;[22] it has been estimated that late in the nineteenth century, less than 10% of large employers came from a working class background.[23] Few came from a landowning background, although some aristocrats had become involved in early industrial activity,[24] while in sharp contrast to Britain, civil servants constituted an important source of new entrepreneurs.

Accurate figures on the origins of German businessmen are notoriously difficult to obtain, but there is a general consistency in the picture produced by those that have been reported (Table 2.3).

It is clear from these figures that most entrepreneurs came from the ranks of those in which the father was economically independent, especially a

Table 2.3. Occupations of fathers of business elite in Germany (%)

Occupation of father	1800–1870	1871–1914	1918–1933[a]
Businessman	54	53	53
Master craftsman, retail dealer	24	20	16
Civil servant	15	16	12
Large landowner	2	2	4

Source: Kaelble (Long-Term Changes), p. 409.

[a] The 1918–33 figure is for 'All business leaders'; for 'owners', respective figures are 63%, 13%, 7%, and 3%. These figures do not match those cited by Charles Maier, who states that by 1930 10% of business leaders came from working class or petty bourgeois backgrounds, 29% from middle levels of society, 23% from old aristocracy or officialdom, and 38% from fathers already engaged in big business. Charles S. Maier, *Recasting Bourgeois Europe. Stabilization in France, Germany and Italy in the Decade After World War I* (Princeton, Princeton University Press, 1975), pp. 40–41.

businessman, artisan, small-scale manufacturer, or shopkeeper; civil servants were sometimes also the fathers of entrepreneurs, but clearly on a lesser scale to businessmen and pre-industrial manufacturers and artisans. Jurgen Kocka[25] claims that some three quarters of businessmen in Berlin during the first phase of industrialisation were the heirs of people in business. He identifies four types of business backgrounds that the fathers were involved in: a craft/artisan background, especially in the metals or engineering fields; mercantile activity; graduates and technicians, including former factory supervisors; and pre-industrial entrepreneurs. Small numbers of entrepreneurs came from the landed aristocracy or working class: according to one study,[26] 69.7% of German entrepreneurs came from the upper middle class, with only 3.5% and 1.9% respectively coming from the aristocracy and the working class. Although there were regional variations on this pattern,[27] the general picture is clear: entrepreneurs came overwhelmingly from among the economically active and independent sections of the urban classes, with very little in the way of aristocratic landowning origins.

Youssef Cassis[28] provides some comparative figures on the social origins of businessmen in these three countries (Table 2.4).

These figures are generally consistent with those cited above in their clear picture of new businessmen coming from families already involved in business or commercial activities of some sort. This is also consistent with the information available about the origins of businessmen in the United States.

Table 2.4. Occupations of fathers of businessmen (%)

	Businessmen	Senior civil servants	Landowners	Professionals
Britain	59	—	11	7
France	52	10	—	16
Germany	53	9	2	3

Table 2.5. Occupations of fathers of businessmen in the United States (%)

Father's occupation	19th Century iron and steel manufacturers Ingham	American businessmen Gregory & Neu
Manufacturer	55	
Merchant	12	
Banker	3	
Total business	70	51
Professional	15	16
Worker	10	8
Farmer	5	25

Source: Ingham (Rags to Riches), p. 617.

The debate about the merchant versus artisanal roots of the emergent American business class noted above has been paralleled by a similar discussion over whether the new industrialists were 'new men' (and they were overwhelmingly men) from lower social origins who worked their way up by dint of hard work, or whether there was much more continuity of control and status. In his famous study of American businessmen in the last half of the nineteenth century, Matthew Josephson[29] argued that the new industrialists were mainly new men who were able to work their way to the top. Similarly, Gutman[30] pointed to lower class social origins and the fact that many new businessmen migrated into the area in which they became prosperous to argue that they were new men from outside the existing social structures. In contrast, Gregory and Neu[31] argue that there was much greater continuity of control with most businessmen coming from upper middle class social origins. What these different explanations may reflect is the different foci of analysis of these studies. This is consistent with the findings of John Ingham[32] who studied the backgrounds of iron and steel manufacturers in six nineteenth century cities and found that in the larger, more established cities with entrenched status hierarchies, industrialists mainly came from the pre-industrial upper social classes, while in the newer cities where such a hierarchy had not become as established, most manufacturers came from outside the upper levels of the pre-industrial social system. However even this finding for the newer cities does not mean that the emergent working class was a potent source of capitalist businessmen. The new businessmen came in large part from among those groups that were already involved in manufacturing or some other kind of business activity (Table 2.5).

According to Ingham, more than half of all businessmen in these studies came from families that were already engaged in manufacturing while 70% were engaged in business of some sort; more than two thirds came from upper level occupational backgrounds in urban areas. Both studies show very little mobility from the working class into capitalist leadership,[33] although

Table 2.6. Occupations of fathers of businessmen in the United States (%)

	Businessmen born 1820–49	Businessmen born 1850–79	Businessmen born 1879–1907
Professional	22.6	18.7	12.6
Business	35.5	47.7	63.1
Public official	3.9	4.7	—
Farming	23.2	21.5	7.6
Skilled craft	10.6	2.8	7.9
Un/semi-skilled	2.6	3.7	2.7
Clerical & salesman	1.6	0.9	6.1

Source: C. Wright Mills, 'The American Political Elite: A Collective Portrait', Irving Louis Horowitz (ed), *Power, Politics and People. The Collected Essays of C. Wright Mills* (London, Oxford University Press, 1967), p. 124.

the Gregory and Neu study does show a surprisingly high proportion from a farming background. But even this does not gainsay the overwhelmingly urban and business origins of the group.

This conclusion is supported by the work of C. Wright Mills (Table 2.6).

The growing importance of business as the major source of new businessmen is evident from these figures, reflecting the self-reproductive nature of the business class, although Mills' data also point to both professional and farming backgrounds as important sources of businessmen. This is consistent with his analysis in class terms (Table 2.7).

A study of the Chicago business elite confirms Mills' general findings.[34] In terms of birth cohort, of those born 1821–40, 31.6% had fathers in business; 1841–60, 53%; and 1861–80, 71.4%. Overall 47.8% of fathers and 42.5% of grandfathers were in a commercial occupation, while 37.4% of fathers and 32.4% of grandfathers were bankers, merchants, or in transport or manufacturing. Businessmen in Chicago (and more generally) thus came disproportionately from upper- and middle-class stock, and each birth cohort seemed to have had less humble origins, thereby reflecting a narrowing of the social origins of the emergent business class.[35]

Table 2.7. Class origins of businessmen in the United States (%)

	Businessmen born 1820–49	Businessmen born 1850–79
Upper class	19.8	41.3
Upper middle class	37.2	29.4
Lower middle class	29.6	18.1
Lower class	13.4	11.2

Source: Mills (American Political Elite), p.122.

Despite the mythology, the shaping of an American business class was not a rags-to-riches story. Very few of those who became prominent businessmen came from working class or poor farming, not to mention black, families. Their origins were overwhelmingly more privileged (even if not as privileged as the larger landowning and social elite which dominated American society prior to the onset of major industrialisation in the 1870s–80s), from families with people already active in business or the professions. As such, the businessmen came from established positions in society; they were not total outsiders even if they were not part of the leading elite.

In all four countries (although the French data are not as definitive), the principal source of the emergent industrial bourgeoisie was that section of the population that was already involved in industrial, commercial, or business activities. In all countries, this constituted more than 50% of the businessmen in the respective samples, and meant that as industrial capitalism emerged, it was seen as being rooted in the established social structure. Its social origins were among that section of the population which was perceived as being firmly based in the notion of private property and which, if for no other reason than economic self-interest, would have been expected to have shared with their social betters an opposition to increased power and autonomy on the part of the lower orders of society. The relatively small proportion in all societies of businessmen coming from the working class was consistent with such a view. There was a logic to the emergence of the industrial capitalists from the small-scale entrepreneurs of the pre-capitalist era, in that large-scale industrialisation involved the pursuit of similar sorts of activities as earlier, only at a significantly higher level, viz. the transformation of small-scale industrial activity into large-scale industrial activity, mainly through the introduction of new technologies and means of organising production. But it was still industrial production, not the transfer from one sort of economic activity, such as agriculture, to another. For the people involved, this would have been a much smaller jump than would have been required had it involved a shift between economic sectors.

Moreover, involvement in pre-industrial manufacturing potentially gave these people three characteristics that would have facilitated their transformation into industrialists. First, experience with the processes that were involved in industrial development. Familiarity with what was involved in, for example, smelting steel, must have been an advantage in the case where someone sought to establish a major steel-making enterprise. Knowledge of what was involved must have eased the initial development and have provided the individual with the confidence that it could be achieved. Second, involvement in manufacturing could have been instrumental in the capacity of the individual to accumulate the necessary natural resource inputs to get the larger scale operation off the ground. It could also have provided him with the contacts needed to ensure a continuing supply of the raw materials required for the new, enhanced enterprise, and the experience in conducting a business. Entrepreneurial skills would thereby have been honed. Third, it could have put the person in a position where they were able to acquire the financial backing needed to undertake the new enterprise. The acquisition of such backing was more likely to be forthcoming if it was for an already successful enterprise than if there was nothing there except a dream.

But within this general pattern, there were some differences between the countries, albeit mainly at the margins. Nowhere were large landowners a significant source of businessmen, but in Germany and France the number coming from such a social group was significantly lower than in the United States and Britain. The same pattern applies with regard to middle-sized and small farmers, with the result that the emergent bourgeoisie was much less closely attached to agricultural pursuits in Germany and France than in the United States and Britain. The professional segment of the bourgeoisie was a much more substantial source of the business class in France and the United States than it was in Germany and Britain while civil servants were much more prominent in France and Germany than in Britain and the United States.

These differences in patterns of social origins may be important for the question of the integration of the new class into the social and political hierarchies of these societies. At an individual level, the fact that some of the new entrepreneurs came from among the traditional landowners or the civil servants may have eased their relations with these groups more broadly. Personal acquaintance could have eased the entry of individual entrepreneurs into the relevant social hierarchy. But more important is probably what these patterns tell us about the mindset of different corporate groups. The higher profile of landowners, both large and small, in the origins of British and American entrepreneurs may reflect the fact that both of these landed groups were more oriented toward commercial relations and economic development than the sort of classic, feudal, orientation usually attributed to such groups. The prominence of civil servants in France and Germany may reflect a more dynamic, developmental approach to the economy on the part of the state and its agents, an approach in which industrialisation was seen as a process to be encouraged both materially and spiritually, than it was in either Britain and the United States where the philosophy of the state was much more laissez faire. In this sense, business origins may be a hint to where the areas of flexibility and flux in the social hierarchy lay.

Open and Closed Hierarchies

While individual members of these emergent national bourgeoisies may have had some personal connections with the leading establishment classes in these societies, generally there was a structural division between the parvenus and those groups already at the peak of the social structure. However as industrial growth stimulated wealth accumulation and as new patterns of urban living began to emerge, the established status hierarchies came under direct challenge. The predominant place of 'old money', based overwhelmingly on the land, was confronted by the new wealth arising from industrial and commercial activity. With this went pressures for increased standing on the part of the emergent bourgeoisie.

Britain

Before the major industrial expansion, Britain was already a commercial society in which the networks and infrastructure of a market economy had been well developed.[36] Indeed, one scholar believes that, in contrast to absolutist France, a type of agrarian capitalism had developed in England whereby the imperative of the market was already driving and structuring economic (including agricultural) life;[37] there was already widespread 'market dependence' by the seventeenth century, including among the traditional nobility, many of whom preferred to lease much of their land to tenant farmers than to farm their estates themselves.[38] Money as the medium of exchange, the growing standardisation of weights and measures, the emergence of rudimentary credit facilities and the development of a network of markets linked by roads, facilitated the growth of a commercially based economy. The basis of this economy was agrarian, in that the bulk of what was traded both by quantity and value was produce from the land. Certainly there was a trade in luxury goods, which was in part internationally connected, but a small minority of the population was engaged in this. A much larger number of people were engaged in the trade and exchange of small-scale manufactured items, most of which were produced in the small workshops to be found in the towns and villages noted above. By the time industrial expansion took off, therefore, commercial principles were already strongly embedded and were eroding the primacy of the traditional, land-based value system.

On the eve of the major industrial expansion beginning in the late eighteenth century, Britain remained a land dominated by the traditional landed, upper class.[39] Although many of these families were in fact of relatively recent ennoblement,[40] the position of the great landowners at the top of the status hierarchy was entrenched by tradition. They dominated the public life of the local communities of which they were part and, through their residence in the towns and cities for part of the year, they were prominent in the social and political life of the developing cities, including the capital. They benefited from an established tradition of deference which acknowledged them as the natural local leaders. This was reinforced by a dominance of local government and the control of many of the local seats gaining representation in the Parliament. Much of their wealth and influence rested upon the produce of their land (although incomes from this source tended to either fall or stagnate in the second half of the nineteenth century[41]), something that was strengthened by the particular nature of English inheritance laws which enabled them to pass accumulated wealth across the generations largely intact. For some of the wealthiest landowners, an important source of income (and one which increased over the nineteenth century) was investment in urban property, especially in London. Many landowners owned large tracts of land in the growing cities and received significant income from the rentals thereby generated. Some even engaged in substantial urban redevelopment.[42] Such landowners were little involved in the major upsurge of industrial development, despite some involvement in commercial activities in the century before the Civil War.[43] A partial exception to this is the way that some had become involved in mining in the early stages,[44] and by the end of the nineteenth century many had become active on the stock exchange and in the taking up of directorships (see below). This sort of involvement in generally small-scale industrial undertakings meant that although the landed upper class was not heavily involved in industrial development, it was not averse either to aspects of industrialisation or to some of the values that went with it, even if its members often looked askance at this new wealth and some of the trappings enjoyed by economic parvenus; in the words of Barrington Moore:

> The strong commercial tone in the life of the landed upper classes, both gentry and titled nobility, also meant that there was no very solid phalanx of aristocratic opposition to the advance of industry itself...the most influential sector of the landed upper classes acted as a political advance guard for commercial and industrial capitalism.[45]

According to Mosse,[46] contacts between the 'haute bourgeoisie' and the nobility were easier in England than in either France or Germany.

But if traditional landowners did not often seek to become involved in industrial and financial activity, the new bourgeoisie, at least its most wealthy circles, did aspire to social integration with their established social 'betters'. In Britain newly rich industrialists sought to enter the world of the landed nobility, often through the purchase of an estate[47] and the adoption of the habits and practices of their models: living at least part of the time in the country, following the London (or local major town) season, and setting some distance between themselves and industrial production.[48] The marriage of eligible sons to landed heiresses also became common by the end of the nineteenth century.[49] While there has been some dispute about the extent of land acquisition by newly rich industrialists, especially in the last part of the nineteenth century,[50] the entry of industrialists into the 'establishment' dominated by the landed nobility was a continuing process during this century, even if it may have been slowing toward the end.[51] The 'ruralification' of the industrialists and the emergence of so-called 'gentlemanly capitalism'[52] was an important development, not just because of its potential implications for Britain's longer term economic development,[53] but because of the remoulding of the traditional elite which it constituted. By the end of the nineteenth century, there was an overlap between aristocracy and industrialists; in 1896 about a quarter of the peerage, some 167 noblemen, were directors of companies,[54] while from 1885 individuals with commercial and industrial connections constituted a significant proportion of newly created peers.[55] According to Moore, 'the lines between wealthy nobility and gentry and the upper reaches of business and the professions were blurred and wavering',[56] while for Perkin, between 1880 and 1914 'The rich, both great landowners and millionaire capitalists, drew together in a consolidation of that new plutocracy which was already beginning to emerge during the mid-Victorian age'.[57]

But even more important than industrialists in this remoulding of the traditional elite was the bankers. In contrast to the model of finanzkapital proffered by Rudolf Hilferding and others, in Britain there was no merger between the highest levels of banking and finance on the one hand and of industry on the other. While the small county banks did play a part in financing some aspects of industrial development, this was not a major activity on the part of the larger banks and finance houses located in the City during the nineteenth century.[58] These had emerged mostly in the eighteenth century, and their gaze tended to be fixed more on investment abroad than at home. As befits an aspirant colonial power, the big banks sought their profits principally in external commercial activities, backing the merchants which were so important in the development of empire, rather than in under-writing fledgling industries at home. Furthermore, as the importance of London as an international financial centre grew, and therefore financial flows came to play a major role in the country's balance of payments, this external focus was strengthened. This meant that not only was there not a strong economic link between the City and domestic industry, but nor was there any social merging between the men who dominated these two spheres. The British financial and industrial elites did not merge, and although they came to overlap at the edges, they remained substantially distinct entities. The financial elite represented by the City was much closer socially to the landed nobility than to the industrialists, with family links between bankers/financiers and landed nobles more common than between the former and industrialists.[59] At the end of the nineteenth century, some 24% of leading City bankers had aristocratic fathers-in-law and another 20% had married into other banking or adjacent occupations; only 1% were married into industrialist families.[60] The City financiers and bankers were much closer, socially and sociologically, to the landed elite than they were to the industrialists.[61] This is a curious situation. The merging of industrial and financial capital would seem to have been a logical development, but it did not come about. This legendary gap between the manufacturing North and the City of London was not simply one of geography. Cultural values were different, in terms of the relative strength of Anglicanism in the City and non-conformism in the North, the sons of well-to-do businessmen tended to prefer a life of leisure among the landed gentry rather than entering the world of finance, and the historical profits to be gained from foreign commerce and finance posed a real disincentive for bankers to become involved in domestic industrial undertakings;[62] few industrial directorships were held by bankers in the late nineteenth century.[63]

Thus in Britain the emergent bourgeoisie was characterised by a divide between industrial and financial fractions. As the nineteenth century progressed, both fractions of the class gained in power and importance,[64] simultaneously reworking the patterns of life and social existence for the higher reaches of society. As the cities grew and became more differentiated with the development of working class suburbs and suburbs where the better off lived, the wealthy bourgeoisie took on some of the elements of the lifestyle of the traditional landowners, often giving them a new twist.[65] Major industrialists and financiers added large, even ostentatious, city residences to the landed estates that many of them bought. Furnished expensively and run by employed staff, these houses were symbols of the new wealth that was becoming evident in the upper reaches of society. Frequenting the same private men's clubs and patronising the same cultural and social events, the upper levels of the new bourgeoisie created a new set of patterns of life that were distinct from those of the working class. Those members of the bourgeoisie of more modest means also followed a lifestyle separated from that of their employees, but at a much more modest scale than that of their wealthy colleagues. In doing so, the bourgeoisie were major shapers of the patterns of life that came to dominate British society. The patterns of life associated with the wealthy had some attraction to the landed aristocracy, and these two groups came together at the edges. In this way, the social prestige and dominance of the traditional landowner was not so much displaced by that of the urban-based wealthy bourgeois as supplemented by it. In the emerging status hierarchy of the late nineteenth century, the bourgeois shared a place of prominence with the traditional aristocracy.

France

Just as Britain was a commercial society before significant industrial expansion, so France had also taken major steps in this direction, especially following the French Revolution of 1789. This event is commonly perceived as ushering in the dominance of the bourgeoisie, or perhaps more specifically, 'la grande bourgeoisie'.[66] Some have argued that each regime after the Restoration period based itself upon a new rising class: the July Monarchy of Louis Philippe (1830–48) on 'la grande bourgeoisie', especially high finance, the Second Empire of Louis Bonaparte (1852–70) on big business, and the Third Republic (1871–1940) on 'the middle bourgeoisie', especially those with academic qualifications graduating from the technical colleges and schools. The bourgeoisie is seen as the class leading the Revolution against the ancien régime, and with its peasant and working class (sans culotte) allies, overthrowing that regime. Stemming mainly from the Marxist perspective, this view sees the Revolution as the means of the clearing away of the feudal fetters on capitalist development and thereby as creating the conditions for the upsurge of capitalist industrialism. In so doing, the Revolution laid the economic basis upon which bourgeois political and social control could emerge and displace the dominance of the landed nobility and its feudal political form, the monarchy. One form this view took was that France was run by the '200 families' whose financial power enabled them to pull the strings behind governments of all sorts. Resting on control of the banks, big business and public administration, these were seen as the controllers of society.[67]

This conception has been very powerful in shaping our understanding of the Revolution. But this view is not sustainable in the bald form in which it is stated here without qualification. Its limitations have been shown by Alfred Cobban.[68] He argues that in the pre-Revolution period there was rising prosperity in the finance and business worlds, with finance seen as becoming increasingly influential and members of the wealthier commercial class able to buy their way into state office, especially at the municipal level. Through the purchase of office, many from the commercial world were able to diversify their power bases and gain a noble title. Generally in the lead up to the Revolution, a struggle for influence and position was occurring in the towns between the business world and the liberal professions. In terms of the actual Revolution itself, leadership was exercised by members of the liberal professions rather than the business world; financiers, merchants, and industrialists were not major players in shaping the course of revolutionary developments. Nor was there a single, influential, coherent Girondist party that represented the interests of the wealthier middle class.[69] Thus while it may be true that members of the bourgeoisie led the Revolution, it was that wing of liberal professionals rather than the commercial/financial/industrial sector that was important.

While many recognise this fact, they still argue that the Revolution represented the interests of the rising commercial, financial, and industrial class because it opened the way to capitalism by overturning the feudal fetters upon it.[70] The Revolution certainly eliminated a range of monopolies and privileges that had shackled would-be entrepreneurs, and abolished those corporations and trading companies that had done much to strangle commerce and industry before the Revolution, although these had been breaking down before 1789.[71] The Revolution led to the fostering of free trade, but it is too simple to see this as a clear capitalist measure. Different economic actors reacted differently to the demand for free trade; generally manufacturing interests supported and commercial interests opposed it. Ultimately the demand for free trade was linked to the century-old call for the abolition of internal customs barriers, and it was ushered in by reforming officials rather than commercial and industrial interests.[72] Rather than seeking a broad-based reform of economic structures, business and mercantile interests sought a larger domestic market and protection from foreign competition, as they had been doing for some time. Nor did the Revolution stimulate industrial upsurge. While the nineteenth century saw the steady growth and development of industry, there was no industrial revolution along the lines of what has been identified as happening in Britain; it was mainly in the Second Empire (1852–70) that industrial development really took off. The Revolution did not unleash industrial forces arbitrarily held in check by ancien régime structures, even though it did remove some of the restraints upon economic development. The limits of the Revolution's economically liberating power can be shown in its effect upon landholding. The Revolution did not lead to a general redistribution of noble landholdings. Those aristocratic landholders who fled at the time of the Revolution did lose their land, which was generally given to the local peasants who divided it up and put it to use through small-scale farming. However those nobles who remained were usually able to retain control over their land and, provided they behaved sensibly, also to retain leadership positions in the local community; in Cobban's words, the 'new ruling class was above all one of landowners'.[73] This does not mean that the dominance of the nobility remained intact, but it does suggest a continuing prominence of the basis upon which power traditionally rested in France, landholding.[74] Thus while some of these nobles did divest themselves of their land, the result of the Revolution was not similar to the enclosures of England and did not lead to the generation of either an efficient farming sector or a newly emergent class of displaced peasants cum proletarians.

But even if the Revolution did not bring about immediate change in the economic structures of the French economy, it did bring fundamental change to its political structures. The Revolution destroyed the structure of power that saw the court as its focus resting upon a social basis of noble landholding. Although the Restoration period (1814–30) and the July Monarchy (1830–48) both saw the restoration of formally royal rule and in the eyes of some presaged the return to power of the traditional landholders, in neither case did these appearances displace the reality of a shift of power in a bourgeois direction.[75] What the Revolution did was to abolish the aristocratic monopoly of key posts, seigneurial dues and tax exemptions, and thereby to destroy the basis of aristocratic distinctiveness compared with other wealthy sections of French society.[76] While the aristocracy retained high social status and considerable landholdings, it lost all semblance of both a prescriptive right to and pre-emptive advantage in the exercise of power. This combination of high status and the loss of control over access to power was to be crucial in shaping social and political development during the nineteenth century, and in the place in French society that the emergent economic bourgeoisie was able to attain. Furthermore, the nineteenth century did see a shift in the locus of wealth. Up to the middle of the century, the very wealthy were overwhelmingly landowners with only a few bankers (principally the Rothschild and Perier families), but by the 1870s the balance of wealth had shifted to 'the great financiers and industrialists'.[77]

Despite the Restoration period and the July Monarchy, the Revolution also destroyed the intellectual basis of noble power. Henceforth claims to power based upon traditional lineage and status were overwhelmed by the conviction that access to power should be open to much broader ranks of the populace. The rhetoric of the Revolution had been very radical in this regard, although as subsequent events were to show, this rhetoric was not realised in practice. The imposition of what was effectively a military dicta-torship by Napoleon clearly undercut the thrust of this rhetoric, while the restoration of the monarchy was also symbolically significant in this regard. However, such developments could not blunt the strength of the conviction arising out of the Revolution that this was to usher in the dominance of the bourgeoisie in the society. The assumption of the appropriateness of bourgeois dominance was clearly held in leading bourgeois circles, but to the extent that considerations about things like the importance of law and the need for development were widely held, these also implied a leading role for members of the bourgeoisie. This was given public affirmation in Gambetta's notion of 'les nouvelles couches socials' (new social strata).[78] The liberal professions—lawyers, teachers, doctors, scientists, writers, and artists— were all seen as having a crucial role to play in the shaping of a modern society, while industrialists and financiers too had an important role here through the economic developments that their activities embodied. So too, it could be argued, did the middle and upper levels of the growing state bureaucracy. In this sense, the prevailing ethos in the society throughout most of the nineteenth century was not hostile to increasing bourgeois influence and status, and as part of that diverse group, the economic segment of the bourgeoisie benefited. This was despite the fact that, especially in the first half of the century, there was suspicion of the possible effects of industrialisation, and especially the way in which it threatened to destabilise agricultural-based society. Even though the structural barriers to the rise of business-men had fallen, they still had to overcome snobbery and petty jealousy; businessmen had little social standing, at least until the time of the Second Empire.

Charle's study cited in Table 2.2 shows that more businessmen generally came from established backgrounds than from elsewhere.[79] He argues that in terms of the trajectory of their careers, new men in business did not differ substantially from those who inherited wealth and opportunity; the only real difference was that the new men started from a lower position.[80] Those who inherited, he categorises as coming from the 'financial aristocracy', the 'ancient aristocracy' or the 'established bourgeoisie'; the new men came from entrepreneurial families or, especially in the second half of the century, engineers, and technocrats. The important point about this is that much of the emergent business sector came from within sections of society that in the mid-nineteenth century were socially accepted in established circles. The basis for this began in the pre-Revolution period, when wealth was increasingly becoming the source of influence, as reflected in the venal nature of most state offices and the propensity of wealthy bourgeois to use their money to acquire such status and power as state office and noble status could bring, emergent businessmen were not universally seen as social outsiders; there was, as one scholar has put it, 'a process of fusion between established elites and the *nouveaux riches*... during the Ancien Regime',[81] as manufacturers sought to use their wealth to manoeuvre their way into the established social hierarchy through the purchase of government office and noble status.[82] These processes accelerated in the nineteenth century, especially its second half.

Important too was the generation of what may be seen as a 'bourgeois style of life'. This has been much studied[83] and constituted an important reshaping of the structures of French society. Through the salons, the clubs[84] and the social occasions which came to dominate the calendar in the larger towns, allied to the urban redevelopment programs of the second half of the nineteenth century which both generated speculative profits for many[85] and provided new living conditions for those with the means to take advantage of it, a specific bourgeois lifestyle emerged. Importantly, one part of this was connected to the traditional landowners, many of whom in their search for a role sought to gain entry to these bourgeois circles on a social basis.[86] Many values were shared by both groups, including the desire to live off private income and to have a house in the country as well as the town.[87] Furthermore, for those bourgeois with surplus cash available, the purchase of land (and often the seeking of a noble title) became an important mechanism of social acceptance.[88] This was particularly the case for industrialists and financiers who often purchased estates in the country. Although they did not always go and live on these estates, this was consistent with the ideal shared by many at that time: to make enough money to be able to give up active work and go and live life as a country gentleman. They sought such landholdings not only for speculative purposes or as a hedge against other investments, but as, in the words of one scholar, a 'symbol of more enduring values. In this respect, as in others, capitalists felt a nostalgia for the way of life and the social role of the former nobility.'[89] In this way, businessmen looked to the traditional landholding nobility and the social status they had as models for their own behaviour.[90] This sort of coming together of business and traditional landholding was reinforced by the way in which many nobles sought to become involved in business activity, especially following the depression beginning in the 1870s. For many, such activity was long established. Many nobles before the Revolution had been involved in mining and small-scale manufacturing on their estates, and this interest in industrial development was maintained by many of these people in the nineteenth century.[91] This was especially so given the ending of the former dominance this group had exercised. Increasingly over the century, such people became involved on boards of companies, especially 'banks, insurance, railways, mines, and steel, where the boards of directors often contained between a third and a quarter of noblemen';[92] in 1840, 20.4% of the members of boards of directors of the fifteen largest joint stock companies were landowners,[93] while in 1902 some 30% of directors of railway companies and 23% of large steel and banking companies were nobles.[94] Thus by destroying the unique basis of noble power while leaving substantially intact the social status that they enjoyed, the Revolution opened the way for the emergent bourgeoisie to enter the French social system, with the upper reaches of that bourgeoisie becoming closely integrated with the traditional landed nobility.[95] They did not, however, integrate as closely with that other major segment of the French national elite, the government functionaries, whose growing sense of corporate identity (see Chapter 4) constituted a major barrier to the penetration of this group by other social elements.

Members of the economic bourgeoisie of more modest means remained socially distant from their wealthier colleagues and less connected to the traditional landowning class. The common pattern was for most French entrepreneurs to work in partnership with relatives, with the family providing much of the capital and some of the labour to get enterprises off the ground and keep them going.[96] Sons often succeeded fathers, and marriage was often with the daughters or sons of similarly placed business families. But although these people did not aspire to the same status as the traditional nobility, they became integral parts of the developing French social structure and at the heart of the emerging middle-class culture which came to dominate French society.

The gap that existed between industrialists and financiers/bankers in Britain was much less marked in France. Although the members of the major banking houses located in Paris were distanced from many industrialists (and bankers) located elsewhere in France, the continued status of the nobility and its achievement was a common aspiration among many in both groups. The bankers were clearly a major component of the emerging dominant group in French society. The merging of the traditional landowners with the emergent bourgeoisie thus embraced both industrialists and financiers and moderated the differences of interest that existed between them.[97]

Germany

The unification of Germany in 1871 saw a country in which the patterns of domination that had been evident in Prussia were maintained in the new state. Industrial development had begun in the Rhine provinces in the 1820s and 1830s based on the coal resources there and had experienced a spurt in the 1850s, but until the onset of major industrialism later in the century, the economy remained primarily agricultural.[98] West of the Elbe River,[99] agriculture was based mainly on small peasant farms held in hereditary tenancy and in which the peasant cultivators had effective control over cultivation. But east of the Elbe, the domination of large seigneurial estates run by traditional landowners, the Junkers, was maintained. Unlike in England where much of the land of the estates was cultivated by tenant farmers, the Junkers generally maintained direct control (albeit often exercised through managers) over their estates, working them on the basis of servile labour; despite formal peasant emancipation between 1806 and 1817, the peasants remained in a state of effective economic subjection. The Junkers dominated the society, occupying the key posts in political life and monopolising the ranks of the officer corps and the army general staff. Their general dominance was reinforced by the victory over France in 1871, and it was this group of conservative landowners who dominated state and society and set the tone for the latter; commercial values were much less important than those associated with the honour and virtue of the traditional lifestyle of the Junkers. They were sustained in this by the increasing value of Junker estates in the decades before 1914, a fact due in part to the official policy of protectionism but also to the way in which large landowners (including both bourgeois landowners and Junkers) had engaged in significant agricultural improvement during the nineteenth century.[100] Unlike in England, urban property ownership was not a major source of income, while most Junkers were little involved in early industrial enterprise;[101] although large landowners were more important in Silesia, and many had diversified some of their capital into shares by the end of the century. Politically, the large landowners dominated local government and had a powerful voice in the national government. It was into this sort of society, dominated by a conservative landed class with strong roots in the military, that the emergent bourgeoisie was born.

The role and position of the German bourgeoisie has been a major issue of controversy in scholarship on both German development and the broader issue of democracy and the state. The crux of this controversy has been the so-called 'sonderweg', or special path, that Germany has been claimed to have followed. The essence of this is a particular view of the German bourgeoisie and the role it has played in German development. Proponents of the sonderweg thesis[102] start, at least implicitly if not explicitly, from the view that elsewhere but especially in Britain, the bourgeoisie was a powerful force which was able to challenge the rule of traditional landed elites, open the formerly closed system and securely establish bourgeois primacy both politically and ideologically. In contrast, the German bourgeoisie was weak. As a result of Germany's late industrialisation[103] and the important role the state played in fostering it, bourgeois failure in the 1848 Revolution, and the unification of Germany from above by Bismarck, the bourgeoisie was never a powerful social force and never fought let alone won a struggle against the Junkers. Rather than challenging the dominance of this traditional landed elite, they compromised through the famous 'alliance of iron and rye' consummated through the tariff reforms of 1879 and the later program of naval rearmament. In this way they continued to pursue their economic interests within the framework of continuing 'feudal' political rule; German economic modernisation was therefore not accompanied by commensurate political development. Furthermore, rather than asserting its own values, the bourgeoisie adopted those of the landed elite, and was therefore not characterised by the liberal values that its Western counterparts were assumed to possess. Proponents of the sonderweg thesis pointed to bourgeois acquisition of estates and adoption of a landed lifestyle, entry of sons to the Prussian reservist forces and the state bureaucracy, and the prevalence of things like duelling to point to the so-called 'feudalisation' of the bourgeois value structure. By capitulating to the Junkers in this way and not recasting politics in a bourgeois fashion as in Britain, the German bourgeoisie are accused of leaving intact the power of traditional pre-industrial elites which, in turn, facilitated the rise of Hitler and the Nazis.

This has been a very fruitful framework, at least in the sense that there have been many stimulating studies of German development that have used it to provide the basic structure of the narrative. However, it is by no means clear that it is the most satisfactory way of studying German development in the last half of the nineteenth century and the first third of the twentieth. The sonderweg conception has been subjected to significant criticism on both methodological and empirical grounds;[104] nevertheless many have continued to maintain that the bourgeoisie became encapsulated by Junker culture in the way that the sonderweg thesis assumes.

Usually taken as evidence of this is the bourgeois adoption of Junker lifestyles, social mixing with the landed elite, and the acquisition of noble titles. The adoption of Junker lifestyles was most clearly reflected in the purchase of landed estates, particularly if the businessman then used that as his chief place of residence. Wealthy businessmen did purchase landed estates in the late nineteenth century; according to one survey,[105] 25% of the wealthiest businessmen who were not of aristocratic lineage were also large landowners, but in a statistic that shows the limits of the view that businessmen were transformed into Junkers, only 6% of the sons became full-time landowners. For the businessmen, landholdings were mainly holiday spots, investments, or status symbols. For many, they were means of flaunting wealth, ways ostentatiously of signalling that they had 'arrived' in society. In this way they were symbolic not of the adoption of Junker values or lifestyle, but of the craving for social respectability and acceptance that they believed landholding brought. In this sense, they were accepting part of a value system that had its roots in the pre-industrial society of feudal Prussia, but this sat awkwardly with many of the values that they were promoting at the same time.

The acquisition of noble titles has often been seen as evidence for the feudalisation of the bourgeoisie, for the propensity of this group to seek to ape its social betters by acquiring the sorts of titles that traditionally had denoted social distinction in Prussian society. Some businessmen did acquire titles, but this seems to have been a small minority. A study of 502 multi-millionaires involved in industry, banking and commerce between 1890 and 1918 showed that 17.4% were raised to a title in their lifetime.[106] This is a much higher rate of entitlement among the very wealthy than among businessmen of more modest means; the same study cites two other surveys showing lower levels of entitlement: among Westphalian textile manufacturers it was said to be 0.4% and among heavy industrialists of Westphalia it was said to be 1.2%.[107] In a study of Commercial Councillors (a title bestowed on businessmen by the state) in the Rhineland and Westphalia, only nine of the 673 councillors in the survey were ennobled, and five of these came from a family whose noble status went back to 1569 and was confirmed in 1903.[108] In Hamburg and Berlin the figures for post-1870 entitlement were said to be respectively 11% and 15%.[109] These figures are consistent with the view that only a small minority of businessmen gained noble title; indeed, some even rejected such an award.[110] By the end of the nineteenth century, state awards and titles may have been more attractive to businessmen than those emanating from Prussian traditions,[111] but even so those bankers and industrialists who were ennobled were almost invariably in the lower ranks of the nobility, with the upper levels dominated by those with traditional landholding connections.[112]

There does not appear to have been a high level of social mixing between the economic bourgeoisie and the traditional landed elite.[113] Given that their main spheres of economic activity were geographically distinct, with the bourgeoisie mainly active in the urban areas and the Junkers in the countryside, this may not surprise, but by the same token, the continuing hegemony that the Junkers had exercised in Prussia and that they sought to maintain under the Empire involved a substantial physical presence in the capital if not in other cities. The capital was the seat both of the royal court and of the government, both of which were institutional arenas attracting members of the traditional landowning class. Neither of these attractions was present in the other cities of the German Empire, with the result that the social circles which leading businessmen frequented did differ depending upon their geographical location. In Hamburg, where the business elite comprised old patrician families in banking, international commerce and shipping with industrialists becoming more prominent towards the end of the nineteenth century, businessmen met socially among themselves and with other members of the local elite. In a city like Hamburg, this comprised principally politicians, administrators, and leading members of the professions, most of whom were bourgeois in terms of social extraction. In Berlin, where the business elite was mainly involved in banking (47% of the wealthiest entrepreneurs were bankers), industry, and commerce and where 60% of it was Jewish, businessmen again mixed socially among themselves and with other members of the local elite.[114] But in the capital that elite included many with an aristocratic background.[115] In the salons and clubs of the capital, and at the court, members of the bourgeoisie met and mixed with representatives of the Junkers, but this does not seem to have led to either enduring social ties or easy social acceptance by the Junkers of businessmen, especially when they were Jewish. Some businessmen had personal access to Emperor Wilhelm II; among these were financier Max Esser, Hamburg bankers Max Warburg and Max von Schinkel, director of the North German Lloyd shipping line Heinrich Wiegand, owner of the Schultheiss Brewery in Berlin Richard Roesicke, AEG's Walther Rathenau and his brother Emil, heavy industrialist Fritz von Friedlander-Fuld, Berlin bankers James Simon, Franz von Mendelssohn, Paul Schwabach, Arthur von Gwinner and Carl Furstenberg, and merchant Eduard Arnhold. Three businessmen who were described as 'particularly intimate friends or personal advisers of the Kaiser'[116] were the heavy industrialists Carl Ferdinand Baron von Stumm-Halberg and Friedrich Alfred Krupp, and the director of the HAPAG shipping line, Albert Ballin.[117] While this sort of personal access may have enabled these people to have some influence with the Emperor, it did not signify general acceptance into polite society. Most of these people were not able to gain acceptance into and membership of the highest social circles; the success of a few people like Rathenau and Krupp in gaining such access simply highlights the inability of most businessmen to replicate their success. The biographer of Albert Ballin summarises the position of leading businessmen when he asserts that Ballin 'and his colleagues in the business world, were not absorbed into this [Junker] aristocracy, but rather that they were allowed to coexist in a socially inferior and politically officeless position, one which—whatever its irritations and humiliations—did not prevent their continuing amassment of still greater wealth'.[118]

Nor was there much Junker involvement in business activities separate from their estates; the Junkers largely avoided industrial investment and encouraged their sons to enter the army, bureaucracy, or agriculture rather than business. As indicated above, the German bourgeois industrial class was largely self-recruiting, both in its origins and maintenance, with little infusion of fresh blood from among the traditional landowners. Looking at multi-millionaires (and therefore a possibly atypical minority of busi-nessmen), one scholar[119] has found that some 75% of the sons of these wealthy businessmen went into business, while only 11.4% entered the aristocratic professions (large landholding, and those holding court posts, military officers, diplomats, and civil servants holding the office of Landrat). Another study has suggested that almost 75% of the sons of Berlin business-men and 66% of those of Hanseatic businessmen became entrepreneurs.[120] Furthermore, a majority of wealthy businessmen married the daughters of businessmen; according to one survey, this amounted to more than 85% of businessmen.[121] The emergence of businessmen from business families, a characteristic which declined in importance as the twentieth century rise of large corporations made technical and bureaucratic factors more important, was an important characteristic of the business class in Germany. In their origins and subsequent development, the German bourgeoisie was largely endogenous, born of itself and reproducing itself.

There was therefore no merging of the bourgeoisie with the traditional, aris-tocratic, landowning, Junker elite in Germany.[122] While both groups touched one another in various arenas of German society, there was very limited overlap and no sustained and deep interaction. There was no social merging into a single integrated ruling elite, with the boundaries between traditional landowners and emergent businessmen much higher and more extensive in Germany (especially Prussia) than in France and Britain.[123] Although the Junkers could no longer be classed as 'feudal' by the late nineteenth century,[124] with many having become capitalist farmers by that time, their ideology remained different from that which characterised the growing eco-nomic bourgeoisie; the cores of the value systems of both groups remained distinct, with the Junkers still very much associated with the militarist values emanating from the state, as did their major networks of social interaction. The bourgeoisie did adopt many of the commercial values of their coun-terparts elsewhere in the attempt to advance their business interests, but the political dominance exercised by Junker interests and their control of the state ensured that commercial values did not dominate the society in the way they did in the other countries being surveyed here. This does not mean that commercial values were not present. Eley[125] points to various German 'institutional forms' that were the 'classical embodiment' of bourgeois values:

the constitutionalizing of public authority via the parliamentary institutions of 1867–71; the recodifications of commercial, civil, and criminal law; the reigning models of administrative efficiency, particularly at the level of the city; and the growth and elaboration of public opinion in the form of an institutionally complex and legally guaranteed public sphere.

But such factors were balanced against more traditional elements in the culture of German official life. The significant role played by the state in industrial development, and the consequent reliance upon it of the emergent bourgeois class (see Chapter 6) served to ameliorate the potential clash between the conservative values of the landowning class and the commercial aspirations of the bourgeoisie; neither surrendered their values nor were assimilated by the other.

United States

The pre-industrial United States differed from the West European case studies in the absence in the former of a traditional, aristocratic, land-based nobility that dominated the main structures of the society and whose values overwhelmingly shaped the prevailing ideology. This absence meant that both structures of power and the ideology that sustained them were more open than their pre-industrial European counterparts, and there was therefore less of a block to the rise of a new class based upon the development of industrial capitalism. Pretensions to nobility had been punctured by the Revolution which rejected the continuing predominance of the full British models of society and politics, while the status revolution constituted by the Jacksonian emphasis upon the 'common man' ended any pretensions to a monopoly of descent by the old New England families.[126] However the degree of openness should not be exaggerated. In the first half of the nineteenth century, different trajectories of social development had occurred in different parts of the country.[127] In the South, society was dominated by a landed class whose position rested overwhelmingly upon the labour of slaves. In the Northeast, traditional landed interests jostled with urban professionals, merchants, and manufacturers at the upper levels of society, with industrial capitalism emerging as the dominant economic form. In the expanding West, the development of small-scale family homesteads was paralleled by the growth of large-scale holdings concentrating primarily upon livestock rather than farming. It was these groups that dominated politics, but it was a dominance that rested less on inherited and noble title than upon economic resources and social prestige. In this sense, despite the primacy of the privileged sections of society, the structure was more open to aspirant newcomers based on new commercial sources of wealth than their European predecessors.

The Civil War had a significant impact on the social and political hierarchy in the United States. It effectively destroyed the society based on the plantation worked by forced labour. In so doing, it undercut the position of the Southern planters and left the emergent commercial/industrial establishment in the Northeast dominant. Comprising principally industrialists and merchants but also including some landowning elements, this group became socially dominant and, in association with Southern propertied interests, blunted the effect of the more radical Reconstruction proposals being voiced soon after the end of the war. But importantly for our purposes, this meant that in the emerging hierarchy of power, privilege, and esteem in the late nineteenth century, those involved in the ownership and development of industry held a central place.

The upper levels of the social structure had always been more open to personal wealth than had been the case in Europe, reflecting the prominent place occupied by commercial values in the prevailing ideology of American life. The limits to long-established inherited privilege and the strengthening of the myth about and the capacities for people to accumulate wealth through their own efforts meant that the established upper reaches of American society were both based on considerations of wealth and more open to entrants who gained the required resources. The rejection of inherited privilege embedded in the Revolution meant that ideologically (if less completely so in practice) there were few barriers to high-level social acceptance of newly wealthy industrialists and financiers. And given that these people originated from sections of society that were considered solid and respectable, their general integration into the existing social hierarchies was relatively easy, notwithstanding the bitter criticism of much business practice in the later nineteenth century (see Chapter 6). The sort of personal entrée into the leading political circles of the American state was facilitated not only by the relative openness of the political system and the economic power of leading businessmen but also by that web of social relationships and commonalities that together helped to sustain establishment America. Many of the leading figures in business and politics knew one another, and even when they were not personally acquainted, they frequently shared interests, economic investments, and social circles. Many belonged to the same clubs and societies, attended the same social functions, lived in the same areas and sent their children to (and themselves attended) the same schools. They interacted easily, without the social distance that was present in Britain.[128] This sort of commonality underpinned the greater access to high political levels enjoyed by business in the America of the early twentieth century.

This was a crucial difference between the United States and the other countries under review. The absence of an aristocratic lifestyle and culture to which emergent classes might seek to assimilate meant that these new classes were relatively free to create their own cultures and patterns of life unencumbered by hierarchical holdovers from the past. The industrial capitalists that came with the wave of industrial development in the last decades of the nineteenth century could thereby build upon the foundations that existed as a result of the earlier dominance of American society by those whose experience had generated the myth that hard work alone led to material reward and ascent of the ladder of opportunity. This myth was confirmed for many by the experience of this new wave of bourgeois entrepreneurs. Through their own efforts (at least this was the public message), they were able to amass significant wealth and exercise substantial power, thereby demonstrating the truth of the myth and the openness of American society. This image was part of the culture that they created, a culture that in practice distinguished them as much from their working class employees as was the case in other capitalist countries. They stimulated urban redevelopment and thereby created geographical space differentiated from much of the rest of the population. Similarly the lifestyle that emerged, sustained by the increased wealth to which they had access and characterised by comfort and sometimes opulence, not only differentiated them from their social inferiors but also created a standard to which other groups aspired. Thus rather than being a group which sought to achieve the status of a traditional ruling class, the emergent bourgeoisie simply took over and moulded that which they inherited from the earlier dominant elites.

***

Thus in all four countries, the emergent bourgeoisie stemmed principally from among those sections of society involved in manufacturing activity before the onset of large-scale industrialisation. This means that all four national bourgeoisies were always an organic part of the social structure, even if there was some initial reserve about them on the part of dominant class groups. Although the emergent bourgeoisie had some access points into their respective countries' hierarchies of power and privilege, they were not, with the probable exception of the United States, immediately perceived by the extant upper classes as worthy sharers in the benefits to be gained from dominating that hierarchy. But the power that flowed to them as a result of the expansion and prospering of their economic activities enabled leading industrialists to gain entry to leading circles in the respective societies, while those of more modest means gained full integration into the developing middle class.

All national bourgeoisies sought to acquire some of the social and cultural trappings of the acknowledged upper-class status groups in their respective societies. In the European cases, this was principally through the acquisition of landed estates and the adoption of a lifestyle that in part emulated those of the traditional landowners. In the United States, the lifestyle that had emerged around those of substantial economic means was adopted and reshaped by the emergent bourgeoisie. This was a principal mechanism of social integration for the new class. This sort of integration of the new class was really only available to the wealthier sections of that class, and generally this seems to have meant that financial elites were more able to become socially integrated in this way with old money than were the industrialists. Certainly this was the case in Britain, where links between the traditional nobility and the financiers of the city seem to have been closer than those between the industrialists and nobility. And according to Cassis,[129] the banking and business elite was much less integrated into the upper class in Germany than it was in Britain, while unlike in Britain and France, there was no real financial aristocracy in Germany, where most large bankers were Jewish. Where the social hierarchies were relatively open—Britain, France, and the United States—the bourgeoisie was able to attain a high degree of social integration with the dominant class groups (although there is a significant qualification with regard to the relationship with state officials in France; see Chapters 4 and 6), but where that hierarchy was more closed, as in Germany, the degree of such integration was significantly less.

However the emulation of the traditional landowning class was really only possible for those very wealthy businessmen[130] who could afford to purchase landed estates and maintain a genteel lifestyle. For the vast majority of the emergent bourgeoisie, this was not really a practical option. For many, their margins were too narrow and their attention too focused on their businesses to engage in such activities. But this group was just as important as the very wealthy in shaping the development of a new, 'bourgeois' lifestyle that transformed society. Initially, many of the new businessmen lived virtually on site, literally within sight of the smokestacks of their new factories. However, as they began to accumulate wealth and as the areas around the factories came to be taken up with working class housing to accommodate the new work forces, many factory owners moved to new, more lavish houses in better parts of town. Often this involved substantial urban renewal, as parts of the cities were remodelled to accommodate the demands of the new residents; in many cases this involved the creation of whole new areas of high-quality housing which was out of the price range of the working class. In this sense, the bourgeoisie created a physical separation between themselves and their workers to match the cultural separation that was also emerging.

Increasingly, the lifestyles of the emergent bourgeoisie became differentiated from that of their working class employees. Not only the patterns of housing noted above but also the daily rhythm of life took on a different form. Especially among the wealthy, the women did not go out to work, the children often received education in the home, there were often domestic servants, and the men often belonged to clubs of differing degrees of exclusivity in the city, all characteristics that clearly separated this class from their working class employees. These people, generally, also had more money to spend, and conspicuous consumption was often the result. Grand houses, expensive clothes, high-quality means of transport (initially carriages, later cars), a greater array of consumer goods (made possible by the growth of industrialism), holidays by the sea, large parties and ostentatious funerary arrangements were characteristic of many of these newly made bourgeois families. Furthermore, they mixed together, both professionally and socially, with many of these families becoming linked through ties of marriage. Of course the degree of participation in this sort of lifestyle differed enormously; some were only modest participants while others took part in a full-blown

51

fashion. But even those who were at the lower end of the ostentation scale, were participating in a style of life that was very different from that of the working class and that also differed from that which the solid, respectable section of society would have followed before industrialisation.

An important part of this new lifestyle was the generation of a new ideology consistent with the newly developing material conditions of society. The growing dominance of bourgeois, or perhaps better middle class, values was a marked feature of all of the societies at this time, but that does not mean that the value structures of all societies were identical, although they all had common elements. The new ideologies were urban rather than rural oriented, were driven by the material production of new industrial and consumer goods (with the obvious consequences for the presentation of a new style of life characterised by such goods), and emphasised the important role played by the innovator/industrialist/entrepreneur; this was urban-based entrepreneurialism. It emphasised the value of individual achievement, and promoted the importance of education and the need for independence from state control. Such values were not always unchallenged in the emergent ideology; for example, the growth in Britain of recognition of the need for state intervention to protect working conditions. But the important thing is that the ideology both reflected and legitimated the changing material structure of society.

Two further aspects of this are significant: national differences, and the role of the emergent middle-class ideologists. The ideology that emerged in each country was a product not just of the class that was emerging, but also of the society into which they were entering and the other forces present in it. Thus while all came to be characterised by a dominant bourgeois ideology, in each case it was an ideology with national characteristics.[131] In Britain, the retention of a dominant place by the traditional aristocracy injected into the ideology those elements, including the value of notions of amateurism, leading to what has been called 'gentlemanly capitalism'. In France, the focus on the role of the individual capitalist was blurred by a continuing emphasis on the importance of the state in economic production. In Germany, the continued strength of the militarised landowner Junker class meant that the prevailing ideology retained significant elements of this traditional culture. In the United States, the myth of the rugged individual was supreme. Although these national differences were significant and reflect the different legacies from the past, they do not detract from the fact that these ideologies ushered in a new stage in each society's development, and that was shaped overwhelmingly by the forces set in train by the economic bourgeoisie.

The second significant aspect of the emergence of such ideologies is that their production was due in large part to the ideologists identified in Chapter 1. The increased wealth in the society made it possible for greater numbers of people to be released from direct involvement in production, thereby leading to an increase in the ranks of the professional bourgeoisie, including lawyers, intellectuals, and educators. These people were at the forefront in generating ideas and theories which served the new circumstances. The emergence of socialism, liberalism, and conservatism and even nationalism, as coherent bodies of ideas, and especially the first two, was the intellectual product of the industrialisation powered by the bourgeoisie. Individual thinkers in each of these ideological spheres generally came from within the middle class, but not the economic bourgeoisie, and they were therefore the intellectual counterparts of that bourgeoisie. If the economic bourgeoisie built the material structures of modern society, the ideological segment of the middle class, or professional bourgeoisie, built its intellectual structures. And as we will see, they were very important in shaping the political forms that emerged from the industrialisation of society.

The generation of these new patterns of life was probably the principal achievement of the emergent bourgeoisie because it involved the reshaping of the societies into which they were born. In doing so, the class was a major driver in the reshaping of the major hierarchies in the society. This was done not through a frontal assault on the old structures, but through integration into the existing structures and, through this, their transformation. At the middle levels of society, it was driven by the aspirations of those bourgeois of modest and comfortable means who lacked the wealth realistically to aspire to the highest social echelons. At the higher levels of society, the wealth and power of the 'big' bourgeoisie enabled them to achieve social integration, but in our case studies the relationship with established dominant groups and classes was different. In the United States where the established class structure lacked a traditional land-based aristocracy and was underpinned by an aspirational ideology of personal achievement, this integration was most fully developed, principally through a substantial merging of lifestyles and involvement in business activities by many of the pre-industrial elites. In France, the basis of traditional power had been destroyed but the social status of the landowners remained high, thereby creating a hierarchy which was relatively open and which enabled a significant level of integration of the emergent bourgeoisie into the upper levels of the social structure; although the self-contained nature and high prestige of the state elite was a complicating factor here (see Chapter 6). In Britain where the hierarchy was relatively open even though traditional landowners retained a dominant political and social presence, newly emergent bourgeois elites were integrated into the society, but those elites themselves were both divided between the industrial and financial sectors and overlapped with the traditional landowning class (although this was more so for the financial than for the industrial wing); the maintenance of many aspects of the traditional landowning culture has been a feature of British life. In Germany where the traditional hierarchy not only remained in place but also was strengthened by German unification, the emergent bourgeoisie did not integrate with the traditional landowning class, but its integration into society was mediated principally through the state (see Chapter 6). Thus in the United States, France, and Britain, the bourgeoisie has been at the same time both socially integrated and transformative; in Germany, its entry did change the social and value structure of the country, and it did gain a place in the social hierarchy, but it was never integrated with established class groups and therefore its presence continued to be a source of tension within the system as a whole.

Notes

1. For an excellent survey of the situation in Europe, see Fernand Braudel, *Civilization and Capitalism 15th–18th Century. Volume II. The Wheels of Commerce* (London, Fontana Press, 1982).
2. Charles Post, "The American Road to Capitalism", *New Left Review* 133, May–June 1982, pp. 30–51, citing Marx's Capital III, pp. 334–335. For an argument about the rural roots of capitalism in America, see A. Kulikoff, "The Transition to Capitalism in Rural America", *William and Mary Quarterly* 46, 1, 1989, pp. 120–144. For a review of some of the literature, see M. Merrill, "Putting Capitalism in its Place: A Recent Review of the Literature", *William and Mary Quarterly* 52, 2, 1995, pp. 315–326.
3. For a discussion of the theory, see Sheilagh C. Ogilvie & Markus Cerman (eds), *European Proto-industrialization* (Cambridge, Cambridge University Press, 1996). On England, see Pat Hudson, "Proto-industrialization in England", Ogilvie & Cerman, pp. 49–66. For studies of individual sectors of the British economy during the period 1540–1640, see J.W. Gough, *The Rise of the Entrepreneur* (London, B.T. Batsford Ltd, 1969). Also Richard Grassby, *The Business Community of Seventeenth-Century England* (Cambridge, Cambridge University Press, 1995). For an argument that this was a form of capitalism based on merchant capital, see Pauline Gregg, *A Social and Economic History of Britain 1760–1965* (London, George G. Harrop & Co., 1965), pp. 36–40. Also see Maxine Berg, "Small Producer Capitalism in Eighteenth-Century England", *Business History* 35, 1, January 1993, pp. 17–39. On France and Germany, see Pierre Deyon, "Proto-industrialization in France", Ogilvie & Cerman, pp. 38–48 and Sheilah C. Ogilvie, "Proto-industrialization in Germany", Ogilvie & Cerman, pp. 118–136.
4. For a contrasting argument which emphasises the importance of a national market, see Ellen Meiksins Wood, *The Pristine Culture of Capitalism. A Historical Essay on Old Regimes and Modern States* (London, Verso, 1991), ch. 6. For an argument that Marx did not argue that capitalist enterprises could grow gradually from the putting out system, see Paul Sweezy, "The Debate on the Transition. A Critique", *The Transition from Feudalism to Capitalism* (London, New Left Books, 1976), p. 54.
5. For example, L. Davis, "The New England Textile Mills and the Capital Markets: A Study in Industrial Borrowing", *Journal of Economic History* xx, 1, 1960, 1–30.

in *American Economic History* (London, Edward Elgar, 1969). For a similar focus on merchants, see Olivier Zunz, *Making America Corporate 1870–1920* (Chicago, University of Chicago Press, 1990), pp. 13–14.

6. For example, Louis M. Hacker, *The Triumph of American Capitalism. The Development of Forces in American History to the Beginning of the Twentieth Century* (New York, McGraw Hill, 1947), pp. 257–266; and Herbert Gutman, "The Reality of the Rags to Riches 'Myth': The Case of Patterson, New Jersey Locomotive, Iron and Machinery Manufacturers, 1830–90", Herbert G. Gutman, *Work, Culture and Society in Industrializing America: Essays in American Working Class and Social History* (New York, Knopf, 1977), pp. 211–233.

7. Post (Agrarian Road to Capitalism), p. 47.

8. Francois Crouzet, *The First Industrialists. The Problem of Origins* (Cambridge, Cambridge University Press, 1985), p. 19.

9. Crouzet (First Industrialists), p. 36.

10. For an argument that entrepreneurs tended to come from the upper reaches of society, see David J. Jeremy, "Anatomy of the British Business Elite, 1860–1980", *Business History* XXVI, 1 March 1984, pp. 3–23. For the conclusion that the chief executives of leading British railways came mainly from upper middle and upper class origins, see Terence R. Gourvish, "A British Business Elite: The Chief Executive Managers of the Railway Industry, 1850–1922", *Business History Review* 47, 3, Autumn 1973, pp. 289–316. These arguments relate to a later period than that discussed above.

11. Charles More, *The Industrial Age. Economy and Society in Britain 1750–1985* (London, Longman, 1989), p. 81.

12. Theodore Koditschek, *Class Formation and Urban Industrial Society. Bradford 1750–1850* (Cambridge, Cambridge University Press, 1990), p. 172. For the view that in the cotton industry, most were "men of modest or moderate capital", see Katrina Honeyman, *Origins of Enterprise: Business Leadership in the Industrial Revolution* (Manchester, Manchester University Press, 1982), p. 81.

13. T.S. Ashton, *The Industrial Revolution 1760–1830* (London, Oxford University Press, 1948), p. 16. Court has said "that the capitalist entrepreneurs were not a class or an homogenous group in the society of their day; that many variations of education and family upbringing and religion and social position and individual personality were to be found among them; that they were representative of the nation, as much as of a class or a social group." W.H.B. Court, *A Concise Economic History of Britain From 1750 to Recent Times* (Cambridge, Cambridge University Press, 1964), p. 88.

14. P.L. Payne, *British Entrepreneurship in the Nineteenth Century* (Basingstoke, Macmillan, 1974), pp. 28–29.

15. Mansel G. Blackford, *The Rise of Modern Business in Great Britain, the United States and Japan* (Chapel Hill, University of North Carolina Press, 1998), p. 71.

16. Although younger sons who were unable to inherit because of the laws of entail and primogeniture were often encouraged to enter profit-making activity, a practice which was instrumental in keeping the aristocracy much more open to social mobility than its counterparts on the continent. Harold Perkin, *The Origins of Modern English Society* (London, Routledge & Kegan Paul, 1969), pp. 60–61.

17. The adoption of improved techniques and the search for non-agricultural supplementation reflects the need to innovate to stay afloat in the competitive market environment that had emerged in post-restoration England.

18. P.L. Cottrell, *Industrial Finance 1830–1914: The Finance and Organization of English Manufacturing Industry* (London, Methuen, 1980), p. 12.

19. For example, see the discussion in David Spring, "English Landowners and Nineteenth Century Industrialism", J.T. Ward & R.G. Wilson (eds), *Land and Industry. The Landed Estate and the Industrial Revolution* (Newton Abbott, David & Charles, 1971), pp. 18–38. Other chapters in this volume provide a series of case studies. For a study of one estate, see Eric Richards, "The Industrial Face of a Great Estate: Trenthan and Lilleshall, 1780–1860", *Economic History Review* XXVII, 1974, pp. 414–430. For a general discussion of the position of the landed nobility, see David Cannadine, "The Making of the British Upper Classes", David Cannadine, *Aspects of Aristocracy: Grandeur and Decline in Modern Britain* (Harmondsworth, Penguin, 1995), pp. 9–36. For an argument about the possibility that funds from this sector played an important role in financing the industrial revolution, see M.W. Flinn, *Origins of the Industrial Revolution* (London, Longman, 1966), p. 47.

20. For a good discussion of the tasks confronting the early entrepreneurs, see Peter Mathias, *The First Industrial Nation: An Economic History of Britain 1700–1914* (London, Methuen, 1969), pp. 151–165.

21. Martin J. Wiener, *English Culture and the Decline of the Industrial Spirit 1850–1980* (Harmondsworth, Penguin, 1985), p. 8. The limited nature of the business activities of the gentry is suggested by the review of the business interests of the gentry in the Parliament of 1841–47. While it is not clear that these people were representative of the broader gentry as a whole, the figures are suggestive. Only some 14% of these people could be classed as businessmen (i.e. those for whom business took up a major part of their time) while a further 22% had minor connections with business. W.O. Aydelotte, "The Business Interests of the Gentry in the Parliament of 1841–47", G.Kitson Clark, *The Making of Victorian England* (London, Methuen, 1965), pp. 290–305, esp. p. 305.

22. Christophe Charle, *A Social History of France in the Nineteenth Century* (Oxford, Berg, 1994), pp. 77–79.

23. Charle (Social History), p. 190. Also see the argument in Hartmut Kaelble, "Long-Term Changes in the Recruitment of the Business Elite: Germany Compared to the US, Great Britain, and France Since the Industrial Revolution", *Journal of Social History* 13, 3, Spring 1980, pp. 404–423.

24. Pamela M. Pilbeam, *The Middle Classes in Europe 1789–1914: France, Germany, Italy and Russia* (Basingstoke, Macmillan, 1990), p. 31. Also see David D. Bien, "Manufacturing Nobles: The Chancelleries in France to 1789", *The Journal of Modern History* 61, 3, September 1989, pp. 445–485.

25. Jurgen Kocka, *Industrial Culture and Bourgeois Society: Business, Labor, Bureaucracy in Modern Germany* (New York, Berghahn Books, 1999), p. 78. At the same time, about one third inherited the business they operated, showing that that there was much greater family continuity than there was institutional continuity.

26. H. Berghoff & R. Moller, "Tired Pioneers and Dynamic Newcomers? A Comparative Essay on English and German Entrepreneurial History, 1870–1914", *Economic*

History Review XLVII, 2, 1994, pp. 267–268. The corresponding figures they cite for Britain are 74.6% for upper middle class, 6.8% for aristocracy, and 5.3% for working class. Also see Pilbeam (Middle Classes), pp. 30–31, who argues that aristocratic involvement in industry varied greatly by region, with the Junkers little involved.

27. For example, see Toni Pierenkemper, "Entrepreneurs in Heavy Industry: Upper Silesia and the Westphalian Ruhr Region, 1852–1913", *Business History Review* LIII, 1, Spring 1979, pp. 65–78, where it is argued that entrepreneurs came mainly from those who were involved in traditional occupations—official, military officer, farmer, innkeeper, clergyman, doctor, lawyer, notary, pharmacist and architect, with craft and technical background of only limited salience.

28. Youssef Cassis, "Businessmen and the Bourgeoisie in Western Europe", Jurgen Kocka & Allen Mitchell (eds), *Bourgeois Society in Nineteenth Century Europe* (Providence, Berg Publishers, 1993), p. 111.

29. Matthew Josephson, *The Robber Barons: The Great American Capitalists, 1861–1901* (London, Eyre & Spottiswood, 1962, originally published 1934), pp. 32–33.

30. Gutman (The Reality of the Rags to Riches 'Myth').

31. Frances W. Gregory & Irene D. Neu, "The American Industrial Elite in the 1870's: Their Social Origins", William E. Miller (ed), *Men in Business: Essays in the History of Entrepreneurship* (Cambridge [Mass], Harvard University Press, 1952), pp. 193–211.

32. John N. Ingham, "Rags to Riches Revisited: The Effect of City Size and Related Factors on the Recruitment of Business Leaders", *Journal of American History* 63, 3, December 1976, pp. 615–637, esp. p. 616.

33. Although Ingham does show that in Wheeling 20% were the sons of working men; however, 63% were the sons of businessmen and 15% of professionals.

34. Jocelyn Maynard Ghent & Frederic Cople Jaher, "The Chicago Business Elite: 1830–1930. A Collective Biography", *Business History Review* L, 3, Autumn 1976, pp. 288–328, esp. pp. 301–303.

35. On the privileged origins of the wealthy, regardless of where that wealth came from, see Frederic Cople Jaher, "The Gilded Elite: American Multimillionaires, 1865 to the Present", W.D. Rubinstein (ed), *Wealth and the Wealthy in the Modern World* (London, Croom Helm, 1980), pp. 189–276.

36. For a discussion of the medieval antecedents of this, see Richard H. Britnell, *The Commercialisation of English Society, 1000–1500* (Manchester, Manchester University Press, 1996).

37. This view sees the leases whereby land was held as being dependent upon capacity to pay the rent, which in turn stimulated productivity and the need to sell one's produce. The essential dynamic was therefore economic exploitation, in contrast to France where it was primarily political and administrative, through the struggle for expanding tax powers and the drive of landowners and 'bourgeois' elements to consolidate their wealth and position through jobs in the state. Ellen Meiksins Wood, *The Origin of Capitalism* (New York, Monthly Review Press, 1999), esp. ch. 4.

38. According to Woolf, the aristocratic willingness to engage in risk-taking and innovation was due to the "diffusive influence of a commercially and industrially minded environment which originated outside the ranks of the nobility" and

which was much stronger in England than on the Continent. Stuart Woolf, "The Aristocracy in Transition. A Continental Comparison", *Economic History Review* XXIII, 3, 1970, p. 527.

39. For an excellent comparative survey of the landed upper classes in Britain, Germany and Russia over the nineteenth century, see Dominic Lieven, *The Aristocracy in Europe 1815–1914* (Basingstoke, Macmillan, 1992).

40. See the discussion in Cannadine (Aspects), pp. 29–32.

41. Such incomes had been stimulated by the Napoleonic Wars, but their position deteriorated with the flow of US grain following the end of the Civil War. Barrington Moore Jr, *Social Origins of Dictatorship and Democracy. Lord and Peasant in the Making of the Modern World* (Harmondsworth, Penguin, 1969), p. 38.

42. For example, the Portlands, Bedfords and Grosvenors in London, Norfolks in Sheffield, Calthorpes in Birmingham, and Ramsdens in Huddersfield. Eric J. Evans, *The Forging of the Modern State: Early Industrial Britain 1783–1870* (London, Longman, 1983), p. 168. Also see Lieven (Aristocracy), pp. 109–111; David Cannadine (ed), *Patricians, Power and Politics in Nineteenth-Century Towns* (Leicester, Leicester University Press, 1982); and David Cannadine, *Lords and Landlords: The Aristocracy and the Towns, 1774–1967* (Leicester, Leicester University Press, 1980).

43. Lawrence Stone, *The Crisis of the Aristocracy 1558–1641* (London, Oxford University Press, 1967), ch. 7.

44. Lieven (Aristocracy), pp. 119–122.

45. Moore (Social Origins), p. 30. Moore also argues that while the connection between the bourgeoisie and the landed aristocracy in the eighteenth century was "very close", it was even closer under Elizabeth and the early Stuarts. Moore (Social Origins), p. 23.

46. Werner Mosse, "Nobility and Bourgeoisie in Nineteenth Century Europe: A Comparative View", Jurgen Kocka & Allan Mitchell (eds), *Bourgeois Society in Nineteenth Century Europe* (Oxford, Berg, 1993), pp. 79–84. He argues that such contacts were more difficult in Germany because of the preservation of a stronger caste spirit among the Prussian nobility, while in France contacts were rare.

47. For the argument that most land purchases emanated not from "narrowly economic calculations of yield, profit and security" but from "the social aspirations of the purchasers for landed status or country retirement" or from established owners seeking to consolidate their holdings, see F.M.L. Thompson, "Business and Landed Elites in the Nineteenth Century", F.M.L. Thompson (ed), *Landowners, Capitalists, and Entrepreneurs: Essays for Sir John Habakkuk* (Oxford, Clarendon Press, 1994), p. 140. According to Lieven (Aristocracy), p. 26, there was little purchase of such estates by non-aristocrats in the first half of the nineteenth century.

48. For the discussion of this in a regional centre, see Koditschek (Class Formation), pp. 135–153.

49. Lieven (Aristocracy), p. 57.

50. For example, compare the views of W.D. Rubinstein, "New Men of Wealth and the Purchase of Land in Nineteenth Century Britain", *Past and Present* 92, August 1991, pp. 125–147 (and his other works listed below) and F.M.L. Thompson, "Life after Death: How Successful Nineteenth-Century Businessmen Disposed of their Fortunes", *Economic History Review* 2nd series, XLIII, 1, 1990, pp. 40–61; Thompson

(Business and Landed Elites), pp. 139–140; and F.M.L. Thompson, "English landed society in the nineteenth century", Pat Thane, Geoffrey Crossick & Roderick Floud (eds), *The Power of the Past: Essays for Eric Hobsbawm* (Cambridge, Cambridge University Press, 1984), pp. 209–211. Also see Tom Nicholas, "Businessmen and Landownership in the Late Nineteenth Century", *Economic History Review* 52, 1, 1999, pp. 27–44; Julia A. Smith, "Land Ownership and Social Change in Late Nineteenth Century Britain", *Economic History Review* 53, 4, 2000, pp. 767–776; Tom Nicholas, "Businessmen and Land Ownership in the Late Nineteenth Century Revisited", *Economic History Review* 53, 4, 2000, pp. 777–782.

51. Rubinstein argues that the scale of land acquisition was much lower than generally thought (only 10–20% of wealthy businessmen set themselves up as landed gentlemen), and that therefore the "aristocracy was increasingly becoming a caste-like and socially isolated group, distancing itself from, and distanced from, the newer business magnates, who found it nearly impossible in many cases to gain full acceptance into the inner circle of high landed society". W.D. Rubinstein, *Men of Property. The Very Wealthy in Britain Since the Industrial Revolution* (London, Croom Helm, 1981), p. 219.

52. P.J. Cain & G. Hopkins, "Gentlemanly Capitalism and British Expansion Overseas. I. The Old Colonial System, 1688–1850", *Economic History Review* 2nd series, XXXIX, 4, 1986, pp. 501–525. For a vigorous critique of the notion of "gentlemanly capitalism", see Geoffrey Ingham, "British Capitalism: Empire, Merchants and Decline", *Social History* 20, 3, October 1995, pp. 339–354.

53. For the view that this was an important factor in Britain's declining levels of economic performance during the twentieth century [in Wiener's terms, "the radical ideal of active capital was submerged in the conservative ideal of passive property", Wiener (English Culture), p. 14], see Paul Warwick, "Did Britain Change? An Inquiry into the Causes of National Decline", *Journal of Contemporary History* 20, 1, January 1985, pp. 99–133; Geoffrey Ingham, *Capitalism Divided? The City and Industry in British Social Development* (Basingstoke, Macmillan, 1984); Cain & Hopkins (Gentlemanly Capitalism); M.J. Daunton, ' "Gentlemanly Capitalism" and British Industry, 1820–1914', *Past and Present* 122, February 1989, pp. 119–158; Perry Anderson, "Origins of the Present Crisis", *New Left Review* 23, January-February 1964, pp. 26–53, and for a reworking of this, Perry Anderson, "The Figures of Descent", *New Left Review* 161, January-February 1987, pp. 20–77; E.P. Thompson, "The Peculiarities of the English", E.P. Thompson, *The Poverty of Theory & other essays* (London, Merlin Press, 1978), pp. 35–91 (originally published in *Socialist Register*, 1965). For one review of the debate, see Wood (Pristine Culture) who argues that far from being anti-capitalist in their effect and orientation, the political, social and value structures of British society may have been perfectly suited to the emergence of the first case of capitalist industrialisation. Also Colin Mooers, *The Making of Bourgeois Europe: Absolutism, Revolution, and the Rise of Capitalism in England, France and Germany* (London, Verso, 1991), pp. 171–176. For a review of Ingham's book, see Colin Leys, "The Formation of British Capital", *New Left Review* 160, November-December 1986, pp. 114–120.

54. Perkin (Origins), p. 435. The gradual erosion of the economic base of the traditional landed ruling interests facilitated this sort of shift of capital.

55. Between 1885 and 1911 they constituted 32% of all new peers compared with 10.3% between 1837 and 1885; 21.4% of those created after 1885 came from non-noble and non-gentry backgrounds compared with 2.9% prior to 1885. Ralph E. Pumphrey, "The Introduction of Industrialists into the British Peerage: A Study in Adaptation of a Social Institution", *American Historical Review* LXV, 1, October 1959, p. 9. Lieven (Aristocracy), p. 56 dates this from the 1870s. For similar figures ('some 70' out of '200 or so'), see Harold Perkin, *The Rise of Professional Society: England Since 1880* (London, Routledge, 2002), p. 43. He argues that the Conservatives ennobled more of the big corporate bankers, brewers and newspaper owners, the liberals more from traditional manufacturing. According to Rubinstein, levels of businessman ennoblement were lower than elsewhere; he cites 15 out of 60 (25%) new non-royal peerages going to businessmen in the 1880s, 22 of 65 (33%) in 1890–99, 27 of 66 (41%) in 1900–09, and 45 of 117 (39%) in 1910–19. W.D. Rubinstein, *Capitalism, Culture and Decline in Britain 1750–1990* (London, Routledge, 1990), p. 161.
56. Moore (Social Origins), p. 36.
57. Perkin (Rise), p. 27.
58. For one discussion, see Forrest Capie & Michael Collins, "Industrial Lending by English Commercial Banks, 1860s-1914: Why Did Banks Refuse Loans?", *Business History* 38, 1, January 1996, pp. 26–44.
59. W.D. Rubinstein, *Elites and the Wealthy in Modern British History. Essays in Social and Economic History* (Brighton, Harvester, 1987), pp. 39–40. On the link between family firms in merchant banking, conservatism and investment in land, see Stanley Chapman, *The Rise of Merchant Banking* (London, Allen & Unwin, 1984), p. 176. Also on the increasing linkages between City, aristocracy and state in the late nineteenth century, see Ingham (Capitalism Divided?), pp. 136–137. However Daunton ("Gentlemanly Capitalism"), pp. 146–151 sees the City as not homogenous but comprising a variety of interests which came into conflict over policy. Also see Chapter 6.
60. Jose Harris & Pat Thane, "British and European Bankers 1880–1914: an 'aristocratic bourgeoisie'?", Thane, Crossick & Floud (The Power of the Past), p. 226.
61. For a discussion of this, see Y. Cassis, "Bankers in English Society in the Late Nineteenth Century", *Economic History Review* 38, 2, 1985 pp. 210–229.
62. W.D. Rubinstein, *Wealth and Inequality in Britain* (London, Faber & Faber, 1986), p. 58.
63. Cassis (Bankers), p. 227.
64. There is a debate about which of these fractions of the bourgeoisie was best able to generate personal wealth. Rubinstein argues that the dominance of industry in the first half of the nineteenth century was supplanted by that of commerce and finance later in the century, while Nicholas argues that there is no evidence to show that industrial wealth was inferior to that of finance and commerce. Rubinstein (Capitalism, Culture and Decline); Tom Nicholas, "Wealth Making in Nineteenth- and Early Twentieth Century Britain: Industry v. Commerce and Finance", *Business History* 41, 1, January 1999, pp. 16–36; W.D. Rubinstein, "Wealth Making in the Late Nineteenth and Early Twentieth Centuries: A Response", *Business History* 42, 2, April 2000, pp. 141–154; Tom

Nicholas, "Wealth Making in the Nineteenth and Early Twentieth Century: The Rubinstein Hypothesis Revisited", *Business History* 42, 2, April 2000, pp. 155–168. For an earlier exchange, see Hartmut Berghoff, "British Businessmen as Wealth-Holders 1870–1914: A Closer Look", *Business History* 33, 2, April 1991, pp. 222–240; W.D. Rubinstein, "British Businessmen as Wealth-Holders 1870–1914: A Response", *Business History* 34, 2, April 1992, pp. 69–81; Hartmut Berghoff, "A Reply to W.D. Rubinstein's Response", *Business History* 34, 2, April 1992, pp. 82–85.

65. See Richard Trainor, "The Gentrification of Victorian and Edwardian Industrialists", A.L. Beier, David Cannadine & James Rosenheim (eds), *The First Modern Society: Essays in English History in Honour of Lawrence Stone* (Cambridge, Cambridge University Press, 1989).

66. For example, Jean Lhomme, *La grande bourgeoisie au pouvoir (1830–1880); essai sur l'histoire sociale de la France* (Paris, Presses universitaires de France,1960). Also see the discussion in Roger Magraw, *France 1815–1914. The Bourgeois Century* (Oxford, Fontana, 1983), ch. 2.

67. For the argument that post-revolutionary France was run by a cohesive bourgeoisie with organised business as its leading element, see L. O'Boyle, "The Middle Class in Western Europe, 1815–1848", *American Historical Review* LXXI, April 1966, pp. 826–845. The notion of "200 families" seems to have come from the fact that the statutes of the Bank of France said that only the 200 largest shareholders could attend its meetings and therefore control the bank, disenfranchising all other shareholders. Theodore Zeldin, *France 1848–1945. Volume 1. Ambition, Love and Politics* (Oxford, Clarendon Press, 1973), p. 53.

68. Alfred Cobban, *The Social Interpretation of the French Revolution* (Cambridge, Cambridge University Press, 1965).

69. Cobban (Social Interpretation), pp. 55–65.

70. For example, see Georges Lefebvre, *The French Revolution from Its Origins to 1793* (London, Routledge & Kegan Paul, 1962, trans. Elizabeth Moss Evanson) and *The French Revolution from 1793 to 1799* (London, Routledge & Kegan Paul, 1964, trans. John Hall Stewart and James Friguglietti). This is a translation of his classic *La Revolution Francaise* (Paris, Presses universitaires de France, 1957).

71. Cobban (Social Interpretation), p. 62.

72. Cobban (Social Interpretation), pp. 70–71.

73. Cobban (Social Interpretation), p. 86.

74. For an argument about an erosion of the nobles' local sense of pre-eminence, see Robert Forster, "The Survival of the Nobility During the French Revolution", Douglas Johnson (ed), *French Society and the Revolution* (Cambridge, Cambridge University Press, 1976), pp. 132–147.

75. Napoleon I had looked down on businessmen and sought to exclude them from positions of prestige, but the system he ushered in relied on the bourgeois class more generally for its staffing and social basis. Cobban (Social Interpretation), p. 85.

76. For this sort of formulation of aristocratic distinctiveness and its destruction, see R. Magraw, "The Making of Post-Revolutionary France", *The Historical Journal* 31, 4, 1988, p. 991.

77. Roger Price, *A Social History of Nineteenth Century France* (London, Hutchinson, 1987), p. 98.
78. R.D. Anderson, *France 1870–1914. Politics and Society* (London, Routledge & Kegan Paul, 1977), p. 36. On Gambetta, see J.P.T. Bury, *Gambetta and the Making of the Third Republic* (London, Longman, 1973).
79. Charle (Les Elites), p. 89.
80. Charle (Les Elites), pp. 152–168.
81. Price (Social History), p. 103.
82. Michael Mann, *The Sources of Social Power. Volume II. The Rise of Classes and Nation-States, 1760–1914* (Cambridge, Cambridge University Press, 1993), p. 173.
83. For example, Adeline Daumard, *Bourgeois de Paris au XIXe siecle* (Paris Flammarion, 1970) and Adeline Daumard, *Bourgeois et la Bourgeoisie en France depuis 1815* (Paris, Aubier, 1987).
84. On the clubs, see Guy P. Palmade, *French Capitalism in the Nineteenth Century* (Newton Abbott, David & Charles, 1972), p. 218 and their membership Charle (Les Elites), p. 394
85. Palmade (French Capitalism), pp. 167–168.
86. For an argument about the indistinct nature of the divisions between ancien regime nobility and bourgeoisie, see Colin Lucas, "Nobles, Bourgeois and the Origins of the French Revolution", Douglas Johnson (ed), *French Society and the Revolution* (Cambridge, Cambridge University Press, 1976), pp. 88–103.
87. See the discussion in Zeldin (France 1848–1945), p. 17.
88. The capacity to realise this fully was, however, quite limited. If we accept that the economic segment of the bourgeoisie ranged from a narrow elite of financiers and industrialists with national interests through prosperous traders to retailers, clerks and minor functionaries [Magraw (France 1815–1914), p. 53.], for most of these categories the purchase of a landed estate was a pipedream. Most industrialists did not belong to the social elite. Price (Social History), p. 130.
89. Palmade (French Capitalism), p. 165. For the argument that the English middle class was more 'bourgeois' than its French counterpart because there was less opportunity for its members to invest in land than in France, see Tom Kemp, *Economic Forces in French History* (London, Dennis Dobson, 1971), p. 110. For Price, "the purchase of land and a chateau continued to mark success in business". Price (Social History), p. 100.
90. Price (Social History), p. 103.
91. See Charle (Les Elites), p. 154. For the absence of a clear line between industrial capital and landed society, see Louis Bergeron, *Les Capitalistes en France, 1780–1914* (Paris, Gallimard, 1978), pp. 27–36. According to Anderson, by about 1900, "landed and industrial wealth were integrated with each other...the topmost strata of French society formed a cohesive and powerful social group." Anderson (France 1870–1914), p. 34.
92. Zeldin (France 1848–1945), p. 17.
93. Bankers and merchants constituted 37.7%, industrialists 10.3%, senior government officials 15.7% and members of the liberal professions 10.9%. Price (Social History), p. 106.
94. Zeldin (France 1848–1945), p. 405.

95. Moore suggests that the extent of the osmosis between landed and industrial interests in France may have been as extensive as in England. Moore (Social Origins), pp. 36 & 56. Also see Jurgen Kocka, "The Middle Classes in Europe", Kocka (Industrial Culture), pp. 236–238.

96. For the argument that the average entrepreneur remained a small businessman relying significantly on family banking and aiming to preserve rather than create wealth, see David Landes, "French Entrepreneurship and Industrial Growth in the Nineteenth Century", *Journal of Economic History* IX, 1, May, 1949, pp. 45–61 and David Landes, "French Business and the Businessman: A Social and Cultural Analysis", Edward Mead Earle (ed), *Modern France: Problems of the Third and Fourth Republics* (Princeton, Princeton University Press, 1951), pp. 334–353. Also in the same volume, John B. Christopher, "The Desiccation (sic) of the Bourgeois Spirit", pp. 44–57. For a discussion of the argument about low productivity levels and the nature of French development, see Magraw (France 1815–1914), pp. 55–62 & 231–234. On marriage patterns, see Palmade (French Capitalism), p. 165.

97. That the industry-finance distinction was not clear cut is reflected in the comments of one scholar that during the Orleanist period, although there was some tension between the financial and landed elite which controlled public office, and the embryonic bourgeoisie, this should not be exaggerated because many were simultaneously financiers and industrialists; he refers to "constant osmosis" between industry, finance, land and bureaucracy. Magraw (France 1815–1914), p. 53.

98. In 1871, 49% of the national labour force worked in agriculture and 29% in manufacturing. Mann II, p. 693.

99. Lieven (Aristocracy), pp. 75–76 & 81–88 emphasises regional differences in the nature, power, economic position, and profile of large landowners.

100. Lieven (Aristocracy), pp. 88–90.

101. Although Evans argues that Prussian landowners did become industrial entrepreneurs if the opportunity arose. Richard J. Evans, "The Myth of Germany's Missing Revolution", Richard J. Evans, *Rethinking German History: Nineteenth Century Germany and the Origins of the Third Reich* (London, Allen & Unwin, 1987), p. 109.

102. For example, see Ralf Dahrendorf, *Society and Democracy in Germany* (New York, W.W. Norton & Co., 1967); Eckart Kehr, *Economic Interest, Militarism, and Foreign Policy. Essays on German History* (Berkeley, University of California Press, 1977, trans. Greta Heinz); Moore (Social Origins).

103. A powerful manufacturing and commercial bourgeoisie emerged only in the second half of the nineteenth century, with the initial economic take off occurring in coal, iron and steel, engineering, and textiles in the 1850s and 1860s, followed by a second surge beginning in the 1890s and based on chemicals, optics, electrics, automobiles, shipping, insurance, and retailing. David Blackbourn, "The German bourgeoisie: An introduction", David Blackbourn & Richard J. Evans (eds), *The German Bourgeoisie: Essays on the Social History of the German Middle Class from the Late Eighteenth to the Early Twentieth Century* (London, Routledge, 1991), p. 6.

104. See in particular, David Blackbourn & Geoff Eley, *The Peculiarities of German History. Bourgeois Society and Politics in Nineteenth-Century Germany* (Oxford, Oxford University Press, 1984) and Thomas Ertman, "Liberalization and Democratization

in Nineteenth and Twentieth Century Germany in Comparative Perspective", Carl Lankowski (ed), *Breakdown, Breakup, Breakthrough. Germany's Difficult Passage to Modernity* (New York, Berghahn Books, 1999), pp. 34–50. Also Sheri E. Berman, "Modernization in Historical Perspective. The Case of Imperial Germany", *World Politics* 53, 1, April 2001, pp. 431–462.

105. Dolores L. Augustine, "Arriving in the Upper Class: The Wealthy Business Elite of Wilhelmine Germany", Blackbourn & Eley (Peculiarities), p. 54. According to Richard J. Evans, "Family and Class in the Hamburg Grand Bourgeoisie 1815–1914", Blackbourn & Evans (German Bourgeoisie), p. 121, there was a low level of business acquisition of landed estates.

106. Dolores L. Augustine-Perez, "Very Wealthy Businessmen in Imperial Germany", Youssef Cassis (ed), *Business Elites* (Aldershot, Edward Elgar, 1994), p. 599.

107. Augustine-Perez (Very Wealthy Businessmen), p. 615, fn.31.

108. Karin Kaudelka-Hanisch, "The Titled Businessman: Prussian Commercial Councillors in the Rhineland and Westphalia During the Nineteenth Century", Blackbourn & Evans (German Bourgeoisie), p. 104.

109. Dolores L. Augustine, "The Business Elites of Hamburg and Berlin", *Central European History* 24, 2, 1991, p. 134.

110. See Augustine-Perez (Very Wealthy Businessmen), p. 601.

111. On state honours, see Alastair Thompson, "Honours Uneven: Decorations, the State and Bourgeois Society in Imperial Germany", *Past and Present* 144, August 1994, pp. 171–205. For the increased bourgeois interest in acquiring the title "Commercial Councillor", see Kaudelka-Hanisch (The Titled Businessman), pp. 96 & 105–106.

112. Arno J. Mayer, *The Persistence of the Old Regime. Europe to the Great War* (London, Croom Helm, 1981), pp. 95–96.

113. Although Charles Maier argues that "business leaders had married into the aristocracies of the German states, and their kin comprised an important component of the civil service, which had developed into a noble-bourgeois aristocracy of office". Maier (Recasting Bourgeois Europe), p. 40.

114. The business elite in Rhineland-Westphalia is reported as being socially isolated. Augustine (Arriving in the Upper Class), p. 72. Regional variations in the situation of the bourgeoisie were considerable.

115. Augustine (Business Elites), pp. 138–146.

116. Augustine (Arriving in the Upper Class), p. 58.

117. For a study of Ballin, see Lamar Cecil, *Albert Ballin. Business and Politics in Imperial Germany, 1888–1918* (Princeton, Princeton University Press, 1967).

118. Cecil (Albert Ballin), p. 350.

119. Augustine-Perez (Very Wealthy Businessmen), p. 604.

120. Augustine (Business Elites), p. 137.

121. Cited in Evans (Family and Class), p. 117. For the general point, see Augustine-Perez (Very Wealthy Businessmen), p. 601, who claims that only 8.5% married into aristocratic families.

122. For the view that the extent of merging between industrial and landed elites may have been as great in Prussia as in England, see Moore (Social Origins), pp. 36–37. It is here that Moore is most explicit on the sonderweg, declaring that

in Prussia the industrialists adopted the habits and outlook of the aristocracy, in England vice versa. For closer links between French nobles and bourgeoisie than in Germany, see Hartmut Kaelble, "French Bourgeoisie and German Burgertum, 1870–1914", Kocka & Mitchell (Bourgeois Society), p. 284.

123. See Jurgen Kocka, "The Middle Classes in Europe", Kocka (Industrial Culture), pp. 236–238.

124. Evans (Myth), pp. 109–110. Evans prefers to consider the Junkers "as the landowning faction of the bourgeoisie by the late nineteenth century". p. 110. Between 1879 and 1885, more than 65% of Junker estates were reliant on industrial sources of income. John M. Hobson, *The Wealth of States. A Comparative Sociology of International Economic and Political Change* (Cambridge, Cambridge University Press, 1997), p. 61.

125. Geoff Eley, "Society and Politics in Bismarckian Germany", *German History* 15, 1, 1997, p. 116.

126. C.Wright Mills, *The Power Elite* (New York, Oxford University Press, 1959), p. 13.

127. This is based on Moore (Social Origins), p. 136.

128. On the lifestyles of the rich, see Alexis Gregory, *The Gilded Age. The Super-Rich of the Edwardian Era* (London, Cassell, 1993).

129. Youssef Cassis, "Financial Elites in Three European Centres: London, Paris, Berlin, 1880s-1930s", Cassis (Business Elites), pp. 413–414.

130. Just as we acknowledge distinctions between wealthy and less wealthy sections and industrial and financial sections of the bourgeoisie, we should also not assume that the bourgeoisie constituted a single, national community. Right through this period, there were clear regional communities in each of these countries. On France, see Michael S. Smith, "Thoughts on the Evolution of the French Capitalist Community in the XIXth Century", *Journal of European Economic History* 7, 1, Spring 1978, pp. 139–144.

131. This characterization can only be done in very abbreviated fashion. It summarises very baldly a vast subject.

3

The Making of a Social Class: The Post-Soviet Bourgeoisie

In Britain, France, Germany, and the United States, the origins of the new bourgeoisie lay in those sections of the existing class structure already involved in commercial, principally small-scale manufacturing, activity. This gave them access to skills and resources that were instrumental in the development of industrialism on a larger scale, and facilitated their entry into the existing social structure. However, in contrast to the cases in the West, the emergence of the Russian bourgeoisie was directly shaped by the state. Reflecting the immediate past when the state dominated economic production and when industry already constituted the chief sector of the economy, one path to the development of a new bourgeoisie was through the privatisation of state assets, or the transfer of existing productive capacity from state into private hands. This was a path that was found in none of the other countries under review. Another path was more similar to that in the West, the creation of new enterprises. However, this too generally relied for its success upon the ability to use state resources for private ends. Thus like in the West large sections of the new bourgeoisie came from among those already linked with economic activity, but the role of the state in Russia gave this process an inflection of its own. Similarly, the collapse of the earlier, Soviet, structure of status, position, and power made social integration of the new Russian bourgeoisie a very different process to that in the West.

The Emergence of the Russian Bourgeoisie[1]

The emergence of the new post-Soviet bourgeoisie differs from the classical paths of class emergence noted in Chapter 2 in one very important respect: it was not propelled by new methods of production, but by juridical changes in ownership provisions driven by the decline and collapse of the Soviet regime. While, as indicated below, this process was well in train by the time private property became legal, the stimulus for the emergence of the new class was the collapse of the notion of state ownership. The importance of this is reflected in the major location of origin of the new Russian business class, the Soviet politico-administrative structure. Official position in that structure has been crucial for large numbers of people to make the switch from Soviet bureaucrat to entrepreneur.

The role of official position in the generation of the new class has been widely noted. Sometimes it has been discussed in terms of elite reproduction versus elite circulation,[2] while others have emphasised the basic continuity of the elite.[3] Such studies have produced a variety of conclusions, in part because of the looseness of the categories they use and, in some cases, the lack of clarity (at least in the published version) about the methodology used to identify and locate individuals. For example, the notion of a business elite is itself unclear, with many students failing to define clearly the boundaries of this group. Furthermore, most focus upon the nomenklatura as the concept used to denote occupation of official Soviet position, but given the range and varying levels of positions within the Soviet system that were part of the nomenklatura, without modification this is a blunt instrument of analysis. However, by acknowledging the differences that exist within the nomenklatura, a more nuanced analysis is possible. Ol'ga Kryshtanovskaia[4] is one who has used the notion of nomenklatura in this way.

She suggests that, overall, 61% of the business elite came from the nomenklatura. Of that group, 13.1% came from the party nomenklatura, 37.7% from the Komsomol (Young Communist League, YCL) nomenklatura, 3.3% from the Soviet (legislative) nomenklatura, 37.7% from the economic nomenklatura, and 8.2% from other parts (e.g. cultural, scientific) of the nomenklatura.[5] These figures suggest a high level of continuity between post-Soviet businessmen in 1993 and both the Soviet economic establishment (principally enterprise managers and high-level bureaucrats in the economic ministries and organisations) and people who were able to take advantage of the favourable circumstances in the Komsomol in the latter part of the 1980s–early 1990s (see below). The importance of work in the Soviet economic establishment is also attested by other studies. According to one study, prior to becoming entrepreneurs, 26.2% were leaders of Soviet enterprises and 41.9% headed sub-divisions within enterprises.[6] Another study calculated that in 1994, 56% of industrialists were former cadres of the Soviet or Russian ministries and state committees, and 26% were directors of major industrial structures.[7]

Szelenyi and Szelenyi[8] provide some comparative figures between the economic and political elites and the elite in general in 1993 (Table 3.1).

These figures show a high level of continuity (and higher levels of continuity in Russia than in either Poland or Hungary which the authors also

Table 3.1. Class origins of 1993 elite (%)

Class position in 1988	Economic elite	Political elite	Elite (total)
Nomenklatura member	52.6	51.0	51.0
Other official	33.4	29.4	33.4
Non-elite	14.0	19.6	15.6

compare), with slightly higher levels in the economic elite than in either the political elite or the broader elite more generally. They suggest that just over half of the economic elite had nomenklatura backgrounds, while 86% had official backgrounds.

The importance of work in the Soviet economic establishment is also evident in the analysis produced by Hanley et al.[9] This analysis distinguishes between the state economic elite (those running state firms) and the private economic elite in 1993, and gives a more differentiated view of occupational position during the late Soviet period (Table 3.2).

These figures suggest that 66.6% of the state economic elite and 37.6% of the private economic elite came from the nomenklatura, with by far the largest proportion of these coming from the economic nomenklatura; if we include economic managers and other officials, these figures rise to 92.1% and 79.6%, respectively. Although it is not clear how these figures relate to those in the table, Hanley et al. also argue that '78.3% of the directors of state firms in 1993 were either enterprise directors or their deputies in 1988', while in the new state elite 27.8% were either directors or deputies of state enterprises in 1988; if enterprise directors who entered state office in Gorbachev's first years are included, this figure would rise to 37.3%.[10] The continuity between the Soviet economic establishment is clearly much greater for the 1993 state economic than the private economic elite, although in the latter it remains substantial. Despite uncertainty about the occupational categories (e.g. most economic managers would have been on the economic nomenklatura) the

Table 3.2. Soviet occupation of state and private economic elites (%)

Occupation in 1988	State economic elite 1993	Private economic elite 1993
Party nomenklatura	5.2	5.5
State nomenklatura	3.4	2.9
Economic nomenklatura	58.0	28.1
Cultural nomenklatura	—	1.1
Economic managers	20.3	24.5
Other officials	5.2	17.5
Professionals	3.1	10.6
Other occupations	2.7	5.8
Out of labour force	2.1	4.0

level of continuity between the Soviet and post-Soviet economic elite remains significant.

Such elite reproduction is the main conclusion of Golovachev et al.[11] as well. They find that 40% of the leaders of major state enterprises had fathers who had been in the Soviet nomenklatura,[12] while 70% of the 1993 economic elite had been leaders of enterprises or held high posts in ministries or departments in 1988.[13] Most of those who had been able to make the transition from Soviet officialdom to post-Soviet business had come from second rung or deputy positions in the Soviet hierarchy. The 1988 occupations of the post-Soviet business elite were said to be the following: party elite, 6%; state elite, 1%; administration of state economy, 9%; culture and science, 1%; leaders and deputies of state enterprises, 45%; party/state bureaucrats, 11%; specialists, 16%; and others, 11%.[14] Despite the difficulty in marrying up all of these figures, they suggest a significant level of continuity between Soviet officialdom, especially economic officials at the enterprise level, and new businessmen.[15]

The high levels of Soviet officialdom in the new bourgeoisie are also evident in the work of David Lane and Cameron Ross.[16] They see five major sectors of the post-Soviet economic elite: banking and finance, oil and gas, industry and building, other entrepreneurs (retail, services, communications), and politico-economic executives (heads of associations of industrialists, members of the stock exchange, and government representatives on company boards). These different sectors exhibit different patterns of involvement in the Soviet politico-administrative structure (Table 3.3).

The proportion of each of the post-Soviet sectoral elites who held responsible positions (i.e. were officials) is very high relative to the proportion that was simply party members in all sectors except Industry and building and Other. Furthermore, this understates the proportion who were officials because it does not include those holding responsible positions in official bureaucracies other than the party, Komsomol and the economic apparat, such as the non-economic ministries of the state. But Lane and Ross' work also highlights the importance of the type of work that the future

Table 3.3. Party and Komsomol membership per business sector (%)

Sector	Communist Party member	Holding responsible post in CP/YCL/economic apparat
Banking and finance	35	25
Politico-economic executives	51	37
Industry and building	41	16
Oil and gas	32	20
Other	54	12

Source: Lane & Ross (Transition), p. 173.

Table 3.4. Soviet occupation of origin by business sector (%)

Soviet occupation	Banking	Industry/building	Oil/gas	Executives	Other	Total
Industrial executive[a]	11	46	54	19	17	27
Economic official	21	—	4	11	2	10
Post in CP/YCL apparat	8	2	6	9	2	6
Govt. post	10	5	8	11	2	8
Entrepreneur	5	17	7	1	13	8
Professional	14	4	9	10	18	12
Researcher	9	12	—	22	12	10
Student	14	5	7	9	11	10

[a] Including factory director.

Source: Lane & Ross (Transition), p. 177.

bourgeoisie was involved in during the Soviet period. They have looked at the occupations held from 1981 to 1988 from which these people came (Table 3.4).

The most striking thing about these figures is that they show the relatively high level of carry over of Soviet industrial executives into the two sectors most like what they were doing in Soviet times, Industry and building and Oil and gas. A similar point can be made, although more weakly, concerning Soviet economic officials and the Banking and finance sector. However, those in the Banking and finance sector tended to have much longer careers and at higher levels of the Soviet politico-administrative structure than those in Industry and building and Oil and gas, who had significantly less experience in the Soviet hierarchy.[17]

Despite the difficulty in making all of these figures comparable, what they suggest is that a substantial proportion of post-Soviet businessmen gained their start through the positions they occupied in the Soviet politico-administrative structure and the advantages that accordingly accrued to them. Businessmen did not generally come from the working class or peasantry, with most coming from white collar occupations within the Soviet politico-administrative structure. Furthermore, a significant proportion of new businessmen came from the corresponding general sector of life (i.e. economic activity) in the Soviet period.[18] Those involved in the management of the Soviet economy seem to have been significantly more likely to go into business than those in other areas of administration. This point applies with particular force to those who filled managerial roles at the enterprise level. This in part reflects the nature of privatisation and the associated opportunities (see below), but it probably also shows the importance of experience in the economic sector as a factor encouraging people to seek out a life in business when the future of the established administrative hierarchies began to look problematic. It is also consistent with views about the bifurcation of Soviet officialdom into political and economic wings.

The emergence of businessmen from the state structures has been conceptualised in a number of different ways. According to David Lane and Cameron Ross,[19] an 'ascendant acquisition class' took advantage of the push for radical economic reform under Gorbachev to seek power, which they gained in the post-Soviet period. They argue that under socialism, there were two organising principles, administrative and market. The former was the basis of the administrative class and the latter the acquisition class. The latter possessed marketable skills while the former had administrative position. It was those with marketable skills, which essentially meant higher education and intelligentsia origins, that were the ascendant class, and it is this class which was strengthened as a result of the Gorbachev reforms, while the administrative class was weakened. Indeed, Lane suggests[20] that this latent acquisition class had been kept in check by the administrative class prior to Gorbachev, but that he had used the intelligentsia to undermine state socialism ideologically in 1988–89, thereby encouraging many in 'ambiguous class positions' to shift their support in favour of the acquisition class and capitalism. An alternative view of this is to be found in the work of David Kotz and Fred Weir.[21] Citing a survey by Judith Kullberg[22] that showed high-level elite support for capitalism in 1991, Kotz and Weir argue that increasingly within Soviet officialdom, individuals came to recognise that their best interests economically were no longer bound up with defence of the existing administrative command system, but lay with a radical shift towards capitalism. As a result, sections of the party–state elite began to support the pro-capitalist political coalition that had formed around Boris Yeltsin. These businessmen, argue Kotz and Weir, came predominantly from different parts of the party–state structure at different times: from the Komsomol in 1987–89, and from the industrial and banking sectors in 1989–91. This shift in support away from the politico-administrative structure in the direction of capitalism and personal profit began in 1987, before the system was clearly doomed, and therefore was instrumental in the fall of communism, rather than these people deserting the system because of its demise. Ol'ga Kryshtanovskaia[23] argued that the Soviet nomenklatura comprised two groups, the partocrats who were party and Komsomol functionaries, and the technocrats who were economic managers, cabinet ministers, and enterprise directors. During perestroika these were transformed into a political and an economic elite respectively, and she argues that the post-Soviet political elite came mainly from former party and Soviet officialdom while the economic elite came from Komsomol officials and economic managers. For the ex-prime minister, Yegor Gaidar,[24] a 'bureaucratic' market of 'quasi-private property' began to develop in the post-Stalin period, reflected in the way in which bureaucratic position gave individuals control over state property. In the Gorbachev period (1985–91), these processes of the extension of control over state property and the acquisition of profits from their operation came to the surface and 'open nomenklatura privatization' began. For economist Vitaly Naishul,[25] the officials who had been involved in the exercise of control over state resources increasingly sought to escape the control of the command-administrative system and aspired to open ownership of the property they controlled; a 'significant part of the bureaucracy aspired to convert itself into a bourgeoisie'.[26] Shmatko[27] pointed to this as a 'new class' bearing some similarities to the concept developed by Djilas.

These sorts of analyses have at their heart the view that within the Soviet politico-administrative structure, there were many officials who aspired to transform the practical control they exercised over state resources into personal ownership. We do not know how extensive such sentiments were,[28] nor how strong they were at different stages of the regime's life. For Gaidar and Naishul, as noted above, this was essentially a post-Stalin phenomenon, with its significant strengthening in the last five years of the regime's life. Another view places it in the 1960s–80s when the imperatives of survival for enterprise directors and those in responsible positions in the economy demanded that they interact and negotiate with one another outside the parameters of the plan. In this way they generated a new sense of collective interest that superseded the essentials of the planning process and propelled them into a new, semi-market, context.[29] However, it is clear that this practice of controlling state institutions and appropriating state resources for personal gain was characteristic of the Soviet system from its earliest years. Formally, the nomenklatura personnel system, whereby all leading posts were filled by nomination from above in a strictly graded hierarchy,[30] had attached to it a strict hierarchy of advantage defining what sorts of privileges were to be available to officials at the different levels. In this way, the official administrative structure had built into it a clear association between official rank and differential access to the resources of the state. Informally, the institution of 'family groups' was common at lower levels of the Soviet structure from the early 1920s.[31] These were alliances of local officials who combined together both to exercise better control over their regions and the institutions within them and to protect themselves against potential threats from officials at higher levels. The members of such groups used the control they enjoyed not only to promote the development of their particular regions but also to buttress their own lifestyles. The consequent privileges they enjoyed were of particular importance given the deficit economy within which the vast bulk of the populace existed throughout much of the life of the Soviet system. However, it was not until the Brezhnev era (1964–82) when central controls upon lower level officialdom were relaxed that the wealth and resources accumulated by officials expanded, with the private use of public resources effectively sanctioned by the centre providing individuals remained subservient to the central leadership group and their wealth was not displayed flamboyantly. But within this tradition of the private utilisation of public resources, there were some evident limits. The first was that the privileges gained from position could not be inherited by one's heirs. There was a strict prohibition on the passing on of one's official position to a son or daughter (although this may have been coming under pressure in the late-Brezhnev period), with the result that the source of generating wealth and privilege was not inheritable. Of course some of the material goods acquired as a result of office-holding could be passed on and the advantages of a privileged upbringing could ensure that children would be able to gain their own access to sources of power and privilege, but with office non-transferable, the means of the generation of wealth were also not transferable. Furthermore, given that access to wealth and privilege depended upon office, and incumbency depended upon higher level appointment and continuing support, there were no guarantees of continued access; this could be taken away at the whim of higher level officials. Moreover, wealth accumulated in this way could also be taken away and, within the context of the official prohibition on corruption, could also lead to arrest. This means that the administrative determination of access to wealth, resources, and privilege within the Soviet system retained a significant degree of personal uncertainty.

Given this tradition of the private use of public facilities for personal gain, notwithstanding its limits, it should not be surprising that many Soviet officials were interested in consolidating their personal control over such facilities in order to increase their capacity to generate privilege and wealth. Whether they saw themselves as an ascendant bourgeoisie or a potential alternative capitalist elite is immaterial, they were on the lookout for opportunities to consolidate their privileges. The prospect of transforming public control into private ownership, of privatising state assets in a formal sense, was not a real one for most of the Soviet period. However, with the changes introduced by Mikhail Gorbachev and his supporters in the latter half of the 1980s, this prospect suddenly became real. The most important changes in this regard were[32]

1. Abolition of the monopoly on foreign trade formerly enjoyed by the Ministry of Foreign Trade.[33] This was adopted in August 1986, to come into effect on 1 January 1987. However, it was not until January 1988, with the re-organisation of the state's international trade bureaucracy,[34] that enterprises and other organisations gained the right to become directly involved in foreign trade.

2. A Law on Joint Ventures was adopted in January 1987.[35] This provided for foreign investors to have a 49% share with the majority in Soviet hands. In October 1988, this was revised to allow majority foreign shareholding,[36] and in October 1990, Gorbachev issued a decree authorising the full foreign ownership of Soviet enterprises.[37]

3. The Law on Individual Labour Activity adopted in November 1986 to take effect on 1 May 1987.[38] This enabled individuals to open a variety of businesses, from restaurants to small consumer goods factories, repair services, private lessons, taxi services and a range of other services. The hiring of labour was prohibited, so only groups of family members living under one roof were able to work in such businesses, and they could be run only in the time that employees legitimately had off from their principal place of employment. These were essentially to be part-time businesses.

4. The beginning of radical economic reform was in 1987, when at the plenum of the Central Committee of the Communist Party, a programme was adopted involving partial dismantling of central economic control and of price subsidies.[39] The shift away from central direction was to be combined with greater room for lower level initiative and activity. Although in retrospect, the measures involved in this programme were modest, they did signal that the leadership was intent on more than merely tinkering with the system, an intention justified by Gorbachev's recognition that the economy was in a 'pre-crisis' situation. This was followed by a number of laws seeking to put the June 1987 programme into effect.

5. The Law on the State Enterprise (Association), which was due to come into effect on 1 January 1988.[40] This law provided for the abolition of precise targets and allocations of resources from above (while retaining general control figures relating to production levels and more specific figures on mandatory enterprise contributions to the state budget), enabling individual enterprises to engage in wholesale trade with each other and to set their own prices. Enterprises were to be self-financing. The law also made provision for the establishment of cooperatives under (*pri*) a state enterprise, and for some powers of election of enterprise managers by the workers. In August 1989, such enterprises were given specific approval to deal with foreign firms.[41] This law, in theory, substantially expanded the autonomy of state enterprises. They were no longer under the control of the central state ministries, but were broadly able to function as independent units. They could organise their supplies through trade with other enterprises, set their own production levels, and establish their own prices, except when they were filling state orders. Although in practice, many enterprise managers did not make the most of the opportunities stemming from this law, preferring to remain within the established planned system that purported to offer security of supplies and sales, and enterprise independence was still restricted by the need to meet compulsory state orders assigned by ministries,[42] it did open up legal room for entrepreneurial activity. By 1990, many

enterprise managers were effectively the de facto owners of those enterprises.[43]

6. The Law on Cooperatives of May 1988[44] which legalised small and medium-sized businesses and enabled them to set their own prices, wages, and production levels (unless fulfilling state orders or using state-supplied materials). They could be involved in foreign trade and retain much of the hard currency thereby generated, and could form joint ventures with foreign partners. Although the cooperatives were not in an official sense private businesses, for the first time since the end of the 1920s non-state economic activity was legally possible in all walks of life.

7. A law on leasing was introduced in November 1989[45] which was to encourage leasing in all areas of the economy and enabled workers to buy out an enterprise they had leased from the state with a guarantee against subsequent expropriation.

8. A new property law was introduced in March 1990[46] which gave 'citizens' property the same status as state and cooperative property, and, among other things, permitted private business while still prohibiting the employment of non-family labour.

9. In August 1990, a Soviet law 'Measures to Create and Develop Small Enterprises' gave a new legal status to small enterprises created inside state enterprises.[47]

10. The 'Law on Enterprises and Entrepreneurial Activity' adopted in December 1990 by the Russian Supreme Soviet allowed private businesses, including limited partnerships, joint stock companies, general partnerships, and sole partnerships within Russia.

11. A 'Law on Destatisation and Privatisation' was adopted on 1 July 1991.[48] This declared that the restructuring of state enterprises could proceed along the lines of leasing, collective enterprises, cooperatives, and joint stock companies, and provided for the redemption of leased state property by the lessee and for the sale of enterprises by competitive bid or auction.

Despite these measures, in practice there were still significant barriers to the exercise of individual initiative on a wide scale. For example, concerning the Law on the State Enterprise, although state enterprises were no longer to be subject to state controls, ministries often issued state orders for production, which had the practical effect of central directives; contracting parties lacked the independence envisaged in the Law; and rather than being able to keep their profits, enterprises lost much of this to their supervising ministries.[49] More generally, tax laws were often structured in such a way as to inhibit the exercise of new initiative under these laws. Furthermore, many of these measures were generally viewed with significant suspicion. There was widespread concern that such measures would increase the cost of living and lead to shortages, fears that were realised in practice,[50] and there was a common view that the cooperatives were simply means of laundering money; the latter concern was behind later measures to limit cooperative activity, including a law on speculation.[51] However, by the end of the 1980s, the continuing deterioration of the economy and the radicalisation of the reform programme in general since mid-1988, led to a reconceptualisation of the sort of economic system required. Reformers increasingly began to speak of a 'market' economy, and although there was significant variation in what they seemed to mean by this, it did mark the conceptual shift from central planning to a system in which individual initiative and private ownership were to play a larger role in economic life; large-scale privatisation was a central component of the various reform programmes advanced in the late 1980s. Following a burst of activity including the discussion of various plans for a shift to a market economy, in October 1990 guidelines for the transition to a market economy were introduced.[52]

The range of measures sketched above did not constitute a comprehensive framework making for the introduction of a market economy, or even for a systematic modification of the command economy along market lines. They constituted individual pieces of legislation designed to achieve particular aims rather than to implement an overall vision of what a post-command economy might look like. Many of those things that would have been essential for the emergence of a stable and soundly based private economy were absent. There was no system of property rights or legally codified structures of ownership, and therefore no clear mechanism for the transfer of property between owners. There was no means for obtaining credit, at least in the amounts necessary for commercial operations. There was no system of exchanges that would allow trade in commodities. Many prices remained set by the state. The currency remained non-convertible. There was little in the way of knowledge of advanced business practices, including the sorts of accounting procedures that underpin modern business in the West. None of the measures introduced by Gorbachev and his supporters addressed these issues or established a sound basis for the development of a market economy. But while those measures did not establish a market economy, they did create pathways for small numbers of enterprising individuals to engage in economic activities of a new type. Restricted and operating under difficulties,[53] new types of economic organisation began to emerge in Soviet society, and with them the basis of the new class.

The emergence of a class of Russian businessmen occurred through three main overlapping phases of activity:

1. Komsomol and party establishment of commercial entities, often in the form of cooperatives and joint ventures. The Komsomol played a leading role in 1987–89. According to a 1994 study,[54] 33% of the business elite got their start at this time through the Komsomol or the party.

2. 'Spontaneous privatisation' as commercial, banking and financial institutions were transformed, either in whole or in part, 1988–92. This is when members of the state economic nomenklatura entered private business activities; as ministries, holdings, associations, enterprises, and concerns were transformed into joint stock companies, enterprise directors were drawn into market activity.

3. Mass privatisation through the voucher scheme, 1992–94.

Establishment of Commercial Entities

Crucial for the shaping of the emergent bourgeoisie were not just the formal legislative measures of the Gorbachev administration, but changes to the modus operandi throughout much of the official party–state structure. Central here were changes made in the Komsomol. It may be that the changes that were made and that were to result in the so-called 'Komsomol economy'[55] were motivated by a pre-existing desire to establish a mechanism of shifting public property into private hands, but it is probable that the real source of them was the economic difficulties the Komsomol was beginning to experience in the second half of the 1980s. This was a result not only of the general economic difficulties experienced in Soviet society at this time but also of the fact that with the decline in popular commitment to Soviet institutions that was such a feature of the last part of this decade, membership levels in the Komsomol were falling. As a result, the organisation received fewer membership dues, and since this was a major part of its revenue, this had potentially dire consequences for the life of the institution. This stimulated the search for other sources of income, including the shift into business activities.[56]

The initial measure in this direction was a decision by the Central Committee of the Communist Party of the Soviet Union (CC CPSU) of 25 July 1986 that approved a proposal from the Komsomol to establish a network of scientific and technical centres which were to function for the benefit of the Komsomol's members, to operate on commercial principles, and through agreements with enterprises to provide services that were not otherwise available.[57] An All-Union Coordinating Council of Centres of Scientific and Technical Creativity of Youth (TsNTTM) was established in April 1987, and by the end of that year individual centres (NTTMs) were established widely. In 1988, their scope was expanded considerably: they could turn non-cash funds into cash, including hard currency, become involved in the manufacture of consumer goods, establish economic relations with foreign entities, set their own prices for the goods they imported, and they did not have to pay customs duties.[58] At the same time, during 1987 and 1988, the Komsomol's central organs delegated to subordinate levels control over their own income and expenditure.[59] This meant that local organs of the Komsomol were effectively financially independent of the centre and could decide to do whatever they liked with the funds they had without approval from either higher Komsomol organs or from party bodies. This liberation of local Komsomol officials from financial oversight added to the creation of the NTTMs and the expansion in their competence gave the opportunity and the means for such officials to use the funds of the organisation to pursue commercial activities,[60] and this is just what many of them did. Officials used Komsomol funds to invest in new commercial ventures, including cafes, video bars, discos, and travel bureaux.[61] They used the capacity to transfer funds between cash and credit accounts, a facility awarded only to them, to underwrite new commercial ventures, like Bank Menatep.[62] Even the CC of the Komsomol was engaged in this practice. From 1988, officials began to shift CC assets into a wide range of new commercial ventures which, by 1990, employed hundreds of former CC staff. Komsomol involvement in the banking sector was especially prominent: Menatep has been noted above, but also important was Finistbank which the CC created in 1988 and between then and 1990 shifted 750 million rubles into it; by 1990 it was the second largest commercial bank in the USSR.[63] This shift of assets took place at all levels as, in Solnick's words, 'committees began investing assets in the rapidly growing network of commercial banks or venture funds, and many gorkom and obkom officials began careers in finance with assets that once belonged to Komsomol committees'.[64] The flow of funds accelerated from early 1990. The range of Komsomol-sponsored businesses was very extensive; one official estimated that by mid-1991, 20% of private businesses in Moscow were linked to the Komsomol.[65]

Similar sorts of measures occurred in the Communist Party. In 1987 the party sponsored and funded to the tune of 12 million rubles the first Soviet-American joint venture, Dialog.[66] This showed the way to further party sponsorship of a range of ventures, some funded at the CC level and others by regional party bodies. Following the February 1990 CC plenum, there were instructions from the party leadership to invest party money in commercial structures.[67] The first private, party-funded bank emerged in June 1990, receiving more than 580 million rubles over the following eight months.[68] A Politburo resolution of August 1990 authorised the creation of several new commercial ventures, including a consulting firm to provide foreign brokerage services and a bank to look after the party's hard currency reserves and investments overseas.[69] In October 1990, party organisations, which like the Komsomol gained formal control over their own budgets, were called upon to become involved in commercial enterprises as a means of dealing with the party's financial crisis.[70] In June 1991, another Politburo resolution authorised the transfer of 600 million rubles to commercial organisations and banks, principally to seed investment in economic activity.[71] According to one report, by 1991 the party had established some 100 joint ventures and coops 'ranging from hotels to trading companies to security companies staffed by ex-KGB generals'.[72] The party became a major source of funds and resources for members seeking to enter private economic activity, especially towards the end of its life as the ruling party; according to one observer,[73] more than 600 enterprises were started with communist party funds, while another has said that the CPSU established 1,453 joint enterprises and companies with a combined capital of 14 billion rubles.[74]

Spontaneous Privatisation

The succession of laws noted above, the changing practices of major institutional structures like the party and Komsomol, the continuing process of radicalisation of the course of economic reform, and the growing conflict of sovereignty between central and republican authorities created an environment within which issues of property rights became increasingly problematic. Building upon the intrinsic uncertainty within the Soviet property structure—did property actually belong to the people or the state?—this situation facilitated attempts to transform collective, Soviet, property into personal possession. In the words of two students of this process, the new business forms that emerged during perestroika, joint ventures, cooperatives and joint stock companies, provided 'a quasi-legal means for managers of state enterprises to appropriate state property for their own use'.[75] This was clearly true, as is shown below, but it only captures part of the process of the emergence of a private economy. Private (or at least, non-state) enterprises emerged not only as a result of the appropriation of state property but through the establishment of new enterprises, not only enterprise managers were involved in appropriation, and some of the forms of property legalised through legislation in practice actually preceded that legislation; the first joint stock companies emerged in late 1986 and early 1987 as employees of state enterprises formed them as a means of generating more capital for the enterprise.[76]

The first sphere where non-state activity became evident on the streets of the capital was the retail sphere. There was, during late perestroika, a mushrooming of small kiosks on the streets selling a range of goods, including many small consumer items imported from abroad. Such kiosks seem to have been part of networks, offering the same broad range of goods for similar prices, and often reliant upon supplies brought into the country illegally. Rumours abounded of the connection between such networks and criminal organisations, but there is little firm evidence on this one way or another. More important was the emergence of the cooperative sector. Sometimes these were based on existing Soviet enterprises, but often they were developed independently.[77] They emerged principally in the services sector: domestic services, restaurants, catering, repair work, and similar pursuits,[78] although much of what many of them produced was sold to state organisations and enterprises, reflecting the fact that many coops were created within existing enterprises (see below). Many, especially in the catering sector, were failed state enterprises. By January 1990, there were estimated to be 193,100 coops in the Soviet Union employing some 4.9 million people.[79]

Cooperatives were often the first step in the 'spontaneous privatisation' of an enterprise.[80] Managers, often in collaboration with workers,[81] would lease space and equipment from the enterprise[82] and convert part of the enterprise into a producers' cooperative. This enabled these coops to function independently from the central controls contained in the Law on Cooperatives while continuing to make use of the centralised supply system; they could also continue to exploit the financial, logistical, personal (chiefly in the way of political contacts) and political advantages enjoyed by the enterprise.[83] In the short term this could be advantageous for the enterprise as a whole: the autonomy of the cooperative meant that the inputs it used would not be included in the overall calculation of enterprise performance, while its cost structure was more flexible, including its profit generation capacity. The existence of the state parent enterprise alongside the leased entity created significant room for the manager to asset strip the state enterprise. He could formally lease the most productive part of the enterprise or the most modern and efficient technology to the autonomous entity, thereby enabling it to prosper while the parent enterprise continued to struggle. Under the Law on Leasing, the manager and workers could then purchase the leased entity, thereby transforming what had been state property into private hands. A similar process could occur from 1990 whereby state enterprises could be reorganised into open or closed (respectively stocks available to people outside the enterprise or only those who worked within the enterprise) joint stock companies on the decision of the employees and a state organ created for this purpose.[84] Often separate entities were established and assets simply transferred to them, either at no cost or at knockdown prices.[85] By 1991, 80% of coops had been established in state enterprises.[86]

Such 'spontaneous privatisation'[87] also occurred within state ministries and their agencies. If a ministry was abolished or combined with other ministries, enterprises operating under that ministry's supervision could, from 1989, form themselves into independent quasi-corporate entities, a practice often formalised by government decree.[88] Gazprom is an example of this. Similarly state ministries and agencies could turn themselves into independent corporations and concerns. For example, the USSR Ministry of Metallurgy was replaced by Roschermet (iron and steel) and Rostsvetmet (non-ferrous metallurgy), run respectively by the former minister and his deputy.[89] These ostensibly new entities usually retained the same building, furniture, and personnel as their official source organisations. This sort of transformation was common practice. Ministries became 'concerns', usually joint stock companies, often with the minister becoming a consultant to the new entity, the deputy minister becoming the president, and either the enterprises subordinate to the ministry or, in some cases, the senior management of the ministry becoming shareholders. In this way the property of the ministry was privatised by those who were formally responsible for running it in Soviet times.[90] Similarly Gossnab, the Soviet organ responsible for the supply of goods, was the basis upon which the first stock exchanges emerged.[91] Leading officials were thus able to use their positions to transfer state assets into their own pockets.

The origin of many of the banks is also to be found in formal state/party structures; according to one estimate by 1989 there were 224 new commercial and cooperative banks and by early 1991 more than 700, with about 40% founded by ministries or associations.[92] The genesis of such banks was twofold. First, the 1987 decision to break up the State Bank into five specialised banks, for agriculture (Agroprombank), foreign trade (Vneshekonombank), industry (Promstroibank), housing (Zhilsotsbank), and household savings (Sberbank). Except for Sberbank, all passed into private hands. Second, permission by the State Bank (Gosbank) for any organisation to create its own commercial bank, combined with a very low threshold: any organisation or group with start-up capital of 500,000 rubles could establish a cooperative bank or 5,000,000 rubles for a commercial bank.[93] Accordingly, many institutions established their own banks, often called 'pocket banks'.[94] Examples of such banks include Aeroflotbank (established by the Ministry of Aviation), Stankinbank (the State Supply Committee), AvtoVAZ-bank (AvtoVAZ automotive works), Finistbank (Komsomol), Profsoiuzbank (trade union organ), Mozbisnesbank (Moscow City Soviet), Menatep (Komsomol), Bank Rossiiu (Leningrad obkom of the CPSU), and Glavmosstroibank (Moscow gorkom of the CPSU).[95] Such banks were used to further the activities of their founders. For example, according to Hellman,[96] 'Ministries, enterprises and other powerful organizations continued to borrow money from the state banking sector at 0.5% interest rates which they reinvested in their own commercial banks that were lending at rates from 15 to 20%'. For ministries, such banks were also useful as a destination for the channelling of funds, which could then be used regardless of the dictates of the plan, as well as retaining any income thereby earned. Ministries, party organs, the Komsomol, trade unions, and other organisations shifted often significant amounts of resources into the commercial banks, using them to hide assets and launder money. According to one analysis in 1992, the party shifted 34.4 million rubles into the creation of the Kazakh Communist Party Bank, 1 billion rubles into Avtobank, 500 million into the USSR Trade Union Bank, 150 million into Tokobank, 500 million into Unikombank, 90 million into Glavmosstroibank, plus other cash movements.[97] These banks were established with start up funds gained from the institution sponsoring them, and most of those that survived soon shifted away from control by those institutions. Thus the initial banking sector was in large part a product of the machinations of middle-ranking bureaucrats in official Soviet structures; in the words of one scholar, banks resulted from manipulation by privileged insiders and were created 'from pieces of former state banks; from finance departments of enterprises; and with resources from Soviet state and party agencies, enterprises, and organizations'.[98]

Voucher Privatisation

'Spontaneous privatisation', or what Kryshtanovskaia has called the 'privatization of the state by the state',[99] marked the second stage of the privatisation process. It was followed by a third stage, voucher privatisation, beginning in 1992. The new programme was adopted in June 1992[100] and its aim was to transform medium-large state enterprises into open joint stock companies.[101] The principle was that the enterprises were to turn themselves into joint stock companies and issue shares that could be bought by those outside the enterprise.[102] With a view to enabling large sections of the populace to become owners of the new entities, the state distributed to all citizens a voucher with a nominal face value of 10,000 rubles; 148,000,000 vouchers were issued.[103] Such vouchers were distributed at the end of the year. Vouchers could be sold for cash, passed to a private investment fund to be invested on the owner's behalf, or used to buy shares in a company.[104] This proposal was designed by a small group around Yeltsin and Gaidar, with some input from Western experts, and sought to exclude the broader populace and sections within it from exercising any influence.[105] Chubais and those around him wanted to avoid passing ownership to the workers of the enterprise, so the method they chose for privatisation involved: 25% of non-voting shares were to go to the workers in the enterprise, who also could purchase a further 10% at 30% discount; managers could buy 5% of shares at full price; the remainder would go to individual citizens through public auction. Such a scheme seemed to ensure that control over the enterprise would be vested in external investors rather than the management or the workers. Accordingly the enterprise managers mobilised through their lobbies, especially the Russian Union of Industrialists and Entrepreneurs (RSPP) and its political arm Civic Union, and their support within the legislature[106] to pressure the government to change this approach.[107] Accordingly, and reluctantly, Chubais and his allies introduced two new options.[108] Option 2 allowed workers' collectives to acquire 51% of full voting shares using either their vouchers or the retained earnings of the firm, thereby enabling the workforce to retain control over the enterprise (by using the enterprise's own capital). A further 20% of the shares were to be retained by the state, with the remaining 29% to be sold at public auction. Option 3 was a form of management buyout when the management assumed control over an ailing enterprise through purchase of up to 40% of shares at low prices in exchange for a promise not to become bankrupt. The workforce in each enterprise was empowered to choose which of these options would be adopted. In addition to these options, some managers were able to negotiate directly with the government for particular modes of privatisation which usually benefited them personally,[109] while some firms (mainly in areas like the military, education, health, railway transport, and space exploration) were excluded from the privatisation process entirely.[110]

The first auction was held in December 1992, and by the time the programme had ended in the middle of 1994, according to official figures 15,052 large and medium-sized firms had been privatised.[111] In these cases of privatisation, the overwhelming majority was achieved by using Option 2; 73% of large enterprises chose Option 2, 25% Option 1, and the remainder Option 3.[112] Furthermore, the general proportion of shares sold through the voucher auctions was closer to 21% than it was to the specified 29%.[113] While formally Option 2 left ownership in the hands of the workforce at large, in practice in many cases effective ownership lay with the management.[114] In some cases this may have reflected the paternalistic traditions of the Soviet enterprise and the willingness of workers to trust the guidance of their managers, especially when the conditions were as confusing as they were. But also important was the ability of managers to manipulate both the situation and the workers to gain control of the company.[115] It was often the managers who organised the workers to band together to take up their shares and who then sought to prevent workers from selling those shares to outsiders. The share register was often kept centrally, under the manager's control,[116] and he would put all sorts of obstacles in the way of workers who sought to dispose of their shares; a common tactic was telling workers there was a notification period before any shares could be sold when no such period existed. In addition, when shares were held on the manager-controlled register, workers often had no proof of ownership of the shares. Sometimes workers were encouraged to invest in the company's voucher fund, then a front man would buy a packet of shares with the vouchers, leaving the workers with a share in the fund but not in the company. Managers could also discriminate against workers who intended selling, such as withholding pay[117] and even threatening to sack such workers.[118] Alternatively, many managers sought to purchase shares from their workers, a course of action that appeared attractive to many workers given the deteriorating economic situation. In many cases, workers sold their shares for considerably less than their market value, and often such managerial purchases were paid for from enterprise funds. In this way, managers gained personal control of the shares for no personal outlay. There were also cases of managers seeking to turn over their workforce in the belief that departing workers would not want to retain shares in an enterprise they no longer worked for. Another pattern was for workers and managers to enter an agreement whereby the workers left the manager to run the enterprise and the manager gave a commitment to maintain the employment of those workers. Managers were thus often able to increase their personal shareholding at the expense of their workers, and even where they could not gain legal property rights, they usually gained effective control.

Managers were also intent on excluding outside ownership, and therefore influence, from the enterprise. The initial means for outsiders to gain equity in a firm was through the share auctions, although there were usually never sufficient shares on offer to enable a bidder to gain a monopoly position. After the share auctions, the only way outsiders could increase their role in an enterprise was by expanding the number of shares they had under their control by purchasing from existing shareholders, and the enterprise workers were usually the single largest category of these.[119] However, managers sought to prevent this from happening. A number of strategies were adopted to achieve this: for example,[120] presentation of data which misled auditors and thereby presented a false picture of the company, exclusion of 'aliens' from shareholders' meetings by holding those meetings with no notice or in inaccessible locations, refusal to allow minority shareholders representation on the board,[121] manipulation of the voting rules, discrimination in the payment of returns to shareholders, redistribution of converted shares only among 'insiders', issuance of new shares only to insiders, revaluation of shares in a way that decreased outsider equity, shifting of assets between mother and daughter companies to dilute the holdings of foreigners, and transferral of resources into pocket banks and firms. In some cases, managers used the support of local authorities[122] to place practical barriers in the way of outsiders; for example, when the representatives of a prominent entrepreneur, Kakha Bendukidze, tried to visit the site of an enterprise he wished to increase his stake in, they were turned away from landing at the airport, arrested by the local police, refused accommodation and food, their telephone was cut off, and they were threatened with physical violence.[123] There were many cases of people standing at the factory gates at knock off time trying to buy the shares of individual workers being physically confronted by supporters of the managers. The measures noted above whereby managers dissuaded workers from selling their shares were of course also important. By attempting to exclude outsiders and either working with their workers or increasing their shareholdings at their expense, many managers were able to consolidate their control over the companies they ran. This was particularly the case given that the state tended to be a silent partner in those companies in which it retained a share.[124] However, we should not exaggerate the weakness of outside involvement in Russian enterprises; between 1995 and 1997, the share of outsiders grew from 31.7% to 45.3%.[125] Especially in those enterprises that were profitable, the original Red Directors were often displaced by outsiders. It is not, however, clear that such an increase in outsider shareholdings always represented an increase in external control; in 1996 outside shareholders were a majority in only 19.8% of companies,[126] and the purchase of shares did not guarantee the effective exercise of ownership rights.

Thus the programme of mass privatisation initially led overwhelmingly to control being gained by enterprise managements, principally the so-called 'Red Directors'. Even though some 41,000,000 Russians became shareholders,[127] in formal terms workforces owned most enterprises, external shareholding did grow over time, and some managers were sacked by their workforces or boards.[128] But privatisation was essentially a programme that passed ownership rights initially to insiders.

Official position was therefore a major source of the new entrepreneurs, with membership of the Soviet economic establishment being the principal location of this new group. Just as the socio-economic location of the nascent Western bourgeoisie provided the logic and gave them skills and resources relevant to the generation of large-scale industrialisation, so official position in the Soviet politico-administrative structure set up this new bourgeois class. By vesting control over public property and resources in their hands as officials, and by implementing permissive legislation, the state gave them the opportunity to transfer public property into private hands, and thereby to become an independent class. Position also gave them both inside knowledge and personal contacts which they could use to consolidate their new positions. Most came from middle to upper levels of the structure and were able to use their insider status to take advantage of the opportunities made possible by the decline and ultimate collapse of the Soviet state. This section of the emergent bourgeoisie was clearly state generated and state shaped. But there was also a part of the bourgeoisie that did not stem from the state.

Non-State Origins

According to one observer,[129] besides those who became rich on the basis of the redirection of state resources, there were two sources of businessmen in the financial sector. The first was those who owed their positions to their own personal circumstances, to wealth, or to personal or family connections, although in practice this often amounted to those who had been able to make use of the NTTM pathway discussed above. An example of this is said to be Konstantin Borovoi. The second was self-made men who do not seem to have made much use of personal contacts. Often they established cooperatives and bought up large quantities of investment vouchers. Examples cited are Uralmash chairman Kakha Bendukidze, banker Mikhail Yurev, and Boris Bere-zovsky. But these people did not spring from thin air; they were embedded in Soviet society. However, the ground from which an indigenous bourgeoisie could spring in post-Soviet Russia was both very different from that in the other countries and did not appear to be as promising. Since the ending of the New Economic Policy and the introduction of a centrally planned command economy at the end of the 1920s, private enterprise had been largely absent from Soviet life. All enterprises in agriculture, industry, trade, services, and finance were formally owned by the people and effectively run by the state. Unlike in Poland, for example, where agriculture remained largely in private hands, the state sector in the Soviet Union encapsulated virtually all aspects of economic life. It was not possible for citizens, legally, to start up private enterprises, so that there was no basis upon which a viable private sector legally could function. Households were able to possess some property that could be used to generate income, most importantly private agricultural plots but also limited numbers of livestock, automobiles, and housing, but resale was restricted and supply difficult. Although the Constitution did provide for individual labour activity and some people pursued this, they could not hire labour. There was therefore only limited room for independent enterprise.

While the dominance of the state sector was unquestioned, at the margins there was always some private activity. The legitimate form of this was the collective farm markets in the big cities. These markets, functioning since the 1930s, were where peasants were allowed to sell the produce from their private plots, and they constituted an important source of supply for urban inhabitants separate from the major state stores. In addition, there was the second economy or black market, private sector activity in which individuals sought to sell their produce or skills and thereby to supplement the basic supply levels provided by the state. A whole range of commercial activi-ties, from pure exchange and barter, trade in goods (often stolen from the workplace), through to the employment of private tradesmen (usually people moonlighting from their regular employment), was common in Soviet society. In the words of one of Gorbachev's economic advisers:

Self-employment, involving hundreds of thousands of people, became widespread on a clandestine level, usually as a second job in addition to work in a state organisation. Individual car repairs, private taxis and production of many goods in strong demand have become particularly widespread.... Since state organisations in commerce and the service sector have not met the demands of consumers, the practice of offering services illicitly using state property has become common. As an example, state drivers often work as private taxi drivers in their free time. Sales assistants with access to goods of which there is a shortage sell them under the counter for extra money. Private cars are repaired for fees paid directly to mechanics in state garages and the garages receive nothing.[130]

The official and the second economy were intertwined; for example, an enterprise manager could divert some of his production for sale in the second economy, using some of the proceeds to purchase resources that were needed but unavailable through the official economy. In this sense, much of the second economy was parasitical upon the bureaucratic–administrative structures of the Soviet state. The extent of such second economy activity cannot be precisely measured, but it became so widespread that during the last decades of the regime's life, some believed that this sort of activity was what actually kept the Soviet economy going and the people passive; it has been estimated that the second economy contributed as much as 25% of the Gross National Product (GNP), and 10% of personal income.[131]

Involvement in the second economy gave many Soviet citizens their first experience of being an entrepreneur.[132] Although such experiences were far from ideal in giving them a sense of how a market economy functioned, they did expose those citizens to the operation of market forces and provide them with some practical know-how about how to operate within such forces. It is not clear what proportion of Soviet citizens were active contributors to the second economy (as opposed to consumers of its products, a category which at one time or another would have included all citizens). It was obviously easier for some sections of the populace to participate than others; those who were employed in occupations which gave them access to scarce resources and those with particular sets of relevant skills were well placed in this regard. But even those with low-level skills could at times utilise them to provide some sort of service to other citizens and thereby increase their income, especially if they had access to state resources which they could siphon off for personal gain. When the restrictions on private activity began to slip during the perestroika period, those with experience of the black market constituted a significant reserve of potential independent entrepreneurs.

If activity in the grey zone represented by the Soviet second economy could be the birthplace of future entrepreneurs, so too could involvement in criminal activity. The scale of criminal operations rose during the last decades of Soviet rule, and exploded in the early years of the post-Soviet period. Involvement in this sort of activity could be a major source of the accumulation of both capital and resources which could be used to underwrite a new business enterprise, while the legal opportunities for establishing legitimate private businesses also created the possibility for the laundering of funds criminally obtained. In this sense, the development of a new legitimate category of 'businessman' enabled some who were engaged in earlier illegal activity to reinvent themselves as legitimate businessmen in the new Russia. Organised crime could also be important through its involvement in the operations of legitimate businesses. The expanded scope for organised crime following the fall of the Soviet Union was in part because of the explosion of new, private businesses beginning in the Gorbachev period, but it was also due to the sorts of conditions that new businesses faced. Security and certainty were lacking in the new post-Soviet conditions, and many had little faith in the state's judicial agencies as a means of bringing these about.[133] One way of seeking to acquire greater security was for businessmen to get the support of a major protection agency.[134] Such protection was called a 'krysha', or roof. There is disagreement over the extent of this practice. According to one scholar writing in the late 1990s, 'an estimated 70–80 per cent of businesses pay 10–20 per cent of their profits for a krysha—while those which do not have to spend on average 30–40 per cent of profits on other forms of protection',[135] while another cites a survey from 1996–97 claiming that 53% of entrepreneurs paid regularly for protection;[136] yet another source has said that 79% of entrepreneurs believed that the use and threat of use of force occurs but that personal experience was modest, while the transaction costs associated with business protection may have amounted to 10–15% of revenues.[137] Whatever the exact figure, it is clear that payment for protection was a significant cost to business at this time.

But possessing a krysha did not, from the early 1990s, necessarily simply involve protection against extortion and demands; organised criminal 'protection agencies' expanded their operations to offer business a range of other services, including[138]

1. assistance in finding and equipping premises;
2. a source of investment using dirty money, thereby effectively using a legitimate enterprise to launder ill-gotten gains;
3. a guarantee that transactions will be carried out; negotiations between businesses will be attended by each one's krysha, and each krysha will guarantee to the other that their partner will abide by the deal;
4. a means of settling business disputes, usually by force or the threat thereof;[139]
5. a means of collecting debts;
6. mediation with the state bureaucracy to obtain various permissions and licences, registration, tax exemption;
7. mediation with state agencies like the police, fire brigade, tax inspectors[140] and sanitary control services to get them either to harass and perhaps close down a competitor, and not to do the same to them.

When pure protection expands in this way, it becomes integral to business. According to Volkov, this gives rise to a stable pattern of development of relations between the business and the krysha that goes through three stages.[141] First, payment of tribute in return for protection, with the cost perhaps US$300–500 per month. Second, the krysha inserts a bookkeeper or auditor into the firm in order to supply information about the firm's transactions and their value, with the krysha receiving a fixed share of some 20–30% of the profits. Third, the krysha invests money into the enterprise, gains a seat on the board, and takes some 50% of the profit. In this way, criminal organisations could become part of the legitimate operation of business, perhaps using this to launder money or even to become transformed into legitimate operations themselves. According to one survey, by the end of 1998, organised crime controlled about half of all commercial banks, 60% of public and 40% of private businesses.[142] At one level, this can be seen as the criminalisation of business. But at another, and in a slightly longer time frame, it may be the means of domesticating the gangs and turning them into reputable business actors; some businessmen actually began their careers through involvement in criminal activity.

As this process implies, involvement in the activities of a firm can be quite lucrative for an organised criminal group, and as a result there was significant competition for such involvement. According to Ministry of Interior figures, the number of organised criminal groups grew from 952 in 1991 to 6,743 in 1996.[143] While it is not clear exactly what this means, these figures do suggest a significant expansion in the population of organised crime gangs and therefore in the potential number of kryshas active in the business world. And in the first half of the 1990s there was a high level of violent conflict between criminal gangs, including the assassination of leading businessmen. What this reflected in part was a struggle by these gangs for position in the business world, and the fact that it died down in the second half of the 1990s would suggest that a general equilibrium was reached. Thus while at one level the extent of criminal activity in business contributed to the prevailing sense of uncertainty within which business had to function, at another level criminal involvement could provide some stability and certainty for individual businessmen.

Criminal gangs were not the only source of a krysha. By the mid-late 1990s there were generically three types of 'protection agencies': criminal organisations, private security firms established under the law, and fragments of the state operating independently. Initially, many of the new entrepreneurs coming from within the state, especially if they controlled large concerns, turned to their state contacts to provide protection. Often this involved the mobilisation of the local police or militia forces, but sometimes it could also involve sections of the state at higher levels, including the FSB (the security apparatus and successor to the KGB), individual officers or sections of which usually operated in an unofficial capacity to provide protection. In contrast, the new entrepreneurs lacking ready contacts in the state, were forced to rely overwhelmingly on protection emanating from non-state sources, mainly the criminal gangs.[144] The role of criminal groups in this regard waned from the middle of the decade beside the expanded role of legalised private security firms (which is in part a reflection of the legalisation of such criminal organisations), activity by state actors, and the development of their own security services by large companies. But the initial difference between the sources of protection sought by state-based compared with new businessmen of more independent origin reflects the varying opportunities open to these different sections of the bourgeoisie.

The mobilisation of criminal organisations into protection and business was not unique to the Russian case. Wherever state capacity to ensure protection was weak, and especially where property rights were poorly defined, the involvement of private protection agencies was likely. Federico Varese has shown how late nineteenth century Sicily was characterised by late transition to a market economy, poor definition of property rights, increased demand for private protection, and a supply of people trained in the use of violence, all of which existed in Russia. In both places there was widespread criminal involvement in business, including the transformation of criminal action into legitimate business activity.[145] The Russia–Sicily parallel is suggestive, highlighting the importance of poorly defined property rights and weak state capacity to provide protection, but where the two cases diverge is in the much larger part played by the Russian state in both the disposition of property and the informal provision of security.

Those entrepreneurs who did not have official origins were therefore generally involved in autonomous economic activity before the Soviet regime ended. Many started from scratch, without inside connections and advantages.[146] By 1996, some 900,000 new small businesses had been established alongside those emerging from the privatisation process,[147] most being in the service and retail sectors. But most entrepreneurs during the first post-Soviet decade had state origins. Their positions, and the contacts they possessed, were crucial in enabling them to take advantage of the opportunities that arose from the decay of Soviet power. In this sense the state was an important determinant of both the contours of the new economic bourgeois class and the economic power it was able to wield. The state therefore played a much greater formative role in the emergence of the new class than in those Western cases analysed earlier. But as the Soviet period receded into the past and successive waves of people entered business activity, position in the Soviet structure became less important as a determinant of career trajectory. However, the Russian state continued to have a crucial influence on the way the new bourgeois class developed (see especially Chapter 7).

A New Social Hierarchy?

The situation confronting the emergent Russian bourgeoisie was very different from that of their counterparts in the other countries under review. In Britain, France, Germany, and the United States, there was an established class structure which was reasonably stable and into which the new class sought to gain entry. In Russia, this was not the case. Because of the absence of private property, the bases of social structure in that country were very different from those in the West, with particular importance residing in the politico-administrative structure and control over administrative resources. However, this structure was undermined by the collapse of the Soviet system and the replacement of the command economy by one based on market principles. This shift meant that the salience of administrative resources as the underpinning for social position was displaced by economic resources; what was important in determining both life chances and the style of life that one could lead was increasingly economic- rather than administrative-based, wealth rather than position. But what is important about this for current purposes is that this was a system in formation. With the old system both breaking down and discredited and the new one not yet established, there was no consolidated structure for the emergent class to break into. Rather the emergence of this class constituted a part of the development of the new structure of inequality in Russia. There was no equivalent of an established upper class based on land or of a state elite with high prestige that could block the entry of such economic parvenus. Thus rather than fitting into an existing social structure, the bourgeoisie could help to shape the new social structure substantially in its image with little opposition from firmly entrenched interests.

Similarly, the Russian context lacked an aristocratic (or equivalent) lifestyle which could play the part of model for the emergent bourgeoisie. Indeed, it was quite the reverse. The prevailing patterns of life that had characterised the Soviet elite, especially the privilege that was associated with the occupation of formal office, was now in general disrepute, at least among those who rejected the former Soviet system. However, the Russian bourgeoisie did have an example upon which they could model themselves, the Western bourgeoisie. In large measure, the emergent Russian class seems to have taken up much of the style of their Western counterparts. For the very wealthy businessmen, this means that they adopted a lifestyle that was in some respects the direct antithesis of that of the Soviet elite: instead of hiding their privilege behind the veils of administrative blandness, they positively flaunted it. Expensive cars, flashy clothes, construction of new and often gaudy houses and dachas,[148] conspicuous consumption, glamorous female companions, and holidays in the playgrounds of the rich and famous in the West created an image of the so-called 'new Russians' that contrasted sharply with the public persona of Soviet era elites. It also generated an image of a lifestyle which, despite widespread popular antagonism because of its contrast with the realities of economic hardship suffered by most people, in some ways set the standard for the new Russia. Thus, rather than aspiring to emulate aspects of the lifestyles of the former dominant class, the new bourgeoisie established the norm for others to aspire to, a norm that was in part copied from their counterparts in the West.

Institutions emerged to cater for this lifestyle. Expensive shops, casinos, restaurants, resorts, exclusive providers of goods and services, and sporting associations all sought to service this new class, for a price. Clubs also emerged in Russia, and although they do not act corporatively as instruments of business interests, they are the site where businessmen may gather to discuss issues and work out common positions. They are, therefore, important both for the immediate formulation of common positions by businessmen, and for the way in which they play a generative role in the growth of a general business-focused culture and assist in social integration. Apart from groups like Lions and Rotary, which have been established in various parts of Russia, more exclusive clubs developed in Moscow. These included Klub-93, Realists, VIP, Vzaimodeistvie, the Moscow Commercial Club, the 2015 Club, and the Logovaz Club, where the oligarchs (see below) used to meet.[149] Such institutions were also important for the generation of a sense of common identity, at least for those most wealthy who frequented them, and this was an identity which set the emergent class and its lifestyle apart from the general populace. The lifestyle that the rich have adopted, while it may not assimilate with that of the traditionally dominant group in Russia/Soviet Union, does shadow that enjoyed by their counterparts in the West.

But the rich businessmen, while maybe the most publicly prominent, are not the most numerous members of this emergent bourgeoisie. Small and medium-sized businessmen far outnumber the rich, and they too are taking part in the reshaping of Russian lifestyles. The shift away from the command economy and towards a market-based economy was accompanied by the growth of a sense of consumerism, at least in the large Russian cities. The supply of goods and services in the big cities expanded dramatically, and by early into the new millennium, they had become within the price range of large parts of the population. The growth of the consumer market, fuelled by the increased exposure to Western standards and styles of life, shaped both the public sphere of the collective consciousness and private aspirations. Although this has not embraced all citizens and not to the same degree,[150] the public culture has become one in which consumer preferences are prominent. The growth of retail advertising has been particularly important in this, as has the growth of retail outlets and the development of niche publications promoting a particular sort of lifestyle; *Domovoi* (Home Spirit), a glossy magazine concentrating on the home lifestyle of the rich, is a good instance of this. The major expansion of new housing areas, consisting principally of 'kottedzhy', is both a further sign of and a stimulant to this development. The promotion of such a consumerist lifestyle is consistent with the basic aim of much of the new bourgeoisie, not only the rich, and constitutes a good instance of the way in which the new class is shaping the society into which it has emerged.

As the emergent bourgeoisie projected many of the sorts of values that their counterparts in the West championed and that dominated in most Western societies—consumerism, limited state role in the economy, the primacy of market principles, and economic concerns above all else—they were part of the impetus which ensured that such values took a strong hold on Russian public life. While many have bemoaned the passing of the values that dominated during the Soviet period and their replacement by a more materialistic public culture, it is precisely this sort of culture that cements the place of the bourgeoisie in the new Russia. As the, in principle at least, generators of the goods upon which this materialistic culture is based, the emergent bourgeoisie is placed right at the heart of the new society and its value structure. The initial links between the bourgeoisie and state officials has consolidated this location. In this sense, rather than the bourgeoisie having to accommodate itself to another class' value culture, in the flux of ideas and values that accompanied the collapse of the USSR and the emergence of independent Russia, it has been able in part to shape society's public culture in its own image. It was, of course, substantially aided in this by the early dominance of reformist politicians around Yeltsin whose vigorous championing of notions of democracy, the market and capitalism helped to shape a public culture consistent with the economic activities of the economic bourgeoisie. In Russia, then, at least in the initial decade and a half of independence and in contrast to the Western cases, politicians were probably more important in articulating the new set of 'bourgeois values' than intellectuals. But it was the activity of the bourgeoisie, as in the West, that established the material underpinnings of this process, and it was therefore the prominent position they achieved that was thereby legitimated.

* * *

The main feature of the post-Soviet bourgeoisie, at least in its first wave, was the extensive role played by the state in its generation. The accumulation of capital and resources, manifested most importantly in privatisation, was directly linked to the state and the relationship with it possessed by members of the new class. Thus, although the Russian bourgeoisie shared with its Western counterparts an origin in the productive sector, it differed substantially in that many of its members had been engaged in the management of production rather than directly in production itself, and this had taken place within a state productive system rather than one of independent small-scale activity. The statist origins of a substantial part of the Russian bourgeoisie therefore clearly distinguishes it from its Western predecessors. There was a difference also in terms of integration into the social hierarchy. In Britain, France, and Germany, the emergent bourgeoisie sought affiliation, even assimilation, with the traditionally dominant class, substantially gaining this in the first two countries but not in Germany; in the United States, integration was largely present from the outset, reflecting the nature of the American social structure at the time. In contrast, in Russia, the emergent bourgeoisie was confronted with a situation in which the established social hierarchies based on the command economy had broken down. Patterns of social interaction and notions of prestige and hierarchy were in flux, so taking their lead from their contemporaries in the West, many of the most wealthy and powerful of the new bourgeoisie sought to create a lifestyle that matched their aspirations. Thus rather than seeking to fit into an existing structure, the Russian bourgeoisie has sought to create a new hierarchy in the context of the uncertainties of the post-Soviet period. Important in this is representation in the political system.

Notes

1. Among the numerous guides to businessmen, see I. Bunin et al., *Biznesmeny rossii. 40 istorii uspekha* (Moscow, OKO, 1994); *Vozrozhdenie elita rossiiskogo biznesa* (Moscow, Institut izucheniia reform, 1994); Anvar Amirov, *Naibolee vliiatel'nye predprinimateli rossii. Biograficheskii spravochnik* (Moscow, Panorama, 1996); Anvar Amirov, *Kto est' kto v bankovskoi sisteme rossii. Biograficheskii spravochnik* (Moscow, Panorama, 1996); Anvar Amirov & Vladimir Pribylovskii, *Rossiiskie biznesmeny i menedzhery. Biograficheskii spravochnik* (Moscow, Panorama, 1997); P. Kozlov, *Bankiry Rossii (Kto est' kto)* (Moscow, SPIK-Tsentr, 1999).

2. For example, Ivan Szelenyi & Szonja Szelenyi, "Circulation or Reproduction of Elites during the Postcommunist Transformation of Eastern Europe", *Theory and Society* 24, 5, 1995, pp. 615–638.

3. For example, Ol'ga Kryshtanovskaia, "Transformatsiia staroi nomenklatury v novuiu rossiiskuiu elitu", *Obshchestvennye nauki i sovremennost'* 1, 1995, pp. 51–65. There is a large literature that emphasises the continuity of communist elites generally. For example, Thomas C. Baylis, "Plus Ca Change? Transformation and Continuity Among East European Elites", *Communist and Post-Communist Studies* 27, 3, 1994, pp. 315–328; John Higley, Judith Kullberg & Jan Pakulski, "The Persistence of Postcommunist Elites", *Journal of Democracy* 7, 2, 1996, pp. 133–147; T.H. Rigby, "New Top Elites for Old in Russian Politics", *British Journal of Political Science* 29, 3, 1999, pp. 323–343; also see below. For one discussion of both theoretical and empirical issues, see M.I. Kodin, *Obshchestvo-politicheskie ob'edineniia i formirovanie politicheskoi elity v Rossii (1990-1997)* (Moscow, FSRSPN, 1998).

4. Kryshtanovskaia (Transformatsiia), p. 65. The same results are reported in Ol'ga Kryshtanovskaia, "Finansovaia oligarkhiia v Rossii", *Izvestiia* 10 January 1996. For different, lower, figures, see Olga Kryshtanovskaya & Stephen White, "The Rise of the Russian Business Elite", *Communist and Post-Communist Studies* 38, 3, September 2005, p. 301.

5. Nearly 50% of entrepreneurs' fathers were members of the communist party compared with 35% for non-entrepreneurs. Simeon Djankov, Gerard Roland, Edward

Miguel, Yingui Qian & Ekaterina Zhuravskaya, "Russian Entrepreneurs: Tell Me Who Your Friends and Family are...", The World Bank, *Beyond Transition* 16, 1, January-March 2005, p. 4.

6. Vad. Radaev, "Novye predprinimateli: sotsial'nyi portret", V.V. Radaev et al. (eds), *Stanovlenie novogo rossiiskogo predprinimatel'stva* (Moscow, RAN, Institut ekonomiki & Mezhdistsiplinarnyi akademicheskii tsentr sotsial'nykh nauk (Intertsentr), 1993), p. 69.

7. N.Iu. Lapina, *Formirovanie sovremennoi rossiiskoi elity (Problemy perekhodnogo perioda)* (Moscow, Rossiiskaia akademiia nauk, Institut nauchnoi informatsii po obshchestvennym naukam, 1995), p. 32.

8. Szelenyi & Szelenyi (Circulation or Reproduction), pp. 623–629.

9. Erik Hanley, Natasha Yershova & Richard Anderson, "Russia—Old Wine in a New Bottle? The Circulation and Reproduction of Russian Elites, 1983-1993", *Theory and Society* 24, 5, 1995, p. 657.

10. Hanley et al. (Russia), p. 659.

11. B.V. Golovachev, L.B. Kosova & L.A. Khakhulina, "Formirovanie praviashchei elity v Rossii", *Informatsionnyi biulletin' monitoringa*, November–December 1995, pp. 18–24 & January-February 1996, pp. 322–38.

12. Golovachev et al. (Formirovanie), p. 21.

13. Golovachev et al. (Formirovanie), p. 36.

14. Golovachev et al. (Formirovanie), p. 37.

15. Although the level of continuity is not as high in the survey by T.H. Rigby, with only 45.7% entering business from an official Soviet background, his work also shows the higher level of continuity in the economic than in other spheres of life. T.H. Rigby, "Russia's Business Elite", *Russian and Euro-Asian Bulletin* 8, 7, August–September 1999, pp. 1–9.

16. David Lane & Cameron Ross, *The Transition from Communism to Capitalism. Ruling Elites from Gorbachev to Yeltsin* (Basingstoke, Macmillan, 1999), ch. 9. Also see David Lane, "The Russian Oil Elite. Background and Outlook", David Lane (ed), *The Political Economy of Russian Oil* (Lanham, Rowman & Littlefield Pubs Inc., 1999), pp. 75–96.

17. Lane & Ross (Transition), pp. 172–174. The graph will be found on p. 179.

18. But not all of them. For example, Berezovsky was a research mathematician and Gusinsky worked in the theatre. David E. Hoffman, *The Oligarchs. Wealth and Power in the New Russia* (New York, Public Affairs, 2002), chs 6 & 7.

19. Lane & Ross, (Transition), chs 8 & 9, esp. pp. 163–164. This is also noted, briefly, in David Lane, *The Rise and Fall of State Socialism* (Cambridge, Polity Press, 1996).

20. Lane (Rise and Fall), pp. 164–172.

21. David Kotz with Fred Weir, *Revolution from Above. The demise of the Soviet system* (London, Routledge, 1997), esp. ch. 7.

22. Judith Kullberg, "The Ideological Roots of Elite Political Conflict in Post-Soviet Russia", *Europe-Asia Studies* 46, 6, 1994, pp. 929–953. The survey showed that in 1991, more than 75% of the sample of officials supported capitalism, although this was not a random sample.

23. Kryshtanovskaia (Finansovaia oligarkhiia).

24. Yegor Gaidar, *Gosudarstvo i evoliutsiia* (Moscow, Evraziia, 1995), pp. 107–108. He also argued that although they followed their instinct for property rather than a well-considered plan, the nomenklatura acted coherently to appropriate assets and legalise their property. Yegor Gaidar, "How Nomenklatura Privatized Its Power", *Russian Politics and Law* 34, 1 January–February 1996, p. 35.

25. Cited in Aleksandr Shubin, *Istoki perestroika 1978–1984gg* (Moscow, Institut etnologii i antropologii RAN, 1997), Vol.1, pp. 61–62.

26. Shubin (Istoki), p. 62.

27. N.A. Shmatko, "Stanovlenie rossiiskogo patronata i biurokraticheskii kapital", *Sotsiologicheskie issledovanie* 6, 1995, pp. 24–36.

28. For the view that party apparatchiki had no such "longing for private property", see Vladimir Shlapentokh, "The Soviet Union: A Normal Totalitarian Society", *The Journal of Communist Studies and Transition Politics* 15, 4, 1999, p. 11.

29. For a similar argument, see Lapina (Formirovanie), pp. 10–14.

30. On the nomenklatura as a personnel system, see Bohdan Harasymiw, *Political Elite Recruitment in the Soviet Union* (London, Macmillan, 1984). On the privileges, see M. Voslenskii, *Nomenklatura. Gospodstvuiushchii klass Sovetskogo Soiuza* (London, Overseas Publications Interchange Ltd, 1985).

31. See Graeme Gill, *The Origins of the Stalinist Political System* (Cambridge, Cambridge University Press, 1990). On their importance in post-Stalin times, see Graeme Gill & Roderic Pitty, *Power in the Party. The Organization of Power and Central-Republican Relations in the CPSU* (Basingstoke, Macmillan, 1997).

32. Many of these were subsequently revised and changed in some respects. For a good overview of the changes under Gorbachev, see Andrew Barnes, *Owning Russia. The Struggle Over Factories, Farms and Power* (Ithaca, Cornell University Press, 2006), ch. 3.

33. "O merakh po sovershenstvovaniiu upravleniia vneshneekonomicheskimi sviazi-ami. O merakh po sovershenstvovaniiu upravleniia ekonomicheskim i nauchno-tekhnicheskim sotrudnichestvom s sotsialisticheskimi stranami", *Spravochnik partiinogo rabotnika* (Moscow, Izdatel'stvo politicheskoi literatury, 1987), pp. 488–492.

34. *Pravda* 17 January 1988.

35. "O voprosakh, sviazannykh s sozdaniem na territorii SSSR i deiatel'nost'iu sovmestnykh predpriiatii, mezhdunarodnykh ob'edinenii i organizatsii s uchastiem sovetskikh i inostrannykh organizatsii, firm i organov upravleniia", *Vedomosti Verkhovnogo Soveta Soiuz Sovetskikh Sotsialisticheskikh Respublik* 2 (2388), 14 January 1987, p. 35.

36. See the discussion of problems faced by foreign investors in Anders Aslund, *Gorbachev's Struggle for Economic Reform* (Ithaca, Cornell University Press, 1991), pp. 140–141.

37. "Ob inostrannykh investitsiiakh v SSSR", Vedomosti . . . 44, 31 October 1990, pp. 1149–1150.

38. "Ob individual'noi trudovoi deiatel'nosti", Vedomosti . . . 47 (2381), 19 November 1986, pp. 905–914. The rules were later relaxed.

39. "O zadachakh partii po korennoi perestroike upravleniia ekonomikoi", *Pravda* 27 June 1987. See Gorbachev's speech of the same name, M.S. Gorbachev,

Izbrannye rechi i stat'i (Moscow, Izdatel'stvo politicheskoi literatury, 1988), Vol 5, pp. 129–185, esp. pp. 157–185.

40. "O gosudarstvennom predpriiatii (ob'edinenii)", Vedomosti...26 (2412), 1 July 1987, pp. 427–463.

41. *Pravda* 11 August 1989.

42. In 1988 state orders took up 90% of industrial output, before being wound back from 1989. Simon Johnson & Heidi Kroll, "Managerial Strategies for Spontaneous Privatization", *Soviet Economy* 7, 4, 1991, p. 286.

43. Kathryn Stoner-Weiss, *Local Heroes. The Political Economy of Russian Regional Governance* (Princeton, Princeton University Press, 1997), p. 39.

44. "O kooperatsii v SSSR", Vedomosti...22, 1 June 1988, pp. 375–421.

45. "Osnovy zakonadel'stva Soiuza SSR i soiuznykh respublik ob arende", Vedomosti...25, 29 November 1989, pp. 641–654.

46. "O sobstvennosti v SSSR", Vedomosti...11, 14 March 1990, pp. 197–208.

47. *Izvestiia* 9 August 1990.

48. "Ob osnovnykh nachalakh razgosudarstvleniia i privatizatsii predpriiatii", Vedomosti...32, 7 August 1991, pp. 11324–1334.

49. Richard Sakwa, *Gorbachev and His Reforms1985-1990* (New York, Philip Allan, 1990), pp. 279–280.

50. See the discussion in, among other places, Stephen White, *Gorbachev and After* (Cambridge, Cambridge University Press, 1991), pp. 121–127.

51. On limits on cooperative activity, see "O proekte Postanovleniia ob uporiadochenii torgovo-zakupochnoi deiatel'nosti kooperativov i tsenoobrazovaniia na tovary (uslugi), realizuemye kooperativami naseleniiu", Vedomosti...18, 11 October 1989, pp. 478–479. On speculation, "Ob usilenii otvetstvennosti za spekuliatsiiu, nezakonnuiu torgovuiu deiatel'nost' i za zloupotrebleniia i torgovle", Vedomosti...45, 7 November 1990, pp. 1167–1169.

52. *Izvestiia* 27 October 1990. On the discussion surrounding these plans, see Jerry F. Hough, *Democratization and Revolution in the USSR 1985-1991* (Washington, Brookings Institution Press, 1997), ch. 11. More generally, see Anthony Jones & William Moskoff (eds), *The Great Market Debate in Soviet Economics* (Armonk, M.E. Sharpe Inc., 1990) and Aslund (Gorbachev's Struggle).

53. For a discussion of official restraints upon them, see Anthony Jones & William Moskoff, *Ko-ops. The Rebirth of Entrepreneurship in the Soviet Union* (Bloomington, Indiana University Press, 1991), ch. 4.

54. Cited in Lapina (Formirovanie), pp. 30–31.

55. The term is attributed to Yegor Ligachev. See Kryshtanovskaia (Transformatsiia), p. 55. Also Ol'ga Kryshtanovskaia & Stephen White, "From Soviet *Nomenklatura* to Russian Elite", *Europe-Asia Studies* 48, 5, 1996, p. 716.

56. For this link between declining income and the search for business activities, see Stephen Solnick, *Stealing the State. Control and Collapse in Soviet Institutions* (Cambridge [Mass], Harvard University Press, 1998), pp. 113–114.

57. Kryshtanovskaia & White (From Soviet *Nomenklatura*), p. 716; Kryshtanovskaia (Finansovaia oligarkhiia). For a profile of Komsomol businessmen, see I.V. Kukolev, "Formirovanie biznes-elity", *Obshchestvennye nauki i sovremennost'* 2, 1996, pp. 15–16. An alternative form was the Youth Housing Cooperative, originally begun in

1971 to assist in the provision of housing through the voluntary construction of new housing stock. These were sometimes the basis of later construction companies. For a study of how the Chinese party handled new entrepreneurs, both party members who became entrepreneurs and entrepreneurs who became party members, see Bruce J. Dickson, *Red Capitalists in China. The Party, Private Entrepreneurs and Prospects for Political Change* (Cambridge, Cambridge University Press, 2003), esp. chs 3, 4, & 5.

58. Kryshtanovskaia & White (From Soviet *Nomenklatura*), p. 716.
59. Solnick (Stealing the State), pp. 111–112.
60. After the legalisation of the cooperatives in 1988, these tended to displace NTTMs as the main vehicle for business activity.
61. Solnick (Stealing the State), p. 116.
62. On this, and the Komsomol's role in supporting the early activities of Mikhail Khodorkovsky, see Hoffman (Oligarchs), pp. 100–119; also Manfred F.R. Kets de Vries, Stanislav Shekshnia, Konstantin Korotov & Elizabeth Florent-Treacy, *The New Russian Business Leaders* (Cheltenham, Edward Elgar, 2004), ch. 5.
63. Solnick (Stealing the State), pp. 119–120.
64. Solnick (Stealing the State), p. 121.
65. Cited in Solnick (Stealing the State), p. 290.
66. Kryshtanovskaia (Transformatsiia), pp. 55–56. For a study of Dialog-Troika, see Kets de Vries et al. (New Russian Business Leaders), ch. 8, and for other joint venture successes, chs 7 & 9.
67. Citing Vadim Bakatin. Stephen Handelman, *Comrade Criminal. Russia's New Mafiya* (New Haven, Yale University Press, 1995), p. 101. Also see Gordon M. Hahn, *Russia's Revolution from Above. 1985–2000. Reform, Transition, and Revolution in the Fall of the Soviet Communist Regime* (New Brunswick, Transaction Publishers, 2002), pp. 218–220.
68. Handelman (Comrade Criminal), p. 101. However there was a report that as early as 1989 the party was establishing cooperatives and banks as commercial ventures to bolster party resources. Radio Liberty, *Report on the USSR* 2 42, 19 October 1990, p. 48.
69. Handelman (Comrade Criminal), p. 102 citing *Komsomol'skaia Pravda* 7 December 1991.
70. *Izvestiia Ts.K. KPSS* 10, 1990, p. 100. The speaker was CC Secretary Shenin. For the party's financial crisis, see Graeme Gill, *The Collapse of a Single-Party System. The disintegration of the Communist Party of the Soviet Union* (Cambridge, Cambridge University Press, 1994), pp. 155–158.
71. Solnick (Stealing the State), p. 232. Also on this process, see Shmatko (Stanovlenie), p. 28.
72. Rose Brady, *Kapitalizm. Russia's Struggle to Free Its Economy* (New Haven, Yale University Press, 1999), p. 56. For a party instruction to Aleksandr Smolensky to establish a coop in 1987, which was an important stage in his development into an oligarch, see Hoffman (Oligarchs), pp. 41–42.
73. Shmatko (Stanovlenie), p. 28.
74. Hahn (Russia's Revolution from Above), p. 219.
75. Johnson & Kroll (Managerial Strategies), p. 285.

76. These were a form of joint venture between the state and shareholder employees. Aslund (Gorbachev's Struggle), p. 134.

77. On the cooperatives, see Jones & Moskoff (Koops). For some of the difficulties they faced, see Vladlen Sirotkin, *Mark Masarskii: put' naverkh rossiiskogo biznesmana* (Moscow, Mezhdunarodnye otnosheniia, 1994), pp. 50–83. For a case of a coop being the means for the generation of funds that were then used to expand and diversify business operations, see the study of Russian Standard in Kets de Vries et al. (New Russian Business Leaders), ch. 4.

78. For a list of the types of coops, see Jones & Moskoff (Koops), p. 21.

79. White, (Gorbachev and After), p. 113. According to another source, by 1991 there were 135,000 officially registered coops producing 3% of consumer goods and 18.4% of services. Thane Gustafson, *Capitalism Russian-Style* (Cambridge, Cambridge University Press, 1999), p. 116. There were also 1,274 officially registered joint enterprises.

80. For one case study, see John Logue & Olga Y. Klepikova, "Restructuring Elinar: A Case Study of Russian Management Reform, Decentralization, and Diversification", M. Donald Hancock & John Logue (eds), *Transitions to Capitalism and Democracy in Russia and Central Europe. Achievements, Problems, Prospects* (Westport, Praeger, 2000), pp. 67–93.

81. For a case study of such cooperation, see Kathryn Hendley, "Legal Development and Privatization in Russia: A Case Study", *Soviet Economy* 8, 2, 1992, pp. 130–157.

82. On leasehold and its development, see Igor Filatotchev, Trevor Buck & Mike Wright, "Privatization and Buy-outs in the USSR", *Soviet Studies* 44, 2, 1992, pp. 274–278. On the role of coops in an enterprise, see Michael Burawoy & Kathryn Hendley, "Between *Perestroika* and Privatization: Divided Strategies and Political Crisis in a Soviet Enterprise", *Soviet Studies* 44, 3, 1992, pp. 371–402. On the importance of leasing, see N. Iu. Lapina, *Rukovoditeli gosudarstvennykh predpriiatii rossii v protsesse formirovaniia rynochnykh otnoshenii* (Moscow, Rossiiskaia akademiia nauk, Institut nauchnoi informatsii po obshchestvennym naukam, 1995), pp. 16–17.

83. Johnson & Kroll (Managerial Strategies), p. 287.

84. Johnson & Kroll (Managerial Strategies), p. 290.

85. Joseph R. Blasi, Maya Kroumova & Douglas Kruse, *Kremlin Capitalism. Privatizing the Russian Economy* (Ithaca, Cornell University Press, 1997), p. 34.

86. V.N. Berezovskii, *Obshchestvennye ob'edineniia delovykh krugov Rossii: lobbitskii resurs i politicheskaia rol'* (Moscow, Tsentr politicheskoi kon'iunktury Rossii, 1994), Part I, 1, p. 7.

87. For the argument that such "nomenklatura privatisation" was part of the struggle between Russian and Soviet authorities for control over state resources, see Hahn (Russia's Revolution from Above), pp. 217–220.

88. For some cases of this in 1992, see Barnes (Owning Russia), pp. 84–85. This is how both Gazprom and UES were created.

89. Johnson & Kroll (Managerial Strategies), p. 291. For a list of ministries that were privatised in this way and the 'new' entities that they became, see Barnes (Owning Russia), p. 60.

90. Kryshtanovskaia (Transformatsiia), p. 57.

91. Kryshtanovskaia (Transformatsiia), p. 58.

92. Joel Hellman, "Bureaucrats vs Markets? Rethinking the Bureaucratic Response to Market Reform in Centrally Planned Economies", Susan Gross Solomon (ed), *Beyond Sovietology. Essays in Politics and History* (Armonk, M.E. Sharpe Inc., 1993), p. 71. According to a study in 1989, 20% of private banks were the result of the reorganisation of state specialist banks, 20% were established by the heads of major branches and enterprises, and 50% by new people. Lapina (Formirovanie), p. 30.

93. Hellman (Bureaucrats), p. 71.

94. Juliet Johnson, *A Fistful of Rubles. The Rise and Fall of the Russian Banking System* (Ithaca, Cornell University Press, 2000), pp. 37–44. Enterprises often transformed their own financial departments into cooperative banks, which provided one means of privatising state assets.

95. Hellman (Bureaucrats), p. 71. For the list of banks, Hellman cites "Kommercheskie banki: igra bez pravil", *Delovye liudi* 3, July–August 1990. Johnson (Fistful), pp. 52–53, refers to a Stankobank stemming from the Riazan branch of Promstroibank. The Alfa group, Inkombank, SBS-Agro and Rossiiskii Kredit were all rooted in enterprises formed under CPSU auspices. Peter Rutland, "Putin and the Oligarchs", Dale R. Herspring, *Putin's Russia. Past Imperfect, Future Uncertain* (Lanham, Rowman & Littlefield Publishers Inc., 2003), p. 135. On the Komsomol as a source of funds, see Gaidar (Gosudarstvo i evoliutsiia), p. 150. Also see Hahn (Russia's Revolution from Above), p. 554, fn.55.

96. Hellman (Bureaucrats), p. 77.

97. "Supreme Soviet Investigation of the 1991 Coup. The Suppressed Transcripts: Part 3. Hearings 'About the Illegal Financial Activity of the CPSU' ", *Demokratizatsiya* 4, 2, 1996, p. 275. Some 700 million rubles also went to the All-Army Party Commission, the new body designed to direct party work in the military. On the proposal for its establishment, see William E. Odom, *The Collapse of the Soviet Military* (New Haven, Yale University Press, 1998), p. 193.

98. Johnson (Fistful), p. 58.

99. Kryshtanovskaia (Finansovaia oligarkhiia). For similar formulations, see Vladimir Brovkin, "Fragmentation of Authority and Privatization of the State: From Gorbachev to Yeltsin", *Demokratizatsiya* 6, 3, 1998, p. 504.

100. "Gosudarstvennaia programa privatizatsii gosudarstvennykh i munitsipel'nykh predpriatii RF na 1992 god", *Delovoi Mir* 2 July 1992, pp. 6–7. This program was updated in 1993. For the legislative background and an analysis of the program, see Roman Frydman, Andrzej Rapaczynski & John S. Earle et al., *The Privatization Process in Russia, Ukraine and the Baltic States* (Budapest, Central European University Press, 1993), ch. 1.

101. On this, see Michael McFaul, "State Power, Institutional Change, and the Politics of Privatization in Russia", *World Politics* 47, 2, January 1995, p. 230. For 'official' discussions of the implementation of the program, see A.B. Chubais (ed), *Privatizatsiia po-rossiiskii* (Moscow, Vagrius, 1999); Maxim Boycko, Andrei Shleifer & Robert Vishny, *Privatizing Russia* (Cambridge [Mass], MIT Press, 1995); and Blasi et al. (Kremlin Capitalism). For an alternative view, sector by sector, see V.A. Lisichkin & L.A. Shelepin, *Rossiia pod vlast'iu plutokratii* (Moscow, Algoritm, 2003), ch. 4.

102. All assets except the land were valued at book value, the total divided by one thousand rubles to produce the number of shares in the enterprise and these were passed to the Russian Property Fund, at the time an arm of parliament, until they could be sold. Blasi et al. (Kremlin Capitalism), p. 40. For some of the technical difficulties facing privatisers, see Filatotchev et al. (Privatization), pp. 270–272.

103. A payment of 25 rubles was needed to collect a voucher. By the end of January 1993, 144,000,000 vouchers had been collected. Boycko et al. (Privatizing Russia), pp. 99–100.

104. An opinion poll in 1994 found that 8% of respondents used their vouchers to buy shares in the firm in which they worked, 6% bought shares in other firms, 30% invested their vouchers in a mutual fund, 39% sold or gave away their vouchers, and 17% did not reply. Robert Cottrell, "Russia's New Oligarchy", *The New York Review of Books* 27 March 1997, p. 29.

105. Roi Medvedev, *Chubais i vaucher. Iz istorii rossiiskoi privatizatsii* (Moscow, Izdatel'stvo "IMPETO", 1997), pp. 6–8.

106. Many deputies favoured giving shares away to insiders. Pekka Sutela, "Insider Privatization in Russia: Speculations on Systemic Change", *Europe-Asia Studies* 46, 3, 1994, p. 423. On the views of enterprise directors, see Lapina (Rukovoditeli), pp. 20–31.

107. For the argument that the reformers around Chubais found themselves in the position of having to buy the support of major groups in society for their reforms, hence the compromises within the privatisation program, see Hilary Appel, "The Ideological Determinants of Liberal Economic Reform. The Case of Privatization", *World Politics* 52, 2, 2000, pp. 520–549. In an attempt to undercut dispersed ownership and enable it to be concentrated, Chubais ensured that shares were transferable and were individually owned by the workers rather than being held by the enterprise workers' councils or trade union. Boycko et al. (Privatizing Russia), pp. 87–88.

108. For some economic reasons for favouring insiders in privatisation, see Sutela (Insider Privatization), p. 419.

109. McFaul (State Power), p. 233. In the later privatisation of the oil industry, general managers of some of the oil companies were major shapers of the form privatisation took. See the discussion in Li-Chen Sim, "The Changing Relationship between the State and the Oil Industry in Russia (1992-2004)", Oxford University, D.Phil. thesis, 2005, ch. 2.

110. There was a separate privatisation scheme for small businesses like shops and cafes. Most were bought for a nominal sum by the workforce, and this level of privatisation occurred quickly. Blasi et al. (Kremlin Capitalism), p. 80. For the different levels of permission required for the privatisation of different types of firms, see Boycko et al. (Privatizing Russia), pp. 73–74.

111. By early 1996, 17,937 large and medium-sized industrial enterprises producing 88.3% of industrial production, employing 79.4% of industrial workers and constituting 77.2% of medium-sized and large industrial enterprises had been privatised. Blasi et al. (Kremlin Capitalism), p. 2. For a figure of 110,000 companies privatised by mid-1994, a figure which must include small enterprises, shops, cafes and the like, see Michael McFaul, "The Allocation of Property Rights in Russia.

The First Round", *Communist and Post-Communist Studies* 29, 3, September 1996, p. 287. For monthly details of voucher auctions, see Barnes (Owning Russia), p. 76.

112. McFaul (Allocation), p. 293. According to Rutland, the respective figures were 77% and 21% for options one and two. Peter Rutland, "Privatisation in Russia: One Step Forward: Two Steps Back?", *Europe-Asia Studies* 46, 7, 1994, p. 1113. On the lack of popularity of Option 3, see Boycko et al. (Privatizing Russia), p. 79.

113. Rutland (Privatisation in Russia), pp. 1116–1117.

114. For four case studies of enterprises privatised before this program was instituted but which clearly shows continuing managerial power, see Simon Clarke, Peter Fairbrother, Vadim Borisov & Petr Bizyukov, "The Privatization of Industrial Enterprises in Russia: Four Case-studies", *Europe-Asia Studies* 46, 2, 1994, pp. 179–214.

115. See the discussion in Hilary Appel, "Voucher Privatisation in Russia: Structural Consequences and Mass Response in the Second Period of Reform", *Europe-Asia Studies* 49, 8, 1997, pp. 1433–1449.

116. For example, see the case of Uralmash. Lapina (Rukovoditeli), p. 23.

117. This occurred during the takeover battle for Norilsk Nickel in 1996. Appel (Voucher), p. 1438.

118. In the early 1990s this could have involved loss of privileges such as housing, health, and child care facilities.

119. This represents the failure of the managers to be able to prevent the shares from becoming freely negotiable, and thereby enabled those with capital to gain control of enterprises.

120. L. Makarevich, "Struktura sobstvennosti i bor'ba za ee peredel v Rossii v 1992–1999gg", *Obshchestvo i ekonomika* 10–11, 1999, pp. 233–235.

121. For a discussion of the legislative response to the abuse of minority shareholders' rights, see Stephen Fortescue, "Privatisation, Corporate Governance and Enterprise Performance in Russia", *Russian and Euro-Asian Bulletin* 7, 5, May 1998, pp. 6–8.

122. Local authorities wanted to ensure that control of resources remained local. See the discussion in Darrell Slider, "Privatization in Russia's Regions", *Post-Soviet Affairs* 10, 4, 1994, pp. 367–396.

123. *Kommersant* 30 May 1995, cited in Fortescue (Privatisation, corporate governance), p. 9.

124. The government part of share-holding capital fell from 9.5% in 1995 to 2.7% in 1997, with private owners growing from 90.2% to 96.6%. Makarevich (Struktura), p. 235. For some other figures, see Fortescue (Privatisation, corporate governance), p. 2. On state interests being ignored in those firms in which the state retained a stake, see Marina Aleksandrovna Deriabina, "Privatizatsiia v Rossii: dolgii put' k chastnoi sobstvennosti", *Biznes i politika* 4, 1997, p. 46.

125. Makarevich (Struktura), p. 235. Although the distinction between inside and outside was not always clear; sometimes managers used external companies as means of buying shares in their own enterprises. Also see figures in Fortescue (Privatisation, corporate governance), p. 3.

126. Blasi et al. (Kremlin Capitalism), pp. 67 & 193.

127. Blasi et al. (Kremlin Capitalism), p. 78. For case studies of some individual firms, see Sheila M. Puffer, Daniel J. McCarthy & Alexander I. Naumov, *The*

Russian Capitalist Experiment. From State-owned Organizations to Entrepreneurships (Cheltenham, Edward Elgar, 2000).

128. For a study of 123 firms conducted in the early-mid-1990s that claims that in a majority of privatised firms there had been a change in manager, see Susan J. Linz & Gary Krueger, *Pilferers or Paladins? Russia's Managers in Transition*, (The William Davidson Institute Working Paper No.17, November 1996, University of Michigan), p. 20. It is not clear how representative this sample is given the basis on which the selection of participating firms was made.

129. Virginie Coulloudon, "Elite Groups in Russia", *Demokratizatsiia* 6, 3, 1998, pp. 535–549.

130. Abel Aganbegyan, *The Challenge: Economics of Perestroika* (London, Hutchinson, 1988), p. 26.

131. Respectively, Marshall I. Goldman, *USSR in Crisis. The Failure of an Economic System* (New York, W.W. Norton & Co., 1983), p. 55 and Paul R. Gregory & Robert C. Stuart, *Soviet and Post-Soviet Economic Structure and Performance* (New York, Harper Collins, 1994, 5th ed.), p. 203.

132. On people being active in artels before the establishment of legal cooperatives, see Vozrozhdenie, p. 198 and Sirotkin (Mark Masarskii), pp. 50–83. Also see Gustafson (Capitalism Russian Style), pp. 114–115. For reports of a survey of 1,000 entrepreneurs claiming that 40% had black market experience, see Leonid Fituni, "Economic Crime in the Context of Transition to a Market Economy", Alena V. Ledeneva & Marina Kurkchiyan (eds), *Economic Crime in Russia* (The Hague, Kluwer Law International, 1999), p. 21.

133. A 1997 survey of managers of new firms showed that only 56% said they could appeal to the courts to enforce a contract with a trading partner. John McMillan & Christopher Woodruff, "The Central Role of Entrepreneurs in Transition Economies", *Journal of Economic Perspectives* 16, 3, 2002, p. 164. On the role of law, see the differing views in Vadim Volkov, *Violent Entrepreneurs. The Use of Force in the Making of Russian Capitalism* (Ithaca, Cornell University Press, 2002), pp. 46–49, and Kathryn Hendley, Barry W. Ickes, Peter Murrell & Randi Ryterman, "Observations on the Use of Law by Russian Enterprises", *Post-Soviet Affairs* 13, 1, 1997, pp. 34–37.

134. By 1997 there were 10,200 registered (and therefore legal) private protection and detective agencies employing 140,600 people. Vadim Volkov, "Organized Violence, Market Building, and State Formation in Post-Communist Russia", Ledeneva & Kurkchiyan (Economic Crime), p. 56. For one study of their role in commercial life, see V. Radaev, "O roli nasiliia v rossiiskikh delovykh otnosheniiakh", *Voprosy ekonomiki* 19, 1998, pp. 81–100.

135. Mark Galeotti, "The Russian Mafiya: Economic Penetration at Home and Abroad, Ledeneva & Kurkchiyan (Economic Crime), p. 36.

136. Volkov (Organized Violence), p. 53. Also see Hahn (Russia's Revolution from Above), p. 543.

137. Vadim Radaev, "Corruption and Violence in Russian Business in the Late 1990s", Ledeneva & Kurkchiyan (Economic Crime), pp. 75–76. According to Brady, 25% of revenue was spent on protection. Brady (Kapitalizm), p. 188. For the view that nearly 70% of commercial firms pay off armed groups, see V. Radaev, "Malyi

biznes i problemy delovoi etiki: nadezhdy i real'nost"', *Voprosy ekonomiki* 7, 1996, p. 77.

138. Galeotti (Russian Mafiya), p. 35, and Volkov (Organized Violence). For some case studies, see David Satter, *Darkness at Dawn. The Rise of the Russian Criminal State* (New Haven, Yale University Press, 2003), ch. 8. Radaev refers to this as 'relational contracting'. V.V. Radaev, *Formirovanie novykh rossiiskykh rynkov: transaktionnye izderzhki, formy kontrolia i delovaia etika* (Moscow, Tsentr politicheskikh tekhnologii, 1998), p. 68.

139. Disagreements between competing ownership groups, for example when the purchase of a company's shares shifted managerial control but the incumbents were reluctant to acknowledge this, were often resolved forcefully. For examples of the problems faced by new, Western, owners, see Matthew Brzezinski, *Casino Moscow. A Tale of Greed and Adventure on Capitalism's Wildest Frontier* (New York, The Free Press, 2001), pp. 169–175, and Chrystia Freeland, *Sale of the Century. The Inside Story of the Second Russian Revolution* (London, Little, Brown & Co., 2000), pp. 74–90.

140. For a study by the former first deputy director of the Federal Tax Police Service of the role of the taxation police in struggling with tax crimes, see Vasili Volkovskii, *Bor'ba s organizovannoi prestupnost'iu v ekonomicheskoi sfere* (Moscow, Russkii biograficheskii institut, 2000).

141. Volkov (Organized Violence), p. 46.

142. United Nations Office for Drug Control and Crime Prevention, *Russian Capitalism and Money-Laundering* (New York, United Nations, 2001), p. 13. There has been much exaggerated reporting on the extent of criminal control of Russian business and the Russian economy. See the discussion in Volkov (Violent Entrepreneurs), pp. 97–98. On the spread of criminal interest, see Svetlana Pavlovna Glinkina, "Vlast' plius biznes ravniaetsia fiktivnaia ekonomika", *Biznes i politika* 2, 1997, pp. 33–35. On criminal control of banks, see Johnson (A Fistful of Rubles), pp. 132–133.

143. Volkov (Organized Violence), p. 49.

144. Volkov (Violent Entrepreneurs), pp. 167 & 180. Also see Federico Varese, *The Russian Mafia. Private Protection in a New Market Economy* (Oxford, Oxford University Press, 2001), chs 2–3; and Galeotti (Russian Mafiya), p. 36.

145. Federico Varese, "Is Sicily the Future of Russia? Private protection and the rise of the Russian Mafia", *Archives europeannes de sociologie* XXXV, 2, 1996, pp. 224–258. Also see Clotilde Champeyrache, "Changement de regime de droits de propriete et infiltration mafieuse dans l'economie legal. Une comparison entre la Russie actuelle et la Sicile du XIXe siecle", *Revue d'etudes comparatives Ost/Oest* 31, 4, 2000, pp. 183–208, and for a more theoretical discussion which accepts the Russia-Sicily parallel, see Stefan Hedlund & Niclas Sundstrom, "Does Palermo Represent The Future For Moscow?", *Journal of Public Policy* 16, 2, 1996, pp. 113–155.

146. For a survey of cooperators in the late 1980s that shows them as not substantially different from the rest of the population, see Jones & Moskoff (Koops), pp. 27–31. For the exaggerated claim that the seemingly independent entrepreneurs were officially authorised to act as the "fiduciary agents" of the nomenklatura, see Kryshtanovskaia (Finansovaia oligarkhiia).

147. Blasi et al. (Kremlin Capitalism), p. 26.

148. On this see Caroline Humphrey, *The Unmaking of Soviet Life. Everyday Economies after Socialism* (Ithaca, Cornell University Press, 2002), ch. 9.

149. On some of these see I.M. Bunin & B.I. Makarenko, *Formirovanie elity: problemy, puti, napravlenie evoliutsii* (Moscow, Tsentr politicheskikh tekhnologii, 1995), p. 13.

150. For example, see Humphrey (Unmaking), ch. 3.

4

Bourgeois Representation
in Political Life

If the bourgeoisie played a major role in shaping a state's political trajectory, that role is likely to be reflected in bourgeois involvement in the state's public institutions. Historically, such institutions have been a medium through which conflicts over power and control of both resources and the state itself have been waged. Such institutions have been both one site of major political conflict, of the playing out of political differences between contending forces in the state's public life, and also a weapon wielded in those conflicts. They can also act as a marker of the course of those struggles. If one group cedes political dominance to another, for example, the traditional landowners to an emergent bourgeoisie, we would expect to see it mirrored in the composition of at least some of these public institutions; the newly dominant group and its interests may be expected to have a much higher profile in many of these bodies than they previously had and than is possessed by other groups in the society. Moreover, one would expect that such representation and involvement would be greater the more important the individual institutions were in the public life of the country.

There are six types of institutions in which bourgeois representation would be expected, although we will treat the first two together because they constitute the formal law-making part of the state: legislature and executive, political parties, civil service, local/regional government, and structured interest groups. The executive and legislature are the major formal law-making bodies in the state, and from them emanate the principles which give formal structuring to public life, including such things important to the bourgeoisie as property rights and the regulation of commercial relations. Political parties are important because, increasingly as the time periods in each country advanced, these became the principal avenues for entry into the legislature and, in Britain, the executive. The civil service was, in practice through its role in implementing the formal decisions made in the legislature and executive, a major defining influence on life in the country, including the conduct of commercial life. Local or regional government could also be a focus of interest for an emergent bourgeoisie because of its responsibility for determining many of the immediate conditions under which bourgeois-owned enterprises had to function, and therefore the capacity of the bourgeoisie to accumulate the sort of capital that was the raison d'être of that class. Structured interest associations were, like the parties, an important potential channel linking government with groups in society, in this case commercial or business interests seeking to press their concerns on government. These institutions were all ones in which we would expect an emergent bourgeoisie to have an active interest. This chapter will analyse the patterns of bourgeois involvement in these institutions and show how they differed from one country to the other, depending principally upon the institutional contours of the respective political systems that were in place at the time the bourgeoisie sought to enter political life.[1]

State Legislature and Executive

The state legislature was a natural place for the emergent bourgeoisie to seek representation. Principally this was because the legislature was an important law-making organ and many issues of relevance to the business interests of the bourgeoisie were likely to pass through this chamber. The degree to which such issues were actually resolved in the chamber is variable, depending in part on the particular circumstances surrounding each issue. But also important here was the relationship with the executive. In Britain, the political (as opposed to the administrative, the civil service) executive was embedded in the parliament, but in the other three countries the executive was separate and therefore a power centre in its own right. It was in these countries to a degree immune from what went on in the legislature, and as the century wore on and the British cabinet became increasingly powerful,[2] Britain too began to go down this route. The power vested in these bodies, legislature and executive, was sufficient reason for the emergent bourgeoisie to take an interest in them. But also relevant here was the historical legacy in place at this time. The legislatures that existed in the early part of the nineteenth century in Europe had a history stemming at least from medieval times of representing what were seen as the principal interests in the society, including commercial interests. This tradition had also been inherited in the United States. Accordingly, as the acknowledged site of the political representation of society's interests, the legislature was a natural arena within which the new class should seek representation.

The levels of representation of businessmen in the national legislatures varied in the different countries, as the following tables demonstrate. All figures

Table 4.1. Britain (%)

1831	1841–47	1865	1885	1885–1906
24	22	23	38	c30

W.L. Guttsman, *The British Political Elite* (London, Macgibbon & Kee, 1963), p. 41; John Garrard, 'The Middle Classes and Nineteenth Century National and Local Politics', John Garrard, David Jarry, Michael Goldsmith & Adrian Oldfield (eds.), *The Middle Class in Politics* (Farnborough, Saxon House, 1978), p. 35; and H. Berghoff & R. Moller, 'Tired Pioneers and Dynamic Newcomers? A Comparative Essay on English and German Entrepreneurial History, 1870–1914', *Economic History Review* XLVII, 2, 1994, p. 280. Also, see W.O. Aydelotte, 'The House of Commons in the 1840s', *History* xxxix, 1954, p. 254.

are percentages and relate to the proportion of legislators from a business background (Tables 4.1–4.5).

In Britain, bourgeois representation in the legislature increased towards the end of the nineteenth century at much the same time that the suffrage was widened. The electorate was initially relatively small compared with the population, but it was opened up considerably as a result of the three reform acts of the nineteenth century.[3] The Great Reform Act of 1832 extended the franchise, giving most middle-class citizens (including industrial capitalists) the vote and increasing the electorate by 64% to 806,000. The 1867 act enfranchised much of the urban working class (and also merchants, manu-facturers, and industrialists), increasing the electorate by 82.5% and bringing it to 2,476,745. The 1884/85 acts standardised adult male householder and lodger franchise across the country, with the result that by now, most adult men had the vote (women did not receive the vote until 1918 when full adult suffrage was introduced for men over 18 and for women over 30 who were either ratepayers or ratepayers' wives).[4] All of the acts introduced a redistribution of seats, but it was not until 1884/85 when constituencies came to be based roughly on population that the clear imbalance of power between the rural constituencies of the south and east on the one hand and the growing industrialised cities of the north on the other was rectified to give the latter satisfactory representation.[5] It may be that the changes introduced in 1884/85 strengthened the political support base of businessmen given the prominent place that many of them held in the local community, but it was actually the 1867 act which enfranchised their major support base in the urban areas (a support base resting in part on the paternalistic relationships and attitudes that pervaded British work structures). The 1884/85 act was important because of the redistribution of seats it brought in, which thereby gave these new businessmen more local constituencies they could win to gain representation. The mid-1880s is also the time when there is the dramatic turn around in the representation of bourgeois interests in the Liberal and Conservative parties, with the latter taking over as the major site of bourgeois

Table 4.2. France (%)

1815	1816	1827–31	1831–34	1848	1852–70	1871	1876	1877	1881	1885	1889	1893	1898	1902	1906	1910	1914
10	18	16	17	14	24	14.1	12.4	11.2	13.6	12.4	14.1	12.9	12.1	12.9	12	16.5	15.1

Reed G. Geiger, *Planning the French Canals. Bureaucracy, Politics, and Enterprise under the Restoration* (Newark, University of Delaware Press, 1994), p. 188; Theodore Zeldin, *The Political System of Napoleon III* (London, Macmillan, 1958), pp. 62–63; and Mattei Dogan, 'Les Filieres De La Carriere Politique En France', *Revue Francaise De Sociologie VIII*, 4, 1967, p. 472. Another source gives the following percentages of elected deputies of bourgeois social status, a category wider than simply businessmen: 1815 15%, 1816 21%, 1819 29%, 1824 16%, 1830 (October) 44%, 1834 45%. Roger Price, *A Social History of Nineteenth Century France* (London, Hutchinson, 1987), p. 114.

Table 4.3. Germany (%)

1871	1874	1877	1878	1881	1884	1887	1890	1893	1898	1903	1907	1912	1919	1920	5/1924	12/1924
7.2	8.1	9.2	12	14.7	13.2	17.4	16.4	12.6	10.2	10.6	10.4	5.5	4.0	6.7	8.8	10.8

Heinrich Best, 'Recruitment, Careers and Legislative Behavior of German Parliamentarians, 1848–1956', *Historical Social Research* 23, 1982, p. 26. Two other sets of figures for businessmen, broadly consistent with those cited in the text, are produced by James Sheehan:

1871	1887	1912
8.0%	17.4%	8.8%
6.5%	16.9%	4.8%

The second set of figures has a tighter definition than the first set. James S. Sheehan, 'Political Leadership in the German Reichstag, 1871–1918', *American Historical Review* 74, 2, December 1968, p. 520. For other, higher, figures, see Youssef Cassis, 'Businessmen and the Bourgeoisie in Western Europe', Jurgen Kocka & Allen Mitchell (eds.), *Bourgeois Society in Nineteenth-Century Europe* (Providence, Berg, 1993), p. 117. For some lower figures, see Berghoff & Moller (Tired Pioneers), p. 281. They cite figures of 14.5% in 1887–90 and 4.6% in 1912–18. According to Berghoff & Moller (Tired Pioneers), p. 281, the number of German businessman MPs was less than 10% of the English contingent.

Table 4.4. US House of Representatives (%)

1851–60	1861–70	1871–80	1881–90	1891–1900	1901–10	1911–20	1921–30	1931–40
16	21.7	19.5	21.8	20.2	23.8	22.8	21	24.4

Allan G. Bogue, Jerome M. Chubb, Carroll R. McKibbin & Santa A. Traugott, 'Members of the House of Representatives and the Processes of Modernization, 1789–1960', *Journal of American History* 63, 2, September 1976, p. 284. According to another study, in the House of the fifty-ninth Congress, 1905–07, 20.2% were businessmen, mostly with local rather than national interests. Robert Harrison, *Congress, Progressive Reform, and the New American State* (Cambridge, Cambridge University Press, 2004), pp. 14 & 15. The corresponding figure for 1990–92 was 30% from 'business and finance'. Pippa Norris, 'Legislative Recruitment', Laurence Le Duc, Richard G. Niemi & Pippa Norris (eds.), *Comparing Democracies. Elections and Voting in Global Perspective* (Thousand Oaks, Sage, 1996), p. 190.

interest representation and, for some time dominating the political process (see below).

In the United States, bourgeois representation was considerable in the House, and at least until the change in mode of selection of the Senate (see below), it was also significant in that house. In the United States, both presidency (indirectly) and the House of Representatives were elected by universal, adult, white male suffrage (female suffrage was guaranteed at the national level only with the Nineteenth Amendment of the Constitution in 1920, while the legal provisions regarding black voting did not really become effective nationally until after the middle of the twentieth century). Until 1913 when popular election was introduced, senators were chosen by the state legislatures. But until this time, the rules about elections were less important than the control of the local political machines. Although this will be discussed in greater detail in Chapter 6, local politics in many parts of the United States was dominated by informal political machines which chose who to send to Washington as congressman and senator. There were close connections between these machines and local businessmen, meaning that the interests of the latter were a major concern of the former, and these

Table 4.5. US Senate (%)

	1860	1900	1905	1940
Senators' fathers' occupation, business	5	5	NA	4
Businessman senators	10	16	21.6	10
Business interests	18	30	NA	26

Ari Hoogenboom, 'Industrialism and Political Leadership: A Case Study of the United States Senate', Frederic Cople Jaher (ed.), *The Age of Industrialism in America. Essays in Social Structure and Cultural Values* (New York, The Free Press, 1968), p. 59. Hoogenboom also provides a breakdown of the different branches of business from which these people came. Hoogenboom (Industrialism), pp. 55–56. The 1905 figure comes from Harrison (Congress), p. 29, who also shows that 70.5% had legal backgrounds.

were instrumental in bringing about substantial bourgeois representation in Washington.

The German Reichstag was elected by near universal, equal, male (over 25 years of age) suffrage through a secret ballot, although the unpaid nature of service was a restriction on access. Bourgeois representation in the Reichstag reached a peak in the late 1880s and then declined, with that decline evident in the initial years of Weimar. Although it began to rise again in the early 1920s, the low level of representation reflects the bourgeoisie's marginal place in the overall political structure.

In France, the electorate during the Bourbon monarchy (1815–30) was highly restricted—there were some 90,000 electors in a population of over 26,000,000 and given the tax requirements to stand, potential candidates could come only from among the 15,000 wealthiest men.[6] This was widened in the Orleanist period (1830–48), and by 1841 it constituted some 2.8% of the male population over the age of 21.[7] Given that taxation fell overwhelmingly on real estate and taxation level was the criterion for voting, it has been calculated that some 90% of the electorate qualified as a result of landholding, with only 10% representing commerce, industry, and the professions.[8] In the Second Empire (1852–70), although the lower house of parliament, the Legislative Body, was to be elected by universal suffrage (introduced in 1848) from single member districts, the prefects and sub-prefects in the regions were able to ensure that official candidates usually were successful; for example in 1857, official candidates were elected in all except thirteen constituencies.[9] Nevertheless, it was in this period of the Second Empire that bourgeois representation reached its peak in the legislature. This was a period when the emperor, Louis Napoleon, pursued a policy of economic development encouraging the growth of industry and sought the advice of members of the economic bourgeoisie. But much of this generally took place outside the bounds of the formal political institutions. During the Third Republic (1871–1940), the absence of clearly defined programmatic parties with fixed membership meant that there was a high level of governmental instability; election relied more on relationship with local notables than party affiliations. Governments came and went, but beside this there was a high level of stability of personnel. Despite changes in government, the same people often reappeared holding office and in the legislature,[10] and businessmen remained a small cohort in the chamber.

The national experiences reflected in these tables are divided into two patterns: the general level of bourgeois representation in Britain and the United States is higher than in France and Germany, and in the former two countries that level has generally increased over time, while in the latter countries it has fluctuated much more. Why has the economic bourgeoisie been much more prominent in the legislative arena in Britain and the United States than in France and Germany?

One factor in this is historical. In both Britain and the United States, the period preceding the rise of the new economic bourgeois class saw the stable functioning of the Parliament and Congress with economic interests well-represented. In both legislatures, mercantile, manufacturing, and banking interests played an established role in the deliberations that took place in the respective chambers. Commercial interests had enjoyed representation in the House of Commons since medieval times. With the growing power of Parliament rooted in the monarch's need to gain access to resources to finance his projects, the representation of the commercial elements of the population in this body was a natural development; as Clark argues, 'one of the reasons for the rising power of the Commons in the late Middle Ages was its claim to speak for the commercial sector'.[11] Such urban commercial interests came to include not just merchants, but those engaged in small-scale manufacturing as well. Furthermore, by the end of the eighteenth century, the pocket borough provided a means for new wealth to purchase political representation. Consequently, when the new style of industry emerged in the nineteenth century, with new men seeking to project and look after their interests, the precedent already existed for their representation in the Parliament; industry in the form of manufacturing was already present and activity to represent its interests well established. This tradition was inherited by the United States, but it was not prominent in either France or Germany. In France, the Estates General had provided scope for the representation of economic interests, but it had had little power and in any event did not meet between 1614 and 1789. Although the imagery and rhetoric of the Revolution had projected the legislature and its representative function into a prominent place in the polity, in practice there was only a weak recent tradition of economic interests having an important role in national deliberations in such a chamber. In Germany prior to unification, state assemblies had been composed of notables, or honoratioren, who had gained office because of their local connections rather than any sense of mass support. Businessmen had not been particularly active in the honoratioren assemblies, so there was little in the way of a strong tradition of representation at this level that could be carried forward into the new national arena.

Also important in this may be that the legislatures in Britain and the United States have been constitutionally more powerful than those in France and Germany over this longer period, and therefore had greater attraction for their national bourgeoisies. In Britain, before the growth of executive authority loosened parliamentary shackles on the cabinet, Parliament was supreme in the political system and by then the House of Commons was the more important chamber; in any case, given the restrictions on entry to the House of Lords, the Commons was the house most readily available to the emergent bourgeoisie. In the United States, the Constitution provided for a broad balance of power between President and Congress, with in practice that balance significantly affected by the personality of the President. During the late nineteenth century, the Congress was a more dominant institution than the presidency, with both House of Representatives and Senate exercising significant power.

The French political system experienced a series of upheavals during the nineteenth century: Bourbon monarchy 1815–30, Orleanist monarchy 1830–48, Second Republic 1848–51, Second Empire 1852–70, and Third Republic 1871–1940.

The political system had initially been restructured as a result of the Revolution and thereby made more open to access by wider sections of the population. The keys to such access were the legislature and the bureaucracy. The legislature had been re-established in 1814, despite widespread concern that it would be unable to function effectively because of the continuing power of the central bureaucracy. Furthermore the king was unreconciled to parliamentary government, and while the legislature could discuss and vote on laws and taxes, executive power and the right of initiative in legislation lay with the king. The legislature remained weak, parties were undeveloped, majorities were frequently shifting, and governments answered to the king. Following the revolution that ended the reign of the Bourbons in 1830, a king from the Orleanist branch of the ruling family came to power, Louis-Philippe. This marked the definitive end of a privileged place for the old aristocracy, symbolised by the suppression of the hereditary peerage and the transformation of the upper chamber into a house of royal nominees. The parliament became more powerful, with the right of initiative in legislation being shared with the king. The fall of the July Monarchy in 1848 led to the dominance of Louis Napoleon and, in December 1852, the proclamation of the Second Empire. The new political arrangements saw power concentrated in the person of the emperor. The deputies were meant to assist the head of state rather than to be representatives of the country's will, while ministers were not to have their own policies but to carry out those of the emperor.[12] Thus not only was the parliament for much of the life of the Empire subject to the emperor but the personnel of which it consisted was generally reluctant to challenge imperial prerogative. However from 1860, the position of the Legislative Body was strengthened and the growth of an opposition within it became apparent. The fall of the Empire and subsequent suppression of the Paris Commune in 1871 ushered in the Third Republic, and in the new political arrangements, the parliament was supreme. For the first time, from 1877 governments became responsible to the legislature. Parliamentary primacy was thus a late development in France.

The polity that was established with the creation of the German Empire through unification of the German states in 1871 was a national system grafted onto the existing Prussian structure. The lower house of the legislature, the Reichstag, was, as explained above, popularly elected. It was balanced by the Bundesrat or Federal Council, which was composed of delegates appointed by the state governments. Legislation had to pass both bodies before it became law. Importantly, the government was not responsible to the legislature but to the Emperor, or Kaiser, who formally headed the executive, made all personnel appointments, headed the military, and retained the power both to declare war and to impose martial law domestically. In practice, the executive powers of the state were exercised by the Chancellor, who was appointed by the Emperor. The 1871 Constitution thus contained a formal balance between three types of elements: democratic, federal, and authoritarian. The democratic element, the Reichstag, was not without power in this structure, but the balance was tilted heavily in favour of the executive: the Reichstag generally acted only on matters brought before it, it could reject important legislation only at the cost of its own dismissal, and it had no power over the Chancellor and his government.[13] It was a system characterised by an insulated executive and limited popular participation. During the Weimar period, the legislature was more powerful, but it was still overshadowed by the executive in the form of the President.

Despite the constitutional limitations on these assemblies, the power they possessed was still sufficient reason for the bourgeoisie to seek representation in them. But in none of these legislatures did the bourgeoisie gain a majority. The entry and growth of bourgeois power was always at the expense of existing dominating groups. Part of this growth was the replacement of the former small-scale manufacturing and commercial interests[14] by the larger-scale, new industrial, and financial interests, but the entry of this new group also had an impact on other groups in the chamber. In Britain, this marked the gradual decline of the dominance of the traditional landowners;[15] according to Perkin,[16] the parliament of 1880 was the last in which landowners had a clear majority, and 1885 the first in which they were outnumbered (they retained a majority in the Lords until the inter-war period of the twentieth century). The professional bourgeoisie was also a significant and growing force in the chamber. In France, there was a similar story of the erosion of landowning power in the assembly with a rise of bourgeois, both economic and professional, representation, but in Germany during the Imperial period at least the proportion of deputies that came from among the landowners was close to double that of the businessmen.[17] But in both countries, and in contrast to both Britain and the United States, the chambers usually also had significant representation by state functionaries; for example, in the 1840s in France state, officials constituted 45% of deputies and in the Second Empire, 26% of all deputies in the legislature.[18] This reflects the important role played by local officials in structuring elections and the prominent role of the state in fostering economic development (see below). In the United States, the levels of business representation seem mainly to reflect the replacement of their smaller-scale manufacturing predecessors, although a general decline in the prominence of purely landed interests had also been in train for some time.

Given the continuing minority position in the chamber possessed by business interests, the question arises, how did they manage to get pro-business legislation passed? There are two aspects of this question. First, the number of businessmen in the chamber is not the same as the number of parliamentarians who had business interests. Increasingly over the nineteenth century, people who were not immediately and directly involved in the new forms of economic production were drawn into contact with it. Share ownership was a major form in which this occurred, with many established landowners taking either an active or a passive interest in the new enterprises that were developing. For example in Britain, according to one author,[19] by the end of the century at least 25% of the House of Lords and 30% of the Commons held company directorships; in 1895, 60 directorships were held by ministers.[20] This representation of interests shaped the way the House operated, especially given the lack of concern about questions of conflict of interest.[21] As a result, many who were not strictly speaking businessmen had a direct interest in facilitating the development of business;[22] the passing of much canal- and railway-enabling legislation in the still landowning dominated British Parliament in the mid-nineteenth century is a good instance of this. This situation, of people other than businessmen having business interests, was replicated in all of the countries.

Second, the task of people in the national legislatures was to govern in the national interest rather than narrow sectional interests. It soon became clear to most in these legislatures that support for economic development, including industrialisation, was a national interest even though it may have some negative effects on other sectors of the domestic economy. Accordingly, general support for measures promoting economic development was forthcoming, even if at times this was moderated by a continuing concern for partial interests. The pursuit of state policies of laissez faire, for example, shows the way a conception of national interest was taking hold, and this was favourable to support for continuing industrial expansion. So too was the presence in the French and German legislatures of a cohort of state functionaries who saw the state as having an important role to play in fostering economic development and who therefore interpreted their parliamentary role as being to promote this.

This propensity of the legislature to look beyond established narrow sectional interests was also strengthened by the growth of representation in these bodies of the professional bourgeoisie. With the growth of a white collar, urban middle class and professional sector, representatives of this group sought entry to the national legislature in increasing numbers. Their outlook was oriented around building the new society of which they saw themselves the heart, and this of necessity involved support for many of those issues favoured by business. While this group could also be harsh critics of business practice and corruption, as in the Progressive period in the United States, they were also solid supporters of the advance of those interests that they saw as crucial to the development of the new, 'bourgeois' society, and these included business.

In Britain, this broader perspective was associated with the notion of 'virtual representation'[23] which held sway (increasingly uncertainly) until politics took on a mass base following the reforms of 1884/85. Virtual representation assumed that MPs represented communities of interest rather than individual constituents. Such communities were envisaged in two ways, functional and local. Functionally, communities were conceived of as comprising, for example, all of those elements in the society which performed basically the same function or carried out the same operations. In this sense, a community could be conceived of as comprising aristocratic landowners, merchants involved in foreign trade, financiers, or industrialists. What this meant practically was that the interests of all members of these virtual communities could be represented by one or a few representatives even if those representatives had no tangible direct links to many of the individual members of the communities. Thus the industrial interests of the whole country could, for example, be represented by an MP from London or Birmingham; geographical propinquity was unnecessary in the light of the presumed sharing of interest. In local terms, the community was conceived of as comprising all of those interests in the local residential/labouring community. The local community could thus comprise a variety of interests (e.g. landowning, trading, industry), all of which combined to bind the community together and turn it into an integral entity. This meant that an MP from a particular district represented all of the interests within the geographical bounds of that district, regardless of that individual's personal background or status. Even if the MP came from an aristocratic landowning family, he was considered to be able to represent the interests of the industrial worker living and working in the local town.

There was clearly tension between these two conceptions of virtual representation, but in practice this does not appear to have been a major problem. Individual MPs did employ both forms of representation when appropriate. When issues of national significance for their putative functional community came up, they were willing to argue on a nation-wide functional basis. For example, issues relating to factory inspection that had relevance right across the country were addressed on that basis by MPs from areas in which factories would be affected. In this sense, MPs did act as advocates of the national community of which their own local constituency was a part. Similarly, when issues came up related to local matters, MPs were willing to pursue them on a local-geographical basis regardless of their personal profiles. A good instance of this is the important role played by landowners in the pieces of legislation that paved the way for railway development in the middle of the century.

More generally, it is reflected in the key role played by landed elites in the adoption of parliamentary legislation facilitating industrial development. The role of landowners in promoting industrial development had been significant and was not restricted to the early establishment of mining operations. Members of the nobility often played a very active part in Parliament in getting bills promoting things like canal construction through the legislature.[24] The lobbying of noble MPs was often essential to the successful passage of such measures. While such projects may have had some of their own money invested in them or been designed to facilitate the movement of resources or produce from their estates, often they had no personal stake at all; they were acting in support of local interests. In this sense, as McCahill argues, they often came to extend a form of patronage to emergent industrial concerns. The activities of noble MPs in this regard was facilitated by the fact that rules relating to conflict of interest were vague and weak throughout the eighteenth and nineteenth centuries; it was not until 1906 that ministers had to surrender their directorships while the practice of declaring an interest did not emerge until the inter-war period of the twentieth century.[25] Thus landowners often acted in the Parliament as representatives or defenders of local business interests, thereby enlarging the weight of pro-business sentiment in the chamber.

The association of business interests with national interests is one reason why the bourgeoisie did not need to create a higher profile through greater representation in the legislature. But also important was the fact that in none of these countries was business a united, coherent group. Business interests were divided along size, sectoral, and regional lines, and this meant that there was often conflict within the business community over the appropriate policies to follow; debates over protectionism versus free trade were a common illustration of this. Such differences were also often reflected in changing patterns of representation in the legislative chamber. For example, in Britain it is clear[26] that the balance between the different components of bourgeois interests changed over time. In 1832, commercial interests were more prominent in the Parliament, comprising just short of half of all bourgeois interests, with industrialists and financiers approximately evenly balanced. Over the following seventy years, commercial interests declined in significance while the other two increased. From 1835, industrial interests were always more weighty than financial, with the former comprising about a quarter of the House from the mid-1860s, while from the early 1850s their representation exceeded that of the commercial and financial sectors combined. Thus as bourgeois interests became more prominent in the House, industrial interests became dominant within them. Similar arguments about the shifting of the weight of interests can be made for the other national legislatures as well. What is common to all cases is the greater representation of industrial than financial interests in these chambers.[27]

The minority position that the economic bourgeoisie continued to occupy in the respective national chambers was not just a function of resistance on the part of established class groups. Many of the new businessmen did not want to get into political life in this way.[28] Many felt unable to devote sufficient time and effort to politics without jeopardising their economic livelihood, especially when the economy experienced periods of expansion, while others were alienated from the parliamentary process by the alien ritual and cumbersome nature of the proceedings and by the education deemed necessary to fully partake in parliamentary debate.[29] Some may also have been dissuaded by the rise of parties like the Labour Party in Britain and the Social Democratic Party (SPD) in Germany which threatened to break any paternalistic influence that employers had over their employees and to mobilise a hostile constituency, thereby leaving them open to electoral rebuff. Such people often preferred to rely upon lawyers to represent their views in the chamber.[30] Furthermore many businessmen who did enter politics did not do so until they had made their fortunes and were quite elderly. In no country did the most prominent businessmen become closely involved in legislative politics, or if they did, it was usually not for very long. But also business found it increasingly effective to work through other channels to influence policy. With the growth in size of industrial concerns and the increasing importance of business organisation, lobbying and the use of personal contacts became a more important means of seeking to influence policy than through the legislative arena (see Chapter 6).

Turning to the executive, the displacement of landowners by the emergent bourgeoisie is less evident in the British executive than in the legislature. Guttsman[31] charts the continuing importance of landowning interests beside increasing middle class (and therefore much wider than the economic bourgeoisie) interests in the changing composition of the different Cabinets prior to the outbreak of the First World War (Table 4.6).

The economic middle class did not achieve a breakthrough into office until Russell's second administration (1865–66) when the businessman George Goschen was made Chancellor of the Duchy of Lancaster with a seat in cabinet, and under Gladstone, who was always attuned to the commercial world of his father and whose brother was a businessman and source of advice from the commercial sector while Gladstone was Chancellor. The first manufacturer to enter the cabinet was Joseph Chamberlain in 1880, while between 1900 and 1919, only 7.7% of Conservative cabinet ministers were the sons of businessmen compared with 50% from a landowning background.[32] Although the dominance of landowners over the post of prime minister was shaken from the middle of the nineteenth century, this post was not dominated by the emergent bourgeoisie. Sir Robert Peel, who was prime minister in 1834–35 and 1841–46, was from a quintessentially bourgeois background, being the son of a Lancashire mill owner. Disraeli was a true outsider but owed much

Table 4.6. Social origins of British cabinet 1830–1914 (numbers)

Year and administration	Landowners	Middle class	Working class	Total
1830–68	68	35		103
1868 Gladstone (Lib)	7	8		15
1874 Disraeli (Cons)	7	5		12
1880 Gladstone (Lib)	8	6		14
1885 Salisbury (Cons)	11	5		16
1886 Gladstone (Lib)	9	6		15
1886 Salisbury (Cons)	10	5		15
1892 Gladstone (Lib)	9	8		17
1895 Salisbury (Cons/Unionist)	8	11		19
1902 Balfour (Cons)	9	10		19
1906 Campbell-Bannerman (Lib)	7	11	1	19
1914 Asquith (Lib)	6	12	1	19

Abbreviations: Lib: Liberals; Cons: Conservatives.

to aristocratic patronage.[33] Between 1780 and 1914, seventeen of twenty-five prime ministers were peers or sons of peers.

Nor were businessmen strongly represented in the French executive. During the Orleanist period, of sixty ministers, only seven were businessmen,[34] although the first two prime ministers (Lafitte and Casimir-Perier; they were formally presidents of the Conseil) were both bankers; they were the last bankers to hold that position for 50 years.[35] Under the Second Empire, Louis Napoleon appointed some businessmen to ministerial office, usually commerce or finance. The most influential of these was the banker Achille Fould who became minister of finance in 1861; others included Duclos from a family of Bordeaux shippers and merchants, and Behic who was manager of the Forge de Vierzon and chairman of the board of the Messageries-Maritime. According to Charle,[36] prior to the Seize Mai crisis in 1877, some 40% of conservative ministers were involved in big business; after that crisis, the number dropped to less than 30%. During the Third Republic, of 631 ministers, only thirty were industrial entrepreneurs and eleven were merchants with a further twelve directors of business societies.[37] According to Cassis, between 1871 and 1914, 26% of ministers were the sons of businessmen.[38] While some businessmen became prime minister —for example, Waddington in 1879, Rouvier in 1887, Casimir-Perier in 1893—generally businessmen gained little representation in the executive.

In Imperial Germany, there were few businessmen in the executive; according to one study, only 11.4% of ministers were the sons of businessmen.[39] Business involvement in the executive was much more common early in the Weimar period than later. A prominent early instance of this was Walther Rathenau, who became Minister of Reconstruction after the war and Foreign Minister for a short time in 1922. But the most important case was that of Wilhelm Cuno who was asked to form a government in November 1922.

The government's economics minister was also a former businessman. At this time, business was opposed to many of the measures that the government was considering on the reparations issue, but if it was thought that Cuno would be able to bring them on board, this view was sadly mistaken. Cuno, who was removed in August 1923, was unable to get industry to agree to anything which they felt would restrict their freedom of action,[40] while his unofficial cabinet of business advisers (which included Stinnes, Warburg, Melchior, and Vogler[41]) would not agree on sacrifices for business and could not agree on the advice to give him. While at this time there was much rhetoric about 'business' in government, there is no evidence that Cuno pursued his own business interests but his government did seek to assist the business sector; many have argued that in the immediate post-Versailles period, the business sector was able to exercise a virtual 'veto power' over state economic policy.[42] More generally, businessmen were reluctant to take on formal government positions.[43]

Business representation in the executive seems to have been much more extensive in the United States.[44] All of the presidents between Reconstruction and the New Deal had business connections prior to entering the presidential office.[45]

- Grover Cleveland (1885–89, 1893–97) was a lawyer representing corporate clients including Standard Oil, Merchants' and Traders' Bank, the Buffalo, Rochester and Pittsburgh Railroad, and the LeHigh Valley Railroad.

- Benjamin Harrison (1889–93) was a lawyer with corporate clients.

- William McKinley (1897–1901) had been a member of the House of Representatives 1876–91 where he had fostered tariff protection and his general attitude towards business had led to strong support for him by the rich businessman Mark Hanna, and he had briefly been on the Board of Directors of the Savings Bank, Canton; McKinley's father had been a manufacturer of pig iron, had rented and owned several furnaces alone and in partnership with his brother, and had invested in mining.

- Theodore Roosevelt (1901–09) inherited wealth from his father, who ran the family glass importing business and engaged in banking; Roosevelt himself invested in banks and railways.

- William H. Taft's (1909–13) siblings were on the boards of a number of insurance, travel, and utility companies.

- Woodrow Wilson (1913–21) had been on the Board of Trustees of the Mutual Life Assurance Company of New York City.

- Warren Harding (1921–23) had owned his own pro-business newspaper in Marion, Ohio, had been on the board of directors of a number of companies, and had married the daughter of the richest businessman in town.

- Calvin Coolidge (1923–29) was a lawyer who had corporate clients.
- Herbert Hoover (1929–33) was a director of many mining and extractive concerns.
- Franklin D. Roosevelt (1933–45) was a partner in a law firm that had Standard Oil and American Tobacco among its clients; he was a director of First National Bank of Poughkeepsie, New York, vice-president of the Fidelity and Deposit Company of Maryland, and had investments in banks, investment companies, bond corporations, trust companies, oil companies, airlines, merchandising corporations, a lobster company, and an automatic camera company.

The range and nature of business contacts of these presidents varied greatly, from those like Harding who had been personally embedded in the business community, through people like Coolidge whose legal practice had included business clients, to those like Taft whose connection to the business world was only through family members. But none came from an anti-business background, and all would have been sensitised by their non-political experiences to business needs and concerns.

There was also significant business representation in the administrations of successive presidents. A survey of leading domestic (secretaries) and ambassadorial (to Britain, France, and Germany) positions in successive administrations gives the proportions coming from a business background (see Table 4.7).[46]

The proportion of business people who went into leading positions in the administration fluctuated, but the general trend of a rise in such representation over time (at least into the 1920s) is clear. What is also clear is the dominance of big business interests rather than people coming from small business; this latter category is hardly represented at all, with at most one person from this background in any administration. There was a change in the types of business backgrounds from which people came over time. In the last decades of the nineteenth century, railway interests dominated in the cabinet; of the six major posts in the Garfield and Arthur cabinets, five were filled by people with railway links. From 1897 to 1913, financial interests became more important.[47] Throughout this period, many of those businessmen who became personally involved in political office did not divest themselves of their economic holdings or cease to play a role in the business sphere. For example, in 1894 when the Democratic Cleveland Administration used troops to break the Pullman strike and appointed special counsel to bring legal proceedings against the strike leaders, the Attorney General was Richard Olney who was a director and general counsel of two

Table 4.7. Business representation in American presidential administrations

Presidency	Big business	Small business	Total business
Hayes 1877–81	7.7		7.7
Garfield 3–9/1881	—		—
Arthur 9/1881–85	25.0		25.0
Cleveland 1885–89	8.3		8.3
Harrison 1889–93	35.7	7.1	42.8
Cleveland 1893–97	15.4		15.4
1877–97	17.1	1.4	18.5
McKinley 3/1897–9/1901	31.3		31.3
T. Roosevelt 9/1901–3/1909	30.8		30.8
Taft 1909–13	33.3		33.3
1897–1913	31.6		31.6
Wilson 1913–21	25.0		25.0
Harding 1921 to 7/1923	53.8		53.8
Coolidge 8/1923–29	40.0		40.0
Hoover 1929–33	47.1		47.1
1913–33	39.2		39.2
F. Roosevelt 1933–40	25.0	0.4	25.4
1877–1940	34.0	1.4	35.4

railway companies (the Chicago, Burlington and Quincy Railroad and the Boston and Main Railroad; the former was involved in the strike activity) and on the board of Pullman.[48] As one observer says, many of those in public office 'unabashedly used political office to advance their business interests'.[49]

The biggest category of people who took up cabinet-level office in the successive administrations was lawyers. Some 47.7% of people holding office from the Hayes to Franklin D. Roosevelt presidencies were lawyers. Many of these had had business clients and were attuned to the needs of business. They added to the very strong business cast of these administrations and reflect the primacy of business interests and concerns in the outlook of the American government. A significant proportion of positions, including all of those at the top levels, were filled by political appointments, and as the above discussion shows, these were often filled by people with business experience. Many such appointees came into office and, while serving the country, also sought to look after their business concerns. Without a clear official check on conflicts of interest, this sort of situation was common.

The significantly higher business representation in the American executive compared with those of Britain, France, and Germany is explained in part by the fact that the person choosing the members of the executive, in this case the president, tended to choose people from a business background more frequently than in the other countries. This is related to the more central place business had in both the fundamental institutional bases and the ideology of American public life. These are discussed more fully in Chapter 6.

Political Parties

Political parties could be significant in those countries where the legislature was most important, Britain and the United States, as vehicles the emergent bourgeoisie could use to gain access to the legislature. This is because parties initially emerged as vehicles for the protection of interests defined overwhelmingly in functional rather than territorial terms. Tending to see themselves as representative of landed interests or commercial concerns or some such, they appeared as natural vehicles through which new interests could seek their representation in the councils of power. However in none of the countries did a specifically business party emerge, a fact reflecting in all countries both the absence of a constituency sufficiently large to sustain such a party and the divisions within the business community.

In Britain, political parties were important as vehicles for the representation of bourgeois interests in Parliament. In the early part of the nineteenth century, there were no disciplined parties. The parties were broad agglomerations of people who may have agreed upon general policy directions and some specific policy issues, but which did not act as a disciplined machine to either garner the vote or create stable majorities in the House. Ministers were chosen by the monarch from either House, and the prime minister usually had a majority in the Commons principally as a result of the Crown's patronage. In the 1830s, the identification of parties with both government and opposition began, leading to the emergence of party governments. This encouraged increased organisation and discipline in the parties, while the 1867 Reform Act forced the parties to restructure and become more mass-based. The greater resultant stability in the House encouraged the Parliament to become more active in legislating on general economic and social relations. But this greater scope of interest was also instrumental in the beginning of a shift of real power out of the chamber and into the executive, including the civil service departments.

According to Thomas, the main concentrations of bourgeois interests were to be found in the two major parties (Table 4.8).[50]

As the representation of bourgeois economic interests in the House increased in the seventy years after the Great Reform Act, there was a significant shift of those interests away from the Liberals and to the Conservatives. Bourgeois interests remained more substantial in the 'natural governing party', the Liberal Party, than in the Conservative Party until the mid-1880s (and again from 1892 to 1895) when the 1886 split of the Liberal Party marked the shift of business interests towards the Conservatives.[51] Perkin[52] has done some calculations based on people (rather than Thomas' interests) and argues that up until the early 1880s Liberal governments had the support of two thirds or more of businessmen in the Commons and Liberal oppositions more than half, while by the 1890s the Conservative Party had two thirds

Table 4.8. Interest representation in British parties 1832–1900

	Whig-Liberals					Tory-Conservatives				
	Total bourgeois interests (n)	Bourgeois % of party MPs interests	Industry (n)	Commerce (n)	Finance (n)	Total bourgeois interests (n)	Bourgeois % of party MPs interests	Industry (nos)	Commerce (nos)	Finance (nos)
1832	168	27.6	50	63	55	46	21.8	5	32	9
1835	156	38.7	55	56	45	61	18.7	7	35	19
1837	121	27.9	43	45	33	91	20.4	20	43	28
1841	115	31.1	44	40	31	100	19.7	29	43	28
1847	170	36.9	84	50	36	112	23.3	57	27	28
1852	180	37.7	94	50	36	107	22.2	55	27	25
1857	233	39.0	135	51	47	70	20.5	43	14	13
1859	204	35.2	126	39	39	80	21.0	44	12	16
1865	358	51.1	185	57	116	146	32.7	88	18	40
1868	487	66.0	305	61	121	121	30.9	70	10	41
1874	324	54.2	175	54	95	196	34.3	103	19	74
1880	422	55.0	230	61	131	168	39.6	77	14	77
1885	355	58.3	202	47	106	218	49.5	112	14	92
1886	248	59.2	145	33	20	312	49.1	156	24	132
1892	302	61.3	183	38	81	274	47.2	136	15	123
1895	188	57.3	113	26	49	344	49.8	165	22	157
1900	190	57.2	128	22	40	356	51.6	177	26	153

This excludes figures for the Liberal-Conservative group which split over the repeal of the Corn Laws in 1846 and the Liberal Unionists which split over home rule in 1886. Bourgeois representation was prominent in both splinter groups, especially after 1874, but the total numbers were significantly less than in the two major parties. Industrial interests were more strongly represented than either commercial or financial. For some other figures, see Martin Pugh, *The Making of Modern British Politics 1867–1939* (Oxford, Basil Blackwell, 1982), pp. 41–44.

of businessmen when in government and about half when in opposition. Between the 1870s and 1890s the Liberals lost parliamentary representation among all groups,[53] with a temporary revival in 1906. According to Perkin,[54] this shift from the Liberals was not due to working class mobilisation as some have argued, which was not revolutionary but conducted in part through the existing parties, but because of the perceived challenge to propertied interests contained in the views of radical sections of the Liberal Party. He attributes the flow back to the Liberals in 1906 to concerns about the moves towards protectionism and away from free trade, although by this time, some of those industrialists in the Liberal Party were supporting old age pensions, graduated taxation, and state investment in sections of the economy that the private sector had not developed.[55] What this suggests is that business interests were less attracted to individual parties by the general ideological stances they adopted than by their attitudes to the particular interests of the businessmen at this time. When a party seemed to threaten the basis upon which private enterprise rested, as sections of the Liberals were accused of doing in the 1880s, the balance of business forces shifted to the Conservatives. Neither party was purely the vehicle of bourgeois interests; in each Parliament over the whole period, bourgeois interests constituted more than a quarter of interests represented in the Liberal Party reaching a peak of almost two thirds in 1868 and remaining more than half from 1865–1900, while in the Conservative Party, bourgeois interests never constituted less than one fifth of interests, and from 1874 never less than a third rising to over a half in 1900.[56] According to one calculation, over the period 1868–1910, MPs from industry and trade went from 31% to 53% of Conservative MPs and 50% to 66% of Liberals.[57] So despite the shift of business interests towards the Conservative Party towards the end of the century, bourgeois interests remained prominent in both parties.

Both parties also contained representation from the three sectors of bourgeois economic interests, industrial, commercial, and financial, but here too there was some shifting of patterns over time. Commercial interests were the largest in both parties in 1832, but in both cases they lost this position in the 1840s and henceforth were reduced to a minor position. In the Liberal party, commercial interests lost their primacy to industrial interests who went on from 1852 to 1895 to make up more than half of the interests represented in the party. Industrial interests were also dominant in the Conservative Party up until 1900 (except for 1880–85). Financial interests were more strongly represented in the Liberal than the Conservative Party until 1886, when these positions were reversed as, in the words of one observer, there was 'the transformation of the City of London from a Liberal into a Conservative stronghold'.[58] There was therefore no clear and unambiguous continuing link between either the bourgeoisie as a whole or the different components of it on the one hand, and a particular party on the other. Part of the general shift in

Table 4.9. Reichstag deputies with business origins in political parties (% & numbers)

	1898	1903
SPD	1.9 (1)	3.8 (3)
Freisinnige Volkspartei	10.0 (3)	18.2 (4)
FVer	38.5 (5)	37.5 (3)
Centre Party	10.3 (11)	6.2 (6)
National Liberal Party	27.1 (13)	26.5 (13)
Free Conservative Party	4.5 (1)	10.0 (2)
Conservative Party	1.9 (1)	—

Abbreviations: FVer: Freisinnige Vereinigung; SPD: Social Democratic Party.

favour of the Conservatives from the mid-1880s was the decisive shift of financial interests towards the Conservative Party at this time; the shift of industrial interests was also considerable, although for the remainder of the century the industrial balance remained less heavily in favour of the Conservative Party than it was in the financial sector. The Liberals lost much more ground to the Conservatives among financiers and industrialists (despite retaining significant industrial representation) than among commercial elements.[59] This shift of bourgeois interest representation to the Conservatives was consolidated in the twentieth century by the decline of the Liberal Party and the rise of the Labour Party.

In France, there was no political party with a clear program until the twentieth century; political parties were unimportant until the Third Republic. Businessmen did not congregate in any particular party, but generally were found in those groups in the centre of the political spectrum; in Dogan's terms, between 1898 and 1940, 20.8% were members of the Radicals, 21.0% of the Centre Left, and 26.8% in the Moderates.[60] There was no single 'business party' as such in French politics.

As elsewhere, in Germany rather than uniting in a 'business party' which clearly set out to represent their interests in the national debate and to pursue policies designed to improve their position, businessmen were divided in their political allegiances. Many businessmen congregated in the National Liberal Party. According to one estimate, 'economic elites' increased as a proportion of the National Liberal Party delegation to the Reichstag from 11.2% in 1874 to 41.5% in 1890.[61] Some sense of the party spread of businessmen can be gained from the following figures, which show the percentage and total number (in brackets) of Reichstag deputies in the major parties who came from business backgrounds in the late imperial period (Table 4.9).[62]

The main vehicle for the representation of business interests was the National Liberals,[63] followed by the mainly Catholic Centre Party; despite the high percentage of business deputies in the left liberal Freisinnige Vereinigung

(FVer), the number involved was quite small. From the outset of the Empire, the National Liberals were closer to heavy industry [and to the Central Association of German Industrialists (CdI)—see below], while left liberals represented the more export-oriented machine-tool industry.[64] But none of these parties could be considered as representative of business, because they all consisted of diverse constituencies which each had different interests to pursue. As a result, party operations were often characterised by some tension between the constituent parts of the party and by the need for compromise on party positions. Accordingly, parties could not take an unambiguously pro-business orientation without upsetting the other constituencies upon which they relied. The instability of party politics throughout the Empire is a clear reflection of this tension.

In line with their lower profile in the Reichstag under Weimar, business activity through the parties remained at a modest level, and was spread among a number of parties rather than being concentrated in one. The sort of disunity among business evident before the war continued after it.[65] There was a feeling among some in business circles that party attachment was less important than business affiliation, and that what was needed was to have more people from business playing a part in the running of the country. This conformed with the views of many businessmen, that what was important was the protection of business and its interests rather than ideology. This was behind the establishment in 1918 by Carl Friedrich von Siemens of a Curatorium for the Reconstruction of German Economic Life, which was designed to give financial support to practising businessmen of all political persuasions who wanted to enter the Reichstag. Accordingly, funding was given to people in the Democratic, Centre, German People's, and German National People's parties.[66] Generally it was in the latter two parties that most industrialists clustered; exporters (including the chemical and electrical industries) tended to concentrate in the German People's Party (DVP) while other industrialists (especially the steel industry) joined the Junker landowners in the German National People's Party (DNVP); smaller numbers joined the Centre Party and the German Democratic Party (DDP).[67] However big business dominated no party. Neither major party was strongly supportive of the republic, and by 1928 the DNVP was actively supporting the notion of a dictator to replace the lost Kaiser, and ultimately under the leadership of conservative industrialist Alfred Hugenberg, allied with the Nazis.[68] An attempt was made in the early 1930s to overcome these partisan divisions and form a single united, anti-socialist party based upon business, but it gained little support among the established parties and politicians, and the businessmen were unwilling to invest the effort and resources to overcome this.[69] During the late 1920s and early 1930s, business generally did not support the rise of Hitler and the Nazis. Some, like Thyssen, did give money to the Nazis, but for many businessmen this was more an insurance policy and part of the process of spreading their support through a number of party groups, than it was an indication of firm support for the Nazis and their program.[70] Very few businessmen joined the Nazi Party, although they were more numerous among the party leadership at the national and regional levels; but even here they were greatly outnumbered by professionals and public employees.[71] Levels of business support did rise after the Nazis gained power in 1933, with part of this being a prudential response to a new government in power.

German businessmen did choose to use their economic resources in an attempt to realise their interests through the legislative chamber. Purchase of a deputy's mandate, either through a donation which enabled a businessman to gain a place on a party's election list or placement of an existing deputy on a company's payroll or board so that that person would represent the company's interests, was common.[72] Donations were shared among the parties. But it is not clear that such efforts bore much fruit. Business and its interests remained only weakly represented in the Reichstag.

Throughout the post–Civil War period in the United States, the American political scene was dominated by the two major parties, the Republicans and Democrats. At times third parties did emerge, but these were never able to become major continuing political forces. The parties were neither highly centralised nor disciplined; in effect, the national parties constituted little more than federations of the state parties, which in turn were amalgams of the political machines at lower levels (see below). Even though the parties in the late nineteenth century remained largely alliances of local and state machines, and therefore contained a diversity of (often competing) views and interests, they were important in shaping the broad policies of industrialisation of the country,[73] and business was active in them, especially at state and local levels where much of the regulation was based and where the membership of leading national institutions was shaped. Business provided significant financial support both for parties and for individual candidates during elections,[74] such support effectively underwriting party activities in some areas. While support was given to both parties, most big business support went to the Republicans. The level of business representation in the cabinet was lower during the Democratic presidencies (Cleveland, Wilson, and F. Roosevelt) than it was under the Republicans, and most businessman senators were Republicans. This reflects the fact that the financial–industrial elite was much more supportive of the Republicans than it was of their rivals. The Republicans privileged manufacturing interests with their emphasis upon protectionism[75] and the gold standard, leading one scholar to argue that the Republicans' strength 'lay in the nation's industrial core among the country's financial and corporate leadership'.[76] Wealthy elements have continued to dominate the Republican Party.

Civil Service

The civil service, or state bureaucracy, was the locus of administrative power in the state and was traditionally staffed by emergent professional bureaucrats, members of the traditional aristocracy, or a combination of both. Because of the role the civil service played in administration of the country, and in particular the autonomy that it had in practice from the government, this would seem to be an obvious place for the emergent bourgeoisie to seek to gain representation. But generally, the class has not been well-represented in state administration.

In Britain, the landowners did not simply sit back and accept the erosion of their position in the key organs of the state. As their position eroded in the Parliament, they sought to buttress their influence at the upper levels of the civil service. In 1853, a report on administrative reform was produced which recommended, inter alia, a lifetime civil service recruited on the basis of competitive examinations based on the curricula of Oxford and Cambridge.[77] This proposal, the Northcote-Trevelyan Report which thereby sought to restrict entry to those educated in the still nobility-dominated 'ancient universities', was finally adopted in 1870 by Gladstone and structured civil service recruitment thenceforth. While the scions of the middle class did increasingly come to fill positions in the expanding civil service, many of the leading positions continued to be filled from among establishment groups in the society.

Businessmen were not strongly represented in the bureaucracy of the French state. The civil service was always highly centralised, riven with favouritism and nepotism, and characterised by an enormous gulf between those at the top, the so-called hauts fonctionnaires,[78] and those at lower levels of the structure. The former had high prestige and were well paid, the latter were clearly much more lowly paid but their positions did give them a sense of status within the community generally. At all levels, at least in the first three quarters of the nineteenth century, appointments and promotions were dependent on patronage and family political relations. This remained the situation until the introduction of entry exams in the Third Republic. At the level of the hauts fonctionnaires, this was accompanied by the development of career pathways that led through new special academies or institutes, the most important of which was the Ecole libre des sciences politiques established in 1871, into the higher levels of the bureaucracy.[79] These were private institutions charging fees, so only those with wealth could attend, thereby confirming the narrow social base of recruitment to the upper levels of the state service. Furthermore this sort of career path, added to the ideology of French national development and the projection of French greatness to which state officials were wedded, helped to generate among this group a strong esprit de corps and sense of collective identity. The civil service was never formally closed to business, and during the Restoration period increasing numbers of sons of businessmen did enter, but this trend stopped under the July Monarchy.[80] Despite the dramatic expansion of the civil service in the second half of the nineteenth century,[81] the scions of businessmen were not prominent. Charle has shown that there was no real movement out of business and into the administrative field in the last part of the century, although senior bureaucrats did move into business and others had personal investments in industry and commerce.[82] Nevertheless, the upper levels of the bureaucracy remained largely closed to French businessmen.

The weakness of the German parties as powerful vehicles of business interest reflects in part the more general point behind declining business represen-tation in the Reichstag, that businessmen could pursue their interests more effectively through other channels. One of these was the state bureaucracy. The upper levels of the state administration remained dominated by the aristocratic old elite, although over the course of the nineteenth century this had been eroded. [83] Nevertheless, the old elite was represented at these levels out of all proportion to their numbers in the society, and generally they were able to hold onto the most important parts of the bureaucracy. But as the state machine expanded,[84] the Junkers could not provide sufficient sons to staff its growing needs.[85] This, plus the increased demand for education as a requirement for employment and advancement in state service, opened the way to members of the bourgeoisie. The professional and educated part of the bourgeoisie, the so-called 'bildungsburgertum', in particular was well placed to take advantage of such opportunities. But the economic bourgeoisie could also exploit this growing need for civil servants. According to one study, by the end of the century, between 20% and 33% of judges and senior state officials came from the families of businessmen.[86] According to Tipton, between 1876 and 1900, the percentage of higher bureaucrats who were sons of wealthy industrialists rose from 12% to 21%.[87] In the Rhine Province, one observer has talked about a 'bourgeois-noble aristocracy of office' arising from the increased connections between business and bureaucracy. This was reflected in the fact that, in 1905, 30% of higher officials had fathers coming from the business and industry sector (cf. 37% of fathers who were officials), while 48% of women married to officials had fathers from the business and industry sector.[88] Of Augustine-Perez's 502 multi-millionaires, 10.9% of their sons became civil servants.[89] Conversely, Spencer has found that of thirty-six managers of heavy industry firms in the Ruhr in the two decades before 1914, twelve had originally been trained as state officials.[90] These figures suggest that by the end of the century there was a significant overlap developing between business and the civil service, and with the simultaneous decline in the position of the aristocracy in the state machine and the growth in recruitment from the bildungsburgertum, the machinery of the state was becoming more bourgeois than traditional in its nature.

In the United States, as noted in the discussion of the executive, business was a rich resource for the staffing of the leading positions in the state structure. At the lower levels of that structure, recruitment was relatively open, in the sense that it was not monopolised by any particular social group. This means that the emergent business class did provide recruits for the civil service, and given the nature of the American class structure (see Chapter 2), this was unproblematic.

Local Government

In all of these countries local government was very important. In part this was because of the limitations of the reach of the central government, at least during the early years of industrialisation. This meant not only that much of concern to local communities was left in the hands of the local authorities, but also that the implementation of central rules and directives was left up to local officials who could act substantially independently of the central government. Furthermore this was the authority which often had most direct power over the immediate conditions within which the new bourgeoisie sought to establish and develop their businesses. This seems like a logical site for the emergent bourgeoisie to seek to control, and this they did.

In contrast to the national level of government in Britain, at the local level in many of the growing towns and cities, industrialists were prominent in government in the nineteenth century.[91] Although aristocrats continued to dominate much of the administration in the countryside through the position of Lord Lieutenant of the county, at least until the 1887 County Councils Act,[92] industrialists often entered the town councils and became mayor. This was an area of government of immediate relevance to them because this level had direct jurisdiction over many of the conditions under which factories had to function. Important here was the Municipal Corporations Act of 1835 which replaced unelected local corporations by councils elected by adult male ratepayers[93] and enabled the local business elite to dominate the cities and towns; between 1835 and 1860, 33% of Lancastrian councillors were textile masters,[94] while in Glossop over forty-three years, all but three mayors were mill owners and in the 1860s of eighteen on the town council, twelve were mill owners and one was a mill manager.[95] In Salford between 1846 and 1890, those classed as manufacturers and merchants averaged 45.7% of the council, in Bolton 1843–90 42.4%, Blackburn 1856–90 40.5%, and in Rochdale 1856–90 55.7%.[96] But there was an interesting paradox here: the more individual industrialists withdrew from entrepreneurial activity and entered the gentlemanly sphere of the county gentry, the more they became encapsulated within a traditional Tory establishment culture of oligarchy and privilege at odds with the culture emerging around urban-based entrepreneurialism.[97]

This was generally a second or third generation development. The first generation of industrialists possessed few family linkages or commonalities with the Anglican Tory elite which had dominated local affairs, and to the extent that they emphasised the image of the self-made man, they exaggerated the differences between them; rather than seeking assimilation, they sought distinction.

French businessmen often played a leading role in local affairs, dominating the towns where they lived and worked. In many places, the local factory or mill was the major source of employment, with the result that the owner wielded significant power over the lives of the town's inhabitants. Often the relationship was highly paternalistic, with the industrialist providing a range of services for those who worked for him.[98] Some entered the departmental conseils generaux, with the proportion of businessmen in these bodies remaining at about 15% during the Orleanist and Second Empire periods.[99] Many took on the mayor's office, which had wide-ranging powers, the better to be able to run affairs to suit their own needs. During the Orleanist period, businessmen were said to be 'the bulk of mayors of major towns',[100] but this situation changed under the Second Empire when the position was more closely integrated into the appointed hierarchical structure of the state.[101] Until late in the Second Empire, it was the mayor who had a preponderant role in determining the outcome of elections because of the way in which they were able to guide those who lived under them.[102] This gave those businessmen who held this position significant influence, but it may also have inhibited the opportunities other businessmen had for gaining national office. Under the Third Republic, some industrialists held the mayoral position, for example, in Le Creusot the Schneider family which owned the local iron and steel works provided the mayor for much of this period, but this was unusual; French local government remained mainly in the hands of state officials.

From at least the early decades of the nineteenth century, German businessmen dominated local politics, especially in those towns where industrial development was most pronounced,[103] and such direct dominance lasted until the end of that century.[104] Such dominance rested in part on a franchise weighted according to income, and in some areas the highest taxpayers were given a part in local budget discussions.[105] Such dominance occurred not only in the smaller towns but also in the major cities. In Hamburg, bankers, financiers, merchants, and industrialists maintained control of the city both by sending sons into city government and by using the network of family ties to exert influence over other members of the municipal administration.[106] But more important than their physical presence in municipal government was probably the influence that they were able to exert because of their importance in the local society and economy, their close professional and social contacts. As one student of the Ruhr at the turn of the century declares: 'It was through such direct, personal contacts, rather than through their sizable representation in the relatively unimportant provincial Landtage, that the entrepreneurial elite exercised their most telling influence on provincial affairs.'[107] Industrialists and the local politico-administrative elite shared a concern to stimulate local economic development (for many administrators this boosted promotion prospects), and to stabilise the status quo against the rise of the socialists. When such administrators were promoted to Berlin, they took with them the associations they had made while in local government, and thereby could act as a continuing channel into the centre for the locally based business interests. Although this sort of local orientation became less important for many businessmen as the process of expansion and cartelisation discussed below shifted their horizons well beyond the local level, local government was a significant channel through which many businessmen sought to realise their aims. But increasingly it was the central level of politics in Berlin that was of most importance to business.

Business was well-represented in the United States at the local and state levels of government. With both levels of government playing an important role in shaping the conditions in which business operated, businessmen were anxious to ensure that their influence was felt in both fora. Furthermore, given that until 1913 senators were chosen by the state legislature, an active business part in this was seen by many as essential for getting 'their' senators into office in Washington (see Chapter 6). Accordingly many businessmen entered politics at the municipal and state levels, taking positions as state legislators and town councillors. But perhaps more common was effective business sponsorship of individual politicians at both levels, with business interests thereby being advanced by professional politicians in the employ of private business. Such business involvement often took a particularly malign form, discussed in Chapter 6.

Structures of Interest Representation

With the structure of state power in these four countries based on acceptance of the right of organisation to press one's views, the principle underlying the growth of electoral politics and political parties, it was a logical inference to accept the legitimacy of organisation for the pursuit of particular interests outside the electoral system. For the emergent bourgeoisie, especially where the level of their representation in the national legislature was low, the organisation of bodies to press their interests directly on government, the legislature, and the civil service was a logical development. This was manifested mainly in the form of employers' associations. The development of these bodies was part of the more general process taking place at this time of the growth of associative societies accompanying industrialisation in these countries. Importantly many of the employers' organisations united large and small businesses within the one structure, although given the greater opportunities available to large businesses to exercise influence in other ways, these associations were generally of more importance for small and medium than for large businesses.

In Britain, business lobbying activity became more organised in the second half of the nineteenth century. Up until the middle of the century, Parliament's view of its role, and in particular the MP's conception of his role as the trustee or representative rather than the delegate, made pressure groups appear illegitimate, except for those 'naturally arising interests'[108] like land and trade. Pressure groups appeared as narrow and selfish, following their own partial interests rather than the broader national interests. However this conception began to change over the course of the nineteenth century. A major part of the reason for this was the mushrooming of civil associations that occurred in the middle years of the century. Such associations took a wide range of forms, from charitable and voluntary associations through to religious and professional bodies and the sorts of workers' associations that were eventually to give way to trade unions. Their emergence and subsequent activity marked the flowering of a vibrant civil society and a vigorous public culture in which political activity and interest became an important component. The transformation of political parties into more mass-oriented organisations following the 1884/85 reforms was part of this process. So too was the development of business associations.

Initially, business associations saw their role principally in terms of the self-policing of business practices. Given the laissez faire approach of the central government, and widespread business support for this, self-regulation was seen as the best way of both ensuring some regularity (and possibly restriction) in competition and of keeping the government out of interfering in their activities. Business organisations also sought to coordinate action at first against the development and activities of trade unions, and then to negotiate with them.[109] But as the century wore on and the prejudice against pressure group activity waned, and as the government became more interested in seeking to become involved in economic matters, these organisations became more intent on influencing government policy. They were particularly interested in seeking to block state regulation of the conditions under which they operated, including the regulation of factories and mines, working conditions, smoke pollution, and regular inspection; issues of public health and housing were also important. Business organisations and businessmen more generally seem to have had significant success in limiting such measures, in part through their capacity to shape the political agenda and to dominate local government, but also because their apparent power discouraged potential reformers from attacking them.[110]

These organisations generally remained localistic and fragmented until well into the twentieth century. There was a proliferation of organisations and associations designed to cater for the interests of particular sectors of the economy. Examples include the General Shipowners' Society (1831), the Central Association of Employers of Operative Engineers (1851), the Mining Association of Great Britain (1854), the General Builders' Association (1865), the Railway Industries Association (1868), the Iron and Steel Institution (1869), the Iron Trades Employers' Association (1872), the National Association of Master Builders (1878), and the Central Association of Bankers (1895). Many of these groups were transitory, established to meet a particular challenge (often in the form of labour unrest), and dissolving once that challenge had disappeared.

Chambers of Commerce could be important vehicles for the projection of bourgeois interests, especially at the local level. Unlike those noted above, the chambers sought to unite all industry and commerce on the basis of territorial propinquity. As such, they could constitute arenas within which local issues could be sorted out, but the different interests of their members (e.g. production versus retail) meant that they often had a fragile unity. Nevertheless, they could have national influence, as in the Manchester Chamber's role as the progenitor of the Anti-Corn Law League, and in the 1880s the Board of Trade was instructed to consult with them on all important matters. In an attempt to increase business influence on Parliament and government, in 1860 some of the provincial chambers of commerce headed by those in Bradford, Hull, and Birmingham formed a federation, the Association of British Chambers of Commerce (ABCC). By 1874, fifty chambers were affiliated with this body.[111] Although it mainly focused upon technical matters of commerce (e.g. bankruptcy provisions), it also provided a channel for the post-Cobden generation of businessmen into national politics. Most active members in the 1860s and 1870s were Liberals, a fact which reflects Liberal dominance in the major industrial and commercial centres where such chambers were to be found.[112] Generally though, the ABCC eschewed political issues, partly because of the tension both between economic sectors and local/regional and national concerns, and it was not very influential. Its refusal to take a stance on political issues and the divisions between different parts of its constituency weakened its capacity for action. Particularly important here was the lack of support for the ABCC among leading financial circles; it was very much an industrially focused organisation.[113] However the establishment of a peak organisation for the chambers created a precedent for later attempts to create similar organisations for employers. It was not until the last decades of the nineteenth century and early twentieth century that nationally organised associations emerged—the National Association of Federated Employers of Labour (1873),[114] the Employers' Parliamentary Council (1898),[115] and the Manufacturers' Association of Great Britain (1905). But such attempts to establish a peak organisation were unsuccessful until the creation of the Federation of British Industries in 1916.[116] Generally, many of the new bourgeoisies remained sceptical about the role and importance of such bodies and unsympathetic to trade organisation, except perhaps insofar as they saw it as a potential counter to the trade unions. Accordingly, despite the network of organisations that emerged, they remained throughout the nineteenth century mostly weak and locally focused until the end of the century when the perceived challenge posed by the strengthening of the trade union presence, the emergence of an avowedly socialist political party, and increased competition on the international scene made collective organisation appear both useful and timely;[117] by the early 1920s, there were some 2,500 employers' associations in Britain.

An important dimension of business activity in France at this time was work through specific business organisations.[118] A law of 1791 had banned all economic associations, but this no longer applied to associations representing one industry from 1884 and to inter-industry associations from 1901.[119] However in practice, this had not prevented such associations from emerging. One of the most important of these was the chamber of commerce. Originally close to official bureaucracy,[120] these had increased in number steadily over the nineteenth century, from twenty-three in 1812 to sixty-two in 1864 and 155 in 1914.[121] These tended throughout much of the century to be dominated by local businessmen and their concerns were correspondingly often local in nature.[122] They could also be characterised by internal conflict and dissension as tensions between different businessmen and different economic sectors were played out within these bodies.[123] There was little coordination between these bodies. In part this was because prior to 1898 they could not meet jointly without specific governmental authorisation, but also important was the fact that the Paris Chamber of Commerce seems consciously to have eschewed a leadership role. Given the different concerns of the local economies, and the differences between sectors of those local economies, it is little wonder that a coherent movement did not develop. Only towards the end of the century, when efforts were made more generally to develop an employers' movement, did the chambers of commerce move in the direction of greater coordination of their activities and the assertion of leadership over the movement more generally. A law in April 1898 recognised the chambers of commerce as 'the representatives, in relation to the public authority, of the commercial and industrial interests in their area'[124] and called for one to be established in each department of the country, thereby giving them a formal status that they had hitherto lacked. In response to this, an Association of Presidents of Chambers of Commerce was established in 1899 as a form of general council of commercial interests, an organisation which had some success in coordinating the employer response to industrial unrest. Ten years later, the Paris Chamber of Commerce coordinated the eight largest national employer associations, 500 syndicates/organisations, and all chambers of commerce to guarantee postal deliveries during the 1909 postal strike.[125] Although the chambers claimed to represent the small and provincial companies better than the sectoral organisations, larger companies tended to dominate the larger chambers of commerce, and these chambers tended to dominate the national association.[126]

Also important were sectoral organisations, seeking to bring together the interests and views of employers in particular sectors of the economy. One of the most important of these during the debate over protection in the last part of the nineteenth century was the Comite des Forges. Founded in 1864 to combine the interests of the iron and steel industry, it always suffered from divisions based on the geographical location of its members: centre versus north versus east. Nevertheless, it was an important mobilising mechanism during the protection debate,[127] and its membership included leading iron and steel industrialists. Also active at various times in the protection debate were such bodies as the Comite Central des Houilleres (founded in 1840) and the Chambre Syndicale des Fabricants de Sucre, and on the other side, the Association pour la Defense de la Liberte Commerciale. Beside such organisations seeking to unite employers in particular industries, there were also bodies which sought to bring together the leaders in various industrial sectors. An even earlier organisation was the Association pour la Defense du Travail National. Founded by the iron magnate Eugene Schneider, cloth manufacturer Victor Grandin, and the iron and railway entrepreneur Leon Talabot in 1846,[128] this organisation disappeared under Louis Napoleon but was revived, with twenty-eight members, in 1878 by the prominent protectionist Augustin Pouyer-Quertier. In the face of rising labour unrest, attempts were made to unite industrial and agricultural employers through the transformation of the Association de l'Industrie Francaise (founded 1878) into the Association de l'Industrie et de l'Agriculture Francaise in 1892. By 1884, there were 185 employers' associations uniting about 25,000 members in Paris with a further 100 organisations in the provinces.[129] Levels of organisation increased late in the century in the face of growing labour unrest.[130]

But many of the business organisations were weak; they had few resources, limited infrastructure, sometimes a shifting membership, often limited horizons, and their role as local representative was often undermined by the propensity of French legislative deputies to act vigorously as representatives of local interests. However they were important in the way that they integrated the French business class into the French polity. They were vehicles through which businessmen could seek to advance their interests, and by enabling some success in this, they acted as means of keeping those businessmen largely within the accepted rules of the system.

At the local level in Germany, paralleling their dominance of local government, many businessmen were active in chambers of commerce. While such bodies often were able to exercise considerable influence in local affairs to the benefit of their business members,[131] they could also play an advocacy role on the national stage; support for the navy laws at the end of the nineteenth century by the Hamburg and Bremen chambers is a case in point.[132] But mostly these bodies concentrated their attention on local matters. More important as vehicles for business activity were the regional and national associations.

German unification followed by the depression beginning in 1873 provided a stimulus for business organisation. An important issue in the early 1870s was that of free trade versus protection, and in an endeavour to mobilise against the currently dominant free trade ethos in the Reichstag, in 1871 the iron industry formed the Association to Protect the Common Economic Interests in Rhineland-Westphalia (the Langnamverein). This united iron and textile industrialists,[133] but was soon overshadowed by the Association of German Iron and Steel Industrialists (VdESI). This was established in November 1873 on a national basis, and soon developed a network of regional groupings representing 214 iron and steel concerns.[134] The aim of the organisation was to represent all parts of the industry, including finishing and manufacturing, in all economic matters and to resolve inter-regional and inter-industrial differences; it thus sought not only to generate common policies but also to prevent conflict within the industry.[135] The VdESI was dominated by the iron and steel producers, especially those of the Northwest, whose leaders also dominated the Langnamverein. They were also present in the peak association established to represent all German industry, the CdI. Established in January 1876, the CdI, although from the start dominated by heavy industry, came to include leading textile, paper, leather, and soda interests.[136] One of the founders of the CdI was industrialist and leader of the Free Conservatives Wilhelm von Kardoff. This body, originally founded in opposition to the prevailing policy of free trade, was instrumental through its negotiations with a corresponding agricultural association[137] in establishing a basis of commonality between heavy industry and major agricultural interests which underpinned the so-called 'alliance of iron and rye' and resulted in the tariff reform of 1879. However the dominating position that heavy industry enjoyed came under challenge before the war, both within the CdI and from other groups. Among these were the small and medium-sized light industries organised in the Federation of German Industrialists (which represented mainly the non-Prussian finishing industry[138]), the emergent chemicals industry, the Association of German Machine Builders (VDMA), and local sectoral organisations.[139]

These employers', or industry, associations were significant actors in the political landscape.[140] Not only were they public advocates for policies that favoured their particular constituencies but they also engaged in behind the scenes lobbying and sought to intervene at all levels of government; according to one scholar, 'by 1914 there was hardly a significant sector of society... that did not have an association claiming to represent it.'[141] Their members and officials often were appointed as experts on committees, where they not only proffered advice but also drafted reports and even on occasions bills;

for example, in the 1890s, representatives of business and the chambers of commerce were brought into the tariff advisory council to design a new tariff regime.[142] They negotiated with leading bureaucrats and could have what one observer has called 'decisive influence' on legislation. They could even exert some hold on party politics by selecting and controlling their own candidates for party and public office.[143] On particular issues, businessmen also often put their support and resources behind other organisations designed to pursue policy aims with which these businessmen agreed; for example, Krupp's funding of the Navy League. But these organisations, their number and the cases of competition between them are testament to the lack of unity within business as a whole. What was good for heavy industry was not necessarily good for other industry sectors. There was a clear division between heavy industry which was overwhelmingly domestically oriented and in favour of protection, and light and machine-tool industry which was more export- oriented and in favour of free trade. The social and economic characteristics of different regions were also different, and this created a variety of interests that were not always easily compatible.[144] This tension, reinforced by a broader sense of resentment at the propensity of the Ruhr industrialists to assume that what was in their interests was in the interests of all others as well and their aspiration to dominate the business sector, was a continuing factor throughout the Empire and was one reason why business was unable uniformly to present a united front on issues.

Under Weimar, business was more organised outside government than inside. The perceived threat to business interests posed by the government's plans to maintain wartime controls stimulated leading businessmen[145] to establish two new peak organisations, the National Association of German Industry (RddI) and the Confederation of German Employers Associations. These were seen as being the instruments for big business to ensure that the economy did not move under state control. The former was to deal with broad issues of economic policy, the latter with labour-management issues. The RddI was the most active of the peak bodies, with its officials having access to high level administrative and political officials in the government, and being able to exert some sense of coherence over some of the business representatives in the Reichstag.[146] But business remained divided. The VdESI remained in existence and, at least from the mid-1920s, under the strong influence of the Ruhr industrialists, but it acted only as an interest group, leaving regulation of the competition in the industry up to the emergent cartel structure.[147] The VDMA revived after 1924, and the Working Community of Iron Finishing Industries (AVI) was established at that time. The perennial conflicts between different sectors of the economy were, in part, played out through these different sorts of institutional configurations.

But many industrialists sought to act independently of these organisations, taking their complaints, requests, and suggestions direct to the authorities.

Many were assisted in this by the continuing processes of growth and cartelisation during this time, and by the way in which German foreign policy was so overshadowed by the reparations issue. This gave businessmen extra leverage with the government and enabled them often to get their way on crucial issues. Cartelisation had been underway before the institution of Weimar, and what it did was to establish large structures of business power, often intimately linked with the state in a mutually beneficial relationship (see Chapter 6). Heavy industry in particular was very powerful for much of the Weimar period.[148] What is important about this is that that power was exercised outside the formal, democratic structures of the system. The process of negotiation and conciliation occurred between major interest blocs, and usually behind closed doors with no democratic controls upon it. As a result, the Reichstag became increasingly irrelevant to the disposition of power in Germany, more a reflector than an initiator of decisions, with business groups and the state engaging through corporatist and lobbying channels on a far more systematic basis than they were through public channels. Thus the importance of business for the collapse of the Weimar Republic was not so much its manoeuvrings around the government and its fall as the structural position it gained and therefore the politico-administrative structure that it helped to create that bypassed the formal institutions; it was part of the emergence of a corporatist-style set of arrangements that bypassed the democratic institutions of the polity. Thus business organisation and the way that sector of life chose to organise its affairs effectively helped to undercut the Weimar system.

Business organisation at the national level in the United States developed rather late; at the local level, chambers of commerce and boards of trade were common during the upsurge of industrialisation, but it was not until the twentieth century that there was a peak employers body with widespread support. Lobbying had taken on a new importance in the last quarter of the nineteenth century[149] as business used all methods at its disposal to influence government. Apart from having one's own people in the leading institutions of the state, the most regular form this took was through the use of special agents in the capital employed to press particular business demands. This could take the form of acting through the existing business associations, of purchasing some of the time of professional lobbying agencies, or individual corporations could employ their own people to do this job.

Thus at the beginning of the twentieth century, the United States lacked an effective national organisation of business associations with close ties to government.[150] This was remedied early in the century. An early step in this regard was the creation of the National Civic Federation (NCF) in 1900, a formally tripartite (business–labour–public) organisation that became the principal organisation of politically conscious corporate leaders up to the First World War.[151] Initially, the NCF saw its main role to be in the mediation of labour disputes, but soon in alliance with politicians like Theodore Roosevelt, Taft, and Wilson, it saw its task as being one of stabilising the socio-economic situation.[152] With this in mind, it supported conservative unionism, a range of welfare-type measures including minimum wages, workers' compensation, public utilities regulation, and limits on child labour, as well as encouraging federal and state action. Federal politicians in particular relied on the NCF for advice and for some policy initiatives; the NCF devised draft bills on workers' compensation, minimum wages, the regulation of public utilities, and treatment of monopolies (the Hepburn Bill), and it drafted principles for the new Federal Trade Commission.[153] In this way, the NCF projected big business right into the process of devising law that was meant to regulate the conduct of business itself.

Much of what the NCF pursued was opposed by small business acting through the National Association of Manufacturers (NAM), which was established in 1894. This opposition was based principally on the fact that smaller businesses felt less able to afford the costs implied by the 'new liberalism', a constant theme in the relationship between big and small business. This is reflected in the support of the NAM for the establishment of a Bureau of Corporations which, they believed, would check the development of trusts and thereby strengthen the economic position of small business in competition with larger entities.

Also important as a form of business organisation was the Chamber of Commerce. This was established in 1912, principally at government stimulus, with the aim of it becoming the major commercial lobby group. It had to overcome a variety of hurdles to become established, including the opposition of existing business organisations,[154] but because of its close links with the government and its more broadly based membership than any competitor business organisation, it soon became 'the recognized voice of the American business community'.[155] Its expertise and its members were effectively co-opted into government service on many issues through the advice-giving role that it played. All of these organisations carried out classic lobbying activities with the government in the defence of business interests.

* * *

The four national patterns of bourgeois representation show some commonalities and some clear differences. In all countries, business interests gained representation in the national legislatures, but this was at significantly higher levels in Britain and the United States than it was in France and Germany. Bourgeois representation in the executive was extensive in the United States, but limited in the other three countries, with Germany, where the executive was strongest vis-à-vis the legislature over the entire period, having the lowest level of this. The absence of a business party which alone represented business interests is a common feature, although there are different dynamics of party representation; in particular, the way in which business interests shifted from the Liberals to the Conservatives in Britain and the superseding of the National Liberal and Centre parties by the People's Party and National People's Party in Germany contrasts with the continuing primary place as business representative occupied by the Republicans in the United States. Representation in local government was strongly developed in Britain and the United States, significant in France, and growing in Germany. Representation in the bureaucracy was extensive in the United States, but much more limited elsewhere. In all countries there was an array of employers organisations, but in Britain these remained weak and locally oriented until into the twentieth century, in France the local focus of these bodies remained significant although their view was becoming more 'nationalised' by the end of the century, they were a strong presence in Germany and took on a corporatist tone under Weimar, while such organisations were well developed in the United States but only took on a national hue in the twentieth century.

It is striking that only in the United States was there a high level of bourgeois involvement in all components of the state; according to one scholar, 'It would seem that every industrial group and every great monopoly was almost directly represented in the political councils of the nation, the better to 'enrich themselves and the country'.'[156] The significantly more prominent place in the legislature in Britain and the United States may reflect the fact that in both countries the legislature was historically a very powerful body in the political system; in both Britain and the United States, the national legislature played a central role in the creation of the conditions for the emergence of industrial capitalism. It was important not only for the setting of broad macro-economic policy but also in many of the more micro issues, like the granting of charters for the establishment of railways. But the power of the legislature alone cannot explain the higher levels of representation because even if in France and Germany the legislature was less powerful than the executive, the legislature could still take decisions of crucial importance for business interests. Important too was the recent, pre-industrial, history of the British and American legislatures acting much more as arenas for the vigorous representation of economic interests at the national level than their counterparts in France and Germany. In France and Germany, where there was more limited access to both the legislature and the political executive, bourgeois interests had to rely principally on other avenues, and, especially in Germany, they sought these through extensive use of trade and industry organisations. Given the extensive role of the state in development in these two countries (see below), this encouraged state cooptation of a more corporatist style of activity than in Britain or in the United States.

New businessmen were therefore active in the political systems that they found. Their wealth, economic power, and presumed expertise, often allied to the sorts of shared values and social circles discussed in Chapter 2, gave them, and especially the large businessmen, entrée into the political heights. In the United States where the line between new money and old was less distinct, this sort of access was seen as a right virtually from the outset. In the other three countries, it was less secure; in Britain the continued denigration of 'new money' by old engendered an element of insecurity into this relationship, in France the continuing sway of the French state and of officialdom made businessmen appear as outsiders, while in Germany the strength of traditional values and of the Junkers limited the capacity of the economic bourgeoisie to achieve high office. But what this also means is that bourgeois access to the state was structured overwhelmingly by the institutional and social configuration of the state that confronted them. Rather than a direct attack upon the state and its structure, the new class accommodated itself to the state and worked through the opportunities the state afforded; the economic bourgeoisie was generally content to act through the political channels available to it rather than revolutionising the political structures through their entry. They largely accepted the channels as given without trying to overturn them. Where the political systems were relatively liberal and open, as in Britain, the United States (even if wealth was becoming an increasingly important factor in the capacity of an individual to climb the political ladder) and for some of this time France, bourgeois entry to the upper reaches of the political system was more extensive than in Germany where the system was more closed. But the question that follows is how the patterns of representation noted above were manifested in the functioning of politics in each country. This will be discussed in Chapter 6.

Notes

1. The statistics used in this chapter come from a variety of sources, and they are not always consistent. This inconsistency reflects the different categories (and the different ways in which categories are defined) used by different scholars and the different time periods to which the statistics are applied.
2. Although throughout the nineteenth century the cabinet's power increased, it had no formal institutional existence and had nothing like the power and authority it was to gain in the twentieth century.
3. For summaries of the effects of these Acts, see John Garrard, *Democratisation in Britain. Elites, Civil Society and Reform since 1800* (Basingstoke, Palgrave, 2002), pp. ix–xiii.
4. Until 1859, there was a property qualification to be elected to Parliament and given that MPs were not paid, this effectively excluded those without independent means, while the need to take the oaths of supremacy and allegiance was, until 1858, a disincentive to practising Jews and Catholics.

5. These acts were also instrumental in doing away with pocket boroughs (constituencies that were controlled by local magnates, usually landowners) and rotten boroughs (constituencies with few or no inhabitants that were bought and sold in order to gain representation in the Parliament).

6. Alfred Cobban, *A History of Modern France. Volume 2: From the First Empire to the Second Empire 1799–1871* (Harmondsworth, Penguin, 1965), p. 78.

7. Cobban (A History), p. 98.

8. However those landowners were not only the old aristocracy, but included many new men who had made their wealth in various ways under the Ancien Regime and during the Revolution, and had invested that wealth in landholding.

9. Cobban (A History), p. 184. This control broke down in the 1869 election. Alain Plessis, *The Rise and Fall of the Second Empire, 1852–1871* (Cambridge, Cambridge University Press, 1985), p. 36.

10. From 1877, only in 1919 (when the figure was 46%) less than 56% of sitting deputies were returned; in 1846, it had been 41%. Mattei Dogan, 'La Stabilite Du Personnel Parlementaire Sous La Troisieme Republique', *Revue Francaise De Science Politique* III, 1, April–June 1953, p. 322. Also Theodore Zeldin, *France 1848–1945. Volume 1. Ambition, Love and Politics* (Oxford, Clarendon Press, 1973), p. 589.

11. Samuel Clark, *State and Status. The Rise of the State and Aristocratic Power in Western Europe* (Montreal, McGill-Queens University Press, 1995), p. 99.

12. Plessis (Rise and Fall), pp. 20 & 26.

13. Gordon A. Craig, *Germany 1866–1945* (Oxford, Clarendon Press, 1978), p. 45. Political power in the system remained located in the hands of the traditional landowning interests supported by the state. In the words of one student of the period: 'The political system of the German Empire was devised from the first, so as to give maximum protection from parliamentary influence to those institutions that had always been the particular preserve of the conservative elites—the army, the civil service and, above all, the leading agencies of foreign policy—by making them subject to the exclusive prerogative of the King and, later, the Emperor.' Wolfgang J. Mommsen, *Imperial Germany 1867–1918. Politics, Culture and Society in an Authoritarian State* (London, Arnold, 1955, trans. Richard Deveson), p. 42.

14. Prior to 1832 in Britain, some manufacturers were able to gain representation through the purchase of land and pocket boroughs; in no House of Commons elected between 1802 and 1831, were there fewer than 150 businessmen. W.D. Rubinstein, *Capitalism, Culture and Decline in Britain 1750–1990* (London, Routledge, 1990), p. 142. They were sometimes active in political life outside Parliament; many supported proposals for parliamentary reform in the early 1830s, with threats to stop business and create a run on the banks instrumental in persuading the Tories to drop their opposition to the 1832 Reform Act. Pauline Gregg, *A Social and Economic History of Britain 1760–1965* (London, George G. Harrop & Co., 1965), p. 156.

15. In terms of access to political power, the nineteenth century saw the rise of the new middle class, including industrialists, at the expense of the noble landowners. With the emergence of the new class of businessmen, new interests sought to gain entry into the political system. Prior to the Reform Act of 1832, the government

was dominated by the interests of the landed nobility and the old mercantile and financial elite which had dominated through the mercantile system linked with the Empire. In this period, the small, new manufacturing class was largely excluded from the ruling elite, which, in the words of one author, 'was based in a close and harmonious connection between mercantile wealth, especially that based in the Old Empire, City finance, land, the professions, and the government as contractor, loan agent, and originator of 'Old Corruption', the extraordinary system of lucrative perquisites which came to fortunate aristocrats, government employees, and their relatives.' Rubinstein (Capitalism, Culture, and Decline), p. 142.

16. Harold Perkin, *The Rise of Professional Society. England Since 1880* (London, Routledge, 2002), p. 41. For figures on the source of wealth of entrants to the House of Commons, 1700–1879, see E.A. Wasson, 'The Penetration of New Wealth into the English Governing Class from the Middle Ages to the First World War', *Economic History Review* LI, 1, February 1988, p. 36. For social groups in the House, 1831–65, see Guttsman (British Political Elite), p. 41. Unlike in France, the position of the landed aristocracy had not been broken by revolution. Indeed, the 'Glorious Revolution' and the settlement it ushered in had actually consolidated their control even while the basis of their power was shifting with the emergence of agrarian capitalism in the countryside. For this argument, see Robert Brenner, 'Agrarian Class Structure and Economic Development in Pre-Industrial Europe', T.H. Ashton & C.H. Philpin (eds.), *The Brenner Debate* (Cambridge, Cambridge University Press, 1987), pp. 10–63; Ellen Meiksins Wood, *The Pristine Culture of Capitalism. A Historical Essay on Old Regimes and Modern States* (London, Verso, 1991); Ellen Meiksins Wood, *The Origin of Capitalism* (New York, Monthly Review Press, 1999), ch. 4; Colin Mooers, *The Making of Bourgeois Europe. Absolutism, Revolution, and the Rise of Capitalism in England, France and Germany* (London, Verso, 1991), ch. 4.

17. For example, according to one study, the proportion constituted by large landowners in 1912 was 16.2%. Best (Recruitment), p. 26. In another publication, Best gives a slightly different figure when he declared that the proportion from the nobility declined from around 40% at the early stage of the Empire to 15% in the last Reichstag of the Empire. Heinrich Best, 'Elite Structure and Regime (Dis)continuity in Germany 1867–1933: The Case of Parliamentary Leadership Groups', *German History* 8, 1, February 1990, p. 6.

18. Robert Tombs, *France 1814–1914* (London, Longman, 1996), p. 97. Zeldin (Political System), pp. 62–63. In the last Chamber of Deputies of the Restoration period, some 38.5% of deputies were higher officials compared with 14.8% engaged in trade, finance, or industry, 5.2% members of the liberal professions, and 41.5% were large landowners. Cobban (A History), p. 78.

19. G.R. Searle, *Corruption in British Politics 1895–1930* (Oxford, Clarendon Press, 1987), pp. 40–41 & 48–49.

20. Searle (Corruption), pp. 40–41 & 44. In 1899, the number of directorships held by ministers was 41.

21. For example, at the time Gladstone's railway bill was watered down in 1844, there were more than 100 directors of railway companies in the House, with many

others having railway interests. David Mountfield, *The Railway Barons* (London, Osprey, 1979), p. 52. In the late 1890s, Lloyd George held shares in the Royal Niger Company while he was colonial secretary. Searle (Corruption), pp. 48–49. Only in 1906 did ministers have to give up their directorships on taking office, while the general practice of MPs declaring an interest did not come in until the inter-war period. Searle (Corruption), pp. 43–44.

22. J.A. Thomas has sought to give an estimate of the share of interests (not representatives) in the House (%).

	Landowners	Bourgeoisie	Bourgeoisie comprising		
			Industry	Commerce	Finance
1832	52.4	27.0	7.2	12.2	7.6
1835	51.5	27.3	8.0	11.7	7.6
1837	51.5	25.8	7.8	10.8	7.1
1841	52.3	25.6	8.8	10.0	6.8
1847	45.8	30.8	15.4	8.7	6.7
1852	43.7	30.1	15.4	8.4	6.3
1857	42.5	32.3	18.3	7.7	6.3
1859	41.8	29.4	17.4	6.5	5.6
1865	34.8	43.7	24.1	6.5	13.1
1868	33.8	52.6	32.4	6.2	14.0
1874	30.5	45.6	24.7	6.1	14.8
1880	26.4	49.3	25.8	6.3	17.2
1885	17.4	53.3	28.9	6.6	17.8
1886	18.8	51.9	27.5	6.1	18.4
1892	16.6	52.7	28.1	6.0	18.6
1895	15.8	52.2	26.9	5.9	19.4
1900	15.5	52.1	28.2	6.1	17.8

J.A. Thomas, *The House of Commons 1832–1901. A Study of Its Economic and Functional Character* (Cardiff, University of Wales Press Board, 1939). The figures are calculated from the tables on pp. 4–7 & 14–17. The 'Industry' category comprises Cotton and other textiles, Colliery proprietors, Railways, Shipping and transport, Metals, Engineering, Manufacturers (miscellaneous), Brewers and distillers, Contractors, and Newspaper proprietors and editors. 'Commerce' comprises Merchants and East and West India proprietors. The figures are rounded.

23. See Garrard (Democratisation), pp. 10–13.
24. Michael W. McCahill, "Peers, Patronage, and the Industrial Revolution, 1760–1800", *Journal of British Studies* xvi, 1976, pp. 84–107.
25. Searle (Corruption), pp. 43–44.
26. For figures on this, see the data in footnote 22. For an insightful discussion of sectoral and regional differences, see G.R. Searle, *Entrepreneurial Politics in Mid-Victorian Britain* (Oxford, Oxford University Press, 1993), pp. 312–314.
27. For example, in the Legislative Body of Second Empire France, there were seventy-five industrialists, four engineers, two printers, thirty-three merchants, and twenty-two financiers. Zeldin (Political System), p. 63. In the Third Republic, most 'businessmen' deputies were industrial entrepreneurs (603)

cf. 259 merchants; this source does not identify financiers separately. Dogan (Les filieres), p. 479.

28. On Germany, see Berghoff & Moller (Tired Pioneers), p. 281 and Cassis (Businessmen and the Bourgeoisie), pp. 117–119.

29. On Britain, see Searle (Entrepreneurial Politics), pp. 4–9.

30. On France, see Roger Magraw, *France 1815–1914. The Bourgeois Century* (Oxford, Fontana, 1983), p. 52. On Germany, Henry Ashby Turner, *German Big Business and the Rise of Hitler* (New York, Oxford University Press, 1985), p. 22.

31. Guttsman (British Political Elites), pp. 38 & 78. The figures from 1830–68 (from p. 38) combine in the 'Landowners' column figures given in the original for 'Large territorial lords and their sons' (56) and 'Country gentlemen (lesser landowners)' (12); in the 'Middle class' column are combined the two categories 'Mercantile and administrative upper class (mainly rentiers)' (21) and "'New men" of no family (mainly lawyers)' (14). Contrast these figures with the generalisation made in Dominic Lieven, *The Aristocracy in Europe 1815–1914* (Basingstoke, Macmillan, 1992), p. 206. Perkin gives slightly different figures: the 1892 Liberal Cabinet had six landowners, one rentier, two businessmen, and eight lawyers and professional men; 1906 had eight landowners and businessmen, nine lawyers and professional men, and one trade unionist. Perkin (The Rise), p. 524.

32. Cassis, (Businessmen and the Bourgeoisie), p. 112. In the words of John Garrard, those industrialists who did reach Westminster 'remained outside the "exclusive circles"'. Garrard (Democratisation), p. 45. In part, the slow progression to Cabinet was because many businessmen entered Parliament only after they had established their businesses. This means that they tended to be older and have less parliamentary experience than their non-business colleagues. But even those who entered Parliament at a younger age, often on the back of their fathers' business fortunes, were slow in climbing the tree.

33. J.M. Bourne, *Patronage and Society in Nineteenth-Century England* (London, Edward Arnold, 1986), p. 53.

34. Magraw (France 1815–1914), p. 52.

35. For a biographical study of Perier, see Medeleine Bousset, *Casimir Perier. Un prince financier au temps du romantisme* (Paris, Publications de la Sorbonne, 1994). On the role of the Perier Bank and bankers generally during the Restoration, see Richard J. Barker, "The Perier Bank During the Restoration (1815–1830)", *Journal of European Economic History* 2, 3, Winter 1973, pp. 641–656. Baron James Rothschild (the head of the Parisian branch) was a close adviser of King Louis-Philippe. On Rothschild, see Guy P. Palmade, *French Capitalism in the Nineteenth Century* (Newton Abbott, David & Charles, 1972), p. 105.

36. Christophe Charle, *A Social History of France in the Nineteenth Century* (Oxford, Berg, 1994), p. 205.

37. Dogan (Les filieres), p. 479.

38. Cassis (Businessmen and the Bourgeoisie), p. 112.

39. Cassis (Businessmen and the Bourgeoisie), p. 112.

40. Craig (Germany), pp. 445–447.

41. Niall Ferguson, *Paper and Iron. Hamburg business and German politics in the era of inflation, 1897–1927* (Cambridge, Cambridge University Press, 1995), p. 377.

42. W.A. McDougall, "Political Economy versus National Sovereignty: French Structures for German Economic Integration after Versailles", *Journal of Modern History* 51, 1 March 1979, p. 16.

43. Charles S. Maier, *Recasting Bourgeois Europe. Stabilization in France, Germany and Italy in the Decade After World War I* (Princeton, Princeton University Press, 1975), p. 247.

44. Business was also strongly represented in the Supreme Court, although this was often by lawyers with ties to business. According to one study, the post-Civil War years was a period 'in which corporate wealth attained great power on this body, for pro-business, especially pro-railroad, lawyers were appointed to the Court on a sharply increased scale, to the point where they came to dominate most of its proceedings'. Burch argues that from the early 1860s until the late 1880s there were six Supreme Court justices with family or other close ties to business interests. This trend continued into the twentieth century. Philip H. Burch (Jr.), *Elites in American History. The Civil War to the New Deal* (New York, Holmes & Meier Publishers Inc., 1981) vol. 2. p. 108. Burch's figure compares with a figure of thee cited by John R. Schmidhauser, "The Justices of the Supreme Court—A Collective Portrait", *Midwest Journal of Political Science* 3, 1, February 1959, pp. 1–57. Also, see Chester McArthur Destler, "The Opposition of American Businessmen to Social Control During the 'Gilded Age'", *Mississippi Valley Historical Review* xxxix, March 1953, p. 665.

45. For information on the background of the presidents, see Edward Pessen, *The Log Cabin Myth. The Social Backgrounds of the Presidents* (New Haven, Yale University Press, 1984) and Burch (Elites), vol. 2, pp. 328–485 & vol. 3, p. 400.

46. Burch (Elites), vol. 3, pp. 374–375 gives the raw data. The substance of this will be found in vol. 2, pp. 328–485 and vol. 3, pp. 400–409.

47. Burch (Elites), vol. 2, pp. 86 & 131.

48. Burch (Elites), vol. 2, pp. 102–103.

49. Frederic Cople Jaher, "The Gilded Elite: American Multimillionaires, 1865 to the Present", W.D. Rubinstein (ed.), *Wealth and the Wealthy in the Modern World* (London, Croom Helm, 1980), p. 219.

50. The figures are from Thomas (House of Commons), pp. 4–5 & 14–15. There was also bourgeois representation among the Repealers (1832–1852), the Irish Nationalists (1880–1900), and the Radicals; and in the latter two they constituted a considerable proportion of the interests represented in the Parliament. However the numbers were generally much smaller than in the two major parties, and it is likely that members of the bourgeoisie joined these parties primarily because of the particular issues with which the parties were concerned rather than the pursuit of their economic interests.

51. See the discussion in Perkin (Rise), p. 40.

52. Harold Perkin, "Land Reform and Class Conflict in Victorian Britain", Harold Perkin, *The Structured Crowd. Essays in English Social History* (Brighton, The Harvester Press, 1981), p. 124.

53. Liberal Proportion of Interests in the House of Commons (%).

	1868	1874	1880	1885	1886	1892	1895	1900	1906	1910
Land	47.4	33.9	48.6	47.5	25.1	23.8	17.0	16.7	51.7	23.5
Business	71.8	57.3	69.7	61.1	40.9	49.9	32.0	32.3	71.6	52.5
Finance	71.7	51.1	61.4	54.0	31.1	38.0	21.7	20.9	64.1	42.1
Merchants	82.9	72.7	81.0	77.4	57.2	66.2	46.8	39.3	87.1	66.7
Professions	72.7	61.5	77.2	68.7	45.6	56.0	40.8	44.3	82.1	57.7

Perkin (Land Reform), p. 130.
54. Perkin (Land Reform), pp. 124–128.
55. Pugh (Making of Modern British Politics), pp. 117–119.
56. According to Berghoff & Moller (Tired Pioneers), p. 280, 56.3% of business-men born before 1830 supported the Liberals, but only 46.2% of those born after 1860. They also state that this understates the extent of the Liber-als' loss of business support, which they attribute to the Irish home rule crisis.
57. Pugh (Making of Modern British Politics), p. 20.
58. Perkin (Land Reform), p. 123. The Liberals held every parliamentary seat in Lon-don in 1865 and eight of seventy-two in 1900. Perkin (Rise), p. 43.
59. This is reflected in the fact that Liberals were more active in creating peers with commercial and industrial links from non-noble and non-gentry backgrounds than the Conservatives. Ralph E. Pumphrey, "The Introduction of Industrialists into the British Peerage: A Study in Adaptation of a Social Institution", *American Historical Review* LXV, 1, October 1959, p. 9.
60. Dogan (Les filieres), p. 473. For some figures relating to the origin of Republican militants at local level during the Second Republic, see Ronald Aminzade, *Ballots and Barricades. Class Formation and Republican Politics in France 1830–1871* (Prince-ton, Princeton University Press, 1993), p. 37.
61. Sheehan (Political Leadership), p. 521.
62. Woodruff Smith & Sharon A. Turner, "Legislative Behavior in the German Reich-stag, 1898–1906", *Central European History* 14, 1, 1981, p. 9.
63. Berghoff & Moller (Tired Pioneers), pp. 279–280, who claim that 50.9% of busi-nessmen in their sample who were affiliated with a political party were linked to the National Liberals, but only 4.2% of their sample had any party association at all.
64. Michael Sturmer, *The German Empire 1870–1918* (New York, Random House, 2000), pp. 38–39.
65. Bankers generally were prepared to follow the lead of the industrialists, although they were able and willing to defend their interests when required, as, for example, in their blocking (with the assistance of the Reichsbank and Finance Ministry) of the establishment of an Economic Bank in 1921, although following the 1931 crisis, bank directors were purged and closer control instituted. Youssef Cassis "Introduction", Youssef Cassis (ed.), *Finance and Financiers in European History, 1880–1960* (Cambridge, Cambridge University Press, 1992), p. 11

66. Gerald D. Feldman, "The Social and Economic Policies of German Big Business, 1918–1929", *American Historical Review* 75, 1, October 1969, p. 49.

67. Herman Lebovics, *Social Conservatism and the Middle Classes in Germany, 1914–1933* (Princeton, Princeton University Press, 1969), p. 34. In 1930, ten DVP deputies held seventy-seven company directorships between them. Craig (Germany), p. 505. According to Geary, the heavy industrial lobby exerted influence in the DVP at the end of the 1920s. Dick Geary, "Employers, Workers, and the Collapse of the Weimar Republic", Ian Kershaw (ed.), *Weimar: Why Did German Democracy Fail?* (London, Weidenfeld & Nicolson, 1990), p. 102.

68. Lebovics (Social Conservatism), p. 34.

69. See the discussion in Henry Ashby Turner Jr, "Big Business and the Rise of Hitler", *American Historical Review* 75, 1, October 1969, p. 58.

70. See Turner, (Big Business), pp. 56–70; Turner (German Big Business); Geary (Employers), pp. 94–97; Frank B. Tipton Jr, "Small Business and the Rise of Hitler: A Review Article", *Business History Review* LIII, 2, Summer 1979, pp. 235–246. Also Michael Mann, *Fascists* (Cambridge, Cambridge University Press, 2004), pp. 196–197.

71. Mann (Fascists), pp. 378–379.

72. Turner (German Big Business), pp. 23–24.

73. Richard Franklin Bensel, *The Political Economy of American Industrialization, 1877–1900* (Cambridge, Cambridge University Press, 2000).

74. For the efforts by Mark Hanna to regularise corporate donations to the Republicans, see Edwin M. Epstein, *The Corporation in American Politics* (Englewood Cliffs, Prentice Hall Inc., 1969), p. 27. In 1907, the Tillman Act forbade corporate contributions to party and individual campaigns in federal elections, but this was circumvented through personal donations. Epstein (Corporation), p. 29.

75. According to Bensel, tariff protection effectively 'redistributed income from the southern cotton plantation to the northern factory, thus promoting capital accumulation in the coffers of industrial corporations'. Bensel (Political Economy), pp. 463–464.

76. The Democrats privileged commodity exporters of the South, with large sections of the party committed to free trade and opposed to the gold standard. Bensel (Political Economy), p. 285. Bensel gives a good account of the different parties' positions on the various issues to do with industrial development. Also, see John M. Dobson, *Politics in the Gilded Age. A New Perspective on Reform* (New York, Praeger Publications, 1971), p. 50.

77. For one discussion, see Peter Gowan, "The Origins of the Administrative Elite", *New Left Review* 162, March–April 1987, pp. 4–34.

78. On the hauts fonctionnaires, see Christophe Charle, *Les hauts fonctionnaires en France au XIXe siecle* (Paris, Gallimard, 1980), chs. 7–9.

79. R.D. Anderson, *France 1870–1914. Politics and Society* (London, Routledge & Kegan Paul, 1977), p. 81.

80. Clive H. Church, *Revolution and Red Tape. The French Ministerial Bureaucracy 1770–1850* (Oxford, Clarendon Press, 1981), pp. 295 & 304.

81. Different authors give different figures, but all show a major increase. Zeldin (France 1848–1945), p. 114: 250,000 in 1848 and 500,000 in 1914; Plessis (Rise

and Fall), p. 42: 122,000 in 1851 and 265,000 in 1871 (only civilians); Michael Mann, *The Sources of Social Power. Volume II. The Rise of Classes and Nation States* (Cambridge, Cambridge University Press, 1993), p. 807: 90,000 in 1840, 146,000 in 1850, 220,000 in 1870, 331,000 in 1880, 348,000 in 1890, 430,000 in 1900, and 556,000 in 1910 (central officials only). Much of this growth was at the lower levels, especially among teachers and postmen. On one department in the Second Empire, see Howard C. Payne, *The Police State of Louis Napoleon Bonaparte 1851–1860* (Seattle, University of Washington Press, 1966).

82. Christophe Charle, *Les Elites de la Republique (1880–1900)* Paris, Fayard, 1987), p. 123. For some figures, see Cassis (Businessmen and the Bourgeoisie), p. 112.

83. David Blackbourn & Geoff Eley, *The Peculiarities of German History. Bourgeois Society and Politics in Nineteenth Century Germany* (Oxford, Oxford University Press, 1984) pp. 245–247. According to one scholar, the proportion of the administrative elite that was from the aristocracy stayed at around 65%. Best (Elite Structure), p. 7.

84. For some figures on the expansion of personnel, both civilian and military, see Mann II, p. 808.

85. According to Gillis, the composition of the higher administration of the Rhine Province changed as follows:

	Nobles (%)	Non-noble birth (%)
1850	38	62
1875	49	51
1905	13	87

John R. Gillis, "Aristocracy and Bureaucracy in Nineteenth-Century Prussia", *Past and Present* 41, December 1968, pp. 105–129.

86. Richard J.Evans, "Family and Class in the Hamburg Grand Bourgeoisie 1815–1914", David Blackbourn & Richard J. Evans (eds.), *The German Bourgeoisie: Essays on the Social History of the German Middle Class from the Late Eighteenth to the Early Twentieth Century* (London, Routledge, 1991), p. 117.

87. Frank B. Tipton, "Government and the Economy in the Nineteenth Century", Sheilah Ogilvie & Richard Overy (eds.), *Germany. A New Social and Economic History. Volume III. Since 1800* (London, Arnold, 2003), p. 139.

88. Gillis (Aristocracy), p. 125.

89. Dolores Augustine-Perez, "Very Wealthy Businessmen in Imperial Germany", Youssef Cassis (ed.), *Business Elites* (Aldershot, Edward Elgar, 1994), p. 604.

90. Elaine Glovka Spencer, "Rulers of the Ruhr: Leadership and Authority in German Big Business", Cassis (Business Elites), p. 369.

91. For the argument that manufacturers were not particularly prominent in the major civic institutions in Glasgow, see Stana Nenadic, "Businessmen, the Urban Middle Classes, and the 'Dominance' of Manufacturers in Nineteenth Century Britain", *Economic History Review* XLIV, 1, 1991, pp. 72–73.

92. Until their replacement by elected county councils through this Act, they nominated the JPs in whom effective power lay.

93. In 1869, the franchise was extended to include all ratepayers including unmarried adult female ratepayers.
94. Searle (Entrepreneurial Politics), p. 13.
95. Malcolm Pearce & Geoffrey Stewart, *British Political History 1867–2001* (London, Routledge, 2002), p. 20.
96. Garrard (The Middle Classes), p. 42. Also see the longer study, John Garrard, *Leadership and Power in Victorian Industrial Towns 1830–80* (Manchester, Manchester University Press, 1983). For figures for Leicester, Leeds and Norwich for 1899–1914, see Pearce & Stewart (British Political), p. 189.
97. Theodore Koditschek, *Class Formation and Urban Industrial Society. Bradford 1750–1850* (Cambridge, Cambridge University Press, 1990), p. 144. For an earlier study of Hull which showed how parliamentary representatives were expected to look after local commercial interests, see Gordon Jackson, *Hull in the Eighteenth Century. A Study in Social and Economic History* (Oxford, Oxford University Press, 1972), pp. 253, 257–258 & 309.
98. For an example, see Donald Reid, "Schools and the Paternalist Project at Le Creusot, 1850–1919", *Journal of Social History* 27, 1, Fall 1993, pp. 129–143.
99. Price (Social History), p. 102.
100. Magraw (France 1815–1914), p. 55.
101. According to Plessis, at this time the mayor was a delegate of the prefect, who was in turn a delegate of central authority and usually came from a military or civil service family. Alain Plessis, *The Rise and Fall of the Second Empire, 1851–1871* (Cambridge, Cambridge University Press, 1985), pp. 44–45.
102. Zeldin (Political System), p. 85. This was in part due to the absence of a truly secret ballot until 1913.
103. For one discussion, see Jeffry M. Diefendorf, *Businessmen and Politics in the Rhineland, 1789–1834* (Princeton, Princeton University Press, 1980), pp. 254–285. Although Berghoff & Moller (Tired Pioneers), p. 280 assert that German businessmen were less likely than their British counterparts to hold municipal office.
104. George Steinmetz, "The Myth of an Autonomous State: Industrialists, Junkers, and Social Policy in Imperial Germany", Geoff Eley (ed.), *Society, Culture, and the State in Germany, 1870–1930* (Ann Arbor, University of Michigan Press, 1996), p. 265. According to Steinmetz, up to the turn of the century, most liberal councillors in many cities were bankers, industrialists or other businessmen. p. 291. However, the position of mayor (Oberburgermeister) was normally a salaried official appointed from outside the town. Berghoff & Moller (Tired Pioneers), p. 280.
105. Steinmetz (Myth), p. 291.
106. Evans (Family and Class), pp. 119 & 123. For a study which shows this as extending well into the Weimar period, see Ferguson (Paper and Iron). For the situation in Hessen, see Dan S. White, *The Splintered Party: National Liberalism in Hessen and the Reich, 1867–1918* (Cambridge, MA, Harvard University Press, 1976).
107. Elaine Glovka Spencer, "Businessmen, Bureaucrats, and Social Control in the Ruhr, 1896–1914", Hans Ulrich-Webler (ed.), *Sozialgeschichte Heute* (Gottingen, 1974), p. 454.

108. Garrard (Democratisation), p. 87.
109. Garrard (Democratisation), p. 149.
110. Garrard (Democratisation), p. 150.
111. Searle (Entrepreneurial Politics), p. 167.
112. Searle (Entrepreneurial Politics), pp. 167–168.
113. Another body which, although dominated by professionals like doctors, lawyers, and civil servants, gave some businessmen a voice in the 1870–1880s was the National Association for the Promotion of Social Science. Searle (Entrepreneurial Politics), pp. 198–201.
114. This was established to oppose the labour unions' push for the repeal of the Criminal Law Amendments Act; when this was repealed, the Association dissolved. Stephen Blank, *Industry and Government in Britain. The Federation of British Industries in Politics, 1945–65* (Farnborough, Saxon House, 1973), p. 11.
115. Established in response to labour activism and dissolved when that subsided. Blank (Industry and Government), p. 11.
116. Two other peak associations were also established around this time, the National Union of Manufacturers (1916) and the National Confederation of Employers' Organisations (1919). Wyn Grant & David March, *The Confederation of British Industry* (London, Hodder & Stoughton, 1977), pp. 17–19.
117. Arthur J. McIvor, *Organised Capital. Employers' Associations and Industrial Relations in Northern England, 1880–1939* (Cambridge, Cambridge University Press, 1996), p. 14.
118. For one study emphasising the role of organisations, see Richard F. Kuisel, *Capitalism and the State in Modern France: Renovation and Economic Management in the Twentieth Century* (Cambridge, Cambridge University Press, 1981).
119. Richard Vinen, *The Politics of French Business 1936–1945* (Cambridge, Cambridge University Press, 1991), p. 21.
120. And therefore seen more as official organisations than independent representatives of commercial opinion. Arthur Louis Dunham, *The Industrial Revolution in France 1815–1848* (New York, Exposition Press, 1955), p. 405.
121. H.D. Peiter, "Institutions and Attitudes: The Consolidation of the Business Community in Bourgeois France, 1880–1914", *Journal of Social History* 9, 4, June 1976, p. 511.
122. For an argument about the way in which local chambers supported the French colonial effort because of the links between local industries and the colonies, see John A. Laffey, "Municipal Imperialism: The Lyon Chamber of Commerce, 1914–1925", *Journal of European Economic History* 4, 1, Spring 1975, pp. 95–120. Although this relates to a later period, the argument also applied in the late nineteenth century.
123. For a study highlighting the tension between different local groups, see David M. Gordon, *Merchants and Capitalists. Industrialization and Provincial Politics in Mid-Nineteenth-Century France* (Alabama, The University of Alabama Press, 1985). This is a study of Reims and St Etienne.
124. Peiter (Institutions), p. 512.
125. Peiter (Institutions), p. 513.
126. Vinen (French Business), p. 21.

127. On the role of a range of organisations in this debate, see Michael Stephen Smith, *Tariff Reform in France 1869–1900. The Politics of Economic Interest* (Ithaca, Cornell University Press, 1980).

128. They had gained legal exemption from the Minister of the Interior to establish such an organisation to defend their interests, Herman Lebovics, *The Alliance of Iron and Wheat in the Third French Republic 1860–1914. Origins of the New Conservatism* (Baton Rouge, Louisiana State University Press, 1988), p. 57.

129. E. Villey, "Employers' Organisations in France", *International Labour Review* XVI, 1, July 1927, p. 51. Also Pieter (Institutions), p. 511.

130. Charle (Social History), p. 200.

131. On Hamburg, see Ferguson (Paper and Iron), p. 67.

132. Eckart Kehr, *Economic Interest, Militarism, and Foreign Policy. Essays on German History* (Berkeley, University of California Press, 1977, trans. Greta Heinz), pp. 84–87.

133. Craig (Germany), p. 86.

134. Craig (Germany), p. 86.

135. Gerald D. Feldman & Ulrich Nocken, "Trade Associations and Economic Power: Interest Group Development in the German Iron and Steel and Machine Building Industries, 1900–1933", *Business History Review* XLIX, 4, Winter 1975, pp. 417–418.

136. Craig (Germany), p. 86.

137. The Vereinigung der Steuer- und Wirtschaftsreformer. Craig (Germany), p. 88.

138. James C. Hunt, "The Bourgeois Middle in German Politics, 1871–1933: Recent Literature", *Central European History* XI, 1, March 1978, p. 91.

139. For example, in Hamburg the Association of the Iron Industry established in 1888 to counter strike activity, and the United Association of German Metal Industrialists and the Hamburg-Altona Employers Association, both established in 1890. Ferguson (Paper and Iron), p. 69.

140. For the view that they were much more prominent than their English counterparts, see Berghoff & Moller (Tired Pioneers), p. 282.

141. Sheehan (Political Leadership), p. 523.

142. Maier (Recasting), p. 35.

143. Berghoff & Moller (Tired Pioneers), p. 282. Also, see Sheehan (Political Leadership), p. 523.

144. For comparative analysis of two regions, see Toni Pierenkemper, "Entrepreneurs in Heavy Industry: Upper Silesia and the Westphalian Ruhr Region, 1852 to 1913", *Business History Review* LIII, 1, Spring 1979, pp. 65–68.

145. From heavy industry, Hugo Stinnes, Alfred Hugenberg, and Jacob Reichert; from machine construction, Anton von Rieppel and Ernst von Borsig; and from the electro-technical industry, Walther Rathenau, Carl Friedrich von Siemens, and Hans von Raumer. Feldman & Nocken (Trade Associations), p. 427. Stinnes was personally very influential, especially in the early period. Maier (Recasting), p. 210.

146. Turner (German Big Business), pp. 35–36.

147. Feldman & Nocken (Trade Associations), p. 441. The Ruhr businessmen also organised an unofficial committee of twelve leading industrialists, the Ruhrlade to settle important economic and political questions. Feldman & Nocken (Trade Associations), p. 444.

148. David Abraham, "Constituting Hegemony: The Bourgeois Crisis of Weimar Germany", *The Journal of Modern History* 51, 3, September 1979, p. 422. For the argument that heavy industry remained the most powerful industrial sector in the mid-1920s, see Bernd Weisbrod, "Economic Power and Political Stability Reconsidered: Heavy Industry in Weimar Germany", *Social History* 4, 2, May 1979, pp. 241–263.

149. Matthew Josephson, *The Robber Barons: The Great American Capitalists 1861–1901* (London, Eyre & Spottiswood, 1962, originally published 1934), p. 357.

150. Richard Hume Werking, "Bureaucrats, Businessmen, and Foreign Trade: The Origins of the United States Chamber of Commerce", *Business History Review* LII, 3, Autumn 1978, p. 323.

151. James Weinstein, *The Corporate Ideal in the Liberal State: 1900–1918* (Boston, Beacon Press, 1968), p. xv.

152. Weinstein (Corporate Ideal), p. 10.

153. Weinstein (Corporate Ideal), pp. 32–88.

154. Werking (Bureaucrats), pp. 324–339.

155. Werking (Bureaucrats), p. 340.

156. Josephson (Robber Barons), pp. 347–348.

5

Post-Soviet Bourgeois Representation in Political Life

The emergent Russian bourgeoisie faced the same problem as its Western counterparts, that of gaining representation in the leading institutions of the state, if it was to maximise its capacity to shape state policy in its areas of concern. But the standing of those institutions and the nature of the institutional milieu within which they functioned were very different to those of the other four states. The political environment within which the new post-Soviet bourgeoisie emerged was one undergoing momentous change. The Soviet regime was decaying and then, in 1991, fragmented, leaving in place in Russia a political superstructure inherited from the past but widely seen as inappropriate for the future. Part of the building of a new, democratic Russia was seen by many to lie in the construction of a new set of political institutions for the national political system. While there was some public debate about what form this should take in the period surrounding the Soviet collapse, the actual introduction of new forms came about as a result of the political crisis of 1993. The introduction of a new constitution, a new legislature, and new electoral laws did not completely stabilise the situation because there was still considerable uncertainty about how those institutions should function, especially in terms of the powers and prerogatives of the president. This means that the political system into which the new bourgeoisie sought entry was one in considerable flux throughout this period. In seeking to evaluate the progress made by the emergent bourgeoisie in entering the political system, the same institutions as were looked at in the other countries will be analysed.

State Legislature and Executive

For the first twenty-one months of independent Russia's existence, many of the state organs of the former Soviet regime continued to function in something like the way they had before the collapse of the USSR. One such body was the legislature. Representation of leading economic interests had been a feature of the Soviet legislature, with membership of the Supreme Soviet always including managerial personnel from state enterprises. Even when the new Soviet legislature was subject to semi-free competitive elections in 1989, members of the so-called 'directors' corps' gained representation.[1] A similar situation applied in the post-1990 leading organs of the Russian Republic, the Congress of People's Deputies and the Supreme Soviet; in April 1992, a total of 72 deputies in the Congress of People's Deputies (representing about 6.6% of the membership) were members of the parliamentary fraction, Industrial Union,[2] although there were many more representatives from different economic sectors, including agriculture, industry, and fuel and energy. Early in the post-Soviet period, this group was able to wield political influence. During 1992–93 they continually pressed, with some success, for state subsidies and, in 1992, for a change in the principles of the privatisation measures; it was due mainly to their pressure that Chubais introduced option 2 to the privatisation programme, which enabled the maintenance of existing managerial control over privatised enterprises. But with the abolition of the Soviet-era legislative organs in 1993, a new situation was opened up.

The forced closure of the Soviet-era legislative organs by Boris Yeltsin in October 1993 followed by the adoption of a new constitution and legislative elections in December 1993 ushered in a new political system. Characterised by a two-house legislature with the upper house (Federation Council) comprising representatives from the regions[3] and the lower house (State Duma) elected by a combination of first past the post single-member constituencies and a central party list system with a 5% threshold, the system created new openings for access into the legislative arena. But this new structure also imposed significant restrictions on such access. From 1995 the upper house was filled on an ex officio basis by those holding leading administrative positions in the regions. In the lower house, from the outset the electoral system created difficulties for the weak emergent parties on the Russian scene. To maximise the vote in the single-member constituencies, a party needed a broadly based organisational structure extending into those constituencies. To maximise votes under the party list system, a party required a developed central apparatus as well as a list of prominent names to appeal to the voters. Given the short time the emergent parties had between the closure of the Soviet-era legislature and the election, no party could meet these twin demands. Indeed, even when the time has not been so short, these demands have consistently been satisfied by only two parties, the Communist Party of the Russian Federation (KPRF) and the Liberal Democratic Party of Russia (LDPR). But more important as a factor in structuring access to political power was the powerful position accorded to the president in the new constitutional structure. While the legislature did pass important economic legislation,

Table 5.1. Proportion of deputies with a business background (%)[a]

1993–95[b]	1995–99[c]	1999–2003[d]	2003[e]
20.6	20.0	24.3	30.0

[a] The biographical data on which this table is based is not full and often contains information that is difficult to interpret. Accordingly there may be some margin for error in the figures. This is particularly the case when trying to distinguish between managerial positions held in the Soviet and in the post-Soviet periods. It is not always clear in which period a person held the position referred to in the biographical sketches in the sources. Bearing this in mind, I have calculated that the figures in the table include the following proportions of all deputies who held positions in the productive economy during Soviet times: 1993–95, 5.1%; 1995–99, 2.6%; and 1999–2003, 2.5%. The table does not include those with business interests solely in the form of shares. Paul Chaisty gives some generally higher figures for those who were either directors or deputy directors of state or private enterprises before their election: respectively 15.5%, 23.1%, 29.7%, and 33.1%. Paul Chaisty, *Legislative Politics and Economic Power in Russia* (Basingstoke, Palgrave Macmillan, 2006), p. 135. For some different figures, see Olga Kryshtanovskaya & Stephen White, 'The rise of the Russian business elite', *Communist and Post-Communist Studies* 38, 3, September 2005, p. 303.

[b] The figures may understate those with business experience because of their focus on positions held at the time of election. The figures are based on O.G. Gladkikh et al., *Vlast'. Deputaty gosudarstvennoi dumy. Kratkii biograficheskii spravochnik* (Moscow, Institut sovremennoi politiki, 1994), vols 1–4.

[c] The figures are based on information found in the Federal Assembly web site http://www.cityline.ru/politika/fs/gdzalf.html, Gladkikh et al. (Vlast'), and A.A. Bocharnikov et al. (eds.), *Sovremennaia Politicheskaia Istoriia Rossii (1985-1998 gody). Tom 2. Litsa Rossii* (Moscow, RAU Korporatsiia, 1999).

[d] Many of these held managerial or board positions in major companies, but given the nature of the sources, it is impossible to get an exact picture of the type of involvement many of them had. Data are from Mikhail Lukin, 'Spravochnik. Vsia Duma', *Kommersant Vlast'* 3 (354), 25 January 2000, pp. 19–44.

[e] This figure came from a number of sources: http://www.politika.su/fs/gd4dai.html , http://www.duma.gov.ru/, http://www.usrbc.org/government/russian_government/deputies_alphabetical/, and Lukin (Spravochnik). Thanks to Grigory Belonuchkin for guidance here. For a set of figures for so-called 'big business', see Kryshtanovakaya & White (The rise), p. 303.

including laws on taxation, joint stock companies, and land privatisation, the presidency was clearly the most powerful institution in independent Russia, and although in constitutional terms the president could not simply ignore the legislature, his constitutional position was such that a skilful president could usually ensure a compliant legislative organ. Access to the presidency was the key to the exercise of power and influence.

The development of a more open representative political system expanded the opportunities for business representation in the official channels of the state. Although many entrepreneurs argued that they should not be involved in politics, there were also many (including Berezovsky) who favoured such activity.[4] In line with this, some people from business gained representation in the State Duma (Table 5.1).

This is a solid representation of people with some business experience in the Duma with a level throughout that is generally higher than in both France and Germany, and approaches British levels. The jump in the fourth Duma is significant. This may be partly a function simply of the effluxion of time: the longer time has gone on and the more settled the business environment has become, the greater the number of people who are likely to have had some involvement in business activity. But two other factors may also have been important. First, this was the first Duma elected after Putin's attack on the oligarchs, and businessmen may have seen a deputy's mandate and the legal immunity this involved as a defence against such action in the future. Second, the legislature had shown itself adept at acting as a kind of clearing house for rent seeking opportunities on the part of business (see below), and therefore membership of it may have been seen as bringing distinct commercial advantages.

Some prominent people with business connections have entered the legislature. For example, Irina Kakhamada (who with Konstantin Borovoi founded the Moscow Commodity Exchange) held a leading position in the Party of Economic Freedom and was a Duma deputy and from 1997 head of the small business agency.[5] Even some of the 'oligarchs' sought and gained a seat in the Duma; in the 1999 election, Boris Berezovsky (he resigned his seat in July 2000), Roman Abramovich, and Mikhail Gutseriev all gained seats.[6] Generally though, few of the large or more prominent businessmen entered the state legislative arena, with most deputies with business backgrounds coming from small- or medium-sized businesses or, if they did come from large companies, from the second rank within those companies. In a pattern which some have suggested applied generally to many businessmen who became deputies, the director of the pyramid company MMM that went bankrupt in 1994, Sergei Mavrodi, won a seat in the Duma at a by-election in October 1994, in order to gain the immunity from prosecution that this gave him. This reflects Chirikova's view that when they went into politics, businessmen were concerned for their own particular interests rather than for those of business as a whole.[7]

Business interests were often represented by deputies who were not businessmen themselves. Given the dominant positions in the local economies held by particular branches of industry, it is not surprising that representatives from those regions should seek to represent and defend the interests of those particular industries or companies. They often did this by coming together in groups or factions within the chamber (see below), and these could at times have significant influence on the course of legislation. In the Federation Council, where the representatives have been directly linked with the regional administration and therefore involved in management of the local economy and with the local power structure (see Chapter 7), such concern has been common; in 2002, almost a third of the representatives in the Federation Council came from private enterprise.[8]

In contrast to the stability of business representation in the legislature, over time there has been a significant increase in the number of people with business experience in the government ministry. Initially in the post-Soviet period, because there was no independent business sector, the only scope for business-like experience open to people was within the Soviet economic administrative structure, but as the independent business sector expanded during the 1990s, so the scope for such representation also expanded. The

Table 5.2. Government ministers by economic work experience (%)

Government	Soviet enterprise	Soviet oil & gas	Soviet banking	Independent commercial	State corporation[a]	Total
1991–93	7.9	2.6	5.3	—	—	15.8
1/94–7/96	6.6	6.6	2.2	—	—	15.4
8/96–4/2000	1.0	—	—	13.5	5.2	19.7
5/2000–1/04	—	—	—	15.4	7.7	23.1
3/04	—	—	—	31.6	—	31.6

[a] Includes Gazprom, Rosneft, Rosneftegaz, and United Energy Systems (UES). There is no separate figure for these in 3/04.

Source: The figures relate to the whole ministry, not just the cabinet. Principal sources: Iulia Shevchenko, *The Central Government of Russia. From Gorbachev to Putin* (Aldershot, Ashgate, 2004); Bocharnikov et al. (Sovremennaia); www.nns.ru; www.whoiswho.ru; www.government.ru According to another study, in 2001 4.2% and in 2003 20% of government ministers came from big business. Kryshtanovskaya & White (The rise), p. 303.

table refers to individuals having some experience working in economy-related occupations (Table 5.2).

Two features of this table are notable: the decline in representation of those who had substantial Soviet administrative experience (although some of those contained in the Independent commercial and State corporation categories will also have had some experience in earlier Soviet administrative hierarchies[9]), and the growth in representation of those with some business experience in the last government (and this includes the prime minister, Mikhail Fradkov). Nevertheless, it remains a minority. Furthermore, none of those who gained membership of the government had extensive business experience, nor was this the only area of activity in which they had been involved. They were, therefore, not simply businessmen who gained ministerial position, but people with diverse backgrounds that involved some business

Such people often held important positions in the government, including posts that were vital for the industrial sectors from which they came. For example, in 1992 under pressure from the Supreme Soviet, Yeltsin brought into his government as deputy prime ministers Viktor Chernomyrdin, Georgii Khizha, and Vladimir Shumeiko, and later promoted Chernomyrdin to prime minister. Chernomyrdin had been Soviet gas minister and, from 1989–92, director of Gazprom, while Khizha was a former head of the Association of Industrial Enterprises in Leningrad and Shumeiko was a former enterprise director turned people's deputy. Soon after his appointment, Chernomyrdin appointed the director general of the oil company Langepasneftegaz, Yurii Shafranik, as minister for fuel and energy and Gazprom's Vladimir Kvasov as government chief of staff.[10] In August 1996, Shafranik was replaced by the former head of Leningrad Gazprom, Petr Rodionov, while the new minister in March 1998 was Sergei Generalov who had been president of Yukos Oil Co. (and later deputy head of Bank Menatep).[11] In the first half of 1996, AvtoVaz head V. Kadannikov (who had worked with Berezovsky) was first deputy prime minister.[12] In 1996, Vladimir Potanin from Oneksimbank and Berezovsky from Logovaz both briefly took up government posts (see Chapter 7). The Deputy Prime Minister (1999–2000) Ilia Klebanov had been general director of the Leningrad Optical Mechanical Company. As these examples show, people with business backgrounds were not marginal members of the government but often gained very important posts.

Turning to the presidential executive, neither President Yeltsin nor Putin had any personal experience of business, although both brought people into the presidential apparatus who did have such experience. For example, in 1996 Yeltsin appointed two people from Most Bank, E. Sevast'ianov and M. Boiko, deputy heads of the Presidential Administration.[13] Before becoming head of the Presidential Administration in 1999 (a post he retained until 2005), Aleksandr Voloshin had been active in business, including for a time working with Berezovsky,[14] while two deputy chiefs of Putin's Presidential Administration, Vladislav Surkov and Aleksandr Abramov, were formerly senior managers at Al'fa Bank.[15] But most people in the presidential apparatus lacked significant business experience; both presidents sought to staff the apparatus mainly with people from their own bailiwicks, Yeltsin initially from Sverdlovsk, and Putin from St. Petersburg and the security apparatus.

Thus the bourgeoisie was able to gain a solid level of representation in the Duma and, more recently, in the government, but have enjoyed little formal access to the presidency. And it was in the presidency that most power lay.

Political Parties

In the pseudo-democracy that was Russia, political parties presented themselves as vehicles for the representation of popular interests. In the lead up to the 1993 election, a number of parties emerged professing to espouse business interests, but none gained significant representation in the Duma. The most important of these was Civic Union, a body officially formed in October 1993 and headed by Arkady Volsky (see below).[16] The Union hoped to represent the interests of the new entrepreneurs, the managers of state-owned enterprises, and chief executives of local government. However, in the 1993 election, Civic Union polled only 1.93% of the vote and won only one seat. Other groups seeking to represent business interests in the 1993 election— like Konstantin Borovoi's Party of Economic Freedom—did even worse.[17] In part, this poor performance by business-oriented groups reflected the fact that many of those newer entrepreneurs who might have been supportive of their efforts probably gave their support to Russia's Choice,[18] which was directly associated with the continuation of liberal reform; the Party of Russian Unity and Accord (PRES) also sought to defend entrepreneurial interests. Many business groups supported competing candidates to cover all possibilities (see below).[19] A number of groups sought to express business interests in the 1995 election. Among these were Trade Unions and Industrialists of Russia-the Union of Labour, which was established in September 1995 by Volsky among others and supported policies favouring industry and domestic producers,[20] and Borovoi's Party of Economic Freedom. These gained 1.6% and 0.1% of the votes, respectively. The party most associated in many minds with big business was Our Home is Russia (OHR).[21] Supporting the policy views of its patron, Prime Minister Viktor Chernomyrdin, and liberally funded by Gazprom, this party was seen by many to be the political arm of the gas monopoly. But even with all of its financial support and political muscle, OHR could win only 10.1% of the votes and 20% of the seats in 1995. While this was a significant proportion of the membership of the Duma, it was considerably less than many had expected, and it did not act in the chamber as a coherent and consistent representative of business interests; it was more important as a support basis for the Chernomyrdin government. In the 1999 election, following Chernomyrdin's ouster as prime minister, OHR did much worse, gaining only 1.2% of the vote. In the 1999 and 2003 elections, there were new executive-oriented parties which replaced OHR as the so-called 'party of power',[22] Unity in 1999 and United Russia in 2003; both were associated with first prime minister and then President Vladimir Putin. These attracted business support but they were not explicitly business parties. In the December 2003 legislative election, businessmen seem to have been more prominent in the party lists than they had been before. According to one study,[23] businessmen constituted 24% of those on the KPRF list (cf. 7% in 1999) and 27% for United Russia (cf. 8% in 1999 for Fatherland-All Russia, which became part of United Russia). It is clear from these elections that political parties dedicated to the representation of business views were unlikely to gain significant representation in the legislature, and it is therefore little wonder that many resources have not been put into building them, and that no single business party has emerged.

Once in the Duma, businessmen were not concentrated in one particular party (Table 5.3).

A couple of things are striking about this table. The first is the pattern of solid business representation across all four Dumas in both the Communist Party[24] and the LDPR, although the latter's level did decline precipitately in the third Duma when its overall representation fell. While both parties made electoral pitches to business, it is likely that their messages were most effective among the former Red Directors, and these are likely to have been the core of their business constituencies, at least initially. The other side of this is the low levels of business representation in those parties most identi-fied with a free-market line, Russia's Choice in the first Duma and Yabloko throughout. The other major feature of this table is the strength of business

Table 5.3. Business membership of parties by Duma (% of all businessmen in Duma by party/group)

Duma	I	II	III	IV
Russia's Choice	7.1	—	—	—
PRES	7.1	—	—	—
Russia	1.4	—	—	—
Stability	1.4	—	—	—
OHR	—	17.3	—	—
Unity	—	—	21.6	—
Fatherland-All Russia	—	—	12.7	—
People's Deputy	—	—	15.7	—
Regions	18.5	8.7	7.5	—
12 December	4.3	—	—	—
Union of Right Forces	—	—	7.5	—
Yabloko	1.4	2.9	—	—
Women of Russia	8.6	—	—	—
LDPR	11.4	15.4	3.7	10.1
Communist Party of Russian Fedration	8.6	26.9	14.2	9.4
Agrarians	27.1	17.3	11.2	—
Popular Power	—	9.6	—	—
United Russia	—	—	—	73.2
Motherland	—	—	—	5.4
Independent	2.8	1.9	6.0	2.0

Source: Based on figures cited in Chaisty (Legislative Politics), p. 135.

representation in the successive so-called 'parties of power', that is, the parties directly associated with a leading government figure. In the second Duma, OHR associated with Chernomyrdin had the equal second highest level of business representation, while in the third and fourth Dumas those parties associated with Putin, Unity and United Russia, had the highest levels of representation. This reflects the perceived role of the legislature as a means of exploitation of the state: association with the party of the major government figure would be likely to facilitate such exploitation.

Business interests were also to be found in the more informal factions that emerged in the chamber,[25] although again they were not concentrated in one particular faction. Sometimes deputies formed groups on a regional basis, and these were in a position to take up issues affecting the industries in that region, thereby becoming defenders of 'their' regions and companies in the legislature. For example, in 1994 Duma deputies from the oil and gas regions formed an association to support the industry, the Association of Economic Inter-Relationships, comprising representatives from Tiumen, Tomsk, Orenburg, Sakhalin, Khanty-Mansi, Yamalo-Nenets, Bashkortostan, Tatarstan, and Komi. However, this was not really active.[26] In the first Duma (1993–95), a group called New Regional Policy[27] emerged and sought to represent the views of industry.[28] This task was taken on by Regions of Russia in 1996–99, while commercial and financial structures were looked after by three political parties, Russia's Choice, Union of 12 December and PRES.[29] In October 1993, the bankers decided that they needed a professional lobby group in the Duma to ensure the continued exclusion of foreign banks, and they have generally been quite successful in gaining membership of the committees most concerned with their interests.[30] In February 2000, the faction Energy Russia was formed by some 70 deputies, reflecting the success of Lukoil's strategy of providing support for individual candidates in their region;[31] in the same Duma there were also groups called Commodity Producers of Russia and Business Russia.[32] However, membership of a particular faction did not mean that all members acted jointly on matters that came before the house. Neither the parties that were elected to the Duma nor the parliamentary factions that were formed after the election within the chamber acted with a high level of unity. Deputies were more inclined to pursue a personal path of voting on legislation rather than adhering to fixed party positions, with the result that there was no stable grouping of businessmen deputies within the Duma that could consistently pursue what were perceived to be business interests.

Generally, businessmen have eschewed holding legislative office, preferring to provide material support for sympathetic political parties and individual politicians who they believed would serve their interests. The financial under-writing of Yeltsin in 1996 (see Chapter 7) and of Russia's Choice, Russia's Democratic Choice, and OHR in successive elections are major instances of this. In the 1999 election, sections of big business provided support to Fatherland-All Russia, the Union of Right Forces (SPS), and Yabloko.[33] A number of companies, including Gazprom and Lukoil, gave support to large numbers of candidates in single-member constituencies, many of whom were elected, while the oil tycoon Roman Abramovich and these two companies plus Sibneft (owned by Abramovich) funded the pro-Putin Unity.[34] In the 2003 election, it was claimed that business gave US$1.2 billion to United Russia, most oligarchs (except for Deripaska and Abramovich) supported the SPS, while Khodorkovsky and Yukos Oil gave money to both Yabloko (which had originally been supported by Gusinsky) and the Communist Party.[35] There were also many cases of this sort of support at regional level.[36] Support was often spread across a number of parties and individuals.[37] According to Sobyanin,[38] two-thirds of the deputies elected to the Duma in 2003 were the owners of businesses, were sent by business, or were lobbyists for whom business paid to get a place on a party list. This figure seems very, even unrealistically, high.

The dynamics of business use of the legislative chamber in Russia was very different from that in the Western countries analysed above. While in all five countries the economic bourgeoisie was insufficiently powerful in the chamber by itself to advance its interests, the balance of mechanisms used to achieve this aim differed. As noted above, in the four Western cases although the economic bourgeoisie did rely on having their own agents in the chamber and on personal connections with legislators, they also benefited enormously from the growth in representation of the professional bourgeoisie in the chamber. Although, this group was not necessarily committed to the commercial interests of the economic bourgeoisie, their adherence to national goals and their perception of those goals in ways very different to what had been in the past persuaded them to support many measures that had a positive impact on bourgeois economic interests. However, in Russia, this professional bourgeoisie has not been particularly active in political life. There have been individuals who have come from this type of professional background and who have had political careers, including in the Duma—Grigorii Yavlinsky is a prominent example—but there have been few others who have either matched his example or been active in a less prominent way in the political sphere. The weakness of professional bourgeoisie involvement is reflected in the often-noted under-development of civil society in Russia. The absence of a dense network of associative bodies structuring the public sphere, of a vibrant public opinion underpinning public debate, both reflects the weakness of civil society and of the professional bourgeoisie in Russia generally. Thus in the first post-Soviet decades, the interests of the economic bourgeoisie could not gain from the activities of the professional wing of this class because this latter group was largely disengaged from political life. Accordingly, the economic bourgeoisie has had to rely on other sorts of connections into the legislature to advance their interests through this institution.

Even more so than in the West, the legislature in Russia seems to have played a significant role in the disposition of privileges to the emergent economic bourgeoisie. Principally through the Duma's structure of policy committees, business has sought to lobby deputies for decisions on issues like taxation, production-sharing agreements, budgetary appropriations, licences of various sorts, and generally preferable decisions. Using professional associations (see below), political parties, personal approaches, professional lobbyists or their own agents in the legislature, business sought to influence legislators to advance their interests. The oligarchs (see below), especially Khodorkovsky, were very active in this. Much of this was blatant, with from the mid-late 1990s newspapers publishing what purported to be the going rate that business was paying for different types of legislative outcomes.[39] More systematic was the practice that was common until about 2003 of the provision by business of experts to assist in the drafting of legislation. It is clear that business expended significant energies on the attempt to exercise influence through lobbying in both houses of the legislature, especially from the mid-1990s into the Putin era. It also seems clear that in this, those who could utilise personal contacts, often stemming from the Soviet period, tended to be more successful, and these were usually the larger, and often state-controlled, companies.

Civil Service

In the state bureaucracy, few people who had experience with post-Soviet business took up bureaucratic positions, although many economic bureaucrats from the Soviet period retained their positions. This is a natural development given that the newly independent Russian state simply took over many of the bureaucratic structures, with their staff, of its predecessor. However, these people are best seen not as representatives of business, or even the economy, but as holdovers from the former state economic sphere. Given the short life of the free-market system in Russia, it is unrealistic to expect those with extensive direct experience of such a system to have made much headway in a hierarchical structure like the civil service.

Local Government

Businessmen have often been prominent in the power structures in the regions,[40] usually in forming alliances with local authorities. This will be discussed more fully in Chapter 7. In most cases of such politics–business alliances in the regions, businessmen did not seek elected office, and when they did, many were not successful; for example, in the 1996–97 gubernatorial provincial campaigns, only three entrepreneurs were successful: B. Bytov in Nenets AO, L. Gorbenko in Kaliningrad oblast, and V. Tsvetkov in Magadan oblast.[41] There were cases of more successful business involvement in the legislature. For example, in 1994 in Altai some 34% of deputies elected to the local legislature were classed as *khoziaistvenniki* (including company directors and deputy directors), in seven other regions in the same year 38.8% were 'economic leaders', principally from the old Soviet 'economic managerial hierarchies', while in Tiumen the figure was 35.3% in 1994 and 32% in 1999.[42] Businessmen became more active and seem to have had greater success in local politics from the end of the 1990s. One study reports that in regional elections in the late 1990s, representatives from the industrial and financial sectors won 80% of seats in Perm, 70% in Smolensk, 60% in Penza, Tambov, and Tomsk, and more than half in Belgorod, Leningrad, Nizhnii Novgorod, Omsk, Rostov, Stavropol, and Primor'e, while the average across all regions that had elections between 1995 and 1997 was 43%.[43] In Khanty-Mansi in the 1996–2001 Duma, 39.6% came from oil and gas companies, and in 2000–05 the figure was 60%.[44] In Moscow city, the proportion of deputies with a business background in the Duma was 5.26% in 1993, 20% in 1997, and 17.1% in 2001.[45] Such electoral success could involve leading businessmen. For example,[46] in 1993 the local businessman Iliumzhinov in Kalmykia; in 1996–97, Yevdokhimov of Sistema in Murmansk, Gorbenko (local businessman) in Kaliningrad, Bytov (local) in Nenets, and Aleksei Lebed of Base

Element in Khakassia (and again in 2004); in 2000–02, Sibneft's Roman Abramovich in Chukotka, Norilsk Nickel director Alexander Khloponin became governor of Taimyr okrug[47] and later of Krasnoyarsk, Norilsk Nickel's Oleg Budargin replaced Khloponin in Taimyr, Yukos director Boris Zolotarev in Evenkiia (and again in 2004), Tkachev (local) in Krasnodar, Loginov (local) in Koryak, Darkin (local) in Primor'e, Alrosa (the diamond monopoly) head Viacheslav Shtyrov became president of Sakha, and the owner of Polyus gold mining company, Khazret Sovmen, became president of Adygea (he sold his company in 2002); in 2004 Dmitrii Selenin of Norilsk Nickel was elected in Tver. In 1996, Gazprom ran its own candidates in the gubernatorial elections in ten regions, but achieved success only in Yamal-Nenets Autonomous Okrug.[48] However, businessmen usually sought to leave the management of political affairs to the politicians while they continued to concentrate on making money. Businessmen tended to finance election campaigns, with in some cases different corporations supporting different candidates,[49] and underpin the projects of local and regional politicians rather than become office-holders themselves. The most important form of business power in the regions lay outside the official political institutions. This is discussed in Chapter 7.

Structures of Interest Representation

There was also a large range of organisations that emerged in Russia to structure business life and to seek to project business interests into the political system, although their membership does not appear to have been very extensive: while in the second half of the 1990s, there was estimated to be more than 150 associations, leagues, unions, and confederations of entrepreneurs,[50] in 2000 it was said that only 17% of firms belonged to trade associations.[51] Business groups generally have been fragmented and divided over personality, ideology, and programme.[52] Nevertheless, they have been prominent features on the Russian scene and have, in their own ways, sought to structure the activities of Russian business.

Five organisations emerged at the peak industry level: Russian Union of Industrialists and Entrepreneurs (RSPP), Federation of Commodity Producers of Russia (FTR), Association of Private and Privatised Enterprises (AChPP), Russian Business Round Table (KSBR), and the Chamber of Commerce and Industry (TPP).[53] There was also a Coordinating Council of Russian Employer Associations, but this seems to have had little effect.[54]

The RSPP[55] was established in December 1991, and was the continuation of the Scientific-Industrial Union of the USSR. By early 1996, it had 4,133 collective members (in both the centre and the regions; it had specially organised regional branches) ranging across a wide sector of economic and public life,[56] although there was, in the words of one scholar, an 'underlying orientation towards large manufacturing enterprises, formerly state-owned and still run by their Soviet-era managers with a consequent lack of sympathy for new, entrepreneurial business and the financial sector'.[57] The Union thus had a bias toward the heavy industry sector, and along with the deputies in the Supreme Soviet, was influential in gaining the entry of the presumed supporters of this sector, Chernomyrdin, Khizha, and Shumeiko, into the government in April 1992 and the restriction of the Gaidar reform programme. The head of the Union, Arkady Volsky, had personal links with Chernomyrdin and first Deputy Prime Minister Oleg Soskovets,[58] who was associated with the defence of heavy industry inside the government. While the Union was recognised as a supporter of traditional heavy industry, in practice, its membership also included some small businesses and enterprises without a heavy industry, state pedigree, with the result that its message was more mixed as it tried to balance the different interests of its constituent organisations; consequently there was some incoherence in the policy positions it espoused.[59] The RSPP through Volsky established a political party, Obnovlenie, in November 1992, which soon became part of the aforementioned Civic Union for Stability, Justice and Progress, which was itself headed by Volsky and did so badly in the 1993 election. In the 1995 election, Volsky joined with two others to form Trade Unions and Industrialists of Russia-the Union of Labour, which supported policies favouring industry and domestic producers,[60] but it received only 1.6% of the vote. The RSPP's lack of success in the electoral arena meant that it concentrated on seeking to represent the views of heavy industry through lobbying. It sought to stabilise its position with the entry into its governing bureau of a number of the oligarchs in 2000 (see below), its public disavowal of Berezovsky and political activity, and its attempt to present itself as the main organisation representing business in dealings with the government. In so doing, it transformed itself from what was little more than an organisation of the red directors into the major representative of business interests with the government. It became the main 'interface' with the government, participating in the discussion of draft legislation on a wide range of issues. It did this through a network of committees and commissions.[61] It interacted with the Duma and the Presidential Administration on a regular fashion and, more irregularly, its leadership met with Putin. Significantly, following Khodorkovsky's arrest (see Chapter 7), the RSPP conference in November 2003 both confirmed the need for continuing dialogue between business and government, and declared that the organisation would 'stay away from politics'.[62] The Yukos affair beginning in 2003 (see below) changed the climate of the state–business relationship and undercut the position the RSPP had sought to develop. It became sidelined during Putin's second term, and by 2004 was seen as being largely supine in the face of the authorities.[63]

The FTR was in some sense a competitor of the RSPP because, from its birth in August 1992, it sought to represent traditional large-scale heavy industry, especially in the former military industry complex.[64] Its origins lay in the Industrial Union faction in the Russian Supreme Soviet, a source consistent with the pro-heavy industry orientation it has adopted, and from the middle of 1993 it was headed by former head of Yeltsin's Security Council, Yurii Skokov.[65] With associations organised at both national and regional levels, the FTR sought to represent the same constituency as the RSPP; indeed many firms were members of both. However, because of its tighter focus, the FTR was able to project a more coherent, if more marginalised, message. It consistently pursued a more oppositionist line to the thrust of the Yeltsin administration than that followed by the RSPP, and from May 1994 until the end of that Duma sought to act through the New Regional Policy faction in the State Duma.

The Association of Private and Privatised Enterprises (AChPP) was established in 1993 and had some twenty sections. In contrast to the types of organisations discussed above, the aim of this body was defence of the interests of privatised and privatising enterprises, and the generation of support both within Russia and abroad for the broad aims of privatisation.[66] Headed by Gaidar and effectively part of the Russia's Choice party, a number of members of this body (including Chubais) followed Gaidar into government service following Gaidar's appointment as first deputy prime minister in autumn 1993. This body worked principally through the personal contacts into the upper levels of the administration possessed by its principals.

The KSBR was established under the aegis of the Council for the Development of Entrepreneurship attached to the government in late 1993 by the businessman Ivan Kivelidi as a 'public non-political collegial representative organ of the entrepreneurial estate (soslovie) of Russian society'.[67] With more than 100 collective members, its primary concentration was upon business rather than industry narrowly defined, and upon new entrepreneurs and non-traditional industry. Although some leaders of the KSBR became involved in party politics, with Kivelidi the leader of the Party of Free Labour established in 1993,[68] the KSBR concentrated mainly on lobbying activities. It went into decline following Kivelidi's murder in August 1995.

The TPP was the lineal descendant of the Soviet body originally established in 1927. In October 1991, this body was reworked with the aim of creating a structure which would integrate all of the regional chambers into a single structure,[69] and from 1993 it acted on the basis of a special law adopted by the government. This law gave the TPP a privileged position, instructing central state agencies to consult with the Chamber on issues within its areas of competence.[70] The Chamber also had its own media outlets—the newspaper *Torgovo-promyshlennye vedomosti* and the journals *Delovye sviazi* and *Business Contact*—which it could use to press on the issues it considered important. The TPP has concentrated principally upon lobbying activities, utilising a wide range of contacts with the presidential and legislative apparatuses.[71] The coverage of the TPP has been wide, embracing both state and non-state sectors of the economy and firms working in most sectors. Its approach has been overwhelmingly cautious or, as one observer has said, 'careful and restrained'.[72] After his resignation as prime minister, Evgenii Primakov became the head of the chamber, and although the Putin administration gave it some encouragement as a counterbalance to the RSPP, it had little real influence.

Below these peak bodies, there has been a proliferation of organisations designed to cater for firms on a sectoral basis. Among the more prominent of these have been the following:[73]

- Financial sector: Association of Russian Banks (ARB), Association of Small Banks (AMB), Moscow Bank Union (MBS), Association of Small and Medium-Sized Banks (AMSB), Association of Joint Stock-Commercial and Industrial-Construction Banks (AAKPSB), Association of Hard Currency Exchanges (ARVB), the Federation of Fund Exchanges of Russia (FFBR), Association of Cheque Investment Funds (AChIF), All-Russian Union of Insurers (VSS).

- Industrial sector: League for Assistance to Defence Enterprises (LSOP), League of Defence Enterprises (LOP), League of Industrialists and Commodity Producers (LPT), Union of Machine Builders (SM), International Metallurgy Union (MCM), International Union of Builders (MSS), Russian Diamond Union (RAS), Gold Industrialists Union (SZ), Union of Timber Industrialists and Timber Exporters of Russia (SLLR), Union of Aluminium Producers and Exporters (SEAPR).

- Fuel and energy sector: Union of Oil Industrialists of Russia (SNPR), Association of Economic Cooperation (AEV), Oil and Gas Industrialists Union (SN), Union of Oil Exporters of Russia (SNR).

Most of these peak and sectoral organisations performed multiple functions. Many gave advice and assistance to members, with those more established and wealthy organisations setting up research and development departments which could give technical assistance to members. They also, in principle, provided venues in which member companies could raise and discuss issues of interest and common positions could be arrived at and advanced, although this function was limited by the diversity of organisations in each sector and the consequent inability to bring about organisational unity. As indicated above, political parties representing business interests have achieved little success at the polls, so business organisations have, after the early failures, generally spent little time or effort on organising parties. More important as mechanisms of influence have been corporatist strategies and lobbying activity by the organisations.

Corporatist strategies[74] were the most natural ones to adopt for those coming from a Soviet administrative or economic background because the essence of the Soviet system as far as economic control went was the incorporation of the productive enterprise into the administrative structure. Accordingly, many post-1991 enterprise directors saw access into the state's decision-making structures as the most natural way of gaining influence in the new conditions. The post-1991 Russian leadership was not totally opposed to such an arrangement; witness the right of being consulted built into the law on the TPP. Two types of system were used, consultative and delegative.[75] An instance of the former was the Ministry of Foreign Economic Relations which had a special consultative organ, the Council of Branch Associations of Exporters and Importers which united more than twenty unions and associations. A case of the latter was the way in which the Federal Commission for the Securities Market delegated some of its duties to the National Association of Participants in the Funds Market. However, this latter form of arrangement is unusual, with most attempts at incorporation being of the consultative type; most bodies established by the government had this aim.

After the fall of the Soviet Union, the Russian government adopted a tripartite strategy involving representatives of both capital and labour.[76] A series of bodies was established in an attempt to bring this to fruition. The Russian Tripartite Commission on the Regulation of Social and Labour Relations was established in January 1992. It was authorised to prepare legislation and facilitate labour agreements, and it was instrumental in the March 1992 signing of a general agreement whereby the state promised to maintain social welfare provisions, managers to avoid unemployment, and unions to avoid strikes. Another Trilateral Commission was established in November 1996,[77] but like its predecessor, it achieved little. The problem with tripartism was that none of the partners could ensure that the agreements that were made were implemented because none of them could control their constituents.[78] More prominent were attempts to incorporate different sections of society into the administrative process on a narrower, bilateral, basis. For example, soon after the end of the USSR, leaders of a number of unions and associations were included in the Presidential Consultative Council (the predecessor of the Presidential Council established in February 1993) which was to be the venue for weekly meetings between leading government figures and representatives of business, but which achieved little. In 1993, a Council for Entrepreneurship headed by Soskovets was established.[79] In June 1998, a Council for Economic Cooperation comprising ten businessmen and ten ministers was announced, but it never came to fruition.[80] In autumn 2000, the government established a new Council for Entrepreneurship attached to the government and headed by Prime Minister Mikhail Kasianov. This was an attempt to institutionalise government–business dialogue, and was different from its predecessors principally by its much higher standing owing to the position of its chairman. Its role was to discuss draft government legislation,[81] but it met infrequently and irregularly and was dissolved in March 2004. In October 2000, following a meeting between Putin and Volsky, the president announced that RSPP would be the 'interface' for dialogue with elite business, and accordingly the RSPP established a bureau of twenty-seven people, including eighteen large entrepreneurs.[82] However, in the Council for Entrepreneurship, which was to take the leading role in such dialogue, the only business representation comprised five members of the RSPP; business representation in this dialogue was thus very narrowly based. This was changed following the January 2001 meeting between Putin and leading businessmen when the latter pushed for a change in arrangements. The new arrangements involved the loss of the monopoly of dialogue by the Council for Entrepreneurship, while the RSPP established a contact group with the Council through which it was able more effectively to press its views on government, the agreement to hold regular quarterly meetings for dialogue between government and business, and governmental readiness to listen to entrepreneurs' views on economic policy.[83] This general aim was enhanced by the creation in October 2001 of Delovaia Rossiia, a body that aimed at the establishment in Russia of 'a strategic alliance between business and government'.[84] However, all attempts to establish a corporatist arrangement and thereby ensure business involvement in governmental decision-making have been unable to usher in a stable system of government–business relations.

More important has been the lobbying activities of business organisations and businessmen individually.[85] Given the way power is structured in the Russian state, with the executive far more powerful than the legislature, most lobbying activity has been directed at the executive branch, the presidency, government, and state ministries.[86] Lobbying differs from incorporation in that it is an attempt to influence governmental bodies from outside rather than from within.[87] Some lobbying has been openly conducted through the press; oligarchs in particular used their press holdings shamelessly to project their own particular interests and views. On occasion, businessmen have signed public letters on particular issues; for example, the letter entitled 'Exit from a deadend' of April 1996 which called for compromise on all sides in the electoral struggle,[88] and that following the June 2000 arrest of Gusinsky. But this has been unusual, with most lobbying being done outside the public eye. In some sectors, like oil, direct contacts with the organs of executive power have been more important than organised lobbying,[89] but even in those cases when lobbying is organised,[90] it has usually relied upon personal contacts and been conducted at the personal level. Former government figures entering business have often acted as primary channels for this.[91]

Generally, lobbying has been in search of individual privileges and benefits rather than changes in general conditions.[92] It was a primary means of gaining the sorts of privileges that were so crucial to the development of business fortunes—export–import licences, quotas, tax concessions, subsidies, and credits (see Chapter 7). But there have also been claimed to be some more general successes, including the entry of the representatives of industry into government in April 1992 and the change in prime minister at the end of that year, both of which were said to have owed much to RSPP lobbying reinforced by enterprise directors and the 'industry lobby' in the legislature at that time. The same group was also successful in ensuring the continued flow of government subsidies into 1993,[93] the commercial banks lobbied the state in the mid-1990s to prevent the entry of foreign banks, to oppose the appointment of Paramonova as head of the Central Bank, and for advantages on the state bond market,[94] and the lobby power of the natural resources sector has long been recognised. But there were also many failures;[95] according to one study, only 30% of firms claimed to be able to influence policy occasionally at some level of government, including only 12% at the federal level.[96] The success of a firm or organisation in lobbying depended upon a range of factors, including the strategic location of the firm in the economy, the level of government it sought to influence, and the size of the firm.[97] There is little evidence that narrow lobbying activity has been able to achieve much success on a continuing basis.[98]

* * *

Russian businessmen have had a prominent place in state organs. They have constituted a significant group in the State Duma, although very few of the more powerful or larger businessmen have chosen to take up deputies' mandates. Business interests in the chamber have been more represented by second rung members of large firms, smaller businessmen, and agents than by major businessmen. Similarly, while their profile in the government has been rising, especially in the new millennium, and while some achieved fleeting notoriety as they held executive positions, they did not usually fill the leading political posts under either the Yeltsin or Putin presidencies. And despite a proliferation of industry and trade associations, none has been able to establish a continuing independent position of primacy in representing business interests to the government. Thus the emergent bourgeoisie has remained largely sidelined in the formal political process; while they, or their agents, have been able to exercise some influence in the Duma in the new millennium, this was at a time when the Duma was of much less importance in the political process than the presidency. Despite the presence of some in the Presidential Administration reputed to be sympathetic to business interests, the new class had no reliable formal channel into the presidency. As a result, business has mainly sought to exert influence through less formal channels. This is discussed in Chapter 7.

The profile that appears here bears significant similarities to those outlined in Chapter 4 for the Western bourgeoisies. In terms of representation in the national legislature, the Russian bourgeoisie is much closer to its British and

American counterparts than to those in France and Germany. The level of involvement in the government also seems to be high compared with the earlier cases, but the time period over which this has been the case is short and it is not clear whether this trend will continue. The situation with regard to political parties—support spread around a number of parties rather than being concentrated in one—is similar to the West, while access to the civil service by the new bourgeoisie may be at the low end of the spectrum of these cases, although again the short time period warrants caution here. The strong involvement in local government in some regions is typical of the other cases, especially Britain and the United States, while the involvement in autonomous structures of interest representation also has parallels with the other cases. However, the trend toward state incorporation of these bodies evident in Russia looks much more like the situation as it developed in Germany than in any of the other three case studies.

Thus in terms of representation in the political system, the Russian bourgeoisie is not greatly different from the range of situations occurring in the other historical examples studied here. What is also apparent is that the emergent Russian bourgeoisie seems simply to have fitted in to the existing institutional structures of the state, again like its earlier counterparts. But the crucial question is how the new class has played out its role in the political structure. This we turn to now.

Notes

1. For some comparative figures, see Jeffrey W. Hahn, "Boss Gorbachev Confronts his New Congress", *Orbis* 34, 2, Spring 1990, p. 173.
2. Richard Sakwa, *Russian Politics and Society* (London, Routledge, 1993), p. 62.
3. In 1993 the seats in the Federation Council were filled by open election, in 1995 the governors and legislative heads of the regions were ex officio members, and from 2002 (the law was adopted in 2000 but was to take effect from the next legislative term) they were to be full-time delegates nominated by regional executives and legislatures.
4. A 1994 survey showed that 38% of entrepreneurs believed that their actions should be restricted to the economic sphere, while 44% said they should be involved in politics. Alla Evgen'eva Chirikova, "Biznes i politika: paradoksy rossiiskoi mental'nosti", *Biznes i politika* 11, 1997, p. 43.
5. She had also headed the strongly liberal and pro-market "Common Cause" bloc in the 1995 election.
6. Respectively from Karachaevo-Cherkessia, Chukotka and Ingushetia, all border districts far from Moscow. Abramovich later became governor of Chukotka.
7. Chirikova (Biznes i politika), p. 44.
8. Andrew Barnes, "Russia's New Business Groups and State Power", *Post-Soviet Affairs* 19, 2, 2003, p. 180. According to Robert Orttung, about 20% of the senators

appointed under the new system introduced in 2000 had "strong ties to big business". Robert W. Orttung, "Business and Politics in the Russian Regions", *Problems of Post-Communism* 51, 2, March-April 2004, p. 58. Also Chaisty (Legislative Politics), pp. 136–137. On links between these senators and particular companies, see Robert Orttung & Peter Reddaway, "What Do the Okrug Reforms Add Up To? Some Conclusions", Peter Reddaway & Robert Orttung (eds.), *The Dynamics of Russian Politics. Putin's Reform of Federal-Regional Relations.* Volume 1 (Lanham, Rowman & Littlefield Publishers Inc., 2004), pp. 284–285.

9. This is because people appear only once in each time period in the table. For some other figures suggesting the replacement of those with Soviet-era experience by those engaged in private business or finance, see Sharon Werning Rivera & David W. Rivera, "The Russian Elite Under Putin: Militocratic or Bourgeois?", *Post-Soviet Affairs* 22, 2, 2006, p. 140.

10. His own chief of staff, Vladimir Babichev, had formerly also worked for Gazprom. Igor Khripunov & Mary M. Matthews, "Russia's Oil and Gas Interest Group and Its Foreign Policy Agenda", *Problems of Post-Communism* 43, 3, May–June 1996, p. 39.

11. Peter Rutland, "Introduction: Business and the State in Russia", Peter Rutland (ed.), *Business and the State in Contemporary Russia* (Boulder, Westview, 2001), p. 13.

12. N. Lapina, *Rossiiskie ekonomicheskie elity i modeli natsional'nogo razvitiia* (Moscow, INION, 1997), p. 16.

13. E. Ya. Vittenberg, "Bankovskoe soobshchestvo rossii: itogi razvitiia i kratkosrochnyi prognoz", M.K. Gorshkov et al. (eds.), *Obnovlenie Rossii: trudnyi poisk reshenii*, vyp. 5, (Moscow, RNISNP, 1997), p. 40.

14. A.A. Mukhin & P.A. Kozlov, *"Semeinye" tainy ili neofitsial'nyi lobbizm v Rossii*, (Moscow, Tsentr politicheskoi informatsii, 2003), p. 179.

15. Ia. Sh. Pappe, *"Oligarkhi". Ekonomicheskaia khronika 1992-2000* (Moscow, Gosudarstvennyi universitet Vysshaia shkola ekonomiki, 2000), p. 227.

16. Initially this had been founded in mid-1992 from the combining of the All-Russian Union for Renewal (Obnovlenie) headed by Volsky, the People's Party of Free Russia (headed by Aleksandr Rutskoi), and the Democratic Party of Russia (headed by Nikolai Travkin).

17. Some parties tried to form organisations that would reach out to economic actors, for example, in late 1993 the Republican Party established the Republican Union of Entrepreneurs, and the Congress of Russian Communities established the League of Russian Entrepreneurs. They had little impact. Aleksei Zudin, "Biznes i politika v postkommunisticheskoi Rossii. Formy organizatsii biznesa", *Biznes i politika* 12, 1995, p. 8.

18. According to one study, 23.3% of entrepreneurs supported Russia's Choice in the 1993 election. This was the highest level of support given to any single party by this group. A. V. Avilova, "Politicheskie predpochteniia rossiiskogo malogo biznesa", M.K. Gorshkov et al. (eds.), *Obnovlenie Rossii: trudnyi poisk reshenii* Vyp. 4, (Moscow, RNISiPP, 1996), p. 190. The Association of Private and Privatised Enterprises (see below) was part of Russia's Choice.

19. V.N. Berezovskii, *Rossiiskie delovye krugi: novye i starye kanali vliianiia na politiku* (Moscow, Tsentr politicheskoi kon'iunktury Rossii, 1994), pp. 1–2.

20. Stephen White, Richard Rose & Ian McAllister, *How Russia Votes* (Chatham, Chatham House Publishers Inc., 1997), p. 208.
21. Although businessmen also appeared in the lists of other parties. For some examples, see Peter Reddaway & Dmitri Glinski, *The Tragedy of Russia's Reforms. Market Bolshevism Against Democracy* (Washington, United States Institute of Peace Press, 2001), p. 488.
22. This was a term in common use in Russian politics at this time. For a discussion, see Hans Oversloot & Ruben Verheul, "The Party of Power in Russian Politics", *Acta Politica* 35, Summer 2000, pp. 123–145.
23. Francesca Mereu, "Business Will Have Big Voice in Duma", *Moscow Times* 13 November 2003.
24. This seems to reflect a conscious decision on the part of the party to broaden both its base and its image.
25. For details on the initial rules and circumstances surrounding the formation of deputies groups, see Thomas F. Remington, *The Russian Parliament. Institutional Evolution in a Transitional Regime, 1989–1999* (New Haven, Yale University Press, 2000), pp. 131–146.
26. David Lane, "The Political Economy of Russian Oil", Rutland (Business and the State), pp. 121–122.
27. This parliamentary faction emerged in 1994 as a result of the need by deputies to constitute themselves into coherent groups in order to gain official party status and the privileges that went with this. Tiffany A. Troxel, *Parliamentary Power in Russia, 1994–2001. President vs Parliament* (Basingstoke, Palgrave Macmillan, 2003), p. 49.
28. Of those working in private enterprise at the time they were elected to the Duma, only 22.2% joined this group, and they were a clear minority within it. This means that business interests were pushed more by deputies not employed in the private sector immediately before entering the Duma than by those who were. Gladkikh (Vlast').
29. Zudin (Biznes i Politika … Formy), p. 7.
30. V.N. Berezovskii, *Obshchestvennye ob'edineniia delovykh krugov Rossii: lobbitskii resurs i politicheskaia rol'* (Moscow, Tsentr politicheskoi kon'iunktury Rossii, 1994) I, 4, p. 4, and Juliet A. Johnson, *A Fistful of Rubles. The Rise and Fall of the Russian Banking System* (Ithaca, Cornell University Press, 2000), pp. 118–119.
31. Irina Stanislavovna Semenenko, *Gruppy interesov na zapade i v rossii. Konseptsii i praktika* (Moscow, Institut mirovoi ekonomiki i mezhdunarodnykh otnoshenii, 2001) p. 23.
32. For a breakdown of representation by sector in each Duma, see Chaisty (Legislative Politics), p. 136. This shows that, after the first Duma, agriculture, manufacturing, and finance-banking were always prominent, while sub-soil energy became prominent in the third and fourth Dumas.
33. Timothy J. Colton & Michael McFaul, *Popular Choice and Managed Democracy. The Russian Elections of 1999-2000* (Washington, Brookings Institution Press, 2003), p. 35.
34. Respectively, Semenenko (Gruppy), p. 23 and A.A. Mukhin, *Biznes-elita i gosudarstvannaia vlast': Kto vladeet Rossiei na rubezhe vekov?* (Moscow, Tsentr politicheskoi informatsii, 2001), p. 39.

35. Michael Waller, *Russian politics today* (Manchester, Manchester University Press, 2005), p. 154. Waller cites Argumenty i fakty 12, March 2003. Also see Chaisty (Legislative Politics), p. 134.
36. For example, the support by Berezovsky and Bykov's Krasnoiarsk aluminium factory for Lebed's gubernatorial campaign in 1998. Andrew Yorke, "Business and Politics in Krasnoyarsk Krai", *Europe-Asia Studies* 55, 2, 2003, pp. 242–243.
37. On the bankers, see Johnson (Fistful), p. 117.
38. Alexander Sobyanin, "Universal'naia mashina: lobbistskie vozmozhnosti novogo Dumy", *Sliiania i pogloshcheniia* 3, 13 March 2004, pp. 36–40, cited in RFE/RL Newsline 8, 59, Tuesday 30 March 2004.
39. Chaisty (Legislative Politics), p. 139. See Chapter 5 more generally for a discussion of lobbying in the legislature.
40. Although for a study of political developments in Saratov, Nizhnii Novgorod, Volgograd, Riazan, Ul'ianovsk, and Tver which barely mentions business interests and their role, see Vladimir Gel'man, Sergei Ryzhenkov & Michael Brie with Vladimir Avdonin, Boris Ovchinnikov & Igor Semenov, *Making and Breaking Democratic Transitions. The Comparative Politics of Russia's Regions* (Lanham, Rowman & Littlefield Publishers Inc., 2003).
41. Igor Vladimirovich Kukolev, "Pochemu i kak predprinimateli uchastvuiut v vyborakh", *Biznes i politika* 3, 4, 1998, p. 6. Kukolev also claims that many entrepreneurs participated in elections purely to gain publicity for their businesses.
42. Respectively Peter Kirkow, "Regional Politics and Market Reform in Russia: The Case of the Altai", *Europe-Asia Studies* 46, 7, 1994, p. 1183; James Hughes, "Sub-national Elites and Post-communist Transformation in Russia: A Reply to Kryshtanovskaia and White", *Europe-Asia Studies* 49, 6, 1997, pp. 1023–1024; and Pete Glatter, "Continuity and Change in the Tyumen' Regional Elite 1991–2001", *Europe-Asia Studies* 55, 3, 2003, p. 409. They were also said to be well-represented in the legislatures of Yaroslavl, Samara, Sakha and Khanty-Mansi. Harley Balzer, "Managed Pluralism: Vladimir Putin's Emerging Regime", *Post-Soviet Affairs* 19, 3, July-September 2003, p. 211.
43. Kryshtanovskaya & White (The rise), p. 304.
44. Julia Kusznir, "Economic Actors in Russian Regional Politics: The Example of the Oil Industry", Graeme Gill (ed.), *Politics in the Russian Regions* (Basingstoke, Palgrave Macmillan, 2007), p. 171.
45. V.M. Platonov et al., *Moskovskaia gorodskaia duma. Istoriia i sovremennost'* (Moscow, OAO "Moskovskie uchebniki i Kartolitografiia, 2004), pp. 83–101.
46. Barnes (Russia's New Business Groups), p. 181.
47. In the words of one observer, this "marked the final stage in the takeover of political power in the *okrug* by its main employer"; Norilsk Nickel people filled many of the leading political posts. Yorke (Business and Politics), p. 253.
48. Peter Rutland, "Putin and the Oligarchs", Dale R. Herspring (ed.), *Putin's Russia. Past Imperfect, Future Uncertain* (Lanham, Rowman & Littlefield Publishers Inc., 2003), p. 146.
49. For some examples, see Rutland (Putin and the Oligarchs), p. 147 and Semenenko (Gruppy), p. 23.
50. Semenenko (Gruppy), p. 21.

51. Joel S. Hellman, Geraint Jones, Daniel Kaufman & Mark Schankerman, *Measuring Governance, Corruption, and State Capture. How Firms and Bureaucrats Shape the Business Environment in Transition Economies* (New York, World Bank Institute & European Bank for Reconstruction and Development, Policy Research Working Paper No. 2312, April 2000), p. 42.

52. Paul Kubicek, "Variations on a Corporatist Theme: Interest Associations in Post-Soviet Ukraine and Russia", *Europe-Asia Studies* 48, 1, 1996, p. 40. For a discussion of early organisations, see Peter Rutland, *Business Elites and Russian Economic Policy* (London, RIIA, 1992), pp. 17–26.

53. Zudin (Biznes i politika...Formy), p. 3. Also Stephen Fortescue, *Policy-Making for Russian Industry* (Basingstoke, Macmillan, 1997), pp. 116–117.

54. Fortescue (Policy-Making), p. 193.

55. See the discussion of the RSPP in Fortescue (Policy-Making), pp. 136–137. Also see Philip Hanson & Elizabeth Teague, "Big Business and the State in Russia". *Europe-Asia Studies* 57, 5, 2005, pp. 658–665.

56. For details, see N.V. Nazarova & Iu.V. Krasheninnikov, *Obshchestvennye (nekommercheskie) ob'edineniia predpriiatii i predprinimatelei Rossii* (Moscow, Tsentr politicheskikh tekhnologii, 1996), p. 43. It was later claimed by Mikhail Poltoranin, that it was founded with communist party money. Reddaway & Glinski (Tragedy), p. 682, fn.49.

57. Fortescue (Policy-Making), p. 137.

58. Aleksei Zudin, "Biznes i politika v postkommunisticheskoi Rossii. Politicheskie strategii grupp davleniia biznesa", *Biznes i politika* 1, 1996, p. 4.

59. Fortescue (Policy-Making), p. 138. This is well explained in Eric Lohr, "Arkadii Volsky's Political Base", *Europe-Asia Studies* 45, 5, 1993, pp. 811–829.

60. The others were trade union leader Mikhail Shmakov and former deputy prime minister Vladimir Shcherbakov. White, Rose & McAllister (How Russia Votes), p. 208. This also seems to have been called the Russian United Industry Party. Zudin (Biznes i politika... Formy), p. 8.

61. These concerned tax and budgetary policy, social and labour relations, industrial policy, land reform and the agro-industrial complex, pension reform, WTO entry and customs reform, railway reform, banking sector reform, electricity restructuring, gas sector reform, judicial reform, and small and medium business.

62. See the reports in *Izvestiia*, 14 and 15 November 2003. Significantly, the second one was entitled "Sit quietly". Neither Khodorkovsky nor Yukos was brought up in the public sessions with Putin while he was present. Significantly, only six of the 27 RSPP board members spoke out publicly against Khodorkovsky's arrest. Hanson & Teague (Big Business and the State), p. 663.

63. *Vedomosti* 17 November 2004, JRL 8457 17 November 2004.

64. N. Iu. Lapina, *Rukovoditeli gosudarstvennykh predpriiatii rossii v protsesse formirovaniia rynochnykh otnoshenii* (Moscow, Rossiiskaia akademiia nauk, Institut nauchnoi informatsii po obshchestvennym naukam, 1995), p. 70.

65. For discussion of the FTR, see Berezovskii (Obshchestvennye), II, pp. 2–9 & 2, pp. 1–11, and Fortescue (Policy-Making), pp. 116–117.

66. Berezovskii (Obshchestvennye), II, 4, pp. 1–6 and Nazarova & Krasheninnikov (Obshchestvennye), p. 7.

67. Nazarova & Krasheninnikov (Obshchestvennye), p. 15 where it is stated that it was formed in December. According to Berezovskii (Obshchestvennye), II, 5, p. 2, it was formed in October.

68. Zudin (Biznes i politika . . . Formy), p. 6.

69. Nazarova & Krasheninnikov (Obshchestvennye), p. 60.

70. Fortescue (Policy-Making), p. 117. According to Zudin (Biznes i politika . . . Politicheskie), p. 9, the TPP also had the right to initiate legislation and had accreditation at the Cabinet of Ministers.

71. Berezovskii (Obshchestvennye), II, 6, p. 2.

72. Fortescue (Policy-Making), p. 117.

73. For details on these, see Nazarova & Krasheninnikov (Obshchestvennye), passim, and Berezovskii (Obshchestvennye), passim.

74. For scholarly focus upon corporatism as the appropriate way of conceptualising government–business relations in Russia, see Sergei Peregudov, "The Oligarchical Model of Russian Corporatism", Archie Brown (ed.), *Contemporary Russian Politics. A Reader* (Oxford, Oxford University Press, 2001), pp. 259–268; Kubicek (Variations), pp. 27–46; Aleksei Zudin, "Neokorporatizm v Rossii? (Gosudarstvo i biznes pri Vladimire Putine)", *Pro et Contra* 6, 4, Autumn 2001, pp. 171–198.

75. Zudin (Neokorporatizm), p. 177.

76. Semenenko (Gruppy), pp. 69–72.

77. Semenenko (Gruppy), p. 70.

78. Kubicek (Variations), pp. 40–41. Also see Elizabeth Teague, "Pluralism Versus Corporatism: Government, Labor and Business in the Russian Federation", Carol R. Saivetz & Anthony Jones (eds.), *In Search of Pluralism. Soviet and Post-Soviet Politics* (Boulder, Westview Press, 1994), pp. 109–124. Sectoral commissions were sometimes useful in labour relations issues.

79. Aleksei Zudin, "Biznes i politika v postkommunisticheskoi Rossii", *Biznes i politika* 2, 1996, pp. 2 & 4. But also see Fortescue (Policy-Making), pp. 129–130, who argues that a Council for Entrepreneurs (representing new entrepreneurs) was replaced in September 1992 by the Council of Industrialists and Entrepreneurs which two months later was split into a Council for the Development of Entrepreneurship and a Council for Industry Policy. In September 1994 these were combined into a Council for Industry and Entrepreneurship.

80. Mukhin (Biznes-elita), p. 173.

81. Zudin (Neokorporatizm), p. 173. For its membership see Mukhin (Biznes-elita), pp. 5–6.

82. Zudin (Neokorporatizm), p. 176. Membership of the initial bureau comprised Khodorkovsky, Bendukidze, Deripaska, Zimin, Chubais, Fridman, Potanin, Kogan, Kiselev, Mordashev, Pugachev, Mamut, Yevtushenkov, Vardanian, Yurgens, Dombrovsky, Komissar, Koveshnikov, Luzianin, Makarov, Mal'gin, Nikulin, Titov, Tokaev, Shcherbakov, Volsky and Yeremeev. This membership changed in later years.

83. Zudin (Neokorporatizm), pp. 179–180.

84. *Delovaia Rossiia. Ob'ediniaetsia. Materialy Uchreditel'nogo s'ezda obshcherossiiskoi obshchestvennoi organizatsii "Delovaia Rossiia"* (Moscow, Rossiiskaia torgovlia, 2001),

p. 137. This brought together representatives of the traditional industries and of the legislature. Also see Natalia Arkhangel'skaia, "Voprosy k S'ezdu", *Ekspress* 39, 22 October 2001, pp. 15–18.

85. On lobbying, see Semenenko (Gruppy), pp. 55–64.

86. This is where activity on the most important issues has been concentrated. For example, when energy companies lobbied for subsidies (principally in the form of loans for their customers) in 1994 because of the non-payment problem, it was the Ministry of Fuel and Energy upon which they focused. David Woodruff, *Money Unmade. Barter and the Fate of Russian Capitalism* (Ithaca, Cornell University Press, 1999), p. 141.

87. For Fortescue, lobbying takes three forms: the shaping of a climate of opinion in the general community and policy-making circles, influence on the law-making process, and the attempt to gain specific decisions in one's favour. Fortescue (Policy-Making), p. 118.

88. This was signed by Berezovsky, V. Gorodilov (Sibneft), Gusinsky, A. Dondukov, N. Mikhailov (Vympel), S. Muravlenko (Yukos), L. Nevzlin (Rosprom), A. Nikolaev (AvtoVaz), D.Orlov (Bank Vozrozhdenie), Potanin, Smolensky, Fridman and Khodorkovsky. *Segodnia* 27 April 1996.

89. Heiko Pleines, "Corruption and Crime in the Russian Oil Industry", David Lane, *The Political Economy of Russian Oil* (Lanham, Rowman & Littlefield Publishers Inc, 1999), p. 100. The head of the ARB, Vladimir Kuz'min, said in 2002 that the banks were "insufficiently developed" to effectively lobby for common interests, and preferred to "resolve their own problems on an individual basis". *Nezavisimaia gazeta* 28 May 2002, cited in Chaisty (Legislative Politics), p. 125.

90. According to Frye, in his sample only half of those businessmen who had been successful in lobbying had acted through business or professional organisations. Timothy Frye, "Capture or Exchange? Business Lobbying in Russia", *Europe-Asia Studies* 54, 7, 2002, p. 1027.

91. For examples, from the telecommunications industry, see Aleksei Mukhin, *Voiny na rynke telekommunikatsii. Osnovnye uchastniki i gruppy vliianii* (Moscow, Tsentr politicheskoi informatsii, 2001), p. 12. Also see Chapter 7.

92. Rutland (Introduction), pp. 24–26.

93. However, the basis of unity of the enterprise directors was undercut by the relief of the inter-enterprise debt crisis at the end of 1992 and by the change in the way in which such debt was managed by the Central Bank; from July 1992 individual enterprises had to lobby on their own behalf. Woodruff (Money Unmade), pp. 98–99 and Johnson (Fistful), pp. 101–102.

94. On the role of the ARB, see Johnson (Fistful), pp. 114–117.

95. For example, the establishment in December 1992 of a group called Entrepreneurial Political Initiative-92 (including Bendukidze, Vinogradov, Gusinsky, Zatulin, Kivelidi, Masarsky and Khodorkovsky) which sought to broker a compromise between Yeltsin and the Congress of Peoples' Deputies. Mukhin (Biznes-elita), p. 6.

96. Frye (Capture or Exchange?), p. 1024.

97. The type of firm (state-owned, privatised, de novo) is largely irrelevant, except at the regional level. Frye (Capture or Exchange?), pp. 1018–1020.

98. In part this is because of the lack by many firms of anything that they could offer in exchange. Frye argues that those that have been most successful have been those able to deliver returns to the bureaucrat or level of government involved. Frye (Capture or Exchange?), p. 1018. Also see Fortescue (Policy-Making), p. 126; and "Formirovanie tsivilizovannykh mekhanizmov vzaimodeistviia predprinimatelei i organov vlasti: rossiiskii opyt i tendentsii", *Biznes i politika* 5, 1996, p. 3. On the difficulty in getting a law on lobbying passed, see Formirovanie tsivilizovannykh, pp. 5–14. On the lack of success of lobbying by FIG organisations, see Ia. Sh. Pappe, *Finansovo-promyshlennye gruppy i konglomeraty v ekonomike i politike sovremennoi Rossii* (Moscow, Tsentr politicheskoi tekhnologii, 1997), pp. 61–63.

6

Class and State: The Western Bourgeoisie

The classic image of the capitalist entrepreneur of the industrial period is of the rugged individualist who, basically through his own efforts, was able to accumulate capital and resources and thereby to build up his business from nothing. While there were many whose experiences did accord with this model, it is also true that a significant proportion of the new bourgeoisie made their way through substantial reliance upon the state. The state was central to the development of the new class for two reasons. First, the state was the source of many of the resources that the new bourgeoisie required. In those places where the state legally owned tracts of unsettled land or the natural resources found on or under the land, the state controlled significant assets sought by an emergent industrial bourgeoisie. Control over such natural resources could be central to the new industrialists, both in terms of their direct use in manufacturing or more indirectly as the site over which raw materials and manufactured goods had to be transported; for example, the route of railway lines or canals. Second, the state was the chief regulator in society, and therefore the body which played the major part in setting the conditions under which new business ventures could operate. This involved the establishment of the day-to-day regime under which business functioned: the legalisation of new forms of business organisation; taxation levels; regulations regarding things like health, safety, and employment; the sanctity of contracts, weights, and measures; and property rights were among the areas in which the state played a regulative part. But the state was also important in the way in which it could help to shape the opportunities open to business both generally and in particular instances. Through the exercise of its powers over licensing and government contracts, the state could significantly advantage particular firms over others. Its pursuit of particular types of economic policy—for example, protection versus free trade and mercantilism versus laissez-faire—could have direct implications for individual businesses and their owners as well as for some sectors of the economy at the expense of others. Even if the state did not consciously seek to interfere in the economy, aspects of its activity like its purchasing policy, levels of state debt, and the nature of its foreign policy (expansionist cf. status quo) could all directly affect business. The state could be a major factor in shaping the bourgeoisie and the forms it took, and was itself of major interest to that bourgeoisie. This has two aspects: the way the state appeared as a resource to be exploited by the bourgeoisie and the way the state appeared to be an instrument for capture by the bourgeoisie. These two facets of state–class relations were in practice often extensions of each other, but in principle they can be distinguished.

Both of these aspects of class–state relations concern the issue of state autonomy, or the degree to which the state elite was able to maintain its autonomy from other social forces, including the emergent industrial bourgeoisie. If that elite was able to sustain a significant level of autonomy, acting in its own or the state's interests rather than in the interests of some other group, this could pose a barrier to both the exploitation of state-controlled resources by non-state actors and to state capture by outside groups. Alternatively, if the state elite was unable to maintain its autonomy as a result of its domination by other social forces, it may be unable to prevent either the exploitation or the capture of the state by such forces. In the four Western cases, the emergent bourgeoisie clearly set out to use the state for its own ends, but its capacity to do so differed because in each case state officials retained a degree of autonomy from business interests and because each system differed in its degree of openness to new influences. Analysis of these patterns is important for our evaluation of the role played by the bourgeoisie in shaping the trajectory of each state.

The State as a Resource

Britain

The ability of a new industrial bourgeoisie to exploit the state was facilitated by the growing dominance of an ideology which gave precedence to the sorts of values which underpinned private entrepreneurial activity. The strength of this ideology occurred at the expense of the continuing ideological hegemony of the landowning aristocracy. Many have argued that the ideological hegemony of aristocratic pre-capitalist values in Britain constituted a major barrier to industrial development.[1] Encapsulated in the term 'gentlemanly capitalism', this was seen as involving an anti-industrial ideology which idealised aristocratic landowning life. But the situation was not so simple. The commercialisation of economic life had embraced aristocratic landowners in the seventeenth and eighteenth centuries, with the result that the world views of many of them were not restricted to the horizons of their landed estates. Certainly some aristocratic landowners eschewed involvement in much outside their traditional landowning pursuits, but many were involved in industry or in commercial pursuits by the time the industrialists emerged as a major group. With the development of the latter and the increasing importance to the national economy of industry, the ideological environment in society changed to accommodate the image of the individualistic entrepreneur who was best able to create wealth in an atmosphere of state laissez-faire. While the ideal of the 'leisured gentleman' remained strong, the form in which it existed in the second half of the nineteenth century was a 'Victorian invention'[2] and reflected a lifestyle consistent with urban living and the earning of significant wealth from non-agricultural entrepreneurial pursuits. The entrepreneur and the industrial innovator, bolstered by the so-called 'cult of progress', were seen as the key to the creation of a modern society, one which was focused in the towns rather than the landed estates, and which emphasised industrial production as the basis of such modernity.[3] This sort of orientation is also reflected in the general disposition of the state.

In the latter part of the eighteenth century and during the nineteenth century, the state played a crucial role in fostering economic development. Reflecting the policy of laissez-faire that it espoused, the British state played little direct role in industrial development.[4] It did little directly to promote innovation or productive investment or to attract foreign investment, and it did not directly engage in widescale production itself. But laissez-faire did not imply complete state absence from the economy. It implied a 'powerful state framework within which capital could operate freely'.[5] The state was important in the creation of a 'market environment' through the establishment of political stability, administrative unification, common law, and a sympathetic approach to business. Its introduction of protection at the end of the seventeenth century, a policy driven by the state's need for increased revenue, created an environment favourable for the development of new industries, an effect sustained by the establishment of the Empire as a large free-trade area from the eighteenth century and then by the introduction of a general policy of free trade in the middle of the nineteenth century. It introduced statutes and legal repression to suppress those who sought to object to the new order— customary rights were turned into crimes, minor offences against property were vigorously punished, and violence in labour disputes was outlawed.[6] More directly, the Private Act of Parliament was an important means of getting decisions concerning local issues made and given a legislative basis.[7] Such acts were significant in facilitating economic development, including the enclosure of agricultural land (between 1760 and 1845 more than 6 million acres of farm and waste land were enclosed as a result of some 4,464 acts of Parliament), the construction of railways, the growth of ports, and the establishment of water supply. The state intervened to impose some minimum standards in the railways, and in health, housing, and working conditions, and it did run some industries, including the dockyard and arsenal.[8] Such things as the railway acts, enclosure acts, the police force, the royal mail, and the management of money supply to favour commercial activity were all significant means whereby the state contributed to economic development. This could be justified under the general rubric of public interest. Furthermore through its role in representing the interests of the dominant aristocratic landowners, the Parliament's actions had reshaped the conception of what was meant by public interest to embrace the protection and welfare of private interests. This not only projected the state as having a primary supportive role to private economic activity, but could be extended into a task of widening the opportunities and facilities for personal gain. The reverse side of this was the view that direct state control and interference were undesirable. In this way, the commercial culture that had infused British life for some time was underpinned by the conception of a state that left most matters up to the individual entrepreneur rather than taking on major responsibilities itself. The image of the role of the state was therefore ambiguous: on the one hand, laissez-faire seemed to give it little role, on the other, the actual part it played in economic life made it appear quite significant. This combination of an ideology of a limited role for the state along with a more substantial role in practice justified business activism in the political sphere by portraying business as the legitimate representative of the interests of economic development while at the same time acknowledging the reality of the state's role in this.

This ambiguity also legitimised involvement with the state to gain specific economic advantages on the part of private business. Sometimes this took the form of getting sympathetic involvement in or avoiding state action against the illegal and fraudulent practices that were commonly used within business to build up private wealth. Getting around state regulations, and reliance upon state officials to do so, and gaining monopoly positions through state accreditation were common aspects of the modus operandi from the early eighteenth century when, in the words of one observer, '[c]orrupt transactions were embedded in the English economy'.[9] This situation in the nineteenth century reflects the political system of 'Old Corruption' which lasted until the middle of the century and was characterised by the personal control by politicians and notables over government office and privileges such as pensions and contracts. A major currency of political life was connections, and these were used vigorously for personal enrichment.[10] In the decades after 1780, the government was accused of being 'little more than a broker of 'corrupt' privileges to a cast of insiders'.[11] In the economic sphere, personal contacts could give significant advantages; for example, in the American War there were charges that the government awarded war contracts to merchant MPs as bribes, and supply to the army in the French wars was rorted through the provision of shoddy goods and the absence of competitive bidding.[12] The Company Acts of 1856–62 were official recognition of the need to protect shareholders and creditors against the negligence, fraud, and mismanagement of company directors. There were many abuses: the 'fraudulent promotion of companies formed only to collect money from the public and then to be wound up, the formation by directors of separate companies to supply land, buildings or materials at exorbitant prices to the main company or to take its products at cost, the granting of free shares by the directors to themselves or their friends, the spreading of false or withholding of true information to affect the price of shares with a view to profitable dealings on the stock market, the paying of dividends out of capital'[13] were all common. There were also corrupt practices, favouritism, and insider trading in the pursuit and award of government contracts.[14] Competitors got together to fix prices, to limit output in bad years, and to segment the market between themselves. Initially, such activity was organised either informally or through loose trade associations, but another form was the cartel, which involved financial links (e.g. exchange of shares and establishment of a common fund) between independent companies, a practice supported by government.[15] Taxation obligations were regularly minimised or evaded. Business was often active in establishing relations with members of parliament—bribery,[16] retainers, access to goods, and directorships were common—in order to obtain favourable legislation; the passage of railway legislation was one area where many members had financial interests in the bills upon which they were deliberating. Similar sorts of relations were also often established with leading government officials. Early businessmen often also exploited their workforce in order to maximise the capital at their disposal. It was the use of such means of defrauding others that was one factor in stimulating increased government intervention, which in turn stimulated renewed efforts at limiting this. But this should not obscure the fact that, to the extent it was able, business sought to exploit the state for its own advantage.

Businessmen were also active in seeking policy change. The industrial bourgeoisie, along with commercial and banking capital, opposed the reintroduction of the gold standard and stabilisation of the monetary system in the 1820s and 1830s that was sponsored by liberal Tories who wanted to find a way of restructuring the state financial system to enable the state to finance preservation of public order and external defence.[17] Free-trade ideas became increasingly important during the nineteenth century as maritime control of the globe ensured that the prop provided by the Navigation Acts and the Empire were less important. Tariff liberalisation was pressed cautiously in the 1820s, mostly by a small group of intellectuals/publicists, and more vigorously in the 1840s, mainly by the Manchester Chamber of Commerce and the Anti-Corn Law League, in part in response to pressure from the cotton manufacturers (who wanted free access to American cotton) who argued that duties on raw materials and food imports reduced the sale of these to Britain and thereby reduced foreign capacity to buy British goods. By the 1840s many business circles were so keen to have free trade that some businessmen were willing to compromise the principles of laissez-faire which they supported by accepting an income tax to provide a substitute for the revenue the state would forego through the removal of tariffs. Crucial in this, at least at the symbolic level, was the abolition of the Corn Laws in 1846. The Liberal-Tory governments of 1815–30 had been more concerned about stable employment and keeping growth within acceptable bounds than for the expansion of industry and commerce. Leading figures in these governments, like Liverpool, Canning, and Huskisson believed in a 'natural level of activity'. They were ambivalent about free trade; they reduced but did not eliminate a number of duties and refused to do away with the Corn Laws.[18] However, the pressure for free trade escalated with the economic crisis at the end of the 1830s and early 1840s, the emergence of Chartist unrest in 1842, and the growth of criticism of agrarian interests on the part of industrial capital. This focused attention again on the Corn Laws and their effect of keeping food prices high. With the election of Peel and the Conservatives in 1841, fiscal reform moved to the top of the agenda. This included the reduction or abolition of a range of customs duties on manufactured and semi-manufactured goods, a development which highlighted the effects of the Corn Laws. The Anti-Corn Law League was an important organisation supporting the abolition of the laws. From the outset, this was a business-based organisation, created from within the Manchester Chamber of Commerce mainly by Lancastrian businessmen and presenting itself as the spokesman for those interests in the manufacturing centres which had been excluded from both social primacy and political power by the traditional aristocratic establishment. Leading industrialists were among its chief figures: Richard Cobden was a calico printer, John Benjamin Smith a cotton dealer, George Wilson a corn merchant and later glue manufacturer with important railway interests, and John Bright a cotton spinner.[19] The chief figure in the League, Richard Cobden, railed against 'the sinister aristocratic system' and wanted to replace monopoly and traditional hierarchy by competition, merit, 'business methods', and 'the principles of political economy'.[20] The vigour of this attack, recognition by many landowners that they no longer needed the protection provided by the Corn Laws,[21] and the realisation by some Conservative supporters of traditional interests that a concession at this point could save traditional interests from further attack,[22] all combined to lead to the abolition of the Corn Laws in 1846. While a victory for many of the manufacturers, although not all were in favour of free trade, this was not a reflection of their real power. The passing of the Ten Hours Bill in 1847 over the opposition of the cotton manufacturers was seen as in part a payback for and a response to the abolition of the Corn Laws.[23] Nevertheless, with abolition of the Corn Laws and the consolidation of the doctrine of free trade,

Britain was able to establish a position at the heart of the world economy. In the words of two scholars: 'Britain created an international division of labour, increasingly specializing in manufactured goods, business services and financial services, the latter directed by the financial institutions of the City of London, and exchanged these for food and raw materials from the rest of the world'.[24] This focus had significant implications for the future balance of power and influence within the emergent economic bourgeoisie and the country more broadly.

Businessmen were also active in the late 1840s and early 1850s when economic difficulties raised the question again of the competence of the aristocrats to govern. One form this took was the debate over the government's attempt to increase the level and extend the term of income tax. Businessmen were prominent in the organisation of popular protest and dissent, often using chambers of commerce as the organisational vehicles for this. One prominent organisation was the Liverpool Financial Reform Association,[25] but reflecting the way in which businessmen adopted different positions on this question of income tax, this body favoured total reliance on direct taxes. It was at this time that Gladstone, who wanted to free commerce from many of its burdens so it could increase employment, began to present himself as someone with particular insight into industrial communities. The mismanagement of the Crimean War fuelled concerns about the competence of the nation's aristocratic governors and gave an impetus to the view that what was needed was more businessmen in government and the application of 'business principles' (although it was never clear what they were) to public policy. Such sentiment spawned the movement for administrative reform (which led to the Northcote-Trevelyan report), which gained significant (although not unanimous) support from within the City. But the blunting of this push by the Northcote-Trevelyan Report, a blunting supported by Gladstone, represented a shoring up of the position of the aristocracy and aristocratic values. Concern over the competence of the governors again propelled businessmen to national prominence early in the twentieth century when criticism of what was seen as a lack of 'national efficiency' led to the promotion of the so-called 'practical wisdom of businessmen' as a partial answer to this. At this time, the issue of tariff protection was also once again salient in the face of competition from German and American industry.

So British businessmen were very active both in seeking to exploit resources under state control and to alter government policy to benefit their businesses.

France

If the French revolution was a turning point in that country's development, one thing it did not substantially change was the strongly statist ideology that had dominated French society at least since the emergence of absolutist rule. Unlike in England, France had an extensive centralised bureaucracy (even if many posts were privately purchased[26]) reaching to all parts of the country. The existence of a large bureaucracy with formal lines of authority to the centre enabled the French state formally to project itself more prominently into society than its British counterpart. This was also manifested in the state's greater involvement in French life, especially economic, than in Britain. Generally, the French state sought to be a more active participant in economic life than in Britain, with the doctrine of laissez-faire having little practical currency. The tradition of state involvement and the image of the state having a prominent role in society, strengthened by the Napoleonic interlude, extended right through the nineteenth century. This image of a powerful and active state was therefore a major feature of the environment into which the new industrial bourgeoisie emerged, and one which clearly affected the course of the integration of the new class into the polity. It was also the basis upon which the social and political prominence of leading state officials in French society rested. With a strong sense of collective identity and *esprit de corps* at the upper levels, state officials constituted an important centre of power in French public life. And although there was little penetration of this by business, there was a point at which interests and perceptions converged. The strong statist tradition in France generated a drive to expand the power and glory of the state. This was seen, in part, in terms of colonial expansion and the spreading of 'la civilisation Francaise', but it also took the form of a drive to develop the economy at home. This of necessity led French bureaucrats to embrace the aspirations to industrial expansion held by the bourgeoisie. Pro-development policies pursued by the state thus added strength to privately propelled industrial growth to fuel economic development, while at the same time providing a favourable state context for business development.

The view that the state had a major role to play in promoting national greatness through economic development encouraged people to look to the state as a source of support for their economic activities. The function of officials, both local and those in the national legislature, was to ensure the flow of resources into the local economy from the centre. Indeed, the 1852 Constitution considered members of the Legislative Body to be 'delegates' from their particular regions rather than representatives of the nation, as had been affirmed in 1789.[27] Many deputies had a financial interest in local railways or other businesses in their constituencies while many were paid continuing consultancy or legal fees in return for representing the interests of their paymasters in governing circles.[28] Many deputies remained active in their businesses even while carrying out their public functions, often leading to a direct conflict of interest; for example, the general manager of a private canal company both acted for the company in negotiations with the government over projected canal construction and, as a deputy, was the chief reporter on a canal bill before the Assembly in 1821.[29] It was claimed that in the July Monarchy, seventy deputies had a direct financial interest in the bills being debated.[30] This sort of exploitation of the state for the benefit of local business was seen as quite acceptable because of the belief that what served the particular business, served the local community. As a result, businessmen saw nothing wrong in using their positions as deputies to benefit their businesses. Private gain for their businesses (or indeed for their families; ministers could use their positions to get jobs for family members[31]) could always be rationalised in terms of local or national interests: what was good for their industries was good for the nation. Some businessmen even held ministerial office in the sphere that affected their private business concerns and many of these remained active in their businesses while acting as government ministers; for example, Duclos who was from a family of shippers and merchants and acted as Minister for the Navy and Colonial Affairs before 1855, and Behic as Minister of Economic Affairs. But such a situation left the way open to the sorts of arrangements that certainly now and sometimes then would be described as corrupt, or at least as conflicts of interest. Throughout the nineteenth century, there were continuing charges that deputies, especially in the conduct of public works, were involved in a network of corruption that embraced businessmen, speculators, developers, financiers, and the press. A classic case of such advantages being given to private enterprises was railway development which the state was always ready to underwrite financially.

Railway development was sponsored by the July Monarchy in the 1830s and 1840s through the granting of concessions to private companies to construct the lines.[32] Initially, much of the infrastructure development and expropriation of land was done by the state, with concessionary companies laying the track, purchasing rolling stock, paying for maintenance, and running expenses of the lines. This process led to many abuses. Speculators set up phantom companies for sale once the stock price had risen, and different individuals and companies engaged in collusion to affect these prices and to artificially increase the bidding at public auctions. This often involved not just those involved in the companies and financiers, but also ministers, deputies, and state officials. For example, in the late 1830s the state made loans to four companies to encourage them to continue with railway construction despite economic difficulties.[33] By 1852, the companies had built up substantial debts. Accordingly, the government promoted company mergers, extended their concessions for ninety-nine years, and guaranteed a minimum profit on the new lines. The companies built a large number of branch lines, often under the influence of national deputies and local politicians who wanted to advance their particular regions, many of which had no shortterm prospect of turning a profit. As a result, the state was subsidising the losses of the private companies,[34] a result that may in part have been due to the way in which, in the words of one scholar, 'rail tycoons like Mires had greased the palms of key members of the imperial entourage...'[35] When railway companies sought assistance in raising capital, the state would often guarantee the interest on their securities[36]; under the Third Republic through the Freycinet Plan, the state guaranteed railway companies' loans and their dividends.[37] Under this plan, the state was to construct 23,000 km of track, which would then be taken over by private companies with a partial state subsidy. The companies could not lose under this arrangement. In one case, a company received grants of money and interest guarantees but never built any track.[38] Indeed, the Freycinet Plan was a classic case of businessmen using their positions and contacts to consolidate their businesses.[39] In 1877, Republicans in the Chamber wanted to break the power of the monopolist railway companies, with many even supporting nationalisation. However, the government formed by the Duc de Broglie (after the Seize Mai crisis) was composed of many people with strong ties to the railway companies: Minister of Finance Caillaux sat on the board of the Paris-Lyon-Mediterranean Railway, Minister of Interior de Fourtou and his Secretary of State Reille were directors of the Paris-Orleans Co., de Broglie had administered feeder lines to trunk lines in his capacity as chairman of Saint Gobain glassworks, and the Minister of Public Works had been spokesman for the Nord Railway Co. in the National Assembly. State exploitation was a major factor in the development of the railways.

Similar sorts of arrangements had been present during the canal construction of the Restoration period. In 1817, the Didier and Vassal Co. agreed to complete the construction of two canals in exchange for a ninety-nine-year concession on tolls. This involved an investment of some 3 million francs by the company, compared with a past and future capital expenditure of some 27 million francs that the city of Paris 'contracted to turn over to the company'.[40] The following year, the government financed the construction of bridges in Bordeaux and docks in Le Havre by borrowing from local private consortia with the guarantee of repayment at a high rate of interest from concessions on port dues and bridge tolls.[41] These occurred at a time when the government was anxious to see the construction of canals and wanted private involvement.

Bribery was a common feature of business–state relations. For example, in 1847 it came to light that large payments had been made to the then Minister of Public Works with the aim of securing industrial concessions.[42] A more spectacular case was the Panama crisis of the late 1880s and early 1890s. The Panama Canal Co., which sought to replicate the financial success achieved by the builders of the Suez Canal, was in a state of almost chronic shortage of capital. It sought to remedy this by raising a special loan, in which it was strongly supported by politicians and the press. However, it gained this support through bribery; it bribed journalists to conceal its troubles and deputies to gain parliamentary sanction for the issue of lottery bonds. It contributed to various deputies' re-election campaigns and it paid money directly into individuals' pockets. It was alleged at the time that 104 deputies had accepted bribes.[43] It was also common to buy favourable publicity in the financial press about a company's shares or to cover up difficulties.[44] Many newspapers were owned by business and financial interests who used those media outlets to press their partisan cases.[45] Bribery was also common in the course of the urban reconstruction that occurred under the July Monarchy and Second Empire; for example, under Louis-Philippe, the head of the department of highways at the Paris Hotel de Ville sold the plans of future projects to speculators who were then able to buy up the land and buildings destined for future development.[46]

Firms also often gained state assistance in the form of laxness in the enforcement of government regulations, including the minimisation or avoidance of tax obligations, support in cases where there was a clash of interest between business and community, and even turning a blind eye while large firms stamped out the competition of smaller rivals.[47] Companies also could often rely upon the state to send in troops to break strikes.[48] The elimination of competition was reinforced, with state approval, towards the end of the nineteenth century with the development of cartels in many branches of industry. For example, in iron and steel the major companies got together to safeguard profits by stabilising prices, curtailing production, and dividing markets, even though this slowed down economic development more generally.[49]

Exploitation of the state was also central to the functioning of the banks. Throughout much of the nineteenth century, many of the banks sought their profits less through investment in productive enterprise than in lending to the state and purchase of its bonds. For at least the first half of the century (they monopolised state borrowing until 1854), the haute banque's business was principally in the floating of state loans with generous (for the bank) rates of interest and solid guarantees against default.[50] According to one scholar, during the Restoration the banks were more like government stockholders than investors in productive activity.[51] Such involvement in the public sphere meant that rather than stimulating production, banks often were effectively parasitic upon the state.[52] Such a situation could make the bankers involved very powerful, as for example when for a period from 1823 Rothschild had a monopoly over state loans.[53] French business generally thrived on the basis of exploitation of the state.

Germany

In Chapter 2, it was argued that the emergence of commercial values did not displace the more traditional outlook of the Junkers in Germany. Nevertheless, such new values did develop and spread. The imperial period was one in

which the development of the cities continued apace, with increasing pop-
ulations, highly developed social structures and networks, and the growth of
a real urban culture. In popular parlance, this is often referred to as a bourgeois
culture, and it is true that much of this accompanied the growth of that
section of the population that was middle class and increasingly professional.
This was not a specifically economic bourgeois culture, but it was one linked
with the strengthening of the bourgeoisie numerically and in terms of cultural
capital: the growth of education and literacy, the recognition of qualifications
and merit as organising principles of public life, the growth of a public sphere
of discussion and debate, the emergence of a new sense of propriety rooted
in an urban lifestyle, and the development of new legal structures all became
consolidated in the late nineteenth century and early twentieth century.[54]
This culture did not force out the cultural values associated with the Junker
lifestyle, but it did emerge beside them. In some cases it took them over and
gave those values new meaning[55]; in others, the contrasting values coexisted,
sometimes causing friction; in yet others they did not intersect at all. Thus
the continued presence of the Junker tradition did not stifle the development
of bourgeois, urban culture, but it did help to shape it and to create a cultural
milieu that was different from other countries also subject to the imperatives
of industrialisation.

Bourgeois development was strengthened by the circumstances in which
industrialisation occurred. The emergence of the German industrial economy
and the new class that it brought took place in very different geopolitical
conditions from those of Britain, France, and the United States. The early
impetus for German industrialisation had come when the German states
remained politically separate, even if after 1834 they were united in a Customs
Union. Industrialisation accompanied the drive for territorial consolidation
into a nation state. Indeed, part of this process was the perceived unity of
the polity and the economy; political unification was the counterpart of the
creation of a single, German, economic system. This perception is reflected
in the significant involvement of merchants and industrialists in the public
organisations working for German unification.[56] This linking of the aspiration
for political unification with the quest for rapid industrialisation encouraged
an instrumental perception of the latter; industrial growth was seen as central
to the state-building project that the state elite consistently pursued.[57] The
importance of industry was increased in their eyes by Germany's geopolitical
location. Unification had been immediately preceded by successful Prussian
wars against Austria and France, but these victories did not eliminate the
perceived challenge from these two powers to German predominance in
Central Europe. Moreover, this was reinforced by the presence of the Russian
Empire on the eastern border, and of a vigorous and outward-oriented Britain
just across the channel. The perception of the new Germany struggling to
attain its deserved status, a struggle highlighted by the constraints confronted

by Germany in gaining an empire to match those of its rivals, reinforced the view of the centrality of industry to German state-building.

This view is consistent with the Gerschenkron thesis concerning Germany as a latecomer industrialiser.[58] In this view, latecomer industrialisers were able to develop more quickly than those that had gone before, in part because of the lessons learned from the earlier experiences and because of the more substantial positive part played in this process by the state. The state consciously facilitated industrialisation in an attempt to strengthen its competitive position as a latecomer industrialiser. Central to such concerns was not just the economic consideration of the country having to make its way in a commercial world already shaped by the earlier industrialisers, but the political concern of national security. This concern was heightened in the case of a new national state like Germany where pre-unification divisions remained embedded in the collective consciousness. Accordingly, Bismarck sought to strengthen German national power through the creation and consolidation of an authoritarian polity in which the Junker value structure retained primacy, and a developed economy resting on state-stimulated industry and agriculture.

In this context, it is important to recognise that many of the broad aims pursued by the government were compatible with those sought by industrialists. The government's aim was to develop Germany industrially as quickly as possible in order to raise it to the status of a great power alongside its main perceived rival, Britain. This, in part, was also behind the drive for a colonial empire, although this drive did not meet with universal business support; in contrast, Tirpitz's drive to expand and modernise the navy in the late nineteenth century,[59] which was linked to the imperial drive and to great power competition, was much more popular with industry.[60] Rapid, state-supported industrialisation and the imperatives of that policy accorded with the general outlook of business and gave businessmen a sort of leverage that they would otherwise probably not have enjoyed. The protectionist trade policy introduced in 1879 provided protection for heavy industry from foreign competition, and therefore gained heavy industry's support, but was also a positive for the Reich government because it weakened its financial dependence on the states.[61] The trade treaties of 1891 improved opportunities for export of manufactures, the government tolerated cartels which protected the advantages enjoyed by established businesses, and the attempts to suppress the growing workers' movement through anti-socialist legislation and harassment of the SPD and trade unions accorded with industrialists' preferences.[62] Of course, not all that the government did was approved by business: the construction of an elaborate welfare system, the attempt to restore state ownership in the coal industry, and the continued toleration of the SPD were all perceived as counter to business interests. But generally, successive governments prior to the war pursued policies which were consistent with business interests. This is why the claim that the 'alliance of iron and rye', represented by the introduction of tariffs on iron, rye, and wheat in 1879, reflects the subordination of industry and the bourgeoisie to agriculture and the traditional landed interests needs to be treated with care. Certainly, the government supported the Junkers in their opposition to industry expanding into East Prussia where Junker estates remained supreme, but in the trade treaties introduced in the early 1890s, strengthening the export position of the industrialists seemed to be a higher state priority than protection of agrarian interests.[63] In the three-and-a-half decades between the tariff reform and the outbreak of war, the industrial sector of the economy developed and prospered much more than did the agricultural, and state policy was a major factor in this.[64]

From the establishment of a united Germany, the nature of the institutional structure and the channels open to business into that structure facilitated its use for improper, even illegal, means. As one scholar says, following unification, 'entrepreneurial chances for dishonest mobilization of state resources grew',[65] and entrepreneurs took advantage of this at all levels. People used government connections to rent seek, and to use capital thereby gained to buy up resources and property.[66] They used their connections to get around laws, give out false business information, skim off capital, sell stocks at inflated prices in sometimes non-existent enterprises, and manipulate share registers to reduce the equity of investors.[67] This sort of pattern was particularly common in the early 1870s during the speculative boom, when entrepreneurs took a small establishment, set up a distinguished board of directors, issued an exaggerated prospectus, and sold large numbers of shares at inflated prices. Between 1871 and 1873, some 726 such companies were established compared with 276 in the 1790–1870 period.[68] A Rhenish business leader was very critical of the sort of morality that pervaded banking circles at this time when he declared:

In my experience, there is no laxer morality, no weaker conscience to be found in any group in Europe than in that of the Haute-Finance. This laxness of moral standards builds in substantial measure on the adroitness, the skill with which corrupt and fraudulent transactions are concealed, so that the machinations remain undecipherable to all except themselves; in addition, in executing their business they employ such a secretive, devious and roundabout chain of agents and intermediaries that no outsider can perceive the beginning, nor distinguish between principal and agent. It is rare indeed when an outsider is able to penetrate this jungle, able to identify and understand the goals, including those by which they successfully deceive a gullible public.[69]

The joint stock company act (1884) was widely used by entrepreneurs as a means of generating quick profits by bringing in outside investors and, having done so, leave the companies to their fates.[70] Some individuals used their personal connections in an attempt to influence policy. Ballin and his relationship with the Emperor has already been mentioned (see Chapter 2), but perhaps an even more obvious case was that of Gerson Bleichroder who was Bismarck's personal financier and carried out many different tasks for the Chancellor: he showed Bismarck how he could finance his war against Austria in the late 1860s despite opposition from within the Prussian government, he often acted as Bismarck's agent internationally, he arranged financial assistance for Bismarck's allies, and he advised Bismarck on state economic policy and on the Chancellor's own personal finances and management of his estates.[71] He also used his contacts for his own benefit, using government loans to buy up productive companies.[72]

Exploitation of the state for personal gain continued during the Weimar period. For example, industrialists were allowed to borrow at interest rates lower than the currency's rate of inflation, thereby enabling private investment or enrichment at public expense; loans were put into capital goods and repaid with depreciated marks that were accepted at face value.[73] Industries continually sought to evade taxes and get concessions from the state, especially given the difficult economic circumstances following the end of the war and the depression, with payment to individual political figures often part of this.[74] Businessmen who also occupied advisory positions with the government routinely used these positions to advance their business interests.[75] German business was as adept at exploiting the state as its British and French counterparts.

The United States

The American system was much more open to penetration by the emergent industrialists than its British, French, or German counterparts. In part, this was due to the fact that historically the apex of the system had since the revolution been open to those of substantial wealth. This means that while not all parts of society could enter its upper levels—the working class and black and native Americans were excluded—industry's capacity to generate substantial material wealth for its principals effectively opened the upper levels of the system to them. While this was in part a function of the absence of a traditional landed aristocracy, especially with the Northern victory in the Civil War that undermined the dominance of Southern plantation interests, it also reflected the dominance of an ideology of individual achievement based on hard work rather than state support. That this did not exactly mirror reality, because of the state's role in economic accumulation and development, did not matter given the context of the aspirational mythology underpinning the independent American state and its founding and the rhetorical emphasis upon laissez-faire in discussions of subsequent economic development. This was symbolised by the way in which the notion of democracy became equated with economic freedom and the rights of property,[76] thereby transforming a radical concept into a prop for the status quo within which the well-to-do could dominate. This ideology was crucial because what it enabled was the linkage of the symbolism of the public interest with that of business; the aphorism 'what was good for our country was good for General Motors, and vice versa'[77] captures this. Such an ideology, seeing business as the path to individual and national success and enrichment, was a very powerful force buttressing the position of business in American society and political life.

Despite this ideology-linking business with the national interest, businessmen came under considerable public criticism in the late nineteenth and early twentieth centuries. This criticism is captured in the term that has come to be associated with businessmen of this period, 'robber barons'. Initially coined by Kansas farmers to refer to speculative capitalists and those who ran the railways,[78] the term gained widespread currency in the 1870s–90s and was enshrined in the title of a major study of these businessmen and their activities.[79] The essence of the notion of robber barons was, in the words of one scholar, 'that business leaders in the United States from about 1865 to 1900 were, on the whole, a set of avaricious rascals who habitually cheated and robbed investors and consumers, corrupted government, fought ruthlessly among themselves, and in general carried on predatory activities comparable to those of the robber barons of medieval Europe'.[80] The first wave of these were mainly rogue financiers, benefiting from financial manipulation and speculation, while the second wave sought monopoly control of a product or market.[81] It was this general perception[82] that was at the heart of the widespread criticism of business and its corruption of government in the last decades of the nineteenth century[83] and the Progressive movement that emerged in the first decade of the twentieth century.

Progressivism[84] and the public criticism that preceded it was an important political movement. It spawned a significant third candidate in the 1892 presidential race (the populist James R. Weaver), actually captured the Democratic nomination in 1896 and 1900 (William J. Bryan), was the banner under which Theodore Roosevelt ran unsuccessfully in 1912, and was the basis for the most successful showing of the left in American political history: by 1911, some 450 Socialists had been elected to public office, including 56 mayors and 1 congressman, and in the 1912 presidential election the Socialist candidate Eugene Debs won 6% of the vote, the highest tally ever by a Socialist. But Progressivism was also important because it became a major agenda-setting force in American politics. Interpretations of Progressivism differ, while all agree that it involved genuine criticism of the abuses of business and gained widespread popular resonance. Some see it as an attempt by the system to adjust to the changing situation and thereby to bring about further stability.[85] For others, it was the means whereby businessmen took control of the political system, using their positions to enact a range of measures that were designed to pacify the rising protest from the left.[86] But even if this is better seen as a process of partial concession designed to bring about moderation rather than a full-blooded onslaught from below, its public face comprised wide-ranging and stringent criticism of American businessmen and their business practices. Theodore Roosevelt's election in 1900 occurred under the banner of bringing the growth and influence of big business under control and criticism of 'the malefactors of great wealth', although such rhetoric and his reputation as a 'trust buster' were not matched by action.[87]

The Progressive criticism[88] was, at its heart, as much a criticism of government as of business. There were two aspects of this. The first was a general unease about the implications that the closeness between business and government could have. While the ideology that national and business interests were mutually compatible and supportive, if not identical, prevailed, there was also a concern about the possible negative effects of the pursuit by individual businesses of their partial interests. Thus although the business of the United States may have been seen to be business, this did not mean that in every case business interests were acceptable. This perception was probably strengthened by the way the broad ideology had been affected by general developments within the business sphere. Initially, when the ideology had been generated, it was in a Jeffersonian America of small business, where business success could be directly linked to personal achievement and community benefit. However, with the growth in size of business and the loss of Jeffersonian innocence, business was more impersonal and the perception of a unity of business and community interests less evident. This bifurcation of business and community interests could be seen to be symbolised by the corruption of politicians. Second was the perception that business abuses were a result of the weakness of state oversight. This was highlighted by the way in which the Supreme Court had used the due process clause of the Fourteenth Amendment to impose a narrow interpretation of the rights of the states to interfere with business, and with the Federal Government largely inactive in this field, there was little effective restraint on business activity.[89] Thus the weakness of state regulation was seen as one source of business abuses.

The merger movement of the early years of the twentieth century was a major stimulant of criticism.[90] Many in big business saw the concentration of economic power through mergers as desirable both in terms of limiting competition and in terms of increasing economic capacity. The 1880s had seen the rise of pools, trusts, and combinations, attempts by individual firms to reach standing agreements with their competitors to limit competition and thereby create the conditions for higher prices, but generally these seem to have been insufficiently stable to secure the sorts of continuing returns their sponsors desired. Accordingly, they looked to other means to facilitate their operations. Around the turn of the century, large-scale mergers occurred, although these were concentrated in a minority of dominant industries.[91] However, this movement was met with hostility in some quarters. Among small businessmen, the growth of large oligopolistic and monopolistic enterprises often seemed to represent a major threat to their continuing viability. For the ordinary person in the street, the growth of such enterprises seemed to presage a situation in which effective power in the society was not vested in its political institutions which promised an element of democratic accountability, but in the smoky boardrooms of the country's major enterprises. Big business looked like unaccountable business, and this served to increase the popularly based suspicion with which business had become widely viewed.

But the most obvious reason for criticism was the way in which people perceived themselves to be suffering at the hands of rapacious businessmen. Such a perception was often well-founded[92]; indeed it was discontent over railway rates that spawned the 'robber barons' tag in Kansas noted above. But what gave this perception of being at the mercy of unscrupulous business interests a sharp political edge was the widespread view that these greedy and grasping businessmen were particularly able to exploit the people because of the close, and corrupt, relationship they had with the government. From the outset, businessmen approached politics and politicians as a means of advancing their business interests. One railway magnate, Collis P. Huntington, wrote in 1877 'If you have to pay money to have the right thing done, it is only just and fair to do it . . . '[93] Much of the development of American business occurred in this vein. For example, the expansion of the railways relied upon the private acquisition of public resources, often facilitated by considerations like those espoused by Huntington. Between 1869 and 1871, railway companies received ~$100 million in financial aid and 200 million acres of land from the federal and state governments,[94] while between 1850 and 1877 the total acreage of public land awarded to railway companies was 155,499,991 acres.[95] Such land grants sometimes also included access to the resources found on the land (e.g. timber and stone) which could then be used in the construction of the railway. This meant that not only was the public, through the government, formally underwriting the development of the railway system, but it was also paying for its construction.[96] In some cases, such aid and land grants were not even used because the projected railways were not built, with the railway owners resisting pressure to return such public moneys and land.[97] The sorts of advantages gained by the railway companies were often a result of special legislation introduced into state legislatures by legislators acting for those companies (see below).[98] When businessmen sought assistance from government, they could often name their own terms given their earlier purchase of the legislators and the desire of those legislators who were not in business' pocket to promote the development of their particular regions. As well as gaining these sorts of concessions for the start up of companies, once established many firms continued to look to government for assistance. Tax breaks, tariff protection, government contracts at favourable rates, cheap loans and grants, the adoption of legislation giving special permission for deals that were commercially advantageous, the evasion and often complete ignoring of regulations and rules, and the sidelining of various committees of enquiry were common in the business relationship with government. So too was the enjoyment of monopolistic privileges made available through federal charters and regulations.

Businessmen often acted unscrupulously in their dealings with the populace at large (including their customers) and with their competition, and this was usually accepted by the state with equanimity. The railways offered differential rates to different customers depending upon what their opposition was offering rather than anything about the particular service they were offering; for example, it sometimes cost more to ship goods half the distance, simply because the longer route was characterised by competition whereas the shorter one was not. There was a tendency to raise prices to whatever the local market could bear. Goods could be fraudulently labelled to deceive the consumer. When stock options were offered, it was often 'watered stock' with inflated measurements and phantom value.[99] False prospectuses were issued and firms could become highly over-capitalised, thereby creating a stock of cash which the businessman could often mobilise to finance yet more moneymaking ventures. Such practices lasted into the 1930s, as the Senate Committee on Banking and Currency, the so-called 'Pecora Committee', showed. When there was labour unrest, businessmen often turned to the state to keep their labour forces under control. When it came to relations with competitors, the competition was often no holds barred as each sought to drive the other out of business. In such conflicts, each side would use virtually whatever means were at their disposal to emerge victorious. Some of the most bitter fights were between large companies and involved the drive towards monopoly control over a particular region or resource. The state was often mobilised into such conflicts, with local authorities supporting their 'local' entrepreneurs over those from somewhere else. Such conflicts were not only often economically very disruptive, but they were also rarely profitable. In all aspects of their activity, business looked to the state and its officials for advantage, both material and legal.

Business Control of the State?

So in all four countries, business looked to the state as a resource to be exploited in the pursuit of economic success and greater profit. But did members of the bourgeoisie do more than simply exploit the state? Did they seek to control it and use it for its own ends? Class control of the state is not easy to discern. It can depend on the personal interactions between wealthy or powerful members of the class and leading figures in the politico-administrative sphere, and the influence that is assumed thereby to flow. However, that flow of influence is rarely easy to see.[100] Instead of seeking to chart its ebb and flow over a succession of issues in each country, the following discussion focuses on the structural bases for the exercise of influence. Formal office-holding has already been analysed in Chapter 4. The following discussion examines the sociocultural basis upon which the bourgeois class could seek to exert influence at two levels of government, the central and the local (or regional) levels.

Central Government

BRITAIN

Central to this question of bourgeois relationship to the state in Britain was the bifurcation between the industrial and financial sectors. The large banks were not prominent in the financing of early industrial development. Unlike their late nineteenth-century German counterparts, they did not promote industrial expansion and associate themselves with the management of industrial enterprises. Local or country banks, many of which owed their origin in part to the influence of local industrialists, played an important part in providing credit for the working capital required by the small firms. While internal (principally re-investment of profit), and personal/family sources were most important for the supply of fixed capital, working capital often came from the country banks.[101] Generally, the banks were more interested in commercial and financial matters, especially of an international nature, than they were in industrial concerns. This was particularly the case following the amalgamation of the banking system into a few London banks after 1880. The resultant concentration of control strengthened the City's domination of the economy which, given the City's primary focus on Empire and overseas investment, did little to facilitate industrial development. The relationship between the financial and industrial sectors was therefore not close.

The difference between industrial and commercial/financial interests was evident in terms of power. As the general wealth of the country rose during the nineteenth century, this was earned among non-landed wealth disproportionately by commercial and financial circles (merchants, bankers, shipowners, merchant bankers, stock and insurance agents, and brokers) rather than those in manufacturing and industry[102]; by the 1880s, leading bankers were generally wealthier than industrialists not only in Britain but also in France, Germany, Italy, and Central Europe.[103] This was, in the view of many, the reverse side of the fact that, during the development of British capitalism, commercial and financial capital based in the City has been much more important than manufacturing or industrial capital.[104] This view rests principally upon the argument that financial services rather than the export of manufactured goods have been the mainstay of the British balance of payments over much of the last two centuries[105]; by the second half of the nineteenth century, a large proportion of the balance of payments came from shipping, insurance, the financing of world trade and international banking, while by 1913 income from investments was a more important source of revenue than material exports.[106] It also sees the Empire principally in terms of its commercial aspects rather than of any contribution it may have made to domestic industry.

But regardless of the precise balance between financial and industrial contributions to the balance of payments, one thing which has been crucial has been the close link between the financial sector and politics. The City was, in the words of one scholar, a 'gentlemen's club'[107] which was able to assimilate the aristocratic establishment but did not include the industrial elite, and had close links with politicians. Bankers and politicians occupied the same 'social world',[108] with financiers enjoying and utilising personal links with individual politicians and with the government and civil service structures to further their economic interests.[109] Generally, bankers did not seek to use Parliament very much as a vehicle for defending their interests[110]; they had the Bank of England (upon the court of which partners in the leading merchant banks sat) and the Treasury for that and the close and continuing links between central government and the City. The City–Treasury–Bank nexus was a very powerful policy combination, especially as all three operated to a considerable extent outside direct parliamentary control. The Bank of England saw its primary function as stabilisation of sterling and the underwriting of the international financial dealings of the banks rather than the long-term funding of British industry.[111] In this sense, the City was generally able to set the parameters of economic policy and it did so to serve its own interests rather than those of domestic industry.[112] This does not mean that the City was always victorious[113] or sought to damage British industry or to work against its interests; indeed, many of the policies pursued did not substantially disadvantage industry, which shared many aims with the financial sector.[114] Rather its consistent pursuit of national interests, which were defined more in financial and commercial than in industrial terms, meant that government policy frequently was not as favourable to domestic industrial development as it might have been.

This does not mean that manufacturing interests had no influence. British industrialists were able to establish a presence in the legislature and in a much more limited fashion in the executive and, socially, they merged at the edges with the traditional landowners. They thereby gained a voice in leading political councils in the country. Wealthy industrial elites were able directly to contact leading figures in the political and administrative structures, and the latter frequently consulted them on issues of the day relating to their activities. Such a direct approach was both easier and likely to be more effective than working through local politicians. This was facilitated by the social overlap noted above, realised through things like common membership of clubs and mixing in common social circles. But even though throughout the nineteenth century the Northern manufacturing elite was growing in wealth and power, it neither merged with nor substantially won power from the commercial/financial elite in the City. The latter continued to cast its gaze outward, to the Empire and abroad rather than to the fledgling industries of the North. Despite the changing class complexion of the formal institutions of the state, including the growth of representation of industrial interests, those interests continued to be less well catered for in government policy than those of banking and financial circles.[115]

Fundamental to the course of British economic development was therefore its financial–commercial nature, centred on London, and the gulf that existed between this and industry. Financial–commercial activity provided the basis for the development of an urban bourgeoisie in the capital which rested not on domestic industry but on international finance, and which was politically more important than its counterpart based in the factories of the North. But while the emergent economic bourgeoisie was incorporated into the British power structure with little difficulty, it was the tripartite relationship between landowners, industrial capital, and financial capital that was crucial in structuring the disposition of power. While the economic importance of landed interests declined, they were able to maintain much of their politico-administrative power through their positions in the legislative and executive arms of the state. They were confronted by newly emergent interests, but these were interests which were not united. The financial sector had developed, fuelled by the English state's continuing involvement in war between 1700 and 1850, but with the reliance of early industry mainly upon local sources of finance, the banks had been encouraged to look abroad for investment opportunities. The growth of Empire helped this. Through this confluence of the financial/commercial search for opportunities and *raison d'etat*, linkages between the financial sector and the state became close, mediated chiefly through the institutional nexus of the Bank of England, the Treasury, and the City. Government policy remained imperial in focus and supportive of financial pre-eminence, while the financial sector looked primarily outward. This created a symbiosis between state and financial sector which effectively crowded out that other newly emergent interest, industrial capital. While parts of this sector, especially after the winding back of protection, also took up an internationalist stance, seeking to export their manufactures outside Britain, industrial exports remained secondary in importance in the British economy to financial flows. And the industrialists generally remained marginal in the corridors of power and certainly had less influence than the financiers. But even this group did not control the state. They were usually able to exercise significant influence on policy issues when these were important to them, but they did not dominate. The machinery of state continued to be dominated by the sons of the traditional landowners and the emergent, mainly professional, middle class. Certainly as time passed some scions of business were able to reach high political and administrative office, but they were never as a group able to exercise the sort of power which, both constitutionally and to a large extent actually, resided in the hands of officials and politicians, or which could be exercised by the City.

FRANCE

In France, no regime was controlled by business, but some businessmen were able to gain positions of authority and influence which they could use to serve their own interests. During the Restoration (1815–30), despite some representation in the legislature, given that industry developed slowly through this period, the newly emergent business class was not yet in a position economically to dominate and thereby to be able to press for predominant influence politically. Their position was rendered more difficult by the restoration of many of the old noble families to high status; symbolic here was the payment of restitution to those nobles who lost their land during the Revolution. In the struggle both to exert influence on the government and to gain positions in the bureaucracy, the emergent bourgeoisie thus had to struggle with a temporarily revived old aristocracy. During this time, many bankers made massive profits from state loans,[116] and despite conflicts between individual banking houses,[117] bankers were able to establish a prominent place of influence for themselves in the conduct of official business. But this was not reflected in consistent policies supporting their interests.

The revolution of 1830 brought Louis-Philippe to the throne and led to the emergence of landholding as the principal basis for formal representation in the legislature. This has led Cobban to call the July Monarchy (1830–48) an 'oligarchy of landowners' rather than the 'bourgeois monarchy' it has often been designated.[118] Financiers seem to have exercised significant influence over policy at this time,[119] often to their advantage compared with the industrialists. But too much should not be made of this division in France because many individuals were simultaneously financiers and industrialists and, in the words of one scholar, at this time there was a 'constant osmosis between industry, finance, land and bureaucracy'.[120] Despite the conservative, land-based nature of the electorate and of the parliamentary deputies, and the weak and corrupt coalitions that dominated the legislature, there were some moves within government to satisfy industrialists, including measures for speeding up economic development, support against worker demands, and improvement of the transport infrastructure.[121] How-ever, businessmen do not appear to have been particularly active politically; the pressure groups established in 1846 to lobby for moderate tariffs were led by journalists and academics rather than business groups.[122] When busi-nessmen did take an interest in politics, they were often divided; in 1848, the established manufacturers supported the government of Louis-Philippe while many of the newer generation and smaller producers supported the Republicans.[123]

During the Second Empire (1852–70), which in the view of some rested on 'big business',[124] business interests were much more strongly represented in the legislature than they were either before or after this time and some were influential in the councils of Emperor Louis Napoleon. In Zeldin's view,[125] these people were often not highly interested in politics, but 'came to par-liament to put their experience at the service of the state and to defend their interests, which were very much dependent on government policy'. But given the authoritarian power possessed by the Emperor,[126] advancement and favour were subject to his will; as Kemp argues, his power enabled him to endow others, mainly 'privileged insiders', 'with economic privileges and opportunities for material gain which would not have come their way through the normal processes of the market-place'.[127] It was during this period that many MPs took a pecuniary interest in finance and railway concessions. This was facilitated by the acceleration of industrial development during this period plus the widespread uncertainty on the part of the rich as to what they should do with their money, which resulted in considerable speculative activity, especially in urban redevelopment.[128] It was during the Empire that industry moved into a much more prominent place in the French economic landscape.[129] Economic expansion was fuelled in part by the growth of credit facilities as various new financial houses emerged to supplement those established ones that had focused principally upon wealthy, conservative rentiers, who had been more concerned with government loans than with developmental investment. In the 1860s, legal changes did away with the barriers to the establishment of joint stock companies,[130] although in practice many French firms remained essentially family concerns using the joint stock provisions as a more flexible means of raising finance. But the state also played an important role. The regime favoured, and promoted, economic development, insisting that the state had an important role to play in this. Louis Napoleon, who had been influenced by the ideas of the Saint Simonians, was a firm believer in the need for French economic development, and with a weak legislature and the support of business (strengthened by his seeming defeat of the 'red threat' in 1848), he pursued this through interventionist means. He directed some of his energies, and those of the French state, into supporting the development of credit,[131] railway development, industry, trade, and urban redevelopment, especially in Paris. The government asserted control over public works and their financing, approved of newly appointed directors of large companies and of the establishment of new businesses open to public subscription, and promoted the rationalisation of small railway companies and the growth of the railway and telegraph. It also introduced the commercial treaty with England in 1860 over the substantial opposition of parts of the business community (but with the support of others). There was also widespread business opposition to an 1864 law enabling workers to combine and strike, but there was widespread support for a law three years later enabling the establishment of limited liability companies without government approval.[132] The regime was generally seen to be pro-business, while business influence was significant in shaping the Emperor's attempts to develop the French economy.[133] Increasingly bankers, such as for a time the Pereire brothers, came into both political and social prominence and were more influential than industrialists.[134] Industrial expansion, plus the state's role in fostering it, helped to weaken the established view that there was something ethically wrong with business, commerce, and industry.[135] In the words of Palmade, 'It was with the Second Empire that the great masters of industry assumed a social importance and a place of merit as supreme representatives of the capitalist world'[136]; not only did they sometimes occupy leading office—for example, Joseph Eugene Schneider was president of the Corps Legislatif from 1867 to 1870—but Adolphe Thiers (who became president of the Anzin Mine Co.) was described as 'the eminence grise of several generations',[137] and others such as Emile Pereire, Fould, Morny, Rouher, Talabot, Enfantin, Chevalier, Didion, Dubochet, and Arles-Dufour played prominent advisory roles under Louis Napoleon, while many industrial magnates were part of the liberal opposition. The economic expansion propelled industrialists and financiers into a much more prominent position than they had been in before, while the state's support for economic development made those groups valued people in French society. But they did not control the state, which retained its autonomy from major economic forces.

In the Third Republic (1871–1940), although the representation of businessmen dropped back to levels closer to those of the pre–Second Empire period, some did gain leading positions in the political structure; for example, the banker Casimir Perier was president of the Senate 1894–95, and Jules Ferry, who married into the Alsatian industrial plutocracy, was prime minister 1880–81 and 1883–85, a senator 1891–93, and a deputy 1869–89. Parties remained weakly developed, with deputies finding it more advantageous to consolidate a local base in the constituency through the provision of material benefits than to build up national party structures. Because of the local orientation of the deputies, businessmen often spent considerable sums or offered directorships and consultancies to secure pliant deputies. Generally, businessmen divided in the chamber and in other arenas of political life on specific issues according to their personal views and how those issues affected their interests.[138] A clear example of this was the issue of protection. In 1860, over loud protestations from some circles of industry but supported by the financier Emile Pereire who was a trusted informal adviser to the Emperor,[139] Louis Bonaparte had signed a free-trade treaty with Britain. By the early 1870s, this issue had come back onto the agenda where it remained until tariff walls were re-erected in the early 1890s.[140] This issue divided the ranks of the economic bourgeoisie; financiers, wine producers, shipping, railways, and the chambers of commerce of Paris and the great port cities supported free trade while iron and steel, shipbuilders, mining, cotton and textiles (except the Lyon silk weavers), along with grain farmers favoured protection. The former group supported free trade because of their reliance upon exports and the free flow of goods and services across national boundaries, while the latter needed tariff protection in order to be able to compete with cheaper foreign, especially British, goods. Both sides sought to press their cases through the established channels of political life. They participated in debates in the chamber, both staffed and appeared before parliamentary commissions of enquiry, organised public meetings, mobilised in their business organisations (see Chapter 4), and used the press to mount their arguments in an attempt to win the debate; they even sought the cooperation of their workers in pressing their case.[141] They were the main actors in this, and their activity reflects the way in which they saw themselves as having a role in the French policymaking process. But the dispute over protection was generally atypical of the way business operated in politics in the Third Republic. Most issues were not fought out in the open, public arena but were resolved in less open fora between politicians, businessmen, and state officials, while the business organisations that seemed so active at this time were actually generally somnolent; in the words of one observer, 'it has been said that very often the annual banquet was their chief activity'.[142] But throughout the Third Republic, at least up until the First World War, businessmen tended to abstain from political office, which was dominated by lawyers, doctors, journalists, and teachers.[143] Business interests were looked after by sympathetic deputies who were able to use the fluid nature of the legislature and, after 1902, its structure of standing committees to pursue the interests of their business constituents.[144]

In all regimes, businessmen sought to exercise influence whenever they perceived their interests to require such action, and at times such influence could be decisive. According to Bergeron,[145] as a general rule but especially in the second half of the nineteenth century, French businessmen 'chose to intervene at all echelons of administrative and political responsibility—the mairie and general council, national organs of representation, and often in the plurality of offices of public functions'. Throughout the nineteenth century, in every regime the commercial and industrial capitalists 'proved remarkably adroit in occupying positions of authority and influence and in using them for [their] own advantage'.[146] They sought to influence both government policy and appointments.[147] Their capacity to do this was facilitated by the fact that they were not a closed elite. Although there was at times a high concentration of directorships and a strong intermingling of industrialists, merchants, and financiers in the leading positions of major French companies, an interlocking that was reinforced by ties of family and marriage,[148] these circles remained open to new men. Indeed, this intermingling at the top of French business also embraced politicians and civil servants. By the end of the century, both groups were prominent among both the directors and shareholders in a whole range of French companies.[149] This was important because it reflected the acceptance by both of these groups, especially the highly selective and status conscious hauts fonctionnaires, of the acceptability of the sort of enterprise within which the industrial, financial, and commercial bourgeoisie was engaged. But this did not mean integration with leading state officials. Despite some overlap, they remained relatively separate from the emergent business class, insulated by the strong sense of collective identity and *esprit de corps* focused on their perceived role of building the greatness of France.

Although business interests could be influential in policymaking, they did not dominate this process. Accordingly, the claims that France was run by 'the financial magnates' or by '200 families who held most of its wealth, ran its major industries, and bribed its politicians to do their bidding'[150] are exaggerated. It is true that directorships of large firms in France came to be concentrated in 'a narrow circle of men' who each occupied many such positions and whose interlocking nature was reinforced by marriage and family ties. Politicians were sometimes added to these boards, others acted as agents for private companies, and some businessmen did enter politics.[151] So in this sense there was a coming together of political and, primarily, financial elites, with the latter, and especially those in la Haute Banque and based in Paris, often able to exercise significant influence on political life. Bankers were able to use the social contacts that came from their privileged position plus the occasional occupation of ministerial office[152] to further their business interests; for example, bankers acted as minister of finance in 1848 (Goudchaux); 1861–7 (Fould); 1872–3, 1875–7, 1877–8, and 1882–3 (Say); 1889–92 and 1902–05 (Rouvier, who was also prime minister in 1887 and 1905–06[153]); and 1899–1902, 1906–09, 1911, and 1913–14 (Caillaux, who made a fortune out of international banking while in office[154]). Some families remained active in both political and business spheres over the generations.[155] For example, Augustin Perier was a deputy in 1827 and a peer in 1832, Camille Joseph Perier was a prefect under both Napoleon I and Louis XVIII and then a deputy in 1828 and a peer in 1838, the next generation provided a counsellor of the Cour des Comptes while Laurent Casimir-Perier was a minister in 1871;

his son Jean Casimir-Perier became president of the Conseil in 1893–4 and president of the Republic in 1894–5. Throughout, all retained their business interests.[156] The most influential tended to be those of the so-called 'haute banque', a total of about twenty Parisian banks that prided themselves on their honour, reputation, and longevity.[157] These banks were mainly family banks, with sons replacing fathers each generation, but although they were closely knit, they were not a closed group; they often had marriage links to high-ranking civil servants. Such people tended to be over-represented among the directors of the Bank of France, the principal bank and from 1848 the sole regulator of note circulation in France.[158] Of the fifteen directors, six to eight were usually influential bankers,[159] four to six were men of commerce or industry, and three were always senior civil servants.[160] Membership of the board of the Bank of France gave them direct entrée into economic decision-making circles, while the Governor of the Bank of France was appointed by the state.

Thus throughout the nineteenth century, French business, and especially finance, faced an open door in terms of its ability to influence state policy. But in doing so, most influence was directed at achieving short-term economic advantage rather than long-term economic policy. The state remained run by its officials, whose sense of collective identity gave them a powerful mechanism enabling their continuing control over state power. The economic bourgeoisie did not dominate the state, but they could exercise significant influence at different times.

GERMANY

In Germany, the question of business domination of the state is related to the more general issue of the political subordination of the bourgeoisie to the Junkers. It is certainly true that many who held top positions in the Empire came from the Junker culture and retained their links with the East Prussian heartland. However as noted above, it was no longer true that the Junkers could accurately be classed as feudal, while many who entered government service clearly had the interests of the country at heart and put them before any sectional considerations relating to estate agriculture east of the Elbe. Social origins did not always or completely determine positions on policy issues; if they did, and given continuing Junker dominance of the top positions (Junker influence at the top of the bureaucracy was actually strengthened in the 1890s[161]), the pro-industry policies of the Empire would be difficult to explain.[162] The state was not an instrument at the mercy of the Junkers.[163] Rather state elites comprised a mixture of people in which, over time, the Junker element was being eroded by the increasing entry into government service of members of the bourgeoisie. While these were often not from the economic bourgeoisie but from the professional middle class, their recognition of the imperatives of developing an industrialised

Germany made them sympathetic to both the advice proffered by German business and to the growing strength of bourgeois values. And as indicated above, during this period German business, especially heavy industry, was increasingly in a position to be able to take advantage of this. With the legislature much less important than the executive, business relied on its contacts with all levels of the imperial bureaucracy to press its case. The increased size of business during this period along with the state's preference not to meddle too much in society meant that it remained out of most sectors of life as long as nothing was happening to lead to disturbances. This meant that if business could organise its own affairs in a way which did not lead either to instability or popular protest, the state was willing by and large to leave it alone. Only when problems emerged, such as shortages of goods or excessively high prices causing conflict, the waste of national resources, or disruption of the political equilibrium, did the state seek to intervene.[164] In this sense, business emerged almost as the junior partner of the state, united with it in its desire to develop the country industrially and to maintain social stability through the suppression of the working class.

Business influence was related to economic power and wealth, but personal entrée to be able to gain the confidence of a Chancellor or Emperor was also often needed. Chancellor Von Bulow (1900–09), for example, provided such opportunities for an assertive group of entrepreneurs through his belief that government was facilitated by bringing together 'men of quality'.[165] But for such an entrée to be obtained, substantial personal wealth or control over significant economic power through a corporation or company was essential. It was the power of the Krupp corporation and of AEG (Allgemaine Elektrizitat Gesellschaft) that enabled Krupp and Rathenau, respectively, to gain positions of personal influence in the imperial power structure. But such a role was beyond most businessmen, and the influence even these people could exercise was limited; according to Niall Ferguson,[166] even though Albert Ballin and Max Warburg had influential access to the upper levels of the government including the Emperor in 1914, 'they were powerless to influence the process of decision-making' leading to the war.

A more important factor in business access to the political elite was the institutional nexus that emerged between business and the state. Crucial here was the dramatic expansion in size that much of German industry experienced during the late nineteenth and early twentieth centuries. This came about through the processes of vertical and horizontal integration and cartelisation. Kocka[167] offers two measures of this increase in size, average capital and number of employees. The 100 largest enterprises had average capital of 9.4 million marks in 1887, 26.8 million in 1907, and 59.2 million in 1927, with inflation responsible for only a small part of this increase. In order to be among the 100 largest companies, in 1887 3.8 million marks was required, 1907 10 million, and 1927 13 million. In terms of size of workforce, in 1887 Krupp was the largest with 64,000 employees, followed by Siemens with 30,000. In 1927, the largest was United Steelworks with almost 200,000 employees, followed by Siemens with 116,000 and IG Farben 80,000. Growth through backward (integration of the production enterprise with raw materials suppliers) and forward (integration of the production enterprise with distributors) integration was a major means of the creation of the extraordinarily large companies that came to dominate the economic landscape in Germany. Along with this often went the diversification of production as companies moved from narrow specialisation to the production of a broader range of products and with this went increased cooperation between companies in the form of syndicates, bodies designed to coordinate the sale and export activities of the member companies. The creation of major syndicates between 1897 and 1914 represented the emergence of major economic actors with much greater economic power than their enterprises of origin had been able to wield. This increased their potential for political power as well.

Also important here was the development of cartels. Initially, these were associations of producers which sought to protect their positions by reaching agreements on production and pricing levels and market share, and by 1900 they constituted a highly integrated business system. The large banks often played an important role in the formation of cartels, although claims that these organisations were dominated by the banks are exaggerated.[168] However, cartels also began to emerge on the basis of vertical integration which had as its aim less the protection of current position than, in Blackbourn's words, 'seeking the strategic objective of institutionalized market domination'.[169] In the coal industry, for example, by 1908, the whole industry was grouped into regional syndicates.[170] These were potentially powerful bodies, even able to stand up to challenge by state governments, as the Hibernia affair of 1904 shows.[171] By 1920–1, Germany was said to have between 2,000 and 3,000 cartels, of which 300 were considered to be of real significance to the economy and outside the Ministry of Economics' control.[172] This process of enlargement of concerns continued unabated during the Weimar period, in part encouraged by the government, as in the 1926 formation of Deutsche Luft Hansa AG from the unification of a number of smaller companies. The growth of cartel arrangements around the turn of the century allied to the increased size of firms projected business into a new structural relationship with the state. Cartel agreements were legally enforceable contracts, and thereby created very large entities that sought to monopolise the areas with which they were concerned; industrial cartels and investment banks were significant centres of economic power. They formed the economic part of what has been seen as 'organised capitalism', and were the counterpart of the state in the economic sphere. Most sections of the political elite believed that the cartels played an important part in fuelling German economic advance,[173] and therefore in the process German state-making, and reinforced this view by supporting an expansive state role in the economy. Not only did the state support the development of private-sector cartels, but it was itself involved directly in production,[174] much of which was organised in the form of cartels. Furthermore, state bureaucrats sought to guide the national economy, in part through cooperation with large private owners; it was their relationship that was crucial for the direction of 'organised capitalism', and this relationship was played out in the boardrooms and offices of the state bureaucracy, private cartels, syndicates, and companies, not in the open arenas of public life. In this sense, there was a structural locking together of the state and the economy which projected big business into the heart of the German polity.

This locking together was strengthened by the war. Prior to its outbreak, no thought had been given to the economic organisation for war, with the result that when the conflict opened, the government had to scramble to get a structure in place. They turned to those who were most crucial for this, the businessmen. A War Raw Materials Section was established in the War Ministry and headed by the Chief of AEG Walther Rathenau with a staff of close associates from AEG and representatives of other industries which used the raw materials to be controlled. They worked through a system of private stock companies established under government auspices to both direct supplies of raw materials and establish wartime priorities; in effect, these 'war companies' involved 'the delegation of monopolistic controls over the distribution of raw materials to trusts made up of the industrial consumers of raw materials'.[175] The government also established the Exports and Exemptions Office headed by a businessman not linked to the war industries, Richard Sichler, with powers over labour matters. This body also established War Boards, which comprised equal representation of employers and unions to resolve labour disputes. By co-opting industry in this way, business was tied into the state and its concerns much more tightly than had been the case before. By the same token, the involvement of business in the supply side of the war economy strengthened the control exercised over the economy by production cartels. But although individual businessmen often exercised significant power—Rathenau and Sichler have been mentioned, Hugo Stinnes was engaged in secret diplomacy with the Russians—decision-making during the war remained with the politicians, especially the Chancellor and the military, not business.

Business enthusiastically supported the war effort once the conflict had begun, despite its reservations about the prospect in the lead up to it. Some business organisations, especially the CdI and the Association of German Industrialists (BdI), vigorously supported the government's annexationist war aims.[176] Many industries prospered during the war,[177] and business never lost sight of its own interests. In late 1916, the steel companies were critical of War Ministry restrictions on their profits, while all sectors loudly opposed the measures giving unions a say in labour affairs, which they claimed interfered with their rights to manage their businesses. There was also widespread criticism of the prices the state paid for what industry produced for the war effort. Shipowners sought and received compensation for their war-induced losses, while the Hamburg Chamber of Commerce managed to obtain the alteration of proposed tax changes so that they fell mainly on firms that were not members of the Chamber.[178] There was also criticism from some quarters about the government's greater involvement in the economy, which was seen as potentially foreshadowing an expansion of state control after the war. These sorts of worries were manifested organisationally by the way in which many of the established lobby organisations were increasingly bypassed as individual corporations and sectors directly lobbied the political authorities.[179] This was part of the legacy to business of the war: an increase in the disunity and disagreement that characterised business, and in particular industry. But the other part of the legacy was the increased statisation of business through its incorporation into the war economy.

The failure of the German revolution at the end of the war was crucial to the consolidation of the emergent system of bourgeois dominance. What the revolution's failure constituted was a rejection of a radical socialist path of development, but it did not at the same time confirm the precise contours of the future German system. It confirmed private ownership as a central element of that system, but at least in the minds of many businessmen it did not allay their fears that the government might seek to maintain and even expand the sorts of controls over the economy that it had exercised during the war. Behind this was a fear that the government might actually have a socialist agenda which it would seek to implement. The fear of socialism was strengthened by the emergent relationship with the working class.

During the war, employers had been pushed into organisational arrangements with the unions to regulate labour disputes. Towards war's end, this was given a new institutional form through the so-called Stinnes-Legien Agreement. This agreement, which was endorsed by a range of employer and labour organisations, established a formal mechanism for resolving disputes between capital and labour, with a hierarchy of committees and a peak organisation called the Central Working Association (ZAG). In practice, this body, which involved equal participation from both sides, took on a range of quasi-official functions, and effectively constituted a corporatist attempt to remove certain areas of economic decision-making from the state and place them in the hands of the participants. While business remained uneasy about the power this gave organised labour over the management of employment issues, businessmen recognised its value both in blocking further state expansion

213

into this sphere and in moderating the pressures on the left of the political spectrum for socialisation of industry.[180] However, cooperation in this body soured when its trade union constituents softened their opposition to other forms of labour organisation that excluded employers, when industry seemed ambivalent (rather than solidly opposed) to the Kapp Putsch, and when the danger of nationalisation seemed to have passed.[181]

There was also general business opposition to the welfare policies that successive governments implemented. While many saw these as part of a programme objectively aimed at pacifying, and moderating, the increasingly organised working class, as the principal productive sector of the economy, it was business and especially industry that had to carry the weight of this. In the environment of Weimar Germany, where concern for community and the collective good clearly ran second to more partial and immediate concerns, welfare policies were an impost business felt increasingly disinclined to bear. It was disillusionment with the welfare burden that was a significant factor in the erosion of business support for the Weimar system that occurred at the end of the 1920s.

The erosion of the Weimar system was a result of many factors, among them the reluctance of major actors in the society, including business interests, to forego the former patterns of interaction with political elites in favour of the greater openness and transparency that abiding by democratic principles would have demanded. Large business interests continued to prefer to rely on their personal contacts with leading political actors and the established relationships with those parts of the state apparatus that dealt with their particular areas of concern.[182] The interlocking structure of cartels and large professionally staffed trade associations which overlapped and connected with state institutions remained in place. The maintenance of such large structures incorporating sections of government, business, and even working-class organisations through which much of their business and interactions were directed, effectively removed much of national concern from the formal governmental apparatus[183]; decisions on things like taxes, tariffs, currency, and labour conditions were increasingly the product of direct bargaining among major organised interests, with the Reichstag merely ratifying these agreements.[184] This sort of structure was welcomed by business because its reliance on large economic corporative bodies promised to ensure that control over industry remained in industrial rather than government hands; the government was happy to accept such a structure because it believed that such 'organised capitalism' gave the best prospects for the rapid rebuilding of the German economy. Thus it was behind-the-scenes machinations and the established patterns of influence-peddling mediated through the institutional contacts between government and business that continued to characterise the relationship between government and business during this period.

Of course, just as during the Empire, industry was not a single, united bloc.[185] The division between export-oriented light industry (plus the chemical and electrical industries, which unlike much heavy industry were able to export to the developed economies because of the advanced nature of these industrial sectors) and heavy industry which concentrated on the domestic market and continued to support protectionist measures remained important. The bankers, light manufacturers, and shippers concentrated on trying to increase exports and wanted low coal and iron prices at home, while the iron and steel producers wanted unrestricted exports to hard currency countries and a form of rationing by high prices of the quota left for domestic producers.[186] The former remained organised in the BdI and supported some form of collective bargaining with workers' organisations; the latter were in the CdI and opposed unionisation. A measure of coordination was reached between these two sectors between 1924 and 1926 when negotiations carried out between the iron producers and the consumers of their products newly united in the AVI resulted in a series of agreements whereby heavy industry paid a rebate to AVI-linked firms to compensate them for differences between world steel prices and domestic prices for iron and steel exported in the form of finished products. In return, the domestic finishing industries agreed not to oppose the maintenance of pre-war tariffs and domestic and international iron and steel cartels. This agreement effectively consolidated the leadership position of heavy industry domestically while both boosting the AVI and effectively sidelining the government from this major industrial sector.[187]

Weimar was therefore the continuation of a trend whereby business sought to pursue its affairs with government principally through direct contacts of both the institutional and personal kind. One author[188] characterised this in the following terms: 'Businessmen disappeared from parliaments, and they reappeared in government commissions'. They were locked together in a much stronger embrace than was the case in Britain or France. And this had consequences, in that it facilitated the growth of corruption and abuse, by both state officials[189] and businessmen.

German businessmen were generally more willing than their British counterparts to accept regulation as a way of ensuring certainty, and they were more willing to accept restrictions on individual autonomy in order to act collectively.[190] This was crucial to the way business–government relations developed after 1870, and laid the basis for the high degree of bureaucratic interaction between these two spheres. This was what characterised the German situation: a high level of bureaucratic interaction occurring on the basis of lobbying and personal and institutional contacts at the expense of pursuit of interests through the open aspects of the political system. Thus even though with the shift from Empire to Republic and from the more constrained political system to one closer to the democratic form, there were increased opportunities for political parties to play a meaningful role in politics, generally business eschewed this in favour of a continuation of the sorts of corporatist structures and processes that had served it well earlier. Throughout, the government was sympathetic to business interests, but those interests remained subordinate to the state.

THE UNITED STATES

American business was directly and intimately involved in the state at the national level. In the last decades of the nineteenth and the first of the twentieth centuries, the Senate was known as a representative of 'special interests' and a 'millionaires' club'.[191] This sort of view was fuelled by popular recognition of the way in which congressmen acted as representatives of business interests. This was especially true of the Senate, which had extensive power (including equal legislative power with the House of Representatives, the special right of advice and consent on treaties, the responsibility to conduct the trial in cases of presidential impeachment and approval of presidential appointments—by the late nineteenth century, by tradition no appointment was approved to which an individual senator was opposed) and was chosen by state legislatures. Because senators were often dominant in their home states' political machines (or close to the dominant boss), they could also often control their state's legislative representatives in the House of Representatives.[192] Due to its power and central role in government, the Senate had for long been a prime target for forces seeking to shape government policy. Initially in the post–Civil War period, the Senate was dominated by men, sometimes called 'spoilsmen',[193] placed there by the local and state political machines in order to utilise the opportunities for patronage afforded by the state to further build up their wealth and power. By the end of the century, these had been overshadowed by the dominance of business interests in the chamber. Sometimes businessmen themselves became senators,[194] but more commonly they either had their employees or associates in the Senate or they bought/bribed existing senators to look after their interests. According to the *Chicago Daily Tribune* on 10 January 1884, 'The Union Pacific Railroad has several Senators, the Northern Pacific has one, the Pennsylvania Railroad has two, Central Pacific has two, the Georgia Railroads have one...the Chesapeake and Ohio has one...Behind every one of half the portly and well-dressed members of the Senate can be seen the outlines of some corporation interested in getting or preventing legislation, or some syndicate that has invaluable contracts or patents to defend or push'.[195] According to another source, in the 1890s senators were known by their business affiliations; there were 'Standard Oil Senators, sugar trust Senators, iron and steel Senators, and railroad Senators'.[196] The Senate became renowned for being a stronghold of privileged business and acting to serve those interests rather than the nation as a whole. This only began to change with the popular election of senators after 1913. Similar sorts of affiliations and contacts existed between business and congressmen in the House.

Business could also wield considerable influence in the executive through the sorts of positions discussed in Chapter 4. But there were also more informal channels. Presidents sometimes called on wealthy private interests for assistance in times of difficulty. For example, following a major industrial collapse in 1893, President Grover Cleveland sought to return the United States to the gold standard, and in an attempt to stop the resultant run on gold, he turned to the banker J.P. Morgan. Morgan formed a consortium of financiers to assure the government bonds Cleveland sought to sell for gold in an attempt to bolster the government's gold stores, an effort which was eventually successful.[197] This sort of association was very common, especially during the Progressive Era when businessmen played a significant behind the scenes role in helping to shape the government's response to the public unrolling of popular criticism.[198] Many of the government's measures of this period were moulded by their business advisers and friends. Often this was done on an ad hoc, personal basis. For example, J.P. Morgan was able to call Senator Nelson W. Aldrich into his office and present him with a draft bill that Morgan wanted to see introduced,[199] while Roosevelt's annual message to Congress in December 1901 was actually written by a number of businessmen.[200] During Cleveland's presidency, a partner of the legal firm where Cleveland had earlier worked, Francis Lynde Stetson (who was also J.P. Morgan's lawyer) acted as an important channel for business advice to the president.[201] A former leading businessman, Mark Hanna,[202] ran the Republican Party during this time and acted as an effective conduit for business interests and views. If major businessmen wanted an interview with the president, they were usually able to get it, and if they could not get into the Oval Office, they would inevitably be able to talk to one of the president's aides.

A more institutionalised relationship developed between some major corporations and the government during the Progressive Era. This was pioneered by Morgan and Theodore Roosevelt in late 1905. Business was concerned about the high levels of public criticism being directed at it and by the way in which successive presidents seemed to endorse this, and especially after Roosevelt sponsored the Northern Securities Case, which was widely seen (inaccurately) as a major blow against big business combination. Accordingly, in late 1905 US Steel (owned by Morgan), which was about to be the subject of a government enquiry, reached a 'gentleman's agreement with the administration'[203] setting out the guidelines for the enquiry in such a way as to ensure that they posed no real threat to the company. This principle was soon generalised, such that if a company either planned something it believed might be objectionable to the government (e.g. a takeover that might contribute to the establishment of a monopoly) or was actually doing something to which the government objected, it would get a private ruling and then fix the matter itself without official involvement.[204] However, not all who sought to establish this sort of relationship were as successful as Morgan, for example Standard Oil. Similarly, when the Bureau of Corporations was established in 1903, it functioned by relying upon the cooperation of the corporations which saw such a mode of action as the best way of keeping a rein on this body; while Garfield ran the Bureau under Roosevelt, this was underpinned by cordial personal relations with Morgan's associates.[205] Such cooperation was moderated in large part through personal relationships. Both Taft and Wilson were less favourably disposed to such private détentes as that between Morgan and Roosevelt, but both nevertheless pursued lines of activity involving business interests. Under Wilson, draft bills often had significant banker input, sometimes through organisations like the American Bankers' Association; the adoption of the Federal Reserve Act was one important instance.[206]

The Progressive criticism of business and its links with government created a public environment that demanded change. But there was also a sense within the business community that a situation of unbridled competition was one that could not be maintained. Given the weakness of both rules regulating business procedure and the state's powers of enforcement, business activity was characterised by significant levels of uncertainty. As many businessmen realised, it was in their interests to bring about certain forms of regulation that would both limit unbridled competition and bring some stability to the business environment. There was therefore significant support from within business circles for some regulation.[207] These measures built upon a series of earlier measures, including the 1887 Interstate Commerce Act designed to prevent abuses in the railways and the Sherman Anti-Trust Act of 1890 which, although designed to protect commerce and trade (but not manufacturing) from 'unlawful restraints' stemming from moves towards combination, had had its effect undermined by the Supreme Court in 1895.[208] The main measures introduced were the following:

- Establishment in 1903 of a new Department of Commerce and Labor, containing a Bureau of Corporations that was designed to investigate corporate behaviour.
- Hepburn Act of 1906 which sought to strengthen railway rate legislation by expanding the competence of the Interstate Commerce Commission.
- Pure Food and Drug Act and the Meat Inspection Act of 1906 were aimed at adulterated or fraudulently labelled products.

- In 1906, President Theodore Roosevelt proposed income and inheritance taxes, federal licensing of corporations, and prohibition of corporate political funds.

- Sixteenth Amendment of the Constitution in 1913 authorised federal income tax.

- Seventeenth Amendment of the Constitution in 1913 provided for popular election of senators rather than their appointment by state legislatures.

- Creation in 1913 of the Federal Reserve Board to exercise supervisory and regulatory powers, and thereby to provide some stability to the national banking system.

- In 1914 the Clayton Anti-Trust Act was designed to reinforce and supplement the Sherman Act.

- The Federal Trade Commission was established in 1914 to assist in enforcing antitrust laws and to curb unfair competitive practices.[209]

This is an impressive list of measures, all of which in one way or another sought to curb business practice and impose some restraints upon it. It was accompanied, at least during the Roosevelt presidency (1901–09), by a high level of rhetoric (but a lower level of practical action) about 'trust-busting'.

This unrolling of federal regulation was consistently supported by leading circles in finance and industry who saw it as both a means of stabilising their business environment and of curbing the criticism they faced. Such business circles acted to ensure that the new regulations were not too onerous or restrictive, and they used the new measures to protect their basic interests. Kolko summarises the situation as he saw it in the following words: 'Ultimately businessmen defined the limits of political intervention, and specified its major form and thrust. They were able to do so not merely because they were among the major initiators of federal intervention in the economy, but primarily because no politically significant group during the Progressive Era really challenged their conception of political intervention'.[210] This does not mean that business spoke with a united voice. There were significant differences of outlook within the business community based on size, geographical location, industry in which they were engaged, and the nature of their relationship with the political authorities.[211] But notwithstanding such differences, what is clear is that certain elements of the business community saw government regulation as a positive; in the words of one scholar, they sought 'to obtain greater security for non-competitive behavior in return for token governmental supervision'.[212] Many smaller businesses, who could not hope to exercise a monopolistic role, supported federal intervention to aid their commercial positions vis-à-vis the larger concerns with which they had to deal.[213] Through their links with government, many businesses were able to help shape this.

The interlocking between government and business had been occurring on a personal basis for many years before American entry into the First World War. Indeed, its prevalence was an important factor in undermining the efficacy of some business organisations; many corporations were so powerful or their owners/managers so personally well-connected that they did not need to indulge in overt lobbying activities. The First World War saw the expansion of the cooptation of business into government service both individually and institutionally. Individually, reflecting the scarcity of competent and experienced staff in government service, the government turned to individual businessmen and managerial personnel with an understanding of the economy to enter temporary government service and manage the mobilisation for the war effort. American mobilisation was 'to a large extent, planned and executed by businessmen who were in temporary federal government service'.[214] The chief institutional channel for cooptation was the War Industries Board (WIB), which was created at the behest of businessmen concerned that the government's purchase of war material would distort supply and demand and thereby destabilise the price system,[215] and its predecessor, the National Defence Advisory Commission. Industry largely regulated itself during the war through the WIB; the commodity committees of the Commission/Board made policy for and administered industry, and these committees were staffed overwhelmingly by businessmen. These committees were advised by war service committees, which were in reality trade associations or councils elected by the industries themselves.[216] These bodies effectively designed business codes of practice and ethics, which were later promulgated into standards of industry fair practice,[217] but they also made recommendations about government purchases and contracts, and almost always those contracts and prices were being recommended by people who had a direct personal interest in the outcome; for example, the chairman of the Commission's Aluminium Committee was the president of the Aluminium Co. of America.[218] It was this important role played by businessmen in mobilising the nation's resources for the war effort that lay the groundwork for the later close relationship between the military and private industry which served it; the demands of mobilisation brought both the military and industrial imperatives together and gave them a common interest and a basis for cooperation, thereby establishing the foundations for what later came to be called the military–industrial complex.[219]

This sort of cooptation was underpinned ideologically by the prevalence of the emergent view that the government was simply a corporation writ large and that business interests coincided with the public interest. Many businessmen shared this view, and from late in the nineteenth century it also had many proponents within political ranks. The implication was that the government should be run along business lines and that this was the best means of ensuring both efficiency and cost effectiveness. Moreover, it implied that if the government was to be run like a corporation, those best suited to do the running were people with experience in business. As a result, the historical trend of powerful economic interests having a part to play in government received a significant level of ideological rationalisation and justification, reflected in the widespread acceptance of a leading role for businessmen in the governance of the country.

Cooptation continued after the war. An early important manifestation of this was the Industrial Board of the Department of Commerce established in 1919. Formally, it was meant to bring about price reductions by way of industry-wide agreements mediated by the Board, but in practice business saw it more as a means to get around the antitrust laws. It was an illustrative case of the entry of businessmen into government bodies which gave them the power and position to influence policy in their interests.[220] But the government–business relationship cooled somewhat with the depression beginning in 1929, as politicians blamed their business compatriots for not seeing this downturn coming. This is reflected in the decline in business representation in Franklin Roosevelt's cabinet. Corporate political influence reached its nadir during the New Deal, when after initially holding fire, many businessmen publicly criticised much of Roosevelt's programme, even though most of it did not interfere significantly with corporate freedom of action.[221] Through organisations like the NAM, Chamber of Commerce, and National Industrial Conference Board, much of business (especially small business) opposed Roosevelt's welfare measures. However some businessmen realised that welfare measures were necessary to stabilise American capitalism and gave support to Roosevelt's programme through the Business Advisory Council of the Department of Commerce.[222] Indeed, business advice was important for Roosevelt in structuring the reforms he introduced[223]; the National Industrial Recovery Act (NIRA) of June 1933 gave business interests most of what they sought in response to the depression.[224] Some businessmen now became involved in national planning. Thus despite the widespread opposition from within business ranks to the New Deal, and especially the restraints it involved on business activity, this does not mean that business was now out of the political equation. Personal contacts remained important and the power of the large corporations ensured continuing access to the upper levels of politics; in 1938 Franklin Roosevelt was able to get US Steel to agree to a drop in prices while keeping wages stable until after that year's mid-term elections.[225] The early years of the twentieth century had seen business become entrenched in the upper levels of the political system, and there it remained.[226]

Thus in the United States, business was easily able to infiltrate the state, with many businessmen active within its formal and informal arenas. The perceived merging of national and business interests in the ideology underpinning American public life provided a sound basis upon which business interests could exercise a significant level of influence in the political and policy arenas. This does not mean that business was so dominant that it was able easily to have its way on all issues, but it was clearly the dominant interest.

Local Government

Business also turned its attention to local government. For industrialists, local government was the important level of regulation with which they had to deal on a day-to-day basis. Issues like the level of council rates, pollution, housing, and the supply of services were within the purview of local government, and these were of direct relevance to the conditions under which the local factory could function. At the local (and in some cases regional) level, small- and medium-sized businesses were often able to gain the sort of influence which only their much larger counterparts were able to achieve at the national level. This was because of the importance of such businesses in the local communities. As major employers of local labour and significant contributors to local taxation revenue, major industrialists were often able to wield substantial influence in the local town halls without themselves occupying formal office. Utilising all sorts of means from persuasion through bribery to veiled threats, businessmen could get local officials to accede to their wishes. Ultimately, it was their place in the economy that enabled the exercise of this sort of power.

In Britain, local government in some parts of the country became dominated by businessmen.[227] Able to benefit electorally from the feelings of deference arising from the paternalistic relationship that developed between owners and workers in many factories,[228] many businessmen gained election to local councils and often to the mayor's office. A prominent place in local government, especially occupation of the mayor's office, was also an important means of satisfying the urge for prestige, respect, and acceptance that seemed to be so strong among the industrial bourgeoisie. Coming into a society in which the established status hierarchy was clear and long-set, many industrialists sought the sort of social recognition that matched their new-found wealth. Some sought this in the purchase of landed estates and the adoption of a genteel lifestyle, sometimes including a title[229] (see Chapter 2), but another route (not mutually exclusive) was to seek municipal office. This quest to attain municipal office coincided with the substantial expansion of the symbolism of local government. The construction of imposing town halls, the generation of municipal ceremonies and 'events', and the increasingly public activist profile of the mayor,[230] all produced an arena within which industrialists seeking public prestige and recognition could achieve fulfilment. British businessmen were thus prominent in local government in many areas.

In France (except for the Second Empire) and Germany, the same sorts of considerations applied, with businessmen sometimes filling municipal office but more often exercising political influence based on their economic power. Often, business influence in French localities was simply a result of the ability of businessmen to influence the views, and votes, of their workers. Elections were characterised by much buying of votes for money and favours and by the development of clienteles among the voters,[231] with businessmen prominent in these sorts of activities. As one student has argued, big industrialists sought deferential support from those dependent upon them, and 'in factory or mining towns dependent on one employer, who provided not only jobs but houses and welfare benefits, they had the means to enforce it'.[232] In both countries, businessmen were often important in the political life of the localities in which they lived and worked.

Business was also active in local and state government in the United States, but here it took a more structured form. Part of the problem identified in the Progressive Era was the close association that had grown up between business and government at local and state levels. Throughout the nineteenth century, the local conditions within which business had to operate were shaped by municipal and state governments far more than they were by the federal government. The responsibility for chartering business concerns lay with the state legislature, while the municipal authorities had power over licensing regulations; until late in the nineteenth century, the federal government was responsible for tariffs and the currency, but had little other direct concern in business regulation.[233] This meant that, initially, when businessmen turned to politics, it was to the municipal and state levels that they directed their attention. In the latter part of the nineteenth century, many of the largest towns, including those with an expanding industrial economy, were run by informal political machines. These have come to be known by the name of the premises where that machine in New York used to meet, Tammany Hall. Such an urban machine was usually an amalgam of smaller groups located in the precincts or wards of the city, with each of these smaller machines headed by a political boss who was subordinate to the boss of the city machine as a whole. Such machines were built principally upon patronage, and they sought to gain control of all the city offices so as both to maximise patronage opportunities and guarantee immunity from prosecution.[234] At the precinct or ward level, central to these machines were local businessmen—saloon keepers, liquor dealers, contractors, and real estate, insurance and loan brokers—whose business activities put them at the centre of local affairs and gave them an opportunity to interact widely with the local citizenry.[235] Businessmen were also associated with the machines at the city level. Initially in many places this involved the businessmen themselves personally running the cities through their direct involvement in urban politics. However, by the end of Reconstruction (c.1880), they had generally withdrawn from such direct involvement, instead seeking to exercise guiding influence over local politicians through the wielding of their wealth or influence.[236] Many simply established close working relationships that enabled them to conduct their business expeditiously, usually by exchanging financial support for the sorts of favours that could ease the conduct of business operations.[237] Some were able to move easily both ways between politics and business.[238] Business often provided financial support for individual candidates, for teams of candidates, and it sometimes financially underwrote an entire city or state political machine.[239] Such a relationship could extend to include the city authorities actually acting on behalf of 'their' businesses and against those from elsewhere. Not only could this be in terms of the offering of more favourable terms for the conduct of business to 'natives' than to 'outsiders', but the city authorities could actually become active participants together with local businesses in things like national level bidding for contracts.[240] In such cases, there was an effective fusing of business and municipal interests in search of an outcome that would bring benefits to both.[241] The most extreme form of this came in the first decade of the twentieth century when there was a move initiated in Galveston for the replacement of traditional city government by smaller city commissions and managers. The idea was to remove politics from city government and to run the cities like business enterprises through combining administrative and executive functions in the persons of the commissioners. The initiative for this came principally from local chambers of commerce and boards of trade, and by 1913 more than 300 cities had adopted the commission structure initiated in Galveston. The principle behind this was to elect only a few men to office on a city-wide vote, and where it was introduced, it usually ensured the election of businessmen to office, or that municipal government remained under firm business influence.[242] But regardless of whether this system was instituted, business was usually a major player in shaping the course of municipal politics.

American business was also important at the state level around the turn of the century. Earlier in the nineteenth century as development had spread westwards, there were instances of entire territories being governed by companies rather than by publicly endorsed governments.[243] A more common pattern, especially in the settled parts of the country, was for major corporations to try to capture control of state legislatures in order both to direct their legislation[244] and, prior to 1913, to influence the composition of the US Senate.[245] Railway companies were the first to exert such control over state legislatures; the buying of the state legislature was important in the struggle between Jay Gould and Cornelius Vanderbilt for control of New York's Erie Railroad in 1869, while at times in the second half of the nineteenth-century state politics in Wisconsin was controlled by the Chicago, Milwaukee, and St. Paul, and the Chicago and Northwestern railroads, and railways ruled in many other states including California (Southern Pacific), North Dakota (Northern

Pacific), Iowa (Burlington), and New Hampshire (Boston & Maine).[246] Corporations could place their own men in the state legislature, they could provide support for the electoral campaigns of sympathetic candidates,[247] or they could put existing legislators on retainers to protect their interests; in some instances, corporations actually 'cleared' candidates proposed by parties.[248] This sort of practice was not always successful; the purchase of legislators could sometimes be overcome by the determined mobilisation of opposition forces,[249] but this was never easy.

Like politics in the cities, state politics was often dominated by a machine run by a local boss. Often this produced what were effectively single-party states, where state politics was dominated by either the Republican or Democratic Party, and that party was in turn dominated by the political machine of a powerful local figure. As in the cities, such machines often worked closely with powerful business interests, exchanging favours for resources and privileging those interests in the pursuit of their commercial concerns. In the first part of the twentieth century, many such political machines at the city and state levels began to weaken,[250] in part under the glare of criticism associated with Progressivism. However, as the case of Chicago and the Daley family extending well into the second half of the twentieth century shows, such an arrangement lasted in many areas for a considerable time. Business was a dominant force in local and state politics in many parts of the United States at the beginning of the twentieth century.

* * *

In all four countries the emergent bourgeois class looked to the state as a resource to be exploited and pursued that exploitation assiduously. Whether it was acquiring control over physical resources owned by the state or gaining a monopoly position through state licensing, whether benefiting as a result of favourable legislation pushed through a chamber by suborned or tame deputies or through decisions resulting from personal contacts with leading officials, businessmen everywhere sought to use the state to advance the interests of their businesses. But in none of these cases did the new class come to dominate the state completely. Everywhere state officials retained a degree of autonomy from these wealthy interests. In Britain and Germany, this was in part a function of the continuing residual importance of the landed aristocracy, in France of the cohesion of state officialdom, and in the United States of the very openness of the structure which meant that other groups (in particular the professional middle class) were able to provide some balance to business power. In all countries, this was also, paradoxically, aided by the association of industrialisation with national interest, because while this legitimised business involvement in politics, it also provided a sound basis from which state officials could resist business and its demands. The rise of the professional middle class and its involvement in politics, both in terms of the development of an educated public and the growth in formal representation of this group in the arms of the state, also helped to mitigate the rise of business power. Such state autonomy was also strengthened by the fact that business was not a single coherent interest confronting the state, but a variety of interests among which the state could manoeuvre. Moreover, in practice it was only those larger and wealthier businessmen who were able regularly to interact with the national state elite; small- and medium-sized businesses in all countries were generally restricted in their exercise of influence to local and regional government officials.

The capacity of the emergent bourgeois class to become involved in the state differed in the various national cases. In the United States, the structure was traditionally open to both access and influence by those who possessed substantial material wealth, and when the new industrialists came along, they were able to tread a well-worn path. As a result, they encountered little initial opposition to their entry into the political elite, and even when public outcry did occur, they were able to shape the response in such a way as to protect their position. Their ability to do this successfully rested in large part on the dominant ideology that merged national and business interests in such a way that business appeared as a central component of the polity. State elites traditionally had business connections, and the political and business spheres were not distinct. Business dominance of politics was but a reflection of this. In contrast, in Britain where the state elite and the state itself remained more dominated by the traditional landowning aristocracy, the emergence of industrialists seemed to pose a greater threat to established interests than in the United States. However, the tradition of the integration of economic interests into the state's representative organs and the transformation of the traditional landowning culture in a commercial direction, both of which had preceded large-scale industrialisation, facilitated the integration of the new class. There was a relative openness of the structure that belied the appearance of traditional dominance and enabled business, and especially finance, to exercise influence on political actors to achieve their ends. In France, the apparent barrier posed by the traditional nobility in Britain had been destroyed by the revolution, but in its place a strongly statist tradition had been strengthened. The French state elite had its roots firmly planted in the state machine, and that machine had a stronger tradition of direct involvement in economic affairs than in Britain. This latter characteristic of the state meant that although the state elite was very conscious of its own identity, power, and privileges, it also recognised the part that industrialists could play in the pursuit of national economic success. In this way, while the entrance to elite life was not completely open to all who sought entry, nor was it closed to those whose economic power and resources made them significant actors in the economic sphere. In Germany, large parts of the state elite retained substantial social roots in the Junker culture of East Prussia (although there was a significant professional middle class influx at the end of the nineteenth century) and in the dirigiste conception of the state that had prevailed throughout recent German/Prussian history. While the values of the society were changing with industrialisation and the growth of the middle class, and bourgeois values were becoming more important, they did not displace those values stemming from the earlier period. However, the direct conflict that might have occurred between these representatives of a former and the future world was mediated by the way in which the state elite was intent on driving state power through economic performance, and the sharing of this goal (at least in terms of economic performance) by the emergent industrialists. This was mediated through the coming together of state and big business through quasi-corporative type arrangements. In this way, the new class did gain a position within the elite, but without substantial social interaction and merging. This was to have significant ramifications for German development. In all four countries, interaction with and reliance on the state was central to the formation of the bourgeoisie.

How do these patterns compare with Russia?

Notes

1. For the argument that limits on British industrialisation flowed from the fact that Britain was the first country to industrialise rather than the salience of pre-capitalist values, see Ellen Meiksins Wood, *The Pristine Culture of Capitalism. A Historical Essay on Old Regimes and Modern States* (London, Verso, 1991), pp. 100–103.
2. David Judge, *Parliament and Industry* (Aldershot, Dartmouth, 1990), p. 8. Also Paul Warwick, "Did Britain Change? An Enquiry into the Causes of National Decline", *Journal of Contemporary History* 20, 1, 1985, pp. 99–133.
3. See Asa Briggs, *The Making of Modern England. 1783–1867. The Age of Improvement* (New York, Harper & Row, 1965), pp. 394–402. The reformist nature of the labour movement, involving a search to address abuses rather than a drive to replace capitalism, is a reflection of the strength of this ideology.
4. Although a tax system in which the burden mainly fell on landed wealth rather than accumulated capital did facilitate this. Mansel S. Blackford, *The Rise of Modern Business in Great Britain, the United States and Japan* (Chapel Hill, University of North Carolina Press, 1998), p. 37.
5. On the limitations of laissez-faire as a description of state policy, see Arthur J. Taylor, *Laissez-faire and State Intervention in Nineteenth Century Britain* (Basingstoke, Macmillan, 1972), esp. ch. 8.
6. Philip Corrigan & Derek Sayer, *The Great Arch. English State Formation as Cultural Revolution* (Oxford, Blackwell, 1985), pp. 97–98.
7. Peter Mathias, *The First Industrial Nation. An Economic History of Britain 1700–1914* (London, Methuen, 1969), pp. 32–36. More generally, see P.J. Cain, "British

Capitalism and the State: an Historical Perspective", *Political Quarterly* 68, 1, January–March 1997, pp. 95–98.

8. Charles More, *The Industrial Age. Economy and Society in Britain 1759–1985* (London, Longman, 1989), pp. 208–213.

9. Linda Levy Peck, *Court Patronage and Corruption in Early Stuart England* (Boston, Unwin Hyman, 1990), p. 160.

10. On "Old Corruption" and its end, see Philip Harling, *The Waning of "Old Corruption". The Politics of Economical Reform in Britain, 1779–1846* (Oxford, Clarendon Press, 1996) and W.D. Rubinstein, "The End of 'Old Corruption' in Britain, 1780–1860", *Past and Present* 101, November 1983, pp. 55–86.

11. Harling (Waning), p. 1. Also see Philip Harling, "Rethinking 'old corruption'", *Past and Present* 147, May 1995, pp. 127–158.

12. Harling (Waning), pp. 33 & 76.

13. Harold Perkin, *The Origins of Modern English Society 1780–1880* (London, Routledge & Kegan Paul, 1969), p. 442.

14. For a discussion of this at the time of the Boer War, see G.R. Searle, *Corruption in British Politics 1895–1930* (Oxford, Clarendon Press, 1987), ch. 3.

15. Mathias (First Industrial Nation), pp. 386–389, and Frank Dobbin, *Forging Industrial Policy. The United States, Britain, and France in the railway age* (Cambridge, Cambridge University Press, 1994), pp. 205–207.

16. For a case of the railways, see Edward Cleveland-Stevens, *English Railways. Their Development and Their Relationship to the State* (London, George Routledge & Sons, 1915/1988), p. 169.

17. Geoffrey Ingham, *Capitalism Divided? The City and industry in British social development* (Basingstoke, Macmillan, 1984), p. 111.

18. Roger Lloyd-Jones & M.J. Lewis, *British Industrial Capitalism since the Industrial Revolution* (London, UCL Press, 1998), pp. 49–50.

19. G.R. Searle, *Entrepreneurial Politics in Mid-Victorian Britain* (Oxford, Oxford University Press, 1993), p. 17.

20. Searle (Entrepreneurial Politics), pp. 2–3.

21. For the view that enterprising landowners were envisaged as the chief beneficiaries of this, see W.O. Aydelotte, "The Country Gentlemen and the Repeal of the Corn Laws", *English Historical Review* 82, 1967, pp. 47–60.

22. For the view that abolition of the Corn Laws showed the landed upper class the limits of its power, see Barrington Moore Jr, *Social Origins of Dictatorship and Democracy. Lord and Peasant in the Making of the Modern World* (Harmondsworth, Penguin, 1969), p. 33.

23. Searle (Entrepreneurial Politics), p. 36.

24. Jones & Lewis (British Industrial Capitalism), p. 82.

25. Searle (Entrepreneurial Politics), pp. 57–63.

26. Thomas Ertman, *Birth of the Leviathan. Building States and Regimes in Medieval and Early Modern Europe* (Cambridge, Cambridge University Press, 1997), p. 103.

27. Francois Furet, *Revolutionary France 1770–1880* (Oxford, Blackwell, 1992), p. 443. The expectation that officials were there to direct resources into the localities may be part of the reason why official candidates were so prominent during the July Monarchy and the Second Empire; if they were official candidates, they may have been thought to have greater potential leverage at the centre.

28. Theodore Zeldin, *The Political System of Napoleon III* (London, Macmillan, 1958), p. 58. Some were directors of such companies. Also Robert Tombs, *France 1814–1914* (London, Longman, 1996), p. 119.

29. Reed G. Geiger, *Planning the French Canals. Bureaucracy, Politics, and Enterprise under the Restoration* (Newark, University of Delaware Press, 1994), p. 184. In the parliamentary debates of 1821–7, all but one who spoke in favour of the canal bills came from a department which had a direct interest in canals. Geiger (Planning the French Canals), p. 190.

30. Geiger (Planning the French Canals), p. 192.

31. Alain Plessis, *The Rise and Fall of the Second Empire. 1815–1871* (Cambridge, Cambridge University Press, 1985), p. 27. For example Thiers made his father-in-law a general tax collector, a regent of the Bank of France in 1836, and a director of the iron and steel firm Anzin. Guy P. Palmade, *French Capitalism in the Nineteenth Century* (Newton Abbott, David & Charles, 1972), p. 84. Speaking about the late July Monarchy period, Charle said that the filling of many administrative posts by politicians' families led to scandals 'including preferential deals, conditional resignations in order to make a job for a relative and exceptional promotion of those close to power'. Christophe Charle, *A Social History of France in the Nineteenth Century* (Oxford, Berg, 1994), p. 30.

32. On attempts by state officials to blunt the effects of local lobbying for rail facilities, see Dobbin (Forging Industrial Policy), pp. 108–110.

33. Dobbin (Forging Industrial Policy), p. 123.

34. For discussion of this, see Tombs (France 1815–1914), p. 400.

35. Roger Magraw , *France 1815–1914. The Bourgeois Century* (Oxford, Fontana, 1983), p. 160.

36. Plessis (Rise and Fall), p. 65.

37. Palmade (French Capitalism), p. 183. As Magraw (France 1815–1914), p. 215, declares "the rail companies, aided by a venal press, had essentially 'milked [the state]' ". Also see Theodore Zeldin, *France 1848–1940. Volume 1. Ambition, Love and Politics* (Oxford, Clarendon Press, 1973), pp. 635–637.

38. Palmade (French Capitalism), p. 184.

39. Even though its main architects were the politicians Freycinet, Gambetta, and Say.

40. Geiger (Planning the French Canals), p. 86.

41. Geiger (Planning the French Canals), p. 87. For the case of a company unsuccessfully seeking a state subsidy of 400,000 francs per year for 20 years in order to build a canal, see Geiger (Planning the French Canals), p. 158.

42. Alfred Cobban, *A History of Modern France. Volume 2. From the First Empire to the Second Empire 1799–1871* (Harmondsworth, Penguin, 1965), p. 128. For the general point, see John Edward Courtenay Bodley, *France* (London, Macmillan, 1902), p. 506.

43. Tombs (France 1814–1914), p. 457. On the scandal, see Jean-Yves Mollier, *La scandale de Panama* (Paris, Fayard, 1991). For a contemporary view, Bodley (France), pp. 499–506.

44. R.D. Anderson, *France 1870–1914. Politics and Society* (London, Routledge & Kegan Paul, 1977), p. 86.

45. Businessmen who were involved in the publication of newspapers used them as weapons in the conflict of ideas about economic and other policy. When the

Association pour la Defense Travail National was refounded in 1878, it had a weekly newspaper, *L'industrie francaise*, and in 1884 it gained another, *Le travail national*. In November 1893, a number of industrialists (principally the Lille and Vosges textile and manufacturing entrepreneurs, Eugene Resseguier of Carmaux and Henri Schneider of Le Creusot) bought a newspaper, *Republique francaise*, to enable the Association de l'Industrie et de l'Agriculture Francaise to press the interests of national capital and ensure solidarity against what was seen as the rising tide of socialism in the form of worker unrest. The Comite des Forges subscribed 11% of the newspaper's capital. *L'economiste francais* was founded in 1873 to replicate the *Economist* in London and to act as a vehicle for the discussion of economic issues, mainly from a free-trade perspective. By 1881, there were at least 228 financial newspapers (cf. 95 political ones), with several having circulations of almost 100,000.

46. Palmade (French Capitalism), p. 84.
47. Plessis (Rise and Fall), p. 65.
48. For example, at the time of the strikes in Le Creusot in 1869–70, the president of the Corps Legislatif was Joseph Eugene Schneider, whose family owned the iron and steel works at Le Creusot. Palmade (French Capitalism), p. 155. Also Herman Lebovics, *The Alliance of Iron and Wheat in the Third French Republic 1860–1914. Origins of the New Conservatism* (Baton Rouge, Louisiana State University Press, 1988), p. 15. For action by troops against spinners in the late 1830s, see William M. Reddy, *The Rise of Market Culture. The textile trade and French society, 1750–1900* (Cambridge, Cambridge University Press, 1984), pp. 119–125.
49. Palmade (French Capitalism), p. 203.
50. For some figures, see Robert Bigo, *Les banques francaises au cours du XIX siecle* (Paris, Librairie du Recueil, 1947), p. 125.
51. Palmade (French Capitalism), p. 78. For Price, in the first half of the century the banks really acted as merchant bankers, interested in state loans and short-term speculation rather than productive investment. Roger Price, *The Economic Modernization of France* (London, Croom Helm, 1975), p. 153.
52. For this during the Restoration period, see Palmade (French Capitalism), pp. 78–79. For later, Roger Price, *An Economic History of Modern France* (London, Macmillan, 1981), p. 154, and Tom Kemp, *Economic Forces in French History* (London, Dennis Dobson, 1971), pp. 254–256.
53. Palmade (French Capitalism), p. 105.
54. See David Blackbourn & Geoff Eley, *The Peculiarities of German History. Bourgeois Society and Politics in Nineteenth Century Germany* (Oxford, Oxford University Press, 1984), pp. 182–190; Geoff Eley, "Society and Politics in Bismarckian Germany", *German History* 15, 1, 1997, pp. 116–117; and Richard J. Evans, "The Myth of Germany's 'Missing Revolution'", Richard J. Evans (ed.) , *Rethinking German History: Nineteenth Century Germany and the Origins of the Third Reich* (London, Allen & Unwin, 1987), pp. 111–113 & 116–117.
55. See the discussion of duelling in this regard. Ute Frevert, "Bourgeois Honour: Middle Class Duellists in Germany from the Late Eighteenth to the Early Twentieth Century", David Blackbourn & Richard J. Evans (eds.), *The German Bourgeoisie: Essays on the social history of the German middle class from the late eighteenth to the early twentieth century* (London, Routledge, 1991), pp. 255–292.

56. Frank B. Tipton, *A History of Modern Germany Since 1815* (London, Continuum, 2003), p. 116.

57. For one discussion of state policy, see W.O. Henderson, *The Rise of German Industrial Power 1834–1914* (London, Temple Smith, 1975), ch. 17.

58. Alexander Gerschenkron, *Economic Backwardness in Historical Perspective* (Cambridge [Mass], Harvard University Press, 1962), esp. ch. 1. For the view that by the Imperial period, cartelised industry and the banks rather than the state drove industry, see Clive Trebilcock, *The Industrialization of the Continental Powers 1780–1914* (London, Longman, 1981), p. 104.

59. Krupp even funded the Navy League, an organisation established to generate popular support for the navy, and its campaign of support for Tirpitz. Gordon A. Craig, *Germany 1866–1945* (Oxford, Clarendon Press, 1978), pp. 307–308.

60. On business having little expectation of profiting from imperial expansion except through trade, see Wolfgang J. Mommsen, *Imperial Germany 1867–1918. Politics, Culture and Society in an Authoritarian State* (London, Arnold, 1995, trans. Richard Deveson), p. 84. This contrasts with the view of big business support for imperialism as part of the late developer model.

61. John M. Hobson, *The Wealth of States. A Comparative Sociology of International Economic and Political Change* (Cambridge, Cambridge University Press, 1997), ch. 2. The government was instrumental in persuading the Junkers, who up until this time had opposed tariffs on wheat imports, to support them. This measure was a case of the perceived interests of industrialists, Junkers and government coinciding.

62. Although the government favoured arbitration in labour disputes, it did support employers in particular disputes; for example there was official collusion during the coal strike of 1912. Geoff Eley, "Capitalism and the Wilhelmine State: Industrial Growth and Political Backwardness in Recent German Historiography, 1890–1918", *The Historical Journal* 21, 3, 1978, p. 746. Also see Elaine Glovka Spencer, *Police and the Social Order in German Cities. The Dusseldorf District 1848–1914* (De Kalb, Northern Illinois University Press, 1992). For the argument that the bourgeoisie entered the alliance of iron and rye in order to achieve bourgeois interests, see Blackbourn & Eley (Peculiarities), pp. 126–127.

63. Hobson (Wealth of States), pp. 52–56. The Junkers organised in opposition to these, but without success.

64. George Steinmetz, "The Myth of an Autonomous State: Industrialists, Junkers, and Social Policy in Imperial Germany", Geoff Eley (ed.), *Society, Culture, and the State in Germany, 1870–1930* (Ann Arbor, University of Michigan Press, 1996). For the argument that Bismarck introduced much of the bourgeois 'program', see Blackbourn & Eley (Peculiarities), p. 86. For Junkers suffering after 1870 cf. industrial and commercial capital, see Blackbourn & Eley (Peculiarities), p. 232.

65. Richard Tilly, "Moral Standards and Business Behavior in Nineteenth Century Germany and Britain", Jurgen Kocka & Allan Mitchell (eds.), *Bourgeois Society in Nineteenth Century Europe* (Oxford, Berg, 1993), p. 184.

66. Frank B. Tipton, "Government and the Economy in the Nineteenth Century", Sheilah Ogilvie & Richard Overy (eds.), *A New Social and Economic History. Volume III. Since 1800* (London, Arnold, 2003), pp. 131, 139 & 141. Tipton argues

that the Reichsbank seems to have been captured by private banks which were able to paralyse fiscal policy. p. 139.

67. Gordon R. Mork, "The Prussian Railway Scandal of 1873: Economics and Politics in the German Empire", *European Studies Review* 1, 1, 1971, pp. 36–37.

68. Craig (Germany 1866–1945), p. 81.

69. Cited in Tilly (Moral Standards), p. 191.

70. Tilly (Moral Standards), p. 195.

71. For a discussion of his role, see Fritz Stern, "Gold and Iron: The Collaboration and Friendship of Gerson Bleichroder and Otto von Bismarck", *American Historical Review* 75, 1 October 1969, pp. 37–46.

72. Both Bleichroder and the head of Diskonto-Gesellschaft Bank used their government connections to get large government loans which they used to acquire control over railways, banks, insurance companies, and breweries. Tipton (Government and economy), p. 131.

73. Henry Ashby Turner Jr, *German Big Business and the Rise of Hitler* (New York, Oxford University Press, 1985), p. 33.

74. Gerald D. Feldman, "The Social and Economic Policies of German Big Business, 1918–1929", *American Historical Review* 75, 1, 1969, p. 49.

75. Niall Ferguson, *Paper and Iron. Hamburg Business and German Politics in the Era of Inflation, 1897–1927* (Cambridge, Cambridge University Press, 1995), pp. 377–381.

76. Edwin M. Epstein, *The Corporation in American Politics* (Englewood Cliffs, Prentice Hall, 1969), p. 24.

77. Charles Erwin Wilson to Senate Committee on Armed Services, 1952.

78. Kevin Phillips, *Wealth and Democracy. A Political History of the American Rich* (New York, Broadway Books, 2002), p. 39.

79. Matthew Josephson, *The Robber Barons. The Great American Capitalists 1861–1901* (London, Eyre & Spottiswood, 1934).

80. Hal Bridges, "The Robber Baron Concept in American History", *Business History Review* xxxii, 1, 1958, p. 1. This sort of activity is the principal focus of Josephson (Robber Barons).

81. Sean Dennis Cashman, *America in the Gilded Age. From the Death of Lincoln to the Rise of Theodore Roosevelt* (New York, New York University Press, 1984), pp. 34–35.

82. For an attempt to survey popular perceptions, see L. Galambos, *The Public Image of Big Business in America, 1880–1940: A Quantitative Study in Social Change* (Baltimore, Johns Hopkins University Press, 1975).

83. See R. McCormick, "The Discovery that Business Corrupts Politics: A Reappraisal of the Origins of Progressivism", *American Historical Review* 86, 2, 1981, pp. 247–274.

84. The Progressive period is normally considered to be approximately 1900–16. However, it was preceded by the populism and 'muckraking' of the 1890s, which were essential elements in the generation of 'progressive' sentiment and ideas.

85. For example, see Robert H. Wiebe, *The Search for Order, 1877–1920* (New York, Hill & Wang, 1966).

86. Gabriel Kolko, *The Triumph of Conservatism. A Reinterpretation of American History, 1900–1916* (New York, The Free Press of Glencoe, 1963). For another view of this process, see James Weinstein, *The Corporate Ideal in the Liberal State, 1900–1918* (Boston, Beacon Press, 1968). For a more general argument, see A. Tone, *The*

Business of Benevolence: Industrial Paternalism in Progressive America (Ithaca, Cornell University Press, 1997).

87. Philip H. Burch Jr, *Elites in American History. The Civil War to the New Deal* (New York, Holmes & Meier Publishers Inc., 1981), vol. 2, p. 165. In his seven-and-a-half-year administration, only 44 antitrust cases were begun (and fewer than 25% were against large companies) compared with 80 in the four years of Taft.

88. The social basis for such criticism was found in the enormous social transformation being wrought by industrialisation, including the economic differentiation it involved.

89. Edward J. Greenberg, *Capitalism and the American Political Ideal* (Armonk, M.E. Sharpe Inc., 1985), p. 70.

90. On this, see N. Lamboreaux, *The Great Merger Movement in American Business* (Cambridge, Cambridge University Press, 1985). This was an important step in the development of large corporations and their ultimate dominance of the American economy. See W. Roy, *The Rise of the Large Industrial Corporation in America* (Princeton, Princeton University Press, 1997) and D. Whitten, *The Emergence of the Great Enterprise, 1860–1914* (Westport, Greenwood Press, 1983).

91. Kolko (Triumph), p. 19. For some figures, see Cashman (America in the Gilded Age), p. 85.

92. For a study of business outlooks at this time, see A. Thimm, *Business Ideologies in the Reform-Progressive Era, 1880–1914* (Alabama, University of Alabama Press, 1976).

93. Cited in Josephson (Robber Barons), p. 354.

94. Phillips (Wealth and Democracy), p. 41.

95. Burch (Elites in American Society), vol. 2, p. 25.

96. Gustavus Myers, *History of the Great American Fortunes. Volume II. Great Fortunes from Railroads* (Chicago, Charles H. Kerr & Co., 1909), pp. 21–34. For a discussion of the Union Pacific Railroad, see W.D. Farnham, "The Weakened Spring of Government: A Study of Nineteenth Century American History", *American Historical Review* 68, 3, 1963, pp. 662–680.

97. Phillips (Wealth and Democracy), pp. 219 & 234–235.

98. Chester McArthur Destler, "The Opposition of American Businessmen to Social Control During the "Gilded Age", *Mississippi Valley Historical Review*, xxxix, March 1953, p. 642. For a case study of one example, see Sidney I. Roberts, "Portrait of a Robber Baron: Charles T. Yerkes", *Business History Review* xxxv, 3, 1961, pp. 344–371. Also see Chester McArthur Destler, "Entrepreneurial Leadership Among the 'Robber Barons': A Trial Balance", *Journal of Economic History* 6, May 1946, pp. 28–34.

99. For example, see Kolko (Triumph), p. 23 and Phillips (Wealth and Democracy), p. 40.

100. The methodological problems in establishing when power or influence is being exercised are considerable and are the subject of extensive literature. For a sophisticated, short, introduction to some of this, see Steven Lukes, *Power. A Radical View* (Basingstoke, Macmillan, 1974).

101. On the role of country banks, see P.L. Cottrell, *Industrial Finance 1830–1914. The Finance and Organization of English Manufacturing Industry* (London, Methuen,

1980), pp. 13–15; on other sources of funds, pp. 34–35. The operation of local banks could be underpinned by the development of connections with London discount houses (specialist institutions dealing with credit). Perkin (Origins) p. 80. For an argument that early manufacturing received some financial support from continental importers and financiers, see Stanley D. Chapman, "British Marketing Enterprise: The Changing Roles of Merchants, Manufacturers, and Financiers, 1700–1860", *Business History Review* LIII, 2, Summer 1979, pp. 210–211. Reliance on local sources of finance was also encouraged by the weakness of the institutional infrastructure for the conduct of business—slow communications, the difficulty of controlling agents at a distance, the high expense and uncertain outcome of legal processes for debt recovery. On the localised nature of early financing, see John F. Wilson, *British Business History, 1720–1994* (Manchester, Manchester University Press, 1995), pp. 42–44. On the early growth of a credit market, see Neil McKendrick, John Brewer & J.H. Plumb, *The Birth of a Consumer Society. The Commercialization of Eighteenth Century England* (London, Europa Publications Ltd, 1982), pp. 203–230. Also B.L. Anderson, "Money and the Structure of Credit in the Eighteenth Century", *Business History* XII, 2, July 1970, pp. 85–101. W.D. Rubinstein, *Elites and the Wealthy in Modern British History. Essays in Social and Economic History* (Brighton, Harvester, 1987), p. 40. For a study of one industry which sees a greater diversity of sources of capital investment, see Ian Donnachie, "Sources of Capital and Capitalization in the Scottish Brewing Industry, c1750–1830", *Economic History Review* XXX, 2, 1977, pp. 269–283. Public money often underpinned private credit, with tax collectors able to use collected funds for private gain, something which assisted the growth of country banking. Immanuel Wallerstein, *The Modern World System. The Second Era of Great Expansion of the Capitalist World Economy, 1730–1840s* (San Diego, Academic Press Inc., 1989), p. 20.

102. W.D. Rubinstein, *Men of Property. The Very Wealthy in Britain Since the Industrial Revolution* (London, Croom Helm, 1981), p. 61.

103. Jose Harris & Pat Thane, "British and European Bankers", Pat Thane, Geoffrey Crossick & Roderick Floud (eds.), *The Power of the Past;Eessays for Eric Hobsbawm* (Cambridge, Cambridge University Press, 1984), p. 219. In the United States, manufacturing was more important than commerce and finance as a source of fortunes.

104. For example, Geoffrey Ingham, *Capitalism Divided? The City and industry in British social development* (Basingstoke, Macmillan, 1984), and W.D. Rubinstein, "Debate. 'Gentlemanly Capitalism' and British Industry 1820–1914", *Past and Present* 132, August 1991, pp. 150–170. For a work which disputes this, see Michael Barratt Brown, "Away With All the Great Arches: Anderson's History of British Capitalism", *New Left Review* 167, January–February 1988, pp. 22–51.

105. Although see Brown (Away), p. 28 for figures which dispute this. Also Michael Barratt Brown, "Commercial and Industrial Capital in England: A Reply to Geoffrey Ingham", *New Left Review* 178, November–December 1989, pp. 124–128.

106. Mathias (First Industrial Nation), pp. 308 & 315.

107. Wilson (British Business History), p. 124.

108. Harris & Thane (British and European Bankers), p. 223.

109. For a study of an, admittedly atypical, financier who did this, see Pat Thane, "Financiers and the British State: The Case of Sir Ernest Cassel", *Business History* 28, 1, January 1986, pp. 80–99.

110. Y. Cassis, "Bankers in English Society in the Late Nineteenth Century", *Economic History Review* 38, 2, 1985, p. 227.

111. Ingham (Capitalism Divided), p. 10.

112. For an argument along these lines which, although focusing mainly on the twentieth century sees its roots in the nineteenth, see Frank Longstreth, "The City, Industry and the State", Colin Crouch (ed.), *State and Economy in Contemporary Capitalism* (London, Croom Helm, 1979), pp. 157–190.

113. For example, while industry generally favoured free trade in the 1840s, the City opposed the shift to free trade in 1846 and supported protectionism in 1909, but in both cases was defeated when, respectively, Conservative and Liberal governments decided otherwise, in both cases supported by many industrialists. Hobson (Wealth of States), pp. 144–145.

114. And in any case, industry was not itself a unified player with a single interest.

115. Although generally the interests of both developed broadly in parallel rather than conflicting. Cassis (Bankers), p. 210.

116. Palmade (French Capitalism), p. 78.

117. Palmade (French Capitalism), pp. 139–148 and Tom Kemp, *Economic Forces in French History* (London, Dennis Dobson, 1971), pp. 193–195. For a discussion of divisions within business over the entire nineteenth century, see H.D. Peiter, "Institutions and Attitudes: The Consolidation of the Business Community in Bourgeois France, 1880–1914", *Journal of Social History* 9, 4, June 1976, pp. 510–525.

118. Cobban (History), p. 98. Also see the figures in Peter McPhee, *A Social History of France, 1780–1880* (London, Routledge, 1992), p. 119.

119. Kemp (Economic Forces), p. 111. He said that the financiers and bankers exercised 'predominating influence over policy', and (pp. 147–148) that the Orleans monarchy had relied for support on a 'narrow and privileged oligarchy of bankers and financiers'. Also see Palmade (French Capitalism), pp. 105–107.

120. Magraw (France 1814–1915), p. 55.

121. Magraw (France 1815–1914), p. 59.

122. Barrie M. Ratcliffe, "Napoleon and the Anglo-French Commercial Treaty of 1860: A Reconsideration", *Journal of European Economic History* 2, 3, Winter 1973, p. 586.

123. Zeldin (France 1848–1940), p. 479.

124. See Zeldin (France 1848–1940), p. 12.

125. Zeldin (Political System), p. 57.

126. His position was the basis for Marx's notion of Bonapartism. For his early discussion of this period, see Karl Marx, "The Eighteenth Brumaire of Louis Bonaparte", Karl Marx & Frederick Engels (eds.), *Selected Works I* (Moscow, Foreign Languages Publishing House, 1951), pp. 221–311.

127. Kemp (Economic Forces), p. 156. The reference to 'privileged insiders' is on p. 159. He argues that the regime 'operated principally through private interest groups to whom it gave special privileges and support—access to means for appropriating

part of the social surplus under favoured conditions'. The emphasis was on enterprises closely related to public works, p. 160. State orders, along with covert subsidies and privileges were common, p. 182.

128. Although there was general business support for such redevelopment, the financial sector was opposed to the non-standard ways in which this was funded. Zeldin (France 1848–1940), p. 554.

129. From the time of the Second Empire, purchase of stocks and shares became a more popular form of investment than land for both nobles and non-nobles. Roger Price, *A Social History of Nineteenth Century France* (London, Hutchinson, 1987), p. 101.

130. Dennis Sherman, "Governmental Policy Toward Joint-Stock Business Organizations in Mid-Nineteenth Century France", *Journal of European Economic History* 3, 1, Spring 1974, pp. 164–165.

131. On the emergence of new banking institutions during the Second Empire, see Palmade (French Capitalism), pp. 123–138. For the conflict between the Rothschilds and the Pereires, see Palmade (French Capitalism), pp. 139–148. On Pereire's attempt to build a railway network in the 1830s and 1840s, see Barrie M. Ratcliffe, "Railway Imperialism: The Example of the Pereires' Paris-Saint-Germain Company, 1835–1846", *Business History* XVIII, 1, January 1976, pp. 66–84.

132. This was important because during the July Monarchy officials hostile to the effects of industrialisation used their positions in the Bank of France and the Conseil d'Etat to block applications for joint stock companies. Sherman (Governmental Policy), p. 155.

133. Michael Stephen Smith, *Tariff Reform in France 1869–1900. The Politics of Economic Interest* (Ithaca, Cornell University Press, 1980), p. 22. On businessmen who acted as advisers, see Palmade (French Capitalism), p. 123.

134. Lebovics (Iron and Wheat), pp. 14–15.

135. On this see, Dennis Sherman, "Governmental Responses to Economic Modernization in Mid-Nineteenth Century France", *Journal of European Economic History* 6, 3, Winter 1977, pp. 717–736. Also see Palmade (French Capitalism), pp. 11–12.

136. Palmade (French Capitalism), p. 152.

137. His influence lasted into the Third Republic. Zeldin (France 1848–1940), p. 607.

138. For a debate about whether the Parti Colonial in the Third Republic was dominated by big business and its interests, effectively acting as their instrument, or was simply a body within which some people with business interests were to be found, see L. Abrams & D.J. Miller, "Who Were the French Colonialists? A Reassessment of the Parti Colonial, 1890–1914", *The Historical Journal* 19, 3, 1976, pp. 685–725 and C.M. Andrew & A.S. Kanya-Forstner, "French Business and the French Colonialists", *The Historical Journal* 19, 4, 1976, pp. 981–1000. Also see the earlier C.M. Andrew & A.S. Kanya-Forstner, "The French Colonial Party: Its Composition, Aims and Influence 1885–1914", *The Historical Journal* 14, 1, 1971, pp. 99–128 and C.M. Andrew & A.S. Kanya-Forstner, "The Groupe Coloniale in the French Chamber of Deputies 1892–1932", *The Historical Journal* 14, 4, 1974, pp. 837–866.

139. Pereire was a founder of Credit Mobilier. See Ratcliffe (Napoleon), pp. 582–613.
140. On the development of this issue, see Lebovics (Iron and Wheat); Smith (Tariff Reform); and for the early period, Sanford Elwitt, *The Making of the Third Republic. Class Politics in France, 1868–1884* (Baton Rouge, Louisiana State University Press, 1975).
141. For discussion of one case of this, see Sanford Elwitt, "Politics and Social Classes in the Loire: The Triumph of Republican Order, 1869–1873", *French Historical Studies* VI, 1, Spring 1969, pp. 96–98 & 109. Also Lebovics (Iron and Wheat), p. 13. Although for the general argument about the construction of a conservative alliance in the late nineteenth century to exclude the working class, see Lebovics (Iron and Wheat).
142. Anderson (France 1870–1914), p. 83. The Comite des Forges, which was very important in the protection issue, was an exception to this generalisation.
143. Anderson (France 1870–1914), p. 36.
144. Anderson (France 1870–1914), pp. 76–81.
145. Louis Bergeron, *Les Capitalistes en France (1780–1914)* (Paris, Gallimard, 1978), p. 182.
146. Smith (Tariff Reform), p. 22.
147. For example, it has been suggested that Alphonse de Rothschild objected to the nomination of Germain as minister of finance, that Thiers accepted this veto and sought Rothschild's agreement to the nomination of Leon Say. This seems to have occurred in 1871, although no date is given in the source. Bergeron (Les Capitalistes), p. 182. On Rothschild's power, see Palmade (French Capitalism), pp. 126–127, and Niall Ferguson, *The World's Banker. The History of the House of Rothschild* (London, Weidenfeld & Nicolson, 1998), passim.
148. Zeldin (France 1848–1945), p. 54.
149. The growth of shareholding in France was dramatic. By the early 1890s, the value of liquid assets exceeded that of fixed assets in the country, while stocks and shares, which had constituted about 7% of the total value of inherited property declared between 1851 and 1855, constituted 39% between 1911 and 1915. Price (Social History), p. 101. For slightly different figures, see Zeldin (France 1848–1945), p. 59. Although there was much investment in government, including foreign government (especially Russian), bonds, investment in business was also growing.
150. Zeldin (France 1848–1940), pp. 13 & 53.
151. Zeldin (France 1848–1940), p. 54.
152. In comparison with industry, there were very few pressure groups formed to press financial/bank interests. Hubert Bonin, "The Political Influence of Bankers and Financiers in France in the Years, 1850–1960", Youssef Cassis (ed.), *Finance and Financiers in European History, 1880–1960* (Cambridge, Cambridge University Press, 1992), p. 220. It should also be noted that bankers frequently were engaged in other sorts of business activities as well. Bergeron (Les Capitalistes), pp. 114–116.
153. On Rouvier and his actions as government minister and banker, see Palmade (French Capitalism), pp. 183–186. He founded his own bank in 1901 with government support.

154. Anderson (France 1870–1914), p. 193.
155. This was also true of some industrialists. For example, Eugene Schneider was president of the legislature in 1865–70, his son-in-law was a minister under MacMahon, and his grandson entered parliament. Zeldin (France 1848–1945), p. 75.
156. Palmade (French Capitalism), p. 108.
157. Alain Plessis, "Bankers in French Society, 1860s–1960", Cassis (Finance and Financiers), p. 149. On le Haute Banque, see Bigo (Les banques francaises), ch. v.
158. Palmade (French Capitalism), p. 120. On the Bank, see the three volumes by Alain Plessis, *Le Banque de France et ses Deux Cents Actionnaires sous le Second Empire* (Geneva, Librairie Droz, 1982), *Regents et Gouverneurs de la Banque de France sous le Second Empire* (Geneva, Librairie Droz, 1985), and *La Politique de la Banque de France de 1851 a 1870* (Geneva, Librairie Droz, 1985).
159. And the same families often provided the directors over the generations. For example, there were four generations of the Hottinguer and Davillier families, three of the Perier and Pillet-Will families, and two of the d'Eichtal, Rothschild, Heine and Vernes families. Palmade (French Capitalism), p. 106.
160. Plessis (Bankers), p. 150.
161. Trebilcock (Industrialization), p. 79.
162. In particular, see the argument in Steinmetz (Myth), pp. 257–318, esp. pp. 277–293.
163. See the comment by Eley (Capitalism and the Wilhelmine State), p. 745. In one formulation, Calleo argues that the Junkers had a veto over policy, but big business was influential in economic and political policy formation. See David Calleo, *The German Problem Reconsidered: Germany and the World Order, 1870 to the Present* (Cambridge, Cambridge University Press, 1978), pp. 129ff.
164. On this position of the Prussian state government, see Charles Medalen, "State Monopoly Capitalism in Germany: The Hibernia Affair", *Past and Present* 78, February 1978, p. 97.
165. Charles S. Maier, *Recasting Bourgeois Europe. Stabilization in France, Germany, and Italy in the Decade After World War I* (Princeton, Princeton University Press, 1975), p. 40.
166. Ferguson (Paper and Iron), p. 94.
167. Jurgen Kocka, *Industrial Culture and Bourgeois Society: Business, Labor, Bureaucracy in Modern Germany* (New York, Berghahn Books, 1999), pp. 159–163.
168. The argument stemming from Hilferding among others about the supremacy of high finance in the economy before 1914 needs substantial qualification. While banks did provide investment for industry on a much larger scale than in Britain, they did not control that industry; in Mommsen's words, 'the big industrial combines that had emerged in the course of the "second industrial revolution" were able, up to a point, to impose their own policies on the banks. For the most part they could select those banks that were most willing to fall in with their requirements, using them almost as private banks...' Mommsen (Imperial Germany), p. 87. Also see Caroline Fohlin, "The Rise of Interlocking Directorates in Imperial Germany", *Economic History Review* LII, 2, 1999, pp. 307–333. For one discussion of cartels, see Henderson (Rise), ch. 15.
169. Blackbourn & Eley (Peculiarities), p. 208.

170. Pamela M. Pilbeam, *The Middle Classes in Europe 1789–1914. France, Germany, Italy and Russia* (Basingstoke, Macmillan, 1990), p. 51,
171. On Hibernia, see, Medalen (State Monopoly Capitalism), pp. 82–112.
172. Gerald D. Feldman, "Industrialists, Bankers, and the Problem of Unemployment in the Weimar Republic", *Central European History* 25, 1, 1992, p. 86. According to Turner, by 1925 there were more than 1500 cartels in industry alone. Turner (German Big Business), p. xix.
173. Henderson (Rise), p. 185.
174. For example in 1913 the Prussian state government owned 40 coal mines and 13 blast furnaces. Ralf Dahrendorf, *Society and Democracy in Germany* (New York, W.W. Norton & Co., 1967), p. 36. On Bismarck supporting the development of cartels following the economic crisis of 1873, see Henderson (Rise), p. 175.
175. Ferguson (Paper and Iron), p. 107. Craig (Germany 1866–1945), pp. 354–355. Rathenau stepped down in April 1915.
176. Craig (Germany 1866–1945), p. 361.
177. Maier (Recasting), p. 69.
178. Ferguson (Paper and Iron), pp. 130–131.
179. Ferguson (Paper and Iron), p. 144.
180. On this see, Dick Geary, "The Industrial Bourgeoisie and Labour Relations in Germany 1871–1933"; Blackbourn & Evans (German Bourgeoisie), pp. 153–155; and Maier (Recasting Bourgeois Europe), pp. 59–64.
181. On the way in which business helped to subvert this, see Maier (Recasting Bourgeois Europe), pp. 218–225 and Turner (German Big Business), p. 10.
182. On the iron and steel industry having easy access to the top of the ministerial bureaucracy, and the steel industry paying a secret retainer to a state secretary, see Gerald D. Feldman & Ulrich Nocken, "Trade Associations and Economic Power: Interest Group Development in the German Iron and Steel and Machine Building Industries, 1900–1933", *Business History Review* XLIX, 4, Winter 1975, pp. 438–439.
183. In particular, businessmen tried to restrict broad areas of economic decision-making to quasi-official bodies under their general control rather than having such issues politicised by being dealt with in the political arena.
184. James C. Hunt, "The Bourgeois Middle in German Politics, 1871–1933: Recent Literature", *Central European History* XI, 1, March 1978, p. 101.
185. The banking community, much of which was Jewish, was probably less integrated with the industrialists than was the case in Britain. Nor was there a real financial aristocracy in Germany, as there was in Britain and France. See the discussion in Youssef Cassis, "Financial Elites in Three European Centres: London, Paris, Berlin, 1880s–1930s", Youssef Cassis (ed.), *Business Elites* (Aldershot, Edward Elgar, 1994), pp. 400–418.
186. Maier (Recasting Bourgeois Europe), p. 66. The steel industry also favoured rearmament (and therefore the rejection of Versailles) and the expansion of German interests to the east.
187. Feldman & Nocken (Trade Associations), pp. 434–435. Also see David Abraham, "Constituting Hegemony: The Bourgeois Crisis of Weimar Germany", *The Journal of Modern History* 51, 3, September 1979, pp. 422–423.
188. David Blackbourn in Blackbourn & Eley (Peculiarities), p. 210.

189. For example, Tipton (Government and the economy), pp. 140–141 cites the earlier case of Bismarck personally who used his position to further his economic interests.

190. Tilly (Moral Standards), pp. 198–199.

191. Robert Harrison, *Congress, Progressive Reform, and the New American State* (Cambridge, Cambridge University Press, 2004), p. 29. According to Phillips (Wealth and Democracy), p. 240, in 1906 about a third of senators were millionaires. Also see Robert Rienow & Leona Train Rienow, *Of Snuff, Sin and the Senate* (Chicago, Follett Publishing Co., 1965), chs 16 & 17.

192. Rienow & Rienow (Of Snuff), p. 29.

193. On 'spoilsmen', see Matthew Josephson, *The Politicos. 1856–1896* (New York, Harcourt, Brace & Co., 1938), Book One, and Richard Hofstadter, *The American Political Tradition and the Men Who Made It* (New York, Vintage Books, 1948), ch. vii.

194. For example, see Rienow & Rienow (Of Snuff), ch. 14. According to one study of the 'business elite', of those born 1820–49, 38.3% held one or more political offices at one time (17.8% held three or more), and of those born 1850–79, the corresponding figures were 39.2% and 11.45%. C. Wright Mills, "The American Business Elite: A Collective Portrait", Irving Louis Horowitz (ed.), *Power, Politics and People. The Collected Essays of C. Wright Mills* (London, Oxford University Press, 1967), p. 130.

195. Cited in Destler (Opposition), p. 662.

196. Phillips (Wealth and Democracy), p. 46. For the 1880s, see Cashman (America in the Gilded Age), pp. 228–230.

197. Cashman (America in the Gilded Age), p. 244.

198. In particular, see Kolko (Triumph).

199. Robert H. Wiebe, "The House of Morgan and the Executive, 1905–1913", *American Historical Review* 65, 1, October 1959, p. 51.

200. Kolko (Triumph), p. 66.

201. Kolko (Triumph), p. 63.

202. On Hanna, see Rienow & Rienow (Of Snuff), ch. 13.

203. Wiebe (House of Morgan), p. 52.

204. For discussion of a case where such an arrangement with the president was instrumental in the later blocking of a Senate enquiry, see Kolko (Triumph), pp. 120–122.

205. Weinstein (Corporate Ideal), p. 143.

206. Kolko (Triumph), pp. 217–242. On differences between the Wilson administration and Morgan, see R. Dayer, "Strange Bedfellows: J.P. Morgan and Co, Whitehall and the Wilson Administration During World War One", *Business History* 18, 2, 1976, pp. 127–151.

207. For an argument which, although applying to the 1880s was also relevant at this time, showed that business attitudes to state regulation depended upon their experience of it and that general support for regulation did not mean support for specific cases of regulation, see Edward A. Purcell Jr, "Ideas and Interests: Businessmen and the Interstate Commerce Act", *Journal of American History* 54, 3, December 1967, pp. 561–578. For an argument about how business groups

supported many of the measures for the direct effect they would have on these businesses themselves, see Greenberg (Capitalism), pp. 75 & 84–86. Also see Kolko (Triumph), p. 60.

208. The Court ruled that a monopoly in sugar refining was a monopoly in manufacturing rather than trade and therefore did not fall under the Act, that the Act could be used against interstate strikes, and later refused to break up major monopolies like Standard Oil and American Tobacco on the grounds that these were not 'unreasonable' combinations in restraint of trade. Howard Zinn, *A People's History of the United States. 1492—Present* (New York, Perennial Classics, 2001), p. 260. According to Bensel, despite the Sherman Act, industrial consolidations 'remained almost invulnerable to prosecution between 1890 and 1900'. Richard Franklin Bensel, *The Political Economy of American Industrialization, 1877–1900* (Cambridge, Cambridge University Press, 2000), p. 344.

209. For the view that the principles underpinning the establishment of the FTC 'were enunciated by corporate leaders and their lawyers consistently throughout the Progressive Era...', see Weinstein (Corporate Ideal), p. 62.

210. Kolko (Triumph), p. 280. For some individual examples, see Greenberg (Capitalism), pp. 86–87.

211. For one discussion, see Robert H. Wiebe, "Business Disunity and the Progressive Movement, 1901–1914", *Mississippi Valley Historical Review* 44, 4, March 1958, pp. 664–685. Also Robert H. Wiebe, *Businessmen and Reform: A Study of the Progressive Movement* (Cambridge [Mass], Harvard University Press, 1962).

212. Robert H. Himmelberg, "Business, Antitrust Policy, and the Industrial Board of the Department of Commerce, 1919", *Business History Review* xlii, 1, 1968, p. 2.

213. On shippers favouring regulation of railway rates while railway companies opposed it, see Richard H.K. Vietor, "Businessmen and the Political Economy: The Railroad Rate Controversy of 1905", *Journal of American History* 64, 1, June 1977, pp. 47–66. For an earlier study that shows some railway support for regulation, see Purcell (Ideas and Interests), pp. 561–578.

214. Edwin M. Epstein, *The Corporation in American Politics* (Englewood Cliffs, Prentice Hall, 1969), p. 34.

215. Jordan A. Schwarz, *The Speculator. Bernard M. Baruch in Washington, 1917–1965* (Chapel Hill, University of North Carolina Press, 1981), p. 51. This book analyses the politico-administrative career of a former Wall Street financial speculator.

216. Paul A.C. Koistinen, "The 'Industrial-Military Complex' in Historical Perspective; The Inter War Years", *Journal of American History* 56, 4, March 1970, pp. 819–822.

217. Epstein (Corporation), p. 29.

218. Robert D. Cuff, "Woodrow Wilson and Business-Government Relations During World War I", *The Review of Politics* 31, 3, July 1969, pp. 390–391. Wilson sought to coopt businessmen onto many government agencies, and many worked for the government in senior coordinating positions.

219. Koistinen (The 'Industrial-Military Complex'), pp. 823–833.

220. Himmelberg (Business, Antitrust Policy), pp. 1–23.

221. Epstein (Corporation), pp. 31–32.

222. Sanford M. Jacoby, "Employers and the Welfare State: The Role of Marion B. Folsom", *Journal of American History* 80, 2, September 1993, p. 528. Also see

Greenberg (Capitalism), p. 75 and Kim McQuaid, "Corporate Liberalism in the American Business Community, 1920–1940", *Business History Review* 52, 3, 1978, pp. 342–368.

223. Peter A. Swenson, "Varieties of Capitalist Interests: Power, Institutions, and the Regulatory Welfare State in the United States and Sweden", *Studies in American Political Development* 18, 1, Spring 2004, pp. 1–29 and Sar A. Levitan & Martha R. Cooper, *Business Lobbies. The Public Good and the Bottom Line* (Baltimore, Johns Hopkins University Press, 1984), p. 28. For one discussion of the disagreements within business ranks, see Michael Patrick Allen, "Capitalist Response to State Intervention: Theories of the State and Political Finance in the New Deal", *American Sociological Review* 56, October 1991, pp. 679–689.

224. Kim McQuaid, *Big Business and Presidential Power. From FDR to Reagan* (New York, William Morrow & Co. Inc., 1982), pp. 26–27. For the role of one business corporation in the events of this time, including its initial support for and then opposition to the New Deal, see Robert F. Burk, *The Corporate State and the Broker State. The Du Ponts and American National Politics, 1925–1940* (Cambridge [Mass], Harvard University Press, 1990). NIRA was actually designed to reduce competition, raise prices and stabilise profits. Greenberg (Capitalism), p. 101. Big business initially appreciated the replacement of the antitrust legislation by a form of self-regulation through industry codes drawn up mainly by the industries themselves. By the time the Act was declared unconstitutional in May 1935, big business had turned against it and the increased regulation it was seen to embody.

225. McQuaid (Big Business), pp. 11–17.

226. On the debate about the broader question of continuities and discontinuities between the New Deal and earlier, see R. Kirkendall, "The New Deal as Watershed: The Recent Literature", *Journal of American History* 54, 4, 1968, pp. 839–852.

227. On businessmen pushing their sectional interests, see Linda J. Jones, "Public Pursuit of Private Profit? Liberal Businessmen and Municipal Politics in Birmingham 1865–1900", *Business History* 25, 3, November 1983, pp. 240–259.

228. Such feelings could be a potent resource for industrialists, although this only tended to function in small-medium sized towns where there was a limited range of employment and where owners continued to live near the workers. This factor lost its salience as the size of towns expanded and local economies became more diverse, the size of individual factories increased, and political parties became more important as vehicles for election. Martin Pugh, *The Making of Modern British Politics 1867–1939* (Oxford, Basil Blackwell, 1982), pp. 12–13. This was also one reason why many industrialists did not oppose the enfranchisement of industrial workers in 1867. John Garrard, *Democratisation in Britain. Elites, Civil Society and Reform since 1800* (Basingstoke, Palgrave, 2005), p. 47.

229. The increase in the proportion of titles going to industrial and professional men in the last decades of the nineteenth century was related in part to the increased need for funds by the parties given the post-reform electoral situation. Pugh (Making), pp. 20–21.

230. For a short discussion, see Garrard (Democratisation), pp. 108–113.

231. Tombs (France 1814–1914), pp. 106–107 and Zeldin (France 1848–1940), pp. 580–581.

242

232. Tombs (France 1814–1914), p. 108. For the situation at Le Creusot, dominated by the Schneider iron and engineering magnates, see Anderson (France 1870–1914), p. 63.

233. John M. Dobson, *Politics in the Gilded Age. A New Perspective on Reform* (New York, Praeger Publications, 1972), p. 34. According to Moore, in the period after the civil war, the Federal Government instituted a series of measures designed to underpin and protect property, especially large property: growth of the internal market protected by tariff walls, the Fourteenth Amendment which was applied to property, the development of a national banking system and the resumption of specie payments put the currency on a sound footing, the public domain was opened to private development (e.g. the Homestead Act of 1862), and continued immigration (the Immigration Act 1864). Barrington Moore Jr, *Social Origins of Dictatorship and Democracy. Lord and Peasant in the Making of the Modern World* (Harmondsworth, Penguin, 1967), p. 150.

234. Dobson (Politics in the Gilded Age), pp. 27–28. For a portrait of one boss, see Zane L. Miller, "Boss Cox's Cincinnati: A Study in Urbanization and Politics, 1880–1914", *Journal of American History* 54, 4, March 1968, pp. 823–838. Also see Cashman (America in the Gilded Age), pp. 125–136 and Rienow & Rienow (Of Snuff), chs 7 & 17–19.

235. Glenn C. Altschuler & Stuart M. Blumin, *Rude Republic. Americans and Their Politics in the Nineteenth Century* (Princeton, Princeton University Press, 2000), ch. 7, esp. p. 243.

236. See the discussion in T.C. Cochran, "The History of a Business Society", *Journal of American History* 54, 1, 1967, pp. 5–18.

237. Industrialists were not always able to get their way. For a case of them failing to get the support of powerful elements in the town during labour disputes, see Herbert G. Gutman, "Class, Status, and Community Power in Nineteenth-Century American Industrial Cities—Peterson, New Jersey: A Case Study", Frederic Cople Jaher (ed.), *The Age of Industrialism in America. Essays in Social Structure and Cultural Values* (New York, The Free Press, 1968), pp. 263–287. For an analysis of New York and the relationship between ethnic, kinship, and business factors, see Barry E. Supple, "A Business Elite: German-Jewish Financiers in Nineteenth-Century New York", *Business History Review* xxxi, 2, 1957, pp. 143–178.

238. For example see Dobson (Politics in the Gilded Age), p. 31.

239. Dobson (Politics in the Gilded Age), p. 32.

240. For a study of this sort of process, see Roger W. Lotchin, "The City and the Sword: San Francisco and the Rise of the Metropolitan Military Industrial Complex", *Journal of American History* 65, 4, March 1979, pp. 996–1020. Also see Dobson (Politics in the Gilded Age), p. 29.

241. For a discussion of this involving the Platt machine in New York in the 1890s, see Dobson (Politics in the Gilded Age), pp. 177–178. On alliances between businessmen and local governments in New York, Philadelphia, Boston, Baltimore and Charleston, see Phillips (Wealth and Democracy), p. 207.

242. On this movement, see Weinstein (Corporate Ideal), pp. 93–109. Also see James Weinstein, "Organised Business and the City Commission Manager Movements", *Journal of Southern History* 28, 2, 1962, pp. 166–182. For example, in Beaufort,

South Carolina, the offices of city manager and secretary of the board of trade were combined and the manager's salary was split between the city and local businessmen.

243. For the case of Union Pacific in Wyoming, W.D. Farnham, "The Weakened Spring of Government: A Study of Nineteenth-Century American History", *American Historical Review* 68, 3, 1963, pp. 662–680.

244. On the large numbers of pieces of special legislation, which applied to particular and usually local cases, rather than general bills in state legislatures, see Scott Allard, Nancy Burns & Gerald Gamm, "Representing Urban Interests: the Local Politics of State Legislatures", *Studies in American Political Development* 12, 2, Fall 1998, pp. 267–302. Also Destler (Opposition), p. 642.

245. For a discussion of the circumstances, and abuses, that could occur in this regard, see Rienow & Rienow (Of Snuff), Part 3.

246. Phillips (Wealth and Democracy), pp. 304–305.

247. For some details on how much particular offices cost to purchase in the 1870s, see Rienow & Rienow (Of Snuff), pp. 109–110.

248. Epstein (Corporation), p. 26.

249. For an instance of this, see Sidney I. Roberts, "Portrait of a Robber Baron: Charles T. Yerkes", *Business History Review* XXXV, 3, 1961, pp. 354–362.

250. For a guide to some of the studies of the way in which political rule changed in various cities, see David C. Hammack, "Problems in the Historical Study of Power in the Cities and Towns of the United States, 1800–1960", *American Historical Review* 83, 2, April 1978, pp. 323–349.

7

Class and State: The Post-Soviet Bourgeoisie

The development, contours, and nature of the Russian bourgeoisie as well as its capacity to exploit or to capture the state were fundamentally shaped by the state and its actions. Crucial to this was the nature of the state itself, including the degree of autonomy it was able to achieve. The post-Soviet state has often been described as a 'weak state',[1] but in this simplistic formulation, this charge is misleading. A better way of seeing the state is to acknowledge that the state was both weak and strong, but in different aspects of its activity. A useful way of looking at this is through the distinction made by Michael Mann[2] between infrastructural and despotic power. Infrastructural power exists when the state is able to achieve its ends through regularised processes. It involves cooperation with other actors in society as well as the existence of effectively functioning procedures within the state itself. Despotic power is exercised when, in order to achieve its aims, the state must use extraordinary means. Rather than cooperation with other actors in society, this involves the assertion of power over such actors. Inevitably in practice, a state's power will be an amalgam of infrastructural and despotic power, with, in a stable modern state, the balance heavily weighted in favour of infrastructural power. However in post-Soviet Russia, especially in the 1990s, infrastructural power was quite weak.[3] Central to this was the nature of the state's internal regulative regime, or the complex of rules, practices, and principles governing the way the state and its officials carried out their tasks.

Two aspects of this were important in post-Soviet Russia: what the state was to do, and how it was to do it. The former aspect, what the state was to do, was problematic because of the collapse of the Soviet Union. In Soviet times, there was no uncertainty: the state had a legitimate role in all aspects of life, able to intrude into the individual's private sphere on a scale hitherto unprecedented while at the same time structuring all aspects of public life. However with the collapse of communism, this totalistic style was no longer acceptable, but it was not clear what was to replace it. Although the official rhetoric emanating from leading circles in the state emphasised the notion of a market economy and interpreted this in a neo-classical way that left little room for the state, there were always dissenting echoes which accorded the state a larger role, and these had significant public support. In essence, this means that there was no clear conception of the role the state should play in society, including its relationship with the economy.

But if there was confusion about what the state should do, there was also uncertainty about how, internally, it should function. This uncertainty stemmed from the coexistence within the Soviet bureaucracy of two competing principles, bureaucratic and personalist. The former comprised the structure of rules and regulations that are necessary for any large bureaucratic machine to function—rules of process, hierarchy, and procedure. These are the officially mandated rules and procedures which govern the operation of a bureaucratic machine and ensure that it works in an ordered fashion. These rules remained in place regardless of the Soviet collapse because the vast bulk of the bureaucratic structures themselves remained in place and functioning; independent Russia took over the Soviet state machine in Russia, along with most of its employees and the set routines and procedures whereby these institutions had functioned. Such rules, routines, and procedures are the struts of infrastructural power. The latter, personalist, principle had been an intrinsic part of the Soviet polity. It mandated that the key to politico-administrative practice was the elevation of personal loyalty to a superior (sometimes immediate, sometimes more removed in the hierarchy) over the bureaucratic principle of obedience to formal rules. This principle can operate in any structured environment, but in the Soviet system it was a key axis around which politics revolved. Politically, it was reflected in the development of chains of patrons and clients, with the support of the former essential for the promotion and advancement of the latter. This was a key currency of political life. Administratively, it took the form of officials putting personal before institutional interests, with officials using their positions to secure personal advantage. Soviet officials were able to use state property, resources, and equipment for personal advantage, a practice which seems to have escalated considerably from the mid-1960s. The practice of officials using their position to gain access to state resources for personal ends, including the provision of benefits to others, undercut the capacity of the Soviet administrative machine to function along formal, institutional lines. It also raised questions about state autonomy and the capacity of state officials to resist the demands emanating from powerful sectors of society.

How have these aspects of the state shaped the development of the bourgeoisie?

The State as a Resource

During the Soviet period, the state was seen as a vast public utility, providing for the needs and wants of its citizens. Formally this was reflected in the extensive welfare functions it performed; informally it operated through the use of official position to structure access to personal advantage. It continued to perform something of this role in the post-Soviet period, except that instead of providing for the needs of its poorest citizens, which it manifestly failed to do, much of its time was spent servicing emergent business. This involved business gaining access to services, resources, and opportunities. Such access was related to the conditions within which Russian business emerged, and the chief characteristic of these conditions was uncertainty.

Unlike the historical bourgeoisies, the emergence of a Russian business class was sudden and occurred in an environment that was not conducive to private business activity. There was not a slow emergence over decades with the gradual growing out of the new class from existing merchant and manufacturing elements that were involved in private economic activity. Indeed, the whole basis of economic activity was private in these historical cases, with the state playing a role that, while it may have been important, was in terms of bulk less significant than that of the private sector. In Russia, a sizeable bourgeoisie burst forth from an environment within which private economic activity was frowned upon. While there was private economic activity in the Soviet Union, and while it may have played a significant part in keeping the general economy afloat,[4] in terms of its social location, it was marginal to the society as a whole. Most private activity was illegal, conducted around and behind the laws rather than through them, and possible only because state officials decided not to enforce the prohibitions against such activity. This means that the emergent bourgeoisie did not inherit a vigorous tradition of private economic activity, nor a framework within which it could be conducted.

In those places where there was a history of economic life structured on the basis of private ownership and private enterprise, there was an infrastructure in place to support that activity. It may have been incomplete and it may not always have been solidly grounded in clear and precise rules or laws, but it was nevertheless in place, because private activity could not be conducted without it. The problem in post-Soviet Russia was that no such infrastructure existed.[5] The legal basis for private economic activity was almost completely absent. There was no effective property law and no system of land titles, thereby rendering the notion of private property itself problematic.[6] There was no system of contracts between individual economic actors, and no formal means for ensuring that once agreements were made between different parties, those agreements would be fulfilled. The absence of a means of enforcement of contracts was an aspect of the wider lack of an effective legal structure for the protection of individuals in commercial transactions; just as there was no specific protection for consumers in retail transactions, nor was there protection for the parties to an agreement against short-changing or cheating on that agreement. Nor was there an effective and easily available means of cheap credit; Soviet financial institutions did not offer credit in this way, and the new banks also did not see it as being within their interests to play this role. The financial system was not designed to cater to a myriad of independent production units. It was inflexible, tied to the command economy, lacking in the sorts of fiduciary instruments essential to the conduct of modern business, and not sensitive to the needs of the new entrepreneurs. The currency was not convertible. There were no established stock or commodity exchanges. The tax system was not designed to cater to a private enterprise economy, with the result that tax rules seemed, and often were, arbitrary and were certainly seen to be punitive,[7] although given the nature of Soviet taxation, virtually any post-Soviet taxation regime was likely to be seen as excessively heavy.

The perception of the tax system in this initial period was symptomatic of what many businessmen saw as a more general hostility of the state to emergent business. Many officials were perceived to be hostile to business interests in this early period, not just because they used this as a means of personal enrichment through abuse of their positions (see below), but often motivated by continuing commitment to Soviet ideals, because they generally put obstacles in the way of would be entrepreneurs. Difficulties in gaining registration and licences were endemic as local officials dragged their feet and sought to use bureaucratic obstruction to block entrepreneurial development. Harassment through the frequent conduct of official inspections by people like health and sanitation, fire, and tax authorities was also common.[8] The barriers posed by such official conduct were reinforced by the broad regulative regime, which was seen as being predatory, punitive, onerous, and much more intrusive and arbitrary than was good for business development.[9] Excessive and arbitrary regulation and red tape was widely seen to stand in the way of establishing and running a business.

In terms of physical infrastructure too there were clear problems. The Soviet economy had been organised on the basis of units that sought to achieve economies of scale. Most of the units of the economy—factories, farms, retail outlets—were very large, employing many people. As a result, there were very few premises readily available that were suitable for small entrepreneurs to set up in. Nor was there an effective transport system for the distribution of goods, raw materials, and resources. There were no trucking firms, for example, that could transport goods by road over long distances, no courier services or light transport companies for the delivery of goods within the large cities, and there was not even an easy availability of fuel through a network of outlets that could keep private commercial vehicles running easily.

In principle, such transport deficiencies could have been compensated for by the state, which clearly did have the capacity for long haul transport via air and rail in particular. But in practice, by the end of the 1980s, these facilities no longer operated in an efficient fashion. There were question marks over the reliability, not to mention safety, of these services and they were not cheap. Nor were they imbued with an ethic of providing a service to private business, or indeed, to any consumer. But in any case, the state system remained too inflexible to cater for emergent needs. It did not have the capacity to meet the demands of a small-scale business that was decentralised and spread throughout various parts of a city or region. So even if the officials of state transport facilities were personally ready to seek to cater to the new needs, and some were, the facilities were not such as to make this an easy task to accomplish.

In no case of the emergence of a bourgeoisie other than in the post-communist situation, was this combination present. When a new industrial bourgeoisie emerged elsewhere, because that emergence was slower and because it had roots in existing economic practice, the rudiments of a privately oriented legal-economic infrastructure were generally in place. Notions of private property, contract law, exchanges, and even legal regulation underpinned private economic activity from the start, and where these were rudimentary, because of the slow development of the new economy, they were able to develop with it. But in Russia, with the collapse of the old legal structure, there was a void that had to be filled immediately.[10] This was particularly so because of the simultaneous virtual collapse of the old economy. The disintegration of the Soviet Union into fifteen independent republics destroyed the old distribution system and substantially assisted the collapse of the production system, with the result that the country could not drift easily into a new economic phase over time; it had to get up and begin working immediately. Otherwise people would starve.

As well as the absence of solid institutional struts of a market system, there was also a lack of the public beliefs upon which such a system depends.[11] The functioning of a market economy relies fundamentally upon trust, upon the belief that those engaged in production, distribution, and exchange deal with people fairly and not seek to cheat, and that agreements, once made, will be kept. This in turn rests upon acceptance that what these people are doing is legitimate, that the private capital that underpins their operations was obtained in a legitimate fashion and is being used in acceptable ways. This sort of consensus was not available for the new emergent businessmen in Russia. Faith in state institutions had been eroded by the growing cynicism and apathy of the last decades of Soviet rule, a development fuelled by the continuing failure of Soviet institutions not only to measure up against the ideals which had for long underpinned the regime's legitimacy but even to supply on a regular basis many of the fundamental necessities of life. But here, trust was not necessary because the state was always there; whether an individual shopper trusted the management and employees of a store made no difference to that store's capacity to continue trading because of the paucity of alternatives available to potential customers. Paradoxically, there was greater popular trust in the informal economy where the legality of activity was more problematic. Such trust rested on the more personalised nature of the relationships that were the essence of most exchanges in that economy. People bought from a personal trader, technician, or provider of services, and the agreement reached was a personal one. People had to trust the person they were dealing with, otherwise the transaction would not go ahead. Such trust was present even though people knew that the operatives in the informal economy were often operating at the margins of legality and the capital they were able to acquire was gained illegally. But because this was seen as being part of the sort of grafting that most Soviet citizens engaged in at one or other time of their lives (such as taking time off from work to shop when some particular necessity became available, or using work time and equipment for private gain), such activity was considered acceptable, if not strictly legal. In this sense, the small entrepreneur in the informal economy enjoyed a certain degree of popular trust denied to the state outlets. This point should not be exaggerated: people still got swindled and cheated in the informal economy; despite the claims of some of the gangs which controlled some of the sites of informal exchange (like the urban markets, such as Cheremushkinskii) that they ensured a fair deal for all, the consumer was advised to remain wary. But even so, this process rested on a degree of trust, because if this did not exist, the informal economy itself could not have existed.

However, the level of trust in the informal economy seems to have been dissipating in the last years of Soviet rule. This occurred under the impact of the explosion of petty trading on the streets of the large cities in the last years of the 1980s, the perceived growth in crime at this time, and the beginnings of spontaneous privatisation. The old informal economy was swamped, and with it went the set of norms and procedures which had sustained it. All of a sudden, a new economic world was opening up, symbolised by the street kiosks selling a range of, often Western and formerly unavailable, goods for higher prices. This was both a major quantitative advance on the old informal economy, meaning that the number of suppliers and the range of goods both expanded significantly (at least in Moscow), and a qualitative advance as well, signified by the way in which the currency of many exchanges became the US dollar rather than the barter or rubles of the informal economy. This development occurred against a background of increasing economic difficulty for the population, and the growth of begging on the streets, not just by those referred to contemptuously by Russians as 'gypsies' but by ethnic Russians as well. The contrast between the belief that people were getting rich through trading, a view strengthened by the price rises that went with inflation, while others were forced to beg was significant. It tapped into the message that Soviet propaganda had been projecting for seventy years, that capitalists were criminals sucking the blood of the ordinary people, and helped define popular attitudes to this new wave of street-based commerce. For many, the attitude was summed up by the term often used to refer to the new entrepreneurs collectively, 'mafia'. The description of those engaged in private trade as belonging to the 'mafia' was not a positive encomium. The term 'mafia' in Russian did not refer to an organised criminal structure like it does in Italy, but had a broader provenance and, during the late 1980s and early 1990s meant any sort of activity that may have been criminal in nature but was actually merely outside the norm. Thus by using this term, ordinary Soviet citizens were characterising the early development of private trading as criminal activity. They did not like it, but given the collapse of state infrastructure, they had little option but to use it where they could. Of course very often they could not make use of it because they were priced out of the market or did not possess dollars, something which only increased their negative view of it. But what is important here for the emergence of a new economic bourgeoisie, there was a strong popular perception that its activities were illegitimate. Thus 'biznesmen' had low social esteem and were not popularly trusted.[12]

The weakness of trust was one factor that opened the way for the involvement of organised crime in business affairs.[13] There has been significant sensationalism and exaggeration of the extent and scale of Russian criminal activity,[14] but despite this it is clear that organised criminal gangs have been active in Russia in the post-Soviet period. It is not necessary to explore the origins of organised crime here,[15] but it is important to recognise that the end of the USSR created increased opportunities for such activity. Part of this was the general decline in the capacity of the state effectively to police society. As the borders became more porous, internal economic controls broke down, and the scope for private economic activity expanded (initially through Gorbachev's reforms), increased room was created for organised crime to play a part. Smuggling of products made abroad joined theft from workplaces as a major source for goods on the informal market. Organised gangs consolidated territories within which they held sway, and the major cities were informally divided into sectors, in each of which the informal economy was dominated by a different gang. Furthermore, with the emergence of private business, a new arena of criminal activity opened up, the provision of protection and security to the new private sector. This has been discussed in Chapter 3, but what is important here is that it added an extra dimension to the climate of uncertainty within which new business had to function. The prevalence of criminal organisations seeking to extort money from business compounded on itself as business sought their own forms of security through private protection arrangements. This sort of situation increased the uncertainty for business both in terms of its physical survival and its bottom line; such a cost was a real impost on its profit margins.

Within this general context of uncertainty, the natural propensity of businessmen to seek whatever advantage they could get for their businesses was heightened. Given the origins of many of them within the official Soviet structure and the tradition of seeing the state as a public utility, it was only natural that they should look to that structure for support in terms of its provision of services, resources, and opportunities. In principle, there is no reason why state origins should mean a continuing relationship between the state and the former officials and employees now embarked on a business career. However in practice, such links frequently were maintained and were used to help sustain the new businessmen in the difficult environment. Many state officials were likely to respond positively to this because they were used to a situation in which official position involved both the right to determine access to resources and the capacity to use that position to personal advantage. In addition, the difficult economic circumstances encouraged them to seek extra sources of income to their salaries. State officials could thus see themselves as the possible protectors or patrons of emergent business, a view consistent with the continuing importance of personal contacts represented in the Soviet institution of blat.[16] Such contacts often were crucial in gaining access to bureaucratic decision-making and therefore to achieving favourable decisions and concessions, especially from tax, customs, banking, and regional authorities.[17] What is important about this is that state officials were able to use their offices to rent seek, exchanging official permissions, and privileges for personal benefits. There was little incentive for officials to restrain the activities of business because of the expectation that cooperation would lead to kickbacks. A 1993 study of small business showed that their main problems involved obtaining premises and special permits, registering ventures, and submitting tax and financial reports, and that these were resolved overwhelmingly through personal contacts.[18] Business was reliant on state licences and regulations for both its establishment and day-to-day functioning; the establishment and early setting up of a company, where registration and licensing, access to premises, the supply of services like telephone connections, and vulnerability to continued checking by such bodies as health and fire authorities, could be subject to the good will of individual officials. The support of such officials was also often crucial for the ability of a company to make substantial profits. In the early 1990s, many companies benefited from state subsidies and credits, from tax waivers, and from import and export licences and quotas. Such licences were major sources of income for the raw materials producers, who could produce their product cheaply and then sell on the world market at higher international rates. Individual decisions by state officials at all levels could greatly benefit particular companies or groups and disadvantage others; the presidential decree making Ingushetia an off-shore tax haven, the granting to the Orthodox Church of the right to import alcohol and cigarettes duty free, the appointment of some banks as authorised banks, and the agreement to the loans for shares scheme are all examples of such decisions. Also important could be protection. The careers of three of the oligarchs, Khodorkovsky, Potanin, and Gusinsky, were all facilitated by the assistance given to these people by higher level protectors within the political structure. At lower levels, state officials have also often provided protection for business.[19] Businesses subsidised police activities (or the policemen's pockets) or Ministry of Interior forces or the security services in exchange for protection. Sometimes this took the form of the officers moonlighting in their own time, but it could also simply be payment for the officials to actually carry out their formal duties.[20]

Officials could use their offices to make life easy or difficult for would-be entrepreneurs. Indeed, personal relations underpinned the entire framework upon which business rested—access to resources, to information, and to capital, questions of supply, marketing, and financing could often be resolved through personal contacts in the bureaucracy. A survey of bankers showed that they saw social connections as 'the core foundation of doing business in present-day Russia, as a prerequisite for each step of obtaining a licence for business, and as a condition of each successful business operation'.[21] A 1994 study showed that more entrepreneurs saw personal contacts as the most effective means of influencing power than any other form of influence,[22] even if at times this took the form of bribery.[23] Acceptance by officials of bribes from businessmen was often an essential part of the way the businessman–bureaucrat relationship worked, with the passing of money often seen as the only way of getting a satisfactory outcome from the bureaucracy. Although the scale of this is impossible to measure,[24] it is generally acknowledged to be vast; Putin even acknowledged the existence of widespread corruption among bureaucrats in his address to the Duma in April 2005.[25] A survey conducted in mid-1999 showed that some 38% of firms' owners/managers believed that they had been adversely affected by the way in which laws or decrees had been bought by private parties.[26] While personal contacts in the state and decisions that thereby ensue in every country have differential effects upon the business population, what made this so significant in Russia was the size of the profits that could be involved, the blatant way in which influence was often wielded, and the fact that given the harsh business conditions, such privileges could be the difference between business survival and failure. Business reliance upon incentives to gain favours and support from officials, in particular access to state services and resources, was intrinsic to the early development of business and projected the state into a primary role in shaping and sustaining business development.

The capacity of individual businessmen to deal with the state, and ultimately the sort of relationship that developed, was not the same for all entrepreneurs. Initially, all sought to take advantage of whatever privileges and advantages they could get from the state and its officers, but their capacity to do this successfully depended for the most part upon their location within the networks of association and influence that were the legacy of the Soviet period. Those who had particular contacts or who held influential positions at the time of the Soviet collapse were much better placed to extract advantage from the state than those who lacked these qualities. The course of spontaneous privatisation, discussed in Chapter 3, is an obvious reflection of this.[27] So too is the way some businessmen were able massively to enrich themselves through the later processes of privatisation. This also had a dimension related to the origins of the economic bourgeoisie. While those who came from within or had prior contacts with influential circles in the Soviet administrative structure were well-placed to utilise those contacts in pursuing their businesses, those who lacked such an official entrée were forced to negotiate favours or concessions with lower level officials. Lacking personal access to official circles, they tended to be more dependent upon the opportunities and imperatives flowing from the officials' positions unmediated by considerations of past association than were those who possessed contacts stemming from their former careers. This difference between personalised access based on past association and that resting purely on present contingency also often had a link to the size of business. Generally the larger businesses were those that initially got their start from the large-scale acquisition of state resources, which usually went with the existence of high-level contacts within officialdom. It was much more difficult for businesses which began de novo to achieve such size, and most lacked high-level patrons within the state structure. They were more reliant on negotiations with officials, and often those at the local and regional level rather than those at the national level. Personal contacts, although as the period wore on the Soviet provenance of these became less important, have remained significant as the source of extra resources, both administrative and material, from the state.

Movement between business and the state reinforced the potential for such contacts. The movement of figures with a business background into government was noted in Chapter 3. While there is no certainty that people who moved from a particular field of economic life into governmental circles would act as the representative of that field once in government, they would at least bring to their new role an understanding of and presumably sympathy for their former area of work. Many people who made this transition did act consciously as the advocate of the sector from which they came. This does not mean that they pursued its interests to the exclusion of all else, but that they generally sought to ensure that government action did not prejudice the interests of their home sectors but as far as possible benefited them. These people did try to serve the interests of 'their' sectors; for example, it is not surprising that in the early 1990s while Chernomyrdin and successive people from the oil industry held government office that the conditions existed enabling this industry to generate significant resources from the export of its products and through government tax concessions. These people should not be seen as the prisoners of their sectors. As David Lane has declared with regard to the Ministry of Fuel and Power,[28] they were both supervisor and advocate, with the former role often overshadowing the latter. But even though such people did not act as mere ciphers for their sectors, their fundamental loyalty to the sorts of policies that benefited the sectors with which they were associated means that the course of Russian politics has often been interpreted in terms of the changing balance between these different economic forces.[29]

These have been described in a number of ways. Shleifer and Treisman[30] have cited the view that by 1995 the government was 'thoroughly penetrated by the main economic lobby groups, from agriculture to the oil and gas sector'. Kryshtanovskaia[31] has argued that most branches of the economy have their own politician in charge, pointing to Chernomyrdin and the heat and power complex, Soskovets and metals, Davydov and export–import trade, and Gerashchenko and finance. Graham[32] refers to Chernomyrdin and the energy sector, Korzhakov–Soskovets and metallurgy (especially aluminium), and Chubais–Berezovsky and finance. Chervyakov[33] points to Soskovets and industrial capital, Aleksandr Zaveriukha and agro-industrial capital, and Chubais and finance capital.[34] Others have pointed to Chernomyrdin (fuel and energy sector, especially gas),[35] Shafranik (fuel and energy), Chubais (financial sector),[36] Soskovets (heavy industry), Kadannikov (industry), Shumeiko (defence industry), Skokov (defence industry), and Korzhakov (defence industry). Such people often acted as energetic advocates of the interests of 'their' sector, but they did not always introduce measures to further those interests. For example, while Chernomyrdin blocked the attempt in 1993 to break up Gazprom and destroy its virtual monopoly,[37] in 1994–95 Chernomyrdin persuaded the oil and gas executives to freeze their prices on oil and oil derivatives and resume supply to their debtors, and in 1995 the oil industry lost many of its tax concessions, while excise taxes for unprocessed oil and petrol were raised;[38] he also increased the energy sector's tax liability and introduced the ruble corridor (a semi-fixed exchange rate whereby the ruble was to be allowed to fluctuate only within the range of 4,300–4,900 to the US dollar, which was bad for exporters of natural resources) and in 1996 folded Gazprom's tax-free stabilisation fund into the federal budget.[39] Other politicians were, at times, similarly constrained. Nevertheless, their role as advocates for their sectors was generally acknowledged, and even though the shifting power balances within the political elite may have at times limited their capacity to act positively for their sectors' interests,[40] they could act as channels of access for business interests into the government. But they were channels of access into government, not full-blown representatives of business in the governmental process;[41] this movement of businessmen into government did not constitute an integration of business and political circles. There was no pattern of movement, nor was there a real consistency of outcome as one would have expected had this constituted a systematic process. Rather there was a situation of business gaining some representation in the executive arm of the state from time to time as people from business backgrounds entered the government when the opportunity arose.[42] But this was much more random than systematic.

There has also been movement the other way.[43] People who had been active in politics sometimes entered the business world when their political activities had ended, bringing with them the personal contacts in the bureaucracy they had from their earlier career. Leading government figures who have transferred in this way include: former Minister of Foreign Trade Petr Aven entered Alfa Bank,[44] First Deputy Finance Minister Andrei Vavilov became president of MFK Bank, Minister of Agriculture Viktor Khlystun was first vice president of Agroprombank, former privatisation head Anatolii Chubais became the head of United Energy Systems, former government head of privatisation Alfred Kokh became the head of Gazprom-Media, and former first deputy head of the Presidential Administration Aleksandr Kazakov joined the Gazprom management.[45] Among those not holding formal government positions but playing a major political role were Yeltsin's former press secretary Viacheslav Kostikov who became deputy director of Media-Most, and former executive director of Our Home is Russia Leonid Vid who became chair of the board of directors of Alfa Bank.[46] In addition, some government figures have held seats on different companies' boards as representatives of the state (thereby reflecting the state shareholding); for example, while he was first deputy prime minister in 1993 Oleg Soskovets joined bank Menatep and was reportedly influential in bringing about the bank's gains in the investment auctions of 1994–95,[47] while in the mid-1990s, Gazprom's board included First Deputy Finance Minister Vavilov, Deputy Economy Minister Yevsiukov, First Deputy Prime Minister for Fuel and Energy Kostiunin, and Deputy President of the Presidential Securities Committee Vasiliev. Under Yeltsin, there was no pattern or regularised system whereby former political activists have entered business. It appears rather to have been an idiosyncratic process, with individuals taking advantage of opportunities that arose.

This sort of career shift seems to have become more systematic under Putin. During his first term, Putin placed associates in some leading companies: for example, Viakhirev was replaced by Aleksei Miller at the head of Gazprom, while Sviazinvest gained a new head in Valerii Yashin.[48] This process of replacing leading businessmen was taken a step further in Putin's second term. Not content with placing people who had been associated with him in the past into leading positions in business, he now injected members of the presidential administration and advisers (compared with Yeltsin who had mainly sent ministers to hold such positions[49]) into business posts, which they held while continuing to carry out their official functions. Leading examples of this were his chief of staff Dmitrii Medvedev as chairman of the board of Gazprom, Igor Sechin as chairman of the board of Rosneft, Vladislav Surkov as a board member of Transnefteprodukt, Viktor Ivanov as head of the boards of Almaz-Antei and Aeroflot, Igor Shuvalev as a board member of Russian Railways, Yevgeny Shkolov as a board member of Transneft, Aleksandr Voloshin (Medvedev's predecessor) was re-appointed as non-executive chairman of UES, while Putin's press secretary became a member of the board of Russia's leading television company, First Channel. This sort of pattern, which involved political figures from Putin's own administration moving into business while continuing to fulfil their political functions, does represent a significant change and constitutes a much tighter integration between business and government circles.[50] It also expanded the potential for the use of personal contacts to benefit business operations.

The State as Shaper of the Economy

In all systems, the state is directly involved in economic activity. Even when it is not itself a major producer, the state is inevitably a major consumer of goods and services produced in the non-state sector. This may be mediated through some type of administrative structure, like the Soviet planning process, or through market relations, but in either event the level of state demand for products helps to shape the broader, non-state, productive process. Furthermore, states are often involved in an ownership capacity in various sectors of the economy, even when the overriding ideology is one of private enterprise. It is, therefore, little surprise that in Russia, despite its recent background of the attempt to move away from complete state ownership, there should be continuing state involvement in major sectors of the economy. One form of this was that some state agencies and enterprises took on commercial functions and were run on commercial lines (the so-called kontserns). More importantly, throughout the 1990s, the state retained a share of ownership in many of the major companies and corporations that were established during this time; in 1996, it held a 10% share in a third of all privatised companies, more than 20% in a quarter of them, and a third share in the top fifty companies.[51] By 2000, the public-sector share of gross domestic product (GDP) remained about 30%.[52] An example of a sector where the state's presence remained significant under Yeltsin was the oil sector. Lane and Seifulmukov[53] have identified the state's shareholdings in particular companies (Table 7.1).

But if the general trend under Yeltsin was to reduce the state's role in the economy, Putin has sought to strengthen it. This was made explicit in August 2004 by a Putin decree listing 1,063 'strategic enterprises', including energy, resource extraction, and media, in which the state intended to

Table 7.1. State shareholding in oil companies (%)

	1994	1995	1996	1997
Sidanko	100	85	51	—
Vostsibneftegaz	100	85	38	—
Sibneft	—	100	51	—
Yukos	86	53	0.1	0.1
Surgutneftegaz	40.1	40.1	40.1	—
Komitek	100	100	92	<22
Lukoil	42.1	26	16.6	6.6
Norsi-Oil	—	100	85.4	45
Tatneft	46.6	46.6	35.1	20–25
Transneft	100	100	75	51
Rosneft	—	100	100	100
Tiumen Oil	—	100	91	51
Sibur	100	85	85	51
Vostochnaia Oil	100	85	85	51
Slavneft	93.5	92	90.1	56–58
Onako	100	85	85	85

maintain decisive control over ownership and management.[54] But its most remarkable aspect has been the establishment of the state's prominent role in the oil industry, brought about chiefly through the prosecution of Mikhail Khodorkovsky and the takeover of Yukos assets discussed below. This does not mean that Putin has sought re-nationalisation, but the establishment of effective state control over some companies in order to be able to have a decisive influence in key sectors of the economy.[55] By becoming a more important actor in the economy, the state is significantly altering the environment within which much of the emergent bourgeoisie is operating.

The state has also been crucial in shaping the development of business through policies it pursued. Of primary importance here were the policy changes which enabled the development of private enterprise in the first place, discussed in Chapter 3. But a number of other aspects were also significant. First, as a result of policies begun under Gorbachev, the Soviet/Russian market began to be penetrated by Western capital.[56] In particular, the law on joint ventures made provision for the involvement of Western capital in domestic production, distribution, and exchange for the first time since soon after the revolution. In practice, the scale of such involvement was not high.[57] Western enterprises generally were wary of the uncertainties of the Soviet/Russian market, but there was some investment in production. More important, because it was more obvious, was foreign involvement in the retail and service sectors. In one sense, the opening of the first MacDonalds outlet in central Moscow in 1990 is emblematic of this. Occurring as it did before the collapse of the Soviet Union, the opening of what many saw to be a paradigmatic representative of Western capital in the centre of the city seemed to be representative of a coming tide of Western investment in the domestic

Table 7.2. Inflation (%)

1991	1992	1993	1994	1995	1996	1997	1998	1999
161	2506	840	204.4	128.6	21.8	10.9	84.5	36.8

market. The gradual growth of retail outlets in central Moscow bearing the names of leading Western companies—for example, Armani, Versace, Yves St Laurent, Coca Cola, Pepsi, Snickers—presented an impression of a wave of Western involvement that belied the relative small size of that investment. As stores, including food stores selling only Western produce, sprang up, the impression of an increasing Western presence was strengthened. Thus for the emergent domestic bourgeoisie, the prospect of having to compete with established Western companies must have seemed real, and perhaps daunting. This would have reinforced their tendency to look to the state for support.

Second, a series of decisions made under Yeltsin were important for structuring this environment. The first one of these, chronologically and probably in importance, was the decision to free prices which took effect on 2 January 1992. The effect of this decision was to drive prices through the roof and to fuel inflation for years to come. According to the European Bank for Reconstruction and Development,[58] inflation, as reflected in the change in the year-end retail/consumer price level, moved as shown in Table 7.2.

The collapse in the value of the currency is also reflected in the changing ruble domestic exchange rate to the US dollar (Table 7.3).[59]

The high levels of inflation, reinforced by the currency's volatility, wiped out the populace's savings, and thereby eliminated both a potential market for the purchase of goods created by any new Russian industry and potential domestic sources of investment. It also fuelled the dollarisation of the economy early in the 1990s, a fact which automatically excluded that vast mass of the population with no ready access to dollars. Also important was the government's decision to try to dry up domestic credit, in part as an attempt to stabilise the monetary system. This policy was not completely successful because of the government's inability to control the Central Bank

Table 7.3. Exchange rate, ruble to US dollar

	1991	1992	1993	1994	1995	1996	1997	1998	1999
First quarter		179	572	1,582	4,288	4,767	5,656	6,048	23.36
Second quarter	38	134	952	1,877	4,933	4,984	5,155	6,157	24.80
Third quarter	53	177	1,028	2,165	4,469	5,266	5,821	10.36*	24.83
Fourth quarter	110	398	1,207	3,194	4,556	5,483	5,908	21.14#	

* August # December.

which, particularly under the leadership of Viktor Gerashchenko in 1992–93, continued to provide lines of credit to struggling industrial enterprises, but it nevertheless did play a part in ensuring that enterprises throughout Russia had difficulty in gaining the financing to be able to continue to operate. This contributed to a further decline in production, short working weeks, employees not being paid, and considerable hardship. Paradoxically, such economic hardship probably propelled more people to engage in private economic activity, and therefore take a step towards entering the new economic bourgeoisie, than would otherwise have been the case. Furthermore, the impression the government gave was that it was intent on introducing a market system as soon as possible regardless of the costs. The impression this created was that, from the perspective of 1992, there would be likely to be still further upheavals in the economy before it settled down into a stable pattern as the government struggled to achieve the ends it set itself.

The continuing uncertainty did not encourage long-term investment in productive capacity. The high levels of inflation generated by the freeing of prices in January 1992 reinforced by the other elements of uncertainty noted at the beginning of the chapter constituted a clear disincentive to long-term investment. This was a particular problem for heavy industry. Handicapped by their Soviet legacy of soft budget constraints, centralised planning system, and chronic under-investment in infrastructure, most enterprises were ill-prepared to enter a market system and required significant investment. However, even the government did not take the opportunity open to it through the voucher privatisation process to stimulate such investment; the winners of the auctions were meant to invest the equivalent of the purchase price in the newly acquired enterprise, but few did and the government did not enforce this. Usually such enterprises lacked both the resources and the flexibility required to function effectively in the new conditions. As a result, at least until the financial collapse of 1998, and for many of these enterprises after that event as well, Russian industry struggled, and few entrepreneurs whose activity was either restricted to or based largely within this sector made money. Accordingly, enterprise directors during 1992 pressed for continuing state subsidies to their enterprises and for a loose monetary policy. They were successful in this throughout much of 1992 and into 1993,[60] reflecting the strength of their lobby in legislative organs, the convictions of new (from July 1992) Central Bank of Russia head Viktor Gerashchenko, and concerns about the levels of inter-enterprise debt. Such debt levels had been rising astronomically during 1992; in the absence of both investment and a vigorous domestic market, most enterprises had few sources of income, and so in order to continue operating, they had to rely upon credit from those with whom they dealt. Given that this situation applied to all enterprises, the levels of debt rose inexorably. Despite government relief of these debts at the end of 1992, enterprise debt levels once again were rising during 1993. This situation was unsustainable, and was exacerbated by the imposition of a tighter monetary policy from May 1993. By the mid-1990s, much of the arrears in payment took the form of unpaid energy bills;[61] major energy suppliers like Gazprom owed substantial levels of unpaid tax to the state, but the government prevailed upon them not to cut off power supplies to their indebted customers in return for some toleration of their own unpaid taxes,[62] the maintenance of export privileges and tax exemptions, and considerable managerial freedom to run their companies as they saw fit.[63] By August 1995, the fuel and energy complex was responsible for 73% of the debt to the federal budget.[64] In effect, under state pressure, the energy sector was subsidising industry, and thereby keeping it afloat.

The government realised that its policies were contributing to the inability of business to gain the investment it needed not just to grow but actually to survive, and in an attempt to bolster industrial performance, it began from the end of 1993 to promote the development of industry-led financial industrial groups (FIGs). The FIGs were essentially combinations of different types of enterprises combining together in an attempt to strengthen their performance through diversification of activities and concentration of management.[65] They were officially promoted by the government, which enacted a number of programs, laws, and presidential decrees promising, among other things, tax breaks, the transfer of state shares in member companies to the new parent FIG, loan guarantees, lower reserve requirements for participating banks, and privileged involvement in state investment projects.[66] Such groups were of two sorts: bank-led (see below) and industry-led.[67] The industry-led FIGs were generally weak organisations from the outset; in the words of one scholar, they 'typically combined poor regional banks with suffering industrial or agricultural enterprises in an unsuccessful attempt to use their collective power to lobby the government for more money and to attract outside investment'.[68] Through diversification, the FIGs spread the economic risks of operation, and they enabled enterprise owners to maintain their control over the activities of the enterprise. But in practice, many of the FIGs existed only on paper or were very weak and unable to function without access to state resources and privileges, yet many of the government's promises of assistance were not kept.[69] The FIGs typified the fate of much Russian industry prior to the economic collapse of 1998: unable to function effectively in the new economic circumstances without state support. But the small amount of state support that was forthcoming was insufficient to overcome the problems to which other state policies had contributed.

If government policy retarded long-term investment, it positively facilitated another form of economic activity, speculation, and rent seeking,[70] with many firms engaging in this type of activity instead of seeking to make profits in the market. The uncertain economic conditions drove all of those seeking to make money into the search for short-term, quick turn-around profit-making ventures. This favoured export-oriented sectors of the economy like the energy sector and other raw materials exporters, and disadvantaged those operating in the domestic market. A number of forms were significant:[71]

1. Arbitrage, or the taking advantage of different prices for the same commodity in different markets, and in particular buying cheaply at fixed state prices and selling at higher free-market (often international) prices. Purchase of raw materials and natural resources at the cheap domestic price (less than 1% of the world market price) and sale abroad at higher foreign prices was a common strategy. Lukoil, for example, was established just at the time when best use could be made of such opportunities, but all of the oil companies made money through the manipulation of exports.[72] With the information available to different markets incomplete and sometimes contradictory, those who could get inside knowledge or had connections could make substantial amounts on individual transactions. Differences in the official ruble:dollar exchange rate and the market rate was one particularly lucrative avenue for arbitrage, at least until the introduction of the ruble corridor in July 1995.[73]

2. State import subsidies and subsidised credits. In the former, for example, importers of essential foods paid only 1% of the official rate of import duties, while in the latter enterprises were accorded government credits at subsidised interest rates, which virtually amounted to gifts to those enterprises.[74] The fuel and energy sector was especially able to take advantage of this.[75]

3. Use of short-term state loans at nominal interest rates to finance export deals and then repayment of the loans in inflation-fuelled devalued rubles.[76] Banks also used the deposits of state enterprises (usually held without interest) and of the state itself to finance such deals; they also used such money to purchase dollars, invest it short-term, and receive increased payments in rubles as a result of inflation. The absence of a treasury system to handle the revenues and payments of state agencies forced the state to deposit funds in commercial banks, thus creating a continuing source of cheap credit for those banks. As one observer said, 'Tax receipts, customs duties, and pension payments, for example, are typically used as 'free loans' by banks, who hold on to them for as long as several months before passing them along to the treasury.'[77]

Many of the opportunities for such manipulation emerged in 1992, when the government passed out privileges like direct subsidies and credits, tax waivers, and import and export licences; particularly important was the massive reduction in export duties on raw materials in 1993 following Chernomyrdin's appointment as prime minister.[78] The main sectors to benefit

Table 7.4. Number of commercial banks

1991	1992	1993	1994	1995	1996	1997	1998	1999	2000
1,360	1,713	2,019	2,517	2,295	2,030	1,697	1,476	1,349	1,316

from rent seeking were energy, agriculture, trade, and banking, while many former state enterprises were also able to profit.[79] Such rent seeking relied significantly upon the sort of privileged access usually associated with personal connections with state officials.

Currency speculation was so easy and so profitable that it was a major factor fuelling the development of the banks.[80] During the first post-Soviet decade, the number of licensed commercial banks fluctuated as shown in Table 7.4.[81]

Many of these banks were small, under-capitalised, and were not interested in investing in industry,[82] even those that had been established by enterprises with that as their specific aim. Most banks made their early money through what were essentially speculative activities, a form of operation that could only be stimulated by the involvement of the Central Bank in similarly shady activities.[83] With little scope for profitable investment in industry or agriculture,[84] banks sought profits through speculative activity and association with the state. Until 'Black Tuesday' (11 October 1994) when the value of the ruble dropped more than 20% in one day, and the introduction of the ruble corridor in July 1995 brought some stability to the value of the ruble, the fluctuations in the currency created significant scope for speculation. The basic mechanism here was to transform rubles into either foreign currency or goods that could be sold for foreign currency, and then reconvert that currency into rubles at the new, higher exchange rate that would result from inflation. This process could be enacted through a variety of types of activity: currency exchange, trade transactions, inter-bank credit operations, and the contraction of loans.

One particularly important vehicle for bank profits was through their activity as 'authorised banks'.[85] These were banks that were authorised to transfer credits from the Central Bank of Russia or other leading government body to specific enterprises or sectors. As well as gaining a 3% commission on the transaction and perhaps some income as a result of bribery from the recipient, banks could delay passing on the credits while inflation eroded their value, thereby skimming off the difference, invest the credits on the short-term money market, or even re-direct the credits to enterprises co-owned by the bank or its managers.[86] Not all banks gained 'authorised' status, something usually acquired as a result of political contacts; for example, Most Bank and Bank Menatep were the first authorised banks for the Moscow administration of Yurii Luzhkov, reflecting the close links between Luzhkov and Most Bank owner Gusinsky.[87] Furthermore, Russian banks profited from the continuing exclusion of foreign banks from much of their market in the first half of the decade, something the commercial banks lobbied hard to achieve.

The reduction in the easy profits that came from currency speculation after 1995 was in part compensated for by three developments: the growth of the GKO market, the development of bank-led FIGs, and the loans for shares scheme. In May 1993, the government first issued GKOs, or short-term state treasury bills.[88] The government soon became heavily dependent upon the banks purchasing successive issues of GKOs, which were offered at very high interest rates; between 1994 and 1996 the returns from GKOs far exceeded the inflation rate, with the rate at one point at more than 150% in real terms.[89] Access to these GKOs was restricted, and those banks with access invested heavily; some of the authorised banks even used those government funds to invest on the short-term market, thereby effectively lending the state its own money.[90] Although ultimately the way the Russian government financed the GKO scheme was unsustainable, using the revenues generated by the current sale to pay off GKOs coming due from earlier sales,[91] in the interim it was a source of great profits to the banks that were involved. These banks were effectively being subsidised by the state. However, these banks suffered severely at the time of the 1998 default.

Bank-led FIGs were created by leading banks in an endeavour to bolster their already substantial position in the Russian market.[92] These emerged between 1995 and 1997, although banks had been building their holdings in diverse companies since privatisation began in 1992.[93] The major ones were focused on Bank Menatep, Oneksimbank, Alfa Bank, Most Bank, LogoVaz, Rossiiskii Kredit, Inkombank, and SBS-Agro Bank.[94] These banks formed the nucleus of often complicated networks of companies that were tied together by webs of ownership and control that were not always easy to disentangle. They constituted the consolidation of wealth and power, although they do not appear to have resulted in substantial increases in bank investment in production.[95] It was principally the leaders of these bank-led FIGs who were initially known collectively as 'the oligarchs', discussed below.

One of the principal mechanisms for the construction of such combines was the loans for shares scheme beginning in mid-1995.[96] Under this scheme, leading banks gave a loan to the government, as collateral accepting the right to manage the state's large parcels of shares in some of the most blue-chip of Russian companies. If the government did not repay the loan (and there seems to have been no intention that the loan would be repaid), the creditor bank was able to auction the shares. The ensuing auctions were for the most part rigged;[97] the bank which held the shares as collateral usually ran the auctions as well as bidding in them, and was able to see the bids of its competitors before submitting its own bid. Rivals were sometimes barred on a technicality, auctions could be held at times and in locations that gave rivals little chance of attending, and foreign interests were generally excluded from participating.[98] The banks gained control over these companies at knock-down prices, with the winning bids being only marginally higher than the minimum bid. The loans for shares scheme turned the successful banks into giant industrial–financial conglomerates and thereby increased their importance in the economy generally. It was a clear case of the state providing certain businessmen with an opportunity to enrich themselves further by getting state resources at knock-down prices.

What is clear is that the wealth and power of the banks was directly linked to their relationship with the state, and in particular the state's reliance upon the banks and the latter's ability to use this to milk resources from the state. This is reflected most clearly in the way in which the state used the commercial banks as a surrogate treasury system through the notion of 'authorised banks', and, in the absence of a reliable flow of income tax, as a source of operating cash through the GKO and the loans for shares schemes. The government also looked to the banks for political/campaigning support, most spectacularly in the 1996 presidential election. This dependence was important for the banks' power. However, the economic position of some of the banks suffered a severe setback with the financial crisis of 1998.[99] Still heavily reliant on GKOs and deeply in debt, many banks could not withstand the government devaluation and default of August 1998; by spring 1999, 200 banks had lost their licences, including five of the big private banks— Tokobank, Imperial, Inkombank, Oneksimbank, and Bank Menatep. However, the banking sector as a whole survived, principally because most of the second tier, smaller banks had not been so exposed to government debt.

Following the 1998 financial crisis (and the subsequent rise in oil prices), companies resting on the so-called natural monopolies, especially in the energy sector—oil, gas, and electricity—became even more prominent than they had been before, displacing finance as the lead sector of the economy. These companies, all created out of the Soviet supply structure, became major economic forces[100] because of the control they exercised over power supply and, especially in the case of gas and oil, the income they could earn from exports and their consequent potential as a major source of taxation revenues. The most important of these was Gazprom. This was created in 1989 when the minister in charge of this sector, future Prime Minister Viktor Chernomyrdin, brought the whole gas industry into a single state-owned company of which he became the chair.[101] When the company was privatised, the state retained a 40% interest,[102] but under an agreement between the government headed by Chernomyrdin and Gazprom headed by his former deputy Rem Viakhirev,[103] the latter had full management rights over the state's stake.[104] The central place Gazprom occupied in the state's economy (especially in terms of its contribution to the state's tax revenue; Gazprom controls 95% of the extraction and 100% of the distribution of gas) plus the established links into the government, especially while Chernomyrdin was prime minister, meant that Gazprom was a major player on the Russian scene and its director was a leading figure in elite councils. This role was played by Viakhirev until he was replaced in May 2001 by Aleksei Miller, a former deputy energy minister and Putin associate.[105] The gas elite has been highly united and disciplined, and has been referred to as the 'gas generals'.[106] The electricity monopoly, UES, was privatised with the state retaining 53% of the shares, and in 1998 Anatolii Chubais became its head, thereby adding economic resources to the political contacts that had been so important in the power he had been able to wield. The oil sector,[107] in contrast to gas, was not consolidated into one monopoly outfit but was divided by the government into fourteen vertically integrated companies. The so-called 'oil barons', therefore, remained independent and competed against one another, although this has taken place within a common ethos or spirit of corporatism.[108] The largest and most powerful company was Lukoil,[109] established in 1991 by Vagit Alekperov, a former deputy minister of the oil industry. Taking advantage of the break-up of the Soviet oil empire at the end of the Soviet period, he established Lukoil as a vertically integrated company separate from the state, but enjoying special export privileges attributed by some to Alekperov's close personal association with Chernomyrdin.[110] The company was able to exploit its position and propel Alekperov into the circle of powerful businessmen at the apex of Russian business life.[111] Mikhail Khodorkovsky and Roman Abramovich were also powerful figures in the oil industry, resting on, respectively, Yukos and Sibneft Oil Companies. Under Yeltsin, such companies functioned largely outside state control; for example, a major source of income for many oil companies was involvement in transfer pricing, which involved declaring their profits in low-tax regions rather than the regions of production or of the true location of the head office.[112] However as a result of the changes brought about by Putin, the state has become a major (but not monopoly) player in the oil sector (see below).

During the 1990s, the natural monopolies, and major resource companies along with the FIGs, constituted the upper reaches of what was essentially a bifurcated economy. The upper levels of that economy were dominated by integrated business groups and conglomerates, often combining a diversity of interests within the one broad business structure.[113] They held a dominant position in the Russian economy; according to the World Bank, in 2003, twenty-two large business groups controlled some 40% of industrial output, more than all of the other private owners combined.[114] Such groups often held a monopolistic or oligopolistic position within their domestic markets, in part a direct result of government encouragement as, especially under Chernomyrdin, the government encouraged the construction of the integrated business groups.[115] The domestic markets in which such conglomerates have operated have been controlled by the small number of sellers and by a tendency to rely on rent seeking as either a substantial supplement to or a replacement for searching for profits through free-market operations. In this sense, the upper levels of the economy have remained tied closely to the state, since it is in part the relationship with the state that has generated the rent seeking strategies that have been so common. However, many of these conglomerates also operate in international markets where their size does not give them dominance and where the Russian state is more restricted in what it can do. Nevertheless, these international operations remain underwritten by the benefits of state connections at home and by Russian diplomacy abroad; for example, Gazprom and the oil companies have been particularly active in seeking to expand their activities in the countries of the Commonwealth of Independent States (CIS), Eastern Europe and the West with the assistance of the Russian state.[116] The power possessed by these big business conglomerates allied to the close relations that many of them have had with the state have ensured that they have been major shapers of the course of Russian economic development, especially after the economic crisis of 1998 and subsequent rise in oil prices.

The lower levels of the economy have not been characterised by monopolistic or oligopolistic markets but by smaller businesses.[117] In late 2004, there were 920,000 small companies, an increase of 30% since 2000, accounting for 10–12% of GDP.[118] The markets within which these businesses operate tend not to be dominated by single large entities, and although rent seeking is still a feature, they are driven much more by the struggle to make a profit through the market. Where rent seeking does occur, this usually involves relations with middle- and lower-level officials of the sort noted earlier in the chapter rather than those at the apex, and is designed to facilitate business and give a competitive edge rather than to replace competition in the market. While the rhythms of the functioning of this part of the economy are not completely shaped by what happens at the upper levels of the economy, there is obviously an important connection. The 1998 financial crisis is the best indicator of this. Although it was brought on in part by developments in the upper level of the economy, it had a dramatic effect in shaping the way the lower levels operated. The effect of the crisis was to change the balance of advantage between imported and domestically produced goods in favour of the latter. This stimulated Russian domestic production, including industrial production, changed the pattern of retail by substituting many domestic for imported goods, and helped to make small business again appear as a potentially profitable enterprise.

So unlike in most of the other historical cases of bourgeois emergence, in Russia the state was an important shaper of the outlines of Russian business through its role in privatisation (including the formation of vertically integrated concerns like Gazprom, Lukoil, and UES), the part access to the state played in generating profits for the new business class, and through it being a major point of origin of the new business class; with many companies, including major banks, being formed from within state structures, the linkage was explicit. The networks of personalised links and contacts that bound business and state officials together at all levels of the structure generated a high degree of integration between the business and state sectors. With, at one level, both the shape and the nature of the business sector and, at another level, the prospects of success for individual business enterprises, largely moulded by the relationship with the state, the development of business was more strongly determined by the state in Russia than in any of the other countries under review. The relationship with the state was fundamental to the emergence and development of Russian business. This sort of almost organic relationship where businessmen sought their interests substantially through direct relations with state officials was an important factor undercutting the importance of the more formal state and lobby organisations as vehicles for business interests. It also reinforced the continuing weakness of state infrastructural power.

Business Control of the State?

The way in which business has been able to feed off the state has encouraged many to argue that the state was controlled by the upper reaches of business. The principal form in which this argument has been advanced has been in terms of the oligarchs.

Central Government and the Oligarchs

Much of the discussion of the role of business in post-Soviet Russia has been distorted by a focus upon the oligarchs.[119] Accepting at face value Berezovsky's comment in 1996 that seven bankers and businessmen owned half of the economy and were able to get their way in government,[120] many have seen these as the rulers of Russia; one author even referred to the oligarchs during Yeltsin's illness as 'Russia's real rulers'.[121] There were also comments about a 'bankirshchina', or reign of the seven bankers.[122] But just as that financial–industrial elite that has commonly been known as the oligarchs is not typical of the vast mass of the emergent Russian business class, so the political influence they have been able to wield at times has not been typical of business as a whole. Nevertheless, these individuals, at times acting collectively, have been able to exercise significant influence in the political realm at some points during the post-1991 period.

The term 'oligarch' was specifically coined to refer to those businessmen who combined together in 1996 to rescue and sponsor Yeltsin's re-election campaign, but was later broadened to embrace a relatively small number of businessmen who came to head the biggest and most important financial–industrial conglomerates in the country. Membership of the group has been fluid, with different candidates being popularly suggested as belonging to it at different times. Those businessmen initially identified as oligarchs were Boris Berezovsky, Mikhail Fridman (and Petr Aven), Vladimir Gusinsky, Mikhail Khodorkovsky, Vladimir Potanin, Alexander Smolensky, and Vladimir Vinogradov. For most of this initial wave of oligarchs, control over a bank was crucial to the accumulation of their wealth and power: Fridman/Aven and Alfa Bank, Gusinsky and Most Bank, Khodorkovsky and Bank Menatep, Potanin and Oneksimbank, Smolensky and SBS-Agro Bank, and Vinogradov and Inkombank; only Berezovsky was not centrally involved in banking. Berezovsky began his business career by establishing automobile dealerships, and then extended into banking, media, air travel, and oil. Fridman began in import–export and arbitrage and moved into banking and construction. Gusinsky was involved in banking, media, and real estate, Khodorkovsky in banking, oil, petrochemicals, transport, and construction, Potanin in banking, oil, petrochemicals, nickel, transport, and media, Smolensky in banking, agriculture, retailing, construction, and media, and Vinogradov in banking, confectionary, metallurgy, and aircraft. The oligarchs were industrial–financial magnates with diverse interests but, in the case of this first group, based principally upon finance and bank operations. They were also characterised by close, and for some even intimate, relations with the political sphere, discussed more fully below. Indeed, these links were central to their rise, to the wealth they were able to obtain, and to the power they were able to wield in the mid-late 1990s.

The sources of oligarch influence have essentially been twofold. First, the wealth and economic resources that they have been able to accumulate. Most of these oligarchs made their start during the Soviet period, principally through involvement in trade or banking operations in companies spun off from state enterprises or the bureaucracy. During voucher privatisation, many were able to expand their holdings and develop their resource base. Usually by using a combination of insider contacts, skill at manipulating the conditions favourable for arbitrage and speculation, and a bit of luck, the oligarchs were able to build up impressive financial–industrial structures in a relatively short time.[123] What made their wealth and power politically so important was that at the time it was being consolidated, the government was suffering from a chronic shortage of funds because, in part, of its inability to collect taxation revenue. As a result, while these people's economic positions were becoming stronger, that of the state was weakening, a conjunction of trends that significantly enhanced their political leverage. It was this, among other things, that was instrumental in the emergence of the loans for shares scheme in 1995. Another aspect of their resources was the influence that some of them were able to exercise through the media that they either owned or controlled; both major television channels and a range of newspapers and magazines were in oligarch hands by the middle of the decade: Gusinsky's Most Bank had founded NTV Television and the newspaper *Segodnia* by 1993 and by 1997 his broad portfolio of media interests (which now included four major newspapers—*Segodnia, Obshchaia Gazeta, Sem' Dnei,* and *Itogi*) had been consolidated into one company, Media-Most. By 1996, Berezovsky controlled two leading television stations (ORT and TV6) and the newspapers *Nezavisimaia Gazeta, Kommersant,* and *Novye Izvestiia,* while Potanin's Inkombank controlled *Komsomol'skaia Pravda, Izvestiia, Russkii Telegraf,* and *Ekspert.*[124] These magnates used the media they controlled to campaign publicly for their own interests, using biased reporting, one-sided comment, and even outright lies to strengthen their cases and attack their perceived opponents. The one-sided treatment of Yeltsin's 1996 election campaign and the unrestrained attacks during the so-called 'bankers' war' of 1997 were the most egregious instances of what was a common practice.

Second, contacts with the political elite. It is not unusual in most societies for those with economic power and control over significant resources to have personal contacts with the political elite. But in Russia, this propensity was enhanced by the way in which leading oligarchs owed their emergence to patronage and support from within the politico-administrative apparatus; for example, Smolensky entered commercial life by establishing a construction cooperative on party orders in 1987, Khodorkovsky gained high-level support and protection from within the Komsomol and in 1992 became an advisor to the minister of fuel and energy and through this moved into the oil industry, Berezovsky built upon his personal relationship with the director of the AvtoVaz automobile factory and for a time First Deputy Prime Minister Kadannikov, Gusinsky's early activities were protected by officials in the apparatus of the CC and in the KGB and by Moscow mayor Yurii Luzhkov, while Potanin seems to have been assisted by officials in the Soviet Foreign Trade Ministry and banking structure.[125] While these contacts were mostly with people some rungs below the politico-administrative apex, they did give these oligarchs entrée into parts of that apparatus that were important for the development of their businesses. But there were also contacts with the highest levels of politics.[126]

One important contact was Anatolii Chubais, who was a leading economic reformer in the government and held, among others, the posts of deputy prime minister (June 1992–January 1996, March 1997–March 1998), and head of the Presidential Administration (July 1996–March 1997), and who was the driving force behind privatisation. A number of the oligarchs had known Chubais from the earliest part of the post-Soviet period,[127] and as he became more important to the question of economic reform, they sought to strengthen their contacts with him. His support was clearly crucial for the loans for shares scheme, and it was to him that they turned when searching for someone to take up the leadership of Yeltsin's re-election campaign in 1996.[128] Pyotr Aven, who had introduced Chubais to Gaidar and was a former minister of foreign economic relations, was an acquaintance of some of the oligarchs in the early 1990s, and once he left government service became a major banker in his own right (the Alfa Group). But the most important contact was that with Yeltsin himself, manifested most importantly through Berezovsky. Aven was important here too, introducing Berezovsky to Yeltsin's ghostwriter, Valentin Yumashev, who in turn brought Berezovsky into Yeltsin's circle. At that time, Yeltsin was searching for a publisher for his latest volume of memoirs, *Zapiski Prezidenta*, and Berezovsky arranged for publication of the book in Finland.[129] Berezovsky was soon invited to join the Presidents Club, which he used to increase his range of contacts within the presidential entourage.[130] But Berezovsky's main channel to the president came to be Yeltsin's daughter, Tatiana Diachenko, for whom he became a principal unofficial adviser from 1996. Mainly through his friendship with Diachenko, Berezovsky became so close to Yeltsin that he was commonly seen to be part of 'the family', the name given to the intimates of the president in the second half of the 1990s.[131]

But what really propelled the oligarchs into an influential place in the Russian polity was that principally through their efforts led by Chubais, Yeltsin was re-elected president in 1996. Through their wealth and especially the use of their media outlets, they transformed a lack lustre Yeltsin election campaign, and enabled him to leap ahead of his principal challenger, the communist Gennadii Ziuganov, and win the presidency.[132] Without their intervention, Yeltsin would probably have lost. Their involvement therefore not only changed the electoral outcome but enabled them to gain a series of privileges from the state (see below) as well as giving at least some of their number the ear of the president. This was enhanced by the way in which power was structured within Yeltsin's apparatus, and particularly the autonomy enjoyed by some of his subordinates. The roles of Korzhakov until June 1996 and Chubais until April 1998 are illustrative of this.[133] This was, of course, substantially assisted by the state of Yeltsin's health, his frequent absences, and his often limited ability to work even when not absent. The 'family' was particularly important from the mid-1990s, with many of its members having direct personal links with individual businessmen and at times acting in their interests; indeed, a number of businessmen (Berezovsky, Abramovich, Mamut) were at times part of this group. The 'family' was a potent way for some in business to gain access to high-level decision-making and to seek to use it for their own purposes.[134]

The oligarchs used their resources to exercise influence over and within the political elite. It would, however, be mistaken to believe that the oligarchs formed a collective unit or cohesive oligarchy which had a clear view of its own collective interests and acted to realise them. Certainly the oligarchs did at times act in a joint fashion. Their approach to the government over the loans for shares scheme and their insider rigging of that process (the scheme was actually devised by Potanin[135]) and their agreement to support Yeltsin's re-election are the two most obvious instances of this, although there were many other cases of cooperation among them.[136] They did contact one another to discuss issues and coordinate action, and between September 1994 and autumn 1995 many of them met on a regular basis to coordinate their activity in a club on the Sparrow Hills[137]; over the following two years, such meetings continued but on a much less regular basis.[138] However, while at one level the oligarchs had some commonality of interest, at another they were vigorous competitors. Their relationship was characterised by a high level of conflict and competition, as they juggled to achieve their interests in the fluid Russian market. The most obvious manifestations of this were the so-called 'faces in the snow' episode in November–December 1994 when conflict between Berezovsky and Gusinsky over Aeroflot led the former to mobilise the support of Korzhakov and his troops against Gusinsky,[139] and the 'bankers' war' of 1997 over Potanin's winning of the Sviazinvest auction[140]; those excluded from the loans for shares scheme (along with the managers of the enterprises slated to be privatised) also opposed this scheme. Generally throughout this time, the oligarchs mainly acted alone rather than as a single entity in pursuit of their interests; they may have been oligarchs, but there was no oligarchy.[141]

Nevertheless, it is clear that they did exercise influence and have access to the political elite at all levels of the state, where they had networks of contacts and agents. This is clear in the range of special deals, privileges, and advantages that they were able to win from government over and above the general conditions favouring arbitrage and speculation that applied to all. Much of the oligarchs' economic power and position was underpinned by loans from the state (or from statist bodies like Gazprom) on very favourable terms including in many instances the absence of any expectation that such money would be repaid. The loans for shares deal, which may in part have been agreed to by the government as a form of compensation to the banks for the reduction in the scope for speculation stemming from the introduction of the ruble corridor in July 1995, was the most egregious case of oligarch concessions from the government,[142] but others included the agreement to fix the Sviazinvest auction,[143] Berezovsky's acquisition of an effective controlling interest in ORT,[144] the rewards they gained for funding Yeltsin's 1996 election campaign,[145] and state prosecution of Anatolii Bykov to assist Oleg Deripaska's takeover of Krasnoyarsk Aluminium Factory. Oligarch power was also evident in Yeltsin's re-election in 1996 when they put capital, organisational resources and, most importantly, their control over media outlets at the disposal of the re-election forces in a way which, in the eyes of most observers, clearly compromised the integrity of the electoral process.[146] After the 1996 election, two oligarchs actually entered the government:[147] Potanin was first deputy prime minister with responsibility for financial-economic matters from August 1996 until March 1997 (during which time he was instrumental in ensuring a profitable conclusion for the banks in the loans for shares deal because the government did not repay the loans[148]), while Berezovsky was deputy secretary of the Security Council from October 1996 until November 1997 (he was removed officially because of his pursuit of his business activities while in office[149]); from May 1998 until March 1999 he was executive secretary of the CIS.[150] The oligarchs also at various times pressed for changes in the personnel of the government,[151] especially at the time of the changes in prime minister from Chernomyrdin to Kirienko (March 1998) to Primakov (August 1998), but also in the appointment of Chubais as representative to the International Monetary Fund (IMF) in June 1998.[152] Furthermore, the oligarchs were sufficiently powerful with enough support in high places to fend off attacks on their positions mounted by Deputy Prime Minister Boris Nemtsov in spring 1997 when he sought to raise utility prices and crack down on corruption in the name of 'peoples' rather than 'oligarchic capitalism',[153] and Prime Minister Kirienko in spring 1998 when he tried to force major companies, including Gazprom, to pay their tax debts.

It was during Yeltsin's second term as president (July 1996 – December 1999) that the oligarchs were most powerful.[154] Utilising the personal contacts that they had with the elite around Yeltsin, and reinforced by their ability to shape the public sphere through their media holdings, they were able to play a part in moulding the broad political agenda as well as using their position of privileged access to win further concessions for their businesses. The capacity to exercise extensive influence at this time was related to the relative weakness of the state's infrastructural power in the second half of the 1990s. A number of aspects of this are relevant. First, the decision-making process at the apex of the state structure remained fluid and under-institutionalised. While there were constitutional rules about the way institutions were meant both to function and to relate to each other, in practice considerable uncertainty continued to surround this process. Particularly important here was the role of the president and the presidential administration, and his willingness to ignore formal proprieties, to concentrate power in his office, and to make decisions either on his own or with his trusted advisers. Yeltsin's health problems and his absences from work maximised the potential influence and power of those with avenues into the elite. Second, the state was weakened by its inability to collect sufficient taxation. This was due in part to the continuing poor performance of the economy before 1998; as the economy continued to shrink, there was less money around to be collected. But there was also a problem with the state's capacity and its ability to collect those tax revenues which were its due. Chronically short of resources, the state was placed at a disadvantage compared with big business and the resources it controlled. Third, the central government exercised only uncertain leadership over much of regional Russia, with many parts of the country using the collapse of Soviet power to weaken many of their ties with Moscow. These factors all constituted serious constraints on the exercise of state power and therefore made it more vulnerable to powerful economic interests than it would otherwise have been. Such state weakness was exacerbated by Yeltsin's own political weakness, reflected in his continuing low personal popularity levels throughout the middle of the decade. In the absence of popular, and apparent electoral, support, powerful economic interests must have seemed like a good alternative to the president and those around him. So when those interests were able to call in debts incurred as a result of their part in getting Yeltsin re-elected in 1996, there were few barriers to the influence they could gain.

However, the power of the oligarchs should not be exaggerated. There is no hard evidence that their efforts to have people appointed to particular positions were always successful;[155] neither Kirienko nor Primakov was their choice as prime minister in March and August 1998, while Chubais was the obvious candidate if someone was to be sent to the IMF seeking financial assistance. Despite the effect on their interests, the oligarchs could not prevent the government from devaluing and defaulting in August 1998, although they were told in advance of those decisions.[156] In effect, the oligarchs were always powerful interests approaching government in search of measures that would benefit their businesses, and in this sense their influence was restricted to the economy and did not range across all areas of government policy.[157] The basic disunity stemming from their business interests was an important factor inhibiting their capacity collectively to control the political elite and gave that elite a degree of autonomy not reflected in the more extravagant claims for the oligarchs' power. They were better placed than most other businessmen because of their wealth and their contacts, and they were, therefore, better able to get a favourable response to their efforts. Their place is symbolised by the published meetings they held with leading government figures: with Nemtsov in April 1997 and Yeltsin in September 1997 and June 1998.[158] But although they were consulted and gave advice to the president, they did not displace the government, and they did not rule Russia. Their economic wealth and the prosperity of their businesses continued to be dependent upon the state and its officials. Many of the main business interests of the oligarchs (including resource extraction and telecommunications) were subject to state licensing, and therefore within the gift of state officials. All business activity was subject to state regulation and taxation. Question marks still remained over the sanctity of private property, especially that acquired through the shady privatisation deals of the early-mid 1990s, and it was upon such property that the oligarchs' positions depended. With all of these things subject to the potentially arbitrary whim of state officials, the oligarchs' quest for influence at the top was understandable, but it was also quite vulnerable. The oligarchs were powerful interests, not part of the rulers, and much of their economic wealth and power remained dependent upon the government. Although Berezovsky did not agree, many of his colleagues in 1997–98 saw themselves as businessmen with no direct role in politics.[159]

The power of those oligarchs still heavily dependent on banking was severely dented by the August 1998 financial crisis.[160] The economic power of individual oligarchs was reduced substantially as some leading private banks collapsed. Some oligarchs (generally those who had not diversified out of finance) were rendered bankrupt, and those who survived were made even more dependent upon state favours than they had been before: Vinogradov lost control of Inkombank (which in 1999 was declared insolvent), SBS-Agro was declared bankrupt but Smolensky survived on the basis of other assets, Khodorkovsky's Bank Menatep went into liquidation but he survived on the basis of his other interests, Gusinsky was caught up in the Kremlin-Luzhkov struggle and was ultimately a casualty of Kremlin enmity, and Potanin and Berezovsky survived on reduced assets.

The fall of many of the initial oligarchs was also reflected in the way in which the ranks of the oligarchs were transformed. By 2003, one list of oligarchs comprised: Oleg Deripaska, Roman Abramovich, Vladimir Kadannikov, Sergei Popov, Vagit Alekperov, Aleksei Mordashov, Vladimir Potanin, Aleksandr Abramov, Len Blavatnik, Mikhail Khodorkovsky, Iskander Makhmudov, Vladimir Bogdanov, Viktor Rashnikov, Igor Ziuzin, Vladimir Lisin, Zakhar Smushkin, Shafagat Tahaudinov, Mikhail Fridman, Boris Ivanishvili, Kakha Bendukidze, Vladimir Yevtushenkov, and David Yakobashvili.[161] To this group should be added the heads of the state-controlled monopolies, Gazprom's Aleksei Miller and UES' Anatolii Chubais, while Sergei Pugachev, Leonid Reiman, Vladimir Kogan, and Aleksandr Mamut were also prominent.[162] This was a very different group from the initial wave of oligarchs. Rather than being based primarily on banking and finance, for most of this group resource extraction and metallurgy were the underpinning of their wealth and power, and many of them had a regional rather than a Moscow focus.[163] Most of this group got their start during the Gorbachev period and therefore Soviet era contacts may have had some initial importance, but most were able to build up a significant base for their businesses during the 1990s wave of privatisation, including for some the loans for shares deal (Abramovich, Khodorkovsky, Potanin, Alekperov, and Bogdanov). But like the initial wave, the success of their business activities was dependent upon state privileges and concessions, especially in the form of access to both production and export licences, loans on favourable terms, and facilitation of the acquisition of assets. Access to the state and its resources thus remained central to oligarch operation, even if the identity of the oligarchs has changed.

The reduction in oligarch power was reflected in the increased official attacks on the oligarchs. In early 1999, Prime Minister Primakov attacked

Berezovsky, principally through raids on his companies by men in camouflage jackets and carrying guns and the issuance of an arrest warrant for Berezovsky, who was at that time in France.[164] This attack failed; Primakov was dismissed by Yeltsin in May 1999,[165] and in the December 1999 Duma election, Berezovsky's media waged a sustained campaign against the new alliance between Primakov, Luzhkov, and Tatarstan leader Mintimir Shaimiev, called Fatherland-All Russia (Otechestvo-Vsia Rossiia), and in support of the pro-Putin Unity (Edinenie); most business seemed to support Putin in the March 2000 presidential poll. Nevertheless, it was under Putin that attacks on the oligarchs escalated substantially.

From the outset of his presidency, Putin moved to end the privileged position the Yeltsin-era oligarchs had enjoyed. Reflecting Putin's campaign promise to hold the oligarchs at 'equal distance' and to 'eliminate the oligarchs as a class',[166] in summer 2000, the authorities acted threateningly towards a number of major companies: Norilsk Nickel (Potanin), UES (Chubais), and Tiumen Oil Co. (Fridman) were accused of irregularities during privatisation, while Lukoil (Alekperov), AvtoVaz (Kadannikov), Gazprom (Viakhirev), and Sibneft (Abramovich) were investigated by the tax police, but nothing formal came from this; break-up of the natural monopolies was also foreshadowed.[167] In July 2000, Putin held a publicised meeting with leading businessmen (Gusinsky, Berezovsky, and Abramovich were not invited, Chubais declined the invitation), where he clearly appeared as the authoritative figure.[168] There was, however, no public threat to reverse any of the privileges, including from privatisation, enjoyed by the oligarchs, but Putin now laid down new ground rules for them: there would be no questioning of their gains from privatisation as long as they paid their taxes and kept out of politics.[169] In an attempt to give the relationship with the government an institutional base, and probably under pressure from the Putin administration[170], many of the oligarchs (including Bendukidze, Deripaska, Mamut, Potanin, Fridman, Khodorkovsky, and Chubais) now joined the governing bureau of Volsky's RSPP,[171] which emerged as the major institutional means for business to consult with and advise government (see Chapter 5). However, it was always only advisory, and none of the oligarchs has sought to use it as the major vehicle for representation of their business interests. This body was sidelined following the attack on Khodorkovsky (see below).

More importantly, the authorities aggressively pursued Gusinsky and Berezovsky, the two oligarchs who had seemed most publicly active in political life, and in 2003 Khodorkovsky. Gusinsky's NTV network had supported Fatherland-All Russia in the election and, subsequently, had been seen as hostile to the Putin administration's prosecution of the second Chechen war.[172] However, NTV was in a vulnerable position because in the wake of the August collapse it had borrowed US$400 million from Gazprom, which was still 40% state-owned. In May 2000, tax and security police raided Gusinsky's

Media-Most offices, and in June Gusinsky was arrested and held for a short time.[173] In July, Gusinsky agreed to surrender control over NTV in return for the cancellation of debts to Gazprom and the dropping of the criminal charges against him. Once freed, he reneged on this deal, resulting in renewed state pressure on NTV for payment of its tax obligations. Gusinsky went abroad, and in November agreed that Gazprom-Media would take a 46% stake in NTV with a further 19% as collateral; in April 2001, Gazprom-Media took over NTV.[174] Gusinsky remained abroad, with government attempts to have him extradited to Russia failing. It seems clear that Gazprom moved against NTV at the Kremlin's behest, reflecting the continuing power the state wields vis-à-vis even the largest and most powerful of firms.

Putin also attacked Berezovsky, despite the latter's support for his promotion as prime minister in 1999 and his election in 2000. There was tension between the two men virtually from the outset as Berezovsky tried to dictate to Putin who should be a member of the cabinet once he became president.[175] On 31 May 2000, Berezovsky was publicly critical of Putin's attempt to revise the federal structure and to weaken the power of regional leaders,[176] and in July, following his resignation from the Duma, he tried to establish a political movement in opposition to Putin. This flopped. He was already under significant pressure. Financial problems had forced him in June to transfer his 49% stake in ORT to the state, and in July and October he was questioned by the procurators over foreign currency transactions by Aeroflot. In November, like Gusinsky, he went abroad into exile, and has remained in Britain, able to defeat in the courts an attempt by the government to have him extradited to Russia. In January 2002, the television station TV6 was closed down;[177] Berezovsky had held a majority holding in the company that owned it.

The onslaught continued in 2003 with an attack on Yukos Oil and its head, Mikhail Khodorkovsky.[178] Charges were laid against both the company and individual major shareholders. The company was accused of fraud and embezzlement in connection with its 1994 acquisition of a 20% stake in the Apatit mineral fertiliser company (Yukos did not make the investment in the company that it was supposed to), while the shareholders were accused of underpayment of taxes and involvement in the company's fraud. In July 2003, the head of the holding company that owned 61% of Yukos (Platon Lebedev) was arrested, and in October Yukos chairman Khodorkovsky was arrested and 44% of Yukos shares were frozen. Pressure on Yukos continued throughout 2004 and into 2005, including yet more demands for payments of taxes, even when Yukos' assets were frozen. In the subsequent trial, Khodorkovsky was sentenced to nine, later reduced to eight, years in prison. The charges against Khodorkovsky could have been applied with equal justice to virtually all of the oligarchs. But what set Khodorkovsky apart was that he, or Yukos, had been providing financial support for parties critical of Putin, the Union of Rightist Forces, Yabloko, and the Communist Party, and there had been talk of him as a future presidential contender. Furthermore, Yukos had been buying Duma deputies in an attempt to thwart government measures in the chamber if they were hostile to its interests and to create a solid core of support there.[179] Although Yukos was not the only company to do this, it was very aggressive in its actions and was seen as particularly cynical in its use of power.[180] The amount of money Yukos could spend in this way was a matter of particular concern given the approaching Duma elections, Putin's drive to control the political system, and Khodorkovsky's stated preference for a change from a presidential to a parliamentary system.[181] Khodorkovsky had clearly breached the ruling Putin had made about non-involvement in politics, and it seemed was now to pay the price.[182] During these proceedings, in a move that appears related to Putin's plans to expand state involvement in key sectors of the economy, Yukos' biggest production company, Yuganskneftegaz, was put on sale and a majority holding (77%) was purchased by a shelf company, Baikal-finansgroup (which was only registered some two weeks before the auction), which was then bought by the state-owned Rosneft oil company headed by Putin aide Igor Sechin. This was followed by Rosneft's acquisition of the other two of Yukos' main production companies, Tomskneft and Samaraneftegaz, as the final auctions of Yukos' assets liquidated that company in May 2007. In December 2003, at a meeting with businessmen in the Russian Chamber of Commerce and Industry, Putin confirmed that although there would be no major revision of privatisation, those cases of privatisation that did not accord with the law could be revisited.[183] When added to his call at the same meeting for higher taxes on the resources sector and for business help in resolving the country's social problems, it was clear that Putin expected more from the oligarchs than he had been getting and that the earlier ground rules had been substantially reworked in terms of business' obligations;[184] 'corporate social responsibility' became the key phrase in the government's expectations of business. Certainly any notion of a privileged position for the oligarchs was gone.

Putin clearly sought to deal with the most prominent businessmen who had opposed him through their media empires, Berezovsky and Gusinsky, or through their use of their wealth in the case of Khodorkovsky. But this was also a campaign to clearly establish that the president owed nothing to either the old oligarchs who had been popularly seen to be so powerful under Yeltsin or to Yeltsin's family.[185] The charges against all three oligarchs were economic in nature, principally concerning their failure either to repay loan moneys owed to the state or to pay taxes. All of the oligarchs had benefited from access to the state in the form of soft loans or deferred tax payments, and such financing was a major factor in their ability to construct business empires. But this also meant that they, and their empires, were vulnerable. The remaining oligarchs understood their position, and it is not surprising that leading businessmen in RSPP issued a public statement disowning Berezovsky and rejecting the position that business could monopolise control of the country and use the media to force its will on government,[186] or that the RSPP did not protest against the action taken against Khodorkovsky.[187] Putin's meetings with leading businessmen in January and May 2001, May 2002, February 2003, April and July 2004,[188] and March 2005 reinforced this point;[189] they (especially the later ones) were dominated by the president with the attendees clearly there in a subordinate capacity.[190]

How was Putin able to reduce the privileged position enjoyed by the oligarchs under Yeltsin? The chief explanation for this lies in the reversal of those factors that had contributed to the relative lack of power of the state vis-à-vis the oligarchs during the 1990s. Under Putin, much of the uncertainty at the top of the political hierarchy disappeared as the president played a more active and continuing part in the policy-making process. While Putin was not always as decisive as some may have wished, there was no sense of there being any ambiguity or uncertainty about who was making the decisions, a personal status that was symbolically bolstered by continuing high levels of popular support. Furthermore, in financial terms, the state was in a much better position under Putin than it had been under Yeltsin. The economic upturn that followed the 1998 crisis (an upturn that was partly stimulated by the rise in oil prices) added to the reworking of the tax system meant that the state was receiving much more in the way of tax revenues than it had before. As a result, it had greater capacity to carry out its functions than it had before, while at the same time the oligarchs remained vulnerable to the withdrawal of state privileges and benefits.

But also important is the fact that Putin undertook an explicit program of strengthening the state and its infrastructural power. This involved not only strengthening central control over the regions and improving bureaucratic performance generally but also reasserting the state's role in the economy. This is reflected in the government's above-noted declaration of the companies in which it wished to retain a strategic interest, in the moves against Khodorkovsky, in the subsequent state entry into the oil and aircraft production sectors,[191] in the moves to restrict foreign involvement in natural resources projects,[192] and in Putin's expectation that he could approve all major instances of foreign investment, at least in the resources sector.[193] Under Putin, the state wants to retain a predominant role in the key sectors of the economy. The reassertion of the state's role is also clear in the way that Putin and those around him have been a major determinant of which individuals would gain and retain control of economic assets, a practice which effectively gives to the state elite the power to define the identity of the upper levels of the bourgeois class. This reassertion of the state's interest, added to the absence of any effective constraints on the exercise of state power, is a clear expression of the subordinate position of big business and the oligarchs.

Because of the direct involvement of state officers, including Putin's personal advisers, in the most important spheres of the Russian economy, Putin's program of state-strengthening also creates a politics–business nexus characterised by the integration of major spheres of economic activity into the heart of the political process. It also embeds the state in the economy in a structurally dominant fashion. At the level of day-to-day politics it creates a series of power clusters, which are generally referred to in Russia as 'clans', around which much political life turns. With bureaucratic position and economic resources the key currencies of this, not only does it sideline those private economic actors who lack links into the centre of politics, but it is also profoundly undemocratic.

This really highlights the situation that has prevailed throughout the post-Soviet period, that although they were powerful and exercised considerable influence, the oligarchs remained outside the ruling elite.[194] Furthermore, they did not consistently act as a collective group (even the coalition to support Yeltsin in 1996 lasted only for the half year before the election and three to four months after it), with individuals uniting on some issues and coming into conflict over others. On no issue was big business united against the government; they were oligarchs without an oligarchy. And generally they were able to exercise influence in areas that were narrow and policy-defined rather than expansive.[195] While they could at times have victories over particular state agencies, they could not stand up to the state when its leader chose to flex its muscles.

Local and Regional Government

If the oligarchs have not controlled the state at the national level, has business been more important at lower levels? In some areas, this has certainly been the case. In discussing Omsk, Neil Melvin[196] has referred to the way 'a powerful core grouping, formed from the merger of the local state apparatus and leading economic interests, dominated the key positions of power in the *oblast.*' This sort of interlocking of political and economic elites has been a common development in many of the Russian regions. Three scholars have conceptualised this relationship in terms of four different patterns:[197]

(a) patronage, where the political leaders keep tight control over the economy and where business accepts the administrative rules set by the governors in exchange for privileges and access to budget resources, for example, Tatarstan[198] and Bashkortostan;

(b) partnership, where there is cooperation between the two and the governor effectively guarantees the arrangements and deals made between the various business groups active in the region, for example, Nizhnii Novgorod and Khanty-Mansii;

(c) suppression, where a weak political elite is in conflict with business, or maybe there are conflicts within business itself, for example, Kirov oblast;

(d) privatisation of power, where the economic elite seizes political power and oversees the economic and administrative arrangements in the region, for example, Kalmykia and Chukotka.

This pattern is useful for the nuances of the business–politics relationship that it alerts us to, and to the fact that the models of regional power distribution are not standard across the country. But nor are they set in stone; for example, the removal of a local leader or business difficulties of a particular company can result in the recasting of the regional power structure and the shifting of the region from one of the above categories to another.

Businessmen were strongly represented in the regions from the time of the fall of the USSR[199] because that was where many of their main sources of income (such as mines and processing facilities) were located. The origins of closer collaboration between political and business elites in many of the regions lay in the privatisation of the early 1990s when regional assets were drawn together by local officials into holding companies; examples include Sistema in Moscow (see below), Tatneft and Tatenergo in Tatartstan, Bashenergo and Bashneft in Bashkortostan, and Doninvest in Rostov. The same sorts of prudential considerations that stimulated contacts with state officials discussed above also operated in the regions. Businessmen could use their contacts with the local administration not only to exploit the privatisation provisions and capture control of significant state assets but also to gain continuing privileges: favourable local legislation, the soft pedaling of monitoring and legislative oversight, low taxes, cheap rates for power and water supplies, cheap loans, and assistance from the local administration in securing federal resources.[200] In return for building up local business in this way, governors gained support from business that helped to block off the emergence of local political challenges; for example, business, especially when underwritten by the state, could contribute to local social stability and political quiescence by providing jobs rather than shedding labour in accord with strict market principles.[201]

But also important were the broader circumstances confronting regional elites. With local administrations short of funds and local businessmen operating in the sort of business climate sketched above, there was significant incentive for collaboration between political and business elites. Regional administrations and businesses shared the desire to keep more resources in the regions and out of the hands of Moscow, while many of the individuals thus involved sought to direct the resources into their own pockets. Regional governors in particular often developed close associations with the stronger local enterprises, especially those with large export earnings or which could wield significant influence in Moscow.[202] This was a major factor in their opposition in the latter half of the 1990s to the restructuring of the tax system,[203] and saw them collude in a variety of ways to prevent revenues from flowing into federal coffers; for example, in 1999 it was reported that the political leadership of the Komi Republic combined with the management of the regional oil company Komineft to embezzle more than US$10 million from oil exports,[204] while Roman Abramovich used his position as governor of Chukotka and head of Sibneft to create an arrangement which minimised the latter's tax bill.[205] Companies used a variety of ways to keep income off their books, with such resources often being, in part, turned towards local uses. Both political and business elites could be faced by threats emanating from the centre. The desire to keep resources locally rather than send them to Moscow was only one part of the continuing struggle by local elites to maximise their room for independent action vis-à-vis the centre. The difficulties Yeltsin had in the early 1990s in introducing the federal treaty and in the discussions with administrations in places like Tatarstan, Sakha, and especially Chechnya were but the most public manifestations of a tug-of-war between centre and regions that lasted throughout the decade. Even when the danger of the widespread disintegration of the federation had passed and federal relations had become more routinised, regional leaders remained anxious to preserve as much local autonomy as they could. Similarly, local businessmen sought to preserve their positions against challenges posed by competitors based in Moscow or in other regions, and they were assisted in this by local governments. When central officials sought to examine the activities of regional companies or to put pressure upon them, regional political authorities (including the governor) usually stepped in to their defence.[206] Duma deputies could also be recruited in this way. The development of industry-led FIGs in the regions was often also a strategy by regional banks, supported by regional administrations, to defend themselves against the threat posed by the major Moscow-based banks, although by the end of the 1990s the major banks had spread across the country, especially into the wealthier, export-oriented regions.[207]

Such challenges became stronger in the second half of the 1990s as the larger natural resource companies sought to extend their activities into the regions. Furthermore, the 1998 crisis made investment in Russia more attractive and, by drawing local companies into the broader Russian market, made them more obvious as targets for external takeover. Such pressures became even stronger with the weakening of the positions of the governors in 2000. It was at this time that businessmen, including some of the oligarchs, became more prominent in regional affairs, partly in reaction to Putin's increased pressure on them in Moscow but also because of the opportunities they saw in the regions. A few oligarchs even became local governors (see Chapter 5). Both sets of local elites, business and government, saw advantages from cooperating in the face of challenges from without because each brought different resources to the struggle:[208] the administrative capacity of the regional administration could be wielded to hinder the efforts of external companies to become established in the region, while local companies could provide both financial resources and the capacity to mobilise such resources in ways that could assist the regional authorities. Furthermore, the smaller scale of these regional systems of administration and their distance from the more robust political life of the capital and St. Petersburg meant that there was likely to be less public exposure and opposition to close political–business alliances.

Business–politics collusion outside Moscow seems to have been most developed where the particular region was characterised by a single major producer or economic sector.[209] The oil found in Tatarstan and the close links between the local oil company Tatneft and the family of the Local Governor Mintimer Shaimiev were fundamental to the capacity of Shaimiev to chart a semi-autonomous course in the early 1990s. In Sakha, the authorities established a joint-stock company to exploit the massive diamond deposits and, for a time, ran their own extraction and export industry independent of Moscow.[210] The monopoly position in the regional economy possessed by such large concerns gave them considerable political power even if they did not enter an alliance with the local political leaders. Furthermore, where the operations of such concerns were not restricted to one region, they were able to play regional administrations off against one another: regional administrations often competed to attract and retain major companies, offering special deals which could lead to the development of the sort of business–politics alliances under discussion.[211]

Perhaps the most developed system of this sort of interrelationship[212] between business and regional administration was to be found in Moscow where the mayor, Yurii Luzhkov, wielded his political power to shape a quasi-autonomous politico-economic structure associated with the holding company 'Sistema'.[213] This conglomerate was initially directed by a close associate and brother-in-law of Luzhkov (Vladimir Yevtushenkov)[214] and combined more than 100 companies, including banks, electronic firms, media outlets, the Intourist group, and the newly developed Manezh shopping complex;[215] these effectively constituted an FIG. The city owned shares in some 540 companies, with controlling interests in 150 firms and a majority interest in more than fifty others.[216] Luzhkov's family, especially his wife Elena Baturina and her family, also had extensive business interests in the capital.[217] Luzhkov's capacity to shape developments in Moscow is reflected in the way in which he refused to go along with Yeltsin's privatisation plans in the early 1990s and instead instituted a scheme unique to Moscow; rather than selling off former Soviet property, the city retained ownership and leased it out under forty-nine-year-leases. He effectively removed from the capital alternative economic models to his own, a model which has been described as 'state capitalism' through its combination of both public and private interests.[218] The origins of this system lay in the early contacts Luzhkov had in assisting cooperatives to thrive in Moscow, thereby enabling him to establish ties with emerging entrepreneurs across the city.[219] The essence of the politics–business relationship in Moscow was that in return for financial support (support that was crucial in giving the Moscow authorities financial independence from the federal government[220]), Luzhkov provided access to property, privileges principally in the form of contracts and tax breaks, and protection. Luzhkov was an early protector of Gusinsky[221] (and was also associated with Khodorkovsky), and it was Gusinsky's MOST group that was given primary responsibility for the finances of the city and its major departments until Luzhkov created the Bank of Moscow in March 1995. But even when this bank was created, Luzhkov ensured that the other major banks retained authorised status, thereby ensuring their continued support. The fact that Luzhkov claimed to offer a degree of certainty and regularity to business in Moscow[222] as well as privileges that could help companies to succeed,[223] added to the fact that Moscow emerged as the most dynamic and richest business environment in the country, meant that involvement in the city was much sought after by business. But the link between Luzhkov and business has not simply led to the enrichment of the mayor; many of the proceeds generated by this relationship have been used to rebuild Moscow.[224] Indeed, many private businesses have been directly involved in financing city programs. But the relationship could also cause problems; the 'faces in the snow' affair of 1994 caught Luzhkov up in the conflict between Berezovsky–Korzhakov and Gusinsky, while the continuing Luzhkov–Chubais tension[225] was related to the sort of regime that he had constructed in Moscow. But although there was a close relationship between businessmen and the city authorities in Moscow, the former remained subordinate to the politicians.

So in some parts of Russia, business was central to the structuring of local politics, but in other parts it played almost no role at all, with about a third of all regions in the latter category.[226] By 2005, one of the conditions that had enabled the development of fused systems in the regions had been changed. The administrative changes introduced by Putin[227]—especially the right to appoint governors but also the withdrawal of the regional authorities' power to establish special economic areas and give tax concessions, and the subordination of regional tax and internal affairs authorities to the centre— substantially reduced the power of regional authorities and made them less attractive as partners than they had been before. Here was another instance of the way in which the conditions under which business operated could be profoundly altered by political changes.

* * *

The shape of the new Russian bourgeoisie was fundamentally moulded by the nature of the Russian state and the way this was changed over time. The weakness of the state's infrastructural power was important in two ways: the weakness in projecting its power systematically into society increased the uncertainty of the environment within which the bourgeoisie had to work, while the limitations of its internal regulative regime provided scope for its officials to act as virtually free agents on their own behalf. The result was a situation in which the emergent bourgeoisie, in seeking to build up both their personal wealth and their businesses, saw the state less as an independent arbiter and guarantor of the rules of the game and more as a resource to be plundered. And many state officials saw the implications of this for their own personal benefit and acted to take advantage of it. Accordingly, much Russian business developed on the basis of a directly exploitative relationship with the state whereby they gained access to the state's material and legal resources in exchange for benefits to officials; initial capital accumulation was much more at the direct expense of the state in Russia than in any of the other countries, thereby making the Russian state the generator of capitalist wealth much more directly than was the case elsewhere. This modus operandi was common at all levels of the system, from small business working hand in glove with local officials to the large conglomerates cooperating with leading government figures. This sort of situation suited business, providing that the costs were limited and predictable, and state officials, but it was not favourable to either long-term economic development or state power. While rent seeking from the state was more profitable than reliance upon market forces and the development of productive capacity, this mode of economic development was a dead end. The only way of ending this spiral was rebuilding the state's infrastructural power, both internally and externally. Putin has sought to do this, and in the process he has used the coercive arms of the state (or sometimes the threat of them) to rework the relationship between leading business circles and the state. He has neutralised the power enjoyed by many of those businessmen who were prominent before his rise by removing their privileged access and holding over them the threat of judicial investigation of past actions. He has also projected the state more directly into strategic sectors of the economy, seemingly with the aim of constructing an economy within which the state will be a significant counterbalance to big business. This would give the state significant capacity to direct the course of economic development in those sectors and, therefore, in the economy as a whole. In this way the state would be the dominant player in the Russian economy. But it is by no means clear that Putin's changes have displaced the exploitative relationship of the past at all levels; officials still are able to use their powers arbitrarily and businesses still often treat the state as a resource to be exploited. This interrelationship and interdependence[228] between infrastructurally weak state and rent seeking officials on the one hand and the emergent business class on the other has tied business into the state in a structurally powerful way. Both sides gained, but at the top of the structure, it was the state that prevailed.

There are similarities between the modus operandi of the Russian bourgeoisie and that of its counterparts in the West. All saw the state as a resource to be exploited and all sought to gain influence in the leading political circles of the state through the use of informal channels into the political elite. While it is difficult precisely to measure these, the interlocking nature of the businessman–official relationship, especially at levels below the national, in Russia suggests that the Russian bourgeoisie may have been more reliant on the state for its operations than its counterparts in the West. However, it is by no means clear that the sort of influence exercised by the oligarchs in Russia at the national level was any more pervasive or effective than that of some businessmen in the United States and Britain. So although the state is a more important aspect of the bourgeoisie's operations in Russia than elsewhere and the state has been more important in shaping its operations, it is not clear that the essential relationship has been substantially different.

Notes

1. For example, Archie Brown, "The Russian Crisis: Beginning of the End or End of the Beginning?", *Post-Soviet Affairs* 15, 1, 1999, pp. 62–65; Stephen Holmes, "Cultural Legacies or State Collapse? Probing the Postcommunist Dilemma", Michael Mandelbaum (ed.), *Postcommunism: Four Perspectives* (Washington, Council on Foreign Relations, 1996); Moshe Lewin, "Collapse of the Russian State", *Le Monde Diplomatique/The Guardian Weekly* November 1998, pp. 1, 10 & 11; and Roger D. Markwick, "What Kind of a State is the Russian State—If There Is One?", *The Journal of Communist Studies and Transition Politics* 15, 4, December 1999, pp. 111–130.
2. For the original formulation, see Michael Mann, "The Autonomous Power of the State: Its Origins, Mechanisms and Results", John A. Hall (ed.), *States in History* (Oxford, Basil Blackwell, 1986), pp. 109–136.
3. For an argument that discusses this in terms of the 'withering away' or 'structural decay' of the state, see Vadim Volkov, *Violent Entrepreneurs. The Use of Force in the Making of Russian Capitalism* (Ithaca, Cornell University Press, 2002), ch. 6. These formulations are less satisfactory because they assume that such capacity existed in the first place, and this is by no means certain.
4. See Chapter 3. Also for the 1940s, see Julie Hessler, "A Postwar Perestroika? Toward a History of Private Enterprise in the USSR", *Slavic Review* 57, 3, 1998, pp. 516–542.
5. For the argument that the collapse of party rule left intact key elements of the command economy which in the early post-Soviet years shaped economic development and led to the growth of 'merchant capitalism', see Michael Burawoy & Pavel Krotov, "The Soviet Transition from Socialism to Capitalism: Worker Control and Economic Bargaining in the Wood Industry", *American Sociological Review* 57,

1, 1992, pp. 33–37. The argument that 'merchant capital' (as they pointedly called it later; see Michael Burawoy & Pavel Krotov, "The Economic Basis of Russia's Political Crisis", *New Left Review* 198, March–April 1993, fn. 6, p. 54) was the dominant form of capital in the economy could not be sustained from the middle of the 1990s.

6. An important aspect of this was the absence of any protection for minority shareholders' rights.

7. For the argument that the high levels of taxation encouraged economic actors to seek self-regulation rather than turning to the state, see Timothy Frye, *Brokers and Bureaucrats. Building Market Institutions in Russia* (Ann Arbor, University of Michigan Press, 2000). For his case study of the equities market, see Timothy Frye, "Governing the Russian Equities Market", *Post-Soviet Affairs* 13, 4, 1997, pp. 366–395.

8. For some figures on frequency, see Alexander Chepurenko & Tatiana Obydyon-nova, *Development of Small Enterprises in Russia* (Moscow, Russian Independent Institute of Social and National Problems, 1999), p. 29.

9. For example, see the discussion in Timothy Frye & Andrei Shleifer, "The Invisible Hand and the Grabbing Hand", *American Economic Review* 87, 2, 1997, pp. 354–358.

10. For a discussion of the advances made in the legal sphere, see Thane Gustafson, *Capitalism Russian-Style* (Cambridge, Cambridge University Press, 1999), ch. 7. Also see Gordon B. Smith, *Reforming the Russian Legal System* (Cambridge, Cambridge University Press, 1996), esp. ch. 7.

11. This relates not only to a generalised suspicion about or wariness of the private ownership of major economic resources, which was strongly reflected in opinion surveys [see the analysis in A.G. Levinson et al., *Obraz predprinimatelia v novoi rossii* (Moscow, Tsentr politicheskikh tekhnologii, 1998), pp. 6–28], but also to the weakness of market-oriented values. On the ambiguous attitude to entrepreneurs, see M.K. Gorshkov et al., *Rossiiskoe Predprinimatel'stvo: Sotsial'nyi Portret* (Moscow, Obshcherossiiskoi Ob'edinenie 'Krugly stol biznesa Rossii' & Aka-demicheskii tsentr 'Rossiiskie issledovaniia', 1994), Part 2, pp. 15–24. For a study of entrepreneurs' views from 1993, see Ya. Roshchina, "Ekonomicheskaia Situatsiia i Problemy Khoziaistvovaniia v Otsenkakh Predprinimatelei", V.V. Radaev et al. (eds.), *Stanovlenie Novogo Rossiiskogo Predprinimatel'stva* (Moscow, RAN, Institut ekonomiki i mezhdistsiplinarnyi akademicheskii tsentr sotsial'nykh nauk, 1993), pp. 111–118 & 127–129.

12. See the graphs of popular perceptions in Richard Rose & Neil Munro, *Elections Without Order. Russia's Challenge to Vladimir Putin* (Cambridge, Cambridge University Press, 2002), pp. 33 & 226.

13. As Varese shows, this was a characteristic shared with Sicily. Federico Varese, *The Russian Mafia. Private Protection in a New Market Economy* (Oxford, Oxford University Press, 2002).

14. For example, see the following title: David Satter, *Darkness at Dawn. The Rise of the Russian Criminal State* (New Haven, Yale University Press, 2003). This book offers a large number of, largely unsourced, case studies of criminal activity, but no analysis to back up the claim in its sub-title. For a more sober study see Gustafson (Capitalism).

15. On this, see Stephen Handelman, *Comrade Criminal. Russia's New Mafiya* (New Haven, Yale University Press, 1995), Varese (The Russian Mafia), and Volkov (Violent Entrepreneurs).

16. Alena V. Ledeneva, *Russia's Economy of Favours. Blat, Networking and Informal Exchange* (Cambridge, Cambridge University Press, 1998). The essence of this was reliance upon personal relations for the supply of goods and services; it was a type of informal mutual exchange based on personal connections. Although it thrived in a situation of material goods shortage during the Soviet period, in the post-Soviet period the uncertainty of the business environment did much to promote this Soviet tradition. For discussion of various ways in which companies operate in the uncertain environment, see Alena V. Ledeneva, *How Russia Really Works. The Informal Practices That Shaped Post-Soviet Politics and Business* (Ithaca, Cornell University Press, 2006), chs. 5–7.

17. Ledeneva (Russia's Economy of Favours), pp. 178–179.

18. Alexander Chepurenko, "Small Business and Big Politics", *Reforma* 9, September 1993, p. 10.

19. For one discussion of this, see Volkov (Violent Entrepreneurs), ch. 5.

20. Alternatively, many ex-police and military men have established official protection agencies, offering the sort of protection that similar bodies in the West offer. Of course, many such people may also be involved in criminally based kryshas.

21. Natalia (Evdokimova) Dinello, "Forms of Capital: The Case of Russian Bankers", *International Sociology* 13, 3, 1998, p. 299. In an attempt to halt some of these problems, new laws were introduced on inspection, licensing, and registration in 2001–02.

22. Gorshkov (Rossiiskoe predprinimatel'stvo), p. 36. Although only 20.9% saw this means as effective, 38.4% believed that they had no means of influencing power at all.

23. According to one study, 32.2% of entrepreneurs often encountered bribery in their dealings with officials, 48% sometimes and 19.8% never. V. Radaev, "O nekotorykh chertakh normativnogo povedeniia novykh rossiiskikh predprinimatelei", *Mirovaia ekonomika i mezhdunarodnoe otnosheniia* 4, 1994, p. 35. For a fuller discussion and different figures, see V.V. Radaev, *Formirovanie novykh rossiiskykh rynkov: transaktionnye izderzhki, formy kontrolia i delovaia etika* (Moscow, Tsentr politicheskikh tekhnologii, 1998), pp. 35–44.

24. According to a 2005 report from the Indem Foundation, from 2001 to 2005 the 'average number' of business bribes fell by 20% while the average bribe amount increased 13 times. Georgy Satarov et al., *Diagnostika rossiiskoi korruptsii 2005. Predvaritel'nye rezul'taty* (Moscow, Regional'nyi obshchestvennyi fond 'Informatika dlia demokratii'. Trudy fonda INDEM, 2005). It is not really clear how these figures have been arrived at or what they actually mean for a businessman on the ground. For a more extensive discussion, see K.I. Golovshchinskii et al., *Biznes i korruptsiia: problemy protivodeistviia. Itogovyi otchet* (Moscow, Regional'nyi obshchestvennyi fond 'Informatika dlia demokratii'. Trudy fonda INDEM, 2004).

25. *Rossiiskaia gazeta* 25 April 2005.

26. Joel S. Hellman, Geraint Jones, Daniel Kaufman & Mark Schankerman, *Measuring Governance, Corruption, and State Capture. How Firms and Bureaucrats Shape the*

Business Environment in Transition Economies (New York, World Bank Institute, and European Bank for Reconstruction and Development, Policy Research WP 2313, April 2000), p. 21.

27. On the role of personal relations in privatisation, see Ledeneva (Russia's Economy of Favours), pp. 186–190.

28. David Lane, "The Political Economy of Russian Oil", Peter Rutland (ed.), *Business and the State in Contemporary Russia* (Boulder, Westview Press, 2001), p. 116.

29. For example, Nodari Simonia, "Economic Interests and Political Power in Post-Soviet Russia", Archie Brown (ed.), *Contemporary Russian Politics. A Reader* (Oxford, Oxford University Press, 2001), pp. 269–285.

30. Andrei Shleifer & Daniel Treisman, *Without a Map. Political Tactics and Economic Reforms in Russia* (Cambridge, MA, The MIT Press, 2000), p. 45.

31. Ol'ga Kryshtanovskaia, "Finansovaia oligarkhiia v rossii", *Izvestiia* 10 January 1996.

32. Thomas Graham, "From Oligarchy to Oligarchy: The Structure of Russia's Ruling Elite", *Demokratizatsiya* 7, 3, 1997, p. 329. He also points to a Luzhkov group focused on Moscow.

33. Vladimir Chervyakov, "The Russian National Economic Elite in the Political Arena", Klaus Segbers & Stephan De Spiegeleire (eds.), *Post-Soviet Puzzles. Mapping the Political Economy of the Former Soviet Union. Vol.1. Against the Background of the Former Soviet Union* (Baden Baden, Nomos Verlagsgesellschadft, 1995), p. 262.

34. The appointment of Chernomyrdin is widely seen as being particularly important because it crystallised at the top of the political structure an amorphous alliance between forces concentrating on him and representing the interests of the old established industries, raw materials exporters, and conservative enterprise directors on the one hand, and Chubais and the importing and financial sectors on the other, with Yeltsin playing a balancing role. This sort of division split the Yeltsin regime throughout its life. For a discussion of this in terms of a struggle for influence over Yeltsin in 1995–96, culminating in Korzhakov's dismissal, between a Korzhakov-Barsukov-Soskovets-Chernomyrdin-Borodin group (security-heavy industry-natural resources), and a Chubais-Berezovsky-Gusinsky group (financial sector), see V.A. Lisichkin & L.A. Shelepin, *Rossiia pod vlast'iu plutokratii* (Moscow, Algoritm, 2003), pp. 159–160.

35. For a discussion of the people around Chernomyrdin and some of their contacts with business, see Aleksei Mukhin, *Korruptsia i gruppy vliianie Kniga 1* (Moscow, SPIK-Tsentr, 1999), pp. 78–91. For exchanges of personnel between Gazprom and the government, see Ia. Sh. Pappe, *"Oligarkhi". Ekonomicheskaia khronika 1992–2000* (Moscow, Gosudarstvennyi universitet Vysshaia shkola ekonomiki, 2000), pp. 98–99.

36. This association was linked more to the policies he pursued than any earlier career contacts. On Chubais and those around him, see Mukhin (Korruptsiia), pp. 92–121.

37. I. Khripunov & M. Matthews, "Russia's Oil and Gas Interest Group and Its Foreign Policy Agenda", *Problems of Post-Communism* 43, 3, 1996, p. 39.

38. Lane (Political Economy), p. 116.

39. Stephen Fortescue, *Policy-Making for Russian Industry* (Basingstoke, Macmillan, 1997), p. 34. On Chernomyrdin's activity specifically for Gazprom, see Aleksei Mukhin, *"Gazprom": Imperiia i ee imperatory* (Moscow, Tsentr politicheskoi informatsii, 2001), p. 39. On its providing financial support for both Chernomyrdin and Our Home is Russia, see Mukhin (Gazprom), pp. 50–57. Also Mukhin (Korruptsiia), p. 78.

40. For one analysis of the changing balance, see the discussion of bureaucratic capitalism in Simonia (Economic Interests), pp. 269–285.

41. Voloshin, head of the Presidential Administration until his resignation in October 2003, was known as sympathetic to business interests. Many officials were like this.

42. This is also clear in the increase in business representation in the Duma and Government noted in Chapter Five. For example, in 1998–99 the Minister of Fuel and Energy (Sergei Generalov) came from Yukos, and in 2000 (Aleksandr Gavrin) from Lukoil. Olga Kryshtanovskaya & Stephen White, "The rise of the Russian business elite", *Communist and Post-Communist Studies* 38, 3, September 2005, pp. 302–303. For the argument that businessmen were able to use their influence with political authorities to fix the Slavneft auction in 2002, see Andrew Barnes, "Russia's New Business Groups and State Power", *Post-Soviet Affairs* 19, 2, 2003, pp. 178–179.

43. For some details of interchange between the business and political sectors, see the discussion of different conglomerates in Ia. Sh. Pappe, *Finansovo-promyshlennye gruppy i konglomeraty v ekonomike i politike sovremennoi Rossii* (Moscow, Tsentr politicheskoi tekhnologii, 1997). For an argument about the supposed 'privatisation' of the security services by major FIGs, principally through such personnel shifts, see A.A. Mukhin, *Biznes-elita i gosudarstvennaia vlast': Kto vladeet Rossiei na rubezhe vekov?* (Moscow, Tsentr politicheskoi informatsii, 2001), pp. 20–25.

44. E.Ya. Vittenberg, "Politicheskie simpatii rossiiskikh bankirov", M.K. Gorshkov et al. (eds.), *Obnovlenie Rossii: trudnyi poisk reshenii*, vyp.3, (Moscow, RNISiNP, 1995), p. 207.

45. There has also been some circulation through the Central Bank and the commercial banks. For example, former deputy director of the CBR Sergei Rodionov became the head of Imperial Bank, Sergei Dubinin moved from first deputy (and then acting) finance minister to first vice-president of Imperial Bank and then became a director of the CBR, and when Viktor Gerashchenko stepped down from being director of the CBR he became chair of the International Moscow Bank. Anvar Amirov, *Kto est' kto v bankovskoi sisteme Rossii. Biograficheskii spravochnik* (Moscow, OOO Panorama, 1996), pp. 17–19, 29–31, & 61–61.

46. Juliet Johnson, *A Fistful of Rubles. The Rise and Fall of the Russian Banking System* (Ithaca, Cornell University Press, 2000), pp. 183–184. For other examples, see Pappe (Oligarkhi), pp. 138–139.

47. A.A. Mukhin & P.A. Kozlov, *"Semeinye" tainy ili neofitsial'nyi lobbizm v Rossii* (Moscow, Tsentr politicheskoi informatsii, 2003), p. 78.

48. Peter Rutland, "Putin and the Oligarchs", Dale R. Herspring (ed.), *Putin's Russia. Past Imperfect, Future Uncertain* (Lanham, Rowman & Littlefield Publishers Inc., 2003), p. 143.

49. Some of these, like Aleksandr Zhukov on the board of Russian Railways and Viktor Khristenko on the board of Transneft, retained their positions into the Putin era.

50. For an earlier, premature, argument about the coming together of political and financial elites, see E.Ya.Vittenberg, "Bankovskoe soobshchestvo rossii: itogi razvitiia i kratkosrochnyi prognoz", M.K. Gorshkov et al., (eds.), *Obnovlenie Rossii: trudnyi poisk reshenii*, vyp.5 (Moscow, RNISiNP, 1997), p. 41.

51. Joseph R. Blasi, Maya Kroumova & Douglas Kruse, *Kremlin Capitalism. Privatizing the Russian Economy* (Ithaca, Cornell University Press, 1997), p. 168.

52. European Bank for Reconstruction and Development, *Transition report 2001. Energy in transition* (London, EBRD, 2001), p. 188.

53. David Lane & Iskander Seifulmukov, "Structure and Ownership", David Lane (ed.), *The Political Economy of Russian Oil* (Lanham, Rowman & Littlefield Publishers Inc., 1999), p. 35. In 1995 and 1996, some of these holdings were wholly or partly in the hands of pledgeholders in the loans for shares scheme. For a list of state shares in strategically important companies for mid-2004, see Ukaz prezidenta rossiiskoi federatsii, "Ob utverzhdenii perechnia strategicheskikh predpriiatii i strategicheskikh aktsionernykh obshchestv", 4/8/04, No. 1009. *http://document.kremlin.ru/doc.asp?ID=023799*

54. Ukaz prezidenta rossiiskoi federatsii, "Ob utverzhdenii perechnia strategicheskikh predpriiatii i strategicheskikh aktsionernykh obshchestv", 4/8/04, No. 1009. *http://document.kremlin.ru/doc.asp?ID=023799*

55. For example, in September 2004 the government transferred Rosneft to Gazprom in exchange for additional shares to its current holding in Gazprom to give it a controlling interest. *Izvestiia* 15/9/04. A year later Gazprom bought a controlling interest in Sibneft from Roman Abramovich, putting nearly a third of the country's oil output in the state's hands. In 2004, state companies produced 13% of all Russian oil production, while in 2005 this figure had reached 34%. "The Changing Structure of the Russian Oil and Gas Industry", *Russian Analytical Digest* 1, 6 June 2006, p. 8. For the argument that nationalisation of strategic enterprises, especially in the energy sector, was a key aim of the so-called siloviki in Putin's administration, see Ol'ga Kryshtanovskaya & Stephen White, "Inside the Putin Court: A Research Note", *Europe-Asia Studies* 57, 7, 2005, pp. 1071–1072. For the view that Putin is creating a corporate form of state-led capitalism, see David Lane, "What kind of capitalism for Russia? A comparative analysis", *Communist and Postcommunist Studies* 33, 4, December 2000, pp. 485–504.

56. These policies were strongly favoured by Western advisors and aid donors. Not all of this was selfless in either intent or effect. For a particularly egregious case, see the study by Janine R. Wedel, *Collision and Collusion. The Strange Case of Western Aid to Eastern Europe 1989–1998* (New York, St Martins Press, 1998). For a strong criticism of this 'consensus', see Peter Reddaway & Dmitri Glinski, *The Tragedy of Russia's Reforms. Market Bolshevism Against Democracy* (Washington, United States Institute of Peace Press, 2001).

57. For example, foreign direct investment in the 1990s peaked in 1997 at US$3,752,000,000, but this represented only US$25 per capita and 0.8% of the GDP. Of twenty-five countries of the former USSR and Eastern Europe, only in the Slovak Republic was the percentage of GDP lower, although the per capita

figure was lower in eleven of the other countries. This means that unlike the effect Western ideas have had on the course of Russian development, the level of foreign investment in Russian productive capacity has not been high enough to have a decisive effect on the development of the economy. Thus while the Western financial sector has been an important location of the channelling of substantial Russian funds abroad, it has not been a player which has shaped in a major way the contours of the Russian economy. European Bank for Reconstruction and Development, *Transition report 1998. Financial sector in transition* (London, EBRD, 1998), p. 81. On the low levels of foreign investment in the oil industry, see James Watson, "Foreign Investment in Russia: The Case of the Oil Industry", *Europe-Asia Studies* 48, 3, 1996, pp. 429–455. Foreign investment in China has been much more extensive. For some figures, see The World Bank, *World Development Report 1996. From Plan to Market* (New York, Oxford University Press, 1996), p. 64.

58. Cited in Anders Aslund, *Building Capitalism. The Transformation of the Former Soviet Bloc* (Cambridge, Cambridge University Press, 2002), p. 201. Different figures for consumer price inflation have been reported in Zbigniew Brzezinski & Paige Sullivan (eds.), *Russia and the Commonwealth of Independent States. Documents, Data and Analysis* (Armonk, M.E. Sharpe Inc., 1997), p. 811: 1991, 93%; 1992, 1354%; 1993, 896%; 1994, 307%; 1995, 196%.

59. Paul R. Gregory & Robert C. Stuart, *Russian and Soviet Economic Performance and Structure* (Boston, Addison Wesley, 2001, 7th edn.), p. 348.

60. See the graph in David Woodruff, *Money Unmade. Barter and the Fate of Russian Capitalism* (Ithaca, Cornell University Press, 1999), p. 85.

61. Shleifer & Treisman (Without a Map), pp. 71–73.

62. Although Gazprom was forced to repay most of its tax arrears in 1997.

63. This was seen by observers as being more an improvised response than a conscious strategy. Shleifer & Treisman (Without a Map), pp. 77 & 79.

64. Shliefer & Treisman (Without a Map), p. 73.

65. Other strategies included vertical integration (the control of all aspects of production in the one combine), the shifting of operations outside Moscow and of assets abroad, and the appointment of foreign managers. All were seen as means of defending the company against hostile actors within Russia, including the government. The shifting of assets abroad involved significant levels of capital flight. See United Nations Office for Drug Control and Crime Prevention, *Russian Capitalism and Money-Laundering* (New York, United Nations, 2001), p. 1, and Vladimir Tikhomirov, "Capital Flight from Post-Soviet Russia", *Europe-Asia Studies* 49, 4, 1997, pp. 591–615.

66. See Johnson (Fistful of Rubles), p. 162. Also Natalia Dinello, "Financial-Industrial Groups and Russia's Capitalism", John S. Micgiel (ed.), *Perspectives on Political and Economic Transitions After Communism* (New York, Institute on East Central Europe, Columbia University, 1997), p. 197. The initial measure was a presidential decree of December 1993. Pappe (Finansovo-promyshlennye gruppy), p. 17.

67. Johnson (Fistful of Rubles), pp. 8–9. On the development of FIGs, see Hans-Henning Schroder, "El'tsin and the Oligarchs: The Role of Financial Groups in Russian Politics Between 1993 and July 1998", *Europe-Asia Studies* 51, 6, 1999, pp. 957–988. For a full list of registered FIGs as of April 1997, see Andrew Barnes,

Owning Russia. The Struggle Over Factories, Farms, and Power (Ithaca, Cornell University Press, 2006), pp. 123–125.

68. Johnson (Fistful of Rubles), p. 8.

69. Johnson (Fistful of Rubles), p. 164.

70. Retailing was also not hindered in the same way that industry was because of its much shorter turn around times and lower needs for investment. For the argument that the scope for rent seeking was a function of partial economic reform, see Joel S. Hellman, "Winners Take All: The Politics of Partial Reform in Postcommunist Transitions", *World Politics* 50, 2, 1998, pp. 203–234.

71. This in part follows Anders Aslund, "Reform Vs Rent-Seeking in Russia's Economic Transformation", *Transition* 2, 2, 26 January 1996, pp. 12–16.

72. Heiko Pleines, "Corruption and Crime in the Russian Oil Industry", Lane (Political Economy), pp. 97–110.

73. For examples of successful speculative trading, see Rose Brady, *Kapitalizm. Russia's Struggle to Free Its Economy* (New Haven, Yale University Press, 1999), ch. 4, and for arbitrage on privatisation vouchers, see p. 104. On Berezovsky being able to take advantage of arbitrage, see Paul Klebnikov, *Godfather of the Kremlin. Boris Berezovsky and the Looting of Russia* (New York, Harcourt Inc., 2000), pp. 96–101. Such arbitrage was perfectly legal and did not take place through a currency black market, which had disappeared by the middle of the decade.

74. In 1992, import subsidies amounted to 15% and credit subsidies 30% of GDP. Aslund (Building Capitalism), p. 13.

75. Business was not the only sector able to profit from such arrangements. For example, in 1993 Yeltsin gave special privileges to sports and veterans associations, providing them with tax exemption, access to government funds and import and export concessions. The Orthodox Church also benefited in this way. Reddaway & Glinski (Tragedy), pp. 443–444. On the role of Shamil' Tarpishchev, Yeltsin's tennis coach, see Mukhin & Kozlov ("Semeinye"), pp. 69–74.

76. Gustafson (Capitalism), p. 27.

77. Gustafson (Capitalism), p. 85.

78. Duties were reduced on natural gas, rolled steel, aluminium, copper, nickel, tin, and nitrogen fertilizer. This occurred while Soskovets was most powerful as first deputy prime minister and when Yeltsin was seeking support among the industrialists. Peter Rutland, "Introduction: Business and the State in Russia", Rutland (Business and the State), p. 16.

79. Aslund (Building Capitalism), p. 14.

80. For one study of the early development of banks that emphasises the legacy of their Soviet past, see Juliet Ellen Johnson, "The Russian Banking System: Institutional Responses to the Market Transition", *Europe-Asia Studies* 46, 6, 1994, pp. 971–995. On the so-called 'spetsbanks' (Agroprombank, Promstroibank, Sberbank, Vneshekonombank, and Zhilsotsbank) and their lineal descendants, see Koen Schoors, "The Fate of Russia's Former State Banks: Chronicle of a Restructuring Postponed and a Crisis Foretold", *Europe-Asia Studies* 55, 1, 2003, pp. 75–100.

81. The figures apply to the end of the year. Johnson (Fistful of Rubles), p. 6 and Richard Sakwa, *Russian Politics and Society* (London, Routledge, 2002, Third edn.), p. 292.

82. In the first quarter of 1999, 12% of the investment of companies came from banks cf. 79.7% from their own capital sources. Lane (What Kind of Capitalism for Russia?) p. 494. According to one study, commercial banks provided funding for 37% of enterprises established prior to the end of 1991, 33% for those between 1992 and 1993, 17% 1994–95, and 15% 1996–97. Most of this went to large and medium sized enterprises. Radaev (Formirovanie), pp. 250–251.

83. For example, for a discussion of the FIMACO affair in which the Central Bank effectively laundered aid and other funds through an offshore banking affiliate, see Marshall I. Goldman, *The Piratization of Russia. Russian Reform Goes Awry* (London, Routledge, 2003), ch. 8.

84. Nor did the banks cater to individual depositors, hence the growth of pyramid schemes in 1992–93. Johnson (Fistful of Rubles), pp. 112–113. For discussions of banking development, see A.I. Arkhipov & V.E. Kokorev (eds.), *Bankovskaia sistema rossii: novyi etap razvitiia* (Moscow, Nauchnoe izdanie, 1997) and A.A. Maslennikov & A.I. Bazhan (eds.), *Rol' bankov v razvitii Rossiiskoi ekonomiki* (Moscow, Ekslibris-Press, 2000).

85. According to Satter, these were originally the banks that supported Yeltsin in the 1993 crisis. Satter (Darkness at Dawn), p. 48.

86. Shleifer & Treisman (Without a Map), p. 54. In 1997, there were 170,000 authorised accounts, 56% at state banks (Central Bank and Sberbank) and 44% at commercial banks. Schroder (El'tsin), p. 964.

87. Gusinsky was actually the originator of the notion of authorised banks. Brady (Kapitalizm), pp. 100–103.

88. There were also OFZs, or Federal Bonds, which had longer maturity periods than the three and six months of the GKOs. Gustafson (Capitalism), p. 92.

89. Shleifer & Treisman (Without a Map), p. 62.

90. Johnson (Fistful of Rubles), p. 124.

91. And therefore making it into a kind of pyramid scheme. Johnson (Fistful of Rubles), p. 124.

92. Johnson (Fistful of Rubles), p. 8.

93. Gustafson (Capitalism), p. 89.

94. For details, see Johnson (Fistful of Rubles), pp. 174–177. On the development of banks and their involvement in the oil sector, see Valery Kryukov & Arild Moe, *The Changing Role of Banks in the Russian Oil Sector* (London, RIIA, 1998).

95. Johnson (Fistful of Rubles), p. 136.

96. On loans for shares, see Chrystia Freeland, *Sale of the Century. The Inside Story of the Second Russian Revolution* (London, Little, Brown & Co., 2000), pp. 161–181. The basis for the diversification of holdings was often initially in the purchase of privatisation vouchers and their investment in companies in the early 1990s. The measure was brought to Cabinet in March 1995 and its terms set out in presidential decree no. 889, 'On the procedure for pledging shares in federal ownership in 1995' of 31 August 1995. For a survey of mechanisms for expanding control of companies and affiliates, see Stephen Fortescue, *Russia's Oil Barons and Metal Magnates. Oligarchs and the State in Transition* (Basingstoke, Plagrave Macmillan, 2006), pp. 61–71, and Barnes (Owning Russia), ch. 5.

97. This was organised principally by Oneksimbank (Potanin) and Menatep (Khodorkovsky). Fortescue (Russia's Oil Barons), p. 55. For different explanations

of this scheme and the results of the auctions, see Fortescue (Russia's Oil Barons), pp. 55–57, and Barnes (Owning Russia), pp. 112–113.

98. This was a result of oligarch, and especially Khodorkovsky's, influence. Freeland (Sale of the Century), pp. 175–176.

99. For a discussion of this, see Gustafson (Capitalism), pp. 94–100 and Pappe (Oligarkhi), pp. 41–47.

100. By the new millennium, natural resources comprised 80% of Russian exports (oil and gas 55%); 37% of budget revenues came from taxes on oil and gas. Fiona Hill, *Energy Empire: Oil, Gas and Russia's Revival* (London, The Foreign Policy Centre, 2004), p. 13.

101. For rumours about the personal benefits Chernomyrdin gained as a result, see Klebnikov (Godfather), pp. 114–115. On Gazprom, see Pappe (Oligarkhi), pp. 77–100 and Pappe (Finansovo-promyshlennye gruppy), pp. 80–103.

102. By 2001, the state's share had dropped to 38.77%. Mukhin (Gazprom), pp. 5–6.

103. On the involvement of Viakhirev's family and Viakhirev personally, see Mukhin (Gazprom), pp. 16–17 & 44–53.

104. Such rights actually extended over 35% of the total share-holding. Mukhin (Gazprom), p. 16. On Nemtsov's attempt in 1997 to reduce Viakhirev's control over these shares, see Mukhin (Gazprom), pp. 47–48.

105. Although Viakhirev had not been considered one of the oligarchs while head of Gazprom, presumably because Chernomyrdin had been the main link between the political elite and the company, Miller has been seen as an oligarch.

106. See N. Lapina, *Rossiiskie ekonomicheskie elity i modeli natsional'nogo razvitiia* (Moscow, INION, 1997), pp. 6–8.

107. On some of the companies involved, see P. Gazukin, *Vostochnaia neftianaia kompaniia, Neftianaia kompaniia "Rosneft", Neftianaia kompaniia "Slavneft", Tiumenskaia neftianaia kompaniia. Obzor deiatel'nosti* (Moscow, Panorama, 1997) and P. Popov, *Vedushchie neftianye kompanii rossii* (Moscow, TsPI, 2001).

108. Lapina (Rossiiskie ekonomicheskie elity), p. 8.

109. Pappe (Oligarkhi), pp. 100–115.

110. Brady (Kapitalizm), p. 128.

111. For ownership details of the major oil companies at the end of the 1990s, see Lane & Seifulmukov (Structure and Ownership), pp. 19–39.

112. As a reflection of this, when Abramovich sold Sibneft to Gazprom in 2005, Sibneft's business registration was shifted from Chukotka where Abramovich was governor to St Petersburg, where the headquarters of Gazprom was to be located. This left a major tax shortfall for Chukotka. Among these so-called 'domestic off-shore zones' were Mordovia, Kalmykia, Chukotka, Baikonur (actually in Kazakhstan but leased to Russia for use as its space base), and the Urals village of Lesnoe. Fortescue (Russia's Oil Barons), p. 118.

113. The main ones are discussed in detail in Pappe (Oligarkhi) and Pappe (Finansovo-promyshlennye gruppy).

114. Sergei Guriev & Andrei Rachinsky, "Russian Oligarchs: a Quantitative Assessment", The World Bank, *Beyond Transition* 15, 1, October–December 2004, p. 4. For the broader discussion of concentration on which this is based, see The World Bank, *Russian Federation. From Transition to Development. A Country Economic Memorandum for the Russian Federation* (New York, The World Bank, March 2005). For a less

negative view of the oligarchs by two of the authors of the World Bank report, see Sergei Guriev & Andrei Rachinsky, "The role of oligarchs in Russian capitalism", *Journal of Economic Perspectives* 19, 1, 2005, pp. 130–150.For some other figures, see Robert W. Orrtung, "Business and Politics in the Russian Regions", *Problems of Post-Communism* 51, 2, March-April 2004, pp. 49 & 59.

115. Rutland (Introduction), p. 15–18.

116. Hill (Energy Empire), pp. 27–28.

117. On small business, see V.A. Zevelev, *Malyi biznes—bol'shaia problema rossii* (Moscow, Menedzher, 1994); A.V. Avilova, *Finansovye i institutional'nye problemy rossiiskogo malogo predprinimatel'stva (regional'nye aspekty)* (Moscow, Informart, 1996); A.V. Avilova, *Maloe predprinimatel'stvo v kontekste rossiiskikh reform i mirovogo opyta* (Moscow, Informart, 1995); A. Iu. Chepurenko (ed.), *Razvitie malykh i srednikh predprinimatel'skikh struktur i problemy zaniatosti* (Moscow, RNISiNP, 1995); Nonna Barkhatova, "Russian Small Business, Authorities and the State", *Europe-Asia Studies* 54, 2, 2000, pp. 657–676; Andrei Kuznetsov & Olga Kuznetsova, "Institutions, Business and the State in Russia", *Europe-Asia Studies* 55, 6, 2003, pp. 907–922; Nonna Barkhatova, Peter McMylor & Rosemary Mellor, "Family Business in Russia: The Path to Middle Class", *British Journal of Sociology* 52, 2, 2001, pp. 249–269; and Alessandro Kihlgren, "Small Business in Russia—Factors that Slowed its Development: An Analysis", *Communist and Post-Communist Studies* 36, 2, 2003, pp. 193–207.

118. Small companies are defined as having an annual turnover of less than 15 million rubles and fewer than 100 employees. In most economies, the small business sector is two to three times larger than this, and even allowing for the possibility of some under-counting in Russia, this sector is smaller than international comparators. Peter Rutland, "Russian Small Business: Staying Small", *Jamestown Foundation Eurasia Daily Monitor* 15 March 2005.

119. For one discussion of who should be classed as an oligarch, see Mukhin (Biznes-elita), pp. 3–19.

120. *The Financial Times* 1 November 1996.

121. Matthew Brzezinski, *Casino Moscow. A Tale of Greed and Adventure on Capitalism's Wildest Frontier* (New York, The Free Press, 2001), p. 39. For the changing popular view of the influence exercised by the oligarchs, see the table in Kryshtanovskaya & White (The rise), p. 298. Such ratings commonly appeared in the Russian press.

122. They were said to be Berezovsky, Potanin, Gusinsky, Khodorkovsky, Smolensky, Fridman, and Aven, with Vinogradov replacing Aven in some accounts. Schroder (El'tsin), p. 970. For English language studies, see David E. Hoffman, *The Oligarchs. Wealth and Power in the New Russia* (New York, Public Affairs, 2002), Klebnikov (Godfather), Goldman (Piratization), chs. 6 & 7, and Dominic Midgley & Chris Hutchins, *Abramovich. The billionaire from nowhere* (London, Harper Collins, 2004).

123. For studies of the early business trajectories of some of these people, see Hoffman (Oligarchs), chs. 2–7, where he notes the support they received from high levels early in their careers.

124. Rutland (Putin and the Oligarchs), p. 135. Also see Laura Belin with Floriana Fossato & Anna Kachkaeva, "The Distorted Russian Media Market", Rutland (Business and the State), pp. 68–77; O.N. Blinova, *Media-Imperii Rossii. Na sluzhbe*

gosudarstva i "oligarkhi" (Moscow, Tsentr politicheskoi informatsii, 2001); and Pappe (Finansovo-promyshlennye gruppy), pp. 200–223.

125. Hoffman (Oligarchs), pp. 41–42, 100–107, 136–143, 158–161, and 303–304.

126. This is consistent with the claim that some of the oligarchs had special telephones that linked them directly to the Kremlin. These were apparently changed periodically, depending upon who was in favour. *The Financial Times* 25 November 2003.

127. On Berezovsky in this regard, see Klebnikov (Godfather), p. 75.

128. On his role in loans for shares, see Hoffman (Oligarchs), pp. 308–317, and on the oligarchs turning to him in the election campaign, Hoffman (Oligarchs), pp. 328–329.

129. Aleksandr Korzhakov, *Boris El'tsin: ot rassveta do zakata* (Moscow, Interbuk, 1997), pp. 282–283. According to Klebnikov (Oligarchs), p. 119, this provided a means for Berezovsky to give regular payments to Yeltsin in the form of foreign royalties.

130. Korzhakov (Boris El'tsin), p. 283.

131. On 'the family' and its influence, see Mukhin (Korruptsiia), pp. 20–37, and Mukhin & Kozlov (Semeinye). The members of the 'family' changed over time but were said to have included Diachenko, Korzhakov, Berezovsky, Abramovich, Chubais, Voloshin, and Yumashev, with Mamut as the banker. V.A. Lisichkin & L.A. Shelepin, *Rossiia pod vlast'iu plutokratii* (Moscow, Algoritm, 2003), pp. 161–174, Mukhin & Kozlov (Semeinye). On the involvement of Yeltsin's son-in-law, Okulov, in Berezovsky's scheme to milk Aeroflot of funds through a Swiss company, Andava, see Mukhin (Korruptsia), pp. 29–39.

132. On this, see David Remnick, "The War for the Kremlin", *The New Yorker* 22 July 1996, pp. 41–57 and Jack F. Matlock Jr., "The Struggle for the Kremlin", *The New York Review of Books* 8 August 1996, pp. 28–34.

133. For Korzhakov's own discussion of the period and his role, see Korzhakov (Boris El'tsin). For some examples of personal links, see Aleksei Zudin, "Biznes i politika v postkommunisticheskoi Rossii. Politicheskie strategii grupp davleniia biznesa", *Biznes i politika* 1, 1996, pp. 4–5. On the people in Yeltsin's entourage and their activities, see Mukhin (Korruptsiia), pp. 20–77. Mukhin divides these people into the following groups: the family, the Sverdlovsk group, the 'siloviki' (power group), and the 'young favourites'.

134. For a detailed analysis of connections, see Mukhin & Kozlov (Semeinye).

135. Freeland (Sale of the Century), pp. 164–165.

136. The first public instance of cooperation was a letter in late 1992 signed by Bendukidze, Vinogradov, Gusinsky, and Khodorkovsky calling for compromise between President and Supreme Soviet. Schroder (El'tsin), p. 985, n. 40.

137. Hoffman (Oligarchs), pp. 270–275. Gusinsky was excluded because he had conflicts with the other members. Hoffman (Oligarchs), p. 285. The origin of the meetings lay in the oligarchs' desire to agree on some rules of the game for relations between themselves, and in particular to stop the attacks on one another. Hoffman (Oligarchs), p. 272.

138. Hoffman (Oligarchs), p. 274. According to Freeland, referring to 1996, the oligarchs were a 'single club with regular meetings'. Freeland (Sale of the Century), p. 229. The Logovaz Club established by Berezovsky was a common meeting place.

139. On 'faces in the snow', see Hoffman (Oligarchs), pp. 285–292; Korzhakov (Boris El'tsin), pp. 282–290; and Freeland (Sale of the Century), pp. 149–158.

140. On the 'bankers' war', see Hoffman (Oligarchs), pp. 365–396; Freeland (Sale of the Century), pp. 260–283; and Aleksei Badol'skii, "Novye starye lidery peredela sobstvennosti", *Otkrytiia politika* 10, 12, 1997, pp. 36–40. This was over the Sviazinvest auction in which Potanin gained preferential treatment at the expense of Berezovsky and Gusinsky, who then attacked him. Yeltsin had to intervene in September 1997 and, in a conference with the protagonists, demanded a truce. At the same time, the attempts by Nemtsov and Chubais to push through a second wave of liberalisation and to cut subsidies to power consumers increased the tension. Rutland (Introduction), p. 22.

141. For a similar argument, see Aleksei Iu. Zudin, "Oligarchy as a political problem of Russian postcommunism", *Russian Social Science Review* 41, 6, November–December 2000, pp. 4–33. Also see Pappe (Oligarkhi), p. 22.

142. On the oligarchs agreeing which companies would go to which oligarchs, and the protests of those excluded from this deal, see Freeland (Sale of the Century), p. 173.

143. Hoffman (Oligarchs), p. 379. Although it is not clear that Chubais agreed to this, and it became a major issue of discord.

144. Hoffman (Oligarchs), p. 281. Yeltsin signed a special decree privatising Russian Public Television (ORT) without the auction required by law. Also see Klebnikov (Godfather), pp. 147–148.

145. For example, Gusinsky's NTV gained an investment (to the tune of 30% of its shares) and a loan from Gazprom and the right to broadcast for 24 hours per day for a normal fee; Potanin gained a post in government, the go-ahead for the loans for shares scheme and continued access to government funds through his authorised bank, and his business partner received the visa he had formerly been denied. Freeland (Sale of the Century), p. 230. The oligarchs also favoured holding the 1996 election, in contrast to those around Korzhakov.

146. On Yeltsin's re-election and their role, see Hoffman (Oligarchs), ch. 13. The role of the media they controlled was crucial. It had been attacking Yeltsin prior to the agreement to come to his rescue; then it completely changed, giving him full-blooded support. The initial group at the meeting in Davos in February 1996 that agreed to come to Yeltsin's assistance comprised Berezovsky, Gusinsky, Aven, Fridman, Khodorkovsky, Smolensky, and Potanin. Lilia Shevtsova, *Yeltsin's Russia. Myths and Reality* (Washington, Carnegie Endowment for International Peace, 1995), p. 161

147. Deputy Prime Minister Aleksandr Livshits also had links to this group. Shevtsova (Yeltsin's Russia), p. 195.

148. Brady (Kapitalizm), pp. 206–207.

149. Klebnikov (Godfather), p. 274. For a brief time in 1993, Khodorkovsky had been deputy minister of fuel and energy. Gustafson (Capitalism), p. 121.

150. In 1999, he was elected to the Duma, but resigned from that body in July 2000.

151. One former minister reported that the oligarchs could call a new minister into a meeting and there, on the basis of a claim to 'own the country', demand that all appointments and major policy decisions be subject to their approval. Personal communication.

152. For the argument that the oligarchs were instrumental in Chernomyrdin's fall, see Hoffman (Oligarchs), pp. 2–3 & 404–408.
153. Even the energy suppliers were not strong advocates of Nemtsov's course because of the compensation they had been receiving in the way of tax concessions and retention of much of their export earnings.
154. For a similar analysis, see Philip Hanson & Elizabeth Teague, "Big Business and the State in Russia", *Europe-Asia Studies* 57, 5, 2005, p. 661.
155. cf. Klebnikov (Godfather), pp. 291–293.
156. Freeland (Sale of the Century), pp. 10–11 & 308–309.
157. S. Fortesk'iu, "Pravit li rossiei oligarkhiia", *Polis*, 5, 2002, pp. 66–67.
158. The first meeting with Yeltsin was when the president tried unsuccessfully to end the bankers' war. Present were Potanin, Gusinsky, Khodorkovsky, Smolensky, Vinogradov, and Fridman. At the second meeting, when Yeltsin tried to get the oligarchs to come in behind the Kirienko government's economic policy, there were present Viakhirev, Potanin, Gusinsky, Alekperov, Khodorkovsky, Smolensky, Fridman, Chubais, Malkin (of Rossiiskii Kredit Bank), and Bogdanov (of Surgutneftegaz). Berezovsky attended a meeting two weeks later with a second group where discussions were had with Kirienko and head of the presidential administration, Yumashev. According to Fridman, the oligarchs themselves initiated the latter two meetings. Schroder (El'tsin), p. 968. The June 1998 meeting was followed by a 'Declaration of the Representatives of Russian Business' calling for trust in Russian government policies. Schroder (El'tsin), p. 970.
159. Schroder (El'tsin), pp. 974–975.
160. For a short summary, see Mukhin (Biznes-elita), pp. 13–14. According to two scholars, only 15% of the 1993 business elite retained their positions in 2001. Kryshtanovskaya & White (The rise), p. 299. Of course this decline was not solely due to the August crisis.
161. Guriev & Rachinsky (The Role), p. 133.
162. Rutland (Putin and the Oligarchs), p. 144. For a survey of businessmen's personal links with Putin, see Mukhin (Biznes-elita), pp. 26–56. It was reported that Putin would 'meet regularly' with Miller, Chubais, and Deripaska. Harley Balzer, "Managed pluralism: Vladimir Putin's Emerging Regime", *Post-Soviet Affairs* 19, 3, July–September 2003, pp. 210–211. Vladimir Kogan of St Petersburg Banking House has also been mentioned in this regard. Kryshtanovskaya & White (Inside the Putin court), p. 1071. Abramovich is reported to have played a part in organising Putin's cabinet when he became Prime Minister and to have financially underwritten Edinenie. Midgley & Hutchins, pp. 102–103 & 106.
163. Mukhin (Biznes-elita), p. 66. For a study of the so-called 'aluminium kings' (which he lists as the Chernyi brothers, Deripaska, Anisimov and Veksel'berg, Abramovich, and Mamut) and the 'metal barons' (which he lists as Makhmudov, Abramov, Zhivilo brothers, Bendukidze, Mordashov, Potanin, and Prokhorov and Iordan), see Mukhin (Biznes-elita), pp. 66–144 & 145–187. His characterisation of some of these individuals as aluminium kings (e.g. Abramovich and Mamut) and metal barons (e.g. Zhivilo brothers and Bendukidze) is problematic. The different economic basis in the 'real' as opposed to the financial economy reflects in part the effect of the 1998 crisis which stimulated a shift of activity from the latter

to the former. On the diversification of the economic activities of some of these people, see Barnes (Owning Russia), ch. 6.

164. Hoffman (Oligarchs), pp. 259–261, Freeland (Sale of the Century), p. 319. A warrant was also issued for Smolensky. Both were soon withdrawn.

165. Gordon M. Hahn, *Russia's Revolution from Above, 1985–2000. Reform, Transition, and Revolution in the Fall of the Soviet Communist Regime* (New Brunswick, Transaction Publishers, 2002), pp. 520–521.

166. Putin's comments are in *Izvestiia* 25 February 2000 and *Segodnia* 20 March 2000. Thomas Graham, "Tackling Tycoons: Revenge or the Rule of Law?", *Wall Street Journal* 20 July 2000. Although for the view that this was part of an attempt by Putin to smash the Luzhkov-Gusinsky-Primakov opposition, see Mukhin (Biznes-elita), pp. 57–65, esp. p. 60.

167. Rutland (Putin and the Oligarchs), p. 140. Shortly after, two other of Gusinsky's media outlets, *Itogi* and *Segodnia*, were liquidated. Also see Natal'ia Arkhangel'skaia, Ekaterina Drankina, Tat'iana Gurova, Dan Medovnikov, Tigran Oganesyan & Aleksei Khazbiev, "Provokatsiia", *Ekspert* 27, 17 June 2000, pp. 10–12.

168. At the meeting were Alekperov, Kakha Bendukidze, Vladimir Bogdanov, Taimuraz Bolloev, Semen Vainshtok, Viktor Veksel'berg, Viakhirev, Deripaska, Yurii Zapol, Dmitrii Zimin, Anatolii Karachinsky, Oleg Kiselev, Vladimir Kogan, Vladimir Lisin, Aleksei Mordashov, Potanin, Sergei Pugachev, Nikolai Pugin, Fridman, Khodorkovsky, and Yevgenii Shvidler. Two days earlier there had been a meeting between Prime Minister Kasianov and Chubais, Alekperov, Bogdanov, Khodorkovsky, Shvidler, Vainshtok, Potanin, Zelenin, Deripaska, Lisin, Oleg Sysuev and people from other oil and metal companies, and Gazprom. Mukhin (Biznes-elita), pp. 15–16.

169. This injunction was later broadened to business as a whole and its terms expanded. For example, at the RSPP Congress in November 2004, Putin confirmed the 'unshakeable' nature of the outcome of privatisation and called on business to pay its taxes and become involved in helping achieve national (i.e. the government's) aims. This latter point was justified in terms of business' so-called 'social responsibility'. *Vedomosti* 17 November 2004, JRL 8457, 17 November 2004. Various other principles have at times been said to have been part of this deal, including that business should be run transparently, and that business should not enter into sweetheart deals with officials. For a questioning of how solid this deal was and for the argument that there was little in the way of commitment on Putin's part to it, see William Tompson, "Putin and the 'Oligarchs': A Two-sided Commitment Problem", Alex Pravda (ed.), *Leading Russia. Putin in Perspective* (Oxford, Oxford University Press, 2005), pp. 179–202.

170. *Vedomosti* 17 November 2004, JRL 8457, 17 November 2004. Lilia Shevtsova claims that they joined this body at the behest of the Kremlin as it sought to create an organised means of controlling them. Lilia Shevtsova, *Putin's Russia* (Washington, Carnegie Endowment for International Peace, 2005), p. 180. Consistent with this is the fact that the joining of RSPP came about following an attempt by Oleg Kiselev and Mikhail Fridman to develop a collective organisation to represent business interests. But before they did so, they sought and gained the approval of the state, in the form of the Presidential Administration.

Tina Podplatnik, "Big Business and the State in Putin's Russia, 2000–2004: Towards a New Super State Corporatism", Oxford University, D.Phil thesis, 2005, pp. 153–154.

171. For its initial membership, see Chapter 5, fn. 82.

172. Even though there was some moderation of this following a February 2000 meeting between Putin and Gusinsky, the coverage remained critical. Mukhin (Biznes-elita), p. 45.

173. Other oligarchs and businessmen clearly saw this attack on Gusinsky as an attack on them and signed an open letter defending the businessman. Signing the letter were Potanin, Chubais, V. Lisin (Novolipetsk Metallurgy Complex), Fridman, Aven, V. Veksel'berg (SUAL), Bendukidze (Uralmash), Khodorkovsky, Karachinsky (IBS), L. Zimin (Vympelson), A. Kokh (Gazprom-Media), A. Mordashev (Severstal), V. Yevtushenkov (Sistema), V. Mashchitsky (Rosinvestneft), Shvidler, Viakhirev, and O. Kiselev (Impeksbank). Mukhin (Biznes-elita), p. 59. Prominent absentees were Alekperov, Abramovich, Berezovsky, Deripaska, and Bogdanov.

174. Rutland (Putin and the Oligarchs), p. 140. In mid-2005, Gazprom purchased a controlling stake in *Izvestiia*.

175. Midgley & Hutchins (Abramovich), p. 113. Putin's show of independence in rejecting this may have been the trigger for Gusinsky's and Berezovsky's break with the president, who they now realised they would not be able to control.

176. See the interview in *Argumenty i fakty* 22, 31 May 2000.

177. It was shortly after revived, with Putin's apparent blessing, by a group including Abramovich, Mamut, Deripaska, Kokh, and Chubais. Shevtsova (Putin's Russia), p. 227.

178. On Yukos, including its political stances, see Pappe (Oligarkhi), pp. 128–140. On the attack, see Hanson & Teague (Big Business and the State), pp. 677–680, and for a discussion of the institutional context, see William Tompson, "Putting Yukos in Perspective", *Post-Soviet Affairs* 21, 2, April–June 2005, pp. 159–181. Just prior to the attack on Yukos, it was proposed to merge Yukos and Sibneft, thereby creating an oil giant that would have rivaled the largest Western firms. This seemed to have Kremlin approval. Shevtsova (Putin's Russia), p. 276. It was halted during the assault on Yukos. For a May 2003 report by a body called the National Strategy Council that claimed the oligarchs were planning a coup and which some saw as laying the groundwork for the move against Khodorkovsky, see "V Rossii gotovitsia oligarkhicheskii pereverot", *www.utro.ru*, 26 May 2003. For threats against other oligarchs at this time, see Tompson (Putin and the 'Oligarchs'), p. 193. Also on Yukos, see Fortescue (Russia's Oil Barons), ch. 7.

179. Putin's path of structural reform of the economy was hindered by oligarch-sponsored opposition within the Duma. Tompson (Putin and the 'Oligarchs'), pp. 188–191.

180. Shevtsova (Putin's Russia), p. 278.

181. For an argument that this was less about politics than taxation, see Fortescue (Russia's Oil Barons), ch. 7.

182. Khodorkovsky had also favoured private ownership of oil pipelines, which were still in state hands, and there was talk of him selling up to 40% of Yukos to Exxon Mobil or Chevron Texaco, which would have given Yukos a significant edge against any form of hostile state action. In March 2005, presidential aide

Igor Shuvalov said that the Yukos affair was meant as an example to others to get them to pay their taxes, and if it had not been Yukos it would have been another company. *Izvestiia* 31 March 2005. For Khodorkovsky's letter from prison effectively renouncing politics (although his declaration in mid-2005 that he would stand for election in Moscow seemed to contradict this) and supporting Putin, see Mikhail Khodorkovsky, "Krizis liberalizma v Rossii", *Vedomosti* 29 March 2005.

183. *Moscow Times* 24 December 2003. Although in the March 2005 meeting, Putin promised to reduce the period in which legal action over privatisation could be brought from 10 years to three. See the discussion in *Ezhednevnyi zhurnal* 7 April 2005, JRL 9114, 8 April 2005. This form of words may actually have been a way of keeping the issue of the certainty of private property on the agenda and thereby maintaining an element of uncertainty for the oligarchs.

184. But he was not convinced of the need for further attacks on the oligarchs. In mid-2004, there was pressure from Auditing Chamber head Sergei Stepashin to investigate Roman Abramovich, but Putin desisted. Shevtsova (Putin's Russia), p. 369.

185. Although for an argument that the 'family' still exercised significant influence under Putin, see Mukhin & Kozlov (Semeinye), pp. 174–274. These authors declare (p. 275) that the 'family' remains 'the most powerful participant in the political process in Russia'. And certainly key members of the Yeltsin administration remained close to Putin during the early part of his administration. These included Voloshin, head of the presidential administration, and Kasianov, the Prime Minister. For an analysis of the forces in his first administration, see Shevtsova (Putin's Russia), pp. 84–90.

186. Rutland (Putin and the Oligarchs), pp. 141–142. This was also an attempt to reorient the RSPP and turn it into the primary vehicle for relations between business and the executive. Irina Stanislavovna Semenenko, *Gruppy interesov na zapade i v rossii. Konseptsii i praktika* (Moscow, Institut mirovoi ekonomiki i mezhdunarodnykh otnoshenii, 2001), p. 22.

187. Only three prominent businessmen—Chubais, Yurgens, and Zimin—spoke out against his arrest.

188. For the different tenor of the July 2004 meeting compared with its predecessors, with Putin's superiority even more marked than it had been before, see Shevtsova (Putin's Russia), p. 367.

189. Among those attending the first meeting were Fridman, Khodorkovsky, Yevgenii Shvidler (Sibneft), Vladimir Bogdanov (Surgutneftegaz Oil), Chubais, Viakhirev, Vladimir Kogan (Promstroibank-St Petersburg), and Oleg Deripaska (Russian Aluminium). At the second meeting, nine of the twenty-two men came from the oil and gas sector, six from metals and engineering, six bankers, and one from a high-tech company. Rutland (Putin and the Oligarchs), pp. 143–144.

190. If under Yeltsin, the oligarchs had seen the president as a potential arbiter of oligarch conflict, Putin was seen much more as a master of the game than a referee. For an argument about the presidency as a referee in a broader oligarch game, see Fortescue (Russia's Oil Barons), pp. 105–106.

191. On aircraft production, a decree of 21 February 2006 unified all civilian and military aircraft manufacturers into one company—United Aircraft Construction

Corporation—in which the state will retain at least a 75% share. A similar move in the automotive sphere was also foreshadowed. The acquisition of Sibneft by Gazprom in 2005 was also significant for the oil industry.

192. For example, the 2005 announcement that majority foreign-owned companies would not be allowed to participate in the development of a number of oil, gold, and copper deposits, the exclusion of foreign oil companies from the exploitation of the Sakhalin-2 project through Gazprom's purchase of 51% of it from Shell (following sustained pressure from environmental authorities on Shell), and the June 2007 sale to Gazprom at a knock-down price of TNK-BP's 63% stake in the Kovytka gas project (on the back of threats by the Natural Resources Ministry to withdraw TNK-BP's licence to develop the field. State-linked companies now had a majority interest in all major oil and gas projects. "The State has Spoken", *Moscow News* 26 June 2007.

193. Shevtsova (Putin's Russia), p. 366. This is reflected in his approval of the creation of a new joint company, TNK-BP, and the purchase of 7.59% of Lukoil's shares by the US firm ConocoPhillips. Shevtsova (Putin's Russia), p. 436 and Barnes (Owning Russia), p. 222.

194. It may be indicative of the way their status has been reduced that when Putin talked to businessmen following the Khodorkovsky arrest, it was not to Russian businessmen but to the heads of Western investment houses: Allan Hurst (Citibank Russia), Stephen Newhouse (Morgan Stanley & Co), Bill Handel (Goldman Sachs International), Arnie Lindman (Alfred Berg Asset Management), John Carlson (Fideliti Investments), Anatolii Miliukov (Alfa Capital), Roman Filatov (Templeton Asset Management), Nicholas Sandstrom (City Group, London), Charles Ryan (United Finance Group), Evgenii Gavrilenkov (Troika Dialog), Jeffrey Costello (Bransvik UBC), Eli Linnaars (AEG Asset Management), Aleksis Rodzianko (Deutsche Bank), Igor Sagirian (Renaissance Capital), Piers Maynard (UBC Global Asset Management), and Sergei Mikhailov (Management Centre). *Izvestiia* 31 October 2003. Of course this may also reflect Putin's judgement that it was more important to satisfy Western investors than domestic businessmen.

195. Schroder (El'tsin), p. 978.

196. Neil J. Melvin, "The Consolidation of a New Regional Elite: The case of Omsk 1987–1995", *Europe-Asia Studies* 50, 4, 1998, p. 642. On regional alliances between local representatives of the organs of power, major regional bureaucrats and representatives of new business being known as the 'party of power', see V.N. Berezovskii, *Politicheskaia elita sovetskogo proshlogo i rossiiskogo nastoiashchego: priemy i metodi konkurentnoi bor'by* (Moscow, Tsentr politicheskoi kon'iunktury Rossii, unpublished, March 1996), p. 26.

197. S. Peregudov, N. Lapina & I. Semenenko, *Gruppy interesov i rossiiskoe gosudarstvo* (Moscow, Editorial URSS, 1999), ch. 5. A variation on this typology has been given by Robert Orttung, who labels the regions 'state controlled' (e.g. Tatarstan and Bashkortostan), 'corporate' (e.g. Chukotka and Sibneft, Moscow city, and Sistema), 'pluralist' (e.g. Astrakhan, Khanty-Mansii), 'foreign influenced' (e.g. Leningrad and Moscow oblasts), and 'neglected' (e.g. Smolensk and Tambov). He argues that of the eighty-nine regions, twenty were corporate, twenty-nine pluralist, four state controlled, five foreign influenced, and thirty-one neglected. Orttung (Business and Politics), pp. 52–56. The World Bank has identified five principal

actors who dominate in different regions: the federal centre (e.g. Sakha, Nizhnii Novgorod), the regional administration (e.g. Tatarstan, Bashkortostan), regional private companies (e.g. Tiumen oblast, Moscow oblast), federal private companies (e.g. Vologda, Sverdlovsk), and foreign investors (e.g. Udmurtiia, Saratov). The World Bank, *From Transition to Development. A country economic memorandum for the Russian Federation* (New York, The World Bank, 2004).

198. For some examples of local political leaders interfering in the affairs of local companies, including acting to redistribute their property, see Barnes (Russia's New Business Groups), p. 176.

199. This was not true in all regions. For two studies, see Galina Luchterhandt, "Politics in the Russian Province: Revda and Kinel", *Europe-Asia Studies* 49, 1, 1997, pp. 59–87 and Joel C. Moses, "Political-Economic Elites and Russian Regional Elections 1999–2000: Democratic tendencies in Kaliningrad, Perm, and Volgograd", *Europe-Asia Studies* 54, 2, 2002, pp. 905–931. For a list of the regions and the companies prominent in them, see Orttung (Business and Politics), pp. 52–54.

200. Orttung (Business and Politics), pp. 49–50.

201. Orttung (Business and Politics), p. 50.

202. Philip Hanson, "Administrative Regions and the Economy", Wendy Slater & Andrew Wilson (eds.), *The Legacy of the Soviet Union* (Basingstoke, Palgrave Macmillan, 2004), p. 150. For an argument about the governors' capacity to construct political machines which at times combined with local businesses, and about those governors' capacity to use local banks to increase their economic control, see Henry E. Hale, "Explaining Machine Politics in Russia's Regions: Economy, Ethnicity, and Legacy", *Post-Soviet Affairs* 19, 3, July-September 2003, pp. 228–263.

203. Shleifer & Treisman (Without a Map), p. 90.

204. Heiko Pleines, "Corruption and Crime in the Russian Oil Industry", Lane (Political Economy), p. 101.

205. Midgley & Hutchins (Abramovich), pp. 139–143.

206. Shleifer & Treisman (Without a Map), pp. 125–130.

207. Johnson (Fistful of Rubles), pp. 137–172. Increasingly the representatives of Moscow FIGs replaced locals in positions of power in the late 1990s Andrew Yorke, "Business and Politics in Krasnoyarsk Krai", *Europe-Asia Studies* 55, 2, 2003, p. 241.

208. There were also some spectacular cases of conflict; for example, between Krasnoyarsk governor Aleksandr Lebed and Krasnoyarsk Aluminium factory's Anatolii Bykov. Yorke (Business and Politics), pp. 241–262; also Volkov (Violent Entrepreneurs), p. 185. For another example, see Andrei Vin'kov & Nikolai Ul'ianov, "Makhmudov protiv gubernatora", *Ekspert* 22, 11 June 2001, p. 22. Some governors welcomed outside business entry. Orttung (Business and Politics), p. 51.

209. According to Stoner-Weiss, 'the more concentrated the regional economy, the more cooperative were economic and political elites.' She shows this through comparative case studies of Nizhnii Novgorod, Tiumen, Yaroslavl, and Saratov. Kathryn Stoner-Weiss, *Local Heroes. The Political Economy of Russian Regional Governance* (Princeton, Princeton University Press, 1997), p. 165 & esp. ch. 6. Also see the discussion of Tiumen oblast in Pete Glatter, "Continuity and Change in the Tyumen' Regional Elite 1991–2001", *Europe-Asia Studies* 55, 3, 2003, pp. 401–435. For a more qualified view, see Hale (Explaining Machine Politics), pp. 248–250.

210. They also invested heavily in the diamond processing industry. Graham Smith, *The Post-Soviet States. Mapping the Politics of Transition* (London, Arnold, 1999), p. 199. On Tatarstan and Sakha, see Mary McAuley, *Russia's Politics of Uncertainty* (Cambridge, Cambridge University Press, 1997), chs. 2 & 3. On Sakha, Daniel R. Kempton, "The Republic of Sakha (Yakutia): The Evolution of Centre-Periphery Relations in the Russian Federation", *Europe-Asia Studies* 48, 4, 1996, pp. 587–613, and Lapina (Rossiiskie ekonomicheskie elity), p. 18.

211. By shifting profits through transfer pricing, companies could both take advantage of differential tax rates and bestow largesse on one region at the expense of the other. Shliefer & Triesman (Without a Map), pp. 132 & 139.

212. For a similar sort of structure in Primorskii krai, see Satter (Darkness at Dawn), pp. 166–173 and Peter Kirkow, "Regional Warlordism in Russia: The Case of Primorskii Krai", *Europe-Asia Studies* 47, 6, 1995, pp. 923–947, where there was a merging of the political machine of Governor Evgenii Nazdratenko with the joint stock company PAKT.

213. On 'Sistema', see V.N. Berezovskii, V.V. Federov & A.L. Chesnakov, *Moskovskoe pravitel'stvo Iuriia Luzhkova: vlastnyi potentsial, rol', mesto i vliianie v Rossiiskoi politike* (Moscow, Tsentr politicheskoi kon'iunktury Rossii, April 1994, unpublished); Virginie Coulloudon, "Moscow City Management: A New Form of Russian Capitalism?", Rutland (Business and State), pp. 89–100, esp. pp. 84–86; Aleksei Mukhin, *Moskovskie oligarkhi* (Moscow, Tsentr politicheskoi informatsii, 2000), pp. 38–56; and Pappe (Oligarkhi), pp. 183–188. For connections between Sistema and crime, see Satter (Darkness at Dawn), pp. 135–136.

214. Hahn (Russia's Revolution from Above), p. 516.

215. Johnson (Fistful of Rubles), p. 192. On the media, see Blinova (Media-Imperii), pp. 103–120.

216. See the discussion in Donald N. Jensen, "The Boss: How Yury Luzhkov Runs Moscow", *Demokratizatsiya* 8, 1, Winter 2000, pp. 83–122. For different figures, see Mukhin (Moskovskie oligarkhi), p. 9.

217. Mukhin (Moskovskie oligarkhi), pp. 15–24.

218. Hoffman (Oligarchs), pp. 245–249 & 265.

219. In particular, see the discussion of Luzhkov's early steps in Hoffman (Oligarchs), pp. 54–77. The links between Luzhkov and many businesses are outlined in Mukhin (Moskovskie oligarkhi).

220. Berezovskii et al. (Moskovskoe pravitel'stvo), p. 4.

221. Hoffman (Oligarchs), pp. 160–164.

222. A promise strengthened by his willingness to use the Moscow-based security apparatus to provide protection to his associates.

223. Conglomerates were able to use their power to declare losses in the regions but profits in Moscow. Shleifer & Treisman (Without a Map), p. 133. For some examples of Muscovite involvement in business, see Elena Rytsareva, "Kosmos izbavliaetsia ot dolgov", *Ekspert* 8, 26 February 2001, p. 25; Valeriia Selivanova, "Konditerskoe otechestvo v opasnosti!" *Ekspert* 11, 19 March 2001, pp. 18–21.

224. For Luzhkov's own discussion of this, see Yurii Luzhkov, *My deti tvoi Moskva* (Moscow, Vagrius, 1996). For a bland discussion of Luzhkov's role, see V.B. Zotov, *Kak mer Luzhkov upravliaet Moskvoi (materialy lektsii)* (Liubertsy, VINITI, 1998).

225. For details, see Berezovskii et al. (Moskovskoe pravitel'stvo), pp. 10–18.

226. Orrtung (Business and Politics), pp. 52–54.
227. On the role played by the presidential envoys, created by Putin in 2000, in regard to business in the regions, see Robert Orttung & Peter Reddaway, "What Do the Okrug Reforms Add Up To? Some Conclusions", Peter Reddaway & Robert W. Orttung (eds.), *The Dynamics of Russian Politics. Putin's Reform of Federal-Regional Relations. Volume 1* (Lanham, Rowman & Littlefield Publishers Inc., 2004), pp. 292–293. The other chapters in this volume discuss the actions of the envoys in the districts of Russia.
228. This is argued very strongly by Tompson (Putting Yukos), p. 172.

Conclusion: Bourgeoisie, State, and Democracy

The national experiences examined in this book show that the image of the industrial entrepreneur as the self-made man, making his fortune independent of assistance from the state, is largely a myth. Significant sections of the emergent industrial bourgeoisie in each of these countries were substantially assisted in the building of their businesses, and their fortunes, by their capacity to exploit the state. Sometimes in the acquisition and utilisation of the state's material resources, sometimes through the use of its legal powers, and sometimes through a combination of both, members of the bourgeoisie gained significant advantages in pursuit of their business activities. While it is true that, generally, wealthy and powerful businessmen at the head of major business concerns were able to extract resources from the state through personal contacts at a much higher level than small- and medium-sized businesses which often had to deal with middle- and lower-ranking officials (a distinction which in Russia was initially related to the different origins of sections of the emergent bourgeoisie—state origins cf. *de novo*), all members of the bourgeoisie sought to exploit the state in their quest to accumulate wealth and power. Although everywhere this bourgeoisie was critical of what it saw to be the state's petty regulation, it was also reliant on the state for its continued well-being. The state was central to the conduct of the very activities that defined the bourgeoisie as a class. The importance of the state's contribution was such that, rather than independence being seen as the defining characteristic of the capitalist bourgeoisie, perhaps reliance upon the state should be seen in this way.

The extent of this dependence is impossible to quantify across the class, nationally or cross-nationally, but the foregoing analysis suggests that the exploitative class–state relationship was much more extensive in post-Soviet Russia than in any of the other countries under study. In terms of origins, because many of the first wave of businessmen in Russia actually came from within the state itself, the state can be said to have spawned the new bourgeoisie in a way that it did not in the other countries. Furthermore, the subsequent balance of the Russian bourgeoisie's activities appears to be different to the others, in the sense that more of it seems to have involved the direct exploitation of the state and its resources than the generation of productive wealth from scratch. The privatisation of state resources appears to have been a much larger part of the wealth accumulation process for many of the Russian bourgeoisie than it has been elsewhere, including the United States where the state–business link had been so important at the end of the nineteenth century. Similarly, reliance upon personal contacts and informal arrangements with state officials at all levels seems to have been more pervasive in Russia than elsewhere.

But three qualifications are in order. First, notwithstanding Progressivism in the United States, there is today much greater publicity and attention given to business and its activities, including its relationship with government, than in any of these other countries at the time of the emergence of this class. Not only is there a larger and more broadly based enquiring media, but there is also a significantly larger body of scholarly investigation which has focused upon this matter. Accordingly, there is much more information available about contemporary developments than those which occurred in preceding centuries. This could exaggerate in a relative sense the perception of levels of state dependence on the part of the Russian bourgeoisie.

Second, with less than two decades since the fall of the USSR, the new class remains in its infancy, and it may be that such a class is more reliant on the state at this stage of its existence than later in its life. Certainly in the other national cases, such overt reliance upon the state was reduced later in the class' history. How this affects a comparison between the first decade and a half of the post-Soviet bourgeoisie and the similar classes over their entire life spans in Britain, France, Germany, and the United State is not clear.

Third, the yardstick about what is and what is not acceptable has changed. At the time of the onset of industrialisation in Britain, France, Germany, and the United States, conceptions of public interest and the distinction between that and private interest were only weakly developed. Notions of a conflict of interest between private concern and public duty on the part of state officials did not have any real currency in public life for much of this time. Acceptance of the principle that the use of state office for personal enrichment was unacceptable did not really take hold in these four societies until industrial development was well under way. As a result, the sorts of contacts and practices which would today be considered corrupt were not always thus considered at the time; what we would see as unacceptable today was accepted as a matter of course. This changed conception of what constituted 'proper' or 'appropriate' behaviour means that Russian businessmen are being judged according to more demanding standards that did not apply to their predecessors, and are therefore being found wanting in a much more stark fashion. The activity of the Russian bourgeoisie may thus appear much more serious and objectionable and on a greater scale than that of its predecessors even though the actions are basically similar.

Nevertheless, there are clear reasons why the post-Soviet bourgeoisie was more exploitative of the state than its analogues in the West. One is the extent of the state's responsibilities. The Soviet state was dominant, spreading its tentacles into all parts of society and asserting control over all the economic resources in the country. This means that if the emergent bourgeoisie was to get access to or control over those resources, it would have to deal with the state and its officials. There was no alternative given that control was vested here. And for those officials, facing the prospect of economic difficulty and dislocation in a context of the weakening of state power, an approach from members of the bourgeoisie offered opportunities to parlay their control over resources into private benefits. Accordingly, if the bourgeoisie had nowhere to go except to the state to gain access to resources, and state officials were open to their approach, the state was fundamental in the shaping of the new class. Such a situation did not exist in any of the other countries under study. In none of these was the state the controller of economic resources on anything like the scale of the USSR. In Britain, France, and Germany, where most of the national territory was settled prior to industrialisation, resources were already overwhelmingly in private hands. In the United States, where significant parts of the continent were still being settled by Europeans at the opening of the industrial era, the state exercised rights of control over some of the territory, and so it was with such authorities that early entrepreneurs (especially in mining and railways) had to deal. This lower profile of the state in direct resource control meant that in the Western countries, there was less need than in Russia for the exploitation of the state in order to build up new businesses. This also affected the form such exploitation took. Where the state was in direct control of resources (Russia and, in a less extensive fashion, the United States), both material and legal exploitation of it were possible; where there was limited direct state control of resources (Britain, France, and Germany), legal exploitation was the main road that was open to the bourgeoisie.

Another factor which may have increased the likelihood of the Russian bourgeoisie to exploit the state to a greater extent than its Western counterparts was class origins. In Russia, the official positions within the state apparatus from which much of the initial wave of bourgeois entrepreneurs came was important. Such origins gave them a direct line into the state structure, reflected both in personal contacts and in the cast of mind which saw the state as an established legitimate source of resources and provision of benefits. The patterns of mutual dependence that were thereby created could become self-sustaining; they would appear as the 'normal' way of acting both for state officials and for new waves of entrepreneurs, even when the latter lacked personal links into the state stemming from their own past. In the other countries the emergent bourgeoisie did not generally have such direct personal connections into the state. Rather such connections, to the extent that they existed, were mediated through the process of social integration. In Britain, the overlap between industrialists and traditional landowners plus the role the latter played in the state provided the new class with some avenues into the state structure. In France and Germany, the strong statist traditions and the view of the state as having an important role to play in fostering national development created a situation in which some commonality of interests emerged between officials and entrepreneurs, thereby giving the latter an opening into the state which they could exploit. In the United States, bourgeois penetration of the state was much greater. The weakness of traditional social barriers and the strength of the ideology that linked business with the normal activities of state and society projected businessmen into a prominent, and what was considered a legitimate, place in the political structure. Business interests were more strongly embedded in the American state and in state policy than in any of the other countries, including Russia.

The capacity of the bourgeoisie to exploit the state was also related to the pattern of integration into the system which the class was able to achieve. An important factor in this was the social structure and accompanying values dominant in the society at the time of the emergence of the new class. Both Russia and France were undergoing a process of fundamental change at the time of the emergence of the new class, although in the French case this was much further advanced than it was in Russia. In both countries, the former political regime had fallen, a development involving the destruction of the basis upon which social and political domination had rested: in France on landed property, in Russia on politico-administrative office. In France, the Revolution had done away with the *ancien régime* and thereby undercut the position of the traditional aristocracy, although their heirs in the form of major landowners continued to exercise significant influence, especially in local matters, and enjoy high social prestige. But the Revolution, reinforced by the modernising reforms of the Napoleonic period, significantly stimulated the view that France was building a modern state and society, one in which the elements from the past would no longer dominate. Accordingly, it was one in which the representatives of the new economy were acknowledged to have an important part to play. However, there was also a strong tradition regarding entry to the state which was maintained during this period. Entry to political office was largely mediated through state officials, often at the local level, with the result that more so than in the other countries under review, such officials played a central role in public life. This was underpinned by a strong statist ethos which emphasised the building and strengthening of the French state and the projection of its national power, an aim which while encouraging industrial development, placed it squarely subordinate to considerations of *raison d'etat*. Thus the emergent bourgeoisie was not confronted by a declining landed aristocracy but by an ascendant self-conscious and cohesive state officialdom, and against such a group, bourgeois claims to be the representative of the future were not as strong as they would have been had they been confronted by a traditional aristocracy. Bourgeois integration into the system therefore did not seriously challenge the dominant place of the state official.

In post-Soviet Russia, the emergence of the new bourgeois class was taking place at the same time as the overthrow of the old regime and the attempt to create a new one out of its remains. Rather than seeking to enter a structure that was basically stable, the emergent bourgeoisie was confronted with a situation in which both values and social structures were in a state of considerable flux. But while aspects of the old world had been discredited, much of it still remained in place, constituting a significant factor shaping the development of both new values and new social structures. Utilising their experience of working in these structures and the traditions stemming from Soviet times about the role of officials, including the control they could exercise over the disposition of state resources, many of the new bourgeoisie were able to bridge from this old structure into the new using the wealth they accumulated along with the contacts with state officials that they enjoyed as the means for doing this; for those coming from within the state, former position and pre-existing personal contacts were central, while for the 'new men' the propensity of many officials to rent seek in order to bolster their personal financial positions appears to have been paramount. There was little in the way of an established social barrier, while the flux in values meant that ideologically little seemed to stand in the way of the new class; indeed, the strength of the message projected by political elites about the building of a market economy (although challenged by significant elements in the polity) seemed to support an expanded bourgeois role in public life. In this way, both ideologically and structurally Russia seemed to offer good scope for the entry of the new bourgeois class into the developing structure of power. Thus in the fluid situation in France and Russia, the established social and ideological barriers to the new class had been weakened, and it was able to take advantage of this to different degrees to place its imprint on the shape of the new social and ideological structure emerging in the society.

In contrast, in Germany the dominance of the traditional value structure and of the landed Junker class which it reflected had been reinforced through national unification along Prussian lines in 1871. These values, and the class of which they were the expression, were deeply embedded in the Prussian polity and were transferred to the new national polity. This meant that, despite the growth of a new bourgeois ideology along with industrialisation and the new bourgeois class, these traditional values continued to exercise significant influence over German development. These values did not destroy the emergent bourgeois value system, just as the Junkers did not destroy the new bourgeois class. But the continued strength of the traditional class and its values, reinforced by the state's drive to construct a powerful German Reich, a drive which harnessed industrial development to state aims and thereby as in France subordinated the bourgeoisie symbolically to state officials, did impose significant constraints on the development of both bourgeois ideology and the accession to a position of social and political power by the new bourgeois class, which thereby remained less integrated, and therefore more of an outsider, than any of the other bourgeoisies studied here.

As in Germany, in Britain and the United States at the time of the emergence of the new bourgeoisie, the established class and ideological structures had not been fundamentally transformed, but each in their own way was very different from that in Germany. In Britain, the established ideology and class structure were rooted in a society in which landed property remained the principal source of esteem and underpinning of power, but where other sources of wealth, including urban commercial interests, were making severe inroads into this. This was reflected in the widespread belief in the importance and value of material progress, and along with this went an appreciation of the importance of entrepreneurial activity and its incorporation into established institutions.[1] Furthermore, the traditional structure was more flexible than it appeared. Few of the landed magnates were of truly ancient lineage; the institutional structures of the society (especially after the middle of the seventeenth century) enabled a degree of social mobility, while the commercial ethos of the society plus the expansion of empire encouraged the development of alternative sources of wealth to land. Consequently, the established structure did not constitute a serious barrier to the rise of a new class of the sort that the new bourgeoisie was. Thus in Britain, ideological and social structural constraints were less powerful than in France or Germany, but more so than in the United States.

In the United States, in structural terms, there was no hereditary landowning aristocracy that dominated the society. Certainly, from the beginning of the republic, established landowners played a prominent role in public life, but they were by no means dominant. Military men, urban professionals (especially lawyers), and people involved in commercial concerns all played a prominent part in shaping public life both nationally and in the individual states. Where there were electoral restrictions, generally they did not exclude businessmen, and many of the latter were active in political life. This situation was underpinned by an aspirational set of values that welcomed those who were successful (as long as they were not black) and enabled the nouveau riche to enter the highest levels of society regardless of the source of their wealth. The myths surrounding the founding of American society and later its liberation from British rule had a strong element of creating a society of opportunity in which talented hard-working individuals could rise up the ladder to prosperity and social prestige. Important here too was the association in much of the public rhetoric of commercial principles and the national ideology; the image of the unity of America and business was a strong element in public ideology. Even though in practice the 'log cabin to white house' myth was a long way from an accurate description of reality, it succinctly encapsulated the aspirational aspects of American society. Underpinned by the expanding frontier and the apparently limitless opportunities for wealth generation that that involved, American society was open to those with wealth and thereby held few barriers to the rise of the new class. In this sense, the relative openness of the structure reinforced by the ideological foundations of the society meant there were few barriers to the advance of the emergent bourgeoisie.

The prevailing social and ideological structures were therefore clearly central to the capacity of the new class to integrate into the hierarchies of the society. Where those structures remained resistant to the new class, as in Germany, integration remained less complete than elsewhere, the main form it took was through official organisations like the cartels, and the scope for exploitation of the state was more limited. Where that structure was undergoing substantial change, as in France and Russia, the new bourgeoisie found itself knocking against another major social group, the state officials, and it was the relationship between these groups that ultimately decided the shape of bourgeois embeddedness in society and the capacity for exploitation. In both cases, informal, social, relations appeared more important than those mediated through the formal institutions of state. But where those structures were open or sufficiently flexible, as in Britain and the United States, the bourgeoisie was able to attain the highest level of integration in both social and institutional terms. With integration went significant potential for exploitation of the state.

Also important in this question of exploitation of the state was the nature and role of the state, including state autonomy. The issue of autonomy and what it means has been much debated,[2] and this ground will not be covered here. But essential for our discussion is recognition of autonomy in terms of the state not being captured by interests or groups within society. This question has been seen in terms of two principal elements,[3] the pursuit by the state of policies that are in its own interests, or at least not in the interests of leading parts of society, and the social origins of state officials. As an institutional structure, the state clearly had interests of its own. At base, these were to bring in sufficient revenue to enable it to continue functioning and to carry out whatever range of functions was believed appropriate. But above such basic survival interests, states have also taken on responsibility for at least external security and domestically for a range of other functions, including domestic security. At times states have also looked to play a major role in economic development. This is reflected in experiences as diverse as the so-called temple economies of the ancient world, seventeenth and eighteenth century mercantilism, and the role of the state as a driver of

313

economic development in backward twentieth century economies. In those cases when the state has seen itself as having an important driving role in the economy, and among our cases this applies especially to Germany at the end of the nineteenth and early twentieth centuries, increased room was opened up for business–state interaction of various sorts. But as long as the state elite remained united and its ethos of officialdom was strong, and while its commitment to the state's aims remained undiminished, restraints existed on business exploitation of the state. This has sometimes been seen in terms of the developmental state. This is conceived of as a state characterised by a neutral or insulated bureaucracy, effective politicians and the pursuit of consistent trade and development policies, which is able through these substantially to stimulate economic development.[4] This sort of state was often contrasted with the so-called 'predatory' state whose officials sought to exploit business[5] and the weak state which is subject to exploitation by groups within society.[6] The weak state could not be an autonomous state because of the inability of state officials to fend off the demands of powerful actors in society and pursue the interests of the state itself. This issue of whose interests policy is in is also central to the second element in the issue of autonomy, that of social origins. This is underpinned by the assumption that state officials, who come from, for example, the bourgeoisie, will be systematically biased in favour of the interests of that group, or if there is no systematic bias, they will at least be more sympathetic to those interests. This is a logical assumption, and historically there seems to be much evidence to affirm its veracity.

The crucial issue in the question of autonomy is therefore in whose interests state officials make decisions. If they systematically make decisions in favour of one particular social group, or perhaps simply all of the most crucial decisions favour the interests of one group, it may be that the state has effectively been captured by that group. Alternatively, if the decisions made by state officials do not systematically favour one group, instead either supporting different interests on different issues or consistently favouring the interests of those state officials themselves conceived as a group, or consistently favouring the state as an institution, the state may be considered autonomous rather than captured. The key here is the extent to which state officials conceive of themselves as a group separate from other groups in society, whether they have a sense of corporate identity and believe that the state itself has particular interests which should be advanced and protected.

The degree to which state officials conceive of themselves as a corporate group (something which is intrinsic to infrastructural power) separate from society as a whole will depend on a variety of factors.[7] The existence of a form of specialised training, such as that offered through the French academies, can be an important element in the development of a sense of identity for officials. So too can be the symbolism of such things as uniforms and titles. But perhaps the most important factor is the degree to which the officials perceive themselves to work within a structured hierarchy ordered along lines generated and enforced by that hierarchy itself distinct and separate from the society more generally. To the extent to which such things are official-specific, they will contribute to such an identity. But perhaps more important than these sorts of things is that to which these actually contribute, the development of a corporate ethos of officialdom which marks this group out as distinct from other sections of society. Where this sort of ethos is strongly entrenched and it is something to which new members must submit, it can be a powerful factor shaping identity and perception of what sorts of policies are appropriate and what are not. Where it is weak, officialdom is more vulnerable to infection by interests from within the society as a whole.

In today's terms, one aspect of this ethos is the notion of public service: that state officials see themselves as being in office to perform functions that will contribute to the well-being of the community or society as a whole. It is commitment to this ideal that is meant to be the main bulwark against partial treatment by the state; officials are expected to place the public interest above private interests. This ideology of public interest, at least in so far as it pervades all ranks of the state service, is a recent, twentieth century, phenomenon. Throughout the period when the bourgeoisie was emerging in Britain, France, Germany, and the United States, this ideology had not displaced the view that public office was something from which one could benefit personally, while in Russia the reverse process has occurred whereby the doctrine of serving the community embedded in the notion of the construction of communism was eroded, beginning in late-Soviet times, by the growth of the ethos of private profit (including personal profit from office) and by the new market conditions. Such ideological flux left open the possibility for the sorts of arrangements businessmen sought to reach with bureaucrats and politicians to further their business interests discussed above. This opportunity was strengthened when officials were paid badly (or not at all), especially when compared with what they could obtain outside state service. Thus where there was little sense of corporate identity and the ethos of state service was weak, and especially where the rewards from state service were paltry, the temptation for officials to supplement their income could be well nigh irresistible. Under these circumstances, the scope for business to gain concessions from the state was substantial.

Official propensity to become engaged in mutually beneficial relations with business was part of the weakness of state infrastructural power. Although the central bureaucracy of the state was growing in all five countries,[8] and it comprised overwhelmingly full-time employees, the capacity of that bureaucracy to extend its control throughout the country was constrained in the four Western states by the nature of the technical means available to it, and in Russia by the Soviet legacy. In the Western countries in the nineteenth century, there were not the sorts of logistics and communications facilities available that would enable the centre to keep close and continuing control over what happened in all parts of the country. In Russia, bureaucratic institutional norms were weak compared with the strength of the personalist principle in structuring the behaviour of state officials. More generally, the controlling and operating mechanisms within the state bureaucratic structure itself were, to different degrees in the different countries, not sufficiently developed to ensure either that that structure worked efficiently or that the room for independent self-serving initiative on the part of individual bureaucrats was highly restricted. This means that the state structure was insufficiently institutionalised, working less on the basis of formal, regularised rules and norms of behaviour related to making the system work efficiently, than of unofficial practices and patterns of work that were more linked to the individual preferences of officials than of any overall schema of institutional functioning. Indicative of this is the prevalence of patronage in the filling of bureaucratic positions and the acceptance of the legitimacy of the use of those positions for personal gain. This latter reflects the weakness of the sense of public service or of the inadmissibility of conflict of interest.

The point about the weakness and ambiguity of institutional norms in the state structures in these countries is that this weakness made those states permeable to outside influence. The weakness of such norms meant that the boundaries between state and society became indistinct and the capacity of the officials to conceive of themselves and to act in a corporate fashion was reduced. The weakness of effective rules governing the behaviour of officials and the lack of a robust ideology of public service that was underpinned by clear conceptions of the illegitimacy of conflict of interest meant that there was little disincentive for officers of the state to seek to use their positions for personal gain. It is this propensity of those who run the state to use their offices and the resources they control to engage in private economic activity which is at the heart of what has widely been called 'crony capitalism'. The receptiveness of the state to penetration by economic concerns and the strength of the ideology of state service on the part of the state's officers will shape the extent to which the state is dominated by economic interests.

The attempt by business to dominate or exploit the state is a natural strategy for those who seek to build up their businesses and their fortunes. The state's regulatory power and its control over resources make it an obvious target for those whose activities could benefit through changes in the regulative environment or by gaining access to such resources. We should not, therefore, expect business to stop trying to exploit the state. If we want to put limits on this, given that its total eradication is impossible, we need to look to the state rather than to business. Historically, business exploitation of the state was brought under control in the four Western countries principally through the process of strengthening the state. But this has been a particular sort of strengthening: the building up of the state's infrastructural capacity through the development of its internal regulative regime. This has involved both increased oversight of the activities of state officials (including punishment for transgression) and the promotion and embedding within state officialdom of a corporate ethos involving the primacy of service to the community and the inadmissibility of partial interests impinging on the fulfilment of their duties. This has commonly been seen in terms of the development of a professional public service, but what it really means is the consolidation in public life of the principle that state officials (both political and administrative) have a responsibility to act independent of partial interest and with only the interests of the broad community at heart. A professional, impartial bureaucracy of state officials is what has lain behind all of the measures taken against corruption in these countries, including the campaign against 'Old Corruption' in Britain and the Progressive movement in the United States. In the four Western countries, such measures have been successful in helping to reduce unacceptable business exploitation of the state and thereby create a more robust and independent market economy, but it is not clear that the state-strengthening measures introduced by Vladimir Putin in Russia can have this effect. While the increased centralisation of power and the coherence of the state that have come about as a result of his measures were needed, they have not thus far been accompanied by measures to improve the transparency of bureaucratic functioning or to embed an ethos of incorruptible public service among state officials. This is clearly crucial to reducing the exploitation of the state by business and to supplement the measures he has taken against business influence since becoming president.

Also crucial in Putin's strengthening of state power has been the way in which he has projected the state back into the economy in a structural fashion. The takeover of what were private assets by state-controlled companies, most spectacularly in the oil industry but also through the growth of state controls in other sectors, has served fundamentally to shape the development of the Russian economy. Putin does not seek the nationalisation of the economy along Soviet lines. He recognises that the private sector has a crucial role to play in Russia's economic development, including foreign capital, but in his view private actors must at all times be sensitive to state interests. The aim seems to be to ensure that the state has a sufficient direct investment in the major sectors of the economy to ensure that it can shape the way market forces operate in those sectors. The economy will remain capitalist in nature, but it will be a form of state-directed capitalism. This has direct implications for the bourgeoisie: this group will remain in a subordinate position in the economic structure, with its opportunities for development significantly shaped and constrained by state preferences and policies. Furthermore, if the pattern that has emerged under Putin becomes consolidated, the state elite will define who can be a member of the upper levels of the bourgeoisie. Given that this structure also involves the blurring of boundaries between state officials and private businessmen, and that it places such significant economic potential in the hands of those officials, it will encourage the perpetuation of the pattern of businessmen seeking to extract privileges and concessions from the state. If the state is the dominant actor in the economy, it will continue to be seen as a source of resources that can potentially be utilised for private gain. In this sense, Putin's projection of the state even more directly into the economy, and the consequent creation of a new type of Russian political economy, is likely to reinforce the patterns of bourgeois dependence on the state that have been so evident until now.

Bourgeoisie and Democracy

The close linkage with the state, achieved through the integration of the emergent economic bourgeoisie into the prevailing power hierarchies and the role the state has played as the generator of wealth for the bourgeoisie, calls into question an important element of the major theories of democratisation noted in Chapter 1. Moore's argument that a bourgeoisie independent of the state resulted in democracy while dependence on the state led to authoritarian rule is clearly fallacious if in practice no bourgeoisie was independent of the state. Similarly, the respective views of Rueschemeyer et al. and Kurth of the bourgeoisie as responding principally to its location in the class structure or in the particular phase of industrial production, requires modification to take into account its reliance on the state. Respectively, any bourgeois response to democratising pressure from below will be shaped by its relationship with the dominant group in charge of the state (see below), while the imperatives driven by the different phases of production will be moderated by the degree to which the bourgeoisie has ready access to the state's resources. This raises a question: if the bourgeoisie is dependent on the state and embedded to some degree in the existing structure, how has democratisation come about, and what role has that class played in it?

The bourgeoisie's approach to the state historically was motivated by the desire to enhance its wealth-creating capacities. While some individuals may have been prompted to enter politics for idealistic reasons, the overwhelming motivation for most was material gain. Despite its historic designation as a revolutionary class, the bourgeoisie did not set out fundamentally to transform society. The established picture of the bourgeoisie as a revolutionary force bursting onto the scene and changing it in all its aspects clearly needs qualification. The bourgeoisie as a class crystallised slowly, building its wealth and power on the basis of its economic activities, and a sense of its own identity on the basis of the recurring patterns of action, both economic and social, that developed around the newly emergent processes of production, distribution, and exchange. But this was not a single, consolidated class with a unity of interest. Some people developed wealth and power very quickly, within the space of a generation, and were catapulted into a social and sometimes political position very different from those whose process of accumulation was more measured. Different types of activity generated different interests and patterns of action: manufacturers, financiers, and traders were the three basic categories, but within each of these there were also manifold divisions, interests, and priorities. Geography, scale of operation, age, religion, and initially even social origin created cleavages that complicated notions of class identity and the pursuit of common interests. But even while the class was crystallising, society was being changed in a revolutionary fashion.

It is clear that with industrialisation, which was the process that both produced this new bourgeoisie and was driven by it, the structures and patterns of society were transformed. The growth of a large urban working class, usually accompanied by the shrinking of the peasantry, was the most striking demographic effect of this, and this took hold immediately large-scale industrial development was under way. Associated with this was the recasting of the geographical environment: the growth of new towns around emergent industry and the enlargement and restructuring of many existing towns around industrial enterprise. With this went both the social differentiation of the urban environment and the redevelopment of existing urban infrastructure, including the town centre. These changes were obvious and easily seen by anyone who cared to look. Furthermore, they constituted a revolution in the existing structure. Similarly, industrialisation generated a whole new material culture, with standards and modes of living being transformed by the introduction of the products of the industrial revolution. In the public realm from electric street lighting to mass circulation newspapers, and in the private realm from new consumer items to better sanitation, innovations resulting from the industrial revolution rendered people's lives unrecognisable from what they had been before. In the cultural sphere too, the modern age differed substantially from what had gone before it. Not only did modes of cultural activity change, but the development of mass literacy completely changed the nature of the cultural sphere and its products. It was also important in ushering the new classes into the political system and defining the role they were to play in it.

These changes to the society were fundamental in nature and revolutionary in effect, but they did not stem directly from the bourgeoisie itself. They were the product of industrialisation, which the bourgeoisie was central in driving, and they were therefore much more a second stage effect of the class than a direct result of conscious actions on its part. Nevertheless, given the relationship between the bourgeoisie and industrialisation, and the effect of the latter in transforming society, the former was a transformative class. But the issue is what the relationship was between this transformative bourgeoisie

319

and the power structures in the societies in which they emerged, and the implications this had for regime change.

It is important to recognise that the bourgeoisie did not metaphorically storm the existing political institutions, take them over, and transform them in their own image. Rather, the bourgeoisie sought to adapt itself to the existing political structures, to creep into the niches that were available to it, and to work within the structures and processes that were current; their place and role were structured by the institutional configurations, both formal and social, with which they were confronted. Involvement in the legislature and executive, in mainstream political parties, in interest groups and business associations, and in local government were the formal vehicles for this, while personal contacts and social integration were the more informal means whereby the new class became embedded in the existing structures of power and privilege. If the class was a revolutionary force, that revolution was carried out by stealth, from within the institutions rather than from outside by direct assault. The issue for the bourgeoisie was less exclusion from the power structures than making their way within those structures where powerful interests were usually entrenched. In this sense, the story was one of peaceful integration into the existing structures and processes, an integration which did not lead to an immediate fundamental reworking of how those structures and processes operated. When there were changes, these were essentially at the margins, and although ultimately these resulted in the fundamental recasting of the form and content of politics at the national level, this was a gradual rather than an immediate development.

The bourgeoisie were not much concerned to try to bring about change in the political system. There is no evidence that either collectively or individually in large numbers they pushed in a systematic fashion for democratic reform, although many did come to support liberal causes.[9] Most were not interested in democracy as a political system or as an ideal, just as they had no ideological attachment to non-democratic forms of government. It may be that some of the emergent bourgeoisie would have favoured the latter, because of the power it denied to the urban working class, but given the paternalist views that many factory owners had and the associated belief that they could control the votes of their workers, even this is not certain. There is very little evidence that the economic bourgeoisie as a class uniformly supported one type of political form over another. There was certainly no 'democratic project' championed by the economic bourgeoisie. They were content to work within the existing system, as long as they were able to benefit from it. Where does this conclusion leave the widely accepted view that the bourgeoisie is the harbinger of democracy? To answer this, we need to distinguish between the economic and the professional bourgeoisie. The latter comprised that group of people who became prominent in the urban public life of industrialising countries, what are now seen as white-collar professionals including most importantly lawyers, teachers, doctors, intellectuals, and state officials. These groups, or at least members of them, were often active in public life; it was from among these that the political activists and party leaders, the pamphleteers, and the organisers who pressed for democratisation of the political system mainly came. But the basis on which they did this was not directly related to the strengthening of private enterprise and the principle of private property, which is what many have seen the bourgeois push towards democracy to be about, but the broader principles associated with democracy as an ideal.

This does not mean that the economic bourgeoisie did not become involved in political issues. They clearly did. The anti-corn law campaign in Britain, the tariff discussions in 1870s–90s France, the post-war campaign against the maintenance of wartime controls in Germany, and business activism surrounding the New Deal in the United States are all instances of businessmen becoming involved in what were essentially political campaigns. But all of these examples related directly to their economic concerns. The question is whether they were major players in bringing about significant change in the political regimes that ruled their countries. Significant changes were introduced in these countries in the periods under review. In Britain, the widening of the franchise transformed the system into a mass-based polity by the end of the nineteenth century, in France regime change occurred in 1830, 1848, and 1871, in Germany there was regime change in 1871, 1918, and (in retrospect) 1933, while in the United States there was some extension of the franchise and attempts to remove the effect of partial interest on politics in the Progressive period. What role did the economic bourgeoisie play in these developments?

In Britain, the accommodation reached between emergent bourgeoisie and traditional aristocratic landowners, mediated through the involvement of some of the latter in industrial and financial pursuits and through the social merging that came about, averted a major struggle for power between these groups. The integration of the emergent class into the power structure thus occurred relatively smoothly and facilitated the emergence of a bourgeois-landowner ruling elite confident in its power and authority and, at least initially, unchallenged in its exercise of these qualities. This was bolstered through the 1832 Reform Act, which effectively replaced the principle of the exercise of influence on the basis of inherited power by that which rested on property ownership. On this basis, the Parliament became a mainstay of the developing capitalist industrial economy, passing a substantial body of legislation designed to consolidate and strengthen that economy and those who played a leading part in it. This does not mean that the interests of the emergent bourgeoisie were always and easily realised; the struggle over the corn laws and the structure of policy on the Empire shows that the emergent industrial bourgeoisie did not have it all its own way. Nevertheless, the ruling elite did stay broadly united on the issue of systemic change. When pressure from below mounted, principally through the growth of social movement activism,[10] especially in the form of Chartism and the trade union movement, this elite gave way, offering a series of compromises that extended both the suffrage and citizenship and that finally provided a range of social welfare measures that underpinned the life experience of the growing urban working class.[11] This process of democratisation through gradual reform was spearheaded by the professional bourgeoisie and broadly supported by the economic bourgeoisie. This does not mean that they favoured the expansion of workers' rights as reflected in the activities of the organised labour movement; there was significant industrial conflict over conditions of work at different times. But they did not stand in the way of the process of gradual democratisation, instead working to shape that in a way which blunted any challenge that it might have constituted to their fundamental position and power.

Regime change in France[12] occurred as a result of revolution in 1830 and 1848, and defeat in war in 1870–1; in Tilly's words, democracy 'flourished temporarily in 1848, receded with the Second Empire (and) recovered through tremendous strife under the Third Republic',[13] and on each occasion democratisation was a result of popular mobilisation and pressure in which the professional bourgeoisie was prominent. In 1830, the attempt at a reactionary restoration by the newly enthroned Charles X[14] mobilised wide sections of society in an attempt to defend the rights stemming from the Revolution of 1789. Following the popular revolts of 1848, the monarchy was replaced initially by the Second Republic (1848–51) and then by the Second Empire (1852–70). The establishment of the Republic was broadly seen as a way of stabilising rule in the face of revolt from below, and therefore gained widespread support by those established interests in society, including the economic bourgeoisie.[15] The Republic's replacement by the Empire, a development which ushered in the major industrial boom, was something that was engineered by the political elite, but because of the pro-industrial development policy followed by the Emperor, it gained solid support from within industrial circles. The Third Republic (1871–1940) was ushered in following defeat in the Franco-Prussian War and the suppression of the Paris Commune. Its introduction was largely a result of the inability of conservative elites to agree on a monarchical solution, and the ensuing republican constitution was constructed by a National Assembly dominated by anti-republicans. The economic bourgeoisie supported the re-establishment of order (reflecting concern at the attacks upon big capital, finance, and the railways) something associated with a desire to limit any strengthening of the power and position of the working class. In none of these cases of regime change did the economic bourgeoisie take the leading role, but it was supportive of the development in each case.

German unification was essentially driven by state elites, in particular in Prussia, but was widely supported in economic circles because of the greater domestic market that it promised to create. Furthermore, the radical nature of the German workers' movement plus the importance of state support in a late industrialising economy were significant factors in persuading the bourgeoisie to support the imperial structure. The collapse of the Empire after the First World War, plus the effect of the abortive socialist revolution, encouraged many elements in German society to look to a restoration of firm central control. Instead they got the Weimar Republic, a polity which proved to be weak and unable to establish the sort of firm central control that many, including many of the economic bourgeoisie, sought. In the face of increasing worker radicalism and government plans for an extensive welfare system, it is not surprising that many among the bourgeoisie rejected the Weimar system and supported a more authoritarian alternative including, on the part of some, the Nazis and the stronger sort of central control that they promised.[16] In this sense, the German bourgeoisie was not a consistent supporter of democratising measures; indeed, if anything, it seems more consistently to have favoured authoritarian political solutions.

In the United States, where there was a closer interlinking between economic elites and those from other sectors of life, including political, and also where members of the professional bourgeoisie were very active in public life, members of the economic bourgeoisie seem to have played a part in all of the major decisions of state. The extension of the suffrage to include male Negroes in 1870 and women in 1920 was a significant democratising measure, even if the former was consistently circumvented in some state jurisdictions until after the Second World War. There is no evidence that the bourgeoisie was particularly opposed to these measures; the existence of universal white male suffrage from the time of the Civil War undercut the objection some made elsewhere that this would involve strengthening the working class at the expense of their employers. Nevertheless, there was strong bourgeois resistance to the strengthening of the labour movement and its attempt to protect its members in their places of employment. In this, the bourgeoisie gained significant support from the state. However, the attempted removal of partial influence on government through the criticism of business and its role in the Progressive Era did evoke some opposition from within business circles. But in this case the bourgeoisie was split. Prominent in the spearhead of the campaign against business influence were professional elements from the bourgeoisie. Also important were many smaller businesses, critical of the sort of influence that large business was able to wield.

This suggests that, in these four countries, the bourgeoisie has not been a consistent supporter of either democratic or anti-democratic change. The position of the class has been shaped by the essential conditions within which they have sought to operate. In Britain, they were assimilated into the power structure and, being confronted by a labour movement which was quickly drained of its revolutionary potential by strategic concessions and compromises and thereby transformed into a reformist force, were able to go along with the gradual move of the country in a democratic direction. While generally they remained opposed to union power, the moderation of the labour movement and its attempt to realise its aims through parliamentary organisation in the form of the Labour Party meant that there was no real challenge to the position and power of the bourgeoisie. Furthermore, the state was constructed in such a way that it facilitated the entry of the bourgeoisie into power and, through its centralism, could be used as an effective tool to realise basic bourgeois interests. Similarly in the United States, the bourgeoisie was assimilated into the power structure and was able to use the state and its resources to consolidate power and achieve its aims. The defeat of the South in the Civil War effectively broke the power of the plantation owners and opened the way for the emergent industrial bourgeoisie to gain primacy in the American state. Although the industrial and financial bourgeoisie shared power with others, most of these people also came from the bourgeoisie, albeit its professional wing. In this sense, the American state was dominated by the bourgeoisie. Masked by democratic rhetoric and ideology, they used the state to consolidate their positions, undermining many democratic practices by the liberal use of appointment and influence peddling, and thereby retarding the further democratisation of the state. However, this position ultimately split the class, with the professional wing and many of the, especially smaller, businessmen throwing their support behind the Progressive measures to eliminate the abuses in government. When this support allied with a labour movement that had no real revolutionary ethos, a sort of reformism in which the state played an important but often unacknowledged role became dominant.

In France, despite some integration with the residual traditional landowners, the bourgeoisie was not as easily assimilated into the upper reaches of the power structure because of the presence of a powerful statist tradition that gave a stronger sense of autonomy to political and administrative elites than existed in either Britain or the United States. A substantial part of these political and economic elites came from the professional bourgeoisie, but given the strength of the statist tradition, the class links between the professional and economic bourgeoisie became more attenuated. As a result, the economic bourgeoisie became a more minor partner in the exercise of power, but one which was reliant upon the state for assistance in the pursuit of its aims. This was especially the case given that there was a tradition of revolutionary activism in France which became embedded in the labour movement and which was a constant reminder to the rulers of the uncertainties of their rule. For the economic bourgeoisie, this reinforced their dependence on the state and compromised any commitment they may have had to widespread and far-reaching democratisation. In Germany too the economic bourgeoisie was less assimilated into the power structure, but here the barrier was the Junkers and the structure of values which they espoused. Confronted with a labour movement with strong revolutionary traditions and a powerful state which, while supporting their development was also pursuing an aggressive external policy prior to the First World War, the German bourgeoisie had little place to go except to tie itself even more securely to the state.[17] Accordingly, it supported the conservative rulers of Germany, took a hard-line stance against the labour movement, and generally eschewed firm democratic convictions.

The economic bourgeoisie has therefore not been a consistent force for either democratic reform or systemic political change. It has sought to fit into the hierarchy of power as it found it, using existing processes and structures to press its concerns and widen its influence. While changes in those processes and structures have come about, they were not propelled primarily by the emergent economic bourgeoisie. A much larger role was played in this by the professional elements of the bourgeoisie who, primarily on ideological grounds, were significant in pursuing changes in the structure of the system within which they were found. But the economic bourgeoisie may have played a role in enabling such democratic trends to become dominant.[18] Democratic political systems were established and at an earlier time where the emergent economic bourgeoisie was most securely embedded as part of the national elite. This was in Britain and the United States, in the former principally through a class alliance with the traditional landowning class, in the latter mainly through collaboration with the professional wing of the bourgeoisie. In these cases, with its position and influence securely grounded in the political and social structure, the economic bourgeoisie felt less threatened by the emergence of an organised working class than their less well-embedded counterparts in France and Germany. Benefiting from an ideology that emphasised common participation in the march of material progress, and secure in the knowledge that their influence in the state was sufficient to ensure that it acted to defend their broad interests, they felt less impelled to seek to block the unrolling of democracy fuelled by the working class. Similar considerations applied to those groups already in power (landowners in Britain and professional bourgeoisie in the United States); the successful integration of the economic bourgeoisie both strengthened the power of this dominant group vis-à-vis society as a whole and ameliorated any fears that the emergent bourgeoisie posed a threat to their continued enjoyment of high office and/or prestige. In Germany and France where integration levels were lower, and therefore where the bourgeoisie was less secure in its power and position, stable democracy was longer in coming; indeed in Germany where the link between bourgeoisie and dominant group was weakest and therefore least stabilising, it was only the result of outside conquest. In both of these cases, the state remained under the control of an elite with which the economic bourgeoisie was far less intimately linked than in either Britain or the United States, and therefore their sense of being able to rely upon that state for support was far more problematic, even given the respective states' drives for economic development. Furthermore, the ideology on which they relied was one of developing state greatness, and although this may have implied a sense of commonality between owners and workers in the greater enterprise, its mediation through the state effectively established a sense of distance (even perhaps 'alienness') between this enterprise and the working class. In this sense, there was less of a unifying ideology at work than in Britain and the United States.

Crucial to the attitude of the bourgeoisie was the sense of threat they were likely to feel emanating from the working class.[19] This sense of threat was lower in Britain and the United States than in France and Germany. Although statistics on strike levels are notoriously difficult to interpret,[20] in the decade either side of 1900 all four countries experienced significant levels of industrial activity. In terms of numbers of strikes and numbers of strikers, Britain and the United States generally experienced higher levels than France and Germany prior to 1900, but after that date such levels were much higher in France, and especially Germany, than in the other two countries.[21] But despite these levels of industrial unrest, the political context of them was different in Britain and the United States to that in France and Germany. In France, with the revolutionary tradition stemming from 1789 and going through 1830, 1848, and 1871, and with the existence of a socialist party rooted in that tradition, the possibility of revolution from below remained prominent in bourgeois consciousness. In Germany too there was a strong socialist movement in the last part of the nineteenth century, and although it had a reformist wing, there were also elements of a more radical disposition, so that the potential threat from below remained tangible and was actually realised in 1919. In contrast in Britain, from an early stage left wing radicalism had been dominated by a strongly reformist tenor, which was embodied in what was to become the dominant party of the left, the Labour Party. In the United States, there was no socialist movement to speak of until its brief emergence early in the twentieth century,[22] so that the political arm of organised labour remained reformist with more radical elements largely sidelined. Thus in those cases where the economic bourgeoisie was most integrated socially and institutionally into the system, the labour movement remained broadly reformist and therefore not a significant challenge to the fundamental interests of that bourgeoisie, chiefly private property. Where the bourgeoisie was not as well integrated into either the political or social elite, and therefore where its influence in the state and dominance of society were much more tenuous, and where a labour movement with revolutionary traditions and leaders seemed to pose a real threat to private property, the country's ruling circles were much less ready to make compromises with democratic demands. Accordingly, the achievement of democracy was much more difficult and uncertain than it had been in Britain and the United States. How does this logic apply to contemporary Russia?

In these terms, the Russian bourgeoisie appears to be in the middle ground between those embedded bourgeoisies of Britain and the United States and those less well integrated in France and Germany. Generally, business consistently supported both Yeltsin and Putin, while their economic success rested heavily on exploitation of the state. However, the attempt to strengthen the state launched by Putin from 2000, marked most spectacularly in our terms by his actions against the oligarchs, seems to propel the Russian case more in the direction of France and Germany than of Britain and the United States; rather than an economic bourgeoisie gaining significant integration with the political elite,[23] the state as represented by the president wanted to keep major elements of that bourgeoisie at a distance while keeping them highly dependent on the state's continuing good will, at the same time ensuring that that part of the bourgeoisie still based in the politico-administrative structure of the state (those state officials who simultaneously took up positions in the economic sphere) remained close to the centre of power in the state, the presidential apparatus. This impression is strengthened by ideological developments in post-Soviet Russia. The initial attempt to generate an ideology of market capitalism was unlikely to act as a force making for coherence and unity between the different levels of Russian society, principally because of the residual effects of the Soviet value structure which had a profoundly negative view of capitalism, something that was reinforced for many people by their experience of economic difficulties in the 1990s. With Putin's state-strengthening policies came a renewed ideology of state power and, despite the strength of Russian nationalism, it is not clear that this will be an effective means of generating an appearance of coincidence of interest between workers and owners.[24] While this has not been much of a problem up until now because of the weakness of the labour movement, any revival of labour militancy would be likely to drive the bourgeoisie into an even more dependent reliance on the state. Such dependence does not bode well for either the establishment of stable democracy or the emergence of an independent business sector much less reliant on exploitation of the state than it has been up until now.

Furthermore, there has not been the committed involvement in Russian political life of significant elements of the professional bourgeoisie, which in other countries has been a carrier of more liberal ideas. While many of those prominent in political life may have belonged to this class group, the generation of that organisational structure of civil society so important for the growth of democratic norms and historically associated with the professional bourgeoisie has been only weakly realised in Russia, something reflected in the continuing failure of liberalism in Russian political life.

The implication for the Russian situation of the location of the bourgeoisie is clear. While the bourgeoisie remains dependent on the state and gains significant benefits from that dependence, it is unlikely to diverge greatly from the political positions and preferences of those who run the state, at least as issues related to regime type and change are concerned. This does not mean that there will not be differences over policies, but on the central issue of regime form, there is unlikely to be a major difference; the economic bourgeoisie is unlikely to be a major advocate of democratisation. There are three circumstances in which this could change. First, if the state elite were to mount a severe and sustained attack on the basis of bourgeois power, that bourgeoisie may believe that it is in their interest to seek changes in the political system, although these may not necessarily be of a democratic nature. This has been the public trajectory of Boris Berezovsky. Second, the balance of the relationship between state and bourgeoisie could shift from one in which bourgeois dependence was the key quality into a relationship of much more clearly defined interdependence between the ruling elite and the bourgeois class, especially its upper levels. This could come about if the state elite sought to create a more stable social basis for the regime, along the lines of some of the developments in the regions. Under such circumstances, if both political and economic wings of this coalition felt more secure in their power, like their counterparts in the West, they might be willing to countenance democratic reform if pressed from below. This second course would make the Russian experience an even closer parallel to that of the Western cases than it has been until now. Third, if the continuing dependence on the state ceased to provide the level of benefits that they expected, the bourgeoisie may look elsewhere in order to bolster their economic position. However, in the absence of any of these sorts of development, the Russian economic bourgeoisie is likely to remain a supporter of the authoritarian trajectory upon which the current regime has embarked.

The bourgeoisie was, therefore, a class which from its emergence in each national context sought to utilise the state for its own purposes. From the time the first entrepreneurs established their businesses, they sought to evade or minimise the effect of state regulation, in part by reaching understandings with state officials, and to use the state to further their economic aims. In what would today be seen as corrupt behaviour, entrepreneurs sought the assistance of officials to further their economic interests. This was a normal, even natural, course of action to pursue, and it was pursued at whatever level of the state was most appropriate; for small entrepreneurs, this may have been at the level of local officialdom, for wealthy and economically powerful interests (including especially many financial interests), it was at the national level. This sort of informal influence buttressed the penetration of state institutions by members of the new class. Access to such institutions, especially the deliberative bodies of the state, provided the opportunity to shape state policy, even though in practice this was probably less important than the effect of the more informal relations wealthy members of the bourgeoisie were able to establish with the political elite. But regardless of the forms it took, bourgeois interaction with, and the search to profit from, the state were central to the development of the bourgeoisie as a class. No bourgeoisie developed independent of the state, while many of their economic activities were dependent upon state support. In this sense, the emergent Russian business class has been acting in a way that is quite consistent with that of its historical forebears; reliance on the state and, at best, agnosticism as regards democracy. Rather than being a case that is unique, they fit into a long line of historically validated practice.

Notes

1. For an argument that British consensus drew outsiders in and emasculated them while preserving their appearance of autonomy and independence, see J.P. Nettl, "Consensus or Elite Domination: The Case of Business", *Political Studies* 13, 1, 1965, pp. 22–44.
2. For example, see Theda Skocpol, *States and Social Revolutions. A Comparative Analysis of France, Russia, and China* (Cambridge, Cambridge University Press, 1979), pp. 24–33; Michael Mann, *The Sources of Social Power. Volume II. The Rise of Classes and Nation States, 1760–1914* (Cambridge, Cambridge University Press, 1993), ch. 3. There is a substantial Marxist debate on this question, much of it discussed in Bob Jessop, *State Theory. Putting Capitalist States in their Place* (Cambridge, Polity Press, 1990), Part I. For a discussion in terms of state coherence rather than autonomy, see David C. Kang, *Crony Capitalism. Corruption and Development in South Korea and the Philippines* (Cambridge, Cambridge University Press, 2002), pp. 13–14.
3. Control over the state is sometimes also seen in terms of the exercise of control through class-based parties, or through the exercise of ideological hegemony.
4. For example, see Peter Evans, *Embedded Autonomy. States and Industrial Transformation* (Princeton, Princeton University Press, 1995), and Alice H. Amsden, *Asia's Next Giant. South Korea and Late Industrialization* (New York, Oxford University Press, 1989).
5. For example, see Margaret Levi, *Of Rule and Revenue* (Berkeley, University of California Press, 1988), pp. 32–45, and Charles Tilly, "War Making and State Making as Organized Crime", Peter B. Evans, Dietrich Rueschemeyer & Theda Skocpol (eds.), *Bringing the State Back In* (Cambridge, Cambridge University Press, 1985), pp. 169–191. Also Peter B. Evans, "Predatory, Developmental, and Other Apparatuses: A Comparative Political Economy Perspective on the Third World State", *Sociological Forum* 4, 4, 1989, pp. 561–587. A variant of this is the so-called rentier state, which collects rent from the sell-off of natural resources rather than the actual creation of wealth in the economy.
6. For example, Joel Migdal, *Strong Societies and Weak States: State-Society Relations and State Capabilities in the Third World* (Princeton, Princeton University Press, 1988). For an interesting and more nuanced discussion, see Paul Hutchcroft, *Booty Capitalism.*

The Politics of Banking in the Philippines (Ithaca, Cornell University Press, 1998). The whole issue of so-called 'crony capitalism', which many have seen in the third world and has occasionally been applied to Russia, is relevant here. The difference between those contemporary states referred to in these terms and the national cases reviewed in this book is a matter of degree, not kind, with 'crony capitalism' a more extreme version of state exploitation and capture than the cases studied here.

7. Seminal in the discussion of this question remains the work of Weber on bureaucracy. Max Weber, *Economy and Society* (Berkeley, University of California Press, 1978, edited by Guenther Roth & Klaus Wittich), vol. 2, pp. 956–1005.

8. This was true even for post-Soviet Russia compared with the USSR. For some figures and discussion, see Richard Sakwa, *Russian Politics and Society* (London, Routledge, 2002, 3rd edn.), pp. 122–123.

9. The pressure for increased representation of their interests in national legislatures was one cause which was at times pursued under the liberal banner.

10. On this, see Charles Tilly, *Contestation and Democracy in Europe, 1650–2000* (Cambridge, Cambridge University Press, 2004), p. 159.

11. Most of these concessions preceded the establishment of the Labour Party and may reflect the willingness to make concessions in the absence of a revolutionary threat from below. See below.

12. For a short survey emphasising the role of the working class, see Tilly (Contestation and Democracy), pp. 121–123.

13. Tilly (Contestation and Democracy), p. 131.

14. The suffrage law he sought to introduce would have left an electorate of only the richest landowners.

15. According to one study, the Paris upper bourgeoisie and financial and railway interests opposed suffrage extension and social reform but supported the overthrow of the monarchy, while the provincial bourgeoisie supported limited extension of the suffrage. Sections of the working class were the main drivers of change. Dietrich Rueschemeyer, Evelyne Huber Stephens & John D. Stephens, *Capitalist Development and Democracy* (Cambridge, Polity Press, 1992), pp. 88–89.

16. See the concise summary in Rueschemeyer et al., pp. 110–111.

17. This is consistent with Kurth's argument that Germany's late industrialisation and its reliance principally on heavy industry (which needed more capital than light industry and thereby increased the state's potential role) was a crucial underpinning of bourgeois reliance on the state–Junker alliance. James R. Kurth, "Industrial Change and Political Change: A European Perspective", David Collier (ed.), *The New Authoritarianism in Latin America* (Princeton, Princeton University Press, 1979), pp. 319–362.

18. It is also possible that if newer generations of the economic bourgeoisie found their path to integration with the ruling elites blocked by bourgeois incumbents, they may have seen their interests well served by throwing in their lot with democratic forces in the hope of opening the system up.

19. On the mobilisation of the working class and its role in bringing about democracy, see Stefano Bartolini, *The Political Mobilization of the European Left 1860–1980. The Class Cleavage* (Cambridge, Cambridge University Press, 2000) and Rueschemeyer,

Stephens & Stephens (Capitalist Development and Democracy). For an earlier argument along these lines, see Goran Therborn, "The Rule of Capital and the Rise of
Democracy", *New Left Review* 103, May–June 1977, pp. 3–41.

20. The comments in the text are based on B.R. Mitchell, *International Historical
Statistics. Europe 1750–1993* (Basingstoke, Macmillan, 1998, 4th edn.), pp. 173–
185; P.K. Edwards, *Strikes in the United States 1881–1974* (Oxford, Basil Blackwell,
1981), p. 254; James E. Cronin, "Strikes and Power in Britain", Lex Heerma van
Voss & Herman Diederiks (eds.), *Industrial Conflict* (Amsterdam, Stichting beheer
IISG, 1988), p. 16; Edward Shorter & Charles Tilly, *Strikes in France 1830–1969*
(Cambridge, Cambridge University Press, 1974), pp. 360–363; and Charles Tilly,
"Theories and Realities", Leopold H. Haimson & Charles Tilly (eds.), *Strikes, Wars
and Revolutions in an International Perspective. Strike Waves in the Late Nineteenth and
Early Twentieth Centuries* (Cambridge, Cambridge University Press, 1989), p. 7.

21. Although the number of workers killed in industrial disputes between 1872 and
1914 was much higher in the United States than in any of the other countries.
Mann II, p. 635.

22. For the level of electoral support for socialists in the national elections in these
countries 1906–14, see Mann II, p. 634.

23. This may be occurring in some parts of the country at the local level, although it is
still too early to tell whether this sort of arrangement will stabilise.

24. Indeed, at times Putin appealed to the Russian population, and particularly the
working class, in his attacks on the oligarchs, thereby seeking to mobilise workers
against part of the bourgeoisie.

APPENDIX

The Tsarist Bourgeoisie

Analysis of the pre-Soviet, tsarist bourgeoisie does not fit in to the main thrust of the argument in this book. This is because this was not a major case study of any of the three theoretical approaches to democratisation around which this book is structured; Moore makes some passing references to Russia, Kurth mentions it three times, while in Rueschemeyer et al. Russia does not even appear in the index. However, it is an interesting case both because of the potential parallels with the post-Soviet situation and in the light of the explanation for democratisation suggested in the final chapter. The comparative question, that is, between the pre- and post-Soviet situations, should not be interpreted to mean that there is any causal impact of the former on the latter. The seventy-three years of the Soviet period eliminated most traces of the pre-revolutionary bourgeoisie; except for some physical infrastructure (houses in the major cities, factory buildings, and railway networks) and the continuing resonance of some of the names, there is little continuing evidence of this disappeared class. Nevertheless, those remnants and the historical memory that is being restored in post-Soviet Russia gives the pre-Soviet bourgeoisie a continuing life in the collective consciousness of society, and can thereby help to structure current development. It is therefore valuable to look at the development of this group in the same terms as the other bourgeoisies have been treated.

Social Origins

The time of greatest industrial expansion, and of the increased importance of indus-trialists, came in the last decade or so of the nineteenth century and early in the twentieth century, so it is the emergent bourgeoisie at this time that is the focus of study. And this really was an emergent rather than an established bourgeoisie. By late in the nineteenth century, the established system of soslovie, or estates, although breaking down,[1] was still formally in existence. Businessmen as we would understand them were found in two soslovie, the *kupechestvo*, which included merchants, industrialists, and financiers and was the term used in the late nineteenth century to refer to the business community generally, and *meshchanstvo*, which included small businessmen.[2] Membership of the *kupechestvo* sosloviia was not hereditary, meaning that the *kupech-estvo* did not constitute a closed caste. People with wealth could buy entry to it and, as long as they paid the annual fee, would retain membership.[3] However if they ceased to pay that fee, they would find themselves relegated to the *meshchanstvo* soslovie, thereby losing many of the rights to engage in commercial activities that adhered to membership of the *kupechestvo*.[4] Although this meant that the rules governing who could engage in commercial activities had been set by the state, and therefore effectively the definition of the business community was dependent upon the state, in practice these rules were being observed less and less systematically, so that membership was increasingly becoming less satisfactory as a means of indicating industrial status.[5]

Nevertheless, studies suggest that most of those businessmen who are to be found in our period of interest came from families who were involved in some form of commercial or productive activity, and therefore were in either of the two identified soslovie but principally the *kupechestvo*. According to one study, by the mid-nineteenth century, upper levels of the ranks of the businessmen were becoming dominated by people who were 'being drawn upward from the middle and lower strata of the *kupechestvo*, chiefly as a result of successful industrial activity, particularly in the textile field'.[6] But it was not restricted in this way. While some also came from the ranks of the artisans in the towns, some families (including, e.g., the Morozovs) had their origins among the peasantry with, according to one study, more seeming to come from among the enserfed peasantry than from those who were free.[7] The former were usually working on the estates of absentee landlords who encouraged their industry, which enabled them to accumulate the capital, purchase their liberty, and enrol in a guild.[8] Some industrialists also came from among the ranks of the *raznochintsy*, a group which emerged in the mid-nineteenth century comprising people not attached to any of the soslovie (such as sons of priests who did not follow in their fathers' footsteps and the children of lower rank non-hereditary civil servants and officers)[9] and the landed nobility,[10] although a section of the elite still came from a small number of old families who had entered industrial activity in the late eighteenth or early nineteenth century.[11] Thus as in the other countries, the origins of the economic bourgeoisie were socially mixed, but came primarily from among those already engaged in productive activity.

Despite the diverse origins of the economic bourgeoisie, they did not integrate easily into the other leading status groups in Russian society, especially the landed nobility and the state bureaucrats. As in the other cases, there was a tendency towards both resentment and snobbishness on the part of established wealth and status towards these parvenus, but what gave this a hard edge was the continuing echoes of the soslovie system which contained a real sense of rank and status in which the *kupechestvo* was not highly regarded. This was reinforced by the prevailing stereotype of the businessman as crude, uncultured, dishonest, and prepared to do anything to gain a profit. This sort of hostility and contempt was widespread among the intelligentsia and, more importantly, the nobility and state officials. It was reinforced in the early parts of the twentieth century by a new stereotype, that of the big industrialist, who was seen as being uncultured, short-sighted, selfish, unenterprising, unable to solve their own problems, and relying upon the state to bolster their activities. Furthermore, they were seen as using the state in order the better to exploit workers, consumers, and farmers, while their increased wealth was seen as underpinning a potential challenge to the continued status of these other groups.[12] This sort of image was a major barrier to the integration of the new business class into the established hierarchies of tsarist society.

Appendix: The Tsarist Bourgeoisie

Table A.1. Business membership in the State Duma (%)

First Duma 27/4/06–21/7/06	Second Duma 20/2/07–2/6/07	Third Duma 1907–12	Fourth Duma 1912–17
0.6	6.0	1.6	10.6

These are based on figures presented by Warren B. Walsh, 'The Composition of the Dumas', *The Russian Review* 8, 2, April 1949, pp. 113–115. For slightly different figures, see C. Jay Smith Jr., 'The Russian Third State Duma: An Analytical Profile', *The Russian Review* 17, 3, July 1958, pp. 202–203 and Rieber (Merchants and Entrepreneurs), pp. 274–275 & 319. In the First Duma, Walsh refers to these as 'industrialists', in the Second Duma 'industrial capitalists' (0.6%), 'mercantile capitalists' (3.3%), and 'kuptsy' (2.1%), while in the Third Duma the six representatives constitute two 'bankers', two 'capitalists' and two 'industrialists'. In the Fourth Duma, the figure actually refers to the number of deputies who associated themselves with the Progressist Party, which was seen as the party of business, so the number of actual members of the economic bourgeoisie may have been less than this figure suggests. The figures do not include noblemen with business interests. In the upper house, or State Council, trade and industry groups were allotted twelve seats.

There was very little inter-marriage between business families and those of the landed nobility and state officials, while very few members of the former gained ennoblement.[13] The social circles remained substantially distinct, with overlap being minimal. Even though many businessmen at the end of the nineteenth century and the beginning of the twentieth century engaged in philanthropic activity and many of the newer generation were both well-educated and culturally sensitive and aware, the barriers between business and these other major groups, the nobility and the officialdom, remained substantial. There was no merging of these classes before the washing away of the whole system in 1917.

Political Representation

Prior to the 1905 revolution, there was no national level legislative body that played the role of a national parliament. The Russian governmental system remained an absolute monarchy, exercised by the tsar sometimes acting on the advice of his appointed advisors. However, in an attempt to dampen the revolutionary wave that had been unleashed in 1905, as part of the so-called October Manifesto of that year, the tsar established a popularly elected State Duma based on a wide but unequal suffrage.[14] This body was to have the power of veto over laws, but in its first two manifestations, it demonstrated too radical a temper and was shut down and the suffrage successively narrowed. The following two dumas were more acceptable and were allowed to serve out their terms. But in all of these bodies, businessmen constituted only a tiny fraction of the membership (Table A.1).

This is a very low level of representation, generally much lower than those of their counterparts in either the West or in the post-Soviet period. This reflects both the weakness of this group in Russian society and a conscious policy on the part of many of them to stay out of political activity for much of this period.

Emergent businessmen had been somewhat more involved in local politics in the last part of the nineteenth century, although even here this had not been on a large scale. A new law of municipal self government of 6 June 1860 had replaced the representation of social estates by a property qualification based on taxable wealth. There was also at this time some lightening of the bureaucratic supervision that the government had exercised over municipal government, two developments which made service in this government a more attractive proposition than it had formerly been. Businessmen now gained what one author has called 'a preponderant voice in the selection of delegates'[15] in the town Duma. In 1870, a new municipal statute strengthened the position of the wealthy by changing the means of election of deputies, a result which was consolidated by further reform in 1892 (although the severe bureaucratic limitations on the duma's legislative power remained[16]). In Moscow, where the business community was one of the strongest in Russia, business representation in the city Duma changed as follows: 1873, 45%; 1877, 80%; and 1893, 61.9%.[17] At this time a number of businessmen also acted as mayor, although not with great success.[18] However, it is not clear that businessmen used this position substantially to further their interests; many were apathetic and only irregular contributors to the Duma's work, and the central government still sought to intervene broadly in municipal affairs.[19] Elsewhere in the country where industry was developing, including St. Petersburg, the southern coal regions, and the Ural Mountains, businessmen also became involved in political life, but as in Moscow, the results of this seemed to be few. While in some areas they challenged the nobility for leadership of the deliberative bodies set up in 1864, the zemstvos, this was principally in order to gain a lightening of their tax burden rather than to introduce measures that might have broader significance.[20] And in any case, their representation in the zemstvo assembly was rarely very extensive, and was reduced even further by the changed zemstvo electoral law of June 1890.[21]

The representation of business interests in political life (as opposed to lobbying and administrative representation) was not possible until political parties became acceptable in 1905, but when the opportunity arose, elements within business actively pursued it. Initial attempts on the part of business to gain representation through political parties were unsuccessful. A number of small parties emerged professing to champion business interests. These included the Trade and Industry Party (founded by the Moscow Exchange Committee[22]), the All-Russian Union of Trade and Industry (in St. Petersburg and comprising mainly small businessmen and merchants), and the Progressive Economic Party (mainly iron and steel and engineering). In the first election, business generally supported the Octobrists,[23] but they won only 13 seats in the First Duma. Nevertheless, the Octobrists seemed to remain the party in which most business interests congregated until the emergence of the Progressists in 1912 (see below); in the Third Duma, 15.3% of the Octobrist fraction were involved in commercial, industrial, or financial activity, a larger proportion than in any other party.[24] But the Octobrists were not a reliable vehicle for business interests because the party was dominated by people with a rural or land-owning background. Business seemed to have a more reliable representative organisation with the establishment of the Progressist Party in 1912. After 1909, a group of industrialists led by P. Riabushinsky tried to transform the small Party of Peaceful Renewal into an industrialist agency. However, this body lacked any national organisation, and by mid-1914, it was wracked by conflict between those older members of the Party of Peaceful Renewal who objected to the takeover by the new industrialist deputies led by A. I. Konovalov, a millionaire textile owner, and these new members. By 1915, the Progressists had lost much of their business support because of their manifest failure to advance business interests in the Duma.[25] The attempt on the part of the business community to project their interests through political parties was largely a failure.

More important as a means of pressing their interests were sectoral or industry organisations. Such organisations developed throughout Russia either where a particular industry was dominant or where businessmen pursuing a diversity of interests decided to organise on a regional level. Examples of the former were the Association of Southern Coal and Steel Producers, the Baku Petroleum Association, and the Russian Society of Sugar Producers,[26] and of the latter the Moscow Exchange Committee.[27] The Moscow exchange was one of a number of exchanges formed in towns throughout the Empire in the wake of the 1867 tariff dispute. Such bodies sought both to organise industry the better to serve its interests and to project those interests to both local and national government; in the 1870s and 1880s, the government actually encouraged the development of organised business interests in order to use them as sources of advice,[28] thereby adopting a quasi-corporatist strategy. However the government, through the Ministry of Finance, also prevented these exchanges from developing into a national organisation by imposing different statutes on each town exchange.[29] The success of these organisations differed, depending on a combination of local conditions and on the nature of the aims they set themselves. Such bodies frequently were able to gain leverage with local, regional, and national state organs because of the attitude to business adopted by the state (see below).

The first national organisation of commercial and industrial interests, the Russian Industrial Society, was created in 1867. It sought to influence the government in favour of a comprehensive program of economic development, but with little success. It was more successful on some issues of tariffs, factory legislation, and the conquest of Central Asia before policy differences among its branches (especially between Moscow and the Polish branches) led to its weakening from the 1880s.[30] It was the major forum for the public discussion of economic policy prior to the establishment of the Association of Industry and Trade (AIT). This was formed explicitly in October 1906 to overcome the effects of the splintering of business representation through a variety of local and sectoral organisations, and effectively acted as an umbrella organisation under which the multiplicity of business and trade bodies sheltered. The AIT was heavily reliant on the state for its continued relevance; in Roosa's words, the government consistently solicited the views of the AIT 'at an early stage in the preparation of all legislation affecting industry and trade'.[31] This sort of access encouraged individual industrial and trade organisations (although the latter seem to have been less enthusiastic than the former about the AIT) to join the AIT. This organisation was generally dominated by large industry, although it remained riven by internal competition and conflict on the basis of both economic interest and geography (especially Moscow vs. St. Petersburg). Generally the AIT remained supportive of the government and of national economic growth, pressing the government to take whatever measures it deemed appropriate to stimulate such growth. However by about 1911, the organisation seems to have become convinced that changes to the governmental structure were needed if growth was to be achieved. Some business figures had reached this conclusion as early as 1905, but this had led nowhere. When the AIT adopted a more critical stance, it seemed as though business was going to loosen its ties with the state, but if this was likely, the outbreak of war changed that. Industry swung in behind the war effort, and with the breakdown of the military supply system, it was co-opted into the state's overall war machine through the creation of the War Industry Committees. The role of the AIT as an autonomous channel into the government was compromised by its more critical stance and then by the absorption through the War Industry Committees. This fate was a miniature version of the history of business–state relations more broadly in the last century of tsarist rule.

Class and State

The relationship that the emergent bourgeoisie had with the state may be described as dependent yet distant. What this means is that the growth and development of Russian industry was highly dependent upon the state, yet those private entrepreneurs who were involved in this did not personally become deeply embedded in the state and its structures.

The state played a major part in Russian industrial development. Even before the main thrust of rapid industrialisation towards the end of the nineteenth century and into the twentieth century, the state had been an important actor in shaping the growth of industry. Throughout the life of the tsarist system, industrial development was highly circumscribed by state regulation and control. The clearest indication of this is the above-mentioned system of soslovie, which effectively meant that if anyone was to engage in industrial activity, they had to become a member of a particular legal category defined by the government. This means that the state actually defined who was to be an industrialist and who was not, a power much greater than that exercised by any of the other countries so close to the onset of large-scale industrialisation. Control was also exercised over how that industrialisation was to take place. Regulations governing all aspects of production, distribution, and exchange structured the environment of industrial production and ensured that its conduct was shaped substantially by the government's vision. The state bureaucracy had extensive powers to interfere in the operations of private companies, reflecting the absence in Russia of a well-grounded infrastructure of administrative and commercial law that would both restrict bureaucratic arbitrariness and provide a solid legal basis upon which private enterprise could rest.

The problem is that the government's view was motivated by two contradictory aims, reflecting differences of opinion within the ranks of high state officials. First, recognition that Russia needed to industrialise, and quickly, if it was to match the economic growth being achieved by potential rivals in Europe, Britain, France, and Germany. This was behind the state's attempts to stimulate industrial development noted below. Second, the fear of the traditional-landed nobility about the challenge posed to their continued dominance by an emergent industrially based bourgeoisie. This was behind the state's continued attempt to highly regulate industrial development, not merely to shape its growth but to keep it under tight control. These two aims, to promote economic growth while containing its social consequences, were behind the amalgam of vigorous state sponsorship of industrial development, especially from the 1890s, and extensive regulation of its growth.[32]

That the Russian state played a major role in fostering industrial development in the last part of the nineteenth century has become a commonplace,[33] although there has been some dispute over whether this was a policy designed simply to stimulate industrialisation, or whether this was a by-product of the attempt to strengthen the state internally and externally.[34] What is clear is that the state did stimulate industrial development through the policies it pursued. Through a combination of state railway building, tariff and subsidy support, state orders and contracts, stabilisation of the currency, and the attraction of foreign capital, especially when Sergei Witte was finance minister (1892–1903), the state drove industrial development at a much faster pace than it had been going before. Given the weakness of legal infrastructure and the role played by the state in development, private entrepreneurs found themselves heavily reliant on the state and its resources for the pursuit of their own aims.

This reliance upon the state and the weakness of the legal infrastructure encouraged Russian businessmen to engage in the same sorts of activities that were characteristic of their earlier counterparts in the West and their later successors in Russia. The traditional picture of the Russian merchant as willing to do anything to turn a profit rang true for the emergent bourgeoisie of the late nineteenth century. They were as willing to perpetrate fraud against their stockholders, creditors, the public, and the state as were their counterparts elsewhere.[35] Syndicates seeking a monopolistic position emerged in the last part of the nineteenth century, with state approval, and distorted markets to the benefit of the partners. Speculation, the falsification of accounts, the misappropriation and misuse of state resources, the short-changing of contracts, overcharging on sales were all common within the business community. And because of the large role the state played in development, much of this involved the state. In this sense, Russian businessmen acted as unscrupulously as their earlier and later counterparts in pursuit of profits.

But while the heavy reliance on the state provided significant opportunities for graft, it also created opportunities for influence. State officials realised that if they were successfully to pursue industrial development, they would need the cooperation of the private entrepreneurs. Accordingly, throughout the entire nineteenth century, the state pursued a course of seeking their advice and opinion on matters related to trade and industry, although they were careful to contain this advice to narrow economic concerns; the state did not consult the emergent business class on matters of broader national interest.[36] Consultation was conducted chiefly through the Ministry of Finance. The business community sought to present its views through submissions to policy-makers, lobbying and through articles in the press; leading businessmen also served as 'experts' on temporary government commissions. They also sought to organise through the sorts of associations discussed above, but here the closeness of government control is evident. All of these organisations had to be chartered by the government, which also had to approve any changes to the statutes of the organisation, they had to supply to the government information on their particular branches of industry, their elected officers were subject to government confirmation, advance approval had to be obtained from the government for the agenda of their conferences and the government could put anything on that agenda it liked, and government representatives attended meetings of these bodies.[37] However, throughout most of the century, the emergent bourgeoisie did not seek to exercise influence on issues other than their immediate economic concerns. They did not have a classically liberal outlook, with many of them tending towards a Slavophile position emphasising the patriarchal tradition of unity and distrust of competing interests, albeit with support for industrialisation (for the Slavophiles this was justified in terms of defence of Russia from the alien West).[38]

By the early years of the twentieth century, under the impact of a depression and a new generation of businessmen coming to the fore,[39] parts of the business community began to become restive under what they saw as the heavy hand of petty officialdom. Within that community, criticism had been growing of the government's failure to develop a comprehensive approach to industrial development. It was seen to be ad hoc and unsystematic, and through its petty regulation to be counter-productive to the longer term development of industry. Indeed, the state's fostering of the Zubatov movement designed to organise workers into trade unions ostensibly to defend their interests,[40] tax, and credit policies which were thought to be designed to move resources from industry into sustaining the financial bases of both the state and the nobility, and tariff treaties with Germany in 1894 and 1904 that were seen as sacrificing industry's interests to benefit agriculture, were all seen as moves directly against the industry sector. With the radicalisation of the situation in 1905, some elements within the business community began to argue that what was needed was not just a reworking of government policy, but broader changes within the society as a whole.[41] Many within business supported the civil liberties and the promise of a State Duma contained in the October Manifesto, but there was also significant opposition, including from within the important Moscow Exchange Committee.[42] Even among supporters, there were differences over whether that Duma should have legislative or merely consultative powers. With this radicalisation of the critique of government coming from within business, there was also a change in tactics away from simply lobbying and seeking to exercise influence that way, into seeking to establish a broader alliance and engage in the new opportunities for electoral politics. However, the attempts to bring unity to business and to establish firm links with the liberal gentry and progressive intelligentsia all failed.[43] Accordingly the efforts made to gain business representation in the Duma achieved only the meagre results noted above. Some elements within business even supported some of the demands of the workers, especially for the franchise if not for improved working conditions.

However, the effect of the 1905 revolution was to isolate the business community even more. State officials were critical of business for its failure to improve workers' conditions, which they felt contributed to the revolutionary outbreak of 1905, and were appalled at the way in which some within the business community had thrown their support behind the demands for a constitutional monarchy.[44] On the other side, the support that some businessmen gave to workers' demands was not sufficient to generate an alliance between these two groups. Furthermore, business was also unable to establish a firm alliance with the liberals through the parliamentary system. Accordingly, the only path left to business was to revert to its former modus operandi, seek to influence government through lobbying and personal contacts. However, it was not until the war and business involvement in the war effort through the War Industries Committees that they could, in a structural sense, get into a position from which they could hope to influence government policy. However, the capacity to do this in a sustained fashion was undermined in part by the continuing chronic disunity within business ranks, especially between Moscow and St. Petersburg.[45]

Conclusion

So the pre-Soviet, Russian bourgeoisie was in a very similar position to the bourgeoisies of Britain, France, Germany, the United States, and post-Soviet Russia in that their development was significantly structured by their relationship with the state and, in particular, their dependence on it. Compared with the British, French, American, and even post-Soviet cases, the tsarist bourgeoisie had to confront much stronger cultural hurdles to integration with the dominant social groups, thereby meaning that in the short time available they were unable to surmount those hurdles and gain close integration with those groups. In this sense, they were closest to the German case. Their inability to penetrate the state and government effectively is also reminiscent of Germany, while their continued subordination to the state is similar to that of both Germany and post-Soviet Russia. In the trajectory of their political views, there was also a similarity with Germany. Like their counterparts elsewhere, they were not innately liberal in outlook and supported the prevailing political structure, seeking to fit into the niches that that structure provided.[46] However, when that structure ceased, in their view, to cater adequately for their interests, they supported a new, more liberal, structure. How they would have reacted had that liberal structure been allowed to develop, and therefore the power of organised labour allowed to grow, is not clear. But it is certain that, when that liberal structure was closed down in 1907, they happily reverted to the position they had been in before. They were clearly not a force for democracy, and only ambiguously and fleetingly a supporter of liberal reform. They were content to operate in a system that denied democracy as long as it served their economic interests. They were therefore consistent with the other national bourgeoisies analysed in this book.

Notes

1. Although for the argument that the soslovie system had not eroded by this time, see Gregory L. Freeze, "The Soslovie (Estate) Paradigm and Russian Social History", *American Historical Review* 91, 1, February 1986, pp. 26–32. These were not like estates in the West, in the words of Ruckman, lacking the 'autonomous self-governing, representative institutions and the juridical rights that enabled them to govern jointly with the ruler' in parts of early-modern Europe. Jo Ann Ruckman, *The Moscow Business Elite. A Social and Cultural Portrait of Two Generations, 1840–1905* (De Kalb, Northern Illinois University Press, 1984), p. xxii.
2. Earlier in the nineteenth century, kupechestvo referred overwhelmingly to merchants. Ruckman (Moscow Business Elite), p. xi.
3. Freeze (Soslovie), p. 22.
4. James L. West, "Merchant Moscow in Historical Context", James L. West & Iurii A. Petrov (eds.), *Merchant Moscow. Images of Russia's Vanished Bourgeoisie* (Princeton, Princeton University Press, 1998), p. 5.
5. See Roger Portal, "Aux origines d'une bourgeoisie industrielle en Russie", *Revue d'histoire moderne et contemporaine* VIII, 1961, p. 42.

6. Ruckman (Moscow Business Elite), p. 16. Italics in original. On ethnic and regional divisions within the emergent group, see Thomas C. Owen, "Impediments to a Bourgeois Consciousness in Russia, 1880–1905: The Estate Structure, Ethnic Diversity, and Economic Regionalism", Edith W. Clowes, Samuel D. Kassow & James L. West (eds.), *Between Tsar and People. Educated Society and the Quest for Public Identity in Late Imperial Russia* (Princeton, Princeton University Press, 1991), pp. 41–56.

7. Portal (Aux origins), pp. 42–43. On the Morozovs, see p. 53. On so-called 'trading peasants', see Alfred J. Rieber, *Merchants and Entrepreneurs in Imperial Russia* (Chapel Hill, University of North Carolina Press, 1982), pp. 45–52. Emancipation facilitated an increase in the merchant soslovie because peasants now had only to purchase entry to the guild, not also buy their freedom.

8. In this context, see Portal's discussion of the textile manufacturers of Ivanovo. Portal (Aux origins), pp. 43–53.

9. Richard Pipes, *Russia under the Old Regime* (London, Weidenfeld & Nicolson, 1974), p. 261. On the activity of commercial elements in the Russian Empire, see Rieber (Merchants and Entrepreneurs), pp. 52–73.

10. For the so-called 'noble industrialists' who emerged in the second half of the eighteenth century, see Rieber (Merchants and Entrepreneurs, pp. 41–45).

11. Ruckman (Moscow Business Elite), p. 16. Although most of those prominent in commercial activity in the early nineteenth century were no longer prominent in business at the end of the century. Ruckman (Moscow Business Elite), p. 16 and Portal (Aux origins), p. 42. For some figures on the erosion of the older group, see Rieber (Merchants and Entrepreneurs), p. 88.

12. For a discussion of perceptions of the bourgeoisie, see Ruckman (Moscow Business Elite), pp. 8–14.

13. Ruckman (Moscow Business Elite), pp. 39–45. Indeed, by the late nineteenth century, few saw the attainment of gentry status as a valuable reward for public service. Thomas C. Owen, *Capitalism and Politics in Russia. A social history of the Moscow merchants* (Cambridge, Cambridge University Press, 1981), p. 148.

14. While the majority of people gained the right to vote, this was neither equal nor direct. The workers in several large cities chose electors who would then elect representatives, while the peasants chose electors who joined electoral colleges comprising themselves and electors chosen by the nobility. There was also an upper house, the State Council, half of which were appointed by the tsar and half elected by the nobility, zemstvos, and university faculties.

15. Owen (Capitalism and Politics), p. 77.

16. Owen (Capitalism and Politics), p. 159.

17. Ruckman (Moscow Business Elite), p. 240. Also Owen (Capitalism and Politics), pp. 77–78.

18. This judgement is partly tempered by the experiences from the late 1870s of Sergei Tret'iakov and Nikolai Alekseev. Rieber (Merchants and Entrepreneurs), p. 103.

19. See the discussion in Owen (Capitalism and Politics), pp. 78–82 and Ruckman (Moscow Business Elite), pp. 121–137.

20. Owen (Capitalism and Politics), p. 99.

21. From 1883–86 to 1890, the proportion of delegates coming from the merchant and urban soslovie in the district zemstvos fell from 16.9% to 13.8% and in the

provincial zemstvos from 11.2% to 8.7%. Rieber (Merchants and Entrepreneurs), p. 97.

22. For its fate, see Rieber (Merchants and Entrepreneurs), pp. 273–280.

23. Peter Gatrell, *Government, Industry and Rearmament in Russia, 1900–1914. The last argument of tsarism* (Cambridge, Cambridge University Press, 1994), p. 82.

24. Geoffrey Hosking, *The Russian Constitutional Experiment. Government and Duma, 1907–1914* (Cambridge, Cambridge University Press, 1973), pp. 47–48.

25. On the Progressist episode, see Raymond Pearson, *The Russian Moderates and the Crisis of Tsarism 1914–1917* (London, Macmillan, 1977), pp. 17–33 & 73–74.

26. For one study of the Association of Southern Coal and Steel Producers, see Susan P. McCaffray, *The Politics of Industrialization in Tsarist Russia. The Association of Southern Coal and Steel Producers 1874–1914* (DeKalb, Northern Illinois University Press, 1996). On some regional associations, see Rieber (Merchants and Entrepreneurs), ch. 6.

27. For discussion, see Owen (Capitalism and Politics), pp. 114–115, and Ruckman (Moscow Business Elite), p. 3, who refers to it as 'in effect the executive committee of Moscow's business elite'. Also Thomas C. Owen, "Doing Business in Merchant Moscow", West & Petrov (Merchant Moscow), p. 34, and Rieber (Merchants and Entrepreneurs), ch. 5. According to Ruckman, from the 1870s it was the chief representative organ of the upper ranks of the Moscow business community. Ruckman (Moscow Business Elite), p. 34.

28. Ruth AmEnde Roosa, *Russian Industrialists in an Era of Revolution. The Association of Industry and Trade, 1906–1917*, Thomas C. Owen (ed.), Armonk, M.E. Sharpe, 1997, p. 2.

29. Rieber (Merchants and Entrepreneurs), pp. 105–111.

30. Thomas C. Owen, "The Russian Industrial Society and Tsarist Economic Policy, 1867–1905", *Journal of Economic History* 45, 3, September 1985, pp. 587–606.

31. Roosa (Russian Industrialists), p. 23.

32. For a study which brings this out, see Thomas C. Owen, *The Corporation Under Russian Law, 1800–1917. A Study in Tsarist Economic Policy* (Cambridge, Cambridge University Press, 1991).

33. For early and late treatments of this, see Alexander Gerschenkron, *Economic Backwardness in Historical Perspective* (Cambridge, MA, Harvard University Press, 1962); Theodore H. von Laue, *Sergei Witte and the Industrialisation of Russia* (New York, Cambridge University Press, 1963); and Tim McDaniel, *Autocracy, Capitalism, and Revolution in Russia* (Berkeley, University of California Press, 1988).

34. See Linda Weiss & John Hobson, *States and Economic Development. A Comparative Historical Analysis* (Cambridge, Polity Press, 1995), ch. 4.

35. For one, brief, discussion of this, see Owen (Corporation), pp. 138–141.

36. Ruckman (Moscow Business Elite), p. 111. Although for the case of Moscow merchants seeking to use the Crimean War defeat to raise broader questions, see Rieber (Merchants and Entrepreneurs), pp. 150–152.

37. Roosa (Russian Industrialists), pp. 1–2, and McCaffray (Politics of Industrialization), p. 32.

38. Owen (Capitalism and Politics), ch. 2. For a discussion of the role of Slavophile beliefs among some of the newer generation, albeit Old Believers, see James L. West, "The Riabushinsky Circle: Burzhuaziia and Obshchestvennost' in Late Imperial

Russia", Clowes et al. (eds.), *Between Tsar and People*, pp. 41–56. For the link between Slavophiles, Old Believers, and the Moscow entreprensurs, see Rieber (Merchants and Entrepreneurs), pp. 137–148.

39. For a discussion of this in relation to Moscow, see Rieber (Merchants and Entrepreneurs), pp. 285–308.
40. On Zubatov, see Dmitry Pospielovsky, *Russian Police Trade Unionism. Experiment or Provocation* (London, Weidenfeld & Nicolson, 1971).
41. On the barriers to the development of a class consciousness among these people, see Owen (Impediments), pp. 75–89.
42. Rieber (Merchants and Entrepreneurs), pp. 266–272.
43. For a discussion of this, see Rieber (Merchants and Entrepreneurs), pp. 308–371.
44. Gatrell (Government, industry, and rearmament), p. 78.
45. On the War Industries Committees, see Lewis Siegelbaum, *The Politics of Industrial Mobilization in Russia, 1914–17* (London, Macmillan, 1983).
46. In the words of Thomas Owen in talking about Moscow, 'the Moscow merchant estate was in fact neither a genuine class nor a bearer of liberalism before 1905, but achieved a rather comfortable place within the Russian old regime'. Owen (Capitalism and Politics), p. ix.

Bibliography

Abraham, D., "Constituting Hegemony: The Bourgeois Crisis of Weimar Germany", *The Journal of Modern History* 51, 3, September 1979, 417–33.

Abrams, L. & D.J. Miller, "Who Were the French Colonialists? A Reassessment of the Parti Colonial, 1890–1914", *The Historical Journal* 19, 3, 1976, 685–725.

Aganbegyan, A., *The Challenge: Economics of Perestroika* (London, Hutchinson, 1988).

Allard, S., N. Burns & G. Gamm, "Representing Urban Interests: The Local Politics of State Legislatures", *Studies in American Political Development* 12, 2, Fall 1998, 267–302.

Allen, M.P., "Capitalist Response to State Intervention: Theories of the State and Political Finance in the New Deal", *American Sociological Review* 56, October 1991, 679–89.

Altschuler, G.C. & S.M. Blumin, *Rude Republic. Americans and Their Politics in the Nineteenth Century* (Princeton, Princeton University Press, 2000).

Aminzade, R., *Ballots and Barricades. Class Formation and Republican Politics in France 1830–1871* (Princeton, Princeton University Press, 1993).

Amirov, A., *Kto est' kto v bankovskoi sisteme rossii. Biograficheskii spravochnik* (Moscow, Panorama, 1996).

——*Naibolee vliiatel'nye predprinimateli rossii. Biograficheskii spravochnik* (Moscow, Panorama, 1996).

—— & V. Pribylovskii, *Rossiiskie biznesmeny i menedzhery. Biograficheskii spravochnik* (Moscow, Panorama, 1997).

Amsden, A.H., *Asia's Next Giant. South Korea and Late Industrialization* (New York, Oxford University Press, 1989).

Anderson, B.L., "Money and the Structure of Credit in the Eighteenth Century", *Business History* XII, 2, July 1970, 85–101.

Anderson, P., "Origins of the Present Crisis", *New Left Review* 23, January–February 1964, 26–53.

——"The Figures of Descent", *New Left Review* 161, January–February 1987, 20–77.

Anderson, R.D., *France 1870–1914. Politics and Society* (London, Routledge & Kegan Paul, 1977).

Andrew, C.M. & A.S. Kanya-Forstner, "French Business and the French Colonialists", *The Historical Journal* 19, 4, 1976, 981–1000.

————"The French Colonial Party: Its Composition, Aims and Influence 1885–1914", *The Historical Journal* 14, 1, 1971, 99–128.

————"The Groupe Coloniale in the French Chamber of Deputies 1892–1932", *The Historical Journal* 14, 4, 1974, 837–66.

Appel, H., "The Ideological Determinants of Liberal Economic Reform. The Case of Privatization", *World Politics* 52, 2, 2000, 520–49.

—— "Voucher Privatisation in Russia: Structural Consequences and Mass Response in the Second Period of Reform", *Europe-Asia Studies* 49, 8, 1997, 1443–9.

Arkhipov, A.I. & V.E. Kokorev (eds), *Bankovskaia sistema rossii: novyi etap razvitiia* (Moscow, Nauchnoe izdanie, 1997).

Ashton, T.S., *The Industrial Revolution 1760–1830* (London, Oxford University Press, 1948).

Aslund, A., *Building Capitalism. The Transformation of the Former Soviet Bloc* (Cambridge, Cambridge University Press, 2002).

—— *Gorbachev's Struggle for Economic Reform* (Ithaca, Cornell University Press, 1991).

—— "Reform Vs Rent-Seeking in Russia's Economic Transformation", *Transition* 2, 2, 26 January 1996, 12–16.

Augustine, D.L., "Arriving in the Upper Class: The Wealthy Business Elite of Wilhelmine Germany", D. Blackbourn & G. Eley (eds), *The Peculiarities of German History. Bourgeois Society and Politics in Nineteenth-Century Germany* (Oxford, Oxford University Press, 1984), 46–86.

—— "The Business Elites of Hamburg and Berlin", *Central European History* 24, 2, 1991, 132–46.

Augustine-Perez, D.L., "Very Wealthy Businessmen in Imperial Germany", Y. Cassis (ed), *Business Elites* (Aldershot, Edward Elgar, 1994), 595–617.

Avilova, A., *Maloe predprinimatel'stvo v kontektse rossiiskikh reform i mirovogo opyta* (Moscow, Informart, 1995).

Avilova, A.V., *Finansovye i institutional'nye problemy rossiiskogo malogo predprinimatel'stva (regional'nye aspekty)*, (Moscow, Informart, 1996).

—— "Politicheskie Predpochiteniia Rossiiskogo Malogo Biznesa", M.K. Gorshkov, et al. (eds), *Obnovlenie Rossii: Trudnyi Poisk Reshenii* Vyp. 4, (Moscow, RNISiPP, 1996), 179–90.

Aydelotte, W.O., "The Business Interests of the Gentry in the Parliament of 1841–47", G.K. Clark (ed), *The Making of Victorian England* (London, Methuen, 1965), 290–305.

—— "The Country Gentlemen and the Repeal of the Corn Laws", *English Historical Review* 82, 1967, 47–60.

—— "The House of Commons in the 1840s", *History* xxxix, 1954, 249–62.

Badol'skii, A., "Novye starye lidery peredala sobstvennosti", *Otkrytiia politika* 10, 12, 1997, 36–40.

Balzer, H., "Managed Pluralism: Vladimir Putin's Emerging Regime", *Post-Soviet Affairs* 19, 3, July–September 2003, 189–227.

Barker, R.J., "The Perier Bank During the Restoration (1815–1830)", *Journal of European Economic History* 2, 3, Winter 1973, 641–56.

Barkhatova, N., "Russian Small Business, Authorities and the State", *Europe-Asia Studies* 54, 2, 2000, 657–76.

—— P. McMylor & R. Mellor, "Family Business in Russia: The Path to Middle Class", *British Journal of Sociology* 52, 2, 2001, 249–69.

Barnes, A., *Owning Russia. The Struggle over Factories, Farms, and Power* (Ithaca, Cornell University Press, 2006).

—— "Russia's New Business Groups and State Power", *Post-Soviet Affairs* 19, 2, 2003, 154–86.

Bartolini, S., *The Political Mobilization of the European Left 1860–1980. The Class Cleavage* (Cambridge, Cambridge University Press, 2000).

Baylis, T.C., "Plus Ca Change? Transformation and Continuity Among East European Elites", *Communist and Post-Communist Studies* 27, 3, 1994, 315–28.

Belin, L., F. Fossato & A. Kachkaeva, "The Distorted Russian Media Market", P. Rutland (ed), *Business and the State in Contemporary Russia* (Boulder, Westview, 2001), 65–87.

Bensel, R.F., *The Political Economy of American Industrialization, 1877–1900* (Cambridge, Cambridge University Press, 2000).

Berezovskii, V.N., *Obshchestvennye ob'edineniia delovykh krugov Rossii: lobitskii resurs i politicheskaia rol'* (Moscow, Tsentr politicheskoi kon'iunktury Rossii, 1994).

—— *Politicheskaia elita sovetskogo proshlogo i rossiiskogo nastoiashchego: priemy i metodi konkurentnoi bor'by* (Moscow, Tsentr politicheskoi kon'iunktury Rossii, March 1996 unpublished).

—— *Rossiiskie delovye krugi: novye i starye kanali vliiania na politiku* (Moscow, Tsentr politicheskoi kon'iunktury Rossii, 1994).

—— V.V. Federov & A.L. Chesnakov, *Moskovskoe pravitel'stvo Iuriia Luzhkova: vlastnyi potentsial, rol', mesto i vliianie v Rossiiskoi politike* (Moscow, Tsentr politicheskoi kon'iunktury Rossia, April 1994, unpublished).

Berg, M., "Small Producer Capitalism in Eighteenth-Century England", *Business History* 35, 1, January 1993, 17–39.

Bergeron, L., *Les Capitalistes en France (1780–1914)* (Paris, Gallimard, 1978).

Berghoff, H., "A Reply to W.D. Rubinstein's Response", *Business History* 34, 2, April 1992, 82–5.

—— "British Businessmen as Wealth-Holders 1870–1914: A Closer Look", *Business History* 33, 2, April 1991, 222–40.

—— & R. Moller, "Tired pioneers and dynamic newcomers? A comparative essay on English and German entrepreneurial history, 1870–1914", *Economic History Review* XLVII, 2, 1994, 262–87.

Berman, S.E., "Modernization in Historical Perspective. The Case of Imperial Germany", *World Politics* 53, 1, April 2001, 431–62.

Best, H., "Elite Structure and Regime (Dis)continuity in Germany 1867–1933: The Case of Parliamentary Leadership Groups", *German History* 8, 1, February 1990, 1–27.

—— "Recruitment, Careers and Legislative Behavior of German Parliamentarians, 1848–1956", *Historical Social Research* 23, 1982, 20–54.

Bien, D.D., "Manufacturing Nobles: The Chancelleries in France to 1789", *The Journal of Modern History* 61, 3, September 1989, 445–85.

Bigo, R., *Les banques francaises au cours du XIX siecle* (Paris, Librairie de Recueil, 1947).

Blackbourn, D., "The German Bourgeoisie: An Introduction", D. Blackbourn & R. J. Evans (eds), *The German Bourgeoisie: Essays on the social history of the German middle class from the late eighteenth to the early twentieth century* (London, Routledge, 1991), 1–45.

—— & G. Eley, *The Peculiarities of German History. Bourgeois Society and Politics in Nineteenth Century Germany* (Oxford, Oxford University Press, 1984).

—— & R.J. Evans (eds), *The German Bourgeoisie: Essays on the social history of the German middle class from the late eighteenth to the early twentieth century* (London, Routledge, 1991).

Blackford, M.G., *The Rise of Modern Business in Great Britain, the United States and Japan* (Chapel Hill, University of North Carolina Press, 1998).

Blank, S., *Industry and Government in Britain. The Federation of British Industries in Politics, 1945–65* (Farnborough, Saxon House, 1973).

Blasi, J.R., M. Kroumova & D. Kruse, *Kremlin Capitalism. Privatizing the Russian Economy* (Ithaca, Cornell University Press, 1997).

Blinova, O.N., *Media-Imperii Rossii. Na sluzhbe gosudarstva i "oligarkhi"* (Moscow, Tsentr politicheskoi informatsii, 2001).

Bocharnikov, A.A. et al. (eds), *Sovremennaia Politicheskaia Istoriia Rossii (1985–1998 gody)* (Moscow, RAU Korporatsiia, 1999).

Bogue, A.G., J.M. Chubb, C.R. McKibbin & S.A. Traugott, "Members of the House of Representatives and the Processes of Modernization, 1789–1960", *Journal of American History* 63, 2, September 1976, 275–302.

Bonin, H., "The Political Influence of Bankers and Financiers in France in the Years, 1850–1960", Y. Cassis (ed), *Finance and Financiers in European History, 1880–1960* (Cambridge, Cambridge University Press, 1992), 219–42.

Bonnell, V.E. & T.B. Gold (eds), *The New Entrepreneurs of Europe and Asia. Patterns of Business Development in Russia, Eastern Europe and China* (Armonk, M.E. Sharpe, 2002).

Bourne, J.M., *Patronage and Society in Nineteenth-Century England* (London, Edward Arnold, 1986).

Bousset, M., *Casimir Perier. Un prince financier au temps du romantisme* (Paris, Publications de la Sorbonne, 1994).

Boycko, M., A. Shleifer & R. Vishny, *Privatizing Russia* (Cambridge [Mass], MIT Press, 1995).

Brady, R., *Kapitalizm. Russia's Struggle to Free Its Economy* (New Haven, Yale University Press, 1999).

Braudel, F., *Civilization and Capitalism 15th–18th Century. Volume II. The Wheels of Commerce* (London, Fontana Press, 1982).

Brenner, R., "Agrarian Class Structure and Economic Development in Pre-Industrial Europe", T.H. Ashton & C.H. Philpin (eds), *The Brenner Debate* (Cambridge, Cambridge University Press, 1987), 10–63.

Bridges, H., "The Robber Baron Concept in American History", *Business History Review* xxxii, 1, 1958, 1–13.

Briggs, A., *The Making of Modern England. 1783–1867. The Age of Improvement* (New York, Harper & Row, 1965).

Britnell, R.H., *The Commercialisation of English Society 1000–1500* (Manchester, Manchester University Press, 1996).

Brovkin, V., "Fragmentation of Authority and Privatization of the State: From Gorbachev to Yeltsin", *Demokratizatsiya* 6, 3, 1998, 504–17.

Brown, A., "The Russian Crisis: Beginning of the End or End of the Beginning?", *Post-Soviet Affairs* 15, 1, 1999, 56–73.

Brown, D. & D.M. Jones, "Democratization and the Myth of the Liberalizing Middle Classes", D.A. Bell, D. Brown, K. Jayasuriya & D.M. Jones, *Towards Illiberal Democracy in Pacific Asia* (Basingstoke, Macmillan, 1995), 78–106.

Brown, M.B., "Away With All the Great Arches: Anderson's History of British Capitalism", *New Left Review* 167, January–February 1988, 22–51.

——"Commercial and Industrial Capital in England: A Reply to Geoffrey Ingham", *New Left Review* 178, November–December 1989, 124–8.

347

Brzezinski, M., *Casino Moscow. A Tale of Greed and Adventure on Capitalism's Wildest Frontier* (New York, The Free Press, 2001).

Brzezinski, Z. & P. Sullivan (eds), *Russia and the Commonwealth of Independent States. Documents, Data and Analysis* (Armonk, M.E. Sharpe Inc., 1997).

Bunin, I. et al., *Biznesmeny rossii. 40 istorii uspekha* (Moscow, OKO, 1994).

Bunin, I.M. & B.I. Makarenko, *Formirovanie elity: problemy, puti, napravlenie evoliutsii* (Moscow, Tsentr politicheskikh tekhnologii, 1995).

Burawoy, M. & K. Hendley, "Between *Perestroika* and Privatization: Divided Strategies and Political Crisis in a Soviet Enterprise", *Soviet Studies* 44, 3, 1992, 371–402.

—— & P. Krotov, "The Economic Basis of Russia's Political Crisis", *New Left Review* 198, March–April 1993, 49–69.

—————— "The Soviet Transition from Socialism to Capitalism: Workers' Control and Economic Bargaining in the Wood Industry", *American Sociological Review* 57, 1, 1992, 16–38.

—— & K. Verdery (eds), *Uncertain Transition. Ethnographies of Change in the Postsocialist World* (Lanham, Rowman & Littlefield Publishers Inc., 1999).

Burch, P.H. (Jr), *Elites in American History. The Civil War to the New Deal* (New York, Holmes & Meier Publishers Inc., 1981).

Burk, R.F., *The Corporate State and the Broker State. The Du Ponts and American National Politics, 1925–1940* (Cambridge [Mass], Harvard University Press, 1990).

Bury, J.P.T., *Gambetta and the Making of the Third Republic* (London, Longman, 1973).

Cain, P.J., "British Capitalism and the State: An Historical Perspective", *Political Quarterly* 68, 1, January–March 1997, 95–8.

—— & G. Hopkins, "Gentlemanly Capitalism and British Expansion Overseas. I. The Old Colonial System, 1688–1850", *Economic History Review* 2nd series, XXXIX, 4, 1986, 501–25.

Calleo, D., *The German Problem Reconsidered: Germany and the World Order, 1870 to the Present* (Cambridge, Cambridge University Press, 1978).

Cannadine, D., *Aspects of Aristocracy. Grandeur and Decline in Modern Britain* (Harmondsworth, Penguin, 1995).

—— *Lords and Landlords: The Aristocracy and the Towns, 1774–1967* (Leicester, Leicester University Press, 1980).

—— *Patricians, Power and Politics in Nineteenth-Century Towns* (Leicester, Leicester University Press, 1982).

—— "The Making of the British Upper Classes", *Aspects of Aristocracy. Grandeur and Decline in Modern Britain* (Harmondsworth, Penguin, 1995), 9–36.

Capie, F. & M. Collins, "Industrial Lending by English Commercial Banks, 1860s–1914: Why Did Banks Refuse Loans?", *Business History* 38, 1, January 1996, 26–44.

Cashman, S.D., *America in the Gilded Age. From the Death of Lincoln to the Rise of Theodore Roosevelt* (New York, New York University Press, 1984).

Cassis, Y., "Bankers in English Society in the Late Nineteenth Century", *Economic History Review* 38, 2, 1985, 210–29.

—— (ed), *Business Elites* (Aldershot, Edward Elgar, 1994).

—— "Businessmen and the Bourgeoisie in Western Europe", J. Kocka & A. Mitchell (eds), *Bourgeois Society in Nineteenth Century Europe* (Providence, Berg Publishers, 1993), 103–24.

—— (ed), *Finance and Financiers in European History, 1880–1960* (Cambridge, Cambridge University Press, 1992).

—— "Financial Elites in Three European Centres: London, Paris, Berlin, 1880s-1930s", Y. Cassis (ed), *Business Elites* (Aldershot, Edward Elgar, 1994), 400–18.

Castles, F.G., "Barrington Moore's Thesis and Swedish Political Development", *Government and Opposition* 8, 3, Summer 1973, 313–31.

Cecil, L., *Albert Ballin. Business and Politics in Imperial Germany 1888–1918* (Princeton, Princeton University Press, 1967).

Chaisty, P., *Legislative Politics and Economic Power in Russia* (Basingstoke, Palgrave Macmillan, 2006).

Champeyrache, C., "Changement de regime de droits de propriete et infiltration mafieuse dans l'economie legal. Une comparison entre la Russie actuelle et la Sicile du XIXe siecle", *Revue d'etudes comparatives Ost/Oest* 31, 4, 2000, 183–208.

Chapman, S., *The Rise of Merchant Banking* (London, Allen & Unwin, 1984).

Chapman, S.D., "British Marketing Enterprise: The Changing Roles of Merchants, Manufacturers, and Financiers, 1700–1860", *Business History Review* LIII, 2, Summer 1979, 205–33.

Charle, C., *A Social History of France in the Nineteenth Century* (Oxford, Berg, 1994).

—— *Les Elites de la Republique (1880–1900)* (Paris, Fayard, 1987).

—— *Les hauts fonctionnaires en France au XIXe siecle* (Paris, Gallimard, 1980).

Chepurenko, A.I., *Razvitie malykh i srednikh predprinimatel'skikh struktur i problemy zamiatosti* (Moscow, RNISiNP, 1995).

Chepurenko, A., "Small Business and Big Politics", *Reforma* 9, September 1993, 9–12.

—— & T. Obydyonnova, *Development of Small Enterprises in Russia* (Moscow, RNISiNP, 1999).

Chervyakov, V., "The Russian National Economic Elite in the Political Arena", K. Segbers & S. De Spiegeleire (eds), *Post-Soviet Puzzles. Mapping the Political Economy of the Former Soviet Union. Vol. 1. Against the Background of the Former Soviet Union* (Baden Baden, Nomos Verlagsgesellschaft, 1995), 205–81.

Chirikova, A.E., "Biznes i politika: paradoksy rossiiskoi mental'nosti", *Biznes i politika* 11, 1997, 43–8.

Christopher, J.B., "The Desiccation (sic) of the Bourgeois Spirit", E.M. Earle (ed), *Modern France: Problems of the Third and Fourth Republics* (Princeton, Princeton University Press, 1951), 44–57.

Chubais, A.B., *Privatizatsiia po-rossiiskii* (Moscow, Vagrius, 1999).

Church, C.H., *Revolution and Red Tape. The French Ministerial Bureaucracy 1770–1850* (Oxford, Clarendon Press, 1981).

Clark, S., *State and Status. The Rise of the State and Aristocratic Power in Western Europe* (Montreal, McGill-Queens University Press, 1995).

—— P. Fairbrother, V. Borisov & P. Bizyukov, "The Privatization of Industrial Enterprises in Russia: Four Case-studies", *Europe-Asia Studies* 46, 2, 1994, 179–214.

Cleveland-Stevens, E., *English Railways. Their Development and Their Relationship to the State* (London, George Routledge & Sons, 1915/1988).

Clowes, E.W., S.D. Kassow & J.L. West (eds), *Between Tsar and People. Educated Society and the Quest for Public Identity in Late Imperial Russia* (Princeton, Princeton University Press, 1991).

Bibliography

Cobban, A., *A History of Modern France. Volume 2: From the First Empire to the Second Empire 1799–1871* (Harmondsworth, Penguin, 1965).

—— *The Social Interpretation of the French Revolution* (Cambridge, Cambridge University Press, 1965).

Cochran, T.C., "The History of a Business Society", *Journal of American History* 54, 1, 1967, 5–18.

Collier, D. & S. Levitsky, "Democracy with Adjectives: Conceptual Innovation in Comparative Research", *World Politics* 49, 3, April 1977, 430–51.

Colton, T.J. & M. McFaul, *Popular Choice and Managed Democracy. The Russian Elections of 1999–2000* (Washington, Brookings Institution Press, 2003.)

Corrigan, P. & D. Sayer, *The Great Arch. English State Formation as Cultural Revolution* (Oxford, Blackwell, 1985).

Cottrell, P.L., *Industrial Finance 1830–1914. The Finance and Organization of English Manufacturing Industry* (London, Methuen, 1980).

Cottrell, R., "Russia's New Oligarchy", *The New York Review of Books* 27, March 1997, 28–30.

Coulloudon, V., "Elite Groups in Russia", *Demokratizatsiya* 6, 3, 1998, 535–49.

—— "Moscow City Management: A New Form of Russian Capitalism?", P. Rutland (ed), *Business and the State in Contemporary Russia* (Boulder, Westview, 2001), 89–100.

Court, W.H.B., *A Concise Economic History of Britain From 1750 to Recent Times* (Cambridge, Cambridge University Press, 1964).

Craig, G.A., *Germany 1866–1945* (Oxford, Clarendon Press, 1978).

Cronin, J.E., "Strikes and Power in Britain", L.H. van Voss & H. Diederiks, *Industrial Conflict* (Amsterdam, Stichting beheer IISG, 1988), 13–29.

Crouzet, F., *The First Industrialists. The Problem of Origins* (Cambridge, Cambridge University Press, 1985).

Cuff, R.D., "Woodrow Wilson and Business-Government Relations During World War I", *The Review of Politics* 31, 3, July 1969, 385–407.

Dahrendorf, R., *Society and Democracy in Germany* (New York, W.W. Norton & Co., 1967).

Daumard, A., *Bourgeois de Paris au XIXe siecle* (Paris, Flammarion, 1970).

—— *Bourgeois et la Bourgeoisie en France depuis 1815* (Paris, Aubier, 1987).

Daunton, M.J., ' "Gentlemanly Capitalism" and British Industry 1820–1914', *Past and Present* 122, February 1989, 119–58.

Davis, L., "The New England Textile Mills and the Capital Markets: A Study in Industrial Borrowing", *Journal of Economic History* xx, 1, 1960, 1–30.

Dayer, R., "Strange Bedfellows: J.P. Morgan and Co, Whitehall and the Wilson Administration During World War One", *Business History* 18, 2, 1976, 127–51.

Delovaia Rossiia. Ob'ediniaetsia. Materialy Uchreditel'nogo s'ezda obshcherossiiskoi obshchestvennoi organizatsii "Delovaia Rossiia" (Moscow, Rossiiskaia torgovlia, 2001).

Deriabina, M.A., "Privatizatsiia v Rossii: dolgii put' k chastnoi sobstvennosti", *Biznes i politika* 4, 1997.

Destler, C.M., "Entrepreneurial Leadership Among the 'Robber Barons': A Trial Balance", *Journal of Economic History* 6, May 1946, 28–49.

—— "The Opposition of American Businessmen to Social Control During the 'Gilded Age'", *Mississippi Valley Historical Review* xxxix, March 1953, 641–72.

Deyon, P., "Proto-industrialization in France", S.C. Ogilvie & M. Cerman (eds), *European Proto-industrialization* (Cambridge, Cambridge University press, 1996), 38–48.

Dickson, B.J., *Red Capitalists in China. The Party, Private Entrepreneurs and Prospects for Political Change* (Cambridge, Cambridge University Press, 2003).

Diefendorf, J.M., *Businessmen and Politics in the Rhineland, 1789–1834* (Princeton, Princeton University Press, 1980).

Dinello, N., "Financial-Industrial Groups and Russia's Capitalism", J.S. Micgiel (ed), *Perspectives on Political and Economic Transitions After Communism* (New York, Institute on East Central Europe, Columbia University, 1997), 197–212.

——(Evdokimova), "Forms of Capital: The Case of Russian Bankers", *International Sociology* 13, 3, 1998, 291–310.

Djankov, S., G. Roland, E. Miguel, Y. Qian & E. Zhuravskaya, "Russian Entrepreneurs: Tell Me Who Your friends and Family are . . . ", The World Bank, *Beyond Transition* 16, 1, January–March 2005, 3–5.

Dobbin, F., *Forging Industrial Policy. The United States, Britain, and France in the Railway Age* (Cambridge, Cambridge University Press, 1994).

Dobson, J.M., *Politics in the Gilded Age. A New Perspective on Reform* (New York, Praeger Publications, 1971).

Dogan, M., "La stabilite du personnel parliamentaire sous la troisieme regime", *Revue francaise de science politique* III, 1, April–June 1953, 319–48.

——"Les filieres de la carriere politique en France", *Revue francaise de sociologie* VIII, 4, 1967, 468–92.

Donnachie, I., "Sources of Capital and Capitalization in the Scottish Brewing Industry, c1750–1830", *Economic History Review* XXX, 2, 1977, 269–83.

Dore, R.P., "Making Sense of History", *Archives europeennes de sociologie* X, 1969, 295–305.

Dore, R., W. Lazonick & M. O'Sullivan, "Varieties of Capitalism in the Twentieth Century", *Oxford Review of Economic Policy* 15, 4, 1999, 102–20.

Downing, B.M., "Constitutionalism, Warfare, and Political Change in Early Modern Europe", *Theory and Society* 17, 7, 1988, 7–56.

Dunham, A.L., *The Industrial Revolution in France 1815–1848* (New York, Exposition Press, 1955).

Earle, E.M. (ed), *Modern France: Problems of the Third and Fourth Republics* (Princeton, Princeton University Press, 1951).

Edwards, P.K., *Strikes in the United States 1881–1974* (Oxford, Basil Blackwell, 1981).

Ertman, T., *Birth of the Leviathan. Building States and Regimes in Medieval and Early Modern Europe* (Cambridge, Cambridge University Press, 1997).

——"Liberalization and Democratization in Nineteenth and Twentieth Century Germany in Comparative Perspective", C. Lankowski (ed), *Breakdown, Breakup, Breakthrough. Germany's Difficult Passage to Modernity* (New York, Berghahn Books, 1999), 34–50.

Eley, G., "Capitalism and the Wilhelmine State: Industrial Growth and Political Backwardness in Recent German Historiography, 1890–1918", *The Historical Journal* 21, 3, 1978, 737–50.

——"Society and Politics in Bismarckian Germany", *German History* 15, 1, 1997, 101–32.

Eley, G., *Society, Culture, and the State in Germany, 1870–1930* (Ann Arbor, University of Michigan Press, 1996).

Elwitt, S., *The Making of the Third Republic. Class Politics in France, 1868–1884* (Baton Rouge, Louisiana State University Press, 1975).

—— "Politics and Social Classes in the Loire: The Triumph of Republican Order, 1869–1873", *French Historical Studies* VI, 1, Spring 1969, 93–112.

Epstein, E.M., *The Corporation in American Politics* (Englewood Cliffs, Prentice Hall Inc., 1969).

European Bank for Reconstruction and Development, *Transition Report 1998. Financial Sector in Transition* (London, EBRD, 1998).

—— *Transition Report 2001. Energy in Transition* (London, EBRD, 2001).

Evans, E.J., *The Forging of the Modern State. Early Industrial Britain 1783–1870* (London, Longman, 1983).

Evans, P., *Embedded Autonomy. States and Industrial Transformation* (Princeton, Princeton University Press, 1995).

Evans, P.B., "Predatory, Developmental, and Other Apparatuses: A Comparative Political Economy Perspective on the Third World State", *Sociological Forum* 4, 4, 1989, 561–87.

Evans, R.J., "Family and Class in the Hamburg Grand Bourgeoisie 1815–1914", D. Blackbourn & R.J. Evans, *The German Bourgeoisie: Essays on the social history of the German middle class from the late eighteenth to the early twentieth century* (London, Routledge, 1991), 115–39.

—— "The Myth of Germany's Missing Revolution", R.J. Evans (ed), *Rethinking German History: Nineteenth Century Germany and the Origins of the Third Reich* (London, Allen & Unwin, 1987), 93–122.

Eyal, Gil, I. Szelenyi & E. Townsley, *Making Capitalism Without Capitalists. The New Ruling Elites in Eastern Europe* (London, Verso, 1998).

Farnham, W.D., "The Weakened Spring of Government: A Study of Nineteenth Century American History", *American Historical Review* 68, 3, 1963, 662–80.

Feldman, G.D., "Industrialists, Bankers, and the Problem of Unemployment in the Weimar Republic", *Central European History* 25, 1, 1992, 76–96.

—— "The Social and Economic Policies of German Big Business, 1918–1929", *American Historical Review* 75, 1, October 1969, 47–55.

—— & U. Nocken, "Trade Associations and Economic Power: Interest Group Development in the German Iron and Steel and Machine Building Industries, 1900–1933", *Business History Review* XLIX, 4, Winter 1975, 413–45.

Femia, J.V., "Barrington Moore and the Preconditions of Democracy", *British Journal of Political Science* 2, 1, 1972, 21–46.

Ferguson, N., *Paper and Iron. Hamburg Business and German Politics in the Era of Inflation 1897–1927* (Cambridge, Cambridge University Press, 1995).

—— *The World's Banker. The History of the House of Rothschild* (London, Weidenfeld & Nicolson, 1998).

Filatotchev, I., T. Buck & M. Wright, "Privatization and Buy-outs in the USSR", *Soviet Studies* 44, 2, 1992, 265–82.

Fituni, L., "Economic Crime in the Context of Transition to a Market Economy", A.V. Ledeneva & M. Kurkchiyan (eds), *Economic Crime in Russia* (The Hague, Kluwer Law International, 1999), 17–30.

Flinn, M.W., *Origins of the Industrial Revolution* (London, Longman, 1966).

Fohlin, C., "The Rise of Interlocking Directorates in Imperial Germany", *Economic History Review* LII, 2, 1999, 307–33.

"Formirovanie tsivilizovannykh mekhanizmov vzaimodeistviia predprinimatelei i organov vlasti: rossiiskii opyt i tendentsii", *Biznes i politika* 5, 1996, 2–14.

Fortescue, S., *Policy-Making for Russian Industry* (Basingstoke, Macmillan, 1997).

—— "Privatisation, Corporate Governance and Enterprise Performance in Russia", *Russian and Euro-Asian Bulletin* 7, 5, May 1998, 1–10.

—— *Russia's Oil Barons and Metal Magnates. Oligarchs and the State in Transition* (Basingstoke, Palgrave Macmillan, 2006).

Fortesk'iu, S., "Pravit li rossiei oligarkhiia", *Polis* 5, 2002, 64–73.

Forster, R., "The Survival of the Nobility During the French Revolution", D. Johnson (ed), *French Society and the Revolution* (Cambridge, Cambridge University Press, 1976), 132–47.

Freeland, C., *Sale of the Century. The Inside Story of the Second Russian Revolution* (London, Little, Brown & Co., 2000).

Freeze, G.L., "The Soslovie (Estate) Paradigm and Russian Social History", *American Historical Review* 91, 1, February 1986, 11–36.

Frevert, U., "Bourgeois honour: middle class duellists in Germany from the late eighteenth to the early twentieth century", D. Blackbourn & R.J. Evans, *The German Bourgeoisie: Essays on the social history of the German middle class from the late eighteenth to the early twentieth century* (London, Routledge, 1991), 255–92.

Frydman, R., A. Rapaczynski & J.S. Earle et al., *The Privatization Process in Russia, Ukraine and the Baltic States* (Budapest, Central European University Press, 1993).

Frye, T., *Brokers and Bureaucrats. Building Market Institutions in Russia* (Ann Arbor, University of Michigan Press, 2000).

—— "Capture or Exchange? Business Lobbying in Russia", *Europe-Asia Studies* 54, 7, 2002, 1017–36.

—— "Governing the Russian Equities Market", *Post-Soviet Affairs* 13, 4, 1997, 366–95.

—— & A. Shleifer, "The Invisible Hand and the Grabbing Hand", *American Economic Review* 87, 2, 1997, 354–98.

Furet, F., *Revolutionary France 1770–1880* (Oxford, Blackwell, 1992).

Gaidar, Y., *Gosudarstvo i evoliutsiia* (Moscow, Evraziia, 1995).

—— "How Nomenklatura Privatized Its Power", *Russian Politics and Law* 34, 1 January–February 1996, 26–37.

Galambos, L., *The Public Image of Big Business in America, 1880–1940: A Quantitative Study in Social Change* (Baltimore, Johns Hopkins University Press, 1975).

Galeotti, M., "The Russian Mafiya: Economic Penetration at Home and Abroad", A.V. Ledeneva & M. Kurkchiyan (eds), *Economic Crime in Russia* (The Hague, Kluwer Law International, 1999), 31–42.

Garrard, J., *Democratisation in Britain. Elites, Civil Society and Reform since 1800* (Houndmills, Palgrave, Basingstoke, 2002).

—— *Leadership and Power in Victorian Industrial Towns 1830–80* (Manchester, Manchester University Press, 1983).

—— "The Middle Classes and Nineteenth Century National and Local Politics", J. Garrard, D. Jarry, M. Goldsmith & A. Oldfield (eds), *The Middle Class in Politics* (Farnborough, Saxon House, 1978), 35–66.

Gatrell, P., *Government, Industry and Rearmament in Russia, 1900–1914. The Last Argument of Tsarism* (Cambridge, Cambridge University Press, 1994).

Gazukin, P., *Vostochnaia neftianaia kompaniia. Neftianaia kompaniia "Rosneft", Neftianaia kompaniia "Slavneft", Tiumenskaia neftianaia kompaniia. Obzor deiatel'nosti* (Moscow, Panorama, 1997).

Geary, D., "Employers, Workers, and the Collapse of the Weimar Republic", I. Kershaw (ed), *Weimar: Why Did German Democracy Fail?* (London, Weidenfeld & Nicolson, 1990), 92–119.

—— "The Industrial Bourgeoisie and Labour Relations in Germany 1871–1933", D. Blackbourn & R.J. Evans (eds), *The German Bourgeoisie: Essays on the Social History of the German Middle Class from the Late Eighteenth to the Early Twentieth Century* (London, Routledge, 1991), 140–61.

Geiger, R.G., *Planning the French Canals. Bureaucracy, Politics, and Enterprise under the Restoration* (Newark, University of Delaware Press, 1994).

Gel'man, V., S. Ryzhenkov, M. Brie, V. Avdonin, B. Ovchinnikov & I. Semenov, *Making and Breaking Democratic Transitions. The Comparative Politics of Russia's Regions* (Lanham, Rowman & Littlefield Publishers Inc., 2003).

Gerschenkron, A., *Economic Backwardness in Historical Perspective* (Cambridge [Mass], Harvard University Press, 1962).

Ghent, J.M. & F.C. Jaher, "The Chicago Business Elite: 1830–1930. A Collective Biography", *Business History Review* L, 3, Autumn 1976, 288–328.

Gill, G., *The Collapse of a Single-Party System. The disintegration of the Communist Party of the Soviet Union* (Cambridge, Cambridge University Press, 1994).

—— *The Nature and Development of the Modern State* (Basingstoke, Palgrave, 2003).

—— *The Origins of the Stalinist Political System* (Cambridge, Cambridge University Press, 1990).

—— (ed), *Politics in the Russian Regions* (Basingstoke, Palgrave Macmillan, 2007).

—— & R. Pitty, *Power in the Party. The Organization of Power and Central-Republican Relations in the CPSU* (Basingstoke, Macmillan, 1987).

Gillis, J.R., "Aristocracy and Bureaucracy in Nineteenth-Century Prussia", *Past and Present* 41, December 1968, 105–29.

Gladkikh, O.G. et al., *Vlast'. Deputaty gosudarstvennoi dumy. Kratkii biograficheskii spravochnik* (Moscow, Institut sovremennoi politiki, 1994).

Glatter, P., "Continuity and Change in the Tyumen' Regional Elite 1991–2001", *Europe-Asia Studies* 55, 3, 2003, 401–35.

Glinkina, S.P., "Vlast' plius biznes ravniaetsia fiktivnaia ekonomika", *Biznes i politika* 2, 1997, 32–8.

Goldman, M.I., *The Piratization of Russia. Russian Reform Goes Awry* (London, Routledge, 2003).

—— *USSR in Crisis. The Failure of an Economic System* (New York, W.W. Norton & Co., 1983).

Golovachev, B.V., L.B. Kosova & L.A. Khakhulina, "Formirovanie praviashchei elity v Rossii", *Informatsionnyi biulleten' monitoringa* November-December 1995, 32–8.

Golovshchinskii, K.I. et al., *Biznes i korruptsiia: problemy protivodeistviia. Itogovyi otchet* (Moscow, Regional'nyi obshchestvennyi fond "Informatika dlia demokratii". Trudy fonda INDEM, 2004).

Gorbachev, M.S., *Izbrannye rechi i stat'i* (Moscow, Izdatel'stvo politicheskoi literatury, 1988).

Gordon, D.M., *Merchants and Capitalists. Industrialization and Provincial Politics in Mid-Nineteenth-Century France* (Alabama, The University of Alabama Press, 1985).

Gorshkov, M.K. et al., *Rossiiskoe predprinimatel'stvo: sotsial'nyi portret* (Moscow, Obshcherossiiskoi Ob'edinenie "Krugly stol biznesa Rossii" & Akademicheskii tsentr "Rossiiskie issledovaniia", 1994).

—— (eds), *Obnovlenie Rossii: trudnyi poisk reshenii* vyp.3 (Moscow, RNISiNP, 1995).

—— *Obnovlenie Rossii: trudnyi poisk reshenii* vyp.4 (Moscow, RNISiNP, 1996).

—— *Obnovlenie Rossii: trudnyi poisk reshenii* vyp.5 (Moscow, RNISiNP, 1997).

"Gosudarstvennaia programa privatizatsii gosudarstvennikh i munitsipel'nykh predpriatii RF na 1992 god", *Delovoi Mir* 2 July 1992.

Gough, J.W., *The Rise of the Entrepreneur* (London, B.T. Batsford Ltd., 1969).

Gourvish, T.R., "A British Business Elite: The Chief Executive Managers of the Railway Industry, 1850–1922", *Business History Review* 47, 3, Autumn 1973, 289–316.

Gowan, P., "The Origins of the Administrative Elite", *New Left Review* 162, March–April 1987, 4–34.

Graham, T., "From Oligarchy to Oligarchy: The Structure of Russia's Ruling Elite", *Demokratizatsiya* 7, 3, 1997, 329–39.

Grant, W. & D. March, *The Confederation of British Industry* (London, Hodder & Stoughton, 1977).

Grassby, R., *The Business Community of Seventeenth-Century England* (Cambridge, Cambridge University Press, 1995).

Greenberg, E.J., *Capitalism and the American Political Ideal* (Armonk, M.E. Sharpe Inc., 1985).

Gregg, P., *A Social and Economic History of Britain 1760–1965* (London, George G. Harrop & Co., 1965).

Gregory, A., *The Gilded Age. The Super-Rich of the Edwardian Era* (London, Cassell, 1993).

Gregory, F.W. & I.D. Neu, "The American Industrial Elite in the 1870's: Their Social Origins", W.E. Miller (ed), *Men in Business: Essays in the History of Entrepreneurship* (Cambridge [Mass], Harvard University Press, 1952), 193–211.

Gregory, P.R. & R.C. Stuart, *Soviet and Post-Soviet Economic Structure and Performance* (New York, Harper Collins, 1994).

Guriev, S. & A. Rachinsky, "The Role of Oligarchs in Russian Capitalism", *Journal of Economic Perspectives* 19, 1, 2005, 130–50.

———— "Russian Oligarchs: A Quantitative Assessment", The World Bank, *Beyond Transition* 15, 1, October–December 2004, 4–5.

Gustfson, T., *Capitalism Russian Style* (Cambridge, Cambridge University Press, 1999).

Gutman, H.G., "Class, Status, and Community Power in Nineteenth-Century American Industrial Cities—Peterson, New Jersey: A Case Study", F.C. Jaher (ed), *The Age of Industrialism in America. Essays in Social Structure and Cultural Values* (New York, The Free Press, 1968), 263–87.

Gutman, H., "The Reality of the Rags to Riches 'Myth': The Case of Patterson, New Jersey Locomotive, Iron and Machinery Manufacturers, 1830–90", H.G. Gutman (ed),

Work, Culture and Society in Industrializing America: Essays in American Working Class and Social History (New York, Knopf, 1977), 211–33.

Guttsman, W.L., *The British Political Elite* (London, Macgibbon & Kee, 1963).

Hacker, L.M., *The Triumph of American Capitalism. The Development of Forces in American History to the Beginning of the Twentieth Century* (New York, McGraw Hill, 1947).

Hahn, G.M., *Russia's Revolution from Above. 1985–2000. Reform, Transition, and Revolution in the Fall of the Soviet Communist Regime* (New Brunswick, Transaction Publishers, 2002).

Hahn, J.W., "Boss Gorbachev Confronts his New Congress", *Orbis* 34, 2, Spring 1990, 163–78.

Hale, H.E., "Explaining Machine Politics in Russia's Regions: Economy, Ethnicity, and Legacy", *Post-Soviet Affairs* 19, 3, July–September 2003, 228–63.

Hall, P.A. & D. Soskice, "An Introduction to Varieties of Capitalism", P.A. Hall & D. Soskice (eds), *Varieties of Capitalism: The Institutional Foundations of Comparative Advantage* (Oxford, Oxford University Press, 2001), 1–68.

Hammack, D.C., "Problems in the Historical Study of Power in the Cities and Towns of the United States, 1880–1960", *American Historical Review* 83, 2, April 1978, 323–49.

Hancock, M.D. & J. Logue (eds), *Transitions to Capitalism and Democracy in Russia and Central Europe. Achievements, Problems, Prospects* (Westport, Praeger, 2000).

Handelman, S., *Comrade Criminal. Russia's New Mafiya* (New Haven, Yale University Press, 1995).

Hanley, E., N. Yershova & R. Anderson, "Russia—Old Wine in a New Bottle? The Circulation and Reproduction of Russian Elites, 1983–1993", *Theory and Society* 24, 5, 1995, 639–68.

Hanson, P., "Administrative Regions and the Economy", W. Slater & A. Wilson (eds), *The Legacy of the Soviet Union* (Basingstoke, Palgrave Macmillan, 2004), 144–68.

—— & E. Teague, "Big Business and the State in Russia", *Europe-Asia Studies* 57, 5, 2005, 657–80.

Harasymiw, B., *Political Elite Recruitment in the Soviet Union* (London, Macmillan, 1984).

Harling, P., "Rethinking 'Old Corruption'", *Past and Present* 147, May 1995, 127–58.

—— *The Waning of "Old Corruption". The Politics of Economical Reform in Britain, 1779–1846* (Oxford, Clarendon Press, 1996).

Harris, J. & P. Thane, "British and European Bankers 1880–1914 an 'aristocratic bourgeoisie'?", Thane, Crossick & Floud, 215–34.

Harrison, R., *Congress, Progressive Reform, and the New American State* (Cambridge, Cambridge University Press, 2004).

Hedlund, S. & N. Sundstrom, "Does Palermo Represent The Future for Moscow?", *Journal of Public Policy* 16, 2, 1996, 113–55.

Hellman, J., "Bureaucrats vs Markets? Rethinking the Bureaucratic Response to Market Reform in Centrally Planned Economies", S.G. Solomon (ed), *Beyond Sovietology. Essays in Politics and History* (Armonk, M.E. Sharpe Inc., 1993), 53–93.

—— "Winners Take All: The Politics of Partial Reform in Postcommunist Transitions", *World Politics* 50, 2, 1998, 203–34.

Hellman, J.S., G. Jones, D. Kaufman & M. Schankerman, *Measuring Governance, Corruption, and State Capture. How Firms and Bureaucrats Shape the Business Environment in Transition Economies* (Washington, World Bank Institute & European Bank for

Reconstruction and Development, Policy Research Working Paper No 2313, April 2000).

Hendley, K., "Legal Development and Privatization in Russia: A Case Study", *Soviet Economy* 8, 2, 1992, 130–57.

—— B.W. Ickes, P. Murrell & R. Ryterman, "Observations on the Use of Law by Russian Enterprises", *Post-Soviet Affairs* 13, 1, 1997, 14–41.

Henderson, W.O., *The Rise of German Industrial Power 1834–1914* (London, Temple Smith, 1975).

Herspring, D.R., *Putin's Russia. Past Imperfect, Future Uncertain* (Lanham, Rowman & Littlefield Publishers Inc., 2003).

Hessler, J., "A Postwar Perestroika? Toward a History of Private Enterprise in the USSR", *Slavic Review* 57, 3, 1998, 516–42.

Higley, J., J. Kullberg & J. Pakulski, "The Persistence of Postcommunist Elites", *Journal of Democracy* 7, 2, 1996, 133–47.

—— & G. Lengyel (eds), *Elites After State Socialism. Theories and Analysis* (Lanham, Rowman & Littlefield Publishers Inc., 2000).

Hill, F., *Energy Empire: Oil, Gas and Russia's Revival* (London, The Foreign Policy Centre, 2004).

Himmelberg, R.H., "Business, Antitrust Policy, and the Industrial Board of the Department of Commerce, 1919", *Business History Review* xlii, 1, 1968, 1–23.

Hobson, J.M., *The Wealth of States. A Comparative Sociology of International Economic and Political Change* (Cambridge, Cambridge University Press, 1997).

Hoffman, D.E., *The Oligarchs. Wealth and Power in the New Russia* (New York, Public Affairs, 2002).

Hofstadter, R., *The American Political Tradition and the Men Who Made It* (New York, Vintage Books, 1948).

Holmes, S., "Cultural Legacies or State Collapse? Probing the Postcommunist Dilemma", M. Mandelbaum (ed), *Postcommunism: Four Perspectives* (Washington, Council on Foreign relations, 1996), 22–76.

Honeyman, K., *Origins of Enterprise: Business Leadership in the Industrial Revolution* (Manchester, Manchester University Press, 1982).

Hoogenboom, A., "Industrialism and Political Leadership: A Case Study of the United States Senate", F.C. Jaher (ed), *The Age of Industrialism in America. Essays in Social Structure and Cultural Values* (New York, The Free Press, 1968), 49–78.

Hosking, G., *The Russian Constitutional Experiment. Government and Duma, 1907–1914* (Cambridge, Cambridge University Press, 1973).

Hough, J.F., *Democratization and Revolution in the USSR 1985–1991* (Washington, Brookings Institution Press, 1997).

Hudson, P., "Proto-industrialization in England", S.C. Ogilvie & M. Cerman (eds), *European Proto-industrialization* (Cambridge, Cambridge University Press, 1996), 49–66.

Hughes, J., "Sub-national Elites and Post-communist Transformation in Russia: A Reply to Kryshtanovskaia and White", *Europe-Asia Studies* 49, 6, 1997, 1017–36.

Humphrey, C., *The Unmaking of Soviet Life. Everyday Economies after Socialism* (Ithaca, Cornell University Press, 2002).

Hunt, J.C., "The Bourgeois Middle in German Politics, 1871–1933: Recent Literature", *Central European History* XI, 1, March 1978, 83–106.

Hutchcroft, P., *Booty Capitalism. The Politics of Banking in the Philippines* (Ithaca, Cornell University Press, 1998).

Ingham, G., "British Capitalism: Empire, Merchants and Decline", *Social History* 20, 3, October 1995, 339–54.

—— *Capitalism Divided? The City and Industry in British Social Development* (Basingstoke, Macmillan, 1984).

Ingham, J.N., "Rags to Riches Revisited: The Effect of City Size and Related Factors on the Recruitment of Business Leaders", *Journal of American History* 63, 3, December 1976, 615–37.

Izvestiia Ts.K. KPSS (Moscow, 1989–91).

Jackson, G., *Hull in the Eighteenth Century. A Study in Social and Economic History* (Oxford, Oxford University Press, 1972).

Jacoby, S.M., "Employers and the Welfare State: The Role of Marion B. Folsom", *Journal of American History* 80, 2, September 1993, 525–56.

Jaher, F.C., "The Gilded Elite: American Multimillionaires, 1865 to the Present", W.D. Rubinstein (ed), *Wealth and the Wealthy in the Modern World* (London, Croom Helm, 1980), 189–276.

Jensen, D.N., "The Boss: How Yury Luzhkov Runs Moscow", *Demokratizatsiya* 8, 1, Winter 2000), 83–122.

Jeremy, D.J., "Anatomy of the British Business Elite, 1860–1980", *Business History* XXVI, 1, March 1984, 3–23.

Jessop, B., *State Theory. Putting Capitalist States in their Place* (Cambridge, Polity Press, 1990).

Johnson, J., *A Fistful of Rubles. The Rise and Fall of the Russian Banking System* (Ithaca, Cornell University Press, 2000).

Johnson, J.E., "The Russian Banking System: Institutional Responses to the Market Transition", *Europe-Asia Studies* 46, 6, 1994, 971–95.

Johnson, S. & H. Kroll, "Managerial Strategies for Spontaneous Privatization", *Soviet Economy* 7, 4, 1991, 281–316.

Jones, A. & W. Moskoff (eds), *The Great Market Debate in Soviet Economics* (Armonk, M.E. Sharpe Inc., 1990).

—— & W. Moskoff, *Ko-ops. The Rebirth of Entrepreneurship in the Soviet Union* (Bloomington, Indiana University Press, 1991).

Jones, L.J., "Public Pursuit of Private Profit? Liberal Businessmen and Municipal Politics in Birmingham 1865–1900", *Business History* 25, 3, November 1983, 240–59.

Josephson, M., *The Politicos. 1856–1896* (New York, Harcourt, Brace & Co., 1938).

—— *The Robber Barons: The Great American Capitalists, 1861–1901* (London, Eyre & Spottiswood, 1962).

Judge, D., *Parliament and Industry* (Aldershot, Dartmouth, 1990).

Kaelble, H., "French Bourgeoisie and German Burgertum, 1870–1914", J. Kocka & A. Mitchell (eds), *Bourgeois Society in Nineteenth Century Europe* (Providence, Berg Publishers, 1993), 273–301.

—— "Long-Term Changes in the Recruitment of the Business Elite: Germany Compared to the US, Great Britain, and France Since the Industrial Revolution", *Journal of Social History* 13, 3, Spring 1980, 404–23.

Kaudelka-Hanisch, K., "The Titled Businessman: Prussian Commercial Councillors in the Rhineland and Westphalia During the Nineteenth Century", D. Blackbourn & R.J. Evans (eds), *The German Bourgeoisie: Essays on the Social History of the German Middle Class from the Late Eighteenth to the Early Twentieth Century* (London, Routledge, 1991), 87–114.

Kang, D.C., *Crony Capitalism. Corruption and Development in South Korea and the Philippines* (Cambridge, Cambridge University Press, 2002).

Kehr, E., *Economic Interest, Militarism, and Foreign Policy. Essays on German History* (Berkeley, University of California Press, 1977, trans. Greta Heinz).

Kemp, T., *Economic Forces in French History* (London, Dennis Dobson, 1971).

Kempton, D.R., "The Republic of Sakha (Yakutia): The Evolution of Centre-Periphery Relations in the Russian Federation", *Europe-Asia Studies* 48, 4, 1996, 587–613.

Kets de Vries, M.F.R., S. Shekshnia, K. Korotov & E. Floreant-Treacy, *The New Russian Business Leaders* (Cheltenham, Edward Elgar, 2004).

Khripunov, I. & M.M. Matthews, "Russia's Oil and Gas Interest Group and Its Foreign Policy Agenda", *Problems of Post-Communism* 43, 3, May–June 1996, 36–48.

Kihlgren, A., "Small Business in Russia—Factors that Slowed its Development: An Analysis", *Communist and Postcommunist Studies* 36, 2, 2003, 193–207.

Kirkendall, R., "The New Deal as Watershed: The Recent Literature", *Journal of American History* 54, 4, 1968, 839–52.

Kirkow, P., "Regional Politics and Market Reform in Russia: The Case of the Altai", *Europe-Asia Studies* 46, 7, 1994, 1163–87.

—— "Regional Warlordism in Russia: The Case of Primorskii Krai", *Europe-Asia Studies* 47, 6, 1995, 923–47.

Klebnikov, P., *Godfather of the Kremlin. Boris Berezovsky and the Looting of Russia* (New York, Harcourt Inc., 2000).

Kocka, J., "The Middle Classes in Europe", *Industrial Culture and Bourgeois Society: Business, Labor, Bureaucracy in Modern Germany* (New York, Berghahn Books, 1999), 231–54.

—— *Industrial Culture and Bourgeois Society: Business, Labor, Bureaucracy in Modern Germany* (New York, Berghahn Books, 1999).

—— & A. Mitchell (eds), *Bourgeois Society in Nineteenth Century Europe* (Oxford, Berg, 1993).

Kodin, M., *Obshchestvo-politicheskie ob'edineniia i formirovanie politicheskoi elity v Rossii (1990–1997)* (Moscow, FSRSPN, 1998).

Koditschek, T., *Class Formation and Urban Industrial Society. Bradford 1750–1850* (Cambridge, Cambridge University Press, 1990).

Koistinen, P.A.C., "The 'Industrial Military Complex' in Historical Perspective; The Inter War Years", *Journal of American History* 56, 4, March 1970, 819–39.

Kolko, G., *The Triumph of Conservatism. A Reinterpretation of American History, 1900–1916* (New York, The Free Press of Glencoe, 1963).

Korzhakov, A., *Boris El'tsin: ot rassveta do zakata* (Moscow, Interbuk, 1997).

Kotz, D. & F. Weir, *Revolution from Above. The demise of the Soviet system* (London, Routledge, 1977).

Kozlov, P., *Bankiry Rossii (Kto est' kto)* (Moscow, SPIK-Tsentr, 1999).

Kryshtanovskaia, Ol'ga, "Finansovaia oligarkhiia v Rossii", *Izvestiia* 10 January 1996.
—— "Transformatsiia staroi nomenklatury v novuiu rossiiskuiu elitu", *Obshchestvennye nauki i sovremennost'* 1, 1995, 51–65.
—— & S. White, "From Soviet *Nomenklatura* to Russian Elite", *Europe-Asia Studies* 48, 5, 1996, 711–33.
—— —— "Inside the Putin Court: A Research Note", *Europe-Asia Studies* 57, 7, 2005, 1065–75.
—— —— "The rise of the Russian business elite", *Communist and Post-Communist Studies* 38, 3, September 2005, 293–307.
Kryukov, V. & A. Moe, *The Changing Role of Banks in the Russian Oil Sector* (London, RIIA, 1998).
Kubicek, P., "Variations on a Corporatist Theme: Interest Associations in Post-Soviet Ukraine and Russia", *Europe-Asia Studies* 48, 1, 1996, 27–46.
Kuisel, R.F., *Capitalism and the State in Modern France: Renovation and Economic Management in the Twentieth Century* (Cambridge, Cambridge University Press, 1981).
Kukolev, I.V., "Formirovanie biznes-elity", *Obshchestvennye nauki i sovremennost'* 2, 1996, 12–23.
—— "Pochemu i kak predprinimateli uchastvuiut v vyborakh", *Biznes i politika* 3, 4, 1998, 3–10.
Kulikoff, A., "The Transition to Capitalism in Rural America", *William and Mary Quarterly* 46, 1, 1989, 120–44.
Kullberg, J., "The Ideological Roots of Elite Political Conflict in Post-Soviet Russia", *Europe-Asia Studies* 46, 6, 1994, 929–53.
Kurth, J., "Industrial Change and Political Change. A European Perspective", D. Collier (ed), *The New Authoritarianism in Latin America* (Princeton, Princeton University Press, 1979), 319–62.
Kuznetsov, A. & O. Kuznetsova, "Institutions, Business and the State in Russia", *Europe-Asia Studies* 55, 6, 2003, 907–22.
Kusznir, J., "Economic Actors in Russian Regional Politics: The Example of the Oil Industry", G. Gill (ed), *Politics in the Russian Regions* (Basingstoke, Palgrave Macmillan, 2007), 161–87.
Laffey, J.A., "Municipal Imperialism: The Lyon Chamber of Commerce, 1914–1925", *Journal of European Economic History* 4, 1, Spring 1975, 95–120.
Lamboreaux, N., *The Great Merger Movement in American Business* (Cambridge, Cambridge University Press, 1985).
Landes, D., "French Business and the Businessman: A Social and Cultural Analysis", E.M. Earle (ed), *Modern France: Problems of the Third and Fourth Republics* (Princeton, Princeton University Press, 1951), 334–53.
—— "French Entrepreneurship and Industrial Growth in the Nineteenth Century", *Journal of Economic History* IX, 1, May 1949, 45–61.
Lane, D., *The Political Economy of Russian Oil* (Lanham, Rowman & Littlefield Publishers Inc., 1999).
—— "The Political Economy of Russian Oil", P. Rutland (ed), *Business and the State in Contemporary Russia* (Boulder, Westview Press, 2001), 101–28.
—— *The Rise and Fall of State Socialism* (Cambridge, Polity Press, 1996).

——"The Russian Oil Elite. Background and Outlook", D. Lane (ed), *The Political Economy of Russian Oil* (Lanham, Rowman & Littlefield Pubs Inc., 1999), 75–96.

——"What kind of capitalism for Russia? A comparative analysis", *Communist and Postcommunist Studies* 33, 4, December 2000, 485–504.

—— & C. Ross, *The Transition from Communism to Capitalism. Ruling Elites from Gorbachev to Yeltsin* (Basingstoke, Macmillan, 1999).

—— & I. Seifulmukov, "Structure and Ownership", D. Lane (ed), *The Political Economy of Russian Oil* (Lanham, Rowman & Littlefield Publishers Inc., 1999), 15–45.

Lapina, N.I., *Formirovanie sovremennoi rossiiskoi elity (Problemy perekhodnogo perioda)* (Moscow, Rossiiskaia akademiia nauk, Institut nauchnoi informatsii po obshchestvennym naukam, 1995).

Lapina, N., *Rossiiskie ekonomicheskie elity i modeli natsional'nogo razvitiia* (Moscow, INION, 1977).

Lapina, N.I., *Rukoviditeli gosudarstvennykh predpriiatii rossii v protsesse formirovaniia rynochnykh otnoshenii* (Moscow, Rossiiskaia akademiia nauk, Institut nauchnoi informatsii po obshchestvennym naukam, 1995).

Lauthier, P., "Les dirigeans des grandes enterprises electriques en France, 1911–1973", M. Levy-Leboyer (ed), *Le patronat de la seconde industrialisation* (Paris, Les Editions ouvrieres, 1970), 101–36.

Lebovics, H., *The Alliance of Iron and Wheat in the Third French Republic 1860–1914. Origins of the New Conservatism* (Baton Rouge, Louisiana State University Press, 1988).

——*Social Conservatism and the Middle Classes in Germany, 1914–1933* (Princeton, Princeton University Press, 1969).

Ledeneva, A.V., *How Russia Really Works. The Informal Practices That Shaped Post-Soviet Politics and Business* (Ithaca, Cornell University Press, 2006).

——*Russia's Economy of Favours. Blat, Networking and Informal Exchange* (Cambridge, Cambridge University Press, 1998).

—— & M. Kurkchiyan (eds), *Economic Crime in Russia* (The Hague, Kluwer Law International, 1999).

Lefebvre, G., *The French Revolution from Its Origins to 1793* (London, Routledge & Kegan Paul, 1962, trans. Elizabeth Moss Evanson).

——*The French Revolution from 1793–1799* (London, Routledge & Kegan Paul, 1964, trans. John Hall Stewart & James Friguglietti).

Levi, M., *Of Rule and Revenue* (Berkeley, University of California Press, 1988).

Levinson, A.G. et al., *Obraz predprinimatelia v novoi rossii* (Moscow, Tsentr politicheskikh tekhnologii, 1998).

Levitan, S.A. & M.R. Cooper, *Business Lobbies. The Public Good and the Bottom Line* (Baltimore, Johns Hopkins University Press, 1984).

Levy-Leboyer, M. (ed), *Le patronat de la seconde industrialisation* (Paris, Les Editions Ouvrieres, 1970).

——"Le patronat francais, 1912–1973", M. Levy-Leboyer (ed), *Le patronat de la seconde industrialisation* (Paris, Les Editions ouvrieres, 1970), 137–88.

Lewin, M., "Collapse of the Russian State", *Le Monde Diplomatique/The Guardian Weekly* November 1998 pp. 1, 10 & 11.

Leys, C., "The Formation of British Capital", *New Left Review* 160, November–December 1986, 114–20.

Lhomme, J., *La grande bourgeoisie au pouvoir (1830–1880); essai sur l'histoire sociale de la France* (Paris, Presses universitaires de France, 1960).

Lieven, D., *The Aristocracy in Europe 1815–1914* (Basingstoke, Macmillan, 1992).

Lindblom, C., *Politics and Markets. The world's political economic systems* (New York, Basic Books, 1977).

Linz, S.J. & G. Krueger, *Pilferers or Paladins? Russia's Managers in Transition* (The William Davidson Institute Working Paper No 17, November 1996, University of Michigan).

Lisichkin, V.A. & L.A. Shelepin, *Rossiia pod vlast'iu plutokratii* (Moscow, Algoritm, 2003).

Lloyd-Jones, R. & M.J. Lewis, *British Industrial Capitalism since the Industrial Revolution* (London, UCL Press, 1998).

Lockwood, D., "Managers and Capitalists: The Emergence of New Class Forces in the Early Post-Soviet Economy", *Russian and Euro-Asian Bulletin* 6, 2, February 1997, 1–12.

Logue, J. & O.Y. Klepikova, "Restructuring Elinar: A Case Study of Russian Management Reform, Decentralization and Diversification", M. Donald Hancock & J. Logue (eds), *Transitions to Capitalism and Democracy in Russia and Central Europe. Achievements, Problems, Prospects* (Westport, Praeger, 2000), 67–93.

Lohr, E., "Arkady Volsky's Political Base", *Europe-Asia Studies* 45, 5, 1993, 811–29.

Longstreth, F., "The City, Industry and the State", C. Crouch (ed), *State and Economy in Contemporary Capitalism* (London, Croom Helm, 1979), 157–90.

Lotchin, R.W., "The City and the Sword: San Francisco and the Rise of the Metropolitan Military Industrial Complex", *Journal of American History* 65, 4, March 1979, 996–1020.

Lucas, C., "Nobles, Bourgeois and the Origins of the French Revolution", D. Johnson (ed), *French Society and the Revolution* (Cambridge, Cambridge University Press, 1976), 88–103.

Luchterhandt, G., "Politics in the Russian Province: Revda and Kinel", *Europe-Asia Studies* 49, 1, 1997, 59–87.

Lukes, S., *Power. A Radical View* (Basingstoke, Macmillan, 1974).

Lukin, M., "Spravochnik. Vsia Duma", *Kommersant Vlast'* 3 (354), 25 January 2000, 19–44.

Luzhkov, Y., *My deti tvoi Moskva* (Moscow, Vagrius, 1996).

McAuley, M., *Russia's Politics of Uncertainty* (Cambridge, Cambridge University Press, 1997).

McCaffray, S.P., *The Politics of Industrialization in Tsarist Russia. The Association of Southern Iron and Steel Producers 1874–1914* (De Kalb, Northern Illinois University Press, 1996).

McCahill, M.W., "Peers, Patronage, and the Industrial Revolution, 1760–1800", *Journal of British Studies* xvi, 1976, 84–107.

McCauley, M., *Bandits, Gangsters and the Mafia. Russia, the Baltic States and the CIS* (Harlow, Longman, 2001).

McCormick, R., "The Discovery that Business Corrupts Politics: A Reappraisal of the Origins of Progressivism", *American Historical Review* 86, 2, 1981, 247–74.

McDaniel, T., *Autocracy, Capitalism, and Revolution in Russia* (Berkeley, University of California Press, 1988).

McDougall, W.A., "Political Economy versus National Sovereignty: French Structures for German Economic Integration after Versailles", *Journal of Modern History* 51, 1, March 1979, 4–23.

McFaul, M., "The Allocation of Property Rights in Russia. The First Round", *Communist and Post-Communist Studies* 29, 3, September 1996, 287–308.

—— "State Power, Institutional Change, and the Politics of Privatization in Russia", *World Politics* 47, 2, January 1995, 210–43.

McIvor, A.J., *Organised Capital. Employers' Associations and Industrial Relations in Northern England, 1880–1939* (Cambridge, Cambridge University Press, 1996).

McKendrick, N., J. Brewer & J.H. Plumb, *The Birth of a Consumer Society. The Commercialization of Eighteenth Century England* (London, Europa Publications Ltd, 1982).

McMillan, J. & C. Woodruff, "The Central Role of Entrepreneurs in Transition Economies", *Journal of Economic Perspectives* 16, 3, 2002, 153–70.

McPhee, P., *A Social History of France, 1780–1880* (London, Routledge, 1992).

McQuaid, K., *Big Business and Presidential Power. From FDR to Reagan* (New York, William Morrow & Co Inc., 1982).

—— "Corporate Liberalism in the American Business Community, 1920–1940", *Business History Review* 52, 3, 1978, 342–68.

Magraw, R., "The Making of Post-Revolutionary France", *The Historical Journal* 31, 4, 1988, 984–1000.

—— *France 1815–1914. The Bourgeois Century* (Oxford, Fontana, 1983).

Maier, C.S., *Recasting Bourgeois Europe. Stabilization in France, Germany and Italy in the Decade After World War 1* (Princeton, Princeton University Press, 1975).

Makarevich, L., "Struktura sobstvennosti i bor'ba za ee peredel v Rossii v 1992–1999gg", *Obshchestvo i ekonomika* 10–11, 1999, 230–53.

Mann, M., "The Autonomous Power of the State: Its Origins, Mechanisms and Results", J.A. Hall (ed), *States in History* (Oxford, Basil Blackwell, 1986), 109–36.

—— *Fascists* (Cambridge, Cambridge University Press, 2004).

—— *The Sources of Social Power. Volume II. The rise of classes and nation-states, 1760–1914* (Cambridge, Cambridge University Press, 1993).

Markwick, R.D., "What Kind of a State is the Russian State—If There Is One?", *The Journal of Communist Studies and Transition Politics* 15, 4, December 1999, 111–30.

Marx, K., "Critique of the Gotha Program", D. Fernbach (ed), *The First International and After. Political Writings*, Volume 3. (Harmondsworth, Penguin, 1974), 339–59.

—— & F. Engels, *Selected Works in Two Volumes* (Moscow, Foreign Languages Publishing House, 1951).

Maslennikov, A.A. & A.I. Bazhan (eds), *Rol' bankov v razvitii Rossiiskoi ekonomiki* (Moscow, Ekslibris-Press, 2000).

Mathias, P., *The First Industrial Nation. An Economic History of Britain 1700–1914* (London, Methuen, 1969).

Matlock, J.F., "The Struggle for the Kremlin", *The New York Review of Books* 8, August 1996, 28–34.

Mayer, A.J., *The Persistence of the Old Regime. Europe to the Great War* (London, Croom Helm, 1981).

Medalen, C., "State Monopoly Capitalism in Germany: The Hibernia Affair", *Past and Present* 78, February 1978, 82–112.

Medvedev, R., *Chubais i voucher. Iz istorii rossiiskoi privatizatsii* (Moscow, Izdatel'stvo "IMPETO", 1997).

Melvin, N.J., "The Consolidation of a New Regional Elite: The Case of Omsk 1987–1995", *Europe-Asia Studies* 50, 4, 1998, 619–50.

Merrill, M., "Putting Capitalism in its Place: A Recent Review of the Literature", *William and Mary Quarterly* 52, 2 1995, 315–26.

Midgley, D. & C. Hutchins, *Abramovich. The Billionaire from Nowhere* (London, Harper Collins, 2004).

Migdal, J., *Strong Societies and Weak States: State-Society Relations and State Capabilities in the Third World* (Princeton, Princeton University Press, 1988).

Miliband, R., *The State in Capitalist Society* (New York, Basic Books, 1969).

Miller, Z.L., "Boss Cox's Cincinnati: A Study in Urbanization and Politics, 1880–1914", *Journal of American History* 54, 4, March 1968, 823–38.

Mills, C.W., "The American Political Elite: A Collective Portrait", I.L. Horowitz (ed), *Power, Politics and People. The Collected Essays of C. Wright Mills* (London, Oxford University Press, 1967), 196–207.

—— *The Power Elite* (New York, Oxford University Press, 1959).

Mitchell, B.R., *International Historical Statistics. Europe 1750–1988* (New York, Stockton Press, 1992 and Basingstoke, Macmillan, 1998).

—— *International Historical Statistics. The Americas 1750–1993* (Basingstoke, Macmillan, 1998).

Mollier, Jean-Yves., *La scandale de Panama* (Paris, Fayard, 1991).

Mommsen, W.J., *Imperial Germany 1867–1918. Politics, Culture and Society in an Authoritarian State* (London, Arnold, 1955, trans. Richard Deveson).

Mooers, C., *The Making of Bourgeois Europe. Absolutism, Revolution, and the Rise of Capitalism in England, France and Germany* (London, Verso, 1991).

Moore Jr, B., *Social Origins of Dictatorship and Democracy. Lord and Peasant in the Making of the Modern World* (Harmondsworth, Penguin, 1969).

More, C., *The Industrial Age. Economy and Society in Britain 1750–1985* (London, Longman, 1989).

Mork, G.R., "The Prussian Railway Scandal of 1873: Economics and Politics in the German Empire", *European Studies Review* 1, 1, 1971, 35–48.

Moses, J.C., "Political-Economic Elites and Russian Regional Elections 1999–2000: Democratic tendencies in Kaliningrad, Perm and Volgograd", *Europe-Asia Studies* 54, 2, 2002, 905–31.

Mosse, W., "Nobility and Bourgeoisie in Nineteenth Century Europe: A Comparative View", J. Kocka & A. Mitchell (eds), *Bourgeois Society in Nineteenth Century Europe* (Oxford, Berg, 1993), 70–102.

Mountfield, D., *The Railway Barons* (London, Osprey, 1979).

Mukhin, A.A., *Biznes-elita i gosudarstvennaia vlast': Kto vladeet Rossiei na rubezhe vekov?* (Moscow, Tsentr politicheskoi informatsii, 2001).

Mukhin, A., *"Gazprom": Imperiia i ee imperatory* (Moscow, Tsentr politicheskoi informatsii, 2001).

—— *Korruptsia i gruppy vliianie Kniga 1* (Moscow, SPIK-Tsentr, 1999).

—— *Moskovskie oligarkhi* (Moscow, Tsentr politicheskoi informatsii, 2000).

—— *Voiny na rynke telekommunikatsii. Osnovye uchastniki i gruppy vliianii* (Moscow, Tsentr politicheskoi informatsii, 2001).

Mukhin, A.A. & P.A. Kozlov, *"Semeinye" tainy ili neofitsial'nyi lobbizm v Rossii* (Moscow, Tsentr politicheskoi informatsii, 2003).

Myers, G., *History of the Great American Fortunes* (Chicago, Charles H. Kerr & Co., 1909).

Nazarova, N.V. & I.V. Krasheninnikov, *Obshchestvennye (nekommercheskie) ob'edineniia predpriiatii i predprinimatelei Rossii* (Moscow, Tsentr Politicheskikh tekhnologii, 1996).

Nenadic, S., "Businessmen, the Urban Middle Classes, and the 'Dominance' of Manufacturers in Nineteenth Century Britain", *Economic History Review* XLIV, 1, 1991, 66–85.

Nettl, J.P., "Consensus or Elite Domination: The Case of Business", *Political Studies* 13, 1, 1965, 22–44.

Nicholas, T., "Businessmen and Land Ownership in the Late Nineteenth Century", *Economic History Review* 52, 1, 1999, 27–44.

Nicholas, T., "Businessmen and Land Ownership in the Late Nineteenth Century Revisited", *Economic History Review* 53, 4, 2000, 777–82.

——"Wealth Making in Nineteenth- and Early Twentieth-Century Britain: Industry v Commerce and Finance", *Business History* 41, 1, January 1999, 16–36.

——"Wealth Making in the Nineteenth- and Early Twentieth Century: The Rubinstein Hypothesis Revisited", *Business History* 42, 2, April 2000, 155–68.

Norris, P., "Legislative Recruitment", L. Le Duc, R.G. Niemi & P. Norris (eds), *Comparing Democracies. Elections and Voting in Global Perspective* (Thousand Oaks, Sage, 1996), 184–215.

O'Boyle, L., "The Middle Class in Western Europe, 1815–1848", *American Historical Review* LXII, April 1966, 826–45.

Odom, W.E., *The Collapse of the Soviet Military* (New Haven, Yale University Press, 1998).

Ogilvie, S.C., "Proto-industrialization in Germany", S.C. Ogilvie & M. Cerman (eds), *European Proto-industrialization* (Cambridge, Cambridge University press, 1996), 118–36.

——& M. Cerman (eds), *European proto-industrialization* (Cambridge, Cambridge University Press, 1996).

Orttung, R.W., "Business and Politics in the Russian Regions", *Problems of Post-Communism* 51, 2, March–April 2004, 48–60.

Orttung, R. & P. Reddaway, "What Do the Okrug Reforms Add Up to? Some Conclusions", P. Reddaway & R. Orttung (eds), *The Dynamics of Russian Politics. Putin's Reform of Federal-Regional Relations*, Volume 1. (Lanham, Rowman & Littlefield Publishers Inc., 2004), 277–301.

Oversloot, H. & R. Verheul, "The Party of Power in Russian Politics", *Acta Politica* 25, Summer 2000, 123–45.

Owen, T.C., *Capitalism and Politics in Russia. A social history of the Moscow merchants* (Cambridge, Cambridge University Press, 1981).

——*The Corporation Under Russian Law, 1800–1917. A Study in Tsarist Economic Policy* (Cambridge, Cambridge University Press, 1991).

——"Doing Business in Merchant Moscow", J.L. West & I.A. Petrov (eds), *Merchant Moscow. Images of Russia's Vanished Bourgeoisie* (Princeton, Princeton University Press, 1988), 29–36.

——"Impediments to a Bourgeois Consciousness in Russia, 1880–1905: The Estate Structure, Ethnic Diversity, and Economic Regionalism", E.W. Clowes,

S.D. Kassow & J.L. West (eds), *Between Tsar and People. Educated Society and the Quest for Public Identity in Late Imperial Russia* (Princeton, Princeton University Press, 1991), 41–56.

——"The Russian Industrial Society and Tsarist Economic Policy, 1867–1905", *Journal of Economic History* 45, 3, September 1985, 587–606.

Palmade, G., *French Capitalism in the Nineteenth Century* (Newton Abbott, David & Charles, 1972).

Pappe, Ia.Sh., *Finansovo-promyshlennye gruppy i konglomeraty v ekonomike i politike sovremennoi Rossii* (Moscow, Tsentr politicheskoi tekhnologii, 1997).

——"Oligarkhi". *Ekonomicheskaia khronika 1992–2000* (Moscow, Gosudarstvennyi universitet Vysshaia shkola ekonomiki, 2000).

Payne, H.C., *The Police State of Louis Napoleon Bonaparte 1851–1860* (Seattle, University of Washington Press, 1966).

Payne, P.L., *British Entrepreneurship in the Nineteenth Century* (Basingstoke, Macmillan, 1974).

Pearce, M. & G. Stewart, *British Political History 1867–2001* (London, Routledge, 2002).

Pearson, R., *The Russian Moderates and the Crisis of Tsarism 1914–1917* (London, Macmillan, 1977).

Peck, L.L., *Court Patronage and Corruption in Early Stuart England* (Boston, Unwin Hyman, 1990).

Peiter, H.D., "Institutions and Attitudes: The Consolidation of the Business Community in Bourgeois France, 1880–1914", *Journal of Social History* 9, 4, June 1976, 510–25.

Peregudov, S., "The Oligarchical Model of Russian Corporatism", A. Brown (ed), *Contemporary Russian Politics. A Reader* (Oxford, Oxford University Press, 2001), 259–68.

——N. Lapina & I. Semenenko, *Gruppy interesov i rossiiskoe gosudarstvo* (Moscow, Editorial URSS, 1999).

Perez-Diaz, V.M., *State, Bureaucracy and Civil Society. A Critical Discussion of the Political Theory of Karl Marx* (London, Macmillan, 1978).

Perkin, H., "Land Reform and Class Conflict in Victorian Britain", H. Perkin (ed), *The Structured Crowd. Essays in English Social History* (Brighton, The Harvester Press, 1981), 100–35.

——*The Origins of Modern English Society* (London, Routledge & Kegan Paul, 1969).

——*The Rise of Professional Society. England Since 1880* (London, Routledge, 2002).

Pessen, E., *The Log Cabin Myth. The Social Backgrounds of the Presidents* (New Haven, Yale University Press, 1984).

Phillips, K., *Wealth and Democracy. A Political History of the American Rich* (New York, Broadway Books, 2002).

Pierenkemper, T., "Entrepreneurs in Heavy Industry: Upper Silesia and the Westphalian Ruhr Region, 1852–1913", *Business History Review* LIII, 1, Spring 1979, 65–78.

Pierson, P., *Politics in Time: History, Institutions and Social Analysis* (Princeton, Princeton University Press, 2000).

Pilbeam, P.M., *The Middle Classes in Europe 1789–1914. France, Germany, Italy and Russia* (Basingstoke, Macmillan, 1990).

Pipes, R., *Russia Under the Old Regime* (London, Weidenfeld & Nicolson, 1974).

Platonov, V.M. et al., *Moskovskaia gorodskaia duma. Istoriia i sovremennost'* (Moscow, OAO "Moskovskie uchebniki i Kartolitigrafiia", 2004).

Pleines, H., "Corruption and Crime in the Russian Oil Industry", D. Lane (ed), *The Political Economy of Russian Oil* (Lanham, Rowman & Littlefield Publishers Inc, 1999), 97–110.

Plessis, A., "Bankers in French Society, 1860s-1960", Y. Cassis (ed), *Finance and Financiers in European History, 1880–1960* (Cambridge, Cambridge University Press, 1992), 147–61.

——*Le Banque de France et ses Deux Cents Actionnaires sous le Second Empire* (Geneva, Librairie Droz, 1982).

——*La Politique de la Banque de France de 1851 a 1870* (Geneva, Librairie Droz, 1985).

——*Regents et Gouverneurs de la Banque de France sous le Second Empire* (Geneva, Librairie Droz, 1985).

——*The Rise and Fall of the Second Empire, 1852–1871* (Cambridge, Cambridge University Press, 1985).

Podplatnik, T., "Big Business and the State in Putin's Russia, 2000–2004: Towards a New Super State Corporatism", Oxford University, D.Phil, 2005.

Popov, P., *Vedushchie neftianye kompanii rossii* (Moscow, TsPI, 2001).

Portal, R., "Aux origins d'une bourgeoisie industrielle en Russie", *Revue d'histoire moderne et contemporaine* VIII, 1961, 35–60.

Pospielovsky, D., *Russian Police Trade Unionism. Experiment or Provocation* (London, Wiedenfeld & Nicolcon, 1971).

Post, C., "The American Road to Capitalism", *New Left Review* 133, May–June 1982, 30–51.

Price, R., *A Social History of Nineteenth Century France* (London, Hutchinson, 1987).

——*An Economic History of Modern France* (London, Macmillan, 1981).

——*The Economic Modernization of France* (London, Croom Helm, 1975).

Puffer, S.M., D.J. McCarthy & A.I. Naumov, *The Russian Capitalist Experiment. From State-owned Organizations to Entrepreneurships* (Cheltenham, Edward Elgar, 2000).

Pugh, M., *The Making of Modern British Politics 1867–1939* (Oxford, Basil Blackwell, 1982).

Pumphrey, R.E., "The Introduction of Industrialists into the British Peerage: A Study in Adaptation of a Social Institution", *American Historical Review* LXV, 1, October 1959, 1–16.

Purcell Jr, E.A., "Ideas and Interests: Businessmen and the Interstate Commerce Act", *Journal of American History* 54, 3, December 1967, 561–78.

Radaev, V., "Malyi biznes i problemy delovoi etiki: nadezhdy i real'nost", *Voprosy ekonomiki* 7, 1996, 72–82.

——"O roli nasiliia v rossiiskikh delovykh otnosheniiakh", *Voprosy ekonomiki* 19, 1998, 81–100.

——"Novye predprinimateli: sotsial'nyi portret", V.V. Radaev, et al. (eds), *Stanovlenie novogo rossiiskogo predprinimatel'stva* (Moscow, RAN, Institut ekonomiki & Mezhdist-siplinarnyi akademicheskii tsentr sotsial'nykh nauk (Intertsentr), 1993), 65–81.

——"Corruption and Violence in Russian Business in the Late 1990s", A.V. Ledeneva & M. Kurkchiyan (eds), *Economic Crime in Russia* (The Hague, Kluwer Law International, 1999), 63–82.

Radaev, V.V., *Formirovanie novykh rossiiskykh rynkov: transaktsionnye izderzhki, formy kontrolia i delovaia etika* (Moscow, Tsentr politicheskikh tekhnologii, 1998).

Radaev, V.V., "O nekotorykh chertakh normativnogo povedeniia novykh rossiiskikh predprinimatelei", *Mirovaia ekonomika i mezhdunarodnoe otnosheniia* 4, 1994, 31–8.
——et al. (eds), *Stanovlenie novogo rossiiskogo predprinimatel'stva* (Moscow, RAN, Institut ekonomiki & Mezhdistsiplinarnyi akademicheskii tsentr sotsial'nykh nauk (Intertsentr), 1993).
Ratcliffe, B.M., "Napoleon and the Anglo-French Commercial Treaty of 1860: A Reconsideration", *Journal of European Economic History* 2, 3, Winter 1973, 582–613.
—— "Railway Imperialism: The Example of the Pereire's Paris-Saint-Germain Company, 1835–1846", *Business History* XVIII, 1, January 1976, 66–84.
Reddaway, P. & D. Glinski, *The Tragedy of Russia's Reforms. Market Bolshevism Against Democracy* (Washington, United States Institute of Peace Press, 2001).
Reddy, W.M., *The Rise of Market Culture. The Textile Trade and French Society, 1750–1900* (Cambridge, Cambridge University Press, 1984).
Reid, D., "Schools and the Paternalist Project at Le Creusot, 1850–1919", *Journal of Social History* 27, 1, Fall 1993, 129–43.
Remington, T.F., *The Russian Parliament. Institutional Evolution in a Transitional Regime, 1989–1999* (New Haven, Yale University Press, 2000).
Remnick, D., "The War for the Kremlin", *The New Yorker* 22 July 1996, 40–57.
Richards, E., "The Industrial Face of a Great Estate: Trenthan and Lilleshall, 1780–1860", *Economic History Review* XXVII, 1974, 414–30.
Rieber, A.J., *Merchants and Entrepreneurs in Imperial Russia* (Chapel Hill, University of North Carolina Press, 1982).
Rienow, R. & L.T. Rienow, *Of Snuff, Sin and the Senate* (Chicago, Follett Publishing Co., 1965).
Rigby, T.H., "New Top Elites for Old in Russian Politics", *British Journal of Political Science* 29, 3, 1999, 323–43.
Rigby, T.H., "Russia's Business Elite", *Russian and Euro-Asian Bulletin* 8, 7, August–September 1999, 1–9.
Rivera, S.W. & D.W. Rivera, "The Russian Elite Under Putin: Militocratic or Bourgeois?", *Post-Soviet Affairs* 22, 2, 2006, 125–44.
Roberts, S.I., "Portrait of a Robber Baron: Charles T. Yerkes", *Business History Review* xxxv, 3, 1961, 344–71.
Roosa, R.A., *Russian Industrialists in an Era of Revolution. The Association of Industry and Trade, 1906–1917* (Armonk, M.E. Sharpe, 1997, edited by Thomas C. Owen).
Rose, R. & N. Munro, *Elections Without Order. Russia's Challenge to Vladimir Putin* (Cambridge, Cambridge University Press, 2002).
Roshchina, Y., "Ekonomicheskaia situatsiia i problemy khoziaistvovaniia v otsenkakh predprinimatelei", V.V. Radaev, et al. (eds), *Stanovlenie novogo rossiiskogo predprinimatel'stva* (Moscow, RAN, Institut ekonomiki i mezhdistsiplinarnyi akademicheskii tsentr sotsial'nykh nauk, 1993), 110–29.
Rothman, S., "Barrington Moore and the Dialectics of Revolution: An Essay Review", *American Political Science Review* 64, 1, March 1970, 61–82.
Roy, W., *The Rise of the Large Industrial Corporation in America* (Princeton, Princeton University Press, 1997).
Rubinstein, W.D., "British Businessmen as Wealth-Holders 1870–1914: A Response", *Business History* 34, 2, April 1992, 69–81.

—— *Capitalism, Culture and Decline in Britain 1750–1990* (London, Routledge, 1990).

—— "Debate. 'Gentlemanly Capitalism' and British Industry 1820–1914", *Past and Present* 132, August 1991, 150–70.

—— *Elites and the Wealthy in Modern British History. Essays in Social and Economic History* (Brighton, Harvester, 1987).

—— "The End of 'Old Corruption' in Britain, 1780–1860", *Past and Present* 101, November 1983, 55–86.

—— *Men of Property. The Very Wealthy in Britain Since the Industrial Revolution* (London, Croom Helm, 1981).

—— "New Men of Wealth and the Purchase of Land in Nineteenth Century Britain", *Past and Present* 92, August 1991, 125–47.

—— *Wealth and Inequality in Britain* (London, Faber & Faber, 1986).

—— (ed), *Wealth and the Wealthy in the Modern World* (London, Croom Helm, 1980).

—— "Wealth Making in the Late Nineteenth and Early Twentieth Centuries: A Response", *Business History* 42, 2, April 2000, 141–54.

Ruckman, J.A., *The Moscow Business Elite. A Social and Cultural Portrait of Two Generations, 1840–1905* (De Kalb, Northern Illinois University Press, 1984).

Rutland, P. (ed), *Business and the State in Contemporary Russia* (Boulder, Westview, 2001).

—— *Business Elites and Russian Economic Policy* (London, RIIA, 1992).

—— "Introduction: Business and the State in Russia", P. Rutland (ed), *Business and the State in Contemporary Russia* (Boulder, Westview, 2001), 1–32.

—— "Privatisation in Russia: One Step Forward: Two Steps Back?", *Europe-Asia Studies* 46, 7, 1994, 1109–31.

—— "Putin and the Oligarchs", D.R. Herspring (ed), *Putin's Russia. Past Imperfect, Future Uncertain* (Lanham, Rowman & Littlefield Publishers Inc., 2003), 133–52.

—— "Russian Small Business: Staying Small", *Jamestown Foundation Eurasian Daily Monitor* 15 March 2005.

Rueschemeyer, D., E.H. Stephens & J.D. Stephens, *Capitalist Development and Democracy* (Cambridge, Polity Press, 1992).

"Russia: The Wild East", *Granta* 64, Winter 1998.

Sakwa, R., *Gorbachev and His Reforms 1985–1990* (New York, Philip Allan, 1990).

—— *Russian Politics and Society* (London, Routledge, 1993 & 2002).

Salamon, L.M., "Comparative History and the Theory of Modernization", *World Politics* 23, 1, October 1970, 83–103.

Satarov, G. et al., *Diagnostika rossiiskoi korruptsii 2005. Predvaritel'nye rezul'taty* (Moscow, Regional'nyi obshchestvennyi fond "Informatika dlia demokratii". Trudy fonda INDEM, 2005).

Satter, D., *Darkness at Dawn. The Rise of the Russian Criminal State* (New Haven, Yale University Press, 2003).

Schmidhauser, J.R., "The Justices of the Supreme Court—A Collective Portrait", *Midwest Journal of Political Science* 3, 1, February 1959, 1–57.

Schoors, K., "The Fate of Russia's Former State Banks: Chronicle of a Restructuring Postponed and a Crisis Foretold", *Europe-Asia Studies* 55, 1, 2003, 75–100.

Schroder, H.-H., "El'tsin and the Oligarchs: The Role of Financial Groups in Russian Politics Between 1993 and July 1998", *Europe-Asia Studies* 51, 6, 1999, 957–88.

Schwartz, J.A., *The Speculator. Bernard M. Baruch in Washington, 1917–1965* (Chapel Hill, University of North Carolina Press, 1981).

Searle, G.R., *Corruption in British Politics 1895–1930* (Oxford, Clarendon Press, 1987).

——*Entrepreneurial Politics in Mid-Victorian Britain* (Oxford, Oxford University Press, 1993).

Semenenko, I.S., *Gruppy interesov na zapade i v rossii. Konseptsii i praktika* (Moscow, Institut mirovoi ekonomiki i mezhdunarodnykh otnoshenii, 2001).

Sheehan, J.S., "Political Leadership in the German Reichstag, 1871–1918", *American Historical Review* 74, 2, December 1968, 511–28.

Sherman, D., "Governmental Policy Toward Joint-Stock Business Organizations in Mid-Nineteenth Century France", *Journal of European Economic History* 3, 1, Spring 1974, 149–68.

——"Governmental Responses to Economic Modernization in Mid-Nineteenth Century France", *Journal of European Economic History* 6, 3, Winter 1977, 717–36.

Shevchenko, I., *The Central Government of Russia. From Gorbachev to Putin* (Aldershot, Ashgate, 2004).

Shevtsova, L., *Putin's Russia* (Washington, Carnegie Endowment for International Peace, 2005).

——*Yeltsin's Russia. Myths and Reality* (Washington, Carnegie Endowment for International Peace, 1995).

Shlapentokh, V., "The Soviet Union: A Normal Totalitarian Society", *The Journal of Communist Studies and Transition Politics* 15, 4, 1999, 1–16.

Shliefer, A. & D. Treisman, *Without a Map. Political Tactics and Economic Reforms in Russia* (Cambridge [Mass], The MIT Press, 2000).

Shmatko, N.A., "Stanovlenie rossiiskogo patronata i biurokraticheskii kapital", *Sotsiologicheskie issledovanie* 6, 1995, 24–36.

Shorter, E. & C. Tilly, *Strikes in France 1830–1969* (Cambridge, Cambridge University Press, 1974).

Shubin, A., *Istoki perestroika 1978–1984gg* (Moscow, Institut etnologii i antropologii RAN, 1997).

Siegelbaum, L., *The Politics of Industrial Mobilization in Russia, 1914–17* (London, Macmillan, 1983).

Sim, L.C., "The Changing Relationship between the State and the Oil Industry in Russia (1992–2004)", Oxford University, D.Phil, 2005.

Simonia, N., "Economic Interests and Political Power in Post-Soviet Russia", A. Brown (ed), *Contemporary Russian Politics. A Reader* (Oxford, Oxford University Press, 2001), 269–85.

Sirotkin, V., *Mark Masarskii: put' naverkh rossiiskogo biznesmana* (Moscow, Mezhdunarodnye otnosheniia, 1994).

Skocpol, T., "A Critical Review of Barrington Moore's Social Origins of Dictatorship and Democracy", *Politics and Society* 4, 1, 1973, 1–34.

——*States and Social Revolutions. A Comparative Analysis of France, Russia, and China* (Cambridge, Cambridge University Press, 1979).

Slider, D., "Privatization in Russia's Regions", *Post-Soviet Affairs* 10, 4, 1994, 367–96.

Smith Jr, C.J., "The Russian Third State Duma: An Analytical Profile", *The Russian Review* 17, 3, July 1958, 201–10.

Smith, G.B., *Reforming the Russian Legal System* (Cambridge, Cambridge University Press, 1996).

Smith, G., *The Post-Soviet States. Mapping the Politics of Transition* (London, Arnold, 1999).

Smith, J.A., "Land Ownership and Social Change in Late Nineteenth Century Britain", *Economic History Review* 53, 4, 2000, 767–76.

Smith, M.S., "Thoughts on the Evolution of the French Capitalist Community in the XIXth Century", *Journal of European Economic History* 7, 1, Spring 1978, 139–44.

—— *Tariff Reform in France 1869–1900. The Politics of Economic Interest* (Ithaca, Cornell University Press, 1980).

Smith, W. & S.A. Turner, "Legislative Behavior in the German Reichstag, 1898–1906", *Central European History* 14, 1, 1981, 3–29.

Solnick, S., *Stealing the State. Control and Collapse in Soviet Institutions* (Cambridge [Mass], Harvard University Press, 1998).

Spencer, E.G., "Businessmen, Bureaucrats, and Social Control in the Ruhr, 1896–1914", H. Ulrich-Webler (ed), *Sozialgeschichte Heute* (Gottingen, Vandenhoeck und Ruperecht 1978), 452–66.

—— *Police and the Social Order in German Cities. The Dusseldorf District 1848–1914* (De Kalb, Northern Illinois University Press, 1992).

—— "Rulers of the Ruhr: Leadership and Authority in German Big Business", Y. Cassis (ed), *Business Elites* (Aldershot, Edward Elgar, 1994), 361–85.

Spravochnik partiinogo rabotnika(Moscow, Izdatel'stvo politicheskoi literatury, 1985–90).

Spring, D., "English Landowners and Nineteenth Century Industrialism", J.T. Ward & R.G. Wilson (eds), *Land and Industry. The Landed Estate and the Industrial Revolution* (Newton Abbott, David & Charles, 1971), 18–38.

Steinmetz, G., "The Myth of an Autonomous State: Industrialists, Junkers, and Social Policy in Imperial Germany", G. Eley (ed), *Society, Culture, and the State in Germany, 1870–1930* (Ann Arbor, University of Michigan Press, 1996), 257–318.

Stern, F., "Gold and Iron: The Collaboration and Friendship of Gerson Bleichroder and Otto von Bismarck", *American Historical Review* 75, 1, October 1969, 37–46.

Stone, L., *The Crisis of the Aristocracy 1558–1641* (London, Oxford University Press, 1967).

Stoner-Weiss, K., *Local Heroes. The Political Economy of Russian Regional Governance* (Princeton, Princeton University Press, 1997).

Sturmer, M., *The German Empire 1870–1918* (New York, Random House, 2000).

Supple, B.E., "A Business Elite: German-Jewish Financiers in Nineteenth-Century New York", *Business History Review* xxxi, 2, 1957, 143–78.

"Supreme Soviet Investigation of the 1991 Coup. The Suppressed Transcripts: Part 3. Hearings 'About the Illegal Financial Activity of the CPSU'", *Demokratizatsiya* 4, 2, 1996, 271–311.

Sutela, P., "Insider Privatization in Russia: Speculations on Systemic Change", *Europe-Asia Studies* 46, 3, 1994, 417–35.

Sweezy, P., "The Debate on the Transition. A Critique", *The Transition from Feudalism to Capitalism* (London, New Left Books, 1976), 33–56.

Swenson, P.A., "Varieties of Capitalist Interests: Power, Institutions, and the Regulatory Welfare State in the United States and Sweden", *Studies in American Political Development* 18, 1, Spring 2004, 1–29.

Szelenyi, I. & S. Szelenyi, "Circulation or Reproduction of Elites During the Postcommunist Transformation of Eastern Europe", *Theory and Society* 24, 5, 1995, 615–38.

Taylor, A.J., *Laissez-faire and State Intervention in Nineteenth Century Britain* (Basingstoke, Macmillan, 1972).

Teague, E., "Pluralism Versus Corporatism: Government, Labor and Business in the Russian Federation", C.R. Saivetz & A. Jones (eds), *In Search of Pluralism. Soviet and Post-Soviet Politics* (Boulder, Westview Press, 1994), 109–24.

Thane, P., "Financiers and the British State: The Case of Sir Ernest Cassel", *Business History* 28, 1, January 1986, 80–99.

——G. Crossick & R. Floud (eds), *The Power of the Past: essays for Eric Hobsbawm* (Cambridge, Cambridge University Press, 1984).

Therborn, G., "The Rule of Capital and the Rise of Democracy", *New Left Review* 103, May–June 1977, 3–41.

Thimm, A., *Business Ideologies in the Reform-Progressive Era, 1880–1914* (Alabama, University of Alabama Press, 1976).

Thomas, J.A., *The House of Commons 1832–1901. A Study of Its Economic and Functional Character* (Cardiff, University of Wales Press Board, 1939).

Thompson, A., "Honours Uneven: Decorations, the State and Bourgeois Society in Imperial Germany", *Past and Present* 144, August 1994, 171–205.

Thompson, E.P., "The Peculiarities of the English", E.P. Thompson (ed), *The Poverty of Theory & other essays* (London, Merlin Press, 1978), 35–91.

Thompson, F.M.L. (ed), "Business and Landed Elites in the Nineteenth Century", F.M.L. Thompson (ed), *Landowners, Capitalists, and Entrepreneurs. Essays for Sir John Habakkuk* (Oxford, Clarendon Press, 1994), 139–70.

Thompson, F.M.L., "English Landed Society in the Nineteenth Century" P. Thane, G. Crossick & R. Floud (eds), *The Power of the Past: essays for Eric Hobsbawm* (Cambridge, Cambridge University Press, 1984), 195–214.

—— (ed), *Landowners, Capitalists, and Entrepreneurs. Essays for Sir John Habbakuk* (Oxford, Clarendon Press, 1994).

—— "Life After Death: How Successful Nineteenth-Century Businessmen Disposed of their Fortunes", *Economic History Review* 2nd series, XLIII, 1, 1990, 40–61.

Tikhomirov, V., "Capital Flight from Post-Soviet Russia", *Europe-Asia Studies* 49, 4, 1997, 591–615.

Tilly, C., *Contestation and Democracy in Europe, 1650–2000* (Cambridge, Cambridge University Press, 2000).

—— "Theories and Realities", L.H. Haimson & C. Tilly (eds), *Strikes, Wars and Revolutions in an International Perspective. Strike Waves in the Late Nineteenth and Early Twentieth Centuries* (Cambridge, Cambridge University Press, 1989), 3–17.

—— "War Making and State Making as Organized Crime", P.B. Evans, D. Rueschemeyer & T. Skocpol (eds), *Bringing the State Back In* (Cambridge, Cambridge University Press, 1985), 169–91.

Tilly, R., "Moral Standards and Business Behavior in Nineteenth Century Germany and Britain", J. Kocka & A. Mitchell (eds), *Bourgeois Society in Nineteenth Century Europe* (Oxford, Berg, 1993), 179–206.

Tilton, T.A., "The Social Origins of Liberal Democracy: The Swedish Case", *American Political Science Review* 68, 2, June 1974, 561–71.

Tipton, F.B., *A History of Modern Germany Since 1815* (London, Continuum, 2003).

Tipton Jr, F.B., "Government and the Economy in the Nineteenth Century", S. Ogilvie & R. Overy (eds), *Germany. A New Social and Economic History. Volume III. Since 1800* (London, Arnold, 2003), 106–51.

—— "Small Business and the Rise of Hitler: A Review Article", *Business History Review* LIII, 2, Summer 1979, 235–46.

Tombs, R., *France 1814–1914* (London, Longman, 1996).

Tompson, W., "Putin and the 'Oligarchs': A Two-sided Commitment Problem", A. Pravda (ed), *Leading Russia. Putin in Perspective* (Oxford, Oxford University Press, 2005), 179–202.

—— "Putting Yukos in Perspective", *Post-Soviet Affairs* 21, 2, April–June 2005, 159–81.

Tone, A., *The Business of Benevolence: Industrial Paternalism in Progressive America* (Ithaca, Cornell University Press, 1997).

Trainor, R., "The Gentrification of Victorian and Edwardian Industrialists", A.L. Beier, D. Cannadine & J. Rosenheim (eds), *The First Modern Society: Essays in English History in Honour of Lawrence Stone* (Cambridge, Cambridge University Press, 1989), 167–97.

Trebilcock, C., *The Industrialization of the Continental Powers 1780–1914* (London, Longman, 1981).

Troxel, T.A., *Parliamentary Power in Russia, 1994–2001. President vs Parliament* (Basingstoke, Palgrave Macmillan, 2003).

Tumin, J., "The Theory of Democratic Development. A Critical Revision", *Theory and Society* 11, 2, 1982, 143–64.

Turner, H.A., *German Big Business and the Rise of Hitler* (New York, Oxford University Press, 1985).

Turner Jr, H.A., "Big Business and the Rise of Hitler", *American Historical Review* 75, 1, October 1969, 56–70.

United Nations Office for Drug Control and Crime Prevention, *Russian Capitalism and Money-Laundering* (New York, United Nations, 2001).

Varese, F., "Is Sicily the Future of Russia? Private protection and the rise of the Russian Mafia", *Archives europeennes de sociologie* XXXV, 2, 1996, 224–58.

—— *The Russian Mafia. Private Protection in a New Market Economy* (Oxford, Oxford University Press, 2002).

Vedomosti Verkhovnogo Soveta Soiuz Sovetskikh Sotsialisticheskikh Respublik (Moscow, 1985–91).

Vietor, R.H.K., "Businessmen and the Political Economy: The Railway Rate Controversy of 1905", *Journal of American History* 64, 1, June 1977, 47–66.

Villey, E., "Employers' Organisations in France", *International Labour Review* XVI, 1, July 1927, 50–77.

Vinen, R., *The Politics of French Business 1936–1945* (Cambridge, Cambridge University Press, 1991).

Vittenberg, E.Y., "Bankovskoe soobshchestvo rossii: itogi razvitiia i kratkosrochnyi prognoz", M.K. Gorshkov, et al. (eds), *Obnovlenie Rossii: trudnyi poisk reshenii*, vyp.5, (Moscow, RNISNP, 1997), 38–44.

—— "Politicheskie simpatii rossiiskikh bankirov", M.K. Gorshkov, et al. (eds), *Obnovlenie Rossii: trudnyi poisk reshenii*, vyp.3, (Moscow, RNISiNP, 1995), 204–10.

Volkov, V., "Organized Violence, Market Building, and State Formation in Post-Communist Russia", A.V. Ledeneva & M. Kurkchiyan (eds), *Economic Crime in Russia* (The Hague, Kluwer Law International, 1999), 43–61.

—— *Violent Entrepreneurs. The Use of Force in the Making of Russian Capitalism* (Ithaca, Cornell University Press, 2002).

Volkovskii, V., *Bor'ba s organizovannoi prestupnost'iu v ekonomicheskoi sfere* (Moscow, Russkii biograficheskii institute, 2000).

von Laue, T.H., *Sergei Witte and the Industrialisation of Russia* (New York, Cambridge University Press, 1963).

Voslenskii, M. *Nomenklatura. Gospodstvuiushchii klass Sovetskogo Soiuza* (London, Overseas Publications Interchange Ltd, 1985).

Vozrozhdenie elita rossiiskogo biznesa (Moscow, Institut izucheniia reform, 1994).

Waller, M., *Russian politics today* (Manchester, Manchester University Press, 2005).

Wallerstein, I., "The Bourgeois(ie) as Concept and Reality", *New Left Review* 167, January–February 1988, 91–106.

—— *The Modern World System. The Second Era of Great Expansion of the Capitalist World Economy, 1730–1840s* (San Diego, Academic Press Inc., 1989).

Walsh, W.B., "The Composition of the Dumas", *The Russian Review* 8, 2, April 1949, 111–16.

Warwick, P., "Did Britain Change? An Inquiry into the Causes of National Decline", *Journal of Contemporary History* 20, 1, January 1985, 99–133.

Wasson, E.A., "The Penetration of New Wealth into the English Governing Class from the Middle Ages to the First World War", *Economic History Review* LI, 1, February 1988, 25–48.

Watson, J., "Foreign Investment in Russia: The Case of the Oil Industry", *Europe-Asia Studies* 48, 3, 1996, 429–55.

Weber, M., *Economy and Society* (Berkeley, University of California Press, 1978, edited by Guenther Roth & Klaus Wittich).

Wedel, J.R., *Collision and Collusion. The Strange Case of Western Aid to Eastern Europe 1989–1998* (New York, St Martins Press, 1998).

Weinstein, J., *The Corporate Ideal in the Liberal State: 1900–1918* (Boston, Beacon Press, 1968).

—— "Organised Business and the City Commission Manager Movements", *Journal of Southern History* 28, 2, 1962, 166–82.

Weiss, L. & J. Hobson, *States and Economic Development. A Comparative Historical Analysis* (Cambridge, Policy Press, 1995).

Werking, R.H., "Bureaucrats, Businessmen, and Foreign Trade: The Origins of the United States Chamber of Commerce", *Business History Review* LII, 3, Autumn 1978, 321–41.

West, J.L., "Merchant Moscow in Historical Context", J.L. West & I.A. Petrov (eds), *Merchant Moscow. Images of Russia's Vanished Bourgeoisie* (Princeton, Princeton University Press, 1988), 3–12.

—— "The Riabushinsky Circle: Burzhuaziia and Obshchestvennost' in Late Imperial Russia", E.W. Clowes, S.D. Kassow & J.L. West (eds), *Between Tsar and People. Educated Society and the Quest for Public Identity in Late Imperial Russia* (Princeton, Princeton University Press, 1991), 41–56.

—— & I.A. Petrov (eds), *Merchant Moscow. Images of Russia's Vanished Bourgeoisie* (Princeton, Princeton University Press, 1988).

White, D.S., *The Splintered Party: National Liberalism in Hessen and the Reich, 1867–1918* (Cambridge [Mass], Harvard University Press, 1976).

White, S., *Gorbachev and After* (Cambridge, Cambridge University Press, 1991).

—— R. Rose & I. McAllister, *How Russia Votes* (Chatham, Chatham House Publishers Inc., 1997).

Whitten, D., *The Emergence of the Great Enterprise, 1860–1914* (Westport, Greenwood Press, 1983).

Wiebe, R., "Business Disunity and the Progressive Movement, 1901–1914", *Mississippi Valley Historical Review* 44, 4, March 1958, 664–85.

—— "The House of Morgan and the Executive, 1905–1913", *American Historical Review* 65, 1, October 1959, 49–60.

Wiebe, R.H., *Businessmen and Reform: A Study of the Progressive Movement* (Cambridge [Mass], Harvard University Press, 1962).

—— *The Search for Order, 1877–1920* (New York, Hill & Wang, 1966).

Wiener, J.M., "The Barrington Moore Thesis and Its Critics", *Theory and Society* 2, 3, 1975, 301–30.

Wiener, M.J., *English Culture and the Decline of the Industrial Spirit 1850–1980* (Harmondsworth, Penguin, 1985).

Williams, R., *Keywords. A vocabulary of culture and society* (London, Fontana Press, 1983).

Wilson, J.F., *British Business History, 1720–1994* (Manchester, Manchester University Press, 1995).

Wood, E.M., *The Origin of Capitalism* (New York, Monthly Review Press, 1999).

—— *The Pristine Culture of Capitalism. An Historical Essay on Old Regimes and Modern States* (London, Verso, 1991).

Woodruff, D., *Money Unmade. Barter and the Fate of Russian Capitalism* (Ithaca, Cornell University Press, 1999).

Woolf, S., "The Aristocracy in Transition. A Continental Comparison", *Economic History Review* XXIII, 3, 1970, 520–31.

World Bank, The, *From Transition to Development. A country economic memorandum for the Russian Federation* (New York, The World Bank, 2004).

World Bank, The, *Russian Federation. From Transition to Development. A Country Economic Memorandum for the Russian Federation* (New York, The World Bank, 2005).

World Bank, The, *World Development Report 1996. From Plan to Market* (New York, Oxford University Press, 1996).

Yorke, A., "Business and Politics in Krasnoyarsk Krai", *Europe-Asia Studies* 55, 2, 2003, 241–62.

Zeldin, T., *France 1848–1945. Volume 1. Ambition, Love and Politics* (Oxford, Clarendon Press, 1973).

—— *The Political System of Napoleon III* (London, Macmillan, 1958).

Zevelev, V.A., *Malyi biznes—bol'shaia problema rossii* (Moscow, Menedzher, 1994).

Zinn, H., *A People's History of the United States. 1492-Present* (New York, Perennial Classics, 2001).

Zotov, V.B., *Kak mer Luzhkov upravliaet Moskvoi (materialy lektsii)* (Liubertsy, VINITI, 1998).

Zudin, A., "Biznes i politika v postkommunisticheskoi Rossii. Formy organizatsii biznesa", *Biznes i politika* 12, 1995, 2–9.

——"Biznes i politika v postkommunisticheskoi Rossii. Politicheskie strategii grupp davleniia biznesa", *Biznes i politika* 1, 1996, 3–10.

——"Biznes i politika v postkommunisticheskoi Rossii", *Biznes i politika* 2, 1996, 2–8.

——"Neokorporatizm v Rossii? (Gosudarstvo i biznes pri Vladimire Putine)", *Pro et Contra* 6, 4, Autumn 2001, 171–98.

Zudin, A.I., "Oligarchy as a political problem of Russian postcommunism", *Russian Social Science Review* 41, 6, November–December 2000, 4–33.

Zunz, O., *Making America Corporate 1870–1920* (Chicago, University of Chicago Press, 1990).

Zwaan, T., "One Step Forward, Two Steps back. Tumin's Theory of Democratic Development: A Comment", *Theory and Society* 11, 2, 1982, 165–78.

Index

Index